JUSTICE DEFERRED

JUSTICE DEFERRED

RACE AND THE SUPREME COURT

ORVILLE VERNON BURTON
AND ARMAND DERFNER

THE BELKNAP PRESS OF HARVARD UNIVERSITY PRESS
Cambridge, Massachusetts & London, England 2021

Printed in the United States of America

First printing

Library of Congress Cataloging-in-Publication Data

Names: Burton, Orville Vernon, author. | Derfner, Armand, author.
Title: Justice deferred : race and the Supreme Court / Orville Vernon Burton and Armand Derfner.
Description: Cambridge, Massachusetts : The Belknap Press of Harvard University Press, 2021. | Includes bibliographical references and index.
Identifiers: LCCN 2020047829 | ISBN 9780674975644 (cloth)
Subjects: LCSH: Race discrimination—Law and legislation—United States. | Civil rights—United States. | United States. Supreme Court—History.
Classification: LCC KF4755 .B87 2021 | DDC 342.7308/73—dc23
LC record available at https://lccn.loc.gov/2020047829

To Georganne Burton and
Mary Giles

Contents

Note to the Reader

We have written this book for general readers, historians, students, and lawyers, and we have tried to accommodate all these audiences while telling the story as comprehensively as possible in a manageable length.

This book is indebted to a vast literature on race and the law in the United States, and we gratefully recognize the thousands of observers and scholars who have studied and chronicled these topics. Because the literature is so extensive, the endnotes in the book are limited to the most essential citations and commentary. A dedicated website supplements the endnotes with added material on many of the cases and historical topics; it also includes links to census reports and relevant web resources. We encourage you to visit the website: http://justice-deferred.clemson.edu.

An Index of Cases provides full case citations along with the pages in the book where the cases are referenced.

We have generally used modern terminology in the book except in direct quotations from earlier times, where readers will see the "n-word" and other offensive epithets. We chose to leave in these terms in order to convey the often grim reality of this history.

I, [NAME], do solemnly swear (or affirm) that I will administer justice without respect to persons, and do equal right to the poor and to the rich, and that I will faithfully and impartially discharge and perform all the duties incumbent upon me as [TITLE] under the Constitution and laws of the United States. So help me God.

—Judicial Oath,
revised after the Judicial Improvements Act of 1990

Introduction

The words "Law—the Guardian of Liberty" are carved high on the east façade of the US Supreme Court building in Washington, DC. Americans typically think of the Supreme Court as the guardian of both law and liberty. Even when we rail against some of its particular decisions, Americans recognize it as the institution that ended segregation, guarantees fair trials, and protects free speech and the right to vote. But the reality is more complicated, especially in the area of race and civil rights. In this area, those accomplishments date from a short period in history, from the 1930s to the early 1970s. Before that time, the Supreme Court spent much of its history ignoring or suppressing those rights, and in the half century since the early 1970s the Court's record on civil rights has retreated far more than it has advanced.

"Race" is a vexing and perplexing concept. DNA has shown that race is a fiction. No gene defines one's race; any random person on earth may be far closer genetically to someone of a "different" race than to someone of the "same" race. Race does not even match up with color, as the Supreme Court declared a century ago when it said "white" meant "Caucasian" and then said maybe it did not. Even though classifying people by race makes no biological sense, it has been common practice for a long time. The artificial social and legal construct of race has been made a very real part of the social and legal system; different combinations of parentage and pigment have been the basis for handing out privileges and disadvantages to people. Artificial or not, race and racism have been given a major role in human life by law and society, including in the United States.[1]

Nor is race just "white" and "Black." Other groups, such as Native Americans, Latinos, and Asian Americans, are part of the story of race and of the US Supreme Court, and they are part of the story of this book. African Americans (the largest minority until the 2000 census) are at the center of this book because so much of US national history and so many Supreme Court cases have focused on slavery and Jim Crow and their aftermath. This book, while covering the entire United States, often looks toward "the South," the place where most African Americans have lived for most of US history.[2]

Just like the notion of race, the Supreme Court can also be vexing and perplexing. Even if its mission were simply to call balls and strikes, as John Roberts suggested in 2005 when he was a nominee to the Court, how does that work when the umpires keep changing, and each new set of umpires can redefine the strike zone, change the number of balls and strikes each batter gets, and even change decisions by previous umpires?[3]

Put together the vexing concept of race with the perplexing Supreme Court, and you have this book. Fusing the perspectives of a historian and a lawyer, the book views US racial history through the lens of the Supreme Court, from slavery in the colonies to the present day, and even projects a glimpse of possible futures.

Race and the Supreme Court are at the center of this drama, but major roles are also played by two other actors—Time and Law. Time is fundamental for understanding race in the United States. African slavery and Jim Crow prevailed for 300 years, and they have been gone for just over 50 years. If we count a generation as 25 years, then American history has consisted of twelve generations of white supremacy and barely two generations of trying, sometimes more aggressively than at other times, to overcome it.[4]

Law, including government action, has always been central in maintaining racial control and racial separation. Law defined enslaved workers as a commodity but also had to grapple with the reality that they were human beings. As a result, both enslaved and free Black people (in all thirteen original colonies and then in the slave states) were regulated by reams of laws—laws that also established a relationship between color and crime. Law also detailed segregation codes and discriminatory rulebooks in twentieth-century federal housing and mortgage agencies. And Law has played a crucial role in events concerning other races, including Native American removal, Chinese exclusion, Japanese internment, Latino discrimination, and more.

In the category of Law, of course, is the work of the Supreme Court, interpreting law and thereby deciding what the law means. The role that law and government action have played in spreading race discrimination and molding attitudes of race prejudice has been virtually erased from public memory by a form of national amnesia. In 1849 this amnesia afflicted a Massachusetts judge who said race prejudice "is not created by law and probably cannot be changed by law." Today it afflicts those—including some Supreme Court justices—who think all-white suburbs just happened by themselves. George Orwell, as usual, had something to say about this: "The past was erased, the erasure was forgotten, the lie became the truth."[5]

But Time and Law can also undo the inequality they created. That undoing is the role of the Thirteenth Amendment, adopted after the Civil War to abolish slavery and bring universal freedom throughout the land. That amendment was not a one-time historical event that became irrelevant once the institution of slavery no longer existed. The Thirteenth Amendment continues its promise to end the badges and incidents of slavery, root and branch, to guarantee equality and, ultimately, to end discrimination and eliminate racial prejudice. Though in recent years it has largely been cast into the shadows of constitutional doctrine, except for occasional appearances, the spirit of the Thirteenth Amendment is at the heart of the Constitution. That spirit animates this book.

The Supreme Court, of course, does not make history or national policy by itself. It is only a single institution interacting with the president, Congress, the states, and innumerable other public and private institutions. Indeed, its overall influence on events, whether involving race or anything else, varies widely. This book is not aimed at magnifying or minimizing the Supreme Court's role in the country's racial history. But the Supreme Court was "there," even when it did not seem to be, so this book is both the story of the Supreme Court's race history and a view from one crucial angle of the overall race history of the nation.

This history of race and the Supreme Court covers more than legal analysis; it is also full of politics, personalities, and high drama: President Buchanan's efforts to "fix" the outcome of the *Dred Scott* case; Booker T. Washington's secret financing of lawsuits challenging various aspects of Jim Crow; Chief Justice Fred Vinson's sudden death and Earl Warren's appointment in time for the segregation cases (regarding which another justice said the timing indicated the possibility of divine intervention).[6]

Thurgood Marshall arrives on the Silver Meteor in May 1951 for the school desegregation case of *Briggs v. Elliott*, the first of five cases that would become *Brown v. Board of Education*. In the heat of the desegregation battle, Marshall remarked, "Sometimes I get awfully tired of trying to save the white man's soul." This picture was taken by thirteen-year-old Cecil Williams, who became a celebrated photographer of the Civil Rights Movement.

There are other examples: the former slaveholder who became the greatest champion of his time for African Americans—but not for Chinese people; the Union soldier, wounded three times in the Civil War, who wrote strong opinions supporting Jim Crow; the former Klansman who as a justice was a vigorous civil rights supporter—until he was not; and the African American lawyer who could not seem to lose a Supreme Court case until he became a justice and soon found himself on the losing side of almost every major civil rights decision for his last two decades on the Court.

We leave it to the reader to explore the "what if" questions: Would Massive Resistance in the 1950s and 1960s have been so massive if the members of the first white mob at Little Rock Central High School in 1957 had all been arrested under the federal law that made it a crime to interfere with exercise of constitutional rights—that is, if the Supreme Court had not thrown that law out in the 1870s and 1880s? Would racial struggles over the right to vote still be so troublesome today if the Supreme Court had not abandoned the Fifteenth Amendment in six cases in a row at the turn of the twentieth century? Would the Civil Rights Movement have been crippled if the Court had decided two cases against the NAACP, as it was preparing to do—until two justices suddenly left the Court within five days, one laid low by a nervous breakdown and the other by a stroke?

The first half of the book, Chapters 1–6, covers the time period from 1619, when the first Africans arrived in Virginia, until 1953, the eve of the Supreme Court decision on *Brown v. Board of Education* and the arrival of Earl Warren as chief justice. This analysis of the past and of past Supreme Court decisions is vital, because the truism that the past creates the present holds especially true for the Supreme Court. The Court has been interpreting the same Constitution and laws, more or less, for generation after generation, and using past precedent, so today really does grow out of yesterday.

The second half of the book is topical rather than chronological. It consists of seven chapters covering recent times, the more than sixty years since the end of the "separate but equal" rule in *Brown v. Board of Education.* Chapters 7–9 cover the Warren Court, 1953 to 1969. Each of these three chapters covers the same years, but the chapters are divided by topic. Also divided by topic are Chapters 10–13, covering the years 1969–2020, the tenures of three chief justices: Burger, Rehnquist, and Roberts.

Chapter 1 begins with slavery in 1619 and Slave Codes. After independence, the new Constitution of 1787 created a weak national government and situated most of the power in the states. The chapter describes several cases on Native American sovereignty and a number of slavery cases, leading up to the *Dred Scott* case and the beginning of the Civil War.

Chapter 2 describes the period when the Civil War brought freedom, and new constitutional amendments radically transformed the US Constitution by giving the national government power to protect citizens from state oppression. The Thirteenth Amendment freed four million enslaved people; the Fourteenth brought citizenship, equal protection, and due process; and the Fifteenth granted the right to vote. These amendments were backed by laws to protect the new freedom. The Founders of the Constitution now included not only George Washington, Thomas Jefferson, and Alexander Hamilton, but also Frederick Douglass, Abraham Lincoln, Charles Sumner, and Thaddeus Stevens.

Chapter 3 focuses on the period when the Reconstruction era ended—and the Supreme Court took apart the Reconstruction constitutional amendments and Congress's laws. Justices who spent their lifetimes under the state-oriented Constitution of 1787 could not, or would not, accept the revolutionary change that gave the federal government a new role and new power. By the end of the 1880s the Supreme Court had largely neutered the new constitutional amendments and the Reconstruction laws designed to protect the freed people.

Chapter 4 begins when proponents of white supremacy were back in control of the former slave states, and political leaders instituted segregation, disfranchisement, and all-white juries. The Supreme Court upheld every such scheme, in *Plessy v. Ferguson* and twenty other cases, some well known, many mostly forgotten. Not merely allowing it, law now mandated segregation. Although the Supreme Court was not alone in its support for Jim Crow, the Court's moral authority gave the stamp of approval to those who wanted to discriminate. In these two decades 1,969 African Americans were lynched—and those were just the recorded lynchings; the actual number was certainly much higher.

Chapter 5 describes a mixed period. Jim Crow was a fixture in the South and spread northward, where audiences, including President Woodrow Wilson, flocked to see the Ku Klux Klan glorified in *The Birth of a Nation.* Beginning in 1911, however, the Supreme Court started striking down the most egregious race laws and, for the first time ever, reversed convictions obtained in grossly unfair trials. However, the Court then followed these advances with subsequent backtracking.

Chapter 6 chronicles the road to *Brown v. Board of Education.* The Court ruled against race discrimination in many forms, including "white primaries," all-white labor unions, and "restrictive covenants" that locked African Americans out of white neighborhoods. The NAACP brought a series of cases in a concerted campaign to end segregation, and the Supreme Court decided in several cases that states were not providing "equal" graduate or professional schools for African Americans. By the close of this period, five cases seeking to strike down segregation were at the Supreme Court's doorstep. Paradoxically, just as the Court was on the verge of ending segregated education, it was already too late to erase patterns of modern-day segregation in housing, especially outside the former Confederacy. Segregated housing flourished with the exponential growth of suburbs, most of which were white by custom with the help of government rules. This chapter also discusses the World War II internment of Japanese Americans.

Chapter 7 begins with the monumental 1954 decision, in *Brown v. Board of Education,* that school segregation is unconstitutional. After this decision, the Court then began ruling against official segregation across the board, ultimately crossing the last frontier by striking down state antimiscegenation laws. School desegregation was less successful, as southern states used the Court's 1955 ruling allowing time to desegregate ("with all deliberate speed") as an excuse and opportunity to do nothing. After a dozen years with little integration in the South, the Court in 1968 said that desegregation must occur "now."

Chapter 8 describes two opposing movements, the southern states' campaigns against the NAACP and the press in the 1950s, and the Civil Rights Movement's sit-ins, demonstrations, and freedom rides in the early and mid-1960s. The Supreme Court issued several dozen decisions in these two campaigns. In this critical period, the Court never upheld a single state attack on the NAACP or the press or a single sit-in conviction.

Chapter 9 covers the Warren Court's interpretation of the Thirteenth, Fourteenth, and Fifteenth Amendments and the new civil rights laws, as well as new interpretations of nineteenth-century civil rights laws. The interpretations were as broad as the nineteenth-century Court's were narrow, especially a new reading of the Civil Rights Act of 1866 that banned private acts of race discrimination, not just official acts, and gave new life to the Thirteenth Amendment. The Supreme Court asserted the constitutional basis for the Civil Rights Act of 1964 and the Voting Rights Act of 1965.

Chapter 10 is an overview of the years since the Warren Court. The Court faced new nationwide issues, especially employment and housing discrimination and non-southern school segregation. Overall, a fractured Court meant a slowdown in momentum for change and enforcement under Chief Justice Burger. Under Chief Justices Rehnquist and Roberts, momentum has stopped altogether and even reversed. Most notably, in 2013 the Court held the heart of the 1965 Voting Rights Act unconstitutional, the first such ruling in more than a century.

As described in Chapter 11, much of the Court's civil rights debate after 1970 has involved whether a discriminatory effect is sufficient to prove a violation of civil rights or whether proof of discriminatory purpose is required. The question is: Are discriminatory *results* of a law enough for the Court to strike it down, or is proof also required that the people who wrote and passed the law *intended* it to discriminate? Not just a technicality, the debate goes to the core of what discrimination is and what the law and the Constitution should address.

Chapter 12 is about affirmative action, ranging from cautious allowance under Chief Justice Burger to very stringent treatment under his successors. The chapter covers the back-and-forth debate and the current status of the issue.

Chapter 13 addresses current issues of criminal justice and law enforcement, focusing on the Supreme Court's role. Topics include the death penalty, jury issues such as race-based peremptory challenges, the war on drugs, and other aspects of the exploding prison population. Most current is the issue of remedies for police misconduct, remedies that the Supreme Court has limited across the board.

July 4, 1776. Thomas Jefferson wrote, "All men are created equal," and those words inspired a dream of justice. Four years later, in May 1787 in Philadelphia, delegates gathered together to "form a more perfect Union." The Constitution they wrote describes the basics of the US government. One of the distinctive features of the Constitution is how it parceled out power and responsibility. In fear of an authoritarian monarchy, the framers divided power between state governments and the "national" or "general" government (not called "federal" until many years later). In the new nation, states retained sovereign power except where the Constitution limited that power, while the national government had only such powers as the Constitution gave it. When the Bill of Rights (the first ten amendments) was added to the Constitution in December 1791, the Tenth Amendment stated, "The powers not delegated to the United States by the Constitution, nor prohibited by it to the States, are reserved to the States respectively, or to the people." The Tenth Amendment still applies, but the Constitution now gives the national government so much power—principally through the Fourteenth Amendment, the twentieth-century reinterpretation of the interstate commerce clause, and the national government's spending power—that in many ways the national government is now dominant.

The power of the new national government was also parceled out among three separate branches. Articles I and II created legislative and executive branches of the national government, and Article III created a judicial branch, headed by the Supreme Court and including such lower federal courts as Congress chose to establish. Trying to protect justice from the thicket of political upheavals, the delegates chose a system where justices were appointed rather than elected and were to serve for life. Congress first set the number of Supreme Court justices at six. In the nineteenth century, that number fluctuated from six to five, back to six to seven to nine to ten to seven to nine, where it has stayed since 1869. The increases were to accommodate the growing number of states, but the decreases were to prevent specific presidents from filling vacancies—in 1801 by the outgoing Federalist Congress to block a possible Thomas Jefferson appointment (a reduction promptly reversed by the new Congress), and in 1866 to keep Andrew Johnson from filling any vacancies (seats restored to nine as soon as Ulysses S. Grant became president).[7]

Congress also promptly created a system of lower federal courts, one or more in each state and all subject to control by the Supreme Court. Each state also had its own system of "state courts" subject to its own state constitution and its own state supreme court. Thus, from the start, there have been two parallel court systems, with state courts and federal courts located in each state, and for federal issues the Supreme Court of the United States at the head of both systems.

In 1788 Alexander Hamilton wrote Federalist Paper No. 78 defending the judicial branch of the new national government. Hamilton wrote that "the judiciary is beyond comparison the weakest of the three departments of power." He added that it would "always be the least dangerous." Within a few years, however, the Supreme Court asserted the authority to decide whether laws and other actions of other branches of the national government or of the states were consistent with the Constitution—that is, whether such actions were "constitutional" or "unconstitutional."[8]

No clause of the Constitution gave the Supreme Court this power. Instead, the foundation stone of that power of constitutional interpretation is the case of *Marbury v. Madison* (1803). William Marbury had been appointed to a federal judgeship in 1801, but outgoing president John Adams ran out of time to complete the necessary paperwork, and incoming president Thomas Jefferson (and his secretary of state, James Madison) refused to do so. Marbury sued Madison and brought his suit in the Supreme Court, as a federal law provided. In an opinion by Chief Justice John Marshall, the Supreme Court dismissed the suit because it was brought in the wrong court. Marshall said a provision in the Constitution required this type of suit to be started in a lower court, not in the Supreme Court. Therefore, the statute Marbury relied on was "unconstitutional" and, as a result, void.

This was the Supreme Court's first exercise of "judicial review," the power to declare laws unconstitutional. The case also confirms that politics, even partisan politics, has never been absent from the Supreme Court's work. In several more cases over the next two decades, the Supreme Court also established its power to declare state laws and other actions of the states unconstitutional and to overrule decisions of state courts on points of federal constitutional law.[9]

Although it made no difference to the outcome, a separate part of Marshall's opinion took a jab at President Jefferson, finding that the Jefferson administration had violated its legal obligations by failing to deliver Marbury's commission. Because Marbury's case was dismissed anyway, this statement was irrelevant to the ruling, not part of the "holding," and thus not precedent to be relied on in later cases. Statements that are not necessary to the actual decision, called "dictum" or "dicta" (meaning "something said" in Latin), are found in many judicial opinions. They sometimes become sources of controversy when there is a disagreement about whether an assertion is "holding"—and thus precedent—or simply "dictum."

With the authority to act as the arbiter of constitutionality, the power of the judiciary has changed beyond Alexander Hamilton's imagination. By the early twentieth century, the reality was expressed by future Chief Justice Charles Evans Hughes: "We are under a Constitution but the Constitution is what the judges say it is." By 2015 the Supreme Court had held federal laws unconstitutional 182 times and state and local laws unconstitutional 1,094 times. In the twenty-first century, the Court is viewed by many as more powerful than ever.[10]

Although constitutional rulings often attract the most attention, a far greater volume of the Supreme Court's work is interpreting the laws of Congress. The Supreme Court is almost entirely an appellate court, limited to "reviewing" decisions of lower federal courts or state supreme courts. For much of its history, the Supreme Court had little choice over what cases it would hear, but since the Judiciary Act of 1925, it has had almost complete choice. Currently the Court is asked to hear thousands of cases every year, and it agrees to hear very few of them—nowadays fewer than 100 per year. In almost all instances, a request that the Supreme Court hear a case is made by a "petition for certiorari" (from the same Latin root as the word "certify"), and if the Court declines to hear the case ("certiorari denied"), the denial is not Supreme Court precedent. Because different routes to the Supreme Court have had many names over the years, this book most often uses the generic term "appeal" for any case going to the Supreme Court, no matter what the technical route was.

The Supreme Court's power to interpret the Constitution and laws inevitably involves choosing among different possibilities; a word or phrase can have more than one meaning, different words or phrases can point in different directions, meanings can change over the years, and interpretations can be broad or narrow. Out of the Supreme Court's almost countless cases that involve or touch on race, we have selected over 200 for this book. We have focused on these cases to describe the issues, alternatives, and consequences of the Court's different possible choices.

Justice Deferred provides a broad-based picture of race in America, past and present, through the lens of the Supreme Court. The sweep of the story touches on the colonies, the Constitution, slavery, Civil War, Reconstruction, Jim Crow, the New Deal, World Wars I and II, the Civil Rights Movement, affirmative action, and today's world. Over that long course, the story of race and the Supreme Court is really a history of the progress of equality—backward or forward, fast or slow. No institution is better suited than the Supreme Court to define the golden ideals of America; that is why this book is so critical of instances when the Supreme Court seems to have fallen short, and why it celebrates the transcendent moments when the Supreme Court carries the nation forward. In charting the progress of Equality, Freedom, and Justice for All, the line is not straight, but the past links to the present. Ultimately the book speaks to the future.

CHAPTER ONE

The Constitution, the Supreme Court, and the Road to Civil War

On July 4, 1854, as the holiday sun rose higher over a sweltering Boston, hundreds of people streamed onto special trains bound for Framingham—sixteen miles and fifty cents away—for a giant rally of the Anti-Slavery Society. Weeks before, many of them had been among the 50,000 people who crowded the streets of Boston watching as 2,000 United States soldiers and Marines forced one "fugitive slave," Anthony Burns, onto a ship returning him to slavery in Virginia. Now, at the July 4 rally, Bostonians were gathering to hear speeches by renowned abolitionists Henry David Thoreau, Sojourner Truth, and William Lloyd Garrison.

By the time Garrison rose to speak, passions ran high. Garrison's words ranged over the Declaration of Independence, the Bible, and the court order that sent Anthony Burns back to his owner. As Garrison spoke, he kept calling out a refrain, "Let the people say," and the response roared back, "Amen!"[1]

Finally, he held up a copy of the US Constitution. Using words from the biblical prophet Isaiah, Garrison called the Constitution "a covenant with death and an agreement with Hell." With these words he lit a match to the document, and as he cried "So perish all compromises with tyranny!" flames engulfed the Constitution of the United States.

Those flames had been smoldering since the birth of the Constitution in 1787. The Supreme Court was about to fan them into a conflagration that would nearly destroy the nation.

Garrison's flames had actually begun more than 200 years earlier, with the arrival of the first Africans to the British colonies. In Point Comfort, Virginia, in 1619, white settlers bought a cargo of "20. and Odd Negras" from Dutch traders. They could not have dreamed of the bitter fruit they were planting and would bequeath to their descendants, including those of the present day.[2]

The story started unremarkably, with little sense of the horrors that lay ahead. The first Africans in the British colonies were treated, somewhat like white arrivals, as bonded or indentured servants held to periods of service followed by freedom. As the seventeenth century progressed, planters turned increasingly to enslaved labor. Enslaving Native Americans was generally not successful; fugitives could find a refuge, and the refuge was often armed. White landowners in both the North and the South turned to captured Africans. In the process, they created a lifetime, hereditary slave system reserved for Africans and their descendants.[3]

The eighteenth century saw the dramatic explosion of the Atlantic slave trade, which dehumanized and "commoditized" captive Africans. Financed by European bankers and by investors in the northern colonies, the Atlantic slave trade brought captives to this country, where they were sold and trafficked in the domestic slave trade.

The numbers were huge. Between 1619 and 1865, more than 400,000 Black captives arrived in what would become the United States (many more died en route)—most directly from Africa, but about 50,000 transshipped from other Western Hemisphere ports. This was actually a small fraction of the astonishing number of Africans—13 million—brought to the Western Hemisphere and enslaved between 1501 and 1875; the largest number of them were taken to Brazil and the Caribbean islands. The first US census, in 1790, recorded 757,208 Black people, 19 percent of the US population; of these, 8 percent were free. By 1810, population growth plus the last frenzied years of the Atlantic slave trade had produced a Black population of 1,377,808—still 19 percent of the US population—of whom 13 percent were free.[4]

Forcing others to do the work that produced wealth was like a drug, powerful and habit-forming. Ownership of this human commodity was a financial investment, an asset good for bank credit. With more enslaved laborers, the colonies began adopting slave laws in the late 1600s, and these morphed into comprehensive Slave Codes in the 1700s. These codes were periodically tightened and made more harsh, especially after major slave revolts in New York in 1712 and in South Carolina in 1739.[5]

In the 1700s the colonies also changed their laws in ways that defined more people as slaves. English law gave a child the status of the father, which would have given freedom to the many children born to a white father and an enslaved mother. The American colonies, however, reversed course and adopted statutes giving a child the status of the mother.[6]

Along with the Slave Codes came other laws drawing a color line between Black people, enslaved or free, and white people. Whether enslaved or free, Black people could not carry arms, testify against white people, or congregate freely without permission. Fleeing slavery was criminal, and patrols enforced rules against traveling without a pass. Lawmakers particularly worked to put a stop to interracial sex and marriage—a likely sign that this human activity was not uncommon; by the mid-1700s eight of the thirteen American colonies barred marriages between white and Black couples, enslaved or free, with harsh penalties for all involved, including the minister performing the ceremony.[7]

The detailed web of Slave Codes and color-line laws throughout the American colonies was designed not only to control the behavior of the enslaved, but to shape attitudes of individuals, communities, and entire colonies. The law in all the colonies defined enslaved people as chattel property. "Free" Black people, though they were not chattel property, were also assigned an official inferior status by law.

The Black Code in New Orleans, which had a substantial free Black population, made "insulting a white person" a crime and further explained that Black persons ought never "strike white people, nor presume to conceive themselves equal to the white; but on the contrary that they ought to yield to them on every occasion, and never speak or answer to them but with respect, under penalty of imprisonment." Laws also restricted white people's ability to contradict or modify the rules governing Black people's lives. Laws rigidly controlled the behavior of every person of every status and every color, and created a color line in people's minds long after the laws themselves were gone. Strangely, though, as the years and centuries passed, a strain of national amnesia settled over Americans, erasing memory of the roles of law and government in establishing the color line. This tended to occur first in states where slavery had ended, and then throughout the country after emancipation and especially after the end of official segregation. The mind retains the color line but forgets that it was created by the web of laws.[8]

America had several opportunities to break its addiction to enslaved labor. The Declaration of Independence in 1776 said that, in addition to equality, all men have an "unalienable right" to "Liberty" (along with life and the pursuit of happiness). At the time of this Declaration, all thirteen colonies had slavery. Over the next decades, some New England and mid-Atlantic states abolished slavery, either outright or gradually.

A decade after the Declaration of Independence, and after the states had tried a loose association under the Articles of Confederation, the Founders met in Philadelphia in 1787 to draft a Constitution. Perhaps it was unrealistic to think the Framers might turn their backs on slavery when the southerners among them were so dependent on it. But when the Framers accepted slavery in the new nation's Constitution, they prepared the tinder for William Lloyd Garrison's match.

A Constitution for a Nation Half-Slave and Half-Free

Southern delegates to the Constitutional Convention in 1787 would not have adopted that document if they had not thought it protected the South's "peculiar institution"—a southern euphemism for slavery. And indeed, slavery, which had already flourished throughout the colonies for more than a century, was formally protected in the fundamental charter of the new nation.[9]

The Constitution contained three clauses dealing directly with slavery: the "three-fifths clause," "slave trade clause," and "fugitive slave clause."

The three-fifths clause was a compromise about balancing political power among the states and regions of the new republic. Seats in the House of Representatives were based on each state's population. This in turn also determined each state's votes in the Electoral College (which chooses the president and vice president), where each state has the number of votes equal to its number of representatives plus two (for its senators). Slave states wanted their enslaved population counted fully, whereas the free states argued that because slaves were deemed to be property, they should not be counted at all. The compromise was Article I, Section 2, which included all free persons ("except Indians not taxed"), plus "three fifths of all other Persons." Throughout the antebellum period, the "slave count" contributed to southern domination of the national government even with a minority of the free population; it may also have made the difference in giving Thomas Jefferson the presidency in 1800 instead of John Adams.[10]

The slave trade clause put a difficult question off to the future. The Constitution gave the new national Congress power over "commerce with foreign nations," which would allow Congress to end the international slave trade. Delegates who wanted to ban the slave trade and those who wanted to keep it compromised on Article I, Section 9, which barred Congress from ending the trade for a twenty-year period. (Article V precluded any amendment of this twenty-year period.)

The fugitive slave clause was not so much a compromise as a free-state agreement demanded by slave states to protect slavery. Unless they were restrained, the free states would be entitled to apply their own laws and treat as free any runaway slaves who managed to reach their borders. To prevent this, Article IV, Section 2, of the Constitution mandated that enslaved fugitives would not become free but must be returned to their owner and slavery.

Having reached these compromises, though, the delegates still felt sufficient unease about them to keep the word "slave" out of the Constitution. Nowhere in the original Constitution do the words "slave" or "slavery" appear. Each of the three slave clauses used different quaint wording: the slave trade clause referred to slaves as "such persons as any of the states now existing shall think proper to admit." The fugitive slave clause called the slave a "person held to service or labor." And in the three-fifths clause, they were simply "other persons," to distinguish them from "free persons." Notably, the new Constitution nowhere differentiated between Black and white, nor did it base privilege simply on race.[11]

The preservation of slavery was accepted as the price of creating a Union, but some nonetheless felt misgivings and even alarm about it. One delegate looked into the future and gave a dire prophecy: "Providence punishes national sins by national calamities."[12]

A Color Line for the New Nation

The Constitution did not have a color line, but the new nation did. In the late eighteenth and early nineteenth centuries, while slavery seemed to be receding outside the South, the color line between white and Black showed no recession. Legal disabilities targeting African Americans filled the laws of the states. Almost all of the thirteen original states (including the free states) had laws that imposed some form of restriction on their Black residents. Some prohibited African Americans from voting, others banned interracial marriage, others prohibited Black witnesses from testifying, and many states imposed more than one legal disability. The same was true of almost all the twenty new states that joined the Union before the Civil War. Some of the new "free" states, like Ohio and Illinois, restricted all African Americans. On the federal level, Congress's first Naturalization Act, passed in 1790, drew a sharp color line by limiting eligibility to become an American citizen to "free white persons of good character." The prejudice created by the color line was manifest in colonial law, thus passed down from generation to generation.[13]

For a few decades the formula of a country half-slave and half-free seemed to proceed as projected. The international slave trade was abolished at the first opportunity—on January 1, 1808—without serious sectional discord. There was also intersectional cooperation between free and slave states. For example, in southern and northern courts alike, enslaved people who sued for freedom on grounds that their slaveholders had taken them to free states usually won when the stay was long but lost when the stay was short. Congress worked to keep the sections balanced by admitting equal numbers of free and slave states to the Union and also by dividing the vast western territories (from which most future states would be carved) into free and slave portions. Division of the territories was done by an 1820 law, commonly called the Missouri Compromise. The law drew a line on the map westward from the Mississippi River—at 36 degrees, 30 minutes north latitude—between a southern portion where slavery was allowed and a northern part where slavery was banned.[14]

The Supreme Court decided dozens of slavery cases, usually involving an individual's claim for freedom. These cases attracted little attention, perhaps because almost all of them supported the slave owner and denied freedom.[15]

Expanding travel and commerce, however, brought growing friction between free and slave states over fugitive slaves. Moreover, the 1830s saw the rise of the abolition movement in the North, led by William Lloyd Garrison's first issue of his antislavery newspaper *The Liberator* in 1831. Nat Turner's slave rebellion in Virginia in the same year stoked fear in white southerners, slaveholder and non-slaveholder alike. One reaction by the slave states was to stiffen existing eighteenth-century laws against teaching enslaved people to read or write, with violators subject to prison (white people) or whipping (free African Americans).[16]

The free and slave states' seemingly easy coexistence was beginning to fray. By the late 1830s the US Congress was receiving myriad petitions to abolish slavery. Senator John C. Calhoun of South Carolina, a former vice president, orchestrated a "gag rule" to stop the flood of antislavery petitions from pouring onto the Senate floor. His friend Henry Laurens Pinckney, of South Carolina, did the same in the House of Representatives. Even though many opposed this infringement of free speech in the US Congress, the gag rule continued from 1836 until 1844.[17]

In February 1837 Senator Calhoun orchestrated a colloquy on the Senate floor about whether slavery was good or evil. His fellow senator and slaveholder William Rives of Virginia gave the usual answer, echoing Washington, Jefferson, Madison, and others that slavery, while necessary, was "a misfortune, and an evil in all circumstances." Calhoun was ready: Slavery, he insisted, was "indispensable to the peace and happiness" of all, and the enslaved workers were in a much better position than were "low, degraded, savage" Africans. He concluded that slavery was "good—a positive good."[18]

The Supreme Court's Early Native American Cases

Before the Supreme Court was caught up in major slavery issues, it decided three important cases involving Native Americans in the 1820s and 1830s. These cases were not typical of race cases; instead, they involved issues of tribal sovereignty and disputes over treaties. Still, they were a forecast of how Native Americans would be treated thereafter.

The first occupants of the North American continent were the Native Americans, or American Indians, and from the beginning of white settlement they had an ambiguous relationship with the European colonists. Overwhelmingly, white settlers wanted the land occupied by the Natives. With state and national governments seemingly consumed by a determination to be rid of Native Americans, Supreme Court rulings could have done little to stem the tide. Nevertheless, the Court's rulings, for the most part, abetted the anti-Indian actions.

The Constitution said little about Native Americans, with only two references, one excluding "Indians not taxed" in the apportionment of seats in Congress and the other giving Congress power to regulate commerce "with the Indian tribes."[19]

Native American tribes were typically considered separate "nations," although not necessarily equivalent to European or other nations. The astute French observer of the early United States, Alexis de Tocqueville, sympathetically described "the Negro and the Indian" as "two unfortunate races."[20]

In 1823 the Supreme Court unanimously ruled that Native Americans had no real property rights to their ancestral land, particularly the fundamental right to sell and dispose of one's property. Two non-Native parties both claimed title to a certain piece of property, one based on purchase from a tribe and the other on a later purchase from the federal government. The Supreme Court ruled for the later purchaser, holding that the one who purchased from the tribe had bought nothing of value because the tribe did not own the land. Treating the Native Americans' status based on their long presence as something unimportant, the Court said, in *Johnson v. M'Intosh* (1823), that Europeans and their government, as discoverers and conquerors of the land, were the owners. In 1831 the Supreme Court refused to issue an injunction against the state of Georgia to prevent its taking Cherokee land to distribute to white citizens of the state. Analyzing Article III of the Constitution, which gives the Supreme Court jurisdiction over suits between a state and a "foreign State," the Court rejected the suit in *Cherokee Nation v. Georgia* (1831) because it said the Cherokee Nation was not a sovereign nation but only a "domestic, dependent nation," a ward of the federal government.

The next year, however, the Court took a different, bold, but ultimately futile step in ruling to limit states' power over Native American lands. In *Worcester v. Georgia* (1832), Georgia claimed authority to enter Indian land and arrest white missionaries who were there without a state license. This time the Court wrote that Indian nations were "distinct, independent political communities retaining their original natural rights." But the Court's seeming turnabout made no difference; Georgia ignored the ruling, and the national executive branch, instead of enforcing the order, sided with the state. President Andrew Jackson vehemently disagreed with the Court's *Worcester* decision, and wrote that the Supreme Court "cannot coerce Georgia to yield to its mandate."[21]

In his State of the Union address in 1829, President Jackson advised that Indians, for their own good, should "emigrate beyond the Mississippi." In 1830 Congress passed the Indian Removal Act in a close vote along sectional lines, with southerners voting overwhelmingly in favor and northerners voting overwhelmingly against (Davy Crockett was the only Tennessee congressman voting no). Senator Frelinghuysen of New Jersey asked, "Do the obligations of justice change with the color of the skin?" From 1831 through 1838, members of many Indian tribes migrated to public lands west of the Mississippi River. By 1838, however, about 16,000 Cherokees had refused all orders to leave, and the US Army then supervised the arrest of the remaining Natives and forced them into internment camps in Alabama and Tennessee. In June 1838 General Winfield Scott announced, "Georgia has been entirely cleared of red population." In October and November, poorly clad and carrying few provisions, most Cherokees walked to Indian Territory in Oklahoma. The death toll on this "Trail of Tears" was in the thousands. In all, about 47,000 Indians were resettled in the West, and white people appropriated millions of acres of land in the East.[22]

Later periods continued the pattern of Indian removal through Indian wars and treaties solemnly made and freely broken by the United States. Of course, the Native Americans were not a racial population in the ordinary sense, but were separate nations with competing claims to land and dominion. Few white people championed the Native American sovereignty that the Indians wanted. White people divided over extinction, migration west, and "Americanizing"—that is, making Indians adopt white culture and norms, with dire consequences for the first Americans.[23]

Thus far the young nation included three races of people—white, Black, and Indian, but the 1840s would soon add two more groups, Mexican and Chinese. The annexation of Texas (1845) and the Mexican-American War (1846–1848) added the Southwest and California, all formerly part of Mexico. The new population included many descendants of intermarriage between Europeans and Latin American natives (also called Indians). The new population, commonly called Mexican American (Latino/a), was not typically called a separate race but in many ways was treated as such.

In 1849 the California Gold Rush brought the first sizable number of Chinese people to the United States, followed in the 1860s by Chinese laborers who came to work on railroads, including the transcontinental railroad, completed in 1869. With the growing population of "Asiatics," as they were listed on the Census, tensions grew. Efforts to restrict this population began in California and intensified in the late nineteenth century into a full-scale federal anti-Asian regime.

Two Supreme Court Cases on Slavery

During the 1840s, growing agitation over slavery drew the Supreme Court into a pair of cases that highlighted the slavery clauses of the Constitution. The results in the two cases pointed in opposite directions—toward freedom in one case but toward slavery in the other—and showed the Supreme Court's broad latitude of choices in deciding cases and interpreting the Constitution and laws.

The first case, *The Amistad* (1841), began when the Spanish schooner *La Amistad* turned up in the waters off New London, Connecticut, in 1839. It carried about forty Black captives, mostly adult men, all speaking a language unrecognizable in Connecticut, a Black cabin boy speaking Spanish, and two Spanish-speaking white men. The white men, Jose Ruiz and Pedro Montez, claimed that the captives were their slaves. As the story was pieced together, the ship was on its way from Havana to another Cuban port when the captives rose up, killed the captain, and seized the ship. Ruiz and Montez were spared on their promise to sail the ship to Africa, which they presumably had no intention of doing. Somehow the ship blundered into northern waters—not Africa where the Black captives wanted to go, but also not a slave port, which was likely the goal of the two white survivors.[24]

A multitude of claims were filed in the local federal court. Ruiz and Montez claimed ownership of what they called their "merchandise." They argued that a treaty with Spain obligated the United States to return their property to them, and in this argument they were supported by the US federal government. The prisoners, besides being claimed by Ruiz and Montez, were charged with murder and piracy but insisted they were Africans entitled to be set free. They said they had been illegally kidnapped in Africa.

Amid all the claims, the case boiled down to one question: Where did the captives originate: Cuba or Africa? In Cuba by this time, as in the United States, domestic slavery was legal but international slave trading was not. Congress in 1820 made international slave trading punishable by death. So the *Amistad*'s prisoners could be slaves if they were really Cubans, but not if they had just been brought from Africa.[25]

This key factual issue involved Cuban government certificates. Ruiz and Montez presented certificates signed by the governor-general of Cuba attesting that the prisoners were slaves native to Cuba. A longtime resident of Cuba, however, testified that the governor-general's certificates could be had for a small price. Another witness was an African seaman who testified that the prisoners spoke no Spanish or English, only a West African language.

The lower court judge in Connecticut ruled that the captives were indeed from Africa, and so were not legally slaves. (The murder charges were dismissed because the acts took place on the high seas, not in Connecticut.) Then in an extraordinary step, the federal government itself appealed to the Supreme Court, where it argued that the treaty with Spain required return of the human cargo to Ruiz and Montez. Former president John Quincy Adams joined in presenting the case for the prisoners' freedom.

Justice Joseph Story of Massachusetts wrote the Supreme Court opinion, which embraced lofty principles. Story said the case involved the "equal rights of all foreigners," so it must be decided "on the eternal principles of justice," especially "where human life and human liberty are at issue." Against this background, the Supreme Court said the evidence was "cogent and irresistible" and "beyond controversy" that the prisoners "are natives of Africa, and were kidnapped there, and were unlawfully transported to Cuba." The Court brushed aside the governor-general's certificates, assuming (or pretending) he was honest but that the certificates had obviously been obtained by fraud. As to the prisoners' violent uprising and killing of the ship's captain, he said, "We may lament the dreadful acts, by which they asserted their liberty, and took possession of the Amistad, and endeavored to regain their native country; but they cannot be deemed pirates or robbers." Story's opinion concluded, "These negroes ought to be deemed free, [with] no obstacle to the just assertion of their rights."[26]

This case was a landmark Supreme Court victory for freedom. The Court could easily have chosen to accept the validity of the governor-general's certificates—the official record of a foreign government—especially when urged to do so by the US government. The Spanish minister, Chevalier de Argaiz, was appalled at the idea that the captives might have rights in court. Why, he wondered, did the US government not "interpose its authority to put down the irregularity of these proceedings"?[27]

The Court's solicitude for the Africans appears to have been more a part of the highly compartmentalized national consensus against the international slave trade, and less a reflection of any skepticism regarding the institution of slavery. The *Amistad* case demonstrated the potential of the Court to make choices and rule for freedom, but it would be followed by very few successful Supreme Court outcomes for Africans or African Americans for the next seventy years.

The following year the Supreme Court faced the explosive issue of fugitive slaves in *Prigg v. Pennsylvania* (1842). As in the *Amistad* case, a certificate issued (or, in this case, not issued) by a government official was an important concern. But in this case the Supreme Court ruled against freedom.[28]

The fugitive slave clause of the Constitution was one of the agreements at the heart of the document, critical for the formation of the Union. The words of the clause in the Constitution were general, simply providing that a fugitive who escaped into a free state did not become free but "shall be delivered up on claim of the [slave owner]." Congress soon adopted the Fugitive Slave Act of 1793 to specify procedures for returning fugitive slaves. One section of the Act required that anyone who captured a supposed fugitive must obtain a judge's certificate (verifying the fugitive's identity and ownership) before removing the fugitive from the state.

The issue grew more controversial as more enslaved people tried to escape to freedom and northern opposition to "slave-catching" began to mount. Northerners accused southerners of invading northern states to kidnap free Black residents; southerners complained that northerners, in violation of the constitutional bargain, obstructed their efforts to recapture actual fugitives. In the 1820s some northern states began passing "personal liberty laws," with various protections (northern view) or obstructions (southern view). At one extreme were southerners who thought a mere statement was enough to establish their ownership; at the other extreme were northerners like the judge who, when asked what proof was needed to show that a captive was indeed a fugitive, reportedly responded, "a bill of sale signed by God Almighty Himself."[29]

Supreme Court involvement came through a case that unfolded along the Mason-Dixon Line, which formed the border between slave Maryland and free Pennsylvania. The sparse history suggests that a young woman named Margaret, although enslaved by a Maryland planter, John Ashmore, seems to have lived and worked essentially on her own. She married Jerry Morgan, a free African American from Pennsylvania, and went into the history books as Margaret Morgan. The couple lived without incident for a dozen years, and at some point they and their children migrated a few miles over the border into York County, Pennsylvania. Several years later their quiet existence came to an end when John Ashmore's widow asked a local man, Edward Prigg, to go to Pennsylvania and bring Margaret Morgan back to slavery in Maryland.

Prigg seized Margaret Morgan in Pennsylvania and took her before a justice of the peace. What happened then is uncertain, but Prigg did not get the certificate. Instead of finding another judge (which might have been difficult), he simply took Morgan and her children back to Maryland and slavery. With that action, Pennsylvania law came into play. Pennsylvania had a "personal liberty law" making it a crime to capture any "negro or mulatto" for the purpose of taking him or her into slavery, unless there was a certificate.[30]

Because the federal Constitution and the federal statute called for returning fugitive slaves, there was a question whether Pennsylvania's law—like other state personal liberty laws—was in harmony or in conflict with the federal statute and the federal Constitution. If the state and federal provisions were in conflict, the federal provisions would win, because Article VI of the Constitution (the supremacy clause) makes the federal Constitution and federal laws "the supreme law of the land."

To help resolve the issue, Maryland agreed that Prigg would return to Pennsylvania for a trial, and Pennsylvania agreed that if he were convicted he would not go to prison. It was a "test case," intended to seek a Supreme Court ruling on the controversial topic of personal liberty laws. Prigg came back for trial in Pennsylvania, was convicted, and appealed to the US Supreme Court.[31]

The Supreme Court thus had three provisions to consider: the federal Constitution with its general language requiring return of fugitives, the federal statute with its certificate provision, and the Pennsylvania law making it a crime to remove an African American for slavery without a certificate.

In *Prigg v. Pennsylvania* the Supreme Court reversed Prigg's conviction. The Court ruled that the federal Constitution authorized Prigg to remove Morgan. Pennsylvania's law was invalid because it punished Prigg for doing what the fugitive slave clause of the Constitution allowed him to do. Regarding the federal statute's certificate requirement that Prigg had ignored, the Court said that was irrelevant; the clause in the Constitution was enough "to execute itself, and to require no aid from legislation, state or federal." The seemingly mandatory provisions of the 1793 federal statute, according to the Court, were simply options that Edward Prigg and others could choose if they wanted judicial assistance, or could freely ignore as they pleased.

The majority opinion was written by Justice Story, the same man who gave a vigorous defense of freedom in the *Amistad* case. Here, however, Story gave a strong endorsement to the slaveholder's rights, saying this clause created "an unqualified, positive right on the part of the slaveholder, which no state law or regulation can in any way qualify, regulate, control or restrain."[32]

Justice John McLean of Ohio was a lone dissenter. In contrast to the majority, he said the federal statute was decisive. Its certificate requirement was a protection for freedom, designed to ensure that the right person was being taken away. According to McLean, because Prigg had not availed himself of the certificate procedure of the federal statute, he had no federal protection and therefore the Pennsylvania prosecution did not interfere with the federal law or the federal Constitution. In his dissent McLean said an enslaved person was not simply property: "The slave, as a sensible and human being," is subject to the law and "bears a very different relation to it from that of mere property."[33]

The opinions of Justices Story and McLean showed that the Court had a choice in this case. McLean treated the federal statute of 1793 as part of the constitutional bargain between the free states and slave states over fugitive slaves, while Story treated the federal statute, and of course any state liberty laws, as interference with the constitutional bargain. The choice made by the majority allowed a man to enter a free state and remove a Black person without seeking anyone's confirmation. Story may have thought he was preserving the constitutional bargain, but the Court's choice in *Prigg v. Pennsylvania* moved the balance far over in favor of the slave states.

The decision and language in *Prigg v. Pennsylvania* enraged many in the North. But there was also a bitter pill for southerners. In giving the federal government primacy over Pennsylvania, Justice Story said that only the federal government, not the states, could pass laws about the fugitives.

That rankled Chief Justice Roger Taney of Maryland. A fervent supporter of slavery, Taney objected that Story's opinion actually weakened enforcement. Taney's preference was a one-way rule: States should of course be barred from hindering the slavecatcher, as the *Prigg* case did, but should be free to pass laws facilitating the work of recapture without federal oversight.

Even with victory in the *Prigg* decision, the South was still embittered because enslaved people continued to escape and a growing abolition movement aided their endeavors. States across the South tightened their already rigid laws, aiming especially at white people, making it even harder to manumit (free) a slave. Southerners also began agitating for an even stronger federal law, which they finally achieved in the Fugitive Slave Act of 1850. It was this more draconian Fugitive Slave Act that struck the match to William Lloyd Garrison's copy of the Constitution on July 4, 1854.[34]

One feature of both Fugitive Slave Acts (1793 and 1850) was that they punished private individuals' misconduct, a provision that was repeatedly upheld by the Supreme Court. The fugitive slave clause of the Constitution, like other sections of Article IV, imposed obligations only upon the states, but Congress implemented that clause with damages and criminal penalties for any person who interfered with the state's obligation to return a fugitive. The Supreme Court upheld this regulation of private conduct under both laws. In *Jones v. Van Zandt* (1847), an Ohio farmer who hid some escaping Kentucky fugitives in his wagon was ordered to pay damages to their owner. In *Ableman v. Booth* (1859), residents of Racine, Wisconsin, were prosecuted under the 1850 Act for freeing a fugitive from custody. In both cases the Supreme Court unanimously upheld Congress's remedy against private individuals. Congress's power to pass laws punishing private individuals was treated as perfectly unremarkable at that time.

Even as antislavery sentiment grew in the North, it represented a range of varying attitudes toward African Americans. Garrison, like many other abolitionists, favored equal justice for all. Much of the national sentiment against slavery, however, was based on antipathy to all African Americans, enslaved or free. Some "free" states (Illinois and Indiana) passed new constitutions that banned all Black people from entering. Prejudice prevailed even in Massachusetts, which abolished slavery in 1780 but still maintained racially segregated schools in the mid-nineteenth century. *Roberts v. Boston* (1849) is an example of amnesia about the longtime web of laws that divided the races and its view that prejudice was the norm. When Charles Sumner, future Massachusetts senator, argued that segregation would perpetuate "prejudice in public opinion," the Supreme Judicial Court of Massachusetts said: "This prejudice, if it exists, is not created by law and probably cannot be changed by law." (The Massachusetts legislature integrated the state's public schools six years later.)[35]

A Missouri Case

During these years, another slavery case was proceeding slowly through the court system. It started in the Missouri courts, brought by an African American couple. Born into slavery, the man was sold in the 1830s to army doctor John Emerson of St. Louis. The enslaved man spent about four years with Emerson at army posts in the free state of Illinois and the free Wisconsin territory. While in Wisconsin, he married an African American woman who had also been sold to Dr. Emerson. Eventually Dr. Emerson returned to Missouri, bringing the couple with him. When John Emerson died, the man tried to purchase freedom for his family, which now included two daughters, but Emerson's widow refused. On April 6, 1846, the man and his wife filed suit in the St. Louis Circuit Court, claiming that residence in free jurisdictions had established a right to freedom.

The couple's names were Harriet and Dred Scott.

The lower court in Missouri ruled in favor of the Scotts, affirming the state's precedent of "once free, always free." This principle, which held that a freed slave could not be re-enslaved, had been followed by the Missouri Supreme Court without exception in all eight cases raising that issue since Missouri became a state thirty-two years earlier. This time, however, when the slaveholder Eliza Irene Emerson, appealed to the Missouri Supreme Court, that Court had something new in mind.[36]

The Court began by recognizing that its previous cases had ruled in favor of freedom for those whose masters held them in slavery in territories or States in which the institution was prohibited. Then, suddenly, the Court changed direction and abandoned precedent simply in response to antislavery sentiment elsewhere: "Times are not now as they were when the former decisions on this subject were made." Some other states, the Missouri court lamented, had become possessed of "a dark and fell spirit in relation to slavery" that would lead to "the overthrow and destruction of our government." The Court overturned its previous cases and removed this path to freedom: "Under such circumstances it does not behoove the State of Missouri to show the least countenance to any measure which might gratify this spirit."[37]

One of the three judges, Missouri Chief Justice Hamilton R. Gamble, disagreed: "Times may have changed, public feeling may have changed, but principles have not and do not change; and, in my judgment, there can

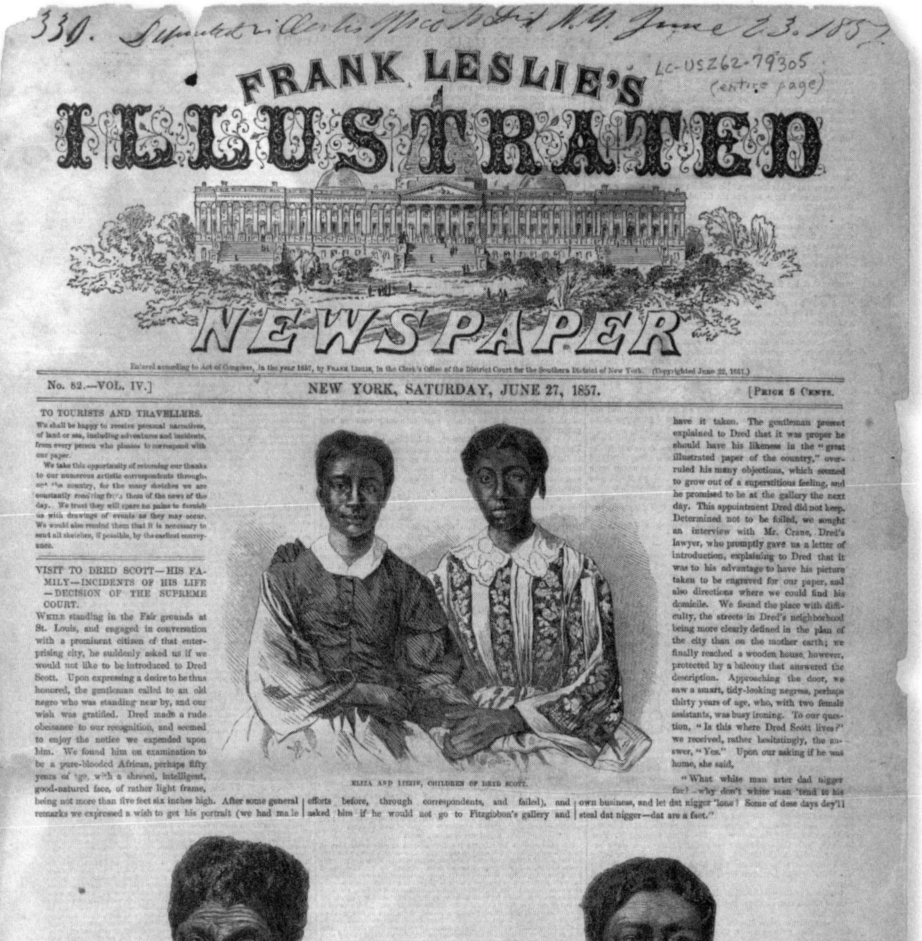

FRANK LESLIE'S ILLUSTRATED NEWSPAPER

Entered according to Act of Congress, in the year 1857, by Frank Leslie, in the Clerk's Office of the District Court for the Southern District of New York. (Copyrighted June 22, 1857.)

No. 82.—VOL. IV.] NEW YORK, SATURDAY, JUNE 27, 1857. [Price 6 Cents.

TO TOURISTS AND TRAVELLERS.

We shall be happy to receive personal narratives, of land or sea, including adventures and incidents, from every person who pleases to correspond with our paper.

We take this opportunity of returning our thanks to our numerous artistic correspondents throughout the country, for the many sketches we are constantly receiving from them of the news of the day. We trust they will spare no pains to furnish us with drawings of events as they may occur. We would also remind them that it is necessary to send all sketches, if possible, by the earliest conveyance.

VISIT TO DRED SCOTT—HIS FAMILY—INCIDENTS OF HIS LIFE—DECISION OF THE SUPREME COURT.

While standing in the Fair grounds at St. Louis, and engaged in conversation with a prominent citizen of that enterprising city, he suddenly asked us if we would not like to be introduced to Dred Scott. Upon expressing a desire to be thus honored, the gentleman called to an old negro who was standing near by, and our wish was gratified. Dred made a rude obeisance to our recognition, and seemed to enjoy the notice we expended upon him. We found him on examination to be a pure-blooded African, perhaps fifty years of age, with a shrewd, intelligent, good-natured face, of rather light frame, being not more than five feet six inches high. After some general remarks we expressed a wish to get his portrait (we had made efforts before, through correspondents, and failed), and asked him if he would not go to Fitzgibbon's gallery and have it taken. The gentleman present explained to Dred that it was proper he should have his likeness in the "great illustrated paper of the country," overruled his many objections, which seemed to grow out of a superstitious feeling, and he promised to be at the gallery the next day. This appointment Dred did not keep. Determined not to be foiled, we sought an interview with Mr. Crane, Dred's lawyer, who promptly gave us a letter of introduction, explaining to Dred that it was to his advantage to have his picture taken to be engraved for our paper, and also directions where we could find his domicile. We found the place with difficulty, the streets in Dred's neighborhood being more clearly defined in the plan of the city than on the mother earth; we finally reached a wooden house, however, protected by a balcony that answered the description. Approaching the door, we saw a smart, tidy-looking negress, perhaps thirty years of age, who, with two female assistants, was busy ironing. To our question, "Is this where Dred Scott lives?" we received, rather hesitatingly, the answer, "Yes." Upon our asking if he was home, she said,

"What white man arter dad nigger for?—why don't white man 'tend to his own business, and let dat nigger 'lone? Some of dese days dey'll steal dat nigger—dat are a fact."

ELIZA AND LIZZIE, CHILDREN OF DRED SCOTT.

DRED SCOTT. PHOTOGRAPHED BY FITZGIBBON, OF ST. LOUIS.

HIS WIFE, HARRIET. PHOTOGRAPHED BY FITZGIBBON, OF ST. LOUIS.

Harriet and Dred Scott and their daughters, Eliza and Lizzie, 1857.

be no safe basis for judicial decisions, but in those principles, which are immutable."[38]

By coincidence, an opportunity arose to start the suit over again in the lower federal court in Missouri, and they did so with a new suit in Dred Scott's name. The coincidence arose because Mrs. Emerson had transferred ownership of the Scott family to her brother, John Sanford, who happened to live in New York. Article III of the Constitution allows federal courts to hear cases "between citizens of different states," which then fit Scott's case because he (a person claiming Missouri citizenship) was then suing a citizen of New York. (An error by the clerk of court listed Sanford's name as "Sandford," and thus his name has remained through the ages.) Although it accepted jurisdiction, the federal court followed the Missouri Supreme Court's ruling leaving Scott enslaved. Scott appealed the lower federal court ruling to the US Supreme Court.[39]

Scott v. Sandford

Dred Scott v. Sandford (1857) is the most reviled case in Supreme Court history, and justly so. The case is universally condemned for its extreme pro-slavery dogma, for twisting the Constitution to incorporate that dogma, and for thereby aggravating sectional divisions and hastening the Civil War. It was also a shoddy piece of judicial workmanship, relying on false statements and fictitious constitutional doctrine.[40]

The Supreme Court in 1857 reflected the long Democratic Party dominance of the federal government. Seven of the nine justices were Democrats and supporters of slavery, including five who owned or had once owned slaves—Chief Justice Taney among them.[41]

Scott's case was entangled with the red-hot issue of slavery in the territories because one of his claims for freedom was based on his time living in the Wisconsin territory. The part of the Wisconsin territory where Scott had lived was designated as free by the line drawn in the Missouri Compromise of 1820. With growing tensions, Congress amended the Missouri Compromise in 1854, but its effort, the Kansas-Nebraska Act, did not relieve tension and even brought on a worse situation in "Bleeding Kansas."[42]

The *Dred Scott* case was argued in 1856; on March 4, 1857, as the Court's decision was awaited, the new president, James Buchanan, was inaugurated. In his inaugural address Buchanan referred to the controversial issue of slavery in the territories, but said that the issue was about to be decided by the Supreme Court. Then he promised, "To their decision, in common with all good citizens, I shall cheerfully submit, whatever this may be."[43]

Two days later, on March 6, 1857, the Supreme Court decision was handed down, ruling against Dred and Harriet Scott. It was almost as if James Buchanan was a seer, or had advance notice.

Well, not "almost." It turned out that President Buchanan had at least two pipelines that kept him informed of the Supreme Court's inner workings—Justice John Catron of Tennessee, and Buchanan's longtime Pennsylvania friend Justice Robert Grier. Buchanan urged Grier to vote with the southerners (which he probably would have done anyway) so the decision would be less of a sectional division.[44]

Chief Justice Taney wrote the majority opinion for the Court, but all nine justices wrote opinions, totaling more than 200 pages. Justices John McLean of Ohio (dissenter in *Prigg v. Pennsylvania*) and Benjamin Curtis of Massachusetts dissented on every issue. To decide the case, the justices needed only to rule on the one issue decided by the lower federal court, which was the same issue decided by the Missouri Supreme Court: Did Scott's residence in the free places of Illinois and the Wisconsin territory entitle him to freedom once he was returned to Missouri?

Precedent dictated following the Missouri Supreme Court's rule, but that court now had two different rules: The thirty-year rule of "once free, always free," and the new Dred Scott decision for slavery. The US Supreme Court also had two different precedents to choose between: Its general practice was to follow a state court's latest decision, but in some cases it had stood by a state court's long-established rule instead of a state court's sudden turnabout. Just a year earlier, a new Michigan state court turnabout had been rejected because the Supreme Court found it was based on "excited public opinion."[45]

Faced with these choices, the majority decided to follow the Missouri court's latest rule, which meant Dred and Harriet Scott remained in slavery. That should have been the end of the case, and if the Supreme Court had stopped there, the case would have attracted little attention. One justice, Samuel Nelson of New York, did stop there, and the internal evidence suggests that his was originally the majority opinion. When Justices McLean and Curtis drafted vigorous dissents, though, Taney and the other southerners responded with their far-reaching opinions.[46]

Instead of a limited decision, the Court chose to make two other momentous decisions: (1) that Scott was not a citizen of the United States because the entire Black race was in a condition so low that no African American, enslaved or free, could be or ever become a citizen of the United States, and (2) that the Wisconsin territory was not free because the Missouri Compromise of 1820 was unconstitutional because Congress had no power under the Constitution to ban slavery anywhere.

Citizenship and the Privilege of Suing in Federal Court

The issue of citizenship had been the basis of the federal court's jurisdiction. The lower court had followed the plain words of Article III of the Constitution, which allowed a citizen of Missouri (as Scott alleged he was because he claimed to be free) to sue a citizen of another state. That did not suit Chief Justice Taney, who insisted—with no support in the Constitution—that, even if Scott were a citizen of Missouri, citizenship of a state was different from citizenship "in the sense in which that word is used in the Constitution of the United States."[47]

Taney's low opinion of Africans *and* their descendants was nothing new. In 1832, as Andrew Jackson's attorney general, Taney had written, "The African race in the United States even when free, are everywhere a degraded class. . . . They were evidently not supposed to be included by the term *citizens*." Now, twenty-five years later, Taney was in a position to write his personal prejudices into the supreme law of the land.[48]

In the *Dred Scott* case, Taney's constitutional theory of African Americans' non-citizenship and non-eligibility rested on the low esteem, as he perceived it, in which the "civilized and enlightened portions of the world" held the entire African race:

> They had for more than a century before [the Declaration of Independence and Constitution] been regarded as beings of an inferior order, altogether unfit to associate with the white race, either in social or political relations; and so far inferior that they had no rights which the white man was bound to respect.[49]

Based on his low opinion of members of the race, and bolstered by the many laws discriminating against all African Americans, even in free states, Taney concluded that the delegates to the Constitutional Convention could not have meant them to be citizens of the United States. In an exercise of what some people today might call "originalism," Taney couched his opinion in historical terms, speaking his understanding of what the Framers were thinking when they wrote the Constitution.[50]

The written Constitution contained nothing to support his theory, but he made up some points that were simply not true. Specifically, he said the slave trade clause and fugitive slave clause of the Constitution singled out all members of the African race, but a simple reading of those clauses shows his statement was obviously false.

The four southerners and Justice Grier of Pennsylvania agreed with Chief Justice Taney. Justice Curtis's dissent, however, skewered Taney's misstatements and noted that in several states, including the slave state of North Carolina, free Blacks had been citizens and voters, and had voted on ratification of the Constitution. Curtis said it was plain that "under the Constitution of the United States, every free person born on the soil of a State, who is a citizen of that State by force of its Constitution or laws, is also a citizen of the United States."[51]

What led Taney to fill twenty-five pages establishing that Dred Scott was not a citizen? Under the Constitution, "citizenship" brings certain "privileges," but the relatively minor "privilege" of suing in federal court was surely not important enough to cause Taney such concern. The answer seems to lie in *other* "privileges and immunities" that Article IV of the Constitution gives to citizens of one state traveling in all the states. Taney openly expressed his fear that if free Black people were citizens, their "privileges and immunities" would give them "the right to enter every other state whenever they pleased, singly or in companies, without pass or passport," "to go where they pleased at every hour of day or night," "full liberty of speech in public and in private," "to hold public meetings on political affairs, and to keep and carry arms wherever they went." All these rights the slave states denied to African Americans, enslaved or free. Taney meant to keep it that way, and the Supreme Court majority agreed.

The Missouri Compromise

The "no citizenship" ruling should have led the Court to go no further. But the Court placed the Missouri Compromise itself on the agenda—just as President Buchanan had known when he gave his inaugural address two days before the Supreme Court's decision.

The territory where Scott had lived was north of the Missouri Compromise no-slavery line. Some southern extremists had previously argued that Congress had no power to ban slavery anywhere, but these voices had largely gone silent after passage of the Missouri Compromise in 1820. Now, nearly forty years later, the Supreme Court took up their cause and destroyed the entire Missouri Compromise with a ringing declaration that "the only power conferred [on Congress by the Constitution] is the power coupled with the duty of protecting the owner in his right."[52]

Chief Justice Taney said, correctly, that a statute, such as the Missouri Compromise, could not violate a person's constitutional rights, for example, freedom of religion. Then he pointed to the Fifth Amendment, a constitutional provision that says no law of Congress may deprive any person "of life, liberty or property without due process of law." According to Taney, a slaveholder had an absolute right to take his slaves, *like any property,* into a territory, so a law that stopped him was depriving him of his property.

But Taney ignored that the Supreme Court had already said slaves were *not* like other property. In *Prigg v. Pennsylvania* (the fugitive slave case), the Court had said: "The state of slavery is deemed to be a mere municipal regulation, founded upon and limited to the range of the territorial laws." Many states could and did keep slaves out, something they could not have done if the slaveholder's property right in slaves allowed him to take them anywhere. It was not only free states that kept slaves out, but some slave states, like Virginia and Mississippi, also barred anyone from bringing enslaved workers into that state. (The Fifth Amendment of the Constitution did not apply to states, but virtually all states had similar provisions in their own constitutions, subject to rulings of their own state courts.)[53]

Taney had another problem. The first Congress had passed a law that outlawed slavery in a territory, the Northwest Ordinance. If the Northwest Ordinance was valid, as all justices, including Taney, agreed, the Missouri Compromise must be valid too. Taney's answer was simply bizarre. The Northwest Ordinance had been enacted under Article IV of the Constitution, which authorizes Congress to "make all needful rules and regulations respecting the territory or other property belonging to the United States." According to Taney, that clause applied only to the Northwest Territory and then stopped working, so it applied to no other territory acquired later. Justices McLean and Curtis demolished Taney's specious wordplay about the Missouri Compromise, but he had the votes, and the Missouri Compromise was gone.[54]

The rulings were illogical. Nevertheless, in a single case, the Supreme Court held that no Black person could ever be an American citizen, and no Congress could ever stop slavery from spreading everywhere. This was the first act of Congress in fifty years to be declared unconstitutional (since *Marbury v. Madison,* 1803).

The *Dred Scott* case has been recognized as infamous for the words that African Americans "had no rights which the white man was bound to respect." Although Chief Justice Taney presented this merely as historical observation, these words were the cornerstone on which Taney built his constitutional doctrine, the unprecedented deed of squarely fastening race discrimination—a color line, not just a slave line—into the Constitution, where it had never been. Instead, the Supreme Court declared in explicit words that the "blessings of liberty" promised by the Preamble to the Constitution were somehow denied to all those of African descent, even if born free of free parents.[55]

Aftermath

The Scotts had lost their case, meaning that Dred and Harriet Scott and their two children were to remain enslaved. Before the case went to the Supreme Court, the widow Mrs. Emerson had married an outspoken abolitionist from Massachusetts, Dr. Calvin Chaffee. When the case became famous, Dr. Chaffee was surprised to learn that his wife had once owned the Scotts. After the Supreme Court decision, Mrs. Chaffee's brother John Sanford sold Dred and Harriet and their two daughters to the Blow family in St. Louis, the family which had brought the enslaved Dred Scott to Missouri years earlier. The Blows then granted freedom to the Scott family on May 26, 1857. Dred Scott died the next year from tuberculosis, but Harriet Scott lived free until she died in 1876 at the age of sixty-one. She lived long enough to see ratification of the Fourteenth Amendment in 1868, which declared that she and every other Black person born in this country were citizens of the United States of America.[56]

Dred Scott jolted national politics. Garrison called the decision "infamous and tyrannical," and Horace Greeley's *New York Tribune* declared it "entitled to just so much moral weight as would be the judgment of a majority of those congregated in any Washington barroom." The new Republican Party was energized; Democrats splintered. More moderate northern Democrats, led by Stephen Douglas of Illinois, tried to hold the party together, but southern Democrats now rejected any compromise. When hard-liners stormed out of the 1860 Democratic nominating convention in rejection of the party platform, one South Carolina delegate announced: "Slavery is our King; slavery is our Truth; slavery is our Divine Right."[57]

In the presidential election of 1860, Republican Abraham Lincoln faced Douglas and two other opponents, and he won the election with 40 percent of the popular vote, with no votes recorded in the nine southern states where the Republican Party was not even on the ballot.

On March 4, 1861, four years to the day after James Buchanan featured the *Dred Scott* case in his inaugural address, Abraham Lincoln was sworn in as the sixteenth president of a nation in which seven states (soon to be eleven) had already committed to secession. Six weeks later the state of South Carolina opened fire on Fort Sumter, a federal facility in Charleston. If the Supreme Court majority had thought its pro-slavery decisions resolved all disputes over slavery, that notion exploded in civil war.

CHAPTER TWO

A New Birth of Freedom

At a cost of more than 700,000 dead and far more maimed or wounded, the Civil War held the United States of America together and ended slavery. The end of slavery was an assertion of freedom, but debate about the meaning of that freedom continued. Was it just the uprooting of chattel bondage, or full first-class citizenship with an end to race discrimination, or something in-between? The debate unleashed by emancipation continues today.[1]

In 1864 President Abraham Lincoln spoke to a group in Baltimore about differing notions of freedom. As was his custom, he told a simple story:

> The shepherd drives the wolf from the sheep's throat, for which the sheep thanks the shepherd as a liberator, while the wolf denounces him for the same act as the destroyer of liberty, especially as the sheep was a black one. Plainly the sheep and the wolf are not agreed upon a definition of the word liberty.[2]

Lincoln professed that freedom meant aiming for equality. In his Gettysburg Address in 1863, midway through the war, he promised "a new birth of freedom" for a nation "conceived in liberty and dedicated to the proposition that all men are created equal." The words "all men are created equal" were only in the Declaration of Independence; if freedom were to have a new birth, the US Constitution would have to be brought into line. The decade following the war witnessed freedom for Black Americans and a redefinition of the role of the national government as a protector of liberty.[3]

Before the Civil War, the US Constitution, particularly the Bill of Rights, protected the people from the national government, but hardly at all from the states. The First Amendment, for example, did not fully protect freedom of speech and freedom of religion, but only protected them against the national government ("Congress shall make no law . . .").

For protection from the states, the people had to look to the states themselves. That may have suited a Thomas Jefferson or James Madison, who were part of the group that controlled their state governments. Many others, however, knew that a state could be as tyrannical as any other government. States were not necessarily trustworthy protectors, especially of African Americans, enslaved or free, and anyone allied with them.

Three amendments to the US Constitution in five years redefined personal freedom in the United States. Often called the Reconstruction Amendments or the Civil War Amendments, they also ensured that personal freedom would be protected by the national government. The Thirteenth Amendment outlawed slavery and decreed universal freedom throughout the land. The Fourteenth Amendment granted citizenship and accompanied it with sweeping federal protections against the states—privileges and immunities, due process, and equal protection. The Fifteenth Amendment granted the right to vote without regard to race—for men, anyway. To emphasize the force of the new provisions, all three new amendments added clauses specifying that "Congress shall have power to enforce." Congress was thus clothed with power to eliminate every badge and incident of slavery, and to make real the grand rights and privileges conferred by the amendments. This alteration in the constitutional role of the states and the national government was revolutionary, a transformation of a core American belief in the need to limit federal governmental power. It was a transformation that many, including some justices on the Supreme Court, were unwilling to accept.

The three amendments were backed up by more than thirty federal statutes enacted by Congress under these enforcement clauses, including laws relating to civil rights, physical security, judicial proceedings, elections, the Freedmen's Bureau, Reconstruction, and others. Four laws in particular were central: Civil Rights Act (1866), Enforcement Act (1870), Ku Klux Act (1871), and Civil Rights Act of 1875. With the three new amendments and the new laws, the original Constitution based on federal restraint and state authority was turned upside down. The new provisions imposed broad obligations on the previously near-autonomous states, and they clothed the national government with power to enforce those new obligations. These amendments and laws did not spring at once from a single grand design, but proceeded one by one, as defiant opponents revealed the limitations of each measure and showed Congress the next needed remedy. The sum was the new birth of freedom.

The cavalcade of amendments and laws from 1865 to 1875 produced a comprehensive structure of freedom, including provisions for racial equality in public and private matters, guarantees of fairness in legal and judicial proceedings, federal protection against public or private invasion of the new guarantees, and—central to all—the right to vote. Efforts to provide economic opportunity faltered, a serious flaw, but overall the various measures helped put four million freed people on an uncertain path toward full citizenship.[4]

And yet slavery's death did not automatically confer any positive rights upon African Americans. It liberated them from ownership by masters, eliminating at the same time the owners' motive for some degree of self-interested concern for their property. Whether the end of slavery would bring economic, political, or social equality was the subject of the events of 1865–1875.[5]

Many areas in the South, especially where battles were fought, were ravaged. White people were poor and Black people were poorer. Yet African Americans, starting from a state of almost universal landlessness and illiteracy, began a steady march of advancement. Countless thousands of former slaves set out to find lost kin and loved ones and to seek employment opportunities. Newly freed people flocked to schools, often taught by northern missionaries. Some African Americans moved to towns and cities, where those with skills opened shops or worked as independent craftsmen. Most, however, had no choice but to work on white-owned land as tenants, sharecroppers, or field hands.

Economic freedom had to come with fair political treatment. A North Carolina minister described his goals: "First, the right to testify in courts of justice; Secondly, representation in the jury box; Third and finally, the black man should have the right to carry his ballot to the ballot box."[6]

Those who had previously ruled the South almost universally thought otherwise, but at the end of the war they no longer were in charge.

Thirteenth Amendment

The bedrock of the new birth of freedom was the Thirteenth Amendment—the end of slavery in the United States. Although the Emancipation Proclamation, issued on January 1, 1863, had struck a blow for freedom, a constitutional amendment was still needed. The Supreme Court might rule that the Emancipation Proclamation was only a wartime measure that would expire after the war. Beyond that, the Emancipation Proclamation applied only to the states under Confederate control and thus did not cover those people enslaved in states that stayed loyal to the United States, or were already under control of the US Army. And it might not pertain to states that would join the Union in the future.[7]

The Thirteenth Amendment was approved in the Republican-dominated Senate in early 1864, by the constitutionally required two-thirds vote. The amendment was sent to the House of Representatives where Republicans did not have two-thirds of the seats, and Democrats opposed the amendment. Republicans all supported the end of slavery, though they ranged over a spectrum from those who favored limited rights, to those who believed in full equality (and were called "Radical" for that reason). In a near-party-line vote, the amendment fell thirteen votes short of the two-thirds needed. The amendment was brought up again in the House during the lame-duck session following the 1864 elections, and this time, on January 31, 1865, it succeeded with 119 votes in favor and 56 opposed; three votes the other way would have meant defeat. The amendment had solid Republican support plus a handful of Democrats whose "aye" votes were secured by President Lincoln's political maneuverings. The vote sent the proposed Thirteenth Amendment to the states for ratification.[8]

Lincoln celebrated with a group in the White House and proclaimed the amendment a "cure for all the evils." The *New York Times* wrote that passage of the Thirteenth Amendment transformed the United States into "what it has never been hitherto, thoroughly *democratic—resting on human rights as its basis*." In jubilation over the passage, Representative George Julian of Indiana wrote in his diary: "Members joined in the shouting and kept it up for some minutes. Some embraced one another, others wept like children. I have felt, ever since the vote, as if I were in a new country." And indeed, he was.[9]

The proposed amendment was personally signed by President Abraham Lincoln before it went to the states. The amendment has two sections:

> Section 1. Neither slavery nor involuntary servitude, except as a punishment for crime, whereof the party shall have been duly convicted, shall exist within the United States, or any place subject to their jurisdiction.
>
> Section 2. Congress shall have power to enforce this article by appropriate legislation.

This was the first time the Constitution was amended in sixty years and only the fourth time in all. The amendment instantly freed 12 percent of the population. The "crime" got little attention, though more so in recent times. Instead, attention focused on the instant freedom of the enslaved people. And yet, instantaneous freedom did not by itself transform the lives of the freedmen or eradicate long-ingrained disabilities and discrimination. That was the message of Section 2, the enforcement clause. The clause, strictly speaking, was unnecessary because Article I of the Constitution already gave Congress the power to pass laws "necessary and proper" for carrying out the federal government's functions. Nevertheless, the eleven words of the enforcement section in the Thirteenth Amendment reflected the changed role of the federal government in securing citizen rights. It also anticipated legislation to fill in the details of the new order—including the eradication of the badges and incidents of slavery.

The promise of freedom shone brightly in those early months of 1865. In mid-January, General William T. Sherman, climaxing his March to the Sea, issued Field Order No. 15, with the approval of President Lincoln, setting aside lands in and near the Sea Islands for settlement in forty-acre plots exclusively by "the negros now made free by the acts of war and the proclamation of the President of the United States." Earlier than that, in November 1861, federal troops had occupied the Sea Island area around Beaufort and Port Royal, South Carolina. The success of the expedition was aided by intelligence from enslaved people living in the area. Planters and other white residents fled, leaving behind their land and 10,000 people still legally enslaved, who continued growing cotton, now on their own behalf. Volunteer teachers and others came from the North to open schools and provide other facilities. Historian Willie Lee Rose christened this Port Royal Experiment a "rehearsal for reconstruction."[10]

In 1861 Congress passed the first income tax to finance the war. In 1862 Congress imposed a direct tax on land in the "insurrectionary" states to make up for tax money that states owed the United States—including the income tax and tariff collections—but which the Confederate states were obviously not paying. When the landowners did not pay, Congress authorized the usual procedure—seizure and public sale of the land. On the Sea Islands, more than 100,000 acres were seized and sold, much of it in twenty-acre parcels to "heads of families of the African race." Between the tax sales and General Sherman's order, more than 40,000 freed men and women eventually lived on 485,000 acres, some with tax deeds and others with "possessory titles" granted by Sherman's order. On March 3, 1865, the outgoing Thirty-Eighth Congress created the US Bureau of Refugees, Freedmen and Abandoned Lands (the "Freedmen's Bureau"), opening additional abandoned, confiscated, and other public land for settlement by freedmen and their families, as well as authorizing temporary shelter and supplies for the newly freed people—as well as other needy people (meaning white people) who had stayed loyal to the Union.[11]

The next day, March 4, 1865, Lincoln began his second term, with an inaugural address promising both healing for the nation ("malice toward none, charity for all") and justice for the African American ("the bondsman's two hundred fifty years of unrequited toil"). A month after that, on April 9, 1865, the promise of the future all came within reach when the war effectively ended with General Lee's surrender to General Grant at Appomattox. By that time, the Thirteenth Amendment had been ratified by twenty states (including four from the former Confederacy) of the twenty-seven needed to make it part of the Constitution and radically change that venerable document of 1787.[12]

Freedom for the former slaves was a new venture, but it had hopeful prospects. Recognizing the urgency of the times, "now if ever," the *Weekly Anglo African* warned that "a century may elapse before another opportunity shall be afforded for reclaiming and holding our withheld rights." Some white southerners were willing to accept the political change, and many just wanted to get on with their disrupted lives. Some joined the Republican Party along with almost all of the freedmen. Opposing voices were weak and disorganized. The rebel states were defeated and in disarray. Secessionist and Confederate leaders had no effective power. Many feared being tried, and even hanged, and some had fled the region or the country. Opponents of freedom also had no useful allies in the North, with Democrats wielding almost no power in Washington. President Lincoln enjoyed vast postwar popularity as "Father Abraham," and Republicans held overwhelming majorities in both houses of Congress, with big victories in the 1864 elections and no southern states represented. The Supreme Court had changed too, with five Lincoln appointments.[13]

Presidential Reconstruction—Abraham Lincoln

President Lincoln did not formulate a detailed Reconstruction plan, but he was clear on the necessary direction for reconstructing the nation. Lincoln was determined not to squander the war victory and to do whatever was necessary to achieve real freedom for the people newly freed. One essential element was preserving order. Lincoln would undoubtedly have vigorously, even ruthlessly, suppressed the outbreaks of disorder like the white riots of 1866 in New Orleans and Memphis. Another essential element was selecting good appointees. They should be people who had been loyal to the Union and who shared his goals for the nation and the freedmen.[14]

Political appointments matter. Perhaps his highest-level appointment came when Roger Taney died in late 1864 and Lincoln replaced him with the famed abolitionist Salmon P. Chase as the nation's new chief justice. One of Chase's earliest acts was to preside when Senator Sumner introduced John Rock as the first Black attorney to qualify for practice before the highest court. *Harper's Weekly* called it "a remarkable indication of the revolution which is going on in the sentiment of a great people." Lower-level appointments also matter, often more so, in the actual lives of people, and Lincoln's appointments at all levels demonstrated this. In 1863 Lincoln, through Salmon P. Chase (then secretary of the Treasury), appointed three people to the critical posts of tax commissioner for the area around Beaufort, South Carolina: Rev. William Brisbane, Judge William E. Worthy, and Judge Abram Smith. Brisbane, a local man, had been a wealthy slave owner and pro-slavery writer, but after long study he had turned strongly against slavery. Worthy was a South Carolina teacher and lawyer before moving to Racine, Wisconsin, where he became a judge. Smith, also a Wisconsin judge, led the Wisconsin Supreme Court in declaring the Fugitive Slave Law of 1850 unconstitutional (mainly for lack of a fugitive's right to jury trial) before that decision was reversed in an opinion by Chief Justice Taney. These commissioners were instrumental in carrying out land reform in the Sea Islands as they secured land titles for African American families.[15]

Two days after Lee's surrender, Lincoln delivered a speech from the White House balcony and spoke about "some new announcement for the people of the South." One listener to this speech, John Wilkes Booth, understood where Lincoln was leading the nation. He told his companion, "That means Nigger citizenship. Now, by God, I'll put him through. That is the last speech he will ever make." And it was. The course of history was changed by a gunshot that killed Abraham Lincoln on April 15, 1865, six days after Lee's surrender.[16]

Lincoln's successor was former senator Andrew Johnson of Tennessee, a Democrat who had been added to the Republican ticket in 1864 as a "unity" measure. It proved a fateful choice. The two men had very different views, especially about the South and about African Americans and their freedom. The Lincoln phase of Reconstruction was over; the new Johnson phase of Reconstruction would fundamentally change the nation's direction and history. Most immediately, it dashed the bright promise of the Thirteenth Amendment as a promise of equality and first-class citizenship, not just formal freedom.

Presidential Reconstruction—Andrew Johnson

The new president wasted little time in showing that his plan for Reconstruction envisioned the rebel states quickly being readmitted to the Union. Johnson vigorously opposed slavery, but, except for the formal abolition of slavery, states would look very much like their prewar selves. He pressed four southern states to ratify the Thirteenth Amendment and thus reached the needed total of twenty-seven states in December 1865. Like other Democrats, however, he believed this was a white man's country. For Johnson, the work of the Thirteenth Amendment was done when the bonds of ownership were broken and the former slaves "achieved" mere second-class status—no more for them and no more for the Thirteenth Amendment. The advent of Andrew Johnson spelled the end of any consensus of the Thirteenth Amendment as a provision capable of dismantling the badges of slavery in their broadest meaning. With President Johnson leading the chorus against equality, the Thirteenth Amendment became an object of conflict and division rather than a pathway forward.

President Johnson quickly began reversing Lincoln's policies. His terms for readmitting the rebel states to the United States were few: ratify the Thirteenth Amendment and amend their own state constitutions accordingly, repeal the secession ordinance, and repudiate Confederate war debt. Johnson quickly began issuing pardons restoring full status, including the right to vote, to secessionist leaders, Confederate officeholders and military officers, and other supporters of the rebel war effort. He directed speedy organization of provisional governments in the South, directing them to hold elections with voter lists based on eligibility as of 1861, thus foreclosing any possibility that they might consider Black suffrage.

Johnson also turned back land reform. After the war, Confederates who had abandoned their land while many of them were bearing arms against the national government wanted their land back. Much of the land, including that covered by General Sherman's Field Order No. 15, was held by "possessory" titles, not formal "deeds." Andrew Johnson gave it back, dispossessing tens of thousands of freedmen, including many who had served in the US Army. In one poignant event, Johnson dispatched General O. O. Howard, head of the Freedmen's Bureau, to a meeting of freedmen at Edisto Island, South Carolina, where some 40,000 acres were going back to the former slaveholding owners. When the crowd asked how their loyalty could be thus punished and secession rewarded, Howard was overcome: "My heart ached." He finally urged the group to send a petition to the government, which of course achieved nothing.[17]

At Port Royal, where many titles, based on formal tax sales, were clear, the former owners could not undo the sale of the land, but they tried to. In 1869 William J. de Treville sued to invalidate one of the Port Royal tax sales of 1863. The current owner of the property was the area's representative in the South Carolina General Assembly, formerly enslaved Robert Smalls. Smalls was a Union war hero. In 1862, while performing forced service on a Confederate ship, the CSS *Planter,* Smalls commandeered the ship, loaded aboard his family and others, and sailed out of Charleston harbor under the Confederates' noses and into Union lines. He became a Union naval officer and toured northern cities to promote the enlistment of African American soldiers in the war. In 1863 he bought the land in Beaufort that de Treville had lost for not paying the tax. De Treville's case went through many procedural steps, including moving from Beaufort to Charleston (on de Treville's plea that jurors in Beaufort would not be impartial because they held the same kind of tax titles). The case was tried in 1875, and a federal court jury (almost certainly biracial) upheld the sale. De Treville appealed to the US Supreme Court (*de Treville v. Smalls*). Four years later, in a dry-as-dust opinion, the Supreme Court upheld the tax sale, the constitutionality of the tax law itself, and the ownership of the property by Smalls, who by then was a US congressman. Even when Reconstruction ended, this legacy remained.

President Johnson, like Lincoln, knew that his appointments would shape Reconstruction, but his appointees as provisional governors were men whose loyalty had been to the Confederacy, not the United States, and who shared Johnson's racial views. For appointment as provisional governor, a petition from 1,456 African Americans in the Sea Islands of South Carolina recommended several white Carolinians, including tax commissioner Brisbane and General John C. Fremont, the Republican candidate for president in 1856. Instead Johnson appointed Benjamin F. Perry, who had served as legislator and judge in South Carolina's Confederate regime. Perry opposed racial equality, announcing, "This is a white man's government, and intended for white men only." In Alabama Johnson appointed as provisional governor Lewis E. Parsons, a Confederate military officer and legislator who presided over "a white man's government in Alabama." When a later governor suggested that Alabama ratify the Fourteenth Amendment as a prudent step that could restore the state's congressional representation, Parsons bitterly denounced him and went on a campaign—ultimately successful—to keep Alabama from taking such a step. It is uncertain whether men like these would have expressed such sentiments aloud while Lincoln was president, but Lincoln would surely not have appointed such men as their states' leaders. Johnson unleashed the bitter-enders, those who hated the North and the freed slaves, and he allowed them—indeed, led them—to express their bitterness and make it the dominant voice of a South that might otherwise have sought true reconciliation.[18]

Through the summer and fall of 1865, the former rebel states carried out minimal compliance, ending slavery primarily in name, barely in substance. One after another, they adopted forms of oppression that left the freedmen vulnerable and subject to legal disabilities and lethal violence. Former Confederate states passed repressive laws, known as "Black Codes" that, for instance, gave white employers the power to administer "moderate corporeal chastisement" (whipping). Traveling without a pass from one's employer was forbidden. In most states it became nearly impossible for African Americans to buy or rent land, to market their own produce, or to seek effective legal redress against white landlords.

More egregious rules were replicas of slave code clauses with the word "freedmen" substituted for "slaves." The system would bind Black workers to the land—uneducated, disfranchised, and impoverished. Mississippi declared that freedmen were not allowed to carry guns or ammunition or Bowie knives. Black workers were not able to quit a labor contract, and if a white person helped them do so, "he or she shall be guilty of a misdemeanor." In Florida, involuntary servitude was the punishment for vagrancy.[19]

In addition to the Black Codes, former Confederate states, fearful of the potential of Black citizenship, began efforts to thwart it. In North Carolina, whipping moved beyond the sadistic control measure of slavery to something with a political motive. Anyone whipped at the community whipping post was henceforth disqualified from voting. In the House of Representatives, Thaddeus Stevens denounced all such corporal punishment and affirmed that the reason for the whippings was "preventing these negroes from voting."[20]

The *Chicago Tribune* typified northern Republican outrage over the Black Codes: "We tell the white men of Mississippi that the men of the North will convert the state of Mississippi into a frog pond before they will allow any such laws to disgrace one foot of soil in which the bones of our soldiers sleep and over which the flag of freedom waves."[21]

Congressional Reconstruction

Congress had been out of session for the tumultuous events of 1865. Under the constitutional rules of that time (changed in 1933 by the Twentieth Amendment), the Thirty-Eighth Congress expired on March 3, 1865, and was not in session when Lee surrendered to Grant and when President

Lincoln was assassinated. The new Thirty-Ninth Congress did not convene until December 4, 1865, and between those dates President Andrew Johnson had free rein. In the new president's seven months without Congress, the nation saw him undermine the results of the war and saw the rebel states restore much of the Old Order.

When Congress convened late in 1865, it set to work undoing the handiwork of President Johnson and the rebel states. The former rebel states had largely selected former Confederate leaders to represent them in Congress, including South Carolina's Benjamin Perry, Alabama's Lewis E. Parsons, and Georgia's Alexander Stephens, former vice president of the Confederacy. Led by the overwhelming Republican majority in each chamber, the Thirty-Ninth Congress swiftly rejected every one of the rebel states' would-be senators and representatives. Then Congress created a Joint Committee on Reconstruction, joint between the House of Representatives and the Senate, and between two wings of the Republican Party, the radicals and the moderates. With co-chairs Rep. Thaddeus Stevens (radical) of Pennsylvania and Senator William Pitt Fessenden (moderate) of Maine, the Joint Committee began considering new laws for the new conditions. Stevens was a firm believer in absolute equality, and said that calling the United States "a white man's government" was "political blasphemy."[22]

The First Civil Rights Act—1866

The idea of freedom is a powerful engine. Whatever meaning the Thirteenth Amendment may have had when the House of Representatives debated it in January 1865, its contours were growing. State intransigence and private terrorism spurred Congress to pass new laws and propose new constitutional amendments for ratification by the states. Thus did the concept of freedom expand.

Congress took the first steps soon after the Thirteenth Amendment was ratified in December 1865. Reacting to the Black Codes, Congress began work on legislation to implement the new amendment and outlaw "badges and incidents" of slavery, a common term for slavery's vestiges. Senator Lyman Trumbull of Illinois set the tone with an opening speech in which he said the enforcement clause of the Thirteenth Amendment empowered Congress to "destroy all these discriminations in civil rights against the black man." According to Trumbull, "These are the rights which the first clause of the [13th] constitutional amendment meant to secure as well. . . . With the destruction of slavery necessarily follows the incidents to slavery." If the amendment did not do that, he said, "the silver trumpet of freedom we have been blowing throughout the land has an uncertain sound."[23]

A measure to enforce the Thirteenth Amendment—to blow that silver trumpet—was quickly introduced and passed by Congress in January 1866. Called the Second Freedmen's Bureau Bill because it extended the life of the Bureau, originally scheduled to expire one year after the war ended, the bill aimed at the Black Codes by prescribing an equal rights code for those states where "the ordinary course of judicial proceedings has been interrupted by the rebellion." In those states, denial on account of race of the "full and equal benefit of all laws" was made a federal crime, and jurisdiction in all such cases was taken away from those states' courts.[24]

President Johnson vetoed this first bill with a lengthy message complaining that the equal rights provision granted special privileges to the freedmen and that the bill singled out certain states. The vote in the Senate to override the veto was 30–18, two votes short of the required two-thirds. This was Johnson's first civil rights veto. He subsequently vetoed more than a dozen civil rights or civil-rights-related bills but never had another of those vetoes sustained.[25]

After the veto, Congress moved forward with two other initiatives: a general equal rights bill to enforce the Thirteenth Amendment, and a proposed Fourteenth Amendment to eliminate any possible questions about whether the Thirteenth Amendment gave Congress power to enact laws for equal rights and against race discrimination.

This new bill, mandating equal rights as an enforcement of the Thirteenth Amendment's ban on slavery, was passed by Congress promptly after the veto of the Second Freedmen's Bureau Bill. President Johnson vetoed the new bill too, but this time three Republican senators who had gone along with him on his first veto gave up on him. The Senate vote was 33–15, one vote more than needed to override his veto, and the House followed with an overwhelming vote along party lines, 122–41. With the veto overrides, the bill became law on April 9, 1866, as the Civil Rights Act. Only later, as more civil rights laws were passed, did it come to be called the Civil Rights Act of 1866.

During the remainder of President Johnson's term (which included his impeachment and acquittal), Congress passed other civil rights laws, almost always over his veto. Many of these laws were far-reaching, or became so in later times, but they have attracted less attention than the first one, the Civil Rights Act of 1866. Other major laws included the Anti-Kidnapping Act of 1866, the Anti-Peonage Act of 1867, the Habeas Corpus Act of 1867, and, of course, the Reconstruction Act of 1867 and its amendments.[26]

The Civil Rights Act of 1866 began with a landmark provision that "all persons born in the United States and not subject to any foreign power, excluding Indians not taxed, are hereby declared to be citizens of the United States." This section declared African Americans to be citizens of the United States, reversing the ruling in the 1857 *Dred Scott* case. The act put the principle of "birthright citizenship" into national law and severed citizenship from race—though not completely, because Native Americans would have to wait until 1924 for full citizenship.[27]

The 1866 act went on to guarantee to "citizens of every race and color" the "full and equal benefit of all laws" and protection against unequal "punishment, pains and penalties." The act applied these guarantees throughout "every State and Territory," not just the states formerly in rebellion. The new law backed up that promise of equality with a specific ban on racial discrimination in making and enforcing contracts, buying and selling property, and suing and testifying in court. To make this new equality enforceable, the law also gave federal courts jurisdiction over cases where "equal rights" might be denied in state courts; the new law even allowed such cases started in state court to be "removed" to federal court if necessary to enforce equal rights. Giving federal courts jurisdiction in these cases may not seem surprising today, when federal courts have jurisdiction over any case alleging a claim under federal law, but no such "federal question" jurisdiction existed until a later Reconstruction Congress created it in 1875. The Civil Rights Act of 1866 was the beginning of the process of expanding federal courts' jurisdiction, a process in keeping with the new federal focus of the Constitution.[28]

The constitutionality of the 1866 act was quickly challenged by an argument that its equality provisions and procedures went beyond Congress's power to enforce the Thirteenth Amendment's ban on slavery. A major challenge, *United States v. Rhodes* (1867), involved several white men in Nelson County, Kentucky, who were tried for "burglariously" breaking and entering into the home of Nancy Talbot, a Black woman. This garden-variety crime was tried not in the state courts of Kentucky but in a federal court with a federal prosecutor under a federal indictment. The federal court had jurisdiction granted by the Civil Rights Act of 1866 because Kentucky law did not allow an African American (like Nancy Talbot) to testify against a white person (like the burglars), so Talbot would be denied her equal right to testify if the case were tried in the Kentucky state court.[29]

This case was decided by Supreme Court justice Noah Swayne, Lincoln's first Supreme Court appointee, but it was not a Supreme Court precedent because he decided it as a lower court judge while "riding circuit" (as Supreme Court justices had to do until the late nineteenth century). Swayne's decision was a ringing affirmation of the broad reach of the new Civil Rights Act and of Congress's power to enforce the Thirteenth Amendment—that is, to eradicate the "badges" of slavery, one of which was being barred from testifying in court.[30]

The defendants argued that the 1866 act was unconstitutional. Swayne rejected that argument, relying on Congress's power to enforce the Thirteenth Amendment: "The constitution, thus amended, consecrates the entire territory of the republic to freedom, as well as to free institutions." Swayne catalogued many of the "mischiefs" of slavery, which were to be remedied. He described how "the shadow of the evil" did not fall only on slaves. Free Black men and women had few rights and wore "many of the badges of the bondsman's degradation." And any white person who might teach a Black person—slave or free—to read or write could be "punished with imprisonment or death." Swayne concluded that when the Thirteenth Amendment banned slavery, Congress's power to annul all these evil manifestations must be "necessary and proper" (Art. I, Sec. 8) and "appropriate" (Amend. 13, Sec. 2). He made it clear that the power granted by the Thirteenth Amendment was not merely to free people from bondage but to guarantee equality: "protection to all persons in their constitutional rights of equality before the law, without distinction of race or color, or previous condition of slavery or involuntary servitude."[31]

Justice Swayne's use of the term "badges of the bondsman's degradation" was familiar. Sometimes rendered as "badges and incidents of slavery" or "burdens and disabilities of slavery," and eventually "badges of slavery," it meant the practices or concepts that were associated with slavery and that remained even after the institution itself was formally abolished. Familiarity with the term still left disagreement over what those badges and incidents were and are. Were "badges and incidents of slavery" limited to those disabilities named in the Civil Rights Act of 1866—disabilities in contracts, property, suing, and testifying? Or did they extend to other acts of race discrimination prompted by generations of an inferior status supported by law?[32]

A year later, another Thirteenth Amendment case came to court, this time before Chief Justice Chase while he was sitting on the circuit court. In late 1864, before the Thirteenth Amendment was adopted, the state of Maryland approved a state constitutional amendment banning slavery. A practice immediately arose, however, of binding some newly emancipated children to be "apprenticed" back to their former owners by means of written "contracts" with their parents.

One such child, Elizabeth Turner of Maryland's Eastern Shore, was eight years old when she was freed on November 1, 1864. She was "apprenticed" back to her former owner two days later to serve until she was eighteen years old, to be taught "the art or calling of house servant." A relative filed a habeas corpus petition on her behalf in 1867, and it came before Chase as *In re Turner* (1867). Under Maryland law Black apprentices need not receive an education and could be transferred to any other person, whereas the laws of Maryland for white apprentices required that they be taught reading, writing, and arithmetic, and also prohibited their transfer. Chase held that the conditions of Elizabeth Turner's apprenticeship amounted to involuntary servitude, but even if not, the law discriminated on account of race. This discrimination violated the "full and equal benefit of all laws" command of the Civil Rights Act of 1866, which Chase held was valid legislation carrying out the Thirteenth Amendment.[33]

The two opinions by Chase and by Swayne were not decisions of the Supreme Court, but these lower court decisions provided a blueprint for interpreting the Thirteenth Amendment and Congress's Section 2 power as broad enough to dismantle every tentacle and vestige of slavery, and to mandate full racial equality in both public and private matters. Soon, however, the Thirteenth Amendment was overshadowed by the more specific commands of the Fourteenth Amendment. And when the Fourteenth Amendment suffered reversals and limitations, the Thirteenth Amendment was already in the shadows, treated as a onetime historical event rather than as the bright promise of an ongoing commitment of freedom and equality. Thus, the Thirteenth Amendment came to be interpreted as narrowly as Andrew Johnson insisted, rather than as broadly as Abraham Lincoln had dreamed.

Fourteenth Amendment

While Congress was enacting the Civil Rights Act in April 1866, it was also working on a new constitutional amendment, which Congress approved 33 to 11 (with 5 abstentions) in June 1866 and sent to the states for ratification as the Fourteenth Amendment. The heart of the amendment was Section 1, which began by repeating the citizenship provision of the Civil Rights Act, with slight rewording. The new wording left out the exclusion of "Indians not taxed" and, very importantly, specified that it conferred or confirmed both federal and state citizenship:

> Section 1: All persons born or naturalized in the United States and subject to the jurisdiction thereof, are citizens of the United States and of the State wherein they reside.

The same section of the amendment went on to guarantee federal protection of "privileges or immunities," "due process" and "equal protection":

> No State shall make or enforce any law which shall abridge the privileges or immunities of citizens of the United States;
> nor shall any State deprive any person of life, liberty, or property, without due process of law;
> nor deny to any person within its jurisdiction the equal protection of the laws.

Section 2 of the Fourteenth Amendment addressed voting rights indirectly, by reducing the number of a state's US representatives if that state denied voting rights "to any of the male inhabitants" otherwise eligible for suffrage. This was the first time "male" was inserted into the Constitution. Sections 3 and 4 were postwar measures, imposing disabilities on Confederate leaders and confirming the Union's war debt while barring states from paying Confederate war debts.

Section 5 was the now-familiar enforcement clause, giving Congress power to enforce the amendment by appropriate legislation.

The Fourteenth Amendment initiated a fundamental redistribution of authority in the United States and gave Congress the power to carry out that redistribution. The majority in Congress wanted the federal government to exhibit its "strong arm of power, outstretched from the central authority." The extent of a citizen's social, civil, and political rights remained open to debate, and the Supreme Court would be called upon to interpret such words of the Fourteenth Amendment as "privileges or immunities" and "due process of law" and "equal protection of the laws." Nevertheless, with the Fourteenth Amendment the Constitution now committed the power of the federal government to the equal extension of those rights.[34]

Congress sent the Fourteenth Amendment to the states, and by the end of 1867, twenty-two states had ratified the amendment, including the former Confederate state of Tennessee. That was six short of the required number of states. Ten states of the former Confederacy rejected the amendment or refused to take a vote. In reaction, Congressman James Garfield of Ohio (who would be president for a brief time in 1881 before being assassinated) declared that military authority was needed to "plant liberty on the ruins of slavery." Congress acted to realize equality before the law. If former Confederate states disagreed, Congress would force the issue.[35]

Over President Johnson's veto, Congress enacted the Reconstruction Act of 1867, putting ten states under federal military control. In addition to dividing the rebel states into five military districts, the Reconstruction Act directed that these states would not be readmitted to the United States until they ratified the Fourteenth Amendment. The Reconstruction Act also required each returning state to call a convention for which all adult males without regard to race could vote for delegates. That convention had to adopt a new state constitution providing for adult male suffrage without regard to race. Applauding the Reconstruction Act, Senator Charles Sumner, ardent supporter of African Americans' rights, thought the ballot would ensure African Americans' citizenship and effective protection against white supremacy. Believing suffrage would be "immortal," he wrote, "The right of suffrage once given can never be taken away."[36]

To prepare for the required state constitutional conventions, US military commanders took charge of registering all male voters to elect the convention delegates. African American men, most of them illiterate, responded overwhelmingly, many of them marching en masse to vote at the very spot where they had been whipped or sold. They cast ballots that would determine the political fate of their families, their fellows, and even their former masters. Louisiana was typical: approximately 90 percent of African American men of voting age registered to vote in 1867. In November 1867 in South Carolina, 80,832 African American men and 46,929 white men registered to vote. Across the South white people who thought the newly freed slaves would not bother voting were proved dramatically wrong.[37]

The newly adopted state constitutions, as required by the Reconstruction Act, all provided for universal male suffrage. These state constitutions, adopted in 1868 and 1869, provided free public school systems, homestead protection, and married women's rights, among others. The new state legislatures also ratified the Fourteenth Amendment, which became part of the Constitution on July 9, 1868. Once they adopted their new state constitutions and ratified the Fourteenth Amendment, a series of Readmission Acts in 1868–1870 restored these states to full status, including representation in the US Senate and House of Representatives.[38]

Fifteenth Amendment

At the outset of the Civil War, only six states in the nation, five of them in New England, permitted African Americans to vote. After the war, Congress had taken several steps toward Black voting: Section 2 of the Fourteenth Amendment (reducing representation for disfranchisement), and two 1867 laws granting African Americans the right to vote in the District of Columbia and in the US territories, and then the Reconstruction Act. The Reconstruction Act enfranchised most of the country's Black male population, but still in only a minority of the states. Extending the vote to African Americans in the other states seemed like a logical step.[39]

Part of the impetus for these measures was a belief that the best way to protect the results of the war (and to help the Republican Party) was to arm the new Black citizens with the ballot. Many Americans came to see African American voting both as a safeguard for African American freedoms and as a principle that should be enshrined in the Constitution. Senator John Sherman of Ohio articulated the view that the United States had to preserve freedom with "universal suffrage." Frederick Douglass, the most prominent Black leader of the nineteenth century, declared that the right to vote was "the keystone to the arch of human liberty."[40]

In 1867 the Democratic Party made significant gains in northern states and helped reject Black enfranchisement in several states. Then in the presidential election of 1868, the war hero Ulysses S. Grant defeated the Democrat Horatio Seymour of New York, who had beaten an unrepentant Andrew Johnson for the Democratic nomination. The election of President Grant gave new impetus to enfranchising African Americans outside the South. In 1868 Iowa Republicans, who had lost two attempts to extend the franchise to African Americans, tried again, enlisting President Lincoln's words calling for "a fair start and an equal chance in the race of life." General Grant, as the Republican presidential candidate, called on Lincoln's legacy to urge Iowa, "the bright Radical star," to grant suffrage to its Black citizens. Iowa met Grant's challenge, and so did Minnesota, which had also rejected Black enfranchisement the previous year. But many preferred a constitutional amendment rather than suffrage state by state.[41]

In early 1869 Congress agreed, and with the enthusiastic backing of the new president, sent to the states a Fifteenth Amendment prohibiting racial restrictions on the right to vote:

> Section 1. The right of citizens of the United States to vote shall not be denied or abridged by the United States or by any State on account of race, color, or previous condition of servitude.
>
> Section 2. The Congress shall have power to enforce this article by appropriate legislation.

This elimination of race discrimination in voting became part of the Constitution on February 3, 1870, when it was ratified by the necessary three-quarters of the states. The ratifying states included all ten states covered by Reconstruction. (The eleventh former Confederate state, Tennessee, was not under the Reconstruction Act because it had promptly ratified the Fourteenth Amendment, but now it rejected the Fifteenth Amendment in

1869.) The short time frame does not mean ratification was easy. The amendment faced opposition from many quarters. Some opposition came from those who thought the amendment should have gone further and should have outlawed particular tactics used against voters. Opposition also came from a segment of the women's suffrage movement, bitterly disappointed that women's suffrage was not part of the Fifteenth Amendment. The various cross-currents led to close division in many states, including some states that voted twice—defeating the amendment and then ratifying it, or, in the case of New York, ratifying it and then trying (unsuccessfully) to rescind its ratification.[42]

The Constitution now defined the new birth of freedom—citizenship and the right to vote. With citizenship secured by the Fourteenth Amendment and the right to vote secured by the Fifteenth, African Americans could protect themselves through the rule of law, could shape those laws by standing for political office, and could choose leaders with free debate and an honest ballot. The effects were greater in southern states, where most African Americans lived, but the right to vote was now nationwide.

With universal male suffrage provided in the new southern state constitutions, and backed by the Fifteenth Amendment, Black political participation mushroomed. Voting was soon followed by local officeholding. Nowhere was an African American elected governor, but they did hold state legislative seats in many states and several statewide offices, particularly in South Carolina and Louisiana. Two Black Mississippians, Hiram Revels and Blanche K. Bruce, were US senators, and fourteen other African Americans served in the US House of Representatives in the 1870s. African Americans in the South were almost all Republicans, and were joined by many white allies in the Republican Party.[43]

In April 1870 Frederick Douglass gave a speech at the last official meeting of the American Anti-Slavery Society. Entitled "A Reform Absolutely Complete," the speech echoed Representative Julian's exhilaration five years earlier over passage of the Thirteenth Amendment: "I seem myself to be living in a new world."[44]

African American progress elicited cooperation from some white people, but it prompted extreme violence from others. Violence has always been a component of US history, but after the Civil War, terrorism exploded. Many formed white terrorist organizations like the Ku Klux Klan and Knights of the White Camellia. Contrary to the stereotypes that portrayed members of these groups as "poor whites" who hated freedmen as economic rivals, Klansmen represented all classes of white society in the South.

Night-riding gangs turned their attention to political activists and appointees, county sheriffs, legislators, and even citizens who attempted to vote. In Hodges, South Carolina, Fletcher Hodges, a prominent landowner, offered a cash reward for the death of African American Benjamin Franklin Randolph, a Methodist Episcopal clergyman and Republican state senator. Soon thereafter, on October 16, 1868, three white men murdered Randolph in broad daylight. The crime took place in front of witnesses, yet no one ever identified the assassins. In 1870 in Sumter County, Alabama, Richard Burke, a prominent Black legislator and educator who had announced that Black men had the same right to carry arms as white men, was "shot all to pieces" by a white gang.[45]

The Klan attacked the fledgling democratic institutions that African Americans and white Republican allies had begun to create. The Klan and its allies struck at African American churches and schools, as well as smaller groups of citizens, but only targeted groups they outnumbered. They avoided any clash with federal troops stationed in the South. White vigilantes determined that the rule of law grounded in constitutional reform would not be allowed to triumph in the South. White southerners often asserted that such terrorism was minimal and that they would take care of the problem, but Supreme Court justice Samuel Miller, appointed by President Lincoln in 1862, challenged his southern brother-in-law in 1867: "Show me a single white man that has been punished in a State court for murdering a negro or a Union man. Show me any public meeting has been had to express indignation at such conduct."[46]

Enforcement Laws

In line with the president on policy, Congress adopted new federal laws designed for enforcement of the Fourteenth and Fifteenth Amendments. Two laws in particular would take center stage in the enforcement battles of the 1870s and 1880s, and they have remained the heart of civil rights enforcement to the present. The Enforcement Act of 1870 guaranteed the right to vote in all elections without racial discrimination. The law also restricted state election officials from specific racially discriminatory practices. Other sections reenacted the antidiscrimination sections of the Civil Rights Act of 1866, which now had the backing of the Fourteenth and Fifteenth Amendments in addition to their original Thirteenth Amendment support.

Section 6 of the new law went beyond protection of the right to vote; it made it a crime to "conspire together or go in disguise upon the public

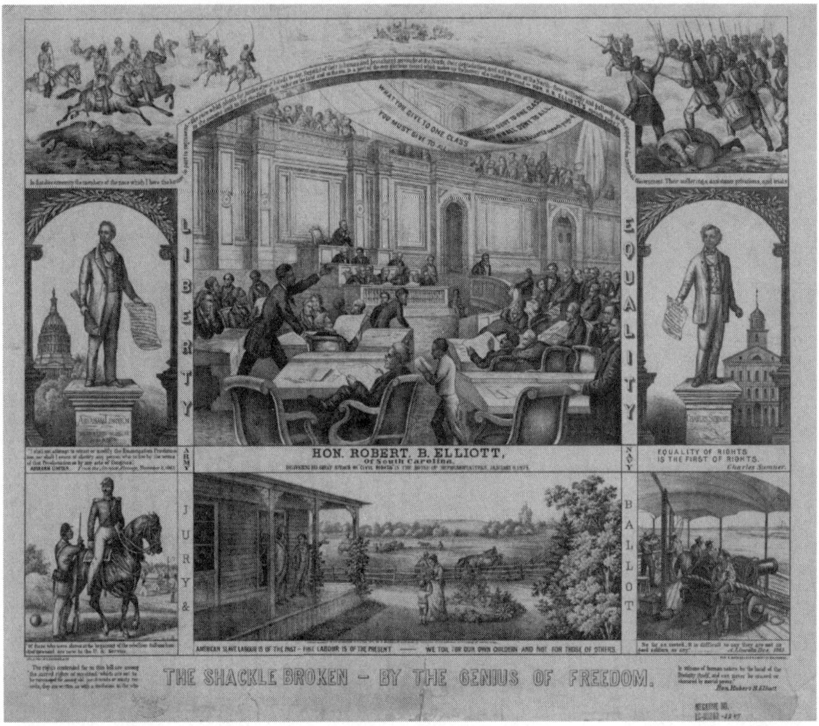

"The shackle broken—by the genius of freedom." The center panel shows South Carolina congressman Robert Brown Elliot urging passage of the Civil Rights Act of 1875.

highway" in order to injure or intimidate any citizen in the free exercise of "any right or privilege granted or secured to him by the constitution or laws of the United States"—not just voting, but *any* federal right. This section would soon become the center of attention in federal prosecutions and in the Supreme Court.[47]

A year later, following extensive hearings about murders and outrages across the South, Congress felt the need for another enforcement law, the Ku Klux Act of 1871. The main target of the Ku Klux Act was organized mob terror that intimidated or overwhelmed the struggling new state or local governments and sometimes even federal officials. The act defined interference with government functioning as insurrection or rebellion, and authorized presidential action to suppress it, including authorization to suspend habeas corpus where needed. Section 2 of the 1871 law again made it a crime for private individuals to conspire for injury to federal rights, and it expanded on the earlier enforcement act by making it a crime for state officials to deny equal protection of the laws to all persons. These companion sections of the 1870 and 1871 legislation were intended to give the broadest protection possible, and were often included together in later indictments. President Grant used the Ku Klux Act of 1871 in a series of prosecutions in South Carolina that broke the back of the Klan in that state.[48]

Other laws supplemented these protections. In particular, Congress authorized the appointment of federal observers to oversee elections and make arrests if necessary. Thousands of observers were sent throughout the South over the next several years. Another innovation of the new laws provided remedies that victims of violence themselves could invoke. These remedies allowed the victim to bring a lawsuit for damages and even make the violator pay for the victim's lawyer—a familiar rule in English law but virtually unprecedented in the American legal system. Finally, a section allowed private individuals to bring federal lawsuits against state or local officials for violation of constitutional rights.[49]

One more law was added to the caravan several years later, the Civil Rights Act of 1875. This law banned racial discrimination on juries, on trains and steamboats, in inns and theaters and other "places of public accommodation" and "places of public amusement." The bill had been repeatedly proposed by Senator Charles Sumner of Massachusetts since 1870 and was finally enacted in 1875, shortly after Senator Sumner's death. The Civil Rights Act of 1875 supplemented the Civil Rights Act of 1866, and the types of race discrimination banned in the 1875 law supplemented the types and categories of discrimination already identified as "badges of slavery" in the 1866 act.[50]

Thus, the new birth of freedom had a constitutional and legal foundation. The guiding principles were citizenship and equality, and there were two modes of protection: prosecutions by the federal government, and self-help through the power of thc vote. As the 1870s began, there was turmoil in the South, but the people had a number of tools to deal with it.

Or so it seemed.

CHAPTER THREE

The Supreme Court in Reconstruction

The new enforcement laws of the 1870s, intended as a wall of protection around the freedmen, were quickly tested. In October 1870 a white mob in Eutaw, Alabama, invaded a political meeting of African Americans, killing two men and wounding several more. John Hall and William Pettigrew were indicted under the Enforcement Act of 1870 for "banding and conspiring together" to keep their victims from exercising federally protected rights—their First Amendment rights to free speech and free assembly. In *United States v. Hall* (1871) the defendants argued that the federal government had no power to prosecute them—private individuals—because the First Amendment, like other provisions of the Bill of Rights, did not apply to the states.

The defendants presented these arguments in the lower federal court to Judge William B. Woods. Woods, an antislavery Democrat from Ohio, had served as a general in the US Army during the Civil War. After the war he moved south, settling in Alabama, and President Grant appointed him federal judge in 1870. (Ten years later, President Hayes appointed him to the Supreme Court.) Because *United States v. Hall* was one of the first cases under the Enforcement Act, Judge Woods wrote for guidance to Joseph P. Bradley, the Supreme Court justice assigned to supervise the lower federal courts in the Fifth Circuit, which covered Alabama and other southern states. Appointed by President Grant, Bradley had just started his service on the Court, in May 1870.

Bradley answered that the Fourteenth Amendment, in his opinion, authorized "direct federal intervention" to protect citizens' fundamental rights. With Bradley's letter in mind and quoting directly from that letter, Judge Woods ruled that the defendants would have prevailed in the past, but no longer. The Bill of Rights originally did not apply to the states, but under the Fourteenth Amendment, he said, "this order of things is reversed." In particular, he said, the Fourteenth Amendment barred a state from abridging a citizen's "privileges or immunities." The Fourteenth Amendment did not define what the "privileges or immunities" of a US citizen were, but Woods asserted that they must include those contained in the First Amendment—free speech and free assembly.[1]

The case never went to the Supreme Court, but Woods's interpretation could have changed history. It read the Fourteenth Amendment broadly to affirm federal power to defend civil rights. It affirmed Congress's power to enforce the amendment and showed that the Enforcement Act of 1870 could be an effective tool against political terrorism.

And for a time the Enforcement Act was effective. The early 1870s saw active federal enforcement of the new laws. In 1873 there were more than 1,200 civil rights prosecutions under the Enforcement Act of 1870 and the Ku Klux Act of 1871. In addition to prosecutions, federal observers ensured honesty at elections.

Republican President Ulysses Grant won reelection in 1872, with the help of African American voters, but the zeal for reform that had animated many in the country after the war was beginning to flag. The depression (then called a panic) that began in 1873 spelled trouble for the Republicans. Labor problems in the North, Indian wars in the West, and accusations of corruption in Washington and the southern states also captured the public's attention. In the 1874 election, the Democrats took the House of Representatives for the first time since the Civil War. They were then in position to prevent any new civil rights legislation.[2]

The Supreme Court's views seemed to reflect these troubling times. Though *United States v. Hall* offered the justices a way forward, they instead chose a retreat and would neuter all three Reconstruction Amendments and Congress's enforcement laws. Ultimately the Court was unwilling to recognize that the new Thirteenth, Fourteenth, and Fifteenth Amendments to the US Constitution had redefined the relationship between the federal and state governments.

The First Supreme Court Case

In 1872, amid the high tide of enforcement, an unsettling decision came from the Supreme Court. Perhaps because the case interpreted a statute, not the Constitution, it is usually overlooked today, but it had all the elements of the Court's later failures during Reconstruction.

The case, *Blyew v. United States* (1872), began with what the Supreme Court later called "a crime of peculiar atrocity." In the summer of 1868 John Blyew and George Kennard, white men in Kentucky, hacked to death a family of African Americans, including an adult couple, a ninety-year-old woman, and a teenage boy. They said they expected "another war about niggers" and wanted to start the killing without waiting for a declaration of war.

There were two witnesses—one of the victims, who gave a statement just before dying, and a thirteen-year-old girl whom the killers apparently overlooked. As African Americans, however, they could not testify in Kentucky courts. Kentucky was a slave state that did not secede. Nevertheless, white animosity against freedmen was widespread, and the no-Black-testimony rule gave white hostility a free license for racial violence and fraud. Laws banning Black testimony were one of the basic "badges of slavery" that the enforcement clause of the Thirteenth Amendment empowered Congress to eliminate. Congress did just that in the Civil Rights Act of 1866, guaranteeing the equal right to testify and making interference with that right a federal crime. Every other state with a law barring African Americans from testifying had eliminated it except Kentucky, where the legislature kept rejecting repeal efforts.

The *Blyew* case, ordinarily a state murder case, was brought in federal court because the Civil Rights Act of 1866 provided federal court jurisdiction if equal rights could not be protected in state court. That issue of jurisdiction was the precise question already decided in *United States v. Rhodes* (1867). In that case, the opinion by Justice Swayne, sitting on a lower court, had been a strong affirmation of federal jurisdiction and of congressional power to outlaw this badge of slavery. The lower court in the *Blyew* case also upheld federal jurisdiction.[3]

Blyew and Kinnard were convicted by a federal jury and sentenced to hang. Officials in Kentucky seethed, and the legislature made a special appropriation to appeal the case to the US Supreme Court.

The literal words of the Civil Rights Act of 1866 authorized federal courts to hear all cases "affecting persons who are denied" their equal rights in state court. The two African American witnesses were obviously denied their equal rights by being ineligible to testify in state court. Therefore, the legal question was whether they were persons "affected" by the case. Because the very purpose of the 1866 act was to allow African Americans to "give testimony," the obvious answer was "yes," they were persons "affected," especially the one who was a victim.

The Supreme Court majority thought differently, holding that only the prosecution and the defendants (the accused murderers) were "affected persons," but not victims or witnesses. This conclusion was based, not on a reading of the Civil Rights Act of 1866, but on the Court's fear that all manner of ordinary cases could be brought into federal court—even civil cases between white people—if victims and witnesses were deemed to be "affected" persons: "We cannot think that such was the purpose of Congress."

The Court's view was contrary to the literal words and obvious purpose of Congress. A flood of cases would end up coming to the federal courts only if judges in Kentucky (or any other state) kept committing the federal crime of refusing to hear testimony from African American witnesses. Congress had very carefully given federal courts jurisdiction for the specific purpose of stamping out such discriminatory laws; removing every case out of the Kentucky courts was the way to end the practice. For this reason the Supreme Court's fear was nonsense. The Supreme Court had a choice, and it chose to read the Civil Rights Act for as little as it could mean, just to accommodate Kentucky's badge of slavery.[4]

Justice Bradley, joined by Swayne, dissented vigorously. He said that to refuse the evidence of the whole race "is to brand them with a badge of slavery, is to expose them to wanton insults and fiendish assaults." He added, "Merely striking off the fetters of the slave, without removing the incidents and consequences of slavery, would hardly have been a boon to the colored race."[5]

The Court's decision to free the murderers of the Black family did not go unnoticed. The federal circuit judge in Kentucky, Bland Ballard, wrote, "If Congress meant what the court says they meant, is not all of their legislation which relates to the negro a mockery?" In 1971 the dean of constitutional historians, Charles Fairman, called this case a "forewarning of things in years to come," and said that "while reconciliation between North and South progressed, the Court would be making some constructions of the law that were anything but benignant toward those for whose protection they had been adopted."[6]

Calling this case a "forewarning of things in years to come" is exactly right. In the next decade, 1873–1883, the Supreme Court decided six major cases that removed essential building blocks from the wall of protection that the Reconstruction Amendments and statutes had erected: in 1873, 1876 (twice), 1880, and 1883 (twice). When these cases were finished, the wall was all but gone.

The Supreme Court that reversed the convictions in the Colfax massacre, *U.S. v. Cruikshank* (1876). Left to right: Joseph Bradley, Stephen J. Field, Samuel Miller, Nathan Clifford, Chief Justice Morrison Waite, Noah Swayne, David Davis, William Strong, Ward Hunt. The Court was the same for the *Slaughter-House Cases*, except the chief justice was Salmon P. Chase.

The *Slaughter-House Cases* (1873)

The *Blyew* case was a warning sign that the Supreme Court might not be ready to accept a strong role for federal law and strong enforcement for the country's Black citizens. Still, it is possible the Supreme Court might have interpreted the new constitutional amendments more expansively if its first major encounter with them had involved an African American claim for protection. Instead, the first case was a business dispute about livestock slaughtering. Equally important, the case was brought by white men and orchestrated by an ex-Confederate zealot to challenge a law enacted by the Reconstruction legislature of Louisiana, which was biracial and dominated by Republicans.

In 1869 the Louisiana legislature adopted a law requiring all livestock slaughtering in New Orleans to be done in one specific location in the city. The law was a response to the city's serious health problems—including yellow fever and cholera—which were aggravated by the haphazard butchering of animals throughout New Orleans. But the state legislature also gave a twenty-five-year license to build and operate a slaughterhouse to only one company, the Crescent City Company. All slaughtering had to be done there, either by the butchers themselves or by the Crescent City Company.[7]

Many New Orleans butchers sued, saying the law created a monopoly and threatened their livelihoods in violation of the new Fourteenth Amendment. The butchers were white, and many had been Confederate soldiers. Their attorney was former Supreme Court justice John A. Campbell, who had left the Court in April 1861 to serve as assistant secretary of war of the Confederacy. After the war Campbell had been imprisoned on suspicion that he was involved in the Lincoln assassination conspiracy. Justice Samuel Miller wrote in 1877 that Campbell was still "saturated" with the rebellion's "spirit."[8]

The butchers' lawsuits went first to the state court, where they lost, and then to the lower federal court, where they were successful. That set the stage for a US Supreme Court appeal, decided under the collective name *Slaughter-House Cases* (1873). The Court's membership had turned over completely since the *Dred Scott* decision in 1857 (in which then-justice Campbell joined in ruling against Scott). Seven of the nine justices were Republicans appointed by Presidents Lincoln and Grant; there were no southerners.

The case presented a conflict between the main purpose of the Fourteenth Amendment, which was to help African Americans, and the literal words of the amendment, which applied to all people. The butchers' main argument was based on the Fourteenth Amendment's first section, which says a state law may not abridge the "privileges or immunities of citizens of the United States." The question to be decided was whether the butchers' right to carry on their business was a "privilege or immunity" under the new Fourteenth Amendment.

The Supreme Court split 5–4. The majority held that the Fourteenth Amendment gave federal protection and jurisdiction only over "privileges or immunities" that were not already protected by the states and in state courts. Because "state privileges and immunities" were many, that meant those covered by the Fourteenth Amendment were very few, and did not include the butchers' desire to carry on a trade or business. The Supreme Court named some privileges and immunities that were covered by the amendment—the right to go to the US capital and participate in federal government functions, the right to protection on the high seas, and not much more.[9]

This ended the butchers' case. Their only recourse was in state court, where they had already lost. It also ended John A. Campbell's crusade against the Louisiana legislature, although he could probably take some satisfaction from having sown confusion about the Fourteenth Amendment.

The New Orleans *Daily Picayune* gloated that the Fourteenth Amendment, rather than being the "odious" measure enacted "in the exclusive interest of the freedman or carpetbagger," could instead be used to "shelter" white people.[10]

In giving the Fourteenth Amendment a narrow interpretation—at least for the "privileges or immunities" clause—the majority justices were influenced by concern that a broader interpretation could allow the national government to overwhelm the states and go far beyond the amendment's original conception primarily as a protection for the freed people. The Court recognized the grave events that had provoked the amendments, but they stuck with the state-dominated Constitution they had always known.

At the same time, the Court's majority opinion seemed to bring the Fourteenth Amendment back to a primary focus on protecting the freedmen. The opinion was by Justice Samuel Miller, who had been outraged by the Black Codes and wrote to a friend in 1866: "The pretence is that the negro wont work without he is compelled to do so, and this pretence is made in a country and by the white people, where the negro has done all the work for four generations and the white man makes a boast of the fact that he will *not* labour."[11]

Miller began his *Slaughter-House* analysis with a sympathetic five-page history of the Thirteenth, Fourteenth, and Fifteenth Amendments, ranging from the valiant service of African American soldiers in the Union Army to the notorious Black Codes. The Court said the "one pervading purpose" in the three amendments was "the freedom of the slave race" and "the protection of the newly-made freeman and citizen." To afford this protection, the Court recognized, the new amendments gave "additional powers to the Federal government," and "additional restraints upon those of the states." The majority opinion seemed to leave ample room in the Fourteenth Amendment for this safeguard, especially under the equal protection clause.

Four justices dissented—including Bradley, who dissented in *Blyew*. Here, Bradley compared the new amendments to the Magna Carta, and said they were responses to "the spirit of lawlessness, mob violence and sectional hate." The dissenters argued that the narrow interpretation imposed too great a limit on the Fourteenth Amendment. Swayne, the other *Blyew* dissenter, wrote that any government unable to protect fundamental privileges and rights was "glaringly defective." He ended his opinion with a doleful premonition: "I can only hope that the consequences to follow may prove less serious and far-reaching than the minority fear they will be."[12]

By holding that the privileges or immunities clause of the Fourteenth Amendment covered only those negligible privileges or immunities that were not already protected (supposedly) by the states, *Slaughter-House* was the first case to remove a building block of Reconstruction's wall of protection—the privileges or immunities clause of the Fourteenth Amendment.

For a time Justice Miller's hopes seemed more likely to be borne out than Justice Swayne's fears. In late 1873, a few months after the *Slaughter-House* decision, as if to show that race cases would be different, the Court ruled in favor of Catherine Brown, an African American woman kept out of a railroad's "white" car, in *Railroad Company v. Brown* (1873).

The Colfax Massacre and *United States v. Cruikshank* (1876)

The consequences of the *Slaughter-House Cases* had already been set in motion by the time of the decision. In the tiny hamlet of Colfax, Louisiana, two groups claimed victory in the elections of November 1872: white Democrats and a Republican coalition of white and Black citizens. By the spring of 1873, the groups were still contesting the election, with the Democrats holding onto the courthouse keys. Late one night a group of Republicans—one African American and the rest white—went to the courthouse, tore off a shutter, and hoisted a young boy into the crevice; he opened the front door, and they occupied the courthouse.

The next morning, white Democrats prepared to besiege the building while two dozen Republicans, mostly African American, stood guard outside the courthouse. As the families of many of those guarding the courthouse joined the contingent inside the building, about 300 people occupied the courthouse, half of them women and children. A force of similar size, mostly former Confederate soldiers from neighboring districts, had gathered in opposition.

On Easter Sunday, April 13, 1873, the standoff boiled over. The Democrats told the people in the courthouse to evacuate all of the women and children because they would be attacking in thirty minutes. Most left. Just after noon the white attackers fired a cannon, and for two hours the two sides exchanged volleys. Eventually the cannon prevailed. Many Republicans fled the courthouse for the nearby forest, while the invaders pursued them on horseback. Then they laid fire to the courthouse to draw the rest of the Republicans out of the building and shot them as they ran from the flames.

After the gunfire ceased, the surviving Republicans were taken prisoner and several Democrats, including William Cruikshank, executed them. Only Levi Nelson survived, by pretending to be dead until Cruikshank and his men left the scene.

The death toll at Colfax was three white Democrats and at least 60 (and possibly as many as 150) African Americans. The grisly slaughter at Colfax led to an indictment of ninety white men under the Enforcement Act of 1870, the same law used in the 1871 Alabama case *United States v. Hall.* That law made it a crime to "band or conspire together" to "injure" or "intimidate" any person for exercising a federal right or to prevent exercise of a federal right (that is, a right protected by the "Constitution or laws of the United States"). Most of the defendants were never found, but nine, including Cruikshank, were arrested and went on trial in 1874 in New Orleans.[13]

Along with Levi Nelson's testimony, James Beckwith, the federal prosecutor in the case, used the body of one of the slain African Americans, Alexander Tillman—who had been found covered in stab wounds, his clothes ripped off, his throat slashed, and his face beaten—as grounds for seeking the death penalty. The wounds on his body, along with its position hundreds of feet from the courthouse, proved that he had been slaughtered while fleeing.[14]

After one trial, in which the jury could not reach a verdict, the jury in a second trial returned guilty verdicts for three men, including Cruikshank. The defendants then filed a motion asking the trial court to overrule the verdict and dismiss the charges. They argued that they should not have been tried at all, claiming Congress had no constitutional power to prosecute private individuals—precisely the line of argument that had been rejected in the Alabama lower-court case of *United States v. Hall* (1871).

According to the procedure of the day, the motion was heard by Circuit Judge William B. Woods and the Supreme Court justice from that circuit, Joseph Bradley. These two judges had agreed in *United States v. Hall* that the Fourteenth Amendment authorized federal prosecution of private individuals who interfered with constitutional rights. This time, however, Bradley took the opposite approach in *United States v. Cruikshank* (Circuit Court, 1874), agreeing with the defendants that the indictment went beyond Congress's constitutional power and was defective in other ways. Woods, perhaps as surprised as everyone else, disagreed. Maintaining the view he had taken in *United States v. Hall,* he voted to uphold the indictment and conviction. Because the two judges disagreed at the circuit level, the case went on appeal to the US Supreme Court.[15]

The indictment charged that on April 13, 1873, in Grant Parish, Louisiana, Cruikshank and the others had "banded" and "conspired" together to injure Levi Nelson and Alexander Tillman. That alone would not have been a federal crime; ordinary injury or intimidation is simply a state crime. The key element needed to make the conspiracy a federal crime under Congress's Enforcement Act of 1870 was to charge that the *purpose* of the conspiracy was tied specifically to a particular federal right or privilege. This was done in eight "counts," each one alleging a particular federal right that the conspiracy was intended to violate.

Cruikshank presented the Supreme Court with an opportunity to interpret the Reconstruction Amendments in the way they were intended to apply; it was a case involving protection of the freed people under a statute exercising Congress's enforcement power. Instead, the *Cruikshank* Court brought the *Slaughter-House* chickens home to roost, with a clear message that the postwar constitutional amendments had little effect on the traditional arrangement of state primacy and federal subordination.

The decision of the Supreme Court in *United States v. Cruikshank* (1876) was unanimous, including all three living justices of the four who had dissented in *Slaughter-House*. The opinion was written by the newcomer on the Court, Chief Justice Morrison Waite, a Grant appointment to replace Salmon P. Chase. Waite's opinion was essentially a summary of Bradley's lower-court decision, reaching the identical result, minus detail.

The opinion began by describing the separateness of state and national power. The national government has only the functions and powers contained in the federal Constitution, so it can only protect (and punish violations of) a right that is "granted or secured by the constitution or laws of the United States." The Court went on to say that the national government could not act beyond its powers, but "within the scope of its powers, it is supreme and above the States," and is "endowed with all the powers necessary for its own preservation and accomplishment of the ends its people had in view."[16]

All this was manifestly correct, but, as it proceeded through the separate counts of the indictment, the Court violated these principles and grossly shortchanged the Reconstruction Amendments and those who should have been protected by them. Upholding any one count would have sustained the conviction, but the Court methodically went through and rejected each one. The true evaluation of the *Cruikshank* case must depend on how the Court actually treated each of the counts of the indictment. Applying this standard, a detailed look at the opinion shows grievous errors; it shows that the Court should have upheld four of the eight counts of the indictment. Furthermore, the Court made other gross errors that blighted the Constitution for generations.

First, two counts of the indictment (Counts 4 and 5) alleged that the conspiracy was intended to injure the victims in order to deprive them of all the rights enjoyed by white people, on account of their race. These counts were fully supported by the Thirteenth Amendment. The Court agreed that the Thirteenth Amendment targeted the "war of race" and that the amendment empowered Congress to punish *public or private* conspiracies motivated by racial animus, as this one was. Nevertheless, the Supreme Court rejected these two counts on the theory that they were too "vague" because they should have specified which particular "rights" the conspiracy was intended to deny. That was seriously in error because the "right" possessed by the victims and violated by the conspirators was equality of rights free of racial discrimination, rather than a particular substantive right like property, education, or free speech. The Court's misunderstanding of this point was shown by the fact that both times the opinion described these counts, it omitted the words of racial purpose that were the heart of the charge.[17]

Next, two of the counts (Counts 1 and 2) alleged that the conspiracy was aimed at the victims' right to assemble and their right to bear arms. The Supreme Court rejected these under the theory of the *Slaughter-House Cases,* holding that these were not "privileges or immunities" covered by the Fourteenth Amendment because they were rights of all state citizens. But here the Supreme Court misunderstood the Fourteenth Amendment. True, Nelson's and Tillman's right to assemble and bear arms were state privileges, not federal privileges, but in this circumstance the federal government was entitled to protect their state privileges. That was because these two counts of the indictment were supported, not by the privileges or immunities clause, but by the citizenship clause in the first sentence of the Fourteenth Amendment. Unlike the white butchers in the *Slaughter-House Cases,* who had the "age-old privileges of state citizenship," Levi Nelson and Alexander Tillman, as African Americans, were not citizens of Louisiana until the first sentence of the Fourteenth Amendment of the US Constitution made them, as native born persons, citizens of the United States "*and of the State wherein they reside.*" Chief Justice Taney's opinion in the *Dred Scott* case singled out "assembly" and "bearing arms" as privileges denied to African Americans, slave or free. Now, however, the first sentence of the Fourteenth Amendment "granted" African Americans the right of being citizens of Louisiana. Thus, by Chief Justice Waite's own words, because the Constitution created those rights, Congress was plainly entitled to protect them and punish interference, which Counts 1 and 2 properly did.[18]

Finally, two counts of the indictment (Counts 3 and 4) rested on the due process and equal protection clauses of the Fourteenth Amendment. Those clauses by themselves regulate only the states ("nor shall any state deprive" any person of due process "nor deny" equal protection), but the question before the Court was whether Congress was allowed to legislate against private individuals who interfered with anyone's entitlement to due process and equal protection. The Court's answer was "no": "The only obligation resting upon the United States is to see that the States do not deny the right. This amendment guarantees, but no more. The power of the national government is limited to the enforcement of this guaranty."[19]

The Court should have held that Congress's enforcement power extended to any act relating to a state providing or failing to provide due process and equal protection to an individual receiving or not receiving those rights. The Colfax conspiracy was probably within that definition because the perpetrators sought to exercise authority over the parish government. The Court might have dismissed these counts of the indictment because they did not specifically allege this Fourteenth Amendment connection, but instead, the Court shut off other cases against anyone but the state. This nullified the constitutional provisions granting Congress both the enumerated power in the Fourteenth Amendment and the very broad reserve power to pass all laws "necessary and proper" to carry out federal responsibilities. The decision was also inconsistent with the Court's cases upholding Congress's power to punish private individuals who interfered with states' obligations to return fugitive slaves. The Court in *Prigg v. Pennsylvania* (1842) had spent pages describing Congress's very broad powers in these and many other categories. In other words, Congress now lacked power to protect the newly freed people in the same way it had time and again protected slaveholders.[20]

Overall, the Supreme Court in *United States v. Cruikshank* should have upheld the convictions based on several counts of the indictment. Instead the Court closed any doors left open in the *Slaughter-House Cases* and largely eliminated the Thirteenth and Fourteenth Amendments as the engines of enforcement and protection they should have been. This cleared the way for a hundred years of murder and mayhem, from the late nineteenth century through the desegregation wars of the twentieth century.[21]

By holding that Congress's power to enforce the Fourteenth Amendment was no broader than the specific prohibitions of the amendment (no power against private interference), the *Cruikshank* case removed a second

This marker glorifying the Colfax massacre of 1873 was erected in 1951 and was still standing in 2020.

building block of Reconstruction's wall of protection, the enforcement clause in Section 5 of the Fourteenth Amendment.

In Louisiana, the history of nineteenth-century white terrorism in the Colfax massacre continues to burden the twenty-first century. In 1951, a time of growing challenges to segregation, the state of Louisiana decided to glorify the massacre by posting a marker that was still standing in Colfax in 2020: "On this site occurred the Colfax Riot in which three white men and 150 negroes were slain. This event on April 13, 1873 marked the end of carpetbag misrule in the South."[22]

The Second Case of the Day

On March 27, 1876, the same day the *Cruikshank* decision limited the Thirteenth and Fourteenth Amendments, the Supreme Court also struck at the Fifteenth Amendment in *United States v. Reese* (1876). While *Cruikshank* weakened one section of the Enforcement Act of 1870, *Reese* took aim at two other sections of the same statute and held them unconstitutional and thus completely void.

Part of the Enforcement Act aimed at schemes that southern election officials used to disqualify African Americans from voting. In one particular tactic, a registrar would refuse to accept an African American's poll tax payment; then, on Election Day, a poll manager would turn the victim away from the polls for lack of a poll tax receipt. The Enforcement Act allowed someone whose poll tax payment was rejected because of his race to vote if he presented a detailed affidavit specifying the racial basis of the rejection. If Election Day officials refused to allow him to vote with the "race-based poll tax rejection" affidavit, they were in violation of Sections 3 and 4 of the Enforcement Act.[23]

The *Reese* case brought this disfranchisement scheme to the Supreme Court in an appeal by two poll managers convicted in Kentucky. On Election Day 1873, they refused to allow William Garner, an African American, to vote, even though he presented the required affidavit that his poll tax payment had been refused because of his race. The election officials argued that these sections of the Enforcement Act were not authorized by the Fifteenth Amendment. The question in the case was whether the statute defined the crime in terms of race, which was a requirement for validity under the Fifteenth Amendment. In this case, that depended on a single word, "aforesaid." The scheme was addressed in three sections of the Enforcement Act. Section 2 specified that the registrar's violation was refusing the poll tax payment *on account of race*. Sections 3 and 4, instead of repeating the phrase "on account of race," used the word "aforesaid." The actual phrase they used referred to that racially discriminatory act as "the wrongful act or omission aforesaid of the person or officer charged with the duty of receiving or permitting such performance or offer to perform."

Even though the word "aforesaid" was in common use in both federal and state statutes, and the Enforcement Act clearly tied these refusals to race, the Supreme Court held that Sections 3 and 4 of the act were not limited to race and were therefore unconstitutional. Chief Justice Waite wrote that these sections did not "in express terms" limit the wrongdoing to race. Then, ignoring the word "aforesaid," he wrote that "it is apparent that it was not the intention of Congress thus to limit the operation of the act." This was patently false, as Justice Ward Hunt made clear in dissent. Hunt stated the obvious: "What do the words 'as aforesaid' mean?" Unless they referred to racial discrimination, he continued, "they are wholly and absolutely without meaning." Waite did not answer him.[24]

The majority opinion's destruction of these sections of the law was outrageous. It would be easier to excuse but for the history of the word "aforesaid" in American law and in Waite's own opinions. He wrote many opinions relying on that word, including, for example, a detailed opinion in the same year as *Reese* in which he explained how the word "aforesaid" gave specific meaning to Section 22 of the Judiciary Act of 1789. In *thousands* of Supreme Court cases where the word "aforesaid" has been used, it does not appear that the Supreme Court had ever found the word to be insufficiently specific in the 90 years before the *Reese* case, nor the 140 years since then. By holding that a statute was not tied to race when it obviously was, the *Reese* case damaged a third building block in the Reconstruction wall of protection—the Fifteenth Amendment.[25]

Technically, the two decisions in *Cruikshank* and *Reese* were not completely fatal—if a prosecution could thread a needle—but probably only in cases involving a federal election. Some of the long-range effects of the cases were even more damaging than the immediate impact. The immediate result of *Reese* affected only one particular election scheme, but procedural rules of the case would thwart major avenues of civil rights protection for nearly a century, until the *Reese* rules were revoked in 1960 and 1971.[26]

By the end of the day on March 27, 1876, the Supreme Court had chosen, in both *Cruikshank* and *Reese,* to dismantle the Enforcement Act, the central law used to protect African Americans against both public corruption and private mob violence. White wrongdoers, in turn, learned what they saw as a valuable lesson: they could harm and even murder African Americans with impunity, and they could use tricks to keep African Americans from voting.

On a much grander scale, former Confederates in Mississippi had already accomplished their goal by violently overthrowing the Republican Mississippi state government in 1875. After *Cruikshank,* white supremacists in South Carolina determined to repeat the Mississippi Plan. They followed a thirty-three-point manifesto written by former Confederate general Martin W. Gary: "There are certain men . . . you must kill. Go in masses, armed, and try to force the Negroes to vote our ticket. . . . Shoot them down and cut off their ears, and I warrant you this will teach them a lesson. If we are not elected we will . . . surround the statehouse, and tear it down, and show them we will rule."[27]

Armed bands of horsemen, attired in symbolically defiant red shirts, threatened, assaulted, and killed Black officeholders and even Black voters and their white allies. They seized control of the state government and put the reins of power in the hands of Gary's Confederate commander, General Wade Hampton. After the successes of Mississippi and South Carolina, like-minded Democrats in every former Confederate state followed suit.[28]

The year 1876 saw the disputed Hayes-Tilden election. It was finally resolved in Hayes's favor, but the result was an end to both Reconstruction and military protection for the remaining biracial state legislatures, while southern Democrats pledged to treat African Americans fairly. Hayes soon saw how naïve he had been to trust the pledge of fair treatment, but history was moving against rights and opportunities for African Americans.

In the national 1878 midterm elections, Democrats took control of both houses of Congress and soon passed a half-dozen bills to eliminate civil rights protections. President Hayes vetoed them all. In his veto message for one of the Democrats' bills, Hayes wrote that its prohibition on federal action was unprecedented and "its design is to render the election laws inoperative and a dead letter."[29]

Of course the Supreme Court's decisions in *Cruikshank* and *Reese* were not the cause or even the main stimulus of the retreat from Reconstruction and the abandonment of the goal of equality. As Gary's manifesto made clear, southern white supremacists were determined to act, whatever the laws. But the cases were important symbols. Moreover, those who tried to enforce equal political rights, like the Republican administrations in the early and late 1880s, found themselves largely without enforcement tools.

As African American political activity increasingly met with violence, some prosecutions continued—at least during Republican administrations, and only regarding federal elections (or any election that coincided with federal elections), where Congress had comprehensive power, not limited to issues of race discrimination. Congress's power over federal elections was contained in Art. I, Sec. 4 of the Constitution.[30]

This power was vindicated in *Ex parte Yarbrough* (1884), a decision that shows how the enforcement of laws to protect African Americans might have flourished if the Supreme Court had read the Thirteenth, Fourteenth, and Fifteenth Amendments fairly. In this case, a group of Klansmen had been convicted of a conspiracy to "go in disguise on the highway" and beat Berry Saunders, an African American, because he voted in a federal election in Georgia in 1883. The defendants challenged their conviction on the same ground that had been successful in *Reese*—that the statute was not limited to race. This challenge was resoundingly rejected because the indictment alleged this was a federal election, so it was a valid exercise of Congress's general power over federal elections.

The Court's description of Congress's power in this case was as sweeping as it had been stingy in the Fourteenth and Fifteenth Amendment cases so recently decided. Justice Miller wrote the unanimous decision:

"A government whose essential character is republican, whose executive head and legislative body are both elective," certainly has the power to secure elections. To say otherwise "is a proposition so startling as to arrest attention."[31]

The power affirmed by the *Yarbrough* case was of waning value. The flight away from Reconstruction was accelerating. State and local governments, increasingly in white supremacists' hands, were free to enact discriminatory laws. Violence grew, with little to check it. In the 1880s two factions of the Democratic Party, known as the Woodpeckers and the Jaybirds, carried on years of struggle for control of the government in Fort Bend County, Texas. The Woodpeckers, a biracial group, were in control in the late 1880s, when the all-white Jaybirds, with the assistance of the governor and the Texas Rangers, drove the Woodpeckers out and took over the government. Many Woodpeckers, white and Black, fled the county for their own safety. Having established an all-white government with the help of a state police force, the Jaybirds were still at it sixty-five years later, holding white primaries nearly a decade after such primaries were outlawed, until the Supreme Court specifically struck down the Jaybird White Primary in Fort Bend County in 1953.[32]

Throughout the former Confederacy, even federal agents were not immune from assassination. And when a witness was murdered because he had testified before a federal grand jury, it was held that this was not a federal crime because Congress had no power to prosecute the killing of a federal grand jury witness. The ruling was issued in the lower court by Justice L. Q. C. Lamar, a former high Confederate official who was Democratic president Grover Cleveland's first Supreme Court appointee. If a prosecution was brought, finding jurors who were not biased and not intimidated was difficult. Finally, if a case could go to trial, conviction was complicated because the jury would be instructed that it could convict only if it found the assault was for voting, not out of any other animus or motive or general race hatred.[33]

In the midst of these dreary developments, however, the Supreme Court ruled in favor of freed people who had acquired land through Reconstruction-era tax titles. The Court first upheld the title of Robert Smalls in *de Treville v. Smalls* (1879) (discussed in Chapter 2). Then, in a case where the Tennessee Supreme Court had rejected a similar tax title and given the land back to its tax-delinquent former owner, the US Supreme Court, in *Keely v. Sanders* (1879), reversed the Tennessee court and upheld the freedman's title.

All-White Juries

Many white people could not abide the prospect of African Americans on juries, occupying positions of such responsibility, especially if a Black person were sitting in judgment on a white person. On a more practical level, all-white juries ensured the "right" verdicts, such as convicting Black defendants but freeing those few white defendants who were prosecuted for crimes against African Americans.

Four years after the decisions in *Cruikshank* and *Reese,* the issue of all-white juries came before the Supreme Court. Three cases decided on the same day, March 1, 1880, showed the strengths and weaknesses of the Fourteenth Amendment as the Supreme Court applied it.

Two of the cases decided that day involved African American defendants indicted and convicted of murder by all-white juries in counties that had never had a Black juror despite having substantial Black populations. One case was in West Virginia, the other in Virginia. Because there was a difference between the laws of the two states, one defendant went free but the other defendant was hanged.

In West Virginia, Taylor Strauder's grand jury and trial jury were all white, by the specific terms of a West Virginia law that limited jury service to "white male persons." Strauder appealed to the Supreme Court which, in *Strauder v. West Virginia* (1880), emphatically declared that under the Fourteenth Amendment the rights of the races must be "exactly the same" and "the law in the states shall be the same for the black as for the white." West Virginia's statute mandating all-white juries, the Court said, was unconstitutional, and Strauder's conviction was reversed.[34]

The Court had an opportunity to reinforce that ruling in a case from the neighboring state of Virginia (*Virginia v. Rives,* 1880) when Lee Reynolds, an African American, was convicted of murdering a white man in Patrick County. Virginia law did not discriminate by race in jury selection—it made all adult males eligible to serve. Nonetheless, both the grand jury that indicted him and the trial jury that convicted him were all white. In fact, no jury in Patrick County had ever had an African American on it, despite a substantial Black population in the county. Instead of using a state law to keep juries all white, county officials used custom to summon only white men. Reynolds turned to a federal judge, Alexander Rives.

Though Judge Rives was from a slaveholding family in Virginia, he had supported the Union. African Americans sat on his juries. He reviewed Reynolds's conviction and found that African Americans had by some means been kept off Patrick County juries, in violation of the Fourteenth

Amendment. He said that even though the state law in Virginia did not call for all-white juries, the fact that no African American had ever been called for jury duty in the history of the county could not "be imputed to chance." Therefore, he accepted jurisdiction under the "removal" provisions of the Civil Rights Act of 1866, and reversed the conviction. The case went to the Supreme Court and was decided on the same day that the Court decisively held that Taylor Strauder's all-white jury was unconstitutional.[35]

To the Supreme Court, unfortunately for Reynolds, this absence of explicit words of discrimination from the Virginia law made all the difference. The justices did not disagree with the facts, but treated the facts as insufficient if the law did not contain words of discrimination. The Supreme Court said that it was not relevant if African Americans had never served as jurors in the county. "[These claims] fall short of showing that any civil right was denied or that there had been any discrimination against the defendants because of their color or race. The facts may have been as stated, and yet the jury which indicted them and the panel summoned to try them, may have been impartially selected."[36]

In contrast to Judge Rives's recognition that the complete absence of Black jurors could not "be imputed to chance," the Supreme Court's statement was preposterous. But with these words, the Court, which had just said the rights of the races must be "exactly the same," went far toward making that impossible. The justices eliminated the most probative—almost the only—type of evidence that could prove African Americans were systematically kept off juries.

For the rest of the century and much of the twentieth century, most of the southern states regularly excluded African Americans from juries, yet they all did so without explicit laws of race. Except for one case where the state admitted it had purposely excluded Black jurors, *Neal v. Delaware* (1881), and another case where the wrong law was used by mistake, *Bush v. Kentucky* (1883), it would be more than half a century and tens of thousands of fraudulent all-white juries before the Supreme Court again reversed a conviction because African Americans had been systematically excluded from a jury.

The *Rives* decision limited the enforcement of equal rights in another way. The case had gone to Judge Rives by "removal" of the state prosecution to federal court under the Civil Rights Act of 1866 because of race discrimination (the all-white jury) in the state court proceeding. *Virginia v. Rives* ended most such removals by establishing a rule allowing such "removal" only where race discrimination in the state court is specified in the words of a state law, no matter how blatant the discrimination.[37]

The third jury case decided on March 1, 1880—*Ex parte Virginia*—had a positive result: it upheld criminal prosecution of state officials who discriminated in selecting juries. The Civil Rights Act of 1875 made discrimination in selecting jurors a federal crime. In 1879, federal grand juries in Virginia indicted state judges in a dozen counties (including the judge in Patrick County, where Reynolds was convicted). Judge Alexander Rives ordered the judges arrested and held for trial. One of the indicted judges, J. D. Coles of Pittsylvania County, supported by the Commonwealth of Virginia, appealed to the Supreme Court to stop the prosecution.

The Court refused. Virginia argued that Judge Coles was not the "state," so the Fourteenth Amendment's equal protection clause ("no state" may deny the equal protection of the laws) did not apply to his actions. The Supreme Court squarely rejected that argument:

> A State acts by its legislative, its executive, or its judicial authorities. . . . The constitutional provision, therefore, must mean that no agency of the State, or of the officers or agents by whom its powers are exerted, shall deny to any person within its jurisdiction the equal protection of the laws.

This proposition seems obvious today, but it was *Ex parte Virginia* that established it.

After the Supreme Court decision, several of the Virginia judges went to trial but were acquitted by biracial juries. Prosecutions for jury discrimination have not occurred since that time, either because the zeal for civil rights prosecutions waned or because the doctrine of *Virginia v. Rives* made the necessary proof almost impossible, or both.[38]

The three jury cases had far-reaching consequences. The *Rives* case gave the states a clear blueprint for race discrimination, well beyond keeping their juries all white. As long as their laws did not explicitly mention race, state governments could discriminate however they chose to. Before long the scheme of using neutrally worded laws to conceal race discrimination spread to other types of laws, especially the disfranchising laws and constitutions that would become a bedrock of Jim Crow starting in the 1890s.

At the same time, the case *Ex parte Virginia* shows it could have been worse. If the Supreme Court had agreed with Virginia that only the state—presumably state law—was covered by the equal protection clause or other parts of the Fourteenth Amendment, the multitudinous actions of state and local officials and subordinate state bodies would go largely unchecked and the Fourteenth Amendment would be of very limited worth.[39]

Nevertheless, by holding that obvious discrimination was essentially irrelevant unless the actual words of a law discriminated, *Virginia v. Rives* was the fourth case to remove one of Reconstruction's protective building blocks—the equal protection clause of the Fourteenth Amendment.

The State Action Doctrine

By the early 1880s the Reconstruction Amendments had been gravely weakened in cases like *Cruikshank, Reese,* and *Rives,* but at least one crucial question had not been conclusively answered: whether Congress could enforce rights contained in the Thirteenth or Fourteenth Amendment against private persons. *Cruikshank* had ruled against charges based on these amendments but did not state an explicit rule. Then in two cases in 1883 the Supreme Court eliminated the doubt. The Court's doctrine of state action essentially eliminated the Thirteenth and Fourteenth Amendments in cases against private misconduct. In this way the Court removed two final blocks in the wall of protection for the new African American citizens.

The first case—*United States v. Harris* (1883)—involved four prisoners jailed in Crockett County, Tennessee. A lynch mob seized the prisoners, killed one, and beat the others. Twenty members of the mob were indicted under the Ku Klux Act, but the Supreme Court said the prosecution of these private individuals was unconstitutional. First, the Court said, as it had in *Cruikshank*, that the Fourteenth Amendment was strictly limited to enforcement against the state itself, not against private individuals, even those in a lynch mob. Second, the Court said that, although the Thirteenth Amendment was not limited to the states and could authorize prosecution of private individuals, it could do so only for race-based violations. The Ku Klux Act was not limited to race-based crimes, and therefore the Thirteenth Amendment provided no support for the prosecution in this case.

Sadly, the Ku Klux Act, rendered all but useless in this case, had been enacted in 1871 following congressional hearings that showed in bloody detail that Congress had to act against private violence or the Reconstruction Amendments would be unenforceable.[40]

By a curious twist, the Supreme Court opinion was written by Justice William B. Woods, who, as a lower-court judge, had upheld prosecutions of private individuals in *U.S. v. Hall* and *U.S. v. Cruikshank*. Whether Woods changed his position on Congress's power to protect African American civil rights or was simply acquiescing to what was now precedent, the result was the same.[41]

By holding that the Ku Klux Act could not be used to prosecute a private mob for kidnapping and lynching a prisoner, the *Harris* case removed a fifth building block from the Reconstruction wall—the Thirteenth Amendment as a weapon against private acts of racial violence.

Civil Rights Cases (1883)

Later that same year, the state action doctrine came again to the Supreme Court in a group of five cases testing the last civil rights law of Reconstruction, the Civil Rights Act of 1875. The cases were decided in a single opinion captioned *Civil Rights Cases* (1883). Although earlier cases had applied or enunciated the principle of "state action," it was this group of cases that firmly established state action as doctrine.

The Civil Rights Act of 1875 was carefully structured to ban discrimination in places of public accommodation (like inns), public conveyances on land or water, and places of public amusement (like theaters). These were well-known categories in the law. For centuries in England, and in the early United States, such quasi-public places of "public accommodation" had been required to accept all orderly travelers or customers. This doctrine should have protected against race discrimination too. Some states had enacted specific laws against race discrimination in places of public accommodation. Nevertheless, such places often discriminated, and enforcement was rare. Now the question was whether the federal government could pass such an antidiscrimination law.[42]

As a measure of the growing presence of African Americans in "society," the places that were charged with excluding African Americans in these cases included the Grand Opera House in New York, the dress circle of Maguire's Theater in San Francisco, and the first-class car of the Memphis & Charleston Railroad. The defendant in each case argued that the Civil Rights Act of 1875 was unconstitutional because Congress had no constitutional power to regulate their private conduct. Supporters of the law argued that such power had been given to Congress by the Thirteenth and Fourteenth Amendments.

Justice Joseph Bradley, writing for an 8–1 majority, held that neither the Thirteenth nor the Fourteenth Amendment provided constitutional support for the Civil Rights Act. In his analysis of the Fourteenth Amendment, Bradley explained the state action doctrine: Neither the Fourteenth Amendment itself, nor Congress acting to enforce it, can apply to "the wrongful acts of individuals, unsupported by State authority in the shape of laws, customs, or judicial or executive proceedings." Where the federal Constitution or laws create certain rights, a hostile individual might "interfere with the enjoyment of the right," for which there is presumably a state remedy, but unless the state has supported the interference, "the right remains in full force." Of course, with widespread discrimination and little enforcement of any such "remedy," Bradley's theory that "the right remains in full force" was more metaphysical than real.[43]

The Court then turned to the Thirteenth Amendment as a possible source of power for the Civil Rights Act. Section 2 of the Thirteenth Amendment, as widely agreed, authorized Congress to enact laws against the "badges and incidents" of slavery. The Civil Rights Act of 1866 defined and banned particular badges and incidents—disability to make and enforce contracts, buy and sell land, sue and testify in court. In the Civil Rights Act of 1875, Congress defined and targeted another category of badges and incidents of slavery: racial discrimination in inns and places of public accommodation, in public conveyances, and in places of public amusement.

Bradley agreed that the Thirteenth Amendment extended to public and private conduct, not just "state action." He also agreed that Congress had power under Section 2 of the amendment to outlaw "badges and incidents" of slavery:

> The power vested in Congress to enforce the article by appropriate legislation, clothes Congress with power to pass all laws necessary and proper for abolishing all badges and incidents of slavery in the United States.[44]

But what disabilities qualify as badges and incidents of slavery, and who gets to decide, Congress or the Supreme Court? Reviewing various factors, the Supreme Court held that refusing service to African Americans in inns and places of public accommodation was not a badge of slavery: it "has nothing to do with slavery or involuntary servitude."[45]

Justice Bradley closed by saying, in effect, that slavery has been finished for almost two decades, so get over it:

> When a man has emerged from slavery, and by the aid of beneficent legislation has shaken off the inseparable concomitants of that state, there must be some stage in the progress of his elevation when he takes the rank of a mere citizen, and ceases to be the special favorite of the law.[46]

This disparaging remark was not the first time, nor far from the last, that white Americans would tell African Americans their quest for equal treatment must be a desire for special treatment.

Dissenting vigorously was Justice John Marshall Harlan. Although he was a Kentuckian and had been a slave owner who disagreed with the Emancipation Proclamation, he opposed secession and was an officer in the US Army during the Civil War. During Reconstruction, Harlan became a Republican, and President Hayes appointed him to the Supreme Court in 1877 (too late for *Slaughter-House, Cruikshank,* and *Reese*).[47]

Over the years, Harlan would write enough important minority opinions about discrimination against African Americans to earn the title "the

Great Dissenter," but this was his first. Harlan believed the law was constitutional based on both the Thirteenth and Fourteenth Amendments. He directly attacked the majority opinion: "The substance and spirit of the recent amendments to the constitution have been sacrificed by a subtle and ingenious verbal criticism."[48]

Harlan emphasized the public character of places covered by the act and the long-standing legal tradition requiring innkeepers and similar "places of public accommodation" to serve all orderly patrons. He said the states' refusal to enforce these age-old laws on behalf of African Americans was both a badge of slavery (Thirteenth Amendment) and state action (Fourteenth Amendment) that Congress surely had a right to legislate against. He pointed to *Prigg v. Pennsylvania* (1842), where the Supreme Court had upheld Congress's power to protect slave owners with exactly the type of legislation it was now saying *could not* protect the former slaves. The majority opinion, he wrote, reduced the Reconstruction Amendments to nothing more than "splendid baubles thrown out to delude those who deserved fair and generous treatment at the hands of the nation."[49]

The Black press expressed outrage at the decision. T. Thomas Fortune editorialized in the *New York Globe:* "Having declared that the colored men have no protection from the government in their political rights, the Supreme Court now declares that we have no civil rights." The newspaper of the African Methodist Episcopal Church wondered if all the rights won since Emancipation might be lost: "Does not this action of the Supreme Court establish a precedent for the interfering with and unsettling the entire legal status of the former slave population in this country," and wondered, "What's next?"[50]

The decision in the *Civil Rights Cases* has gone down in Fourteenth Amendment history as *the* state action case. But there was also a Thirteenth Amendment debate over the meaning of "badges of slavery." Justices Bradley and Harlan agreed that the Thirteenth Amendment decreed "universal freedom." Bradley, though, limited badges of slavery to disabilities directly related to "servitude," whereas Harlan took a broader view, stressing "inferiority" as the crucial element. He said the institution of slavery was founded upon the supposed—and enforced—"inferiority" of the entire African race, but "The Thirteenth Amendment alone obliterated the race line, so far as all rights fundamental in a state of freedom are concerned."[51]

Implicit in Harlan's concept is the recognition that white people's views of African Americans—or racial prejudice against them—is rooted in slavery, a continuing "badge of slavery" that the Thirteenth Amendment was designed to eradicate. And yet, with the *Harris* case and the

Civil Rights Cases the Supreme Court stripped away the power in the Thirteenth and Fourteenth Amendments to prosecute private individuals, no matter how heinous their conduct.[52]

The *Civil Rights Cases* are noted mainly for their state action rule of the Fourteenth Amendment. In addition, however, by holding that the ban on discrimination in places of public accommodation went beyond Congress's power, the Supreme Court removed its sixth and final building block—Congress's power to define the badges and incidents of slavery under its enforcement power contained in Section 2 of the Thirteenth Amendment.

Of course, the Supreme Court was not pursuing a plan in deciding these cases. Courts decide cases as they arrive, and decide one case at a time. Nonetheless, with this succession of cases apparently animated by a skepticism of expanded federal authority, the Court showed a readiness to adopt interpretations that minimized the new amendments and new laws. The succession of cases removed the wall of protection erected by Reconstruction and left those who should have been protected defenseless as a far worse future was arriving.

As noted earlier, the Supreme Court was not alone, and probably not even dominant, in turning back the tide of Reconstruction and enforcement. But if the laws passed during Reconstruction could have advanced the goals of civil rights and equal justice, those laws were not available after the Supreme Court's work of this crucial period.

Of Love and Laundries

In the same year that the *Civil Rights Cases* upheld private individuals' right to reject a person of a different race, the Supreme Court upheld Alabama's right to punish people for *not* discriminating against a person of a different race in *Pace v. Alabama* (1883). Tony Pace (Black) and Mary Cox (white) were convicted and each sentenced to two years in the state penitentiary for violating an Alabama law against interracial sex or marriage. They appealed their conviction based on the equal protection clause, but the US Supreme Court unanimously ruled there was no denial of equal protection because the partners of both races were punished the same.

In another case, *Yick Wo v. Hopkins* (1886), the Court put real teeth in the Fourteenth Amendment by holding that the equal protection clause was violated by unequal administration of a state or local law even if the law as written was not discriminatory. In 1880, San Francisco adopted an ordinance (one of innumerable anti-Chinese measures) prohibiting operation of a laundry in a wooden building without a city permit. Two Chinese operators, Yick Wo and Wo Lee, were fined $10 each for operating wooden laundries without city permits. The evidence showed that all permit applications by Chinese laundry operators were denied while all but one of the applications by white operators were granted.[53]

The Supreme Court unanimously held that the maladministration of the ordinance violated the equal protection clause. In a memorable passage, the Court said:

> Though the law itself be fair on its face, and impartial in appearance, yet, if it is applied and administered by public authority with an evil eye and an unequal hand . . . the denial of equal justice is still within the prohibition of the constitution.[54]

The *Yick Wo* principle is powerful and has had a profound influence in modern times. In the near term, however, as Chapter 4 will show, the case was quickly shunted aside and was ignored as massive race discrimination took hold.

Prelude to Disfranchisement and Segregation

By the end of the 1880s, it was clear that progress toward equality was stalled. In 1890 two events took place in Washington, DC, that were the beginning of far worse to come. The two events involved what are rightly called the "twin pillars" of race discrimination: disfranchisement and segregation.[55]

Disfranchisement: In 1888, Republicans won the White House and both houses of Congress for the first time in fourteen years, running on a party platform that accused the Democrats of "suppression of the ballot by a criminal nullification of the Constitution and laws of the United States." Fully determined to follow through on their election mandate, one of their major goals was passage of the Federal Elections Bill of 1890, also known as the Lodge Elections Bill.

As Representative Henry Cabot Lodge proclaimed, "The Government which made the black man a citizen of the United States is bound to protect him in his rights as a citizen of the United States, and it is a cowardly Government if it does not do it." Federal observers had been authorized under earlier laws and had played a role in elections throughout the South in the 1870s. The Lodge bill expanded the scope of the earlier legislation and also created a mechanism to ensure a fair count in the elections being observed. The bill was long—eighty-five pages designed to surmount various tricks the states might use.[56]

The bill passed the House of Representatives with strong Republican support. Former African American congressman Robert Smalls advocated full support of the Lodge bill. Also in support was Republican attorney-writer-activist Albion Tourgée, who cautioned against the "demand which Slavery always made," that white people in the South should be left alone to deal with racial issues in their own way—with violence and fraud.[57]

Democrats struck back by labeling the bill a "Force Bill" and misrepresenting it as an authorization for military occupation. The nickname was baseless but it stuck. With Southern Democrats filibustering for thirty-three legislative days, the bill stalled in the Senate, and some Republican senators with different priorities (silver coinage and tariffs) let the moment pass. This was an early use of the filibuster tactic, but it would not be the last time Southern Democrats stopped civil rights legislation. In 1890 Democrats took control of the House of Representatives, and chances for the bill ended. The demise of the Lodge bill signaled that Republicans could no longer muster the political support for Black voting rights. White southerners' priorities had not changed, and they were about to have a free hand. More than six decades would pass before a new law to protect African American voters would be approved by Congress.[58]

Segregation: After the *Civil Rights Cases* upheld private individuals' right to discriminate if they chose as far as federal law was concerned, southern states began taking a fateful step further, enacting laws mandating discrimination—not just allowing it. Laws requiring segregation on trains and boats were enacted in Florida in 1887, in Mississippi in 1888, and in Texas in 1889. The Mississippi law went to the US Supreme Court in *Louisville, N.O. & T.R.R. v. Mississippi* (1890) via a fine imposed on a railroad for failing to maintain separate cars for white and Black passengers as the state law required.[59]

The Supreme Court had decided an almost identical case just a dozen years earlier, *Hall v. DeCuir* (1878). The earlier case involved a Reconstruction-era Louisiana law that prohibited segregation on trains and boats. The Supreme Court found that the Louisiana law banning segregation might conflict with the railroad's seating custom outside the state (which could be segregated seating) and therefore could "burden" interstate commerce by forcing a train to stop at the state border to rearrange passengers when entering or leaving the state. Under the Constitution, states are not allowed to place burdens on interstate commerce; thus the Supreme Court found the Louisiana law banning segregation to be unconstitutional.

The Mississippi law that mandated segregation put the exact same "burden" on interstate commerce. That is, a railroad that might choose to have *integrated* seating would have to stop at the Mississippi border and move passengers into segregated seating. That was the same burden as in the earlier Louisiana case; the burden on interstate commerce arose in both states alike—whenever a train entered or left the state. If one violated the interstate commerce clause, then so did the other. Except, suddenly, the Supreme Court said it was not the same. The Court that would not allow integrated railroad service now specifically approved segregated railroad service. One law prohibited segregation and was struck down, while the other law required segregation and was upheld. In 1890 the Mississippi law became the first racial segregation law upheld by the US Supreme Court.[60]

The dissent by Harlan made it clear: "It is difficult to understand how a state enactment [forbidding] the separation of the white and black races on interstate carriers of passengers is a regulation of commerce among the states, while a similar enactment [requiring] such separation is not a regulation of that character." This dissent was joined by Justice Bradley, who had written the devastating lower court opinion in *Cruikshank* (1874) and the Supreme Court *Civil Rights Cases* (1883), bracketed those decisions with stirring pro-civil-rights dissents at the start and end of his career in *Blyew* (1872) and now *Louisville, N.O. & T.R.R v. Mississippi* (1890).[61]

The segregation train was running, and the US Supreme Court was on board. In the 1870s and 1880s the Supreme Court struck down or severely narrowed sections of the Civil Rights Act of 1866, the Enforcement Act of 1870, the Ku Klux Act of 1871, and the Civil Rights Act of 1875. In several cases, the Court had expressed strongly favorable, even noble, sentiments, but—perhaps inexplicably—those expressions did not seem to translate into useful results.[62]

By the close of the 1880s, the federal government was largely out of the business of protecting freedom in the rebel states. With the Supreme Court's surgery on the Reconstruction Amendments and on Congress's enforcement laws, the federal government was incapable of protecting citizens against hostile mobs and increasingly hostile state governments. The Court showed that federal privileges were pitifully few, that the federal government could not protect even those few privileges, and that if state laws avoided explicit words of discrimination, they would meet little judicial resistance. Laws built to protect the newly freed people had been demolished.

But far worse was about to come. African Americans entered the 1890s with no meaningful way to protect their rights.

CHAPTER FOUR

The Supreme Court and the Jim Crow Counterrevolution

By 1890, white supremacists had gained or regained control of the former Confederate states. With legal and governmental machinery now in their hands, they were determined to strip African Americans of the opportunities they earned during Reconstruction, drive them from public life, and restore as much of slavery's caste system as might be allowed.

The counterrevolution of 1890 was about to begin. It was a dizzying descent into Jim Crow. "Jim Crow" is the colloquial term for the regime of mandated white supremacy. The term derives from a Black character in early-nineteenth-century minstrel shows, portrayed—often by white actors wearing blackface—as childlike and foolish. It came to stand for the comprehensive rule of racial inequality that dominated every aspect of legal and social relations from cradle to grave in the band of states stretching from Virginia to Texas, and it spread its tentacles outward from there. Jim Crow was rigidly enforced by law, fraud, and violence, and by the education and socialization that infected the minds of millions of otherwise decent people, white and Black.[1]

Jim Crow was built on two fundamental and related supports, the twin pillars of segregation and disfranchisement. Especially in the early days, southern leaders had to wonder how far the Supreme Court would let them go, but they need not have worried. Segregation and disfranchisement were challenged repeatedly in court by African Americans, but both pillars and other forms of discrimination would receive the Supreme Court's blessing, not once or twice, but in a parade of more than twenty cases over the next two decades.

The story properly begins with two events in the middle of 1890, one in Louisiana involving segregation and the other in Mississippi involving disfranchisement.

Racial segregation was not the norm in the South during slavery, but with the end of slavery, former slave states began instituting segregation as a substitute system of race relations. Separation was less the goal than a mechanism for racial subordination, a caste system. Under Reconstruction, some integrated state legislatures had banned segregation, but the tide turned back toward new segregation laws in the late 1880s. An earlier Mississippi railroad law was the first state segregation law tested in the US Supreme Court. When the law was upheld in early 1890, the Court insisted it was deciding only the railroad's claims, but obviously a test of personal rights would be next. In the end it was Louisiana's 1890 law that would ultimately test segregation in the Supreme Court.[2]

In May 1890, the mostly white Louisiana legislature introduced Act 111. Formally titled "An Act to Promote the Comfort of Passengers on Railway Trains," it was commonly called the Separate Car Law. It required railways in the state to provide "equal, but separate, accommodations for the white and colored races," and said that "no person or persons shall be permitted to occupy seats in coaches other than the ones assigned to them on account of their race." Violating the law was a crime, for which a passenger could be fined or jailed, as could a railroad employee or executive who permitted a violation.[3]

The dozen-plus African Americans who were still in the Louisiana legislature were unsuccessful in fighting the bill, and it became law in July 1890. Opponents quickly organized to challenge the Separate Car Law, but it would be 1896—six years after enactment—before the US Supreme Court decided its fate.

While lawmakers in Louisiana were segregating trains, 133 white men and one Black man were meeting in Jackson, Mississippi, to replace the Reconstruction-era state constitution with a new one whose clear purpose was to deny the vote to African Americans. Everyone acknowledged that fraud and violence were the means by which Mississippi's white minority (a minority in both population and registered voters) had maintained control since the violent overthrow in 1875 of the elected interracial Republican government. Judge J. J. Chrisman, one of the convention delegates, put it most colorfully: "Sir, it is no secret that there has not been a full vote and a fair count in Mississippi since 1875, that we have been preserving the ascendancy of the white people by revolutionary methods." He was candid: "In other words, we have been stuffing ballot boxes, committing perjury, and here and there in the state carrying elections by fraud and violence." Indeed, the instability, fraud, and violence of the previous fifteen years were a significant part of the push for a new way to maintain white control. As Chrisman stated, "No man can be in favor of perpetuating these election methods who is not a moral idiot."[4]

Mississippi's solution to the fraud and violence was to disfranchise the victims, but first the delegates to the constitutional convention had to be elected. African Americans were warned that seeking election as delegates would be "worse than folly." One Black man, Marsh Cook, nonetheless declared his candidacy; shortly thereafter his body was found riddled with bullets.[5]

Still, the people elected one African American delegate, Isaiah Montgomery, a well-to-do planter and businessman who had founded the town of Mound Bayou, virtually all-Black then and now. He was the son of enslaved parents, both of whom were literate. All three worked on the Hurricane Plantation, owned by the older brother of Confederate president Jefferson Davis. The senior Montgomery often managed the plantation, and his son learned at his side how to accommodate his white neighbors. White voters supported this "safe and conservative" delegate, even though a white man ran against him. Recognizing that it was Black equality that most enraged white people, Isaiah Montgomery assumed, incorrectly, that if he sidestepped that issue, African Americans could be left alone and escape the worst excesses of racial strife. He proposed a literacy-based plan that would have disfranchised two thirds of African American voters and a number of white voters, leaving a substantial white majority.[6]

It was a futile effort. The other delegates to the Mississippi state constitutional convention had come to disfranchise not some people but an entire race. S. S. Calhoon, president of the convention, declared, "We came here to exclude the negro. Nothing short of this will answer." Or, as it was later put by future governor and senator James K. Vardaman, perhaps with a touch of campaign hyperbole, "Mississippi's constitutional convention of 1890 was held for no other purpose than to eliminate the nigger from politics; not the 'ignorant and vicious,' as some of those apologists would have you believe, but the nigger." Recalling that in 1880 the Supreme Court had declared that state laws were unconstitutional if their actual wording discriminated against African Americans, the white convention delegates thought they might be on safe ground if they achieved the same result but with slightly veiled language. Time—and the Supreme Court—proved them right.[7]

The new Mississippi Constitution began by removing all voters from the rolls and requiring them to re-register. Then the constitution erected formal barriers to registration, such as the poll tax and literacy test, that were understood to bear more heavily on African Americans than on white voters. The literal requirements, however, would have taken the convention only part way to its goal of an all-white electorate; instead these tests were mere tools to put "discretion" into the hands of local white registrars, who understood their task to be registering white applicants and rejecting African Americans. To facilitate discrimination, the 1890 Mississippi Constitution contained an "understanding test," which allowed an illiterate person to skip the literacy test if he could satisfy the registrar that he "understood" a provision of the state constitution when read to him. Mississippi's leading newspaper, the Jackson *Clarion-Ledger,* reported that "it so happened that no man could devise any test which, fairly and honestly applied," would register all white and no Black voters. "There was a general understanding that the interpretation of the constitution offered by an illiterate white man would be acceptable to the registrars; that of a Negro would not."[8]

Thus, the new disfranchising system maintained white supremacy "by legal rather than illegal means." This was a favorite phrasing of the day, even though "legal" actually meant "pretend legal"—cheating by officials acting in the name of the law. The "Mississippi Plan," as it came to be called, was an immediate success, reducing the number of Black registered voters from 200,000 to 8,000 in just the first two years. Soon there were entire counties with large Black populations where not a single African American was registered to vote.[9]

For the next several years after 1890, efforts to install as official policy the two pillars of white supremacy—segregation and disfranchisement—cautiously moved forward. Five more states adopted separate car laws, but widespread movement to segregate other areas of life lagged. Democrats in Washington reinforced the pillars. When they gained control of the presidency and Congress in 1892, they promptly repealed the federal observer law, which had not been used in recent years, so the southern states could run dishonest elections without oversight. Southern states manipulated voting laws, but uncertainty about how the Supreme Court would react made most of them reluctant to join Mississippi in its total disfranchisement plan.[10]

The only exception was South Carolina, 60 percent Black, which adopted a Mississippi-style constitution in 1895. Governor "Pitchfork Ben" Tillman, nicknamed for threatening to prod that "bag of beef" Grover Cleveland with the farm tool in question, called for white people to preserve "Anglo-Saxon supremacy" and proclaimed, "The only thing we can do as patriots and statesmen is to take from them [African Americans] every ballot we can." Later, in the US Senate, Tillman declared: "We have scratched our heads to find out how we could eliminate every last one of them. We stuffed ballot boxes. We shot them. We are not ashamed of it."[11]

Lawrence P. Mills, an African American voter, quickly sued to block the South Carolina convention. He secured an injunction from a lower-court federal judge who found that the purpose of the convention was "to destroy the greatest number of the ballots of the citizens of African descent, while at the same time to interfere with as few as possible of those of the white race." But the injunction was reversed on dubious procedural grounds by an appeals court headed by US Supreme Court Chief Justice Melville Fuller (selected by Democratic president Grover Cleveland). By the time the case—*Mills v. Green* (1895)—reached the Supreme Court, the convention was already at work and the Court simply dismissed the case, saying it was too late for any effective relief. Thus was the first challenge to a disfranchising state constitution turned away.[12]

Once the era of segregation and disfranchisement began, African Americans had precious little room to maneuver. One of those who tried was Booker T. Washington. Born a slave in Virginia, Washington eventually moved to Alabama, where he founded the Tuskegee Institute in 1881. Preaching a gospel of self-help and uplift by education and work, Washington exerted some limited degree of political influence. In a famed 1895 speech at the Cotton States Exposition in Atlanta, Washington said, "The opportunity to earn a dollar in a factory just now is worth infinitely more than the opportunity to spend a dollar in an opera house." His Atlanta speech is often described as an acceptance of second-class citizenship. His mostly white audience, regarding it in that light, responded with vigorous applause. His point, though, was that African Americans should concentrate on improving their lot through education and labor, without seeking social integration. He believed that prejudice would die out as African Americans made economic and educational progress, ignoring the fact that it was precisely such progress that seemed to ignite white hostility and even fury.[13]

Washington and others hoped that the country's cautious momentum toward segregation and disfranchisement could be halted by the Supreme Court. The Court had not yet squarely ruled on any cases involving the new pillars of white supremacy, but the Court was soon to make a ruling that would propel segregation forward on a lightning-fast track. That case was Homer Plessy's, and he entered the pages of history by taking a ride on a railroad.

Booker T. Washington was a secret sponsor of legal challenges to disfranchisement, all-white juries, the convict leasing system, and other evils.

Plessy v. Ferguson (1896), the Segregation Case

Homer Plessy, born in 1863, had grown up in New Orleans free to vote, engage in politics, and ride any train and streetcar. When he was twenty-seven, however, Louisiana enacted its Separate Car Law, and the reign of Jim Crow began. Plessy's arrest was no accident. As soon as the separate car law passed in 1890, a group of African Americans and white residents in New Orleans formed a Citizens Committee for the Annulment of Act No. 111, and set about planning a challenge to the new law. The first case actually involved not Homer Plessy but an African American named Daniel Desdunes, son of a prominent New Orleans editor and author. Desdunes was arrested for refusing to leave a "white" car, but the charges were dismissed when he went to court. Thus, it was the second volunteer, Homer Plessy, whose case went forward. Seven of Plessy's eight great-grandparents were white, but one was Black, which meant he was "colored" under Louisiana law. Whatever his designation, he looked white enough to buy a ticket for the white car, on June 7, 1892.[14]

After revealing his "true color" to the conductor, Plessy refused the directive to move to the colored car, and he was arrested. He challenged his arrest in the Louisiana Supreme Court, which expressed some indignation at African Americans for their "unreasonable" opposition to segregation. Their "insistence on thrusting the company of one race upon the other, with no adequate motive," said the Louisiana justices, was "calculated . . . to foster and intensify repulsion between them, rather than to extinguish it." Plessy appealed to the US Supreme Court.[15]

To handle Homer Plessy's case, the Citizens Committee recruited the nationally renowned white lawyer Albion Tourgée. Son of a devout Methodist farming family in Ohio, Tourgée fought for the United States in the Civil War and later became a lawyer and author, writing unflinching admonitions against lynching, segregation, and disfranchisement. Based on his experiences in North Carolina during Reconstruction, Tourgée had written a best-selling novel, *A Fool's Errand,* sharply critical of the white supremacy prevalent in the postwar South. Now the *Washington Post* suggested that his representation of Homer Plessy before the Supreme Court might likewise turn out to be another "fool's errand."[16]

The Court handed down its decision on May 18, 1896, just five weeks after the oral argument. The decision rejected Plessy's claims and upheld the Louisiana law. The opinion was written by Justice Henry Brown, a Yale Law School graduate appointed to the Court by Republican president Benjamin Harrison in 1890.

Brown began by dispatching the Thirteenth Amendment argument against the Louisiana law. He said the law could not be a "badge of slavery" because it was simply a distinction based on "color," a distinction "which must always exist so long as white men are distinguished from the other race by color." Of course, that aphorism made no sense in this case because Homer Plessy's color looked "white"; so if the law had really been about color, Plessy would not have been evicted from the white car.

Turning to the Fourteenth Amendment, Brown began with the proposition that "the object of the Amendment was undoubtedly to enforce the absolute equality of the races." But then he took it all back: "but in the nature of things, it could not have been intended to abolish distinctions based on color, or to enforce social, as distinguished from political, equality, or a commingling of the two races upon terms unsatisfactory to either." Brown did not explain what "in the nature of things" meant, or why Homer Plessy's desired result "could not have been intended." Opinions typically use phrases like "it could not have been intended" when the literal words seem to say exactly what the Court is about to deny. The *Plessy* opinion was an exercise in explaining why the Fourteenth Amendment, which required that rights of the races be "exactly the same," allowed Louisiana to make the races sit in separate cars. No explanation could suffice.[17]

One point cited by Justice Brown did provide some support for Louisiana's Separate Car Law: the Congress that had approved the Fourteenth Amendment in 1866 also approved segregated schools in Washington,

The Supreme Court that approved racial segregation in *Plessy v. Ferguson* (1896) and racial disfranchisement in *Williams v. Mississippi* (1898). Front row, left to right: David Brewer, John Marshall Harlan, Chief Justice Melville Fuller, Horace Gray, Henry Brown. Back row, left to right: Rufus Peckham, George Shiras, Edward D. White, Joseph McKenna. McKenna sat in *Williams,* after he was appointed in 1897, succeeding Stephen J. Field, who sat in *Plessy*.

DC, which suggested that the 1866 Congress, at least, found no inconsistency between the Fourteenth Amendment and segregation in schools. The *Plessy* opinion also cited one federal case and several state court cases (some antebellum) that upheld school segregation laws, while not citing contrary cases from other states that rejected school segregation.[18]

In another supposed line of precedent, Brown pointed to a string of eleven cases in which, according to him, "similar statutes for the separation of the two races upon public conveyances were held to be constitutional." This would obviously have been powerful support for segregation laws, except that Brown misrepresented the cases—not a single one of the eleven cases he listed had upheld a law mandating segregation. Rather, the eleven cases all involved suits by African Americans against private transportation companies' segregation policies (not laws), and the African Americans' suits were successful in a majority of the eleven cases.[19]

Perhaps most intriguing was the *Plessy* Court's failure to take account of a case in which a theory of "separate but equal" had already been rejected unanimously by the US Supreme Court itself—*Railroad Company v. Brown* (1873). In that earlier case, Catherine Brown sued for being kept out of the white car on a trip in early 1868 from Alexandria, Virginia, to Washington, DC. The railroad was not subject to the Fourteenth Amendment, which had not yet been ratified, but it was governed by a congressional franchise that said "no person shall be excluded from the cars on account of color." The railroad company contended that Ms. Brown had not been "excluded from the cars" because the white car and the colored car were "equally safe, clean, and comfortable." The Supreme Court unanimously rejected this argument, calling it "an ingenious attempt to evade compliance with the obvious meaning of the requirement." The Supreme Court upheld a $1,500 jury verdict for Ms. Brown.[20]

Of course, the exact wording of the prohibition in Catherine Brown's case (that no person may be "excluded from the cars on account of color") is not quite the same as the prohibition in the Fourteenth Amendment in *Plessy* (that no person may be denied "equal protection of the laws"), but it is hard to see much difference in the meaning of the language. The separate-but-equal theory, which had persuaded not a single justice in 1873, looked different to eight justices in 1896. Brown cited the *Brown* case in his *Plessy* opinion but did not explain or even describe it, and he and the Court paid no attention to its holding and lesson.

Facing mixed precedent, the Court's principal basis for upholding segregated street cars seems to have been its view that race prejudice is the normal order of human behavior, even human instinct. The Court said, "legislation is powerless to eradicate racial instincts" and that social intercourse "can neither be accomplished nor promoted by laws which conflict with the general sentiment of the community." (The Court did not explain how these observations were relevant to a law that eliminated a person's choice not to segregate.)[21]

This thinking was in line with the social Darwinist views of people like William Graham Sumner, a well-known author of the day, who depicted any legislative attempt to rectify racism as a conflict with custom, and concluded that "stateways cannot change folkways." Near the close of the opinion, the Court offered its racially infused contempt in a disparaging comment reminiscent of previous comments offered in the *Dred Scott* case and the *Civil Rights Cases:*

> We consider the underlying fallacy of the plaintiff's argument to consist in the assumption that the enforced separation of the races stamps the colored race with a badge of inferiority. If this be so, it is not by reason of anything found in the act, but solely because the colored race chooses to put that construction upon it.[22]

The Supreme Court's willingness to accommodate private prejudice contrasted sharply with some other courts of that period, such as the Michigan Supreme Court. That court ruled that segregated restaurant tables did not satisfy the "equal treatment" requirement of a Michigan statute, and it eloquently addressed the problem of private prejudice: "The prejudice against association in public places with the negro, which does exist, to some extent, in all communities, less now than formerly, is unworthy of our race, and it is not for the courts to cater to or temporize with."[23]

The ruling in *Plessy* not only accommodated prejudice but mandated it. Whereas the *Civil Rights Cases* (1883) upheld a private citizen's "freedom" to discriminate or not, the new segregation laws took that freedom away, instead ordering every individual—white and Black—to discriminate or go to jail. This conscription of every white person into the army of racial discrimination gave official segregation a totalitarian cast. Jim Crow became anchored in the minds of many later generations of people, such as innkeepers and restaurant owners, who claimed they were exercising their free will or free choice.

The sole dissenter in *Plessy* was Justice John Marshall Harlan. He said the arbitrary separation of the races on the public highways was both a badge of slavery, in violation of the Thirteenth Amendment, and a denial of equal protection, in violation of the Fourteenth Amendment, and had been so intended. His dissent remains vivid to this day. Harlan gave his personal opinion that the white race was the dominant race and likely to remain so. But,

> in view of the constitution, in the eye of the law, there is in this country no superior, dominant, ruling class of citizens. There is no caste here. Our constitution is color-blind, and neither knows nor tolerates classes of citizens.[24]

Harlan called the law's qualifier ("equal") a lie: "The thin disguise of 'equal' accommodations for passengers in railroad coaches will not mislead anyone, nor atone for the wrong this day done." He closed his dissent with a tragically prophetic statement: "The judgment this day rendered will, in time, prove to be quite as pernicious as the decision made by this tribunal in the *Dred Scott* case."[25]

The *Plessy* decision, unlike the *Dred Scott* case, attracted only a moderate amount of press attention outside the South, an indication of the nation's waning interest in race issues. But there was no mystery about what the case involved; the newspapers that did cover the story typically referred to it as "the Jim Crow case." A few newspapers picked up on Harlan's point that the law made no more sense than a law requiring separation "of Protestants and Roman Catholics." The African American press roundly derided the decision, with one Kansas paper saying the Supreme Court had so "wantonly disgraced itself" that it was "time to put an end to the existence of this infernal, infamous body."[26]

Both South and North shared a common expectation: the Court's decision would prompt more segregation laws in the South. One Republican newspaper wrote, "The law may now be expected to spread like the measles in those commonwealths where white supremacy is thought to be in peril."[27]

Starting quickly, and with increasing speed, every aspect of life in the South, and often in the North and Midwest, was racially segregated, immediately or with the spread of new technology, from buses and lunch counters to Coke machines, from movies and parks to water fountains. The city of Baltimore was the first of many to pass an ordinance restricting where African Americans could live. Even the word of God was segregated as courtrooms used separate Bibles to swear witnesses. One young African American captured the absurdities of Jim Crow's oppression: "For trains, it is in the front; on the ship, it is below; on the street car it is in the rear; and in the theatre it is above."[28]

Before long, segregation was the norm in many places and many ways throughout the country, from neighborhood housing patterns to "the national pastime," baseball. It was a deluge and it came with the moral authority of the US Supreme Court.

Disfranchisement

Supreme Court consideration of the other twin pillar of Jim Crow—disfranchisement—was already under way when *Plessy v. Ferguson* was decided. It would come in an attack on the Mississippi Constitution of 1890, brought by way of an African American lawyer's challenge to Mississippi's all-white juries.

By the 1890s, growing numbers of African Americans were engaged in law practice, and one of their constant problems was the universal system of all-white juries. The Supreme Court of the 1880s had ruled that race discrimination in jury selection was unconstitutional but made it almost impossible to prove.[29]

One lawyer who kept challenging the issue was Cornelius J. Jones, who had served one term in the legislature before the disfranchisement constitution. After that term he returned to live in tiny Issaquena County and kept confronting all-white juries as he handled cases throughout Mississippi's overwhelmingly Black Delta region. Before the 1890s were over, Jones would make three trips to the US Supreme Court on behalf of African American defendants indicted, convicted, and sentenced to death by all-white juries. All three trips were to no avail.[30]

The first two cases were on behalf of two Black Delta residents—John Gibson of Washington County, and Charlie Smith of Bolivar County. Both were convicted of murder although Gibson had obviously acted in self-defense. Smith's guilt was unclear.[31]

Jones focused on the fact that neither county had ever had a Black juror even though both had large majorities of African American men eligible for jury service compared to white men (7,000 to 1,500 in Washington County, and 1,300 to 300 in Bolivar County). On appeal to the US Supreme Court, Jones argued for Gibson, and, needing another attorney to argue in Smith's case, hired Emanuel Hewlett, an African American lawyer located in Washington, DC. This was the first time two African American lawyers had ever argued before the US Supreme Court on the same day.[32]

The Supreme Court made short work of the arguments in the two cases, saying the statistics were insufficient by themselves or were barred by state procedural rules. The 1890 constitution was raised indirectly, but the Court noted that the words of the Mississippi Constitution were neutral, not tied to race. In 1898 Cornelius Jones made his third appearance before the US Supreme Court. Jones's client this time was Henry Williams; the charge again was murder in Washington County, and the jury again, like all juries in Mississippi, was all white. This time Jones included a frontal attack on the Mississippi Constitution of 1890. He contended that African Americans' absence from juries stemmed from their disfranchisement as voters, because the 1890 constitution provided that only registered voters could serve as jurors.

Jones had a powerful weapon to use against the Mississippi's Constitution of 1890: a new decision by the Mississippi Supreme Court itself boldly stated that the 1890 Mississippi Constitution *was in fact* a scheme to disfranchise Black voters. The Mississippi court wrote that "within the field of permissible action under the limitations imposed by the federal constitution, the convention swept the circle of expedients to obstruct the exercise of the franchise by the negro race."[33]

This was done, the Mississippi court explained, by picking and choosing requirements for voting that mostly disqualified African Americans but not white voters: "Restrained by the federal Constitution from discriminating against the negro race, the convention discriminated against its characteristics, and the offenses to which its criminal members are prone." One of the Mississippi court's examples was a section disqualifying those convicted of certain crimes—but not a logical list of crimes. Instead, the Mississippi Supreme Court said, the crimes chosen for disqualification were the "furtive offenses" to which "criminal members of the [Black] race were given," but not "the robust crimes of the whites."[34]

Why would the Mississippi Supreme Court justices make such an incriminating statement? The reason was the poll tax. A county sheriff had tried to enforce collection of the poll tax, including from Black residents. But the Mississippi Supreme Court blocked this effort, explaining that, unlike other taxes, which are supposed to be paid, Mississippi's poll tax was intended to *not* be paid, at least not by African Americans—in order to keep nonpayers from voting. All this the Mississippi Supreme Court openly, and amazingly, explained. Armed with the Mississippi Supreme Court's own words, Jones was, if not confident, at least hopeful.[35]

In *Williams v. Mississippi* (1898), Jones attacked the disfranchisement scheme on two grounds—challenging first the 1890 constitution itself, and second, its administration by the county voting registrars. As to the first ground, Mississippi's 1890 constitution did not contain literal words disfranchising Black voters, but the Mississippi Supreme Court filled that gap when it announced that "the convention swept the field of expedients, to obstruct the exercise of suffrage by the negro race." That statement should have produced an instantaneous reversal by the US Supreme Court. Instead the highest court in the land endorsed the lie that the federal Constitution had a "field of permissible action" where deliberate racial discrimination is constitutional.[36]

Then, since the Mississippi scheme relied on voters' "characteristics," the US Supreme Court said Mississippi's picking and choosing characteristics to disfranchise one race did not matter: "It cannot be said, therefore, that the denial of the equal protection of the laws arises primarily from the constitution and laws of Mississippi." This decision shredded the Fourteenth and Fifteenth Amendments. It puts this case—decided unanimously—in the list of the most disgraceful decisions in Supreme Court history.[37]

That still left Williams's second argument, discriminatory administration by the registrars. This argument relied on the 1886 case of *Yick Wo v. Hopkins*. In *Yick Wo* the Supreme Court had condemned a San Francisco city ordinance which, though "fair on its face," had been applied against Chinese-owned laundries "with an evil eye and an unequal hand." In *Williams,* the justices abandoned *Yick Wo*. To reject the rule it had accepted in *Yick Wo v. Hopkins,* the Supreme Court in *Williams* fashioned a barrier it must have known was impossible to overcome. The Court said the evidence was not "definite" enough because Williams should have shown how, when, and by whom the wrongs were committed. The proof in *Williams* was necessarily general, depending on widely scattered registrars throughout the (at the time) seventy-five counties of the state; it certainly did not and could not match the detailed census of laundries within a single city, as had been accomplished in *Yick Wo*. Without those specifics, according to the Court, Williams's huge numbers—including an absolute zero for Black jurors in an overwhelmingly Black county—did not show that Mississippi's constitution and laws were administered with "an evil eye and unequal hand," only that "evil was possible under them."[38]

The *Plessy* case crippled the Fourteenth Amendment. The *Williams* case erased the Fifteenth Amendment. No one seemed to remember the Thirteenth Amendment. Jim Crow was now the law of the land.

Chinese Immigration in the United States

By the late 1800s people from China had increasingly become targets of bigotry in the United States. With the Far East closed to the outside world until the mid-nineteenth century, Chinese immigration to the United States began in 1849 during the California gold rush. In the 1860s more Chinese laborers came to work on the transcontinental railroad. By 1880 the census reported 105,405 Chinese immigrants in the United States, almost all men, mostly laborers or miners.

Chinese residents could not become American citizens. The Naturalization Act of 1790 limited eligibility to white persons. An amendment in 1870 expanded the color line to allow naturalization for people of African descent as well as white people, but no one else. Despite treaties in 1868 and 1880 that promised US protection for Chinese immigrants, white hostility grew, starting with competition for jobs but growing more general and widespread. In 1871 in Los Angeles, where Chinese residents were 3 percent of the population, a mob of about 500 white and Mexican American residents looted Chinese homes and stores and attacked Chinese people, lynching twenty and destroying the Chinese neighborhood. Eight men were convicted, but the convictions were overturned. In the 1880s, white mobs in Tacoma, Washington; Rock Springs, Wyoming; and elsewhere looted and burned "Chinatowns" and forced residents to flee. According to John Higham, a historian of nativism, "No variety of anti-European sentiment has ever approached the violent extremes to which anti-Chinese agitation went in the 1870s and 1880s."[39]

Hostility spread to Congress. The Page Act of 1875 aimed at supposed undesirables, but as carried out it cut all Chinese female immigration to a trickle. Congress then passed the Chinese Exclusion Act of 1882. One legislator who opposed the new law was Senator George F. Hoar of Massachusetts, the man who later would lead the effort to enact the Lodge Elections Bill of 1890. Senator Hoar described the racism involved as "the last of human delusions to be overcome." Reflecting the different temper of the times, the *New York Times* called Hoar's attitude "stupidity," and the *New York Tribune* put him in the class of "humanitarian half-thinkers."[40]

Congress followed up with more laws, repeatedly extending and tightening the 1882 act in 1884, 1888, 1892, and 1894, and making it permanent in 1902. The original law prevented entry of new Chinese immigrants, but it allowed US residents to leave and return. The 1888 law restricted those who were already US residents by eliminating "re-entry certificates," and the 1892 law required US residents of Chinese ancestry to have residence certificates or face deportation.[41]

The Supreme Court was relatively supportive of Chinese immigrants at first. In *Chy Lung v. Freeman* (1876), the Court struck down a California state statute that gave state port officials unlimited power over immigrants, which the Port of San Francisco had used arbitrarily against Chinese women. In 1879 Justice Field, sitting as a circuit judge, held that San Francisco's "pigtail ordinance" (cutting off the "queue" of Chinese jail inmates) was a violation of the equal protection clause. In 1886 the landmark case of *Yick Wo v. Hopkins* struck down San Francisco's wooden laundry ordinance. Even after passage of the Chinese Exclusion Act of 1882, the Court's first two cases interpreted the law favorably for Chinese immigrants.[42]

The first sign of a bleaker day for Chinese immigrants in the Supreme Court involved a civil rights prosecution for anti-Chinese violence. In February 1886 in Nicolaus, California, a white mob forced Chinese residents to abandon their homes and immediately board trains leaving town. The federal government prosecuted the mob leaders under the Enforcement Act of 1870. Even though the treaty with China guaranteed protection for Chinese immigrants, the Supreme Court held that the wording of the Enforcement Act protected only "citizens." Justice Harlan, dissenting along with Justice Field, said, "the language neither demands nor justifies" the Court's interpretation. The indictment was dismissed in *Baldwin v. Franks* (1887) and the mob leaders released. Thereafter, the Supreme Court upheld all of Congress's amendments and extension of the Chinese Exclusion Act of 1882.[43]

The measures, as intended, froze the number of Chinese people in the United States. Few Chinese immigrants were allowed to enter, and, because the number of female Chinese immigrants had always been small, there were few American-born children of Chinese descent. People in this small group were American citizens because the first sentence of the Fourteenth Amendment gives "birthright citizenship" to all those "born or naturalized in the United States and subject to the jurisdiction thereof." The federal government, though, took aim at this small group, contending that they were not "subject to the jurisdiction" of the United States but were instead subjects of the emperor of China.[44]

One of those targeted was Wong Kim Ark, born in San Francisco in 1873 of Chinese parents who were not US citizens. In 1890, amid mounting anti-Chinese sentiment, the family moved to China, but the teenage son returned alone to California. He spoke fluent English, and, like many American children of immigrant parents, he may have felt at home in America and out of place in a homeland where he had never lived. When he returned home from another visit to his parents in 1894, he was excluded and his citizenship was challenged. A lower court ruled in his favor, rejecting the federal government's argument against citizenship for "the rag tag and bob tail of humanity, who happen to be deposited on our soil by the accident of birth." The government did not give up, and on appeal, in *United States v. Wong Kim Ark* (1898), the Supreme Court ruled that the Fourteenth Amendment meant what it said. It may have been a lone victory, but it was a monumental one.[45]

The Chinese Exclusion Act ended only with the Magnuson Act of 1943, and then only because China was a World War II ally of the United States in the war against Japan.[46]

Residents of another Asian country, Japan, observed the Chinese experience and determined to avoid it. Japanese immigration began much later than Chinese immigration; only 148 Japanese people were reported in the 1880 census, but the number rose rapidly to 24,826 by 1900. Japanese immigrants were affected by some immigration restrictions, but they were not singled out by any law comparable to the Chinese Exclusion Act. Rather than repeat the Chinese experience, Japan and the United States entered into the so-called Gentlemen's Agreement of 1907, by which the United States would avoid anti-Japanese legislation and would try to ensure nondiscrimination against Japanese already in the country, while Japan would restrict immigration by refusing passports for travel to work in the United States.[47]

Thus, by the early twentieth century the United States Congress and courts had policies of race discrimination firmly in place. Those policies would spread in the years that followed.

Native American Treaties

After spending much of the century on a policy of Indian extermination, the US government by the late nineteenth century had settled most Indian tribes on reservations, which had been established by treaties between the federal government and the various tribes. But just as had happened east of the Mississippi, as white settlers moved westward, they began to inhabit the lands set aside for reservations.

The Treaty of Medicine Lodge in 1867 asserted that several tribes, including Kiowa, Comanche, and Apache, had possession of more than two million acres of grazing and farm land, with supposed protections built into the treaty. By the turn of the century, however, the land was so valuable that white settlers orchestrated falsified "agreements" to get the land from the tribes. When Congress passed a statute in 1900 approving the agreements, Kiowa chief Lone Wolf brought a lawsuit alleging fraud and violation of the 1867 treaty. When the Supreme Court heard the case, *Lone Wolf v. Hitchcock* (1903), it held that Congress had plenary power over Indian tribes, that Congress was free to violate treaties and approve obvious frauds, and that the Court had no jurisdiction. This case has been called "the Indians' *Dred Scott*."[48]

The Twin Pillars Flourish

As the twentieth century arrived, the last African American US congressman, George White of North Carolina, gave his parting address in 1901: "This, Mr. Chairman, is perhaps the Negro's temporary farewell to the American Congress, but let me say that, Phoenix-like, he will rise up and come again."[49]

What the Supreme Court said, as well as what it did in *Williams v. Mississippi*, seemed to eliminate any doubts about the viability of disfranchising schemes. Looking back in 1907, US Representative John Sharp Williams of Mississippi, Democratic minority leader, said the threat of Black voting did not end with Mississippi's 1890 constitution, but only when the US Supreme Court held it "not to be violative of the US Constitution." Louisiana, Alabama, Virginia, and Georgia joined Mississippi and South Carolina in adopting new disfranchising constitutions, North Carolina and Texas did so with amendments, and Tennessee and Arkansas by statute. Florida's statutes preceded Mississippi's.[50]

Rhetoric became more blatant. Carter Glass, a leader of the Virginia constitutional convention in 1902, used the words approved in *Williams v. Mississippi* to explain how driving African Americans from the voting booth fit perfectly within the Supreme Court's conception of the Fifteenth Amendment: "Discrimination! Why that is precisely what we propose, that, exactly, is what this convention was called for—to discriminate to the very extremity of permissible action under the limitations of the Federal Constitution." Glass stated explicitly that the purpose was "the elimination of every Negro voter who can be gotten rid of legally without materially impairing the numerical strength of the white electorate." In Louisiana the leader of the convention, Ernest B. Kruttschnitt, got to the bottom line in fewer words when he spoke about the literacy test: "What care I whether it be more or less ridiculous or not? Doesn't it let the white man vote, and doesn't it stop the negro from voting, and isn't that what we came here for?"[51]

Not just the language, but the schemes, became bolder. Because disfranchising tactics such as literacy tests and poll taxes might also work against poor white residents, lawmakers needed new maneuvers; the most spectacular of these was the grandfather clause. With slight variations, states imposed strict standards to qualify for voting but exempted white voters by giving automatic eligibility to any man who was eligible to vote—or whose ancestor was eligible—as of, say, 1865, or any other date before the Fifteenth Amendment enfranchised African Americans in 1870. It was thus an exact synonym for "white." Such a daring clause was not included in the early disfranchising constitutions of Mississippi and South Carolina, and when Louisiana proposed one just before the *Williams* decision, the state's two US senators called it unconstitutional. In the end it was adopted in Louisiana only as a temporary measure, for three months. After the *Williams* decision, however, other southern states put a grandfather clause in their constitutions.[52]

The *Williams* case was not the Supreme Court's last brush with disfranchisement and does not stand alone on the list of its worst. The case must share that distinction with a set of Alabama cases that resulted in two despicable Supreme Court decisions.

Alabama adopted its disfranchising constitution in 1901. As alleged in a series of five lawsuits filed in 1902, Alabama relied both on formal eligibility restrictions in the new constitution and on the "evil eye and unequal hand" of county registrars who could be depended on to register white applicants, qualified or not, while turning away masses of African Americans. The Alabama scheme was quickly and hugely successful in clearing Black voters off the rolls.

At this point Booker T. Washington helped organize and finance a group called the Colored Men's Suffrage Association, which in turn hired the experienced African American lawyer Wilford Smith from Galveston, Texas. Smith filed five separate lawsuits, each one with the same plaintiffs (starting with Jackson W. Giles, a US postal employee). Each suit listed the same facts about the Alabama disfranchising 1901 constitution in conjunction with white supremacist registrars. Each of the otherwise identical suits used a different procedure and sought a different remedy; this tactic increased the chances that at least one of the lawsuits would survive procedural hurdles and result in a solid ruling that the Alabama Constitution violated the Fourteenth and Fifteenth Amendments. As Washington secretly wrote to Smith, "I believe there is a way to win, or at least to put the Supreme Court in an awkward position." The end result would not do African Americans any good, and the Court seemed not to notice its "awkward" position.[53]

Two cases made it to the US Supreme Court in 1903 and 1904. In *Giles v. Harris* (1903), the plaintiffs requested an injunction ordering them to be registered, which would remedy the registrars' illegal refusal. In *Giles v. Teasley* (1904), Giles and the others each requested damages of $5,000 for the wrongful rejection of their right to vote.[54]

In the first case, Giles faced a new justice, Oliver Wendell Holmes Jr. of Massachusetts. Holmes was raised in an antislavery family, was wounded three times as a Union soldier in the Civil War, and was named to the Supreme Court in 1902 by President Theodore Roosevelt on the recommendation of Senator Henry Cabot Lodge (sponsor of the Federal Elections Bill of 1890). Despite all these indications, his work on the Court generally—at least for the first dozen years—rebuffed African Americans' claims of civil and constitutional rights.

In *Giles v. Harris,* the Supreme Court denied the request for an injunction, saying quite plainly that Jim Crow was stronger than the US Constitution. Holmes wrote that if "the great mass of the white population intends to keep the blacks from voting," a Supreme Court order placing "a name on a piece of paper will not defeat them." In a ruling that has received harsh criticism over the years, the Court retreated from its jurisdiction and said that relief for the political wrong alleged by the plaintiffs could only come from the state or from "the legislative and political departments of the government of the United States."[55]

The Court had another ground for denying the injunction. Wilford Smith had drafted a careful, detailed complaint specifying how the Alabama Constitution was designed to discriminate, including a version of the grandfather clause, plus detailed allegations (as in *Yick Wo v. Hopkins*) that registrars rejected qualified Black applicants while accepting white applicants who showed no qualifications. Holmes simply disposed of the complaint with sophistry and wordplay: "How can we make the court a party to the unlawful scheme by accepting it and adding another voter to its fraudulent lists?" The Court was not going to stand in Alabama's way.[56]

The first *Giles* case had been unsuccessful, but it seemed to have a possible silver lining. In denying the injunction request, Holmes had said there could be a remedy in "damages to the individual." One of the other cases filed by the Colored Men's Suffrage Association was just such a damage suit.

The claim for damages was denied in the Alabama courts on a bizarre ground. The Alabama Supreme Court said it conceded for purpose of argument that Giles was correct in his claim that the Alabama Constitution violated the federal Constitution. If so, said the Alabama court, the registration board was unconstitutional and therefore had no lawful authority to register Giles or anyone else, which meant he was not injured and was entitled to no damages. The Alabama court followed the same theory in denying another remedy requested by Giles—a "writ of mandamus" (a type of injunction). This was a sham because the Board continued to register white voters and they voted freely.

On appeal, in *Giles v. Teasley* (1904), the US Supreme Court approved this nonsense and took it a step further. The Court said it had no jurisdiction even to hear the appeal, and dismissed it. The Court's theory was that the Alabama court did not really reject Giles's claim that the Alabama Constitution violated the US Constitution. This was not true, but it was enough to get rid of Giles's case.[57]

The logic of the Colored Men's Suffrage Association had proven powerless in the Supreme Court. African American voter registration in Alabama plummeted from a pre-1901 total of 181,000 to 3,742 in 1908, less than 2 percent of the Black adult male population, compared to 250,831 white voters, more than 80 percent of the white adult male population.[58]

The Supreme Court finished its disfranchisement work in 1904 with two cases rejecting African American challenges to the Virginia Constitution of 1902 (Carter Glass's convention). The ground was the same as in the 1895 South Carolina case: although the challenges had been filed in time, they reached the Supreme Court too late.

In a decade starting in 1895, the Supreme Court heard six cases challenging disfranchising constitutions in four states, and the justices rejected every challenge. By 1904 disfranchisement was a fixture, and the message was unmistakable: the US Supreme Court would approve any egregious or farcical scheme to deny African Americans' right to vote.

Separate and Unequal

While upholding state disfranchisement schemes, the justices also expanded the reach of racial segregation. In 1899, in *Cumming v. Richmond County School Board*, the Supreme Court faced the issue of segregated education for the first time. It was an unusual setting in which the plaintiffs accepted segregation but asked for equal schooling. The school board in Augusta, Georgia, closed the African American high school, the only Black public high school in the state, while still operating its white high school. The school board's reason was that the meager amount it was spending for African American students (far less than for white students) could be better spent on Black elementary schools. Even the lower state court in Georgia could see this was wrong and ruled for the African American plaintiffs. But the Georgia Supreme Court disagreed, and so did the US Supreme Court. In a unanimous opinion by Justice Harlan, the US Supreme Court held this was a prudent use of public funds so federal interference was unwarranted "unless in the case of a clear and unmistakable disregard of rights secured by the supreme law of the land." The Court went on, "we have here no such case." If anyone thought that under *Plessy v. Ferguson* "separate" must at least appear to be "equal," the Augusta high school case contradicted that naïve hope.[59]

Local school boards had taken seriously the needs of African Americans when Black men were able to vote. In the Carolinas and Alabama, school funding was close to equal until about 1880, when African American political power was evaporating. Soon the South saw a growing number of well-constructed and better-equipped white schools in districts where African American students attended tarpaper shacks with no desks or toilets. Differences in school funding were extreme across the South. In 1910 the average annual expenditure in the South was $9.45 for a white student and $2.90 for a Black student, a ratio of more than 3:1. In South Carolina, the ratio was 5:1. In many rural areas the disparity was even more appalling—for example, Laurens County, South Carolina, spent $11.33 per white child versus 56 cents for each African American child—a ratio of more than 20:1. This was no surprise, because segregation was intended not simply for the cosmetics of separation, but as a mechanism for the imposition of inequality.[60]

In 1908 the justices extended segregation theory further. One of the underpinnings of *Plessy* was the Supreme Court's concern about "commingling" of white and Black people. Voluntary commingling of the races was what brought students to Berea College in Kentucky. Founded in 1855 by ardent Christian abolitionist John G. Fee, Berea College was a private school that enrolled African American and white students and taught them in classes together. The college chose as its motto "God has made of one blood all peoples of the earth." The state of Kentucky, however, made it a crime for a person or corporation (which Berea College was) to teach integrated classes. Berea College was convicted and fined $1,000. The Kentucky courts upheld the conviction on two separate grounds. One ground was that the segregation law was valid, and the

Students at Berea College, Kentucky, in 1899, before the state made integrated education a crime.

other ground was that states have broad power to impose rules on their corporations.[61]

The US Supreme Court affirmed the Kentucky criminal conviction in *Berea College v. Kentucky* (1908). The Court's affirmance was on the ground that Kentucky was entitled to regulate its corporations, so the Court said it need not review the segregation issue. Kentuckian Harlan, in dissent, argued that there was no procedural basis for avoiding the segregation issue in this case and then denounced the segregation law: "Have we become so inoculated with prejudice of race that an American government . . . can make distinctions between such citizens in the matter of their voluntary meeting for innocent purposes simply because of their respective races?"[62]

Giving the state of Kentucky a free hand to regulate the Berea College corporation was a radical departure from other cases in this era of laissez-faire and "freedom of contract." In the late nineteenth and early twentieth centuries, the Fourteenth Amendment, instituted to protect the freedmen, became instead the preserve of business. The Supreme Court decided about 600 Fourteenth Amendment cases between 1868 and 1912, of which 80 percent were about corporations and fewer than 20 percent were about African Americans. The Supreme Court held that corporations were "persons" entitled to due process, and the Court repeatedly blocked state regulation of everything from railroad rates to working conditions to insurance contracts and other matters. In the *Berea College* case, however, the state was regulating racial integration, and the Court offered no resistance.[63]

Enforcement Stymied

By the start of the twentieth century, federal enforcement of the few remaining Reconstruction-era civil rights laws was sparse. National resolve had faded, and Supreme Court rulings of the 1870s–1880s left few civil rights laws still alive to enforce. Then two cases in the early 1900s all but ended prosecutions for civil rights violations.

In *James v. Bowman* (1903), two Kentucky men were indicted under Section 5 of the Enforcement Act of 1870 for preventing African Americans from voting in a federal election. The Supreme Court dismissed the indictment and held the section of the law unconstitutional. The Court held that neither the Fifteenth Amendment nor the federal elections clause of Article I of the Constitution gave Congress the power to enact this law, one of the few laws that had been left alive after the Supreme Court's decisions of the 1870s.

In *Hodges v. United States* (1906), some white men in Arkansas were convicted of conspiring to drive a group of African Americans off their jobs because of their race, thus depriving the victims of the Thirteenth Amendment right to contract. The Supreme Court reversed the convictions, holding that the Thirteenth Amendment protected against little more than actual servitude. This conflicted with the universal understanding, such as Justice Bradley's majority opinion in the *Civil Rights Cases* (1883), that denial of the right to contract was a badge of slavery that the Thirteenth Amendment protects against.[64]

These two cases thus weakened the Thirteenth and Fifteenth Amendments, held part of the Enforcement Act of 1870 unconstitutional, and cut back on Congress's power over federal elections which had been so vigorously affirmed in *Ex parte Yarbrough* (1884).[65]

All-White Juries, Again

The pillars of disfranchisement and segregation were given important support by all-white law enforcement and court systems, especially juries.

After rejecting C. J. Jones's claims in the 1890s that African Americans were intentionally excluded from Mississippi juries, the Supreme Court denied such claims of "jury exclusion" in a series of cases in 1903 (two cases), 1906, 1908, and 1910. All these cases came from counties with long histories of all-white juries. In each case the Supreme Court, often eloquently, reiterated the rule that such exclusion was unconstitutional, and then proceeded to reject the claim for one reason after another: the defendant had asked for the wrong remedy, or filed the wrong motion, or filed it too late, or even too early, or failed to present proof, or the proof was unclear, or the record was missing, and on and on and on. The bottom line is that during these two decades when southern juries were virtually always all white, the Supreme Court did not reverse a conviction of an African American defendant in a single case.[66]

The grim consequence of all-white "justice" was to turn the legal system into a regime of capricious and brutal enforcement against anyone, guilty or innocent of a crime, who might think to question the social norms of Jim Crow. White society, for its part, suffered the moral corruption—recognized or not—of forcing its leaders into constant lies ("No, we do not keep Negroes off juries") to maintain Jim Crow. And the Supreme Court rewarded those lies.

Two cases involving all-white juries early in the new century were somewhat different. Both cases were handled by Wilford Smith, whose strategy in the *Giles* cases had ultimately proven unsuccessful. In these two jury cases, *Carter v. Texas* (1900) and *Rogers v. Alabama* (1904), the state court had refused even to consider the defendant's motion challenging the jury. Although the Supreme Court did not void either conviction, it reiterated that state courts had a constitutional duty to consider these motions, and returned both cases to the state courts to do so. These had little lasting impact in putting Black jurors in the jury box, but they did show that states needed to be slightly less blatant in their exclusion of African Americans from jury service.[67]

These two Supreme Court decisions also gave some fleeting hope to others. In Mississippi a pair of civil rights attorneys, African American Willis Mollison and white Dabney Marshall, teamed up to campaign against the state's all-white jury system. Mollison had studied law under Elza Jeffords, former Republican justice on the Mississippi Supreme Court. An advocate of bipartisanship with moderate Democrats, Mollison had been elected district attorney of Issaquena County in 1883 and reelected in 1887. Dabney Marshall was a member of a prominent Mississippi family, related to John Marshall, fourth chief justice of the US Supreme Court. In 1895, a political opponent, Rufus Dinkins, had circulated in the press certain rumors about Dabney Marshall, accusing him of "unspeakable acts" that implied homosexuality. Marshall, who felt honor-bound to defend his masculinity, shot and killed Dinkins. Under a plea agreement he was sent to jail but avoided the death penalty. Prison may have given him some empathy for African Americans; after serving his time, Marshall determined to fight for civil rights.[68]

Buoyed by partial victories in Supreme Court jury cases, Mollison and Marshall decided to represent Joseph Hill, a Black man sentenced to death in 1905 by an all-white jury for murdering his wife. They argued that Hill had been denied his constitutional right to question selection of an all-white grand jury. The Mississippi Supreme Court, in *Hill v. State* (1906), agreed, based on its understanding of Supreme Court rulings. Hill, granted a retrial, was again found guilty, but this time he was not sentenced to death, which in those times counted as a significant victory.[69]

Following that trial, in January 1907 the Warren County board of supervisors began adding African American names to the potential jury pools, and for the next ten months some African Americans served on juries in Mississippi. In October of that year, however, the Mississippi Supreme Court clarified its position. According to Justice Robert B. Mayes of that court, "It is a mistaken impression, which seems to have become prevalent, that in order to constitute a valid jury there must be some Negroes in the jury list. Such is not the case." Mayes assured white Mississippians that the US Supreme Court would not necessarily hold juries unconstitutional just because they happened to always be all white. And then juries were back to being all white—again.[70]

More Violence

Even with increasing segregation and more systematic disfranchisement, white hostility grew. White race riots were too common. A major one was in Wilmington, North Carolina, in 1898. Wilmington had a Black majority and an active biracial coalition of Republicans and members of the new political party, the Populists. White Democrats were determined to end "negro domination." Alfred M. Waddell, former colonel in the Confederate Army, was the leader of the white supremacy movement in Wilmington. He declared that "we will not live under these intolerable conditions," and announced intentions to "change it, if we have to choke the current of the Cape Fear river with carcasses." Democrats went on a two-day rampage, murdering African Americans, ransacking their community, and destroying a Black newspaper. They installed themselves in the "elected" positions, and neither state nor federal forces intervened in this coup d'état.[71]

In South Carolina, also in 1898, some white assailants instigated a particularly bloody assault, lynching at least eight Black men over two days near Ninety Six. Ninety Six was the ancestral home of Preston Brooks, a congressman who in 1856 had viciously attacked abolitionist Senator Charles Sumner on the floor of the Senate. It was also the home of Benjamin E. Mays, future president of Morehouse College and renowned civil rights leader. Mays's first childhood memory was of fear and torment during this riot in the neighborhood of Phoenix. Local newspapers as usual blamed African Americans for instigating the Phoenix Riot, but a Charleston newspaper wrote that the white mob was "mad with the lust of blood."[72]

The white mob was indeed mad, enraged that a local coalition of African Americans and their white Republican allies, like the Tolbert family of Ninety Six, challenged South Carolina's disfranchising constitution and persisted in voting. Determined to stop any and all African Americans from voting, the white mob killed the men whom they thought they could kill with the least, or no risk to themselves. The violence, intimidation, and murder continued sporadically for a year, until, in August 1899, US senator Benjamin Tillman, who earlier in his career had boasted about his role in the Hamburg Massacre of 1876, told the local white troublemakers to cease their "devilment" or the federal government might intervene. He suggested instead, "If you want to uproot the snake and kill it, go and kill the Tolberts."[73]

Booker T. Washington continued to have the ear of some white authorities on appointments and policies, and he became one of the few African Americans with political influence. But how inadequate this influence was. He spoke out against lynching and worked tirelessly to make "separate" facilities more "equal," but he had to walk a careful line and follow segregation rules. There was a pretense that African Americans who knew their place were respected, but it was a sham. Then, a simple dinner invitation exposed the harsh truth.

In October 1901 Washington attended a White House meeting with President Theodore Roosevelt; after the meeting, Roosevelt invited Washington to stay for dinner with the family and another guest. Other African Americans had been to the White House for meetings, but this was the first time a president had invited a Black man to his home for dinner. Both men knew it was a groundbreaking event with potentially dire consequences—political considerations for Roosevelt (who had been president less than a month), and death threats for Washington. As they expected, the dinner at the White House unleashed a crescendo of fury across the South.[74]

US senator Ben Tillman of South Carolina spoke for many southern white people when he declared, "The action of President Roosevelt in entertaining that nigger will necessitate our killing a thousand niggers in the South before they will learn their place again."[75]

A variant of a white race riot was the "Post Office Riot." Postal employees were often the only federal appointees in a community, and Republican presidents stirred white rage when they selected African Americans for some of these positions. In 1897 a white mob had murdered Frazier B. Baker and his two-year-old daughter, and also burned their home to the ground—Baker was the Black postmaster in Lake City, South Carolina. Tillman praised the "proud" white people for refusing to accept "their mail from a nigger." Thirteen men were identified and tried in federal court, but an all-white jury deadlocked and the case was never retried. In 1903 white residents forced Minnie Cox, the postmistress at Indianola, Mississippi, to flee town to avoid Baker's fate. Refusing to appoint a successor, President Roosevelt closed the Indianola post office for a year, which forced city residents to travel thirty miles to Greenville for their mail.[76]

Between 1900 and 1908 more white race riots erupted, some in northern cities. In 1906 a race riot engulfed Atlanta, focusing less on voting and more on anger toward the economic stability of the Black community. White mobs inflicted massive property damage and wounded and killed African American businessmen and many others. In 1908 in Springfield, Illinois, an angry white lynch mob raided Black neighborhoods, destroying businesses and committing murder. A Springfield magazine, the *Independent,* declared that the Springfield riot, in the hometown of Abraham Lincoln, was "worse, if possible, than the horrible Atlanta riot."[77]

In an article entitled "Race Wars in the North," labor reformer William English Walling called for a revival of the "spirit of the abolitionists" to seek political and social equality. After reading Walling's article, Mary White Ovington, a New York social worker, suffragist, and writer, organized a meeting to discuss the need for an equal rights association. As a result of that meeting, Oswald Garrison Villard, the grandson of William Lloyd Garrison, called for a National Negro Conference.[78]

Answering the call was a group of sixty prominent reformers and social workers. Mostly white with some African American professionals, including W. E. B. Du Bois, Ida B. Wells-Barnett, and Mary Church Terrell, they met in New York in February 1909. It was on this centennial of Abraham Lincoln's birth that Villard called for "a renewal of the struggle for civil and political liberty." That meeting led to the creation of a new organization to fight against white supremacy: the National Association for the Advancement of Colored People (NAACP). The stated goal was to secure for all people the rights guaranteed in the Thirteenth, Fourteenth, and Fifteenth Amendments to the United States Constitution. Du Bois became the director of publications and established *The Crisis*, a magazine that became the national voice for civil rights. Villard provided early leadership essential to the NAACP's survival.

White Massachusetts attorney Morefield Storey became the association's first president and served from 1910 until his death in 1929. In his younger days Storey had briefly served as secretary for Senator Charles Sumner as Sumner fought for African American civil rights. Storey orchestrated the integration of the American Bar Association. He helped lead the new organization's early legal activities and encouraged local branches to participate in overcoming the worst of Jim Crow.[79]

And there was much to overcome. Southern politicians like Alabama's Tom Heflin, South Carolina's Cole Blease, and Mississippi's J. K. Vardaman (the self-styled "Great White Chief") had joined Ben Tillman as mouthpieces for race hatred. White demagogues who declared that segregation of the races would prevent violence were woefully wrong: between 1900 and 1910, recorded lynchings totaled 962, nearly 90 percent of which were of African Americans.[80]

Court decisions in *Plessy* and *Williams* marked the beginning of a period often called the nadir of race relations in post–Civil War America. For African Americans, life seemed to get worse, as it did for other racial minorities. Federal jobs that had once been a source of opportunity were closed off when southerner Woodrow Wilson became president. "Sundown towns" sprouted in the North and West, with their message of "N——, don't let the sun go down on you" in this town. Some towns excluded almost every Black person (except domestic workers). In others, Black workers were allowed in for a day job, but could not live there. The color line was extended to most walks of public life. In athletics, Black jockeys, who had won the Kentucky Derby in fifteen of the first twenty-eight years, were excluded from Churchill Downs. Professional baseball stars, such as John "Bud" Fowler, Moses Fleetwood Walker, and George Stovey, were cut loose by their major league teams.[81]

As the new century dawned, segregation and disfranchisement were entrenched in the South, and the underlying attitudes were prevalent outside the South too. W. E. B. Du Bois said, "The problem of the twentieth century is the problem of the color-line." Jim Crow was the winner in the counterrevolution of 1890.[82]

CHAPTER FIVE

Beginning the Long, Slow Turnaround

By 1910 more than thirty years of fraud, violence, and corrupt state laws, actively tolerated by the US Supreme Court, had firmly established Jim Crow in the South. The new century saw a flowering of Confederate statues and memorials. Often erected in front of a local courthouse, such monuments were a deliberate message that white supremacy was in charge. In the next quarter century, race relations in the South would be little changed, but a tug of war would begin over African Americans' status in other parts of the country, where some states had enacted civil rights laws in the nineteenth century.[1]

Nationwide, the era saw an explosion of pseudoscientific race theories, with doctored statistics to "prove" African Americans' inferiority and criminality. Writers subdivided various races into categories, complete with cranial measurements and other nonsense metrics. Madison Grant, in his 1916 book *The Passing of the Great Race: Or, The Racial Basis of European History,* urged the preservation of the "Nordic" race. Historians toed the same line of white supremacy, condemning Reconstruction as a time of tyrannical military rule, corrupt and vindictive white turncoats and "carpetbaggers," and ignorant Black former slaves.[2]

In literature, the popular Tarzan of the Apes series was steeped in attitudes of racial superiority. The notorious 1915 movie *The Birth of a Nation,* based on the best-selling novel *The Clansman: A Historical Romance of the Ku Klux Klan* (1905), was lauded by President Woodrow Wilson. The resurgent Klan spread around the country, albeit with less violence outside the South, and was especially strong in some midwestern states. The new KKK added Jews, Catholics, and foreigners to the list of people it hated.[3]

Against this mass tide would swell significant currents. In the early twentieth century, African Americans began leaving the South for better lives. World War I spurred the movement, as industrialization in the North drew large numbers of African Americans to jobs in New York, Chicago, Detroit, and other cities. In these cities, the new arrivals were no longer disfranchised, and the numbers meant voting power.[4]

The Supreme Court's treatment of race discrimination during this quarter century from 1910 to 1935 was mixed—but a mixed record was a great improvement over previous decades. The Court broke important new ground in decisions requiring fairness in state criminal trials. In addition, it struck down extreme forms of state-imposed discrimination. The two most important of these cases, however, were nullified when later Supreme Court decisions upheld the same discrimination in modified forms. With one step forward, then one step back, the Court did not lead a way out of Jim Crow, but it did largely end the downward spiral and suggested a path for the next period.

A boundary of sorts between old and new was a case involving southern lawlessness and faint stirrings of Supreme Court resistance. It was and remains a case like none other in Supreme Court history, before or since: the contempt case of *United States v. Shipp* (1906, 1909).[5]

The Sheriff and the Lynch Mob

On January 23, 1906, a white woman named Nevada Taylor was raped in Chattanooga. An African American man named Ed Johnson was promptly arrested, tried, convicted, and sentenced to death—all within eighteen days. His trial was a circus, held in a rush to beat the lynch mob. Johnson's attorneys told him that if he appealed his conviction he surely would be lynched. He did not appeal.

Then, just before the scheduled execution, Noah Parden and Styles Hutchins, two African American attorneys in Chattanooga, filed a petition in federal court detailing the exclusion of African Americans from the jury and other ways in which Johnson's trial had been unfair. The federal judge denied the petition but stayed the execution for ten days to allow a Supreme Court appeal. Six days later, a telegram arrived saying Justice Harlan had issued an order allowing an appeal to proceed. Notice of Harlan's order was sent to all those involved in the case, including Sheriff Joseph Shipp, who had custody of Johnson in his jail.[6]

Justice Harlan's order was electrifying front-page news. The *Chattanooga News* complained, "Such delays are largely responsible for mob violence all over the country." That same night, as widely anticipated, a huge mob attacked the jail, which had not been reinforced, took Johnson, and lynched him at a downtown bridge. On his mutilated body, they left a note: "To Justice Harlan—here's your nigger now." The Birmingham *Age-Herald* reported, "The Supreme Court of the United States was responsible for this lynching."[7]

News of the lynching shook Washington, and the attorney general met with President Theodore Roosevelt to explore options. A serious prosecution by Tennessee was unlikely. (A state grand jury was later convened, but none of the thirty-five witnesses—some of whom were probably in the lynch mob themselves—could identify anyone involved.) Federal prosecution of private individuals in the lynch mob was barred by the Supreme Court's state action doctrine, and federal prosecution of a sheriff was unknown until the mid-1940s. But the Supreme Court's authority had been flouted. At this point, for the first and only time in its history, the US Supreme Court itself put someone on trial.

Based on charges filed by the US attorney general (after an investigation by Secret Service agents), the Court issued an order that the sheriff, deputies, and fifteen private citizens "show cause" why they should not be held in criminal contempt of court for causing the death of a prisoner whose case was in the Supreme Court's jurisdiction. In a unanimous opinion written by Justice Holmes, the landmark decision said that as long as Johnson's case was on appeal to the Supreme Court, "this court, and this court alone," could decide his fate. Sheriff Shipp, said the Court, was responsible for Johnson's safety while the appeal was pending, and now Shipp and the others would go on trial for interfering with the Supreme Court.[8]

The Court appointed its deputy clerk as a commissioner to conduct the actual hearings and take the testimony (2,200 pages) considered by the Supreme Court, which rendered the verdict. Unsurprisingly, most of the several hundred participants in the mob, who had not earlier been reticent about their presence, could not be identified, but the Supreme Court did find the sheriff and six other men guilty. The sentences were anticlimactic—three months in jail for the sheriff and up to three months in jail for the others. (Holmes had suggested a year in prison plus a $25,000 fine.) A point of some kind was made when the prisoners were taken to the District of Columbia prison instead of the local Chattanooga jail to serve their sentences.

Back in Chattanooga, the Court's rulings made little difference. When Reverend Howard E. Jones, pastor of the white First Baptist Church, gave a strong sermon against lynching, he was threatened with mob retaliation if he did not retract his statements. He refused, and his house was burned. Parden and Hutchins, the two African American lawyers who had filed the Supreme Court appeal, left Tennessee, never to return. In the South, juries remained all white, jury discrimination appeals in the Supreme Court dwindled, and it would be another quarter century before the Supreme Court ever reversed a conviction for systematic exclusion of African Americans from a county's juries. But it was a start.[9]

First Small Steps toward Racial Justice

The Court that decided the *Shipp* case still had a majority, five of nine of the justices who had sat in *Plessy v. Ferguson* (1896); within two years, only one of them remained (Edward D. White, who replaced Fuller as chief justice). All told, President William Howard Taft had six appointments in his single four-year term, tying George Washington's record. Most of the appointees did little by themselves to change the Court, except for one: Charles Evans Hughes. Hughes was a breath of fresh air. Previously the progressive Republican governor of New York, he served as associate justice from 1910 until he resigned in 1916 for an unsuccessful challenge to President Woodrow Wilson's reelection. Then in 1930 he was nominated by Herbert Hoover to return to the Supreme Court as chief justice. Hughes is not well remembered today for his race opinions, but he should be.

Hughes was sworn in as a justice on October 10, 1910, and ten days later the Court heard arguments in *Bailey v. Alabama* (1911), a case that would begin the Supreme Court's long, slow turnaround on issues of racial justice. Alonzo Bailey was convicted of fraud under an Alabama law aimed at people like him—poor, Black, and rural. Bailey was effectively tied to the land in a pattern familiar across the South. He had signed a contract to work at the Scott's Bend farm near Montgomery for the year 1908, at a wage of $12 per month. He received a $15 advance to be repaid monthly, reducing his net monthly wage to $10.75. He worked for January and part of February, and then stopped work. The record does not show why, but the white jury found his leaving was "not justified."[10]

Under the law everywhere, including Alabama, Bailey would have been liable for the unearned advance ($13.75) as damages in a civil case, although it would likely be impossible to collect; it would not be a criminal case unless he had entered into the contract with intent to defraud the grower—

in other words, unless there was proof that from the very beginning he intended to leave early, still owing money.

This general law of fraud was insufficiently stringent to suit Alabama and other southern states, because there was usually no evidence of the farm laborer's initial intent. To get convictions more easily, Alabama amended its law to provide that simply leaving the job early, without justification and still owing money, was itself sufficient proof the laborer had a fraudulent (criminal) intent when he first entered into the contract. That was not all. A general rule in the Alabama courts limited the defendant's ability to testify in his defense. Thus, evidence that Bailey had a bad intent was not necessary, and his testimony that he had a good intent was not allowed. According to Booker T. Washington, the Bailey case involved "flagrant injustice being done to Colored People in Alabama." He explained, "Any white man, who cares to charge that a Colored man has promised to work for him and has not done so, or who has gotten money from him and not paid it back, can have the Colored man sent to the chain gang."[11]

Based solely on the evidence of the contract, the $15 advance, and Bailey's failure to complete the year, he was convicted of petty theft. Under the Alabama law he was sentenced to a $30 fine (half of it to repay the disappointed employer's advance) plus court costs, or 136 days in jail. Behind the scenes, Booker T. Washington quietly put together coalitions of white supporters in the South and the North to support Bailey's challenge in court.

Bailey's appeal arrived at the US Supreme Court about the same time Charles Evans Hughes did. In early 1911 the Supreme Court handed Bailey a ringing victory, written by Justice Hughes. Hughes found that the Alabama law, stripped of all its fictions and presumptions, allowed conviction of a person for the mere act of leaving contracted employment owing money. That, he said, was peonage, which was banned both by the Thirteenth Amendment ("involuntary servitude") and the Anti-Peonage Act of 1867. The decision was a remarkable affirmation of the Thirteenth Amendment, which had been cast aside by the Court for decades.[12]

Then, in a crucial sentence, the opinion charted a new course for the Supreme Court: "What the state may not do directly, it may not do indirectly." If it could, Hughes wrote, the charter of freedom "would become an empty form." This was essentially the same point the Supreme Court had rejected when it upheld the disfranchising schemes in *Williams v. Mississippi* (1898) and the *Giles* cases (1903 and 1904).[13]

The vote was 8–1. The lone dissenter was Justice Oliver Wendell Holmes, whose position, like his view in the disfranchisement case of *Giles v. Harris* (1903), was that Alabama was free to define crimes however it chose.

The *Bailey* case illustrated one form of the notorious convict-leasing system that flourished in the South for decades after Reconstruction until after the turn of the twentieth century. Tens of thousands of men, almost all of them Black, were arrested and convicted—rightly or wrongly—and then leased out to plantations and other private employers in the hardest and most dangerous industries, including coal mines and steel mills. There they were worked to death, figuratively and even literally—with death rates that could reach 20 percent *per year.* Lacking the slave owner's presumed financial interest in keeping his enslaved workers at least moderately healthy, the states and their contractors' lack of concern about the convicts' fate has been described by a court as "you can always find another one, so who cares." John Henry, "the steel-driving man" of folklore, is a sad reminder of how legend can airbrush history. His story has entertained and inspired many, but the real John Henry was a Virginia Black prisoner leased to the railroads, who was worked to death and, like so many others, died from the fine rock dust that lodged in his lungs when he worked tunneling through mountains. And, like so many others, he was buried in an unmarked grave at the penitentiary. The lease system did not directly come before the Supreme Court, but it was involved in lower-court cases, many of which were disputes between states, counties, and contractors over who was entitled to the lucrative income.[14]

Some recent writers argue that the Thirteenth Amendment, which ended slavery, opened up the system of convict labor because of the phrase "except as a punishment for crime." A few supporters at the time of the new amendment, such as Senator Charles Sumner, worried that the phrase could allow states "to re-establish the condition of slavery by a system of crimes and punishments." And some diehard supporters of slavery, like former Confederate general John T. Morgan, seized on this phrase and said it enabled judicial authorities "to sell into bondage again those negroes who shall be found guilty of certain crimes." Virginia's supreme court went so far as to declare in 1871 that a prisoner "during his service in the penitentiary is for the time being a slave of the State."[15]

There seems to be little basis, though, for the view that the Thirteenth Amendment enabled the explosion of convict labor under conditions similar to slavery, or that these conditions—or, for that matter, the mass incarceration of the present day—could not have occurred without the "exception" in the Thirteenth Amendment. The phrase "except as a punishment for crime" was a familiar one in similar charters of freedom at the time, including the Northwest Ordinance, the Wilmot Proviso, the constitutions of all the free states that entered the Union since Ohio in 1803, and the 1862 law abolishing slavery in the territories. The convict lease system thrived in spite of the Thirteenth Amendment, not because of it. It is conceivable that the amendment without that clause could have prevented the most extreme forms of private contractors' control over leased convicts, but incarceration per se, and even mandatory work by prison inmates, would surely not go away even if the exception were deleted from the Thirteenth Amendment. Without question, the amendment was then, and is now, a grand charter of freedom.[16]

The decision in the *Bailey* case came none too soon for Justice John Marshall Harlan. In his thirty-four years on the Supreme Court, almost all his significant votes in favor of African Americans' rights had come in dissent. The *Bailey* case was the first case in years where he was part of a majority ruling for African Americans. Harlan died later that year.[17]

Two years later, the Court revisited the Civil Rights Act of 1875 and found itself straitjacketed by doctrines of the past. Mary Butts, an African American woman, took a steamship voyage along the Atlantic coast between Boston and Norfolk. Even with a first-class ticket, she was shunted off to segregated, inferior accommodations. She sued under the Civil Rights Act of 1875, which banned race discrimination by "inns, public conveyances on land and water, theaters and other places of public amusement." The *Civil Rights Cases* (1883) had struck down the provisions about inns and theaters, saying Congress had no such power under the Thirteenth or Fourteenth Amendment. Here, however, the discrimination occurred on the high seas, where Congress has the power, not the states. In *Butts v. Merchants & Miners Transportation Co.* (1913), the Supreme Court rejected Butts's claim because the public conveyance provision was in the same law as the unconstitutional part about inns and theaters; the Court said the valid could not be separated from the invalid. This contrasted with other cases where state *segregation* provisions were upheld even though they mixed constitutional and unconstitutional provisions. Those segregation laws were upheld on the theory that the valid *could* be separated from the invalid.[18]

In another transportation case, *McCabe v. Atchison, Topeka & Santa Fe Rail Road* (1914), the Court dealt with separate-but-equal. Hughes wrote an opinion that seems obvious today, but only with the benefit of hindsight. The case came from the new state of Oklahoma, which had entered the Union in 1907. The laws of Oklahoma while still a territory had been relatively innocuous on the subject of race, but as soon as it became a state, Oklahoma shifted to some harsher measures. One was a new law allowing separate *and unequal* treatment of railroad passengers. Although the new law required equal treatment for the races in regular (separate) cars, it allowed a railroad to provide dining or sleeping cars for one race (obviously the white race) without providing the same for another race. Just before the law was scheduled to go into effect, five African Americans, including one E. P. McCabe, sued five railroads operating in the state. The lower federal courts upheld the Oklahoma law, saying the equal protection clause did not require the railroads to provide these expensive luxuries for which there was so little demand from African American passengers.

On appeal, the Supreme Court rejected this view. The Court said the argument based on limited demand from members of a race as a whole was irrelevant. Hughes announced a far-reaching principle of individual rights:

> [The argument] makes the constitutional right depend on the number of persons who may be discriminated against, whereas the essence of the constitutional right is that it is a personal one.[19]

Technically, the ruling against the Oklahoma law was not the *holding* of the case. The actual holding denied an injunction because McCabe and his fellow plaintiffs had not been "injured" and thus lacked "standing to sue"—they had simply sued the railroads without actually buying tickets or being denied the sleeping or dining accommodations. But the decision made clear that "separate" must be "equal."

A year later, the Supreme Court rejected another Oklahoma misadventure, its grandfather clause for voters. As with the railroad car law, the Oklahoma territory had a straightforward voting provision before statehood, which made all males at least twenty-one years of age, with a year's residence, eligible to vote. Once it was safely within the Union, the new state promptly abandoned its legitimate voting rule in favor of a pernicious grandfather clause. The clause imposed a literacy test on all voters—with a crucial exemption for those who had been eligible to vote (or whose ancestors had been eligible) as of January 1, 1866. Thus, in the familiar scheme adopted by several former Confederate states, Oklahoma put in a stringent requirement—the literacy test—but made certain that white men would not have to bother with it.

The Taft administration prosecuted and secured convictions of several state election officials who had rejected African American voters. On appeal, the Supreme Court in *Guinn v. United States* (1915) held that the Oklahoma provision was unconstitutional and affirmed the convictions. The opinion was written by Chief Justice Edward Douglass White of Louisiana. White was a former Confederate and had also been a member of the White League, a Klan-like organization in Louisiana. Nominated as associate justice by Democratic president Cleveland in 1894, White was then named chief justice by Republican president William Howard Taft in 1910. As chief justice, White selected the justice who would write the opinion, and he selected himself.

In language unusually blunt for a Supreme Court opinion, White had no difficulty seeing that Oklahoma's selection of a date just before adoption of the Fifteenth Amendment worked to *disfranchise* the very people whom that amendment had *enfranchised:* "We have difficulty in finding words to more clearly demonstrate the conviction we entertain . . . that the provision [is] in direct and positive disregard of the Fifteenth Amendment."[20]

On the same day, the Court also struck down a grandfather clause adopted by the city of Annapolis, Maryland. The grandfather clause was the first southern voting scheme ever to fail a Supreme Court test. The African American press hailed the grandfather clause cases. The *Chicago Defender* foresaw real change: "Nothing in recent years has shaken the solid south so much; they feel themselves slipping."[21]

The ruling on the grandfather clause also broke new ground in constitutional analysis. In the grandfather clause cases, the Court rejected the state's claim that its law had a legitimate purpose. Instead the Court found for itself that the actual, hidden purpose was to discriminate on account of race. The Court said the clause had "no discernible reason other than the purpose to disregard the prohibitions of the [Fifteenth] Amendment." This mode of analysis was a more direct use of an approach suggested in *Bailey v. Alabama* ("what the state may not do directly, it may not do indirectly"). The Court's examination of a law's actual or underlying discriminatory purpose rather than its declared surface purpose is familiar today, but it was novel at the time. It would be sixty years before the Supreme Court adopted a rule against laws having an unstated or hidden discriminatory purpose.[22]

Having finally found a voting restriction it would not allow, the Supreme Court two years later found a segregation law it would not allow, in *Buchanan v. Warley* (1917). The case involved an increasingly popular type of local ordinance. Beginning in Baltimore in 1910, these ordinances were designed to keep or force segregated housing, block by block. The Louisville, Kentucky, version of the ordinance, adopted in 1914, made it illegal for any person, white or "colored," to buy, lease, or move onto a block where a majority of houses were occupied by people of the other race. The ordinance had a bland formal title, "An Ordinance to Prevent Conflict and Ill-Feeling between the White and Colored Races," but the Kentucky Supreme Court minced no words, saying the ordinance was adopted "partly in recognition of the peril to race integrity induced by mere propinquity."[23]

The case that arose was probably arranged as a test case. Charles Buchanan, a white realtor, contracted to sell to William Warley, an African

American and NAACP member, property on a block with eight white families and two Black families. The sale did not go through because of the city ordinance, and a breach of contract suit was brought in which the constitutionality of the city ordinance was the key issue. The Kentucky Supreme Court upheld the ordinance based on the US Supreme Court's own segregation cases—including *Berea College v. Kentucky* (1908), where the US Supreme Court had upheld the Kentucky law barring the teaching of interracial classes.[24]

But the US Supreme Court in 1917 looked at this case in a different way. The Court ruled that this "drastic measure" was an interference with the "fundamental" right to buy and sell property. That right, the Court said, was protected by the Fourteenth Amendment (no deprivation of life, liberty, or property without due process) and the Civil Rights Act of 1866 (no racial discrimination in buying or selling property). The Black press was overjoyed. The *New York Age* declared that the Supreme Court was on the side of justice and that the Constitution was "a vital, living influence for the maintenance of right and the annulment of wrong."[25]

The Court did not rule that the housing ordinance was a segregation tool; it would not be ready for this type of challenge for many years. Nevertheless, the Court's reliance on the due process right to buy and sell property produced a ruling for a form of racial equality. That Supreme Court decision could have led to a nation of open housing and a radically different modern-day America, but it was not to be.

Setbacks

Property owners and public officials instituted ways to maintain residential segregation. In later cases, the Supreme Court stood firmly by its ruling against such ordinances, but by then the alternatives were so effective that the Louisville-style explicit ordinance was unnecessary.[26]

There were two principal alternatives that kept housing separated by race: restrictive covenants and zoning laws. Combined with racial discrimination by the real estate and banking industries and government agencies, the overall effect was a generations-long drive toward racially segregated housing that set seemingly indelible patterns.

One response was segregation by property owners' agreements, called "restrictive covenants." Such covenants were not new. White property owners on a block or in a neighborhood would agree with each other—either permanently or for a set period of years—not to sell to an African

American (or sometimes to a Jew or an Asian or another disfavored category of people), and further, would agree to add this restriction to their property deeds. The same end could be accomplished more easily by a developer who put such a clause in the deed of each new house being sold. Because the agreement was in the deeds, it was called a "covenant running with the land," meaning that the next buyer of the property, and the next and the next and so on, was bound to accept and continue that restriction, like it or not. And once a mutual restriction was in a deed, it could not be removed before the maximum time in the covenant without the agreement of every other owner of property within that covenant group.[27]

While restrictive covenants were mushrooming, another development was emerging that would play an important role in controlling housing and residential choices—the movement toward residential zoning, city planning, and land-use regulation. Modern-day zoning arose in the early twentieth century and spread quickly across the country. Much of the focus was on separating different land uses, especially industrial, but many or most ordinances also regulated residential areas. Although its most extreme form—the explicitly racial ordinance—was struck down in the Louisville case, zoning ordinances often continued to promote racial segregation, either by thinly disguised purpose or as a by-product of lot size, density or other restrictions.[28]

Restrictive covenants and zoning ordinances both came to the Supreme Court in 1926, nine years after the Louisville ordinance was held unconstitutional. Racially restrictive covenants raised the question whether "state action" was present, but in a new form—a combination of private and public acts. The covenant itself was "private," but any enforcement (by one property owner against another owner who had a change of heart and tried to sell to an African American) required state power by way of a court order.

Whether combinations of private and public acts were "state action" was an open question, and the nineteenth-century state action cases had not dealt with this problem. The *Civil Rights Cases* contained some language suggesting that even partial state involvement might be enough to trigger the constitutional protections, but those words had never been applied to real facts.[29]

This type of covenant came to the Supreme Court in *Corrigan v. Buckley* (1926). The case involved twenty-five property owners in Washington, DC, on the block of S Street, NW, between 18th Street and New Hampshire Avenue. They signed a white-buyer-only covenant in 1921. A year later one of the signers, Irene Corrigan, changed her mind and agreed to sell to Helen Curtis, an African American woman. Another signer, John Buckley, sued to prevent the sale. Corrigan and Curtis said the covenant was unconstitutional. They lost in the lower court, which issued an injunction blocking the sale. The Supreme Court, presumably recognizing that the combination of private and public acts (private agreement plus court order) was unlike previous state action issues, chose a route that avoided a decision on whether the combination was state action or not. The Court interpreted the lawsuit as a challenge only to the racial covenant itself and not to its enforcement by court order. Having put aside the real question at stake (court enforcement), the Court proceeded to the question the parties were not really asking: whether the covenant by itself was unconstitutional. As to this question, the Court said there was no constitutional problem because the covenant was merely "the act of individuals." The Court may have avoided direct approval of racial covenants, but the result and the message were the same: racially restrictive covenants survived the challenge, to thrive for another twenty deadly years.

Thus, the challenge to residential segregation, successful in the 1917 Louisville case, was checked or checkmated by an expanded state action doctrine in the *Corrigan* case. More generally, the decision silently opened the way for a future of increasing federal and state government involvement in "private" activity—including race discrimination—while ignoring constitutional protections. The failure of the equal protection clause to "keep pace" with the advancing role of federal and state governments played a major role in succeeding years, especially in the problem of residential segregation and its counterpart, school segregation.

Six months later the Supreme Court had its first encounter with a classic zoning ordinance, in *Village of Euclid v. Ambler Realty Co.* (1926). The Court had decided zoning cases before, but this case in a suburb of Cleveland, Ohio, was its first involving "residential districts, from which business and trade of every sort" were excluded. The crux of the case involved the exclusion of apartment houses from the residential districts. A realty company challenged the ordinance, saying the restriction on its permissible uses lowered the value of its properties.

A lower court had struck the ordinance down, noting among other things the potential of race discrimination. Reversing, the Supreme Court treated apartment houses as threats to neighborhoods of single-family homes. The Court used unusually strong language, saying apartment houses were sometimes "mere parasites" and "almost nuisances." In a sweeping decision the Supreme Court held that state and local governments had broad discretion to adopt zoning ordinances for health and safety, and upheld Euclid's ordinance in full. Zoning was generally viewed as the progressive choice; the Court's three most conservative members—Van

Devanter, McReynolds, and Butler—all dissented, while progressive justices Holmes, Brandeis, and Stone all joined the majority.

The consequences of the two 1926 cases were major. Once the Supreme Court upheld restrictive covenants, they mushroomed throughout the country. Zoning ordinances likewise spread, most with some type of residential restrictions. Whether purposeful or not, zoning could keep African Americans out of desirable (white) areas and locked in crowded areas of substandard housing. That framework of residential segregation was in place as new forces developed in later decades—government money, multiplying suburbs, and growing power of the real estate, banking, and insurance industries. The complicity had fateful consequences for the twentieth and twenty-first centuries.[30]

By this time, the mid- to late 1920s, segregation was so entrenched that when the Supreme Court got a case involving segregated schools, it treated the issue as long-settled. Ironically, the case *Gong Lum v. Rice* (1927) was not a challenge to school segregation. Second-grader Martha Lum, born in the United States to Chinese parents, attended school in Rosedale, Mississippi. The students in her class had various complexions; many were children of immigrants from Europe and the Middle East, and some were perhaps Native Americans. On her first day in third grade, the new principal decided that Martha was "colored" and would no longer be able to attend this "white" school. The alternative was a poorly funded Black school, the only other choice offered by Mississippi. The Lums filed suit, and the county court ruled that Martha Lum should be admitted to the white segregated school. The state appealed the lower-court decision to the Mississippi Supreme Court, which overturned this decision. The US Supreme Court agreed, finding that however Mississippi arranged its segregated schools was a question for Mississippi authorities. The Lum family moved to the Arkansas side of the Mississippi Delta, where Martha was able to attend a white school.[31]

Immigrants and Nativism

A desire to keep white neighborhoods separate from African Americans, Jews, and other ethnic groups was an aspect of a growing movement of nativism. Nativism was fueled by many strains, but especially the influx, between 1890 and 1914, of 17 million immigrants, mostly Italians, Jews, and other eastern and southern Europeans who seemed to be not quite "white." One reflection of growing nativism was the expansion of the Ku Klux Klan, which grew to a million members in the 1920s. In August 1925, and then again in 1926, some 30,000 fully hooded Klansmen marched down Pennsylvania Avenue in the nation's capital. Another reflection was some state antimiscegenation statutes, which added other nonwhite races to the list of those people whose unions with white people were off-limits. To some degree, Prohibition also was an expression of nativist views, fueled in part by rural residents and white Protestants who did not approve of the drinking habits of the new city-dwelling Catholic immigrants. Still another manifestation was an attempt by the Harvard College administration to limit the number of Jews because these supposedly unwelcome immigrants were too successful in gaining entrance to the elite institution.[32]

Congress joined the rush to nativism in the Immigration Act of 1924. The act restricted the number and type of immigrants by imposing a system of quotas based on national origin. The act assigned each European country an annual quota of 2 percent of the US population of that country's ancestry. The catch was that the population base was not that of the most recent census (1920), but instead that of 1890—a census taken before all the Italians, Greeks, and Jews started arriving. People wanting to immigrate from southern and eastern Europe were put on years-long waiting lists, while immigrants from Ireland (previously so despised), England, and Germany never came close to reaching their very large quotas. The quotas for all of Africa and Asia were not based on US population; instead they were near zero. Immigration from the Western Hemisphere, including Mexico, was unrestricted but small.[33]

The Supreme Court had little direct involvement in these developments, but did confront the questions "Who is white?" and "Who can be an American?" in a series of three cases in the 1920s involving the eligibility of certain immigrants for naturalization (US citizenship). The law relevant to these cases was the Naturalization Act of 1790, which limited naturalization to "free white persons." An 1870 amendment added people of African descent. Thus, only white or Black immigrants were eligible for naturalization.[34]

The first case, *Ozawa v. United States* (1922), involved a longtime US resident who had arrived as a child but was born in Japan of Japanese ancestry. Ozawa was represented by George Wickersham, former attorney general of the United States. Wickersham argued that recent statutes that regulated some administrative details on immigration had in effect removed the white-and-Black limit of the naturalization law.

The Supreme Court acknowledged that the literal words of the newer statutes gave some support to Ozawa, but the Court said it must look beyond the words of the law to ascertain the law's "design and purpose, sacrificing, if necessary, the literal meaning in order that the purpose may not fail."[35]

Having determined that the word "white" still remained in the law, the Court found itself in some difficulty in determining what the words "white

Martha and Berda Lum (front row, third and fourth from the left). They attended a "white" school until the state of Mississippi ejected them, with the US Supreme Court's approval, in *Gong Lum v. Rice* (1927).

person" actually meant. The Court said the word "white" could not mean mere "color" because some "white" people are darker than some "non-white" people. In the end, the opinion solved the immediate problem by saying that the word "white" as used in immigration statutes meant "what is popularly known as the 'Caucasian' race." Because Ozawa was not of the Caucasian race, he was not eligible for naturalization.[36]

Very soon the Court learned that using the term "Caucasian" did not solve anything. The next case, *United States v. Thind* (1923), involved an application from a Hindu native of Punjab. Thind claimed "a line of descent" from the Caucasus Mountains region of Europe—in other words, that he was a real Caucasian. To solve the problem it had created by using the word "Caucasian" in the previous case, the Court roamed through many topics, including the Bible, history, the number of races people are divided into (four, five, or twenty-nine, according to different writers), the Aryan race (not white), caste systems, intermarriage, and endless others. The Court finally backtracked, concluding that "Caucasian" really referred to its popular meaning—"white." Therefore, Thind was not eligible for naturalization even if he was Caucasian, because he was not "white," which the Court still did not define. The Court said it was not implying

Marching for white supremacy: A Ku Klux Klan parade on Pennsylvania Avenue, Washington, DC, September 13, 1926.

any racial superiority or inferiority: "What we suggest is merely racial difference, and it is of such character and extent that the great body of our people instinctively recognize it and reject the thought of assimilation."[37]

The third case in this series, *Toyota v. United States* (1925), involved another native of Japan, Hidemitsu Toyota, who had served ten years in the US Coast Guard, including combat duty during World War I. He applied under statutes that made naturalization available to certain nonwhite persons who had served in the US military, but the statutes were ambiguous. To resolve the conflict, the Court applied the "national policy to maintain the distinction of color and race," so it rejected Toyota.[38]

This was the same period when the Supreme Court, in *Buck v. Bell* (1927), upheld the sterilization of a (white) woman classified by Virginia authorities as feebleminded, specifically, an "imbecile." The Supreme Court opinion endorsed sterilization with the words: "three generations of imbeciles are enough."[39]

Steps toward Constitutional Rules in State Criminal Proceedings

In 1923 the Supreme Court began to put life into the due process clause of the Constitution. Tragically, it took horrific racial episodes to get it started. World War I and the postwar period encompassed major changes in the American economy and culture. In the aftermath of Russia's Bolshevik Revolution in 1917, the Red Scare, beginning in early 1919, was a reaction to any challenging ideas. Not all the scare was imaginary; on June 2, 1919, bombs exploded in eight US cities. Other bombs intended for business executives and political leaders were found at post offices, where they were stranded for insufficient postage. US Attorney General A. Mitchell Palmer refashioned the Justice Department and created a new division whose main target was radical agitators and revolutionaries. A young J. Edgar Hoover was placed at the head of the new division. Hoover, hardly alone, thought racial justice was subversive.

When African American veterans of World War I came home, having spent time in countries where they had been treated with dignity and respect, France in particular, they felt a new pride in their patriotic service. According to African American theologian Howard Thurman, each Black soldier knew that "the future of democracy was dependent upon him." In this "breathless, swirling moment," Black people knew they were "part and parcel of the very core of the nation."[40]

And yet their bearing provoked reactions from southern white men who saw the necessity to discipline "uppity" veterans. Reactions were not just in the South. The *New York Times* fretted that "the new negro problem has entered upon a new and dangerous phase" and declared that this problem was "in some respects the most grave facing the country." The *Times* worried about the influence of new Black leaders, such as W. E. B. Du Bois, who was editor of the NAACP magazine *The Crisis*—favoring instead Booker T. Washington and his "policy of conciliation."[41]

The *Times* was correct that the newfound pride of Black people instigated white American paranoia, which then led to white racial attacks in more than three dozen cities across America. For African American James

Weldon Johnson, field officer in the NAACP, the blood spilled brought a name: the "Red Summer of 1919." Starting in Charleston, South Carolina, and spreading to cities in the North and South, including Washington and Chicago, it was a nationwide onslaught of white mobs targeting African American lives, homes, and businesses. Rioting continued over the next several years. In Tulsa, Oklahoma, in 1921, rampaging white gangs destroyed the entire African American neighborhood of Greenwood—more than a thousand homes, churches, schools, and businesses, and even a hospital and library. A report in 2001 from the Race Riot Commission in Tulsa estimates that 100 to 300 people were killed. After all the destruction, the city moved to add insult to injury with city codes that would have prevented residents from rebuilding their homes and businesses, but local African American attorney B. C. Franklin and his law firm worked to block this effort. In Florida in 1922, white rioters from neighboring areas destroyed the small African American town of Rosewood, driving the residents away and leaving the town barely a memory.[42]

One of the 1919 events had been a bloody massacre in Elaine, Arkansas, a plantation community in the Arkansas Delta, on the west side of the Mississippi River. This was the setting for a new departure in Supreme Court doctrine, applying constitutional standards to state trials and law enforcement.

At least since 1868, with the ratification of the Fourteenth Amendment, the Supreme Court had the constitutional power to review state court verdicts for unfairness amounting to denial of due process. Yet despite this power, except for the tiny handful of cases involving exclusion of African Americans from juries, the Supreme Court had never reversed a state criminal conviction for unfair procedure. With the Supreme Court keeping hands off, southern state courts trying African American defendants were unrestrained and often seemed like conviction machines, irrespective of guilt or innocence of the crime. Police lawlessness and brutality were endemic, and many white people in all strata of society considered that white criminal activity—that is, murder by lynching—was a permissible way to handle Black people accused of crime.

The massacre in Elaine, Arkansas, began because some of the thousands of African American plantation workers and sharecroppers, who lived in conditions of near serfdom, began meeting with organizers of the Progressive Farmers Union in hopes of improving their condition. On the evening of September 30, 1919, a white mob invaded a local church meeting of union organizers and Black farmworkers. In the ensuing melee, one white man and a number of African Americans were killed. This gave impetus to a white killing spree. White men formed posses and spent days roaming the countryside, hunting down and killing African Americans. More than 200 Black people died, while five white men were also killed. The local newspaper fanned the flames with incendiary headlines, including: "Negroes plan to kill all whites."[43]

No white man was charged with any crime, but twelve African Americans were charged with first-degree murder and others were charged with lesser crimes. After various trials and appeals in the Arkansas court system, five African Americans were convicted and sentenced to death. Their case went to the Supreme Court, where a grim story was laid out in an opinion by Justice Oliver Wendell Holmes.

Holmes had in earlier years written and joined opinions rejecting African Americans' claims in several significant cases, but he led the way to fair trials here. Eight years earlier the Supreme Court had refused to intervene in the shameful trial of Leo Frank, a Jewish businessman in Atlanta who was accused—falsely, as we know today—of murdering a young girl who worked in his factory. His trial was a farce. Throngs surrounded the courthouse and threatened jury members. The judge told lawyers to keep Frank away from the courtroom when the verdict was to be rendered for fear the mob would kill him.

The US Supreme Court upheld the verdict of Leo Frank's sham trial in *Frank v. Mangum* (1915), but Holmes dissented, joined by Hughes. With doubts about the case, Georgia governor John Slaton commuted the death sentence to life imprisonment. At this point—as if to prove that the mob atmosphere made a fair trial impossible—a gang of men seized Frank from the jail and lynched him. The commutation ended the governor's political career and forced him to leave the state for a decade.[44]

With that travesty in mind, the Supreme Court heard the case of the Elaine Massacre, *Moore v. Dempsey* (1923). The trial of the African American defendants had been as shocking as the Leo Frank trial, but this time Holmes had a majority to rule against the proceedings.[45]

Holmes described the facts as alleged in the defendants' habeas corpus petition, starting with the posses and the systematic hunting of African Americans. Once the African Americans who were still alive were arrested, a vigilante "Committee of Seven" prevented a mass lynching only by promising that if the citizenry refrained from lynching the captives, the committee would see to it that "justice" was done. "Justice" turned out to consist of a forty-five-minute trial with a defense lawyer appointed that day and no defense witnesses called. The jury deliberated five minutes and returned guilty verdicts for all defendants. Holmes's opinion described the belligerent atmosphere:

Marching for America: New York's celebrated "Harlem Hellfighters," the 369th Negro Regiment, march up Fifth Avenue in a parade in their honor following World War I, February 17, 1919.

> The Court and neighborhood were thronged with an adverse crowd that threatened the most dangerous consequences to anyone interfering with the desired result . . . there never was a chance for the petitioners to be acquitted; no juryman could have voted for an acquittal and continued to live in Phillips County and if any prisoner by any chance had been acquitted by a jury he could not have escaped a mob.[46]

By a 7–2 vote, the Supreme Court held that the hysteria and mob spirit surrounding the trial meant that the proceedings were so unfair as to create an unconstitutional denial of due process. This was remarkable—it was the first time the Supreme Court had ever done so.[47]

Scottsboro

The Supreme Court's next step toward guaranteeing fairness in state criminal proceedings came nine years later, when the Court again reversed a state criminal conviction in a highly charged case. This case also involved African American defendants sentenced to death. In the Great Depression of the 1930s, this grisly tale propelled the small Alabama town of Scottsboro into international notoriety forever, while leading the Supreme Court to new landmarks of constitutional law.

In March 1931, separate groups of white and Black teenagers were "riding the rails" on a freight train. There was an altercation and the white boys jumped or were pushed off the train. At the next stop, Paint Rock, Alabama, police and an armed white crowd, alerted by the white teens, were waiting for the Black youths. What the police found were nine African Americans, aged twelve to nineteen. Not all knew each other and not all had been traveling together.

In a surprise turn, police also found two white girls riding the rails, Ruby Bates, age seventeen, and Victoria Price, twenty-one. While the nine boys were being taken to the jail in Scottsboro, the county seat of Jackson County, for their altercation with the white youths on the train, the two girls suddenly said they had been raped by every one of the Black youths. Historically, a report that a Black man had raped a white woman, reliable or not, was often enough to summon a lynch mob. Now, in Scottsboro, the report was not just a rape but a mass rape. Pandemonium erupted.[48]

The arrest took place on Wednesday, March 25, 1931. A grand jury was immediately summoned, and by the following Monday it had indicted all nine defendants for rape. Trial began the Monday after that. In spite of inconsistent testimony by the accusers and the absence of medical evidence to support the accusation of rape, by Thursday, April 9, eight of the nine had been convicted and sentenced to death. A mistrial was declared for twelve-year-old Roy Wright because the jury was divided between execution and life imprisonment. (Wright waited in jail six years for his new trial, which never came. He was released in 1937.) The eight defendants appealed to the Alabama Supreme Court, which upheld seven of the eight convictions, except that of Eugene Williams, a minor at age thirteen.[49]

Under normal circumstances in the southern justice system, this would have been the end of the defendants and the story. It happened, however, that James S. Allen, working for the Communist Party in Chattanooga, Tennessee, heard about the arrests on the radio. The Communist Party, actively engaged in southern racial issues, brought attention to the case, which ultimately saved the lives of the defendants. The Communists provided lawyers through the International Labor Defense and organized national and international protests about Scottsboro, thereby creating a cause célèbre. The NAACP later tried to enter the fray, but was never able to replace the

Communist Party, which had gained the trust of the defendants and, just as important, some of their mothers.[50]

Ultimately, three Scottsboro cases went to the Supreme Court. The Scottsboro Boys' constitutional legacy began with an appeal of these first convictions, *Powell v. Alabama* (1932). There, the Supreme Court held that a defendant has a right to court-appointed counsel in a capital case (a case where a death penalty is possible). Alabama insisted that it had indeed provided counsel, by appointing all the members of the local Bar to represent the defendants, but the Supreme Court brushed this aside as an empty gesture; the appointment had come on the day of trial, so those lawyers had not been available for the important early steps of consulting with their clients, investigating the facts, locating witnesses, and preparing the defense.

This was a new direction for the Supreme Court, and its theory—nowadays called "incorporation"—was dramatic: the Court held that the right to a lawyer, which is guaranteed in *federal* criminal trials by the Sixth Amendment (part of the Bill of Rights), is so important that it is also guaranteed in *state* criminal trials by being "incorporated" into the concept of "due process of law" in the Fourteenth Amendment. *Powell v. Alabama* has been followed by cases, one by one, as late as 2020, which by now apply almost all of the Bill of Rights to the states through incorporation into the due process clause of the Fourteenth Amendment. In a sense, the doctrine that the Fourteenth Amendment includes protections of the Bill of Rights is an undoing of the *Slaughter-House Cases* (1873) and a perhaps fitting vindication of Judge Woods's ruling in an earlier Alabama case, *United States v. Hall* (1871). After the Scottsboro convictions were reversed, the cases were sent back to Alabama and transferred from Scottsboro to Decatur, in Morgan County. Some new participants came on the scene. One was a new judge, James E. Horton Jr. Another was a new lawyer, famed New York defense attorney Samuel Leibowitz, working for no fee. Also new was Ruby Bates's story: she now said there had been no rape.[51]

First to be retried was Haywood Patterson. The atmosphere was just as hostile in Decatur as it had been in Scottsboro at the first trial. The prosecutor whipped up the jury in his closing argument: "Show them, show them that Alabama justice cannot be bought and sold with Jew money from New York."[52]

Notwithstanding the weakness of the evidence, including Bates's testimony for the defense, the jury returned a verdict of guilty and another death sentence in quick order. Leibowitz moved for a new trial, a standard motion that is usually quickly denied, especially in the Alabama of that day.

Charles Evans Hughes, who led the Supreme Court's turnaround with his maj civil rights opinions in *Bailey* (1911), *McCabe* (1914), *Norris* (1935), *Brown v. Mississippi* (1936), *Missouri ex rel. Gaines* (1938), *Mitchell v. United States* (1941), an others.

But Judge Horton took it seriously. First, he postponed all the other trials while he considered the motion. Then, two months later, in a bombshell ruling, he set aside the verdict. With remarkable courage Judge Horton granted Patterson's request for a new trial. The response was swift. The state removed the cases from Judge Horton and transferred them to another judge. Early the next year, Judge Horton was defeated in his bid for reelection, and he never served as a judge again. Like other white leaders before him, Judge Horton learned that even highly placed members of white society would pay a heavy price if they challenged the totalitarian norms of Jim Crow.

Judge William W. Callahan took over. He was the opposite of Judge Horton, antagonistic to outside interference with his form of southern justice, and especially disapproving of a Jewish lawyer from New York City. In late 1933 he conducted trials of two of the defendants, Haywood Patterson (his third trial) and Clarence Norris (his second). Judge Callahan routinely overruled Leibowitz's objections, cut off his cross-examination, and summarily rejected challenges to the all-white jury.[53]

Patterson and Norris were quickly convicted in these mock trials and again sentenced to death. The Alabama Supreme Court again affirmed their convictions and death sentences. This set the stage for new trips to the US Supreme Court, which, on April 1, 1935, would issue two more landmark constitutional rulings protecting the rights of criminal defendants.

The first of these, *Norris v. Alabama* (1935), dealt with the all-white juries, the original Jackson County grand jury that indicted Norris and the Morgan County trial jury that convicted him. The constitutional rule against exclusion from juries on account of race had been laid down in 1880, and then repeated again and again, but not acted on. The *Norris* case brought the rule to life. The opinion was by Charles Evans Hughes, now back on the Supreme Court as chief justice.

This was not Hughes's first look at juries and race discrimination. Soon after rejoining the Court, in *Aldridge v. United States* (1931), he wrote a unanimous opinion overturning a Black defendant's conviction where the judge refused to question jurors about their possible racial bias. The case was from a federal court, not a state court, and involved a different issue, but it reflected an interest in the racial fairness of juries and jurors.

Hughes began the *Norris* opinion with a crucial procedural principle: that the Supreme Court was obligated to question not only the state court's legal rulings but also its factual findings. Without this searching examination, Hughes wrote, "review by this Court would fail of its purpose in safeguarding constitutional rights." The Court's obligation to look at the facts for itself was a familiar one in prior Supreme Court cases on general topics but had been ignored in the Court's all-white jury cases.[54]

Hughes then proceeded to a withering examination of the evidence, which left no doubt that the county jury officials in both Jackson and Morgan Counties had systematically excluded African Americans for years and had lied in court to cover their misdeeds. Despite ample testimony that there were African Americans who were well qualified, everyone, including officials and witnesses as old as seventy-six, swore that they had never known an African American to serve on a jury, or even be called for jury duty, in either Jackson or Morgan County. There was even evidence of an attempted cover-up: the Jackson County jury books for 1931 had been altered by adding the names of six African Americans to make it look as if they had been on the jury roll. This secret conspirator was not very skillful, however, because the names were simply added out of alphabetical order at the end of the alphabetical list, and in ink that did not match the ink on the lines already on the books.[55]

Hughes's opinion made it clear that the Alabama Supreme Court and Judge Callahan knew all this, knew it was routine, and still held that the juries were fairly selected—in other words, that highly respected leaders of the state were habitual liars. The bottom line was that the indictment and conviction were reversed for discrimination in selection of the grand

Postcard sent by Bertha Markowitz of Brooklyn, New York, to Alabama governor B. M. Miller, in 1931, as part of an international campaign urging the governor to free the Scottsboro Boys.

jury and trial jury. This was the first time in more than fifty years that the Supreme Court found that African Americans had been systematically excluded from juries—and the first time in history that the Court's decision was based on controverted evidence rather than a state's concession.[56]

On the same day as *Norris,* the Supreme Court also reversed Haywood Patterson's third conviction. He had been indicted and convicted by the same defective juries as Clarence Norris, so he should have been treated like Norris. The Alabama Supreme Court, however, said Patterson was not entitled to a reversal because his appeal was filed late. Hughes analyzed the Alabama cases and established, without quite saying so, that the Alabama Supreme Court was lying on this point too, about its own rules. The Supreme Court sent the case back for the Alabama court to reconsider, and this time the Alabama court reversed Patterson's conviction, entitling him to a new trial.[57]

The wheels of justice usually roll slowly, but on the same day as the *Norris* and *Patterson* decisions (April 1), another case again showed the Supreme Court's seriousness about juries. Jess Hollins was an Oklahoma Black man convicted of rape and sentenced to death by an all-white jury. The Supreme Court agreed to hear the case and heard oral argument (by

Charles Hamilton Houston of the NAACP) four weeks later (April 29), almost unprecedentedly fast. Two weeks after that (May 13), in *Hollins v. Oklahoma* (1935), the Court reversed Hollins's conviction and ordered the Oklahoma Supreme Court to apply the *Norris v. Alabama* rule.

Altogether, Scottsboro gave rise to three landmark Supreme Court cases involving the right to counsel, all-white juries, and oversight of state court procedural rules. These cases, as well as the Elaine Massacre case, *Moore v. Dempsey* (1923), created a new doctrinal framework in twelve short years. The new doctrine applied the Constitution in reviewing state court criminal cases—not just in the Deep South but everywhere. These landmark cases were not decided based on race, except for the jury exclusion case, but they all involved African American defendants. The new constitutional doctrine of fair trials benefited all defendants and all citizens, but these cases played a special role in the lives of racial minorities, who were so often the victims of tyranny in a perverted criminal "justice" system.

The landmark decisions, unhappily, did little for the Scottsboro Boys. Because reversal of a criminal conviction for an error, even a constitutional error, ordinarily just means a new proceeding instead of outright freedom, Alabama was entitled to keep indicting, retrying, and convicting the defendants. Four were released in 1937, after six years in prison, but the other five stayed in prison into the 1940s. The last Scottsboro defendant, Andy Wright, was not released until 1950—nineteen years later.

Almost a century later, it is generally believed that no rape took place. The younger girl, Ruby Bates, recanted her charge after the first trial, and later testified for the defense, fruitlessly. The older girl, Victoria Price, never changed her story. All of the Scottsboro defendants were eventually released and pardoned. Clarence Norris, the last survivor, was pardoned by Governor George Wallace in 1985, and all nine Scottsboro Boys were pardoned and exonerated by Governor Bob Bartley in 2013.[58]

A Step Forward and a Step Backward on White Primaries

If there was excitement about the Scottsboro cases, which were the twelfth and thirteenth cases announced by the Supreme Court on Monday, April 1, 1935, it was tempered by the dose of sobering reality administered in the fourth case announced by the Court earlier that day. On the day the justices struck down Clarence Norris's all-white jury, they upheld Texas's all-white Democratic primary election. The case was a heartbreaking turnaround from a victory eight years earlier in a previous Texas white primary case.

Primary elections are familiar everywhere, but the "white primary" was the version conducted by state and local units of the Democratic Party throughout the South. Because the Democratic Party was considered a private organization, its activities were not regarded as state action, even though the party was running an election for public office. Therefore, it could and did adopt blanket party rules making only white voters eligible to be members and to vote in the party's primary—hence the name "white primary." Winning the Democratic primary was tantamount to winning the office. The general election was only window dressing and invariably had a sharply lower voter turnout than the primary election.

Since the turn of the twentieth century, the white primary had become the most effective weapon in the southern arsenal against African American voting. Literacy tests and poll taxes were either incomplete (because some Black voters would qualify) or messy (dependent on fraud and intimidation).

An indispensable part of the "private" white primary system was keeping the Democratic Party rules (especially the whites-only rule) out of the state statute books. In Texas, however, that party's white-only rule was written into a state law enacted in 1923. The new law said "in no event shall a negro be eligible to participate in a Democratic Party primary election." This created an opportunity for a legal challenge.[59]

In 1924 Dr. L. A. Nixon, an African American physician in El Paso, Texas, sought to vote in the Democratic primary and was turned away. He brought a damage suit against the local party officials, and the case, *Nixon v. Herndon* (1927), eventually was appealed to the US Supreme Court. Nixon won a unanimous victory, written by Justice Holmes. The Court had no difficulty holding that under the Constitution, Texas could not have a law keeping African Americans out of the Democratic primary: "It seems to us hard to imagine a more direct and obvious infringement of the Fourteenth [Amendment]."[60]

That sensible outcome, however, was not the end. Texas promptly went back to the drawing board and made a technical change, though part of the rule was still in the state statute. Dr. Nixon tried again to vote, was turned away again, and won a Supreme Court decision again, *Nixon v. Condon* (1932), although by only 5–4 this time.

That was not the end, either. Texas went back to the drawing board again, and this time took all its rules, including the whites-only rule, completely out of the statute books. When the case then went back to the Supreme Court, in *Grovey v. Townsend* (1935), this time the Court ruled unanimously for the Democratic Party. The Court held that the party was private and therefore not engaged in state action and not subject to the US

Constitution—even though it was running the same primary in the same way it always had.

The loss, after two victories, was crushing. In other southern states, Democratic Party rules were not governed by state law, and proponents had hoped that the Texas cases would form an entering wedge, allowing an attack on the white primary in other states. *Grovey v. Townsend* blocked that hope.

Thus, in 1935 the state action doctrine snatched away the victory in the 1927 white primary case, just as the state action doctrine had enabled the 1926 restrictive covenant case to snatch away the victory in the 1917 residential segregation ordinance case. These two episodes involving segregation and disfranchisement showed that the twin pillars were still upholding Jim Crow.

By mid-1935 the Supreme Court had begun its long, slow turnaround, taking steps forward and backward toward racial justice. It had two different racial paths before it. One path, with its reliance on a version of the state action doctrine, allowed segregation in housing and schools and disfranchisement in white primaries. The other path, restricting unfair criminal procedures, showed steps the Supreme Court could take as a guardian of justice. Even against a dismal doctrinal background, that path looked to the Constitution to guarantee due process.

A poignant event in 1933 was a bridge to the future. On March 8, four days after his inauguration, President Franklin D. Roosevelt paid a visit to the home of retired justice Oliver Wendell Holmes to honor Holmes's ninety-second birthday. The visit was arranged by Harvard Law School professor Felix Frankfurter, who idolized both men. Six years later, President Roosevelt would name Frankfurter to the seat Holmes had occupied on the Supreme Court. A quarter century after that, on July 26, 1962, Justice Felix Frankfurter, by then disabled and soon to retire, would be honored with a similar visit by President John F. Kennedy.[61]

CHAPTER SIX

Breaking New Ground

On October 7, 1935, the traditional First Monday in October, after nearly a century and a half in borrowed quarters, the Supreme Court opened its new term in its gleaming new building across First Street from the US Capitol. One of the new occupants said the justices in their black robes looked like "nine beetles in the Temple of Karnak."[1]

Chiseled in the marble high above the grand entrance were the imposing words EQUAL JUSTICE UNDER LAW. The inspirational words meant something real to Chief Justice Hughes. When the Supreme Court marshal questioned whether Black people were allowed to eat in the cafeteria, Hughes told him to step outside and accept the chiseled words on the portal.[2]

For racial minorities, the inscription was more a hope for the future than descriptive of the past, and yet in its first decade in the new building, the Court continued its work insisting on fair trials, and it began taking aim at segregation, disfranchisement, and abuse of the state action doctrine. These first steps would take years to arrive at real change, but the Supreme Court was choosing to break new ground.

The 1930s were turbulent times, marked by the Great Depression, the New Deal, and cross-country movement. During the Dust Bowl, farmers, mostly white, moved to California seeking work, and African Americans left the South in growing numbers. From a small start in about 1910, when almost 90 percent of African Americans lived in the South, the Great Migration took six million of them to other parts of the country in the next six decades. These migrants were hoping for a better economic situation and an escape from the worst of Jim Crow. According to *Negro World,* the North had much to offer: "higher farm wages, better housing conditions, better educational facilities, equality in the enforcement of laws, the repeal of contract labor laws, the elimination of mob violence." There was a new type of freedom, symbolized by the Harlem Renaissance and Chicago's South State Street, where poet Langston Hughes found "a teeming Negro street with crowded theaters, restaurants, and cabarets."[3]

In the midst of this geographical Great Migration was the early beginning of a political shift of African Americans away from the party of Lincoln. Symbolic of the shift was Illinois First Congressional District in Southside Chicago. In 1929 voters in the district chose Oscar De Priest, a Republican, as the first-ever African American congressman from a northern state. In 1934 De Priest lost his seat to African American Democrat Arthur W. Mitchell, and that district has elected a Black Democrat in every election since then.[4]

Emerging African American political strength was evident in 1930 when the NAACP helped defeat President Herbert Hoover's nominee for the Supreme Court, Judge John J. Parker of North Carolina. Political strength required good planning. In the early 1930s, attorney Nathan Margold, a Jewish immigrant from Romania, was formulating a plan that led to the legal strategy for the NAACP to fight Jim Crow. Also coming onboard in the early 1930s was Charles Hamilton Houston. The legendary Houston had been valedictorian at Amherst College, and in law school he had been a member of the *Harvard Law Review.* After practicing law briefly with his father in Washington, DC, Houston became dean of Howard Law School in 1929. There he oversaw the law school's accreditation and launched the law careers of graduates who then formed a national civil rights bar, many of whom went on to become renowned judges.[5]

In his first case for the NAACP, Houston represented George Crawford, an African American man who was charged with the double murder of two white women in Virginia. Crawford fled to Massachusetts and fought his extradition back to Virginia on the ground that he could not get a fair trial in Virginia—an argument that initially succeeded in the district court but was ultimately unsuccessful on appeal. The case went to trial in Virginia with Crawford represented by Houston and several recent Howard Law School graduates. An all-white jury found Crawford guilty of the double murder but sentenced him to life in prison rather than death. Given the nature of the crime, this was something of a victory.[6]

In 1935 Houston, now at the NAACP full time, was instrumental in modifying the litigation plan that Margold had developed. Keeping the focus on attacking the inequality of so-called separate-but-equal, Houston refined the plan to concentrate on graduate and professional schools, where facilities provided for Black students were not only unequal but nonexistent.[7]

Presidential politics would soon affect the Supreme Court. In the 1936 presidential election, Franklin D. Roosevelt won 46 of 48 states. The election was a referendum on the New Deal and something of a referendum on the Supreme Court. There had been no Supreme Court vacancies during Roosevelt's first term, which led to his ill-fated court-packing plan. Retirements and deaths soon began opening up seats, and by the end of his second term, in 1940, five of the nine justices were Roosevelt appointees. His first appointee, Hugo Black of Alabama, was a fierce Senate liberal but had been a member of the Ku Klux Klan (a story that broke just after his nomination). Another new justice was Harvard Law professor Felix Frankfurter, who had been mentor to both Margold and Houston. Frankfurter had spent the previous decade in many liberal crusades, such as the murder trial of anarchists Nicola Sacco and Bartolomeo Vanzetti. On the Court in the 1940s and 1950s, Black and Frankfurter would become antagonists on many issues but shared strong support for claims of African Americans. The Court was poised to chart a new course toward racial justice.[8]

One of the first cases decided in the Supreme Court's new building was a continuation of the Court's new insistence on due process in state criminal cases. The case, *Brown v. Mississippi* (1936), involved a confession obtained by torture, and the Court reversed a state conviction on that ground for the first time ever. The opinion spared no details in describing the facts. One defendant was beaten while hanged "by a rope to the limb of a tree, and, having let him down, they hung him again, and when he was let down the second time, and he still protested his innocence, he was tied to a tree and whipped, and, still declining to accede to the demands that he confess, he was finally released, and he returned with some difficulty to his home, suffering intense pain and agony." Later the deputy returned to resume the whippings until "the defendant then agreed to confess to such a statement as the deputy would dictate." The whippings continued until the confessions had the precise details demanded by the deputies. The Supreme Court decision against torture was unanimous. The opinion was written by Chief Justice Hughes, who said the facts sounded like "pages torn from some medieval account." After this case the Supreme Court stepped up its intervention in state criminal cases. In the next five years, the Court overturned convictions in six southern or border states that involved tortured confessions or all-white juries.[9]

In 1937 and 1938 the Supreme Court issued important decisions protecting African Americans' right to speak out against race discrimination. Angelo Herndon was an African American Communist circulating leaflets in Atlanta and planning interracial meetings to protest segregation and poverty. He was convicted and sentenced to eighteen to twenty years on a charge of attempting to incite insurrection, but the Supreme Court, in *Herndon v. Lowry* (1937), held that the Georgia statute violated free speech. The following year, in *New Negro Alliance v. Sanitary Grocery Co.* (1938), the Supreme Court interpreted a federal labor law to protect a group of African American ministers picketing a grocery store for its failure to hire Black employees.[10]

The First Desegregation Case

In 1938 the Supreme Court confronted the case that would start it on the path to ending school segregation. The case involved admission to law school, which for African Americans was out of reach in every southern and border state.

The NAACP's Charles Houston had already gone through a recent dress rehearsal in Maryland, a border state. After Maryland's only law school rejected Donald Murray in 1935 for being the wrong color, Murray sued. Maryland, like other southern and border states, offered a "carfare education" defense, a state fund to pay the tuition and travel expenses for African American students to attend graduate or professional schools in other states. Houston's cross-examination of state officials showed how inadequate that alternative was. A lower-court judge ordered Murray admitted to the University of Maryland Law School, and the Maryland Court of Appeals unanimously affirmed, in *Pearson v. Murray* (1936). The decision did not question the constitutionality of segregated schools and it did not go to the US Supreme Court. Nevertheless, it was a major step forward—a court order integrating a law school in a former slave state, home of Roger B. Taney. Working with Houston in the Maryland case was a young Baltimore lawyer named Thurgood Marshall.

On the heels of the Maryland case, Houston looked to another border state, Missouri, and another rejected African American applicant, Lloyd Gaines. This time, however, the state courts ruled against Gaines, and the NAACP appealed the case to the US Supreme Court in *Missouri ex rel. Gaines v. S.W. Canada* (1938).

Charles Hamilton Houston (second from left) and co-counsel James Buy Tyson, Leon A. Ransom, and Edward P. Lovett, all connected to Howard Law School, in the 1933 murder trial of George Crawford in Loudoun County, Virginia. At far left is the NAACP executive secretary, Walter White.

In the Supreme Court, Missouri's defense was an elaboration of the unsuccessful arguments made earlier by Maryland. Missouri said it was prepared to include a law school at its Black college, but there had been insufficient demand thus far, and so, as a temporary measure, it would pay for African Americans to attend excellent law schools in nearby states.

Hughes wrote for a 6–2 majority, rejecting both of Missouri's solutions. He acknowledged that *Plessy v. Ferguson* (1896) and other cases allowed a state to meet its constitutional obligation under the equal protection clause by furnishing equal facilities in separate schools, but Missouri was not complying with this obligation. The state's willingness to provide a law program for African Americans when the demand was sufficient was rejected because, as Hughes had written in 1914 in the *McCabe* case, Gaines's right was personal to him, not just based on whether or not other Negroes sought the same opportunity. Turning to Missouri's alternative of paying for Black students to go elsewhere, Hughes said, the state must have equal laws in the place "where its laws operate." Hughes thus relied on the concept of federalism to support rather than defeat a claim for equal protection: "The separate responsibility of each State within its own sphere is of the essence of statehood maintained under our dual system." In other words, states' rights come with states' responsibilities. The Supreme Court had taken the first real step away from racial segregation.[11]

Three years later, in 1941, the Supreme Court further tightened the "equal" part of separate-but-equal, and applied the rule to private business, not just state action. The case arose when Arthur Mitchell, US congressman from Illinois, took a railroad trip from Chicago to Texas with a first-class ticket. He was traveling on an integrated, first-class railroad car—until he reached the Arkansas border. There, passengers were segregated, and there was no longer a first-class car for people of Mitchell's color. He was evicted from the car of "modern design" with the new feature of air conditioning, and assigned a seat in the "colored" car with no running water or flush toilets, which Mitchell described as "filthy and foul-smelling." Because the railroad was a private company, the Constitution provided no remedy for Mitchell.[12]

With no civil rights law applicable, Congressman Mitchell instead filed his complaint, in *Mitchell v. United States* (1941), under the Interstate Commerce Act of 1887. That act was based on Congress's power under the Constitution to regulate interstate commerce. One section of the act made it unlawful for any common carrier in interstate commerce (trains, boats, airplanes, and such) to subject any person to "unjust discrimination" or "any undue or unreasonable prejudice or disadvantage in any respect whatsoever." That language was designed to stop railroads from the common practice of charging different freight rates for favored or disfavored shippers. Although the Interstate Commerce Act was aimed at a different problem, the Court chose to apply the language of the act to cover discrimination between races, not just between shippers.[13]

In those years the Court decided several other cases to resolve old problems. In one case, *Lane v. Wilson* (1939), Oklahoma had responded to the end of its grandfather clause by giving affected Black voters only eleven days to register to vote or be disqualified for life. The Supreme Court struck that down, saying that "the [Fifteenth] Amendment nullifies sophisticated as well as simple-minded modes of discrimination." Other states kept trying to enact peonage laws, which the Court likewise struck down, in *Pollock v. Williams* (1944).[14]

The years leading up to World War II witnessed some change in white attitudes toward African Americans—at least outside the South. The rise of Nazism in Hitler's Germany concerned many Americans and led them to think about racism in their own country. Several incidents involving popular African Americans caught the attention of many white people. In 1936 Jesse Owens led a group of Black athletes in winning gold medals at the Berlin Olympics (although the Olympics were marred by the US Olympic Committee's craven removal of several Jewish athletes to appease Hitler). In 1938 heavyweight boxer Joe Louis won huge acclaim as America's Hero when he knocked out the German Max Schmeling in the first round before a cheering overflow crowd at Yankee Stadium.[15]

Perhaps most dramatic was the 1939 concert by Marian Anderson. Acclaimed one of the greatest singers of all time, she was scheduled to complete a world tour in Washington, DC. The premier concert location was Constitution Hall, but the proprietor, the Daughters of the American Revolution, rejected Anderson because of her race. The incident angered many, including First Lady Eleanor Roosevelt, who dropped her membership in the DAR and, with the aid of Interior Secretary Harold Ickes and the approval of President Roosevelt, had the event moved to a then-unprecedented concert venue—the Lincoln Memorial. On Easter Sunday 1939, Marian Anderson made history with a brilliant concert on the steps of the Lincoln Memorial before 75,000 people in attendance and millions more listening on nationwide radio.[16]

Two years later the United States entered World War II. The war fundamentally changed American life, including American race relations. Over the next few years, nearly a million African Americans served in the armed forces, about 9 percent of the total military force. Many African Americans were assigned to segregated units and limited to secondary assignments. For example, the Tuskegee Airmen, an elite corps of African American pilots, at first were restricted to training maneuvers at Tuskegee, Alabama. A visit from Eleanor Roosevelt in March 1941 brought their expertise to the public eye. To demonstrate the absurdity of prejudice against the airmen, the First Lady climbed into the passenger seat of a plane piloted by one of the Black airmen; after the flight, she verified that, indeed, the African American pilot was truly flying the plane. The curbs were lifted, and the Tuskegee Airmen amassed a sterling record of protecting combat missions.[17]

On the home front, African American migration northward increased, pushed by the increasing mechanization of farm work and pulled by attractive jobs for Black men and women in the defense industries. Under pressure from Black labor leader A. Philip Randolph and others, President Roosevelt issued Executive Order 8802, which required defense contractors to agree not to discriminate. Though compliance was limited and enforcement even more limited, the order set a precedent by creating a Fair Employment Practices Committee (FEPC).[18]

State Action in White Primaries and White Labor Unions

In 1944 the Supreme Court took its fifth look at the "white primary" in Texas. The constitutional rule was crystal clear: African Americans could not be kept out of the Democratic Party's primary if the discrimination was in state law, but could be kept out if the discrimination was no longer specified in state law. So said *Grovey v. Townsend* (1935), decided unanimously just nine years earlier, with the votes of liberal Justices Hughes, Brandeis, Stone, and Cardozo.

The white primary battle flared up again when the NAACP filed suit on behalf of Lonnie Smith after he was turned away from the 1940 primary in Houston, Texas. After predictably losing in the lower courts, the case headed to the Supreme Court. By this time Thurgood Marshall had succeeded Charles Houston as the NAACP's chief counsel. Having forged the organization's legal program, Houston had moved on in 1940 but would keep bringing civil rights cases (and later, Cold War cases) until his early death in 1950 at age fifty-five. Now, "all" Marshall had to do was persuade the Court to overrule its nine-year-old unanimous decision. But overruling *Grovey v. Townsend* is exactly what the Court did in *Smith v. Allwright* (1944).[19]

The facts were the same in 1944 as they had been in 1935, but this time the US Supreme Court determined to find the facts for itself—just as it had said in evaluating jury selection in the Scottsboro case *Norris v. Alabama* (1935). When it did review the facts for itself, the Court canvassed more than fifty Texas laws regulating every detail of Texas primaries, from requiring a poll tax to prescribing the dates, places, ballot design, and so on. Based on this review, the Court said Democratic Party *membership* as such might be private, but running the primary election was a *public* or *state* function, and the party could not discriminate. The Court said that "the state makes the action of the party the action of the state." The Court's conclusion was: "*Grovey v. Townsend* is overruled."[20]

The decision outlawed white primaries across the South and caused pandemonium. The states responded with various artifices, but all proved unsuccessful. The most notable response was in South Carolina, where the state repealed all state laws dealing with primary elections. When the Democratic Party again rejected Black voters, US District Judge J. Waties Waring of Charleston issued an injunction and said, "It is time for South Carolina to rejoin the Union. It is time to fall in step with the other states and to adopt the American way of conducting elections."[21]

The South Carolina Democratic Party then adopted a bizarre "states' rights" and segregation oath to be signed by every would-be primary election voter. Judge Waring issued another injunction and warned party officials that any violations would be met, not with the usual fines, but with jail time. White South Carolina complied, but it did not forget.[22]

Just months after the white primary decision, the Supreme Court examined the state action doctrine as it related to another type of private organization—labor unions. Many labor unions had been notorious for excluding African Americans, and the railroad unions were among the worst. But the unions were private organizations and therefore were free to discriminate.

The case that challenged the railroad unions' discrimination involved the job category of railroad fireman. Oddly enough, unlike the usual situation where African Americans were kept out of a trade or job category, railroad fireman was considered a Black job, so African Americans had the seniority and thus the best assignments. The reason was a quirk of industrial history. When the fireman's job was shoveling coal to power the engines, white railroad workers were only too happy to leave those dirty jobs to African Americans. The arrival of diesel engines eliminated the coal and made the position a clean job with no arduous work—a plum position. White railroad workers wanted the fireman's jobs and wanted the African American firemen out.

Federal labor law now came into play. Under the Railway Labor Act, the employees of a company or in a department can vote for a union to represent them, and the union that wins a majority becomes the *exclusive* bargaining representative for all the employees. A majority of diesel firemen for twenty railroads were now white, and they voted for the all-white Brotherhood of Locomotive Firemen, which thus became the exclusive representative for all diesel firemen, members or not. Once installed, the Brotherhood promptly demanded, successfully, that the railroads systematically demote, reassign, or lay off the African American firemen. For hundreds of well-situated Black firemen, this was a disaster. Plaintiff Bester William Steele, for example, was in a pool of one white and five Black firemen on a well-paying, desirable assignment. Suddenly the union and the railroad declared the job vacant, refilled it with four white firemen, and sent Steele to a low-paying, more arduous job, and then demoted him again.

Charles Houston, now in private practice, was the attorney for Steele and others in an Alabama lawsuit. As the US Supreme Court later described it, the Alabama Supreme Court held that the union, as a private organization, had no duty to protect Steele and other African American nonmembers "from discrimination or unfair treatment, no matter how gross."[23]

Houston appealed to the US Supreme Court, which, in *Steele v. Louisville & Nashville Rail Road* (1944), unanimously reversed the ruling. The Court's reasoning was as in the white primary decision. As a private organization, the union was free to discriminate and deny membership to anyone. However, it was federal law (the Railway Labor Act) that made it the exclusive bargaining agent for all firemen—union members and nonmembers alike. The act therefore required the union, in its collective bargaining role, to represent nonunion or minority workers "without hostile discrimination, fairly, impartially, and in good faith," just the way a legislature must provide equal protection. This Supreme Court doctrine of "duty of fair representation" revolutionized the law of labor relations and has become a core principle of labor law, reaching far beyond racial issues.[24]

Amid these forward steps, not all Supreme Court decisions honored the principle of racial justice. On December 18, 1944, the same day the Supreme Court rejected discrimination against African American railroad firemen, the Court upheld race discrimination against Japanese American residents of the West Coast.

Japanese Internment

The Japanese attack on Pearl Harbor on December 7, 1941, thrust America into the war. In the next six months, 120,000 men, women, and children of Japanese descent (two-thirds of whom were US citizens) were put under curfew, corralled into assembly centers, and relocated to internment camps in the country's interior, where they spent more than two years behind barbed wire. The War Relocation Authority had pushback from some states about accepting the Japanese, even temporarily. Governor Nels Smith of Wyoming was typical: "If you bring Japanese into my state, I promise you they will be hanging from every tree." Governor Ralph Carr of Colorado, on the other hand, denounced "the shame and dishonor of race hatred." One official who vigorously supported the program was the attorney general of California—his name was Earl Warren.[25]

The Supreme Court approved key parts of the program. It did not quite approve the actual internment, but its overall treatment of these cases has left the fair conclusion that the Supreme Court bent or broke the Constitution in support of race discrimination.

Pearl Harbor stoked fears of a Japanese attack on the West Coast that could be abetted by domestic espionage and sabotage. The fear led to several presidential executive orders and a series of military orders "excluding" all people of Japanese descent from the West Coast states. The "exclusion" was a comprehensive process. It included a nighttime curfew, followed by an order to report within seven days to a designated "central assembly area" (typically fairgrounds or horseracing tracks), and finally the actual removal to an internment camp in an interior state as far east as Arkansas. Living conditions in the camps varied, but all were grim. People lived mostly in shacks and could bring only what they could carry—

often just two suitcases. The zeal for anti-Japanese action was fueled by racial stereotypes, so the effect of wartime fear had far harsher consequences for the Japanese Americans than for Americans of German and Italian descent.[26]

Japanese exclusion had three parts: curfew, reporting, and internment. The first part of the program, the curfew, was upheld in *Hirabayashi v. United States* (1943). While the Court disavowed racial distinctions, it nevertheless held that the exigencies of war justified the degree of restriction imposed. The decision was unanimous, but it appears that Justice Frank Murphy came close to dissenting. He wrote a concurring opinion pointing out that this was the first time the Court had upheld "a substantial restriction on personal liberty of citizens of the United States based on race or ancestry."[27]

A year later the Supreme Court faced two cases involving more severe restrictions, *Korematsu v. United States* (1944) and *Ex parte Endo* (1944). The cases had both begun in 1942. By the time they were argued, in October 1944, the fears of early 1942 had long since dissipated; indeed, voices had been calling for at least a year to end the internment.[28]

The *Korematsu* case involved the second part of the exclusion program, reporting for internment. The Supreme Court, by a 6–3 vote, upheld Fred Korematsu's conviction for violating the military order that all people of Japanese descent must report to a designated central assembly area. The Court began by describing its constitutional principle: "All legal restrictions which curtail the civil rights of a single racial group are immediately suspect . . . courts must subject them to the most rigid scrutiny. Pressing public necessity may sometimes justify the existence of some restrictions; racial antagonism never can."[29]

The Court then, however, changed direction and described the military necessity that justified this restriction. The Court said it felt compelled to defer, that "exclusion of those of Japanese origin was deemed necessary because of the presence of an unascertained number of disloyal members of the group, most of whom we have no doubt were loyal to this country." This was the same basis on which the Court had upheld the curfew conviction a year earlier, and a majority of the Court agreed that it justified the reporting requirement too.[30]

The Court insisted that it was deciding only the issue of reporting, which was the basis of Fred Korematsu's conviction, and that it was not deciding anything about the internment itself. Justice Roberts, in dissent, said the two parts of the program, reporting and internment, could not be separated, because relocation and internment promptly or immediately followed for all those who reported. In the retrospective of history, Roberts has prevailed,

Fred T. Korematsu (center) and his family, 1939. Korematsu defied the 1942 order for Japanese Americans to relocate, was sent to federal prison, and was then interned in a camp. The legality of the internment was upheld by the Supreme Court in 1944 in *Korematsu v. United States*. Korematsu's conviction was ultimately overturned in 1984.

because the *Korematsu* case is universally cited as the case in which the Supreme Court upheld the internment of Japanese Americans in detention camps. Justices Murphy and Jackson also dissented.

The second wartime case that day, *Ex parte Endo* (1944), was anticlimactic. Mitsuye Endo, a camp internee, sued for release in 1942 on the ground that the internment was unconstitutional. By the time her case reached the Supreme Court, late in the war, officials had certified that she was indeed a loyal citizen. The Supreme Court ordered her release on that ground, without ruling on the constitutional question that Endo had been asking for two years.

By that date, December 18, 1944, it was too late for the Supreme Court to make any difference. One day earlier, Sunday, December 17, 1944, the government formally announced that it would begin emptying the internment camps two weeks later. On January 2, 1945, eight months before the end of World War II, every internee was released with $25 and a train ticket home.

Keeping the camps open to the end of 1944 may have been a political maneuver designed to avoid hurting President Roosevelt's election campaign, particularly in the West Coast states. And the government's closing-the-camps announcement, on a Sunday, one day before a crucial Supreme Court ruling, certainly seemed like someone had inside information from someone at the Supreme Court. All these and other points might be just strange features of history, except for the bitter reality that 120,000 people spent two and a half years in virtual prison, torn from their lives and homes.

Soon after the war ended, the Supreme Court ruled against two anti-Japanese laws of California. Forty years later, after many of those interned had died, the United States delivered some gestures of amends. The Civil Liberties Act of 1988 provided reparations of $20,000 each to some 80,000 camp internees who were still alive. In 1984 and 1987, Gordon Hirabayashi and Fred Korematsu were exonerated when federal courts reversed their wartime convictions and all charges against them were dismissed.[31]

Ironically, the *Korematsu* case has left a lasting Supreme Court doctrine, the rule requiring "strict scrutiny" of laws that distinguish among people based on race. Under strict scrutiny, such laws cannot be upheld unless they are "necessary" to meet a "compelling interest" of the government, which means almost never. That rule, with its roots in *Korematsu*—where it did not prevent the racial division—was formalized in *Loving v. Virginia* (1967), where it doomed antimiscegenation laws (see Chapter 7). The doctrine to scrutinize racial discrimination has come into play in many other cases since then.

The end of World War II saw the return home of millions of military servicemen and servicewomen—white, Black, Native American, Latin American, and Asian American, including Japanese American. Symbolic of change was the arrival and instant stardom of Jackie Robinson, the first African American in organized baseball since Black players were forced out in the 1880s (Indians and Latinos were allowed). Just two years earlier, in mid-1944, as an army lieutenant at Camp Hood, Texas, Robinson was court-martialed for refusing to move to the back of an on-base bus. Luckily for baseball, he was acquitted of all charges. His arrival in the minor leagues in 1946 and joining the Brooklyn Dodgers in 1947 was the beginning of making baseball a genuine national pastime. The enthusiasm he sparked among fans far outstripped the outrage felt by some. For millions around the country, Robinson fully belonged. And if he belonged, why not other African Americans?[32]

America had a new president, too, and African Americans had played an indirect but major role in his selection. In the 1944 process of selecting a vice presidential candidate to run with President Roosevelt, an early favorite for the spot was James F. Byrnes of South Carolina. He was a former US senator and briefly a Supreme Court justice. He was also a protégé of Pitchfork Ben Tillman and an outspoken segregationist who, as senator, had filibustered anti-lynching bills. The NAACP and most labor unions were strongly against him. Northern big-city political leaders expressed horror at putting Byrnes on the ticket, which they said would lose New York and Illinois and hand the presidency to the Republicans. The final blow may have been struck by William Dawson, an African American congressman from the Illinois First District—successor to Oscar De Priest and Arthur W. Mitchell—who, after a lengthy meeting with Byrnes at the convention, said, "You cannot be my candidate." Instead, the vice presidential nominee was Harry S. Truman, and he became president when Roosevelt died on April 12, 1945.[33]

New Federal Civil Rights Prosecutions

Federal prosecution of southern officials was almost unknown before 1940. The high tide of federal civil rights prosecutions of the 1870s had long since ebbed, and those had almost always been against private violence rather than against state officials. What few federal civil rights prosecutions occurred in the twentieth century were mostly for election violations. In 1939, however, under Attorney General (and future justice) Frank Murphy, the Justice Department established a Civil Liberties Bureau, and beginning in 1940 that unit started paying attention to abuses by sheriffs and police officers, particularly, but not exclusively, in the South and against African American victims. Their chief tool was Section 2 of the Civil Rights Act of 1866, which made it a crime for a state or local public official—usually a law enforcement officer—to violate any person's constitutional rights or other federal rights. Section 2 had gone virtually unused for three-quarters of a century before 1940. The Justice Department's new unit brought that section to life.

The then-recent case of *Brown v. Mississippi* (1936), in which the Supreme Court held that a confession gained by torture violated the due process clause of the Fourteenth Amendment, focused attention on police brutality, such as what was commonly called "the third degree." The Justice Department started by bringing a handful of cases in the early 1940s. Indictments of law officers were hard to obtain and convictions were even harder, but cases involving extreme brutality resulted in some convictions. The punishment was often trivial, usually limited to one year in prison and a fine of $1,000, but because no one else was holding these officers to account at all, this was a start.

The Supreme Court test of the new civil rights use of section 2 outside the context of an election came in a case that the Supreme Court called "a shocking and revolting episode in law enforcement." Claude Screws, sheriff of Baker County, Georgia, and two other officers arrested an African American named Robert Hall on a charge of stealing a tire. On the way to jail, they began beating him with fists and a blackjack and did not stop until he was dead. At their eventual federal trial they testified that he had tried to escape, or tried to pull a weapon, or cursed them, or whatever—all allegedly occurring while he was handcuffed and surrounded by three heavily armed officers.[34]

Sheriff Screws and the other men were indicted, tried, and found guilty of the federal crime of willfully violating Hall's federal rights under the Fourteenth Amendment by depriving him of life and liberty without due process of law—that is, by punishing him without a trial. The court of appeals affirmed. In a crucial decision, the Supreme Court upheld the use of this long-dormant law to prosecute misconduct by state officials. The Court's approval, however, came with serious limitation—a requirement to prove "specific intent." Instructions to the jury had to clarify that it could convict only if it found that the sheriff intended to violate the victim's federal constitutional rights; the unjustified beating or killing by itself was not enough. The Supreme Court said this jury instruction was needed in order to preserve the distinction between state crimes and federal crimes. Because that new instruction had obviously not been given to the jury in this case, Sheriff Screws and his companions were entitled to a new trial.

The decision was a new example of a step forward with a half-step back. The jury instruction required by the Supreme Court was so confusing that it was difficult to prosecute state or local officials for misconduct, even if they maimed or killed prisoners in their charge. In fact, Sheriff Screws and his deputies were acquitted in their retrial. While the ruling did not end the Justice Department's civil rights prosecutions, it did mean that only the most aggravated and airtight cases had any chance of success.

Three justices dissented entirely, arguing that any such federal prosecution was an intrusion into the states' domain. The dissenters' legal theory was reminiscent of the 1870s Supreme Court in cases like *Cruikshank,* and their archaic sense of history was an echo of the type of history taught in the early twentieth century: "It is familiar history that much of this legislation was born of that vengeful spirit which to no small degree envenomed the Reconstruction era."[35]

One barbaric incident in 1946 illustrated the difficulty of these cases but also helped galvanize national support for change. Sergeant Isaac

Woodard, a decorated war veteran returning home after being mustered out that day, was apparently not deferential enough to a bus driver. Woodard was savagely beaten by several policemen in Batesburg, South Carolina, who rendered him permanently blind in both eyes. The Justice Department prosecuted Police Chief Lynwood Shull, who was quickly acquitted by an all-white jury, so quickly that it is obvious no instruction to the jury could have made a difference.[36]

Horrified about Woodard's blinding was President Truman, himself a veteran of World War I. In July 1948 Truman ordered the integration of the country's armed forces (carried forward by President Eisenhower), and the Democratic Party began laying the groundwork for changes in civil rights laws and enforcement. In the 1948 Democratic Convention, senatorial candidate Hubert Humphrey introduced the party's first civil rights platform and exhorted Democrats to "get out of the shadows of states' rights and to walk forthrightly into the bright sunshine of human rights."[37]

Reaction in the South was explosive. It led to a third-party presidential run in 1948 by the States' Rights Party (Dixiecrats). The Dixiecrats faded, but these events would begin a shift over the next forty years of southern white voters out of the Democratic Party.

State Action in Housing: Restrictive Covenants

In the 1944 cases involving white primaries and white labor unions, the Supreme Court had held that the Constitution could not be avoided by cloaking state action in private garb. In 1948 a monumental Supreme Court decision again struck at abuse of the state action doctrine, this time in the vital area of segregated housing. The case was a reprise of *Corrigan v. Buckley* (1926), which upheld housing segregation accomplished by private agreement. By the 1940s, racial covenants were widespread, by some estimates affecting as much as 80 or 90 percent of housing in Chicago, Detroit, and Los Angeles. Covenants had been enforced—often with evictions—in hundreds of cases around the country.[38]

A graphic illustration of the breadth of the practice was shown in a Supreme Court case that involved just one of Chicago's many covenants. That one covenant, in the Washington Square area of Chicago, banned the "colored race" throughout a twenty-four-block area (two square miles) containing 500 properties. In that case, *Hansberry v. Lee* (1940), the US Supreme Court ruled for the African American purchaser because the Illinois courts had blocked him from presenting evidence that the covenant lacked necessary signatures. As it happened, when the purchaser, Carl Hansberry, moved his family into the disputed house, his family included ten-year-old Lorraine, who, nineteen years later, wrote a world-famous play about the hostility a Black family faced when they moved into a white neighborhood—*A Raisin in the Sun* (1959).[39]

The 1948 case had farther-reaching consequences. A white property owner in St. Louis had sold a house to a Black couple, J. D. and Ethel Lee Shelley. The sale violated a neighborhood covenant signed in 1911, more than thirty years earlier. The Missouri Supreme Court held the covenant enforceable and ordered the Shelleys evicted. The Missouri court expressed concern that St. Louis's fast-growing Black population was largely restricted to overcrowded housing in limited areas, but said that could not affect its legal judgment.

George Vaughn, the Shelleys' African American attorney in St. Louis, had the support of the local Black press: "Here's hoping the 'Nine Good Men and True' will make his work a complete success when they meet next October." Vaughn called restrictive covenants "the Achilles heel" of democracy, and the Supreme Court, in *Shelley v. Kraemer* (1948), seemed to agree.[40]

The Supreme Court began by reiterating that "so long as the purposes of those agreements are effectuated by voluntary adherence to their terms," there was no state action and no constitutional violation. The Court said this was the only question it had decided in the 1926 case. "But here," the Court said, "there was more," meaning the court order: "It is clear that but for the active intervention of the state courts, supported by the full panoply of state power, [the Shelleys] would have been free to occupy the properties in question without restraint."[41]

The linchpin of the decision was the Court's treatment of judicial action as state action, citing dozens of cases that illustrated that point. The case has been criticized by many, including supporters of the result, for suggesting that any court endorsement of private action—such as administering an individual's will containing a discriminatory provision—might be subject to constitutional restraints. As a general proposition, the concern is a serious one, but the Court's emphasis on the specific nature of the covenant highlights the fact that this case involved a restraint on buying and selling property, a fundamental privilege of citizens.

The opinion in *Shelley v. Kraemer* attracted enormous public attention. Restrictive covenants were widespread throughout the nation and, as noted by the Supreme Court, were widely used not only against African Americans but also against all manner of other racial minority groups and even some groups not usually thought of as "racial," such as Armenians and Jews. The solicitor general filed a brief and participated in the oral argument opposing the restrictive covenants, the first appearance of the federal government as an amicus curiae in support of civil rights.[42]

What the Shelley Case Did Not Accomplish

The 1948 decision in *Shelley v. Kraemer* tried to untie a Gordian knot, but ultimately the end of restrictive covenants could not unravel race discrimination and segregation practiced by the entire housing industry—realtors, banks, insurance companies, appraisers, state and city governments, and even the federal government.[43]

The decades just before and after the *Shelley* decision were years of a gigantic housing boom when millions of Americans became homeowners (35 million new homeowning families from the 1930s through the 1970s). Millions of those homeowners populated a vast new frontier of suburbs in the North and West (nearly doubling the suburban share of the US population in just two decades, from 1940 to 1960). The people who became homeowners were mostly white, and so were the new, mostly segregated suburbs. None of this could have been done without the help of the federal government. As Justice Powell said in discussing nonsouthern schools that were highly segregated even without segregation laws, "Population trends are the product of state action of all sorts." It was in those decades and as a result of that seemingly benign growth of government assistance that the patterns of today's racial segregation in housing and therefore in schools, especially in the suburbs, were deeply set.[44]

Before the 1930s, home ownership was beyond the reach of a majority of Americans. The New Deal changed home ownership by a series of housing initiatives. It pioneered the modern mortgage (low-down-payment, long-term, amortizable) and created agencies that would encourage mortgage lending by guaranteeing those mortgages. Yet from the beginning, those programs allowed, encouraged, and even required segregation and discrimination, not only in existing neighborhoods but also in new developments. One federal agency, Home Owners Loan Corporation, drew four-color maps of cities and towns across the entire country, with African American neighborhoods colored red (denoting high risk) even if they were stable and in good condition—hence the term "red-lining." Another agency, the Federal Housing Administration (FHA), the backbone of the US housing industry, actively and rigidly promoted racial segregation, not only in existing neighborhoods but also in new communities with no previous racial identity. The FHA peppered its operating manual with warnings against infiltration by "inharmonious" racial groups. Until the *Shelley v. Kraemer* decision in 1948, the *FHA Underwriting Manual* included a model restrictive covenant, and the agency gave preferential mortgage treatment to subdivisions with such covenants. The manual also said that homes had higher value if they were covered by racially restrictive covenants, called "protection from adverse influences."[45]

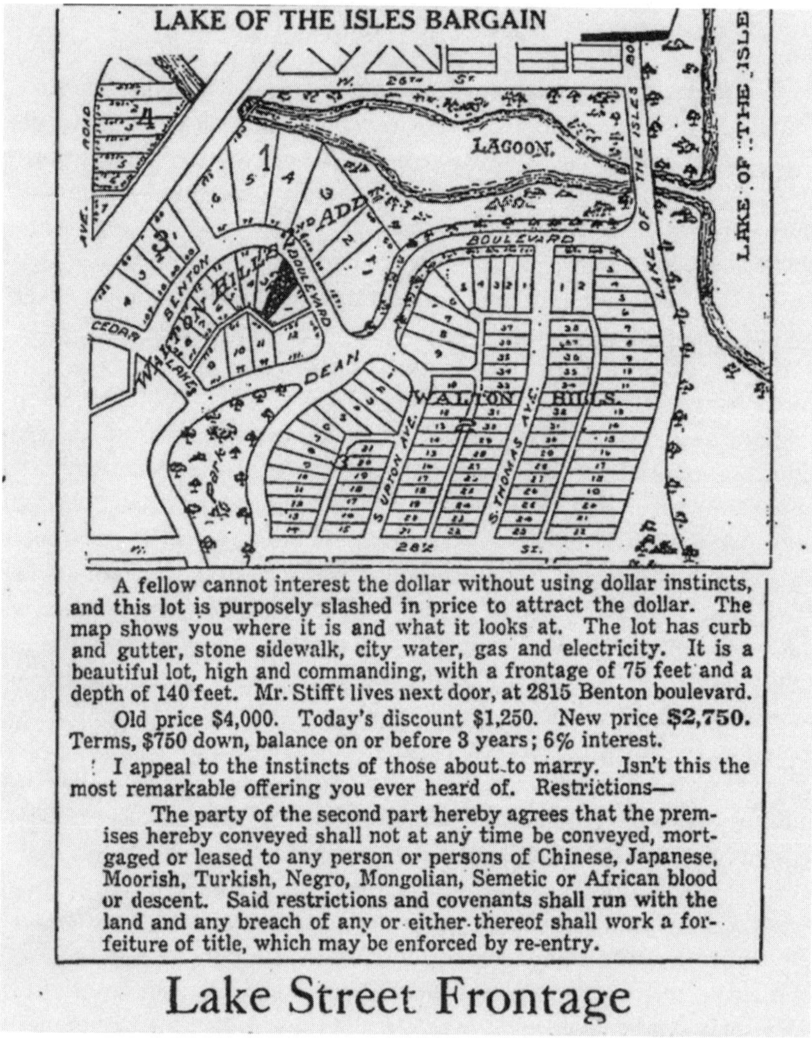

A fellow cannot interest the dollar without using dollar instincts, and this lot is purposely slashed in price to attract the dollar. The map shows you where it is and what it looks at. The lot has curb and gutter, stone sidewalk, city water, gas and electricity. It is a beautiful lot, high and commanding, with a frontage of 75 feet and a depth of 140 feet. Mr. Stifft lives next door, at 2815 Benton boulevard.

Old price $4,000. Today's discount $1,250. New price $2,750. Terms, $750 down, balance on or before 3 years; 6% interest.

I appeal to the instincts of those about to marry. Isn't this the most remarkable offering you ever heard of. Restrictions—

The party of the second part hereby agrees that the premises hereby conveyed shall not at any time be conveyed, mortgaged or leased to any person or persons of Chinese, Japanese, Moorish, Turkish, Negro, Mongolian, Semetic or African blood or descent. Said restrictions and covenants shall run with the land and any breach of any or either thereof shall work a forfeiture of title, which may be enforced by re-entry.

Lake Street Frontage

Advertisement for properties covered by restrictive covenants to prevent sales to "persons of Chinese, Japanese, Moorish, Turkish, Negro, Mongolian, Semetic [*sic*] or African blood or descent." Minneapolis *Morning Tribune*, January 12, 1919.

Another government program, the GI Bill (Servicemen's Readjustment Act of 1944), was also part of the boom in home ownership and college attendance. The GI Bill offered all veterans financial support in education and housing as well as other programs and was a significant benefit for all veterans, both Black and white. Its implementation by local administrators, however, very often reinforced race discrimination.[46]

In short, federal government money helped create the new suburban America. That housing shift affected so many people that it was almost as if two new nations, thoroughly segregated, had arisen. The federal government's well-intentioned efforts to spread the benefits of the middle class—home ownership, higher education, and economic security—mostly left African Americans and other minority people out. As suburbs grew, central cities became more overcrowded, further spurring the division between new homeowning suburbs (white) and old rental-unit cities (Black). The consequences continue to plague the country even decades after segregation as a policy has been disowned.

Two years after it struck down restrictive covenants in *Shelley v. Kraemer,* the Supreme Court was asked to extend the equal protection clause to private developments that received significant public assistance. The case *Dorsey v. Stuyvesant Town Corporation* (1950) involved New York City's Stuyvesant Town apartments. By agreement with Metropolitan Life Insurance Company, New York City condemned eighteen city blocks, including streets, in a blighted area in downtown Manhattan, evicted and relocated 10,000 people of various races (nearly 40 percent Black and Puerto Rican), and then sold the entire parcel to Met Life at cost. Met Life erected thirty-five buildings containing 8,759 apartments that would have below-market rent. Met Life's investment was $90 million, and the city provided a tax exemption worth an estimated $50 million over twenty-five years.[47]

By Stuyvesant Town's policy, the tenants were all white. The chairman of Met Life said, "Negroes and whites don't mix." Robert Moses, longtime park commissioner of New York City, said no company would have invested in a project like this if not for the right to select its tenants—that is, to keep African Americans out. In a lawsuit by Joseph Dorsey and two other African American World War II veterans, a state court ruled 4–3 that the city's role did not amount to state action, so the equal protection clause did not apply.[48]

The US Supreme Court held on to Dorsey's appeal for an unusually long period before finally deciding not to hear the case. Two justices, Black and Douglas, argued that the Court should grant a hearing. The decision not to take the case might have gone another way if the two strongest supporters of civil rights, Justices Murphy and Rutledge, had not suddenly died just months before the case came to the Supreme Court. When the Court chose not to hear the case, it missed an opportunity to curb segregation and promote housing integration during a time of massive national housing development. During the eighteen years between Stuyvesant (1950) and passage of the Fair Housing Act (1968), the housing industry established rules and customs, and the repercussions continue today.

On the same day Dorsey's case was declined, June 5, 1950, the Supreme Court handed down a trio of momentous decisions involving separate-but-equal policies in law schools, graduate schools, and railroad trains.

Separate-but-Equal Again

In the 1938 case involving Missouri's law school, the Supreme Court had established that, if a state provided a certain type of graduate education, African American residents of the state were entitled to receive that category of education within the state. Southern states found various ways to comply or not comply; a few admitted African American students to their existing white schools, while other states established separate "colored" graduate or law schools, which typically were mere subterfuges.

In 1950 the Supreme Court dealt with two of these variations. In a case from Oklahoma, an African American teacher, George W. McLaurin, was admitted, more or less, to the graduate program in education at the University of Oklahoma. The words "more or less" are used here because McLaurin was essentially quarantined—assigned a seat that was initially just outside the regular classroom and separated by a rail and sign marked "Reserved for Colored." He was also restricted to isolated times and places in the library, cafeteria, and other facilities. In *McLaurin v. Oklahoma State Regents* (1950), the Supreme Court held that this regime was not an equal or an adequate education.

The other case, *Sweatt v. Painter* (1950), involved a new law school built by Texas expressly for African American law students. The law school, built very quickly after the University of Texas law school rejected Heman Sweatt because of race, was decidedly a poor excuse for an equal alternative. Whereas the white law school at the University of Texas was well equipped, the substitute school had no independent faculty or library and no accreditation. The Texas courts, of course, held that this was "substantial equality," and so it met the state's constitutional obligation. Sweatt appealed the decision.

By the time the case arrived at the US Supreme Court, the state of Texas had improved its offerings. Its law school for African American students was on its way to accreditation. It had no building of its own but did have a library of 16,000 volumes and a staff of five full-time faculty for twenty-three students, and various other facilities.

The US Supreme Court was not persuaded. Far superior course offerings, faculty, and facilities were offered to white students, but even more

The University of Oklahoma responded to a 1948 court order to integrate its graduate school by admitting George W. McLaurin, but he was forced to sit in an alcove, separated from his white classmates. The US Supreme Court rejected this practice in 1950.

important was the difference in intangibles like "reputation of the faculty, experience of the administration, position and influence of the alumni, standing in the community, traditions, and prestige." The Court found no substantial equality, and indeed, there was clearly no way any ad hoc school for African Americans could achieve substantial equality under the Supreme Court's calculus. This was a landmark ruling—finding "equal" essentially unattainable in a regime of separate but equal.[49]

In the third major discrimination case that day, *Henderson v. United States* (1950), the Court rejected a railroad's separate-but-almost-equal dining car facilities. The railroad company and the federal Interstate Commerce Commission kept proposing alternatives that came closer and closer to equality but never quite arrived there; it was impossible to do so and still achieve their main goal, which was to ensure that people of different colors would not under any circumstances be seated at the same dining-car table at the same time. The Court struck all the alternatives down.

In these three cases, the Supreme Court was not ready to face the larger question of racial segregation itself. Thurgood Marshall, representing Sweatt, did ask for a ruling that segregation was unconstitutional. He was backed up by Justice Department amicus briefs in all three cases, which urged the Court to strike down the separate-but-equal doctrine. The Court noted that "broader issues have been urged for our consideration," but said it would stick to questions actually raised by "the particular case before the Court."[50]

Over the next three years, while the segregation question loomed, the Court broke no new ground but decided several cases blocking attempted evasions of its earlier rulings. One case involved the white-only "Jaybird Primary," a seventy-five-year-old relic of the Jaybird-Woodpecker Wars of Fort Bend County, Texas, of the 1880s. The Court struck it down as just another version of the now-outlawed white primary. In another case, the Court disallowed a different scheme for state court enforcement of racially restrictive covenants in California. Another case, the "yellow-ticket case," rejected a conviction by an all-white jury selected from a list in which white jurors' names were on white slips and Black jurors' names were on yellow slips. Finally, in that same three-year period, the Court banned racial discrimination in restaurants in the nation's capital by resurrecting a nineteenth-century Washington, DC, civil rights ordinance.[51]

In a decade and a half in its new building, the Supreme Court had regained ground lost in earlier periods and had broken new ground in other race cases. The stage was set for the next act. In these postwar years the Supreme Court seems to have adopted the view that race discrimination was a violation of national policy. Indicative is a 1948 case involving race discrimination on a ship traveling between Detroit and Canada. A Michigan agency ordered the ship company to stop discriminating, which by all precedent should have been reversed by the US Supreme Court as an interference with Congress's regulation of interstate and foreign commerce. But the Court upheld the Michigan order. The Supreme Court did not mention the Thirteenth Amendment; actually the decision was a fractured set of opinions without a real explanation. Nevertheless, the decision was consistent with a view of race discrimination and race prejudice as badges of slavery that the Thirteenth Amendment was adopted to eradicate, in the present as well as in 1865.[52]

Clarendon County, South Carolina

Life, of course, happens beyond the austere halls of the courts. In rural Clarendon County, South Carolina, one of the poorest counties in the

United States, African American parents worried over the safety of their children as they walked to school. One pair of six-year-old twins, for example, "used to leave about sun-up to get to school on time; and when they got back, it was almost night." In 1947, having asked and been denied a school bus for the children (the district provided thirty buses for white children), Black parents purchased an old one from the school district, one that, in the meantime, had been used as a chicken coop. They asked Reverend Joseph De Laine, a schoolteacher and local clergyman, to intercede for them to get funds for a driver and for gas and maintenance. The school board said no.[53]

When the bus broke down, the parents had no funds for a new bus. Spurred by returning World War II veterans, the parents had had enough. Working with De Laine, one parent, Levi Pearson, submitted a formal petition asking for a school bus. With the petition ignored, Pearson's African American attorney, Harold Boulware of Columbia, filed a lawsuit on March 16, 1948. Pearson's suit was dismissed on a technicality; his taxes went to School District 5 but his children attended schools in districts 26 and 22.

The next step was a larger group of plaintiffs and a new lawsuit for equal schools—transportation, yes, but also school buildings and supplies. The parents then began a new petition drive and collected 107 names. Every African American who signed the petition lost a job, was denied the ability to trade for necessary agricultural goods, or was threatened with physical violence. Teachers suspected of being members of the NAACP were summarily fired.

African Americans made up roughly 70 percent of Clarendon County's population, and most worked on land that was almost 85 percent owned by white landowners. The segregated public schools of the county had an enrollment of 6,531 African American and 2,375 white students in 1951. Yet total expenditures for white students exceeded that for Black students by $112,379—some 300 percent per pupil—leaving the African American schools in appalling condition and lacking basic facilities. One school used "two-by-eights . . . propped up by two fifty-five gallon cans" for seating; another required that the boys be responsible for maintaining the fire that heated the school while the girls did the cleaning. Another school, serving some 600 Black students, had only two outdoor toilets, and students had to carry drinking water in a bucket from a neighbor's home. This is what "separate but equal" had wrought.[54]

In March 1949 Reverend De Laine suggested they contact Thurgood Marshall of the NAACP. At first Marshall was reluctant to take the case because fundraising would be hard for a county that was pretty much unheard of. But when he met with the group of parents, Marshall had a change of heart. Further retribution followed. One of the parents, Harry Briggs, a Navy veteran and father of five children, was fired from his job of fourteen years. Briggs found it impossible to find employment in South Carolina and finally moved out of state to support his family. Another, William Ragin, a cotton farmer who owned approximately eighty acres of land, could no longer buy motor oil; the store refused to sell to him even though he did not owe any money.[55]

As leader of the group, Reverend De Laine came under special pressure. He was fired from his teaching job (his wife, Mattie, also a schoolteacher, was still employed). Then, in 1950, the bishop of De Laine's AME Church district transferred him out of the county to serve the church in Lake City, South Carolina. After the De Laine family home in Summerton was set aflame on October 5, 1951, the family moved full-time to the parsonage in Lake City.[56]

Planning how the case should proceed, Thurgood Marshall, as chief counsel, had to decide whether the case should be for equalization, which would be easier after the Supreme Court's decision in *Sweatt v. Painter,* or for the end of segregated schools—a much harder battle to overthrow the precedent of *Plessy v. Ferguson* (1896). Marshall was inclined to have the Clarendon County case stay as an equalization case because the integration would not change much in a rural school district that was 70 percent African American.[57]

At the pretrial hearing, however, the district judge in South Carolina, J. Waties Waring, said there had been enough cases about equalization and it was time to attack *Plessy v. Ferguson* head-on. Marshall heeded that advice.

With this encouragement, the two attorneys from the NAACP, Boulware from the South Carolina branch and Marshall from the national office, gathered the parents of Clarendon County together on December 18, 1950, and invited them to join a changed lawsuit, one that explicitly attacked South Carolina's 1895 constitution and *Plessy v. Ferguson* with its doctrine of separate but equal. The NAACP lawyers had expected some hesitation, but after a brief silence one of the group spoke out: "We wondered how long it would take you lawyers to reach that conclusion."[58]

As Marshall planned the case, he decided to concentrate on School District 22 rather than the whole county. The case of *Briggs v. Elliot* had twenty plaintiffs on behalf of forty-six schoolchildren. They filed the new petition in federal court on December 22, 1950. Because the new case attacked the state constitution and laws, however, federal rules provided

School segregation plaintiffs gather in June 1951 at Liberty Hill AME Church in Summerton, South Carolina, to wait for the federal court ruling in *Briggs v. Elliott*.

that it would be heard not before Judge Waring alone, but before a three-judge panel, Waring and two other judges. It was unlikely the Clarendon County parents would win, but the federal rules for a three-judge court provided that any appeal would go directly to the US Supreme Court without stopping in a mid-level court of appeals.

On May 28, 1951, African Americans filled the courtroom in Charleston and thronged the surrounding sidewalk. South Carolina had a new governor, the staunch segregationist James F. Byrnes, elected just months before the trial. Fighting for time, Byrnes had quickly pushed a sales tax bill through the legislature to provide millions of dollars to upgrade African American schools in Clarendon County and elsewhere around the state. Hoping a closer equalization would prevent a ruling for integration, South Carolina admitted its schools were unequal, but argued that the new sales tax would substantially improve Black schools and that the state needed more time.[59]

As expected, two of the three judges on the panel agreed to the state's proposal, asked for a progress report in six months, and noted that the Supreme Court's precedents upheld segregation. Judge Waring, however, penned a scathing dissent: "The system of segregation in education adopted and practiced in the state of South Carolina must go and must go now."[60]

Judge Waring came from a prominent white family in Charleston and was part of the dominant political machine. After becoming a district judge in 1942, he rendered a few mildly progressive decisions, but nothing unusual. Then he tried the case of Sergeant Isaac Woodard's blinding and was outraged. When he rendered the two white primary decisions, it was South Carolina's turn to be outraged. By the time of the segregation case, he had long since been ostracized by his old friends in Charleston but defended by African Americans. A longtime friend, who was asked many years later what turned Judge Waring from a traditional, even racist, Charlestonian into a fearless opponent of racism, said, "You know, it was all about that Sergeant."[61]

After the three-judge court's decision in Clarendon County, the NAACP filed a notice of appeal to the Supreme Court. After nearly two decades of the step-by-step campaign against segregation, the constitutionality of separate-but-equal was at the Supreme Court's door, and a federal district judge, J. Waties Waring, had laid it on the line by stating unequivocally: "Segregation is per se inequality."[62]

CHAPTER SEVEN

The End of Separate but Equal

Thurgood Marshall and the African American parents of Clarendon County, South Carolina, had lost their case in lower court, and *Briggs v. Elliott* was now on appeal in the Supreme Court. The plaintiffs were ready for an all-out ruling on separate-but-equal, but the Supreme Court was not ready for them. On the first trip to the Supreme Court, the Court sent the case back to the lower court for another look because South Carolina, under Governor James F. Byrnes, had been working on equalization of Black and white schools. The district court, now minus Judge Waring, who had retired, said there had been progress toward equalization and again ruled for the state. When the Clarendon County case came back to the Supreme Court in 1952, it was now joined by four other cases challenging school segregation in Virginia, Delaware, Kansas, and Washington, DC. The Court heard oral argument but still could not decide. Instead, it ordered reargument in the fall of 1953, and asked for additional briefs.

Some Supreme Court justices may have been ready to outlaw segregation, but four were from southern or border states, and one was the chief justice, Kentuckian Fred Vinson. Vinson had just written the Court's opinion in *Sweatt v. Painter,* rejecting Texas's vain attempt to create an "equal" law school. Did that mean he knew separate-but-equal could not work? Or was he just pushing the states to make it work?

The reargument was scheduled for October 12, 1953. As the date neared, all eyes were on Vinson. Then, on September 8, thirty-four days before the reargument, Vinson died of a sudden heart attack, at age sixty-three. The acid-tongued Felix Frankfurter told a friend, "This is the first indication I have ever had that there is a God."[1]

Three weeks later, in time to begin the Supreme Court's October term, President Dwight D. Eisenhower named a new chief justice, California governor Earl Warren. The arguments in the segregation cases were pushed back to December.[2]

The arguments in the five cases stretched over three days, December 7, 8, and 9. Six NAACP staff or affiliated lawyers spoke for the challengers, supported by the US assistant solicitor general. Six lawyers represented the school districts in support of segregation. Leading the defense was John W. Davis, dean of Supreme Court lawyers and unsuccessful 1924 Democratic presidential candidate. In *Guinn v. United States* (1915), forty years earlier, the NAACP and Davis, who was then solicitor general, had been allies, successfully challenging Oklahoma's grandfather clause. Davis had become the nation's preeminent Wall Street lawyer and Supreme Court advocate for large corporations (including a record 140 Supreme Court arguments). Now he had come to defend South Carolina. In this last Supreme Court appearance Davis closed his career by serving as the main spokesman for racial segregation.[3]

The decision came five months later, on May 17, 1954. This time the Court was ready to decide. Just before 1:00 p.m., the new chief justice began reading his opinion for the Court in the segregation cases. Within a few minutes, it was likely, then clear, that the Court was ruling against school segregation. Warren said the question was whether racial segregation in public schools, even if the schools were to have equal facilities, deprived minority children of an equal education. He read from the opinion, "We believe that it does."

But what was the vote? One dissent seemed certain, from Stanley Reed of Kentucky, steeped in southern ways. There was also Tom Clark, a Texan with Mississippi roots, as well as some non-southerners whose votes seemed uncertain. Then came the bombshell: "We conclude unanimously that in the field of public education the doctrine of separate but equal has no place."

"Unanimously!" One biographer of Warren reports that at the word "unanimously," Thurgood Marshall's head snapped back and he stared at Justice Reed, who gave an almost-imperceptible nod.[4]

As it turned out, the word "unanimously" was not in the written opinion, and those who look at the official *U.S. Reports* today (under the collective name *Brown v. Board of Education of Topeka, Kansas*) will not find that word. But it was crucial for the Court and the country. Getting to that point was how Chief Justice Warren had spent much of the previous several months.

Earl Warren

The Warren Court almost did not happen at all. Earl Warren's road to the Supreme Court was almost derailed not once, but twice. In 1952 Warren, then governor of California and head of the state's delegation to the Republican National Convention, helped General Eisenhower gain the presidential nomination over Robert A. Taft. Eisenhower promised Warren the first Supreme Court vacancy, but when that first vacancy turned out to be for chief justice upon Vinson's sudden death, President Eisenhower hesitated. Warren stayed firm, and the appointment went ahead.

The appointment then was almost derailed again. Because Fred Vinson's death came in September 1953, with the Senate out of session, there was no time for Senate confirmation before the new Supreme Court term started in October, so Eisenhower gave Warren a "recess appointment." But a recess appointment is only temporary unless Senate confirmation follows. In Warren's case the confirmation was dragged out for six months by the chairman of the Judiciary Committee, Senator William Langer of North Dakota, for reasons that are still not clear but may have had little to do with Warren himself. In the end the Senate confirmed Warren on March 1, 1954, unanimously, ten weeks before the *Brown* decision was announced. If the *Brown* decision had been issued while Warren was still on a recess (temporary) appointment, his confirmation would unquestionably have been blocked by outraged southern senators. His recess appointment would have expired and there would have been no "Warren Court."[5]

Warren joined a Court that was split among strong personalities, particularly between Hugo Black and William O. Douglas on one side, and Felix Frankfurter and Robert Jackson on the other. They were all Roosevelt appointees, but their sharp differences in judicial philosophy had grown into bitter personal animosity. When Chief Justice Harlan Fiske Stone died in 1946, both Black and Jackson wanted to become chief justice, but their relationship was so bad that there were threats of resignation from the Court if one or the other were named chief. President Truman avoided the fray by naming his friend, Treasury secretary and former court of appeals judge Fred Vinson.[6]

The Supreme Court that decided *Brown v. Board of Education* (1954). Front row, left to right: Felix Frankfurter, Hugo Black, Chief Justice Earl Warren, Stanley Reed, William O. Douglas. Back row, left to right: Tom Clark, Robert Jackson, Harold Burton, Sherman Minton.

As Vinson's replacement, Warren was a politically skilled consensus builder. Back in California, Warren had been elected district attorney, attorney general, and then governor of the state three times, with the nomination of both the Democratic Party and the Republican Party in his last election as governor. Now he put his political skills to work again, bringing together this divided Court. Of course, Warren had no judicial experience with segregated schools, but as governor of California in 1947, he signed the bill repealing the state's long-standing law permitting school districts to operate segregated schools for American Indian, Chinese, Japanese, and Mongolian children.[7]

The justices' deliberations in the *Segregation Cases* took a slight turn from the usual path. Rather than voting at the conference that followed the week's oral arguments, Warren orchestrated more time for the justices to simply discuss the cases, still without voting. Meanwhile, the chief justice was walking the halls, talking to each of the justices. Alabamian Hugo Black, who won his first US Senate term in 1926 as the candidate of the Ku Klux Klan, was firm that segregation was unconstitutional and must go without qualification; at the same time, as a southerner, he was certain that people would be killed as a result of such a ruling.

It soon became clear that a majority of the justices would vote to overturn *Plessy,* but that was far from the end. Frankfurter agreed but wanted a detailed opinion, while Douglas might well dissent from anything Frankfurter wrote. On and on the jockeying went. Warren drafted an opinion, as dry as possible, and kept talking to his brethren. Finally, it was down to the last two. Jackson supported a desegregation ruling but wanted to make clear that *Plessy* was being abandoned only because times had changed. Then, he was suddenly hospitalized with a heart attack. Jackson's law clerk read a final draft of Warren's opinion to him in his hospital room, and Jackson added his vote.[8]

That left Stanley Reed. He was preparing a dissent. Since his appointment to the Supreme Court in 1938, Reed had joined almost all of the Court's many decisions requiring racial fairness, and he was the author of the pathbreaking opinion in *Smith v. Allwright* (1944), which ended the white primary. But he was nearly seventy years old; racial segregation was still part of his personal outlook. He and Warren had a warm and respectful relationship, but his support for *Plessy v. Ferguson* did not waver. Finally, in the spring of 1954, Warren made one last visit to Reed's chambers and said, "Stan, you're all by yourself in this now. You've got to decide if it's really the best thing for the country."[9]

Pete Hernandez and John Raymond Rice

Meanwhile, the Supreme Court kept working through the other cases on its docket. As the month of May 1954 began, with the *Segregation Cases* not yet decided, a harbinger of sorts was a decision in a different case—a case that brought the Fourteenth Amendment to life for Mexican Americans in the Southwest. This large ethnic group had been part of the United States for a hundred years, since the 1840s annexation of Texas and the War with Mexico. The inclusion of vast territories of the Southwest into the United States created many questions, such as land disputes, that the US Supreme Court was still addressing forty years later.[10]

Issues of race and its cousins, ethnicity and language, were present from the start. Residents of these lands, once citizens of Mexico, had various degrees of Indigenous and African ancestry, and therefore various degrees of color. Much of the American opposition to the War with Mexico was a fear of adding this population. In 1848 Senator John C. Calhoun of South Carolina declared, "Ours, sir, is the Government of a white race." Worried about "the mixed race of Mexico," he said their influx would be "fatal to our institutions." Even though the Treaty of Guadalupe Hidalgo, which ended the War with Mexico, granted US citizenship to the new residents, that did not prevent widespread discrimination against Mexican Americans, even those who looked white but had Spanish surnames. There was official discrimination, even if unwritten, and even more private discrimination, as well as violence.[11]

One aspect of discrimination against Latinos, at least in Texas, was their exclusion from juries. On May 3, 1954, that issue was the subject for the US Supreme Court's first-ever decision addressing discrimination against Latino people. The case involved Pete Hernandez, indicted and convicted of murder by an all-Anglo grand jury and an all-Anglo trial jury in Jackson County, Texas. The prosecutor in Hernandez's case stipulated that Jackson County, which was 10 percent Latino, had not had a single Spanish-surnamed juror among the 6,000 jurors seated in the county over the previous twenty-five years. The Texas courts rejected Hernandez's jury challenge. As they read the cases, the Fourteenth Amendment protected only the Black race, whereas Mexican Americans are "white."

The US Supreme Court unanimously reversed, in *Hernandez v. Texas* (1954). This was Chief Justice Warren's first significant opinion. He said the Fourteenth Amendment does not reflect just a "two-class theory." The amendment protects distinct classes who, because of community norms and community sentiment, are at special risk of being singled out for unequal treatment and therefore need special protection. In this case, the evidence showed that in Jackson County, Mexican Americans were a distinct and disfavored class, treated as "Colored," even down to the separate toilet at the county courthouse. As for the jury, the Court found that the long absence of any Latinos on any jury proved the claim of systematic exclusion.

This was not the first federal court ruling against anti-Latino discrimination, though it was the first in the Supreme Court. Twice in the 1940s lower federal courts in California had struck down such discrimination—once where a city banned Latino children from a public swimming pool, and again when several school districts put Spanish-surnamed children in separate schools for their elementary grades.[12]

In that spring of 1954 another case came to the Court that showed how pervasive race discrimination was but also showed that blatant discrimination could arouse emotional opposition. On April 12, 1954, the Court

Marine Sergeant John R. Rice, killed in action in Korea in 1950, was denied burial in a Sioux City, Iowa, cemetery because he was a member of the Ho-Chunk (Winnebago) Nation. President Harry Truman ordered his burial with full military honors in Arlington National Cemetery.

granted certiorari in a case it would never quite decide even after two attempts, *Rice v. Sioux City Memorial Park Cemetery* (1954, 1955).

In December 1950 Sergeant John Raymond Rice, a decorated veteran of World War II, was killed in action while leading his platoon in Korea in his second war for this country. His body was shipped back to the United States, and his widow, Evelyn, arranged for his burial in the Sioux City (Iowa) Memorial Park Cemetery. A graveside service took place on August 28, 1951, conducted by a Catholic priest. But there was no burial that day. The problem was that burial in that cemetery was restricted to "members of the Caucasian race," and Sgt. Rice was not one of those members. He was an Indian, eleven-sixteenths Ho-Chunk (Winnebago), and had lived with his wife, who was white, on the nearby Indian reservation. The cemetery management said it had not realized he was an Indian until it saw so many Indians at the funeral. That this happened in a place named Sioux City lent a touch of dreary irony to the story.

Two things happened when he was not buried. One was a lawsuit by Mrs. Rice against the cemetery. The suit was unsuccessful in the Iowa courts, and she then filed a petition for certiorari, which set off a curious sequence of events in the US Supreme Court. The Court granted certiorari, then heard oral argument, then tied 4–4 (Justice Jackson had just died and had not yet been replaced). That technically would affirm the lower court, but with no opinions and no precedent. The Court then granted rehearing (something almost never done). Then the Court issued a 5–3 decision saying that it had decided not to decide the case because the Iowa legislature had passed a law prohibiting cemetery discrimination.[13]

But something else happened. The incident was instant news, nationwide. As a Sioux City history says, "Across the country, people responded with a combination of disbelief and outrage that a war hero and his family could be treated this way." President Truman was asked about it at a press conference the next day and expressed his own anger. On the president's instructions, an Air Force plane flew the body and the Rice family to Washington. There, on September 5, 1951, just eight days after the Sioux City event, Sgt. John Raymond Rice was buried with full military honors in Arlington National Cemetery.[14]

The Decision in *Brown v. Board of Education*

On Monday, May 17, the Supreme Court rendered its decision on school segregation. Justice Jackson was back on the bench for the first time since his heart attack, and Warren read the opinion. Separate-but-equal was finished. Over the coming years, as Hugo Black had predicted, many people would end up dead because of this.

The opinion was just fourteen pages, remarkably short for a major opinion, and it carefully tiptoed through doctrine to avoid openly criticizing *Plessy v. Ferguson*. Instead, emphasizing the vastly different role of education in modern American life, the Court essentially put *Plessy* aside as a product of its time: "We cannot turn the clock back to 1868 when the [Fourteenth] Amendment was adopted, or even to 1896 when *Plessy v. Ferguson* was written." Four years earlier, in *Sweatt v. Painter* (1950), the Court said Texas's new law school for African Americans was not equal because of intangible factors, no matter how many books were in the library. Now the Court said these considerations applied even more to younger children: "To separate them from others of similar age and qualifications solely because of their race generates a feeling of inferiority as to their status in the community that may affect their hearts and minds in a way unlikely ever to be undone."[15]

The bottom line: "Separate educational facilities are inherently unequal," and therefore the conclusion (without the word "unanimously") was: "We hold that in the field of public education the doctrine of separate but equal has no place."[16]

Plessy was not directly overruled. The strongest break was with the *Plessy* Court's statement that if African Americans believed segregation was a badge of inferiority, it was all in their imagination. Now, in 1954, the Court took the opposite tack and said that "a feeling of inferiority" was reality and was generated by racial segregation itself. "Any language in *Plessy v. Ferguson* contrary to this finding is rejected."[17]

The Court's statement about a "feeling of inferiority" was in accord with psychological and sociological knowledge unavailable to the *Plessy* Court in 1896. Such references in the 1954 opinion, however, gave the apologists of segregation a handy stick with which to beat the Supreme Court. A major criticism of *Brown* targeted footnote 11 of the opinion, which cited some of that modern research and ended, innocently enough, with a reference to *An American Dilemma,* the landmark 1944 study of segregation by Swedish economist and sociologist Gunnar Myrdal. Professional segregationists harbored a special grievance toward this work. They spent years complaining that its indictment of white supremacy in the South, so universally acknowledged today, was a fantasy.[18]

Opponents also ridiculed the famous "doll" research conducted by a pair of African American psychologists, Mamie and Kenneth Clark. The two scholars had done research in the 1940s that showed lack of self-esteem in young African American children in Massachusetts and Georgia. Part of their research methodology relied on a pair of dolls, one white and one brown. Some of the children's responses to questions about the dolls were heart-wrenching; the children, who consistently pointed to the white doll as the "pretty" one and the "nice" one and the brown doll as the "bad" one, showed confusion and distress when they had to choose the doll that "looks like me." Kenneth Clark went to Clarendon, South Carolina, in May 1951 to conduct the same tests and found the same results: "These children saw themselves as inferior and they accepted the inferiority as part of reality."[19]

Some defenders of segregation claimed that the decision was illegitimate because the Supreme Court had abandoned law for pseudoscience. Overall, the attacks on the *Brown* decision were little different from John C. Calhoun's antebellum defense of slavery as a positive good.

Black voices, on the other hand, were very positive. Horace Mann Bond, president of Lincoln University, declared after the *Brown* decision: "Mine eyes have seen the glory of the coming of the Lord!" Benjamin E. Mays, president of Morehouse College in Atlanta, was hopeful about white reaction: "The South will adjust in this case. There will be no violence and no revolution down South." Mary McLeod Bethune, educator and president of the Florida chapter of the National Association of Colored Women,

NAACP attorneys Thurgood Marshall, George E. C. Hayes (left), and James M. Nabrit (right) exit the Supreme Court on May 17, 1954, immediately following the landmark *Brown v. Board of Education* ruling against segregated schools.

wanted Thurgood Marshall to know that "The world salutes you for your courage, for your undisputed and efficient presentation. History cannot forget your fight."[20]

Brown II

Beyond reversing the lower-court decisions upholding segregated schools (and affirming the Delaware state court that had itself ruled against segregation), the Supreme Court ended its *Brown* decision with another postponement. The Court scheduled a third set of arguments on the issue of what remedy should be ordered. The Court invited the attorney general of each state with segregated schools to participate.

A year later, in May 1955, the Supreme Court announced another unanimous ruling in what came to be called *Brown II*. The Court was encouraged by steps already taken in the three non-southern cases, Delaware, Kansas, and Washington, DC. While the Court emphasized that school segregation was outlawed everywhere, the justices also recognized that conditions and difficulties varied from place to place. The Court stipulated that steps toward compliance had to begin immediately, but it offered no master timetable. In words that became part of the national folklore, the Supreme Court said simply that further progress must come "with all deliberate speed." One ominous sign of the future was the response of the district court in the Clarendon County case: "The Constitution, in other words, does not require integration. It merely forbids discrimination. It does not forbid such segregation as occurs as the result of voluntary action."[21]

The rule of "all deliberate speed" prevailed for thirteen years, until another Supreme Court case adopted a new rule in 1968. During that period, the Supreme Court stepped back into school integration in several extreme emergencies but otherwise left the lower courts in charge. Many believe that it was an error for the Court to remain absent for so long, from 1955 to 1968. Many believe it was an error for the Court to fail to provide an explicit schedule. These beliefs, of course, are hindsight, and there is little evidence that another policy would have made much difference.[22]

The phrase "all deliberate speed" is only half of the original expression. In one of its earlier uses, an 1893 poem by Francis Thompson titled "The Hound of Heaven," the particular line is "deliberate speed, majestic instancy." Some might wonder if history would have been different if the Supreme Court had added "majestic instancy" to its 1955 opinion. The phrase "all deliberate speed" has been blamed for a process that turned out to be mostly "deliberate," with little "speed." Without that phrase, progress might not have been speedier but intransigent officials would have been less able to claim they were complying with the Supreme Court's requirements. As apprehensive as the justices were, they were still unprepared for the ferocity of the resistance from the South's officials as well as its white citizenry.

The demise of official racial segregation may have been clear in the courthouses, but integration was far from a reality in the schoolhouses. Thurgood Marshall cautioned his team, "Don't any of you fool yourselves, it's just begun, the fight has just begun." Willing compliance was difficult after a history of slavery and Jim Crow and an ideological and moral climate aided by Supreme Court support for white supremacy. African Americans were still in the shadows in American life. Black performers were invisible on television except for caricatures like Amos 'n' Andy or servants like Beulah, who was played in the first season of the show *Beulah* (1950–1951) by the singing sensation of the 1920s, Ethel Waters. Willie Mays and Hank Aaron were aiding the integration of baseball, but progress on all the athletic fields was slow. At the time of the *Brown* decision in 1954, only one African American general served in the armed forces, only two African Americans served in the US House of Representatives, and only two served as federal judges.[23]

At the same time that integration was starting to progress, America emerged from World War II as one of the world's two superpowers, locked in a Cold War with the Soviet Union. As information around the world brought countries closer together, news about America's race relations did not play well on the international scene. Segregated hotels and restaurants were a favorite target of Communist criticism, especially when diplomats from new African nations were regularly denied service in the Virginia and Maryland suburbs of Washington, DC.[24]

A new question emerged: Did the *Brown* decision refer only to segregation in public education? Most observers saw that its logic applied to other activities—just as *Plessy*'s pro-segregation rule applied to schools as much as to the streetcars of New Orleans. Over the next two years, the Supreme Court indicated that the *Brown* rule against racial segregation applied beyond schools, in several cases involving city golf courses, parks, stadiums, swimming pools, and beaches. The Court simply issued summary orders in these cases, rather than writing full opinions, so some observers, including some judges in lower courts and state courts, thought *Plessy* might still survive in some areas outside of schools.[25]

The view that *Plessy* had any sway came to an effective end with the Montgomery bus case, which accompanied the Montgomery bus boycott.

The Montgomery Boycott

Late on December 1, 1955, an African American seamstress was riding home from work on a city bus in Montgomery, Alabama. This was more than a year after the Supreme Court had ruled against segregation in the *Brown* case, but, as in most of the South, nothing had changed on Montgomery buses. State law and city ordinance still required separate rows for the races. As was also typical, actual practice as it was enforced by the bus company and the city inflicted indignities beyond the written law. A particularly vexing part of this so-called separate-but-equal system was Montgomery's system of a "floating line" between the white and Black rows: if a new white passenger found the white rows full, Black passengers in the first Black row had to vacate their seats and the Black row became a white row. Sometimes this meant four African Americans had to stand so a single white passenger could occupy the row in splendid isolation.[26]

Rosa Parks was educated as a stenographer and typist, but there were few office jobs for Black people. She became a seamstress, but more important in her life was her work for civil rights. She was active in the local NAACP, a friend of local and national leaders, and had attended a conference at Highlander Folk School in Tennessee on nonviolent direct action. On that December evening, she was going home when the driver shouted to the African Americans to clear a row because a white passenger needed a seat. Others in her row complied in the usual way, but Parks refused to give up her seat. As Parks described it later, "People always say that I [did not give up] my seat because I was tired but that isn't true. . . . the only tired I was, was tired of giving in." When the driver threatened to call the police, she calmly replied, "You may do that." He did call, and the police came and arrested her.[27]

African American leaders had been waiting for an incident to challenge the bus system's insistence on maintaining segregation. This was it. Jo Ann Robinson's committee of informed and active women, the Women's Political Council, was ready. On Friday, December 2, 1955, the women called for a boycott of the buses on Monday, December 5. Robinson and her committee spent the night mimeographing and distributing the information, and on Monday African Americans in Montgomery stayed off the buses. Days, weeks, months went by; winter turned to spring. Former passengers walked, car pools were organized, and white employers even chauffeured their employees to and fro. It was a mass movement of unprecedented discipline and perseverance. A parallel organization was formed, the Montgomery Improvement Association, which chose as its leader the newly arrived twenty-six-year-old minister of Dexter Avenue Baptist Church, Reverend Martin Luther King Jr.[28]

After five months there seemed to be a breakthrough, but it was short-lived. In Columbia, South Carolina, a lower court had ordered the bus company to desegregate, and on April 23, 1956, the US Supreme Court dismissed the bus company's appeal. The Supreme Court's dismissal was on procedural grounds, without ruling on the segregation issue, but the point was obvious. That same day the Montgomery bus company said it would desegregate. For a brief moment bus segregation had been vanquished in Montgomery, just as in Dallas, Houston, Little Rock, Knoxville, and other cities.[29]

That, however, did not suit the city of Montgomery or a radically white supremacist judge, Walter B. Jones. The city filed a lawsuit in state court, and Judge Jones ordered the bus company to keep obeying the city segregation ordinance. He said the US Supreme Court had not explicitly ruled against segregation on city buses, so authority still rested with Alabama, not the federal government, "and this Court will not be a party to filching the power from the state."[30]

The boycott and the stalemate continued, but meanwhile the boycott had been backed up by a lawsuit. The NAACP and African American lawyer Fred Gray challenged the state and city bus segregation laws. The strong combination of direct action and legal action guaranteed that the city would not outlast the boycott. In June the federal court held the segregation laws unconstitutional but stayed the order, pending the outcome of the appeal, a temporary suspension, which is common. The city and state (though not the bus company) appealed to the US Supreme Court, while the boycott continued into the fall and winter. The Supreme Court, in *Gayle v. Browder* (1956), affirmed the lower court's ruling in November and denied rehearing on December 17, 1956. Only at that point did Montgomery and Alabama give up their segregated city buses, and the boycott ended.[31]

On December 20, 1956, after 380 days of successful boycott, open seating began. The world did not end, but peace did not come to Montgomery either. Gunshots were fired at buses and boycott leaders' homes, and Black churches were bombed. The city defiantly enacted new segregation ordinances. Rosa Parks never got her fine money back, but the success of the boycott was never forgotten.

As the Montgomery bus boycott case showed, the lower federal courts played an important role in enforcing constitutional rights because they were closer to the scene and often better able to respond to problems quickly. Central in this work was the US Court of Appeals for the Fifth Circuit, covering six states including the most recalcitrant and violent states. The Fifth Circuit was indispensable in protecting constitutional and civil rights in that time and place. It had nine members, but its core consisted of an excellent Truman appointee, Richard Rives of Birmingham, and three extraordinary Eisenhower appointees, Elbert Tuttle of Atlanta, John Minor Wisdom of New Orleans, and John R. Brown of Houston. They backed up some outstanding district judges, including Frank Johnson of Montgomery and J. Skelly Wright of New Orleans. Other circuits had some remarkable judges, most notably Fourth Circuit judges Simon Sobeloff and Morris Soper, both of Maryland.[32]

Sidestep and Misstep

Segregation was not simply one case or one doctrine but a way of life that permeated every institution. As the US Supreme Court picked its way forward, there were missteps. Two early cases in particular mar the Court's record. They seem to have been misguided attempts to avoid inflaming the South even more than the Court already had.

In *Naim v. Naim* (1955, 1956), the Supreme Court bent or broke its procedural rules in order to put off deciding the ultra-explosive issue of interracial marriage. In 1955, just a year after *Brown v. Board,* the Virginia Supreme Court of Appeals upheld the state's antimiscegenation law in a case involving the marriage of a Chinese man and a white woman. An appeal to the US Supreme Court asked that the law be declared unconstitutional. Clearly reluctant to address this issue at the dawn of the integration era, the Supreme Court sent the case back to Virginia, asking the state court to clarify an aspect of the decision. The Virginia court stuck to its original ruling, with no changes, and the appeal returned to the US Supreme Court. At this point the jurisdictional rules put the Supreme Court on the spot. If this had been a certiorari case, where the Supreme Court is free to grant or deny certiorari, a denial would have been just a nondecision, setting no precedent. Instead the jurisdictional rules made this one of the less common "direct appeal" cases, which the Supreme Court is ordinarily obligated to decide—in this case, obligated to decide whether the Virginia antimiscegenation law was constitutional or not. Frankfurter wrote to his close friend Judge Learned Hand that he was very anxious to avoid deciding this case: "I shall work, within the limits of judicial decency, to put off decision on miscegenation as long as I can." In the end the Court dismissed the appeal without a decision, saying the Virginia court's nonresponse left the case without a "properly presented federal question," an incomprehensible straddle. In the circumstances, this was simply a made-up excuse to postpone a decision on miscegenation.[33]

In the other case, *Williams v. Georgia* (1955, 1956), the Georgia Supreme Court defiantly challenged the US Supreme Court, and the US Supreme Court shrank from meeting the challenge—at the cost of a man's life. Aubry Williams, an African American on death row, was indicted and convicted by all-white juries that had been selected using the same yellow-ticket system that the US Supreme Court had already held unconstitutional. The Georgia Supreme Court said Williams's motion came too late. The US Supreme Court took the case seriously enough to appoint an outstanding Washington lawyer, Eugene Gressman (former law clerk for Justice Frank

Murphy), to argue the case for Williams. The Court concluded that the Georgia courts sometimes allowed late motions, which would have been a ground for the US Supreme Court to reverse the obviously unconstitutional conviction and order a new trial. Instead of reversing, however, the Supreme Court chose a course that seemed more respectful of the state court. Relying on the "new" fact that, in the argument, the state's lawyer admitted that Williams was denied his constitutional rights, the Court sent the case back for reconsideration by the Georgia Supreme Court: "[We must] reject the assumption that the courts of Georgia would allow this man to go to his death as the result of a conviction secured from a jury which the State admits was unconstitutionally impaneled."[34]

The Georgia court was not buying it. Two weeks after the Georgia Supreme Court received the case back on remand, it told the US Supreme Court, as paraphrased by a law clerk, to "go to hell": "This court bows to the Supreme Court on all Federal questions of law but we will not supinely surrender sovereign powers of this State."[35]

Williams, assisted by his appointed lawyer, of course filed a new petition for certiorari—which the US Supreme Court chose to deny, without comment or dissent. Presumably amazed by the indifference shown to Williams, his attorney filed a petition for rehearing. Such petitions are virtually always denied, and this one was denied too. That was the end of the case. Aubry Williams was soon executed.[36]

School Emergencies—Little Rock and Ole Miss

During the thirteen-year period of "all deliberate speed" after *Brown II* in 1955, the Supreme Court put the task of supervising the transition to desegregated schools in the hands of the lower federal courts. School districts and federal judges struggled with various approaches. Some districts adopted desegregation plans that eliminated dual attendance zones, paired schools, or adopted grade-a-year plans. Others adopted "freedom-of-choice" plans, which typically kept desegregation to a minimum by putting the burden on minority students and forcing them to run a gauntlet of bureaucratic mazes that were designed not to work. The Deep South states rejected such "half-measures" in favor of all-out resistance. They preferred state legislative solutions like ending compulsory education, closing schools that faced desegregation, and diverting public funds and property to newly created private white schools—little different from official embezzlement.

There were people of stature and renown in the South who could have tried—successfully or not—to lead the way forward to peaceful accommodation; instead, the region's political "leaders" were most often found stirring up disorder and racial animosity. Twice in these thirteen years, national insurrections brought the Court back into school desegregation—Little Rock in 1958 and Ole Miss (University of Mississippi) in 1962—and both times the flames were sparked or fanned by state governors—including lies they told to the president of the United States.

On August 28, 1958, the Supreme Court convened a special term to consider whether defiance by a state's governor and legislature could outweigh the Constitution and force abandonment of a federal court desegregation order. Holding the special session was itself an extraordinary step. In the modern era, the Court had gone outside its usual October term schedule in only one case—involving the execution of Julius and Ethel Rosenberg for atomic espionage—and it has done so only twice more since then—in the Pentagon Papers case and President Nixon's secret tapes case.

The 1958 special term was convened to hear a request for a two-year delay in a desegregation plan for the schools of Little Rock, Arkansas. This was actually year two of the Little Rock crisis.

By the 1957–1958 academic year, 740 of the South's 2,300 school districts had desegregated in some fashion or were about to do so. One of those about to do so was Little Rock, whose school board in 1956 had unanimously approved a plan of gradual integration, to be started in the fall of 1957. Although opposed by the NAACP as inadequate, the plan allowed nine African American students to attend Central High School in the 1957–1958 school year, along with its 2,400 white students. The plan was that within six years all the Little Rock schools would allow some integration. Daisy Bates, head of the state NAACP, had been working with the nine students, and local white citizens appeared resigned to the plan as inevitable. There was no sign of impending disorder as the opening day of school approached. On Labor Day, Monday, September 2, the *Arkansas Gazette* reported, "Little Rock Quiet on Eve of Opening Integrated Schools." But then Governor Orval Faubus, with an eye on reelection and persuaded by hardcore segregationists, including Georgia governor Marvin Griffin and Roy Harris, firebrand former Georgia speaker of the House, announced that he would make a television appearance.[37]

That night at 10:15 p.m., Faubus warned of disorder "if forcible integration is carried out tomorrow," and he announced that he was sending the Arkansas National Guard to Central High School to maintain order. The next morning, as if summoned by Faubus, a thousand people gathered. People who might be law-abiding on other days wielded baseball bats and lead pipes, determined to harm children.[38]

When eight of the nine African American students, prearranged by Daisy Bates and her husband, L.C., arrived together at Central High, the

Elizabeth Eckford, one of the Little Rock Nine, is turned away as she tries to enter Central High School on the first day of school, September 6, 1957.

Arkansas National Guardsmen turned them away from school. These eight students had been driven to school together in a caravan and were taken away in safety. The ninth, Elizabeth Eckford, had come separately because, having no telephone, she did not receive the message about transportation. When she saw the soldiers, she thought they were there to help her get inside the school. Instead they blocked her way, and the nation was treated to the spectacle of a crazed white mob threatening a fifteen-year-old girl. Eckford had been worried about what to wear to the first day of class, and had wondered if the dress she and her mother were making would be ready in time. A photograph of this attractive teenager in sunglasses and an impeccably starched dress walking to the bus stop in front of a frenzied mob is now part of the iconography of the nation's history. Sitting on the bench awaiting the bus, an almost motionless Eckford cried silently. Two white people sat with her and tried to offer comfort. One, Benjamin Fine, was the longtime education reporter for the *New York Times*, covering what was supposed to be an education story. The other was local white resident Grace Lorch, who told the crowd, "She's scared. She's just a little girl."[39]

Without question, Governor Faubus called the National Guard not to enforce but to defy a court order. At the urging of the Department of Justice, the district court ordered Faubus to cease interfering with its integration order. Faubus, invited to Newport, Rhode Island, to meet with President Eisenhower, promised the president that he would comply with the *Brown* decision. He stated that it was "the law of the land and must be obeyed." Back in Arkansas, however, he noted, "Just because I said it doesn't make it so."[40]

Faubus dismissed the National Guard, and now only the white mob remained. On September 23, 1957, as the nine Black students prepared to return to school following the federal court orders, Faubus's tactic meant that a huge crowd waited near the main school entrance. The students avoided the crowd, at least for the moment, by entering through a side door. As the mob grew more violent, their rage centered on the journalists covering the story, who had to flee for safety and perhaps for their lives. Inside the school, the students were still in danger. At noon, Black parents and the local NAACP decided that the nine African American students should leave for their safety and to prevent complete chaos. The first half day of integration at Central High came to an ignominious close.

President Eisenhower, though lukewarm about integration, had spent a lifetime in the army giving and following orders. He now understood that Arkansas officials could not be trusted to follow court orders and that Faubus could not be trusted to tell the truth. That night the president issued a proclamation condemning the violence, and he placed 10,000 members of the Arkansas National Guard under federal command. He also ordered units of the integrated 101st Airborne Division, stationed at Fort Campbell, Kentucky, to Little Rock immediately to ensure that the court order would be carried out. On Wednesday, September 25, 1957, the nine students returned to Central High School, escorted by soldiers of the United States of America.[41]

The 1957–1958 school year passed with no open outbreak, but active tension and harassment of the Little Rock Nine continued. Soldiers and guardsmen patrolled the inside and outside of Central High School, most of the white students who had left returned, one of the Little Rock Nine, Ernest Green, graduated, and seven of the other eight finished the year successfully. The one exception was Minniejean Brown. Frustrated by taunts and low-level harassment, she finally reacted and turned a cafeteria tray with a bowl of chili upside-down over the head of her white tormentor. She was suspended. Supporters arranged for her to attend a private school in New York. She moved there, graduated, and went on to a career far from Arkansas.

Southern politicians expressed no concern about the mistreatment of the African American students but ranted about the presence of enemy soldiers in the South for the first time since Reconstruction. Senator Richard B. Russell of Georgia said they were like "Hitler's storm troopers."[42]

The leaders of the mob, armed with bats and lead pipes, were not arrested. They could not be charged under Section 6 of the Enforcement Act of 1870 or Section 2 of the Ku Klux Act of 1871 because the Supreme Court in the 1870s and 1880s had held that the federal government could not prosecute these armed private citizens who were leading a mob, even if they committed serious mayhem or killed someone.

If there was hope that calmer times would come to Little Rock the next year, events soon proved otherwise. Near the end of the 1957–1958 school year, the Little Rock school requested a two-year delay in its desegregation plan. According to the school board, public hostility, which the board itself said was engineered largely by the attitudes and actions of the governor and legislature, made it impossible to maintain a sound educational environment. On June 20, 1958, the federal district court granted the delay over the NAACP's opposition. On August 18, however, the court of appeals reversed, and ordered the plan to go forward for the school year about to begin on September 15. The case was appealed.

In an extraordinary move, the Supreme Court convened in special session to hear oral argument on August 28 and again on September 11. On the next day, September 12, the Court announced that it was unanimously affirming the court of appeals and that the desegregation plan must go forward as scheduled. Its full opinion was issued two weeks later in *Cooper v. Aaron* (1958). The Court rejected any delay, saying, "Law and order are not here to be preserved by depriving the Negro children of their constitutional rights." The Court went further and put the case in the starkest terms. The Court said the case involved "a claim by the Governor and Legislature of a State that there is no duty on state officials to obey federal court orders," specifically, "that they are not bound by our holding in the *Brown* case." The Court treated this as "war against the Constitution," compared it to the discredited notion of "nullification." The Court spoke on the rule of law, the supremacy clause of the Constitution, and the oath that all officials, state as well as federal, take to support the Constitution of the United States.[43]

The opinion in *Cooper v. Aaron* included new justices, John Marshall Harlan and William J. Brennan, who had joined the Court since the *Brown* decision and joined in this decision. The new justices, both Eisenhower appointments, would play important roles on the Court. Harlan, appointed in 1955, was the grandson of the nineteenth-century John Marshall Harlan, the Great Dissenter. The second Harlan supported civil rights but dissented from some of the Warren Court's civil rights decisions. Although not a "conservative" by current standards, he was regarded as the most conservative member of the liberal Warren Court. Brennan, appointed in 1956, was a solid liberal who went on to serve for thirty-four years. He was known for his ability to pull together justices of seemingly different views and was therefore able to gain some surprising majority victories. He wrote some of the most important decisions on the Warren, Burger, and Rehnquist Courts.

Despite the traumatic chapter in the nation's history, the Supreme Court's Little Rock decision was a milestone. Positive lessons came from the president's support of the court order and the Supreme Court's refusal to allow a mob, even a mob of state officials, to destroy constitutional rights.

But if anyone thought the Supreme Court decision would produce swift compliance, that thinking was naïve. The immediate reaction in Arkansas was devastating. Governor Faubus, relying on new state legislation, closed the Little Rock schools, and they stayed closed for the entire 1958–1959 school year, leaving most Black and many white students with no schooling. A lawsuit was filed challenging the state's transparent new laws authorizing the governor to close the schools and authorizing giveaways of school property and funds to "private" schools. The suit moved slowly, though, and by the time the federal court held the laws unconstitutional (with a Supreme Court affirmance), the school year was over.[44]

Faubus, who originally had few prospects for reelection, became a segregation hero and rode the "seg" train to five more terms as governor. The lesson was not lost on other politicians, who saw that they could gain votes by summoning their people to follow them in race hatred and ignorance.

Two years later, in Louisiana, a special session of the legislature tried to block the desegregation of New Orleans schools. To back up the familiar package of obstructionist laws, the legislature also enacted something it called the Interposition Act, announcing that "Louisiana has interposed itself in the field of public education over which it has exclusive control." The lower federal court made short work of the new laws and Louisiana's Interposition Act: "Interposition is not a constitutional doctrine . . . it is illegal defiance of constitutional authority." The Supreme Court affirmed, saying the lower court's rejection of "Interposition" was in line with the Supreme Court's Little Rock decision.[45]

Another effort to determine if Supreme Court decisions had substance involved the University of Mississippi, where James Meredith applied as a student and was twice denied. In 1962, after many hearings and delays, the US Court of Appeals for the Fifth Circuit ruled that he must be admitted, and denied a stay of its order. Suddenly, Judge Ben Cameron, an arch-segregationist who was a judge on the appeals court but was not on the panel in this case, took it upon himself to issue a delay of the order admitting Meredith. The panel assigned to the case, which had already denied any stay, held that Judge Cameron's order was a nullity, but he repeated his adventure four times. Finally, the issue came before Justice Hugo Black, who put a swift end to Judge Cameron's interference.[46]

In Oxford, Mississippi, however, white crowds gathered to block Meredith's admission. As hostility mounted, Governor Ross Barnett promised President John F. Kennedy that he would provide police protection, following the by-then-familiar pattern of southern governors feeling free to lie to the president of the United States. At the height of tension in Oxford, state troopers suddenly vanished, the federal marshals were overwhelmed, and two bystanders, including journalist Paul Guihard, were killed in Governor Barnett's riot at Ole Miss.

The court of appeals cited Governor Barnett and Lieutenant Governor Paul Johnson for civil and criminal contempt of court. By the time trial was approaching, after Barnett's unsuccessful Supreme Court appeal in *United States v. Barnett* (1965), three years had passed and a 4–3 majority of the court of appeals dismissed the contempt charges as a way, they said, of looking forward, not backward.

The riot over James Meredith may have been a sobering experience for southern political demagogues. When 1963 dawned, Governor George Wallace of Alabama did go through the ritual of calling for "Segregation Now, Segregation Tomorrow, and Segregation Forever!" but it was already playacting. When two African American students, Vivian Malone and James Hood, were admitted to the University of Alabama under court order, Wallace did block the schoolhouse door. But it was only a show, and he quietly moved aside after a moment.[47]

Meanwhile, although it largely stayed out of school desegregation, the Supreme Court was busy extending the antisegregation rule to new areas. One such area was voting, where the Court was kept busy rejecting blatant tactics designed to maintain white control. In one such tactic, the Alabama legislature redrew the city boundaries of Tuskegee from a traditional square to "an uncouth, 28-sided figure" that put all but five Black voters outside the city without removing a single white voter. In *Gomillion v. Lightfoot* (1960), the Supreme Court held this exercise unconstitutional, saying that this change was not simply a city boundary change, a routine exercise invariably within a state's power; instead, this law came into the constitutional orbit because "the inescapable effect of this essay in human geometry and geography is to despoil colored citizens, and only colored citizens, of their theretofore enjoyed voting rights."[48]

Then, in *Anderson v. Martin* (1964), the Court rejected a Louisiana law that required each candidate's race to be listed on the ballot—for the obvious purpose of ensuring that white voters would know which candidates *not* to vote for. In a pair of other cases in 1965, the Court reached back, finally, to dismantle parts of the Mississippi and Louisiana disfranchising constitutions of the 1890s. Affirming a sweeping injunction by a lower court, the Supreme Court described the broad obligation to vindicate the Constitution by eliminating injustice:

> We bear in mind that the court has not merely the power but the duty to render a decree which will so far as possible eliminate the discriminatory effects of the past as well as bar like discrimination in the future.[49]

New Directions in the 1960s

As the 1960s began, new allies were joining in a campaign that had been largely driven by the Supreme Court and waged by judges, lawyers, and, of course, brave citizens. One month after 1960 began, the first sit-ins took place, heralding a growing Civil Rights Movement in which people would march, sit in, and go to jail—often singing—to break down the walls of discrimination.

Meanwhile, the other branches of the federal government were coming on board as well. The Civil Rights Act of 1957 created a Civil Rights Commission that began to shine a light on the worst aspects of race discrimination. The new law also empowered the Justice Department to bring suits to protect voters, which greatly upset the segregationist politicians who had benefited for years from keeping potential voters off the rolls. One of them, Senator Sam Ervin of North Carolina, was horrified at the idea that "the only qualifications required of voters," besides age and address, would be "the possession of a physical body, with or without intelligence and character." Moving forward, however, President Eisenhower pressed for and got a new civil rights bill in 1960, to supplement the earlier act. His successors, John F. Kennedy and especially Lyndon Johnson, would each increase the pressure for equal rights.[50]

During the 1960s, the political branches, the president, and Congress combined to enact three landmark civil rights laws: the Civil Rights Act of 1964, the Voting Rights Act of 1965, and the Fair Housing Act of 1968. These laws are discussed in the next two chapters. The year 1965 was a banner legislative year, with the Voting Rights Act (and Medicare), and two other laws that have had an enormous, if indirect, effect on race and civil rights: federal aid to education in the Elementary and Secondary Education Act (sometimes called Title I, for short), and the Immigration and Nationality Act of 1965.

The Aid to Education Act of 1965 and the Civil Rights Act of 1964 dovetailed to put pressure on still-segregated schools to change. The civil rights law contained a provision that banned discrimination in any program or activity receiving federal aid, and the Aid to Education law, suddenly, provided very large amounts of federal funding to America's public schools. The lure of big money from the Aid to Education law and the threat of losing it because of the civil rights law gave the school districts a huge incentive to desegregate.[51]

Another major antidiscrimination law is often overlooked, but over the years it has done more to change the racial demographics of the United States than anyone ever dreamed at the time the law was passed: the Immigration and Nationality Act of 1965. The law completely scrapped the national quota system of the Immigration Act of 1924 and also opened the United States to immigration from the entire world, including non-white countries of Africa, Asia, and the Pacific. Passage in the House of Representatives was led by Judiciary chairman Emanuel Celler, the sole remaining member of Congress who had been in office in 1924, when he voted against that immigration law because of its strict quotas. Many saw the parallel between race discrimination at home and the immigration policy. Labor lobbyist Ken Meiklejohn, for example, condemned "racial and ethnic bigotry . . . in our treatment of those who seek to come to our shores [just as] in the treatment of our own citizens." The new law was expected to have little effect on the size and composition of the country's population, but its effect in future years would be large.[52]

The Warren Court took novel and sometimes controversial approaches in some other areas of the law, for example in criminal law. By the time of the Warren Court, the Supreme Court's constitutional power to require fairness in state criminal cases was established but was exercised only intermittently. Beginning in the 1920s and 1930s the Court reversed several state convictions in egregious cases, and did so slightly more often in the 1940s and 1950s. The advances in guaranteeing fairness involved many

African American and some Latino defendants. Until the 1960s, however, the few cases had little effect on the overall administration of the criminal process at the state and local level. Beginning in 1961, though, the Supreme Court began making the procedural protections in the Bill of Rights binding on the states. The major rulings involved Bill of Rights guarantees relating to search warrants, the right to a lawyer, the right to a jury, and, of course, the universally known rule against uninformed confessions ("read him his rights"). It was not just these individual cases but the frequency and consistency of them that brought change to state courts and state and local police forces, even in those states that previously had the worst records. The cases helped dismantle official Jim Crow because they reduced the states' ability to use the criminal process as a tactic of racial control.[53]

Despite the Warren Court's reputation of ensuring fairness in the criminal justice process, some cases had different outcomes. In one case the Court upheld a state practice excluding women from juries (a practice that soon ended). Another decision upheld racially discriminatory "peremptory challenges" of jurors in criminal trials, an issue that would be revisited by a later Supreme Court. Finally, the Warren Court approved a watering down of the constitutional protection against illegal searches and seizures. The Court upheld police authority to "stop and frisk" a person based on mere "suspicion" without "probable cause" sufficient for an arrest. Perhaps unforeseen at the time, this decision has taken on monumental importance as the years have passed.[54]

The criminal procedure decisions, largely accepted today at least regarding their core, were controversial at the time, and, as the decade wore on, they stirred opposition to the Supreme Court. In a time of anxiety over urban riots and conflict over the Vietnam War, some accused the Court of coddling criminals. Other issues also aroused opposition. Many religious groups opposed Supreme Court decisions limiting prayer in public schools. All the antagonism contributed to an "Impeach Earl Warren" movement.[55]

Adding to that antagonism were Supreme Court decisions restricting governmental power to root out "subversives." After a single day in 1957 when the Supreme Court decided three cases restricting state and federal "anti-subversive" efforts, opponents of those decisions brought on proposed federal legislation to strip the Court of jurisdiction to hear certain types of cases. The bill was defeated in the Senate, but only by a vote of 49–41. The vote was an indication of a deep divide in the approval or disapproval of the Warren Court.[56]

Many billboards, such as this one near Holly Springs, Mississippi, 1968, called for the impeachment of Chief Justice Earl Warren.

Love and Marriage

A decade after the *Brown* case, and eight years after it ducked the miscegenation issue in *Naim v. Naim,* the Supreme Court stepped gingerly into the last taboo of race—love and marriage. The Court began by voiding a Florida law prohibiting interracial, unmarried cohabitation. That case began when a suspicious Miami property owner noticed that a Black man (Dewey McLaughlin) was spending a lot of time, including nights, with her white tenant, Connie Hoffman. She reported her suspicions to the police, who investigated and arrested the couple for the Florida crime of living together interracially. The couple were both convicted, and by this time the Supreme Court was ready to take the appeal. The Court held, in *McLaughlin v. Florida* (1964), that the Florida law was an unconstitutional denial of equal protection because it punished people solely because of their race. The Court recognized that this decision was contrary to *Pace v. Alabama* (1883), but said the theory of that case had long ago been "swept away." The Court also took pains to say it was not ruling on the validity of a law against interracial marriage.[57]

There was a curious dualism to the issue. Sex between a Black man and a white woman enraged some white southerners beyond measure, and reports of such events—real or imagined—sometimes led to a lynching or even a white race riot. But sex between a Black woman and a white man, from slave masters like Thomas Jefferson to twentieth-century political leaders like Strom Thurmond, was quite a different matter.

As of the end of World War II, more than half the states had laws against interracial marriage or interracial sex or both. Then the California Supreme Court, in *Perez v. Sharp* (1948), held that state's law violated the California Constitution. A dozen of the remaining states abolished their bans in the next two decades. By 1967, when the issue returned to the US Supreme Court, interracial sex or marriage was against the law in only sixteen states—all eleven states of the former Confederacy plus four more, all but one bordering the old Confederacy.[58]

The case that brought the issue back to the Supreme Court had started a decade earlier. In 1958 Richard Loving and Mildred Jeter were married in Washington, DC, and then went home to Caroline County, Virginia. Mildred recalled the night of July 11, 1958: "I woke up and these guys were standing around the bed. I sat up. It was dark. They had flashlights. They told us to get up, get dressed." The couple was arrested and indicted for violating one of Virginia's collection of antimiscegenation laws; Richard was white and Mildred was not. At the trial in Virginia, the local judge explained the fundamental principle supporting the law: "Almighty God created the races white, black, yellow, malay and red and he placed them on separate continents. . . . The fact that he separated the races shows that he did not intend for the races to mix."[59]

The Lovings pleaded guilty to being married and were sentenced to a year in prison, suspended on the condition that they leave Virginia and remain away for at least twenty-five years. They moved to Washington, DC, but after several years wanted to go home to Caroline County. They filed a motion to set aside the verdict on the ground that the antimiscegenation law was unconstitutional. When they lost in the Virginia state courts, the issue of race-mixing returned to the Supreme Court.

On June 12, 1967, in *Loving v. Virginia* (1967), the Supreme Court ruled unanimously in the Lovings' favor, rejecting the antimiscegenation laws of Virginia and of the other states with remaining laws. The question at the heart of the case was whether an explicitly racial purpose could ever justify a state law. The "legitimate" purposes of the Virginia laws, according to the Virginia Supreme Court, were to "preserve the racial integrity of its citizens" and to prevent "corruption of blood," a "mongrel breed of citizens," and "obliteration of racial pride." The US Supreme Court wryly noted that the Virginia laws did not preserve all racial integrity, but only *white* racial integrity, or white supremacy, because the laws allowed the various colored races to "mix" with each other as long as none of them mixed with white partners.[60]

In the *Loving* case, the Supreme Court left almost no room for invidious official action based on race. The Court referred to the Japanese internment cases during World War II and repeated that "distinctions between citizens solely because of their ancestry" are "odious to a free people whose institutions are founded upon the doctrine of equality." Then, still referring to the Japanese internment cases, the Court said that racial classifications, like Virginia's, must "be subjected to the most rigid scrutiny," and "if they are ever to be upheld, they must be shown to be necessary to the accomplishment of some permissible state objective." In the early 1970s this would be formalized as the rule of strict scrutiny, which is still applied today. *Loving v. Virginia* is often cited as the origin of the strict scrutiny rule.[61]

The decision in *Loving v. Virginia* was announced on June 12, 1967. Two days before that, the actor Spencer Tracy died, having recently finished filming the movie *Guess Who's Coming to Dinner.* A mirror of the time, this film portrayed the run-up and various reactions to the interracial marriage of a couple played by the actors Sidney Poitier (Black) and Katharine Houghton (white). It was a daring subject even then, but by the time the film was released, the Supreme Court was already on record.

Back to School Desegregation

In the 1960s the Warren Court returned to where it had begun, with the task of dismantling segregated school systems. "All deliberate speed" had been the rule since *Brown II* in 1955. In Prince Edward County, Virginia, site of one of the original 1954 segregation cases, the situation was worse than a decade earlier. The county's public schools had been closed, but the state, county, and school board were financing a new system of white private schools, including state tuition grants and county tax exemptions. The school board misappropriated public funds and assets to the white private school. By contrast, African American children had lost even their poorly supported schools. In *Griffin v. Prince Edward County Bd of Education* (1964), the Supreme Court held that Virginia could not operate schools everywhere but in this county, ordered the schools reopened, and blocked most of the public funds going to the private school. The Supreme Court opinion ended with these words: "The time for mere 'deliberate speed' has run out."[62]

The Court followed up with another Virginia school case in 1968. New on the Court by then was Justice Thurgood Marshall. After Marshall's quarter century leading the NAACP and NAACP Legal Defense Fund, President Kennedy named him to a federal appeals court in 1961. President Johnson appointed him solicitor general in 1965, and in 1967 nominated him for the Supreme Court to succeed Tom Clark.[63]

The case that would end the doctrine of "all deliberate speed" came in Marshall's first term on the Supreme Court. New Kent County was a small rural county in Virginia, with equal numbers of African American and white students. The school board supervised two K–12 schools, New Kent (white) and Watkins (Black). Each school had students of the designated race from throughout the county. When segregation was declared unconstitutional, the school district first used Virginia's "pupil placement" laws and then a freedom of choice plan, but those plans made little difference. No white students started attending Watkins and only a few African American students started attending New Kent School. The school district argued that its obligation was simply to remove the legal structure of segregation laws. In *Green v. School Board of New Kent County* (1968), the Supreme Court flatly disagreed and said school boards had the duty to take "whatever steps might be necessary" to eliminate the long-standing, state-imposed racial discrimination "root and branch." The Court said the school board was obligated to adopt a plan "that promises realistically to work, and promises realistically to work now." The only successful result would be "a system without a white school and a Negro school, but just schools."[64]

As some people already knew, and many others soon discovered, new kinds of serious problems arose, not from segregation but from integration. Where some desegregation did take place, African American teachers, administrators, and coaches paid a heavy price, and African American students, families, and the community did also. When there was consolidation of any kind, invariably white people would get the plums and African Americans the pits. In merged schools, the principal of the former Black school became the assistant principal, the head football coach of the former Black high school became the assistant coach or, worse, was sent down to be a gym teacher at the junior high school. Black teachers who had taught and nurtured African American students were demoted or fired because white educators thought they were poor teachers—certainly not qualified to teach white children. Black students were scattered, often thrown into chilly environments in largely white schools without a network of support. Black schools, even though often physically substandard, had been central to Black community life and were now closed. A great deal was tragically lost.[65]

The *Green* decision was a new direction in school integration. By focusing on the actual effect or result achieved, it could open the way to real equality. The focus of *Green* opened up questions about northern segregation, which was rarely, if ever, based on laws but grew out of attitudes resulting from laws and institutions. The framework of *Green* offered a path forward, albeit still a difficult path. Fourteen years after *Brown v. Board of Education,* segregation by law was largely gone, but segregation in reality remained.

The Supreme Court of the late 1960s had walked far down Freedom Road, inspiring other public and private institutions to take that journey as well. It might have been a hundred years late, but the *Green* ruling beckoned toward a deeper look at solving the problem of the country's racial history.

CHAPTER EIGHT

Opposing Forces

Massive Resistance and the Civil Rights Movement

The Supreme Court's rejection of segregated schools in *Brown v. Board of Education* started a process of dismantling the legal structure of separate-but-equal, one deliberate step after another. Supreme Court rulings were only part of the story. After centuries of slavery and Jim Crow, would the new sense of legal equality be able to transform the nation into a "beloved community," as envisioned by Dr. Martin Luther King Jr.? In the decade following the *Brown* decision, two opposing movements shared center stage in a battle for hearts and minds: Massive Resistance and the Civil Rights Movement. These two forces opposed each other from the time of the *Brown* decision in 1954 until civil rights forces won passage of the Civil Rights Act of 1964 and the Voting Rights Act of 1965.

In that decade, from 1955 to 1965, the Supreme Court's docket was crowded with cases involving the major weapons of the two groups. For Massive Resistance against desegregation, the weapon of choice was an attack on "outside agitators"—the NAACP and the press. The weapon of the Civil Rights Movement was peaceful protest—marches and sit-ins. In dozens of cases between the years 1955 and 1965, the US Supreme Court *never once* upheld a state attack on the press or the NAACP, and *never once* upheld a conviction of a sit-in demonstrator or civil rights marcher.

This could happen only because the southern states adopted the most transparent schemes and carried them out in blundering fashion. Such tactics had always succeeded before, but this was a new era and a new Supreme Court. Nor did the Court tilt the law to favor the NAACP, the press, or the demonstrators; the Court was sensitive to these parties, to be sure, but the cases against them had little or no merit. The states that practiced Jim Crow had typically wielded the legal machinery at will, and now they were not prepared to defend their methods under real scrutiny.

In the process, the Court enforced the equal protection clause of the Fourteenth Amendment and established important constitutional principles under its due process clause as well as the free speech, free assembly, and free press guarantees of the First Amendment.

Massive Resistance

The Supreme Court's ruling in *Brown v. Board* on May 17, 1954, brought hope and some civic acquiescence, but more than anything else it brought hostile opposition. Early on, the Court's decision had support from the religious community. In July a council of white ministers in Atlanta declared that the ruling was "in harmony with Christian principles." Reverend Billy Graham of North Carolina, who denounced racism as a sin, spoke only to integrated audiences, and in 1957 he invited Reverend Martin Luther King Jr. to offer the invocation at a Madison Square Garden rally. The official response of the Southern Baptist Convention (the representative body of Southern Baptist churches) to the *Brown* decision was also supportive. Having already desegregated denominational seminaries in 1951–1952, the convention expressed support for the *Brown* ruling at its annual meeting in June 1954, declaring the decision to be consistent with "the constitutional guarantee of equal freedom to all citizens and with Christian principles of equal justice and love for all men." Three years later the convention reiterated its near-unanimous support for *Brown*, in spite of a prolonged debate led by a small but vocal segregationist contingent.[1]

Moderates throughout the South initially urged compliance with the law. Governors Francis Cherry of Arkansas and Frank Clement of Tennessee supported the decision. Earl Long of Louisiana denounced those opposing the *Brown* decision as "fakers trying to make themselves politically by using the issue to befuddle the people." "Big Jim" Folsom of Alabama accepted the *Brown* decision and remarked that the effort of white supremacists to nullify the Supreme Court's desegregation orders was like "a hound baying at the moon and claiming it's got the moon treed." During the 1954 campaign for governor of Arkansas, the eventual winner, Orval Faubus (later notorious for his defiance of school integration in Little Rock), announced that he would have voted with the Supreme Court justices on the *Brown* decision. Eight of the eleven Democratic governors in the South at the time of the *Brown* decision were considered racial "moderates" who recommended obedience to the law of the land.[2]

The voices of moderates, however, did not prevail. This period of moderation, if it could be called one, was tentative and uncertain, and reasoned self-control quickly dissipated as southern politicians tried to surpass each other in defending segregation and attacking *Brown* and the Supreme Court. Mississippi congressman John Bell Williams denounced *Brown* and branded the day of the Supreme Court decision "Black Monday," a term that caught on in local newspapers throughout the South. Thomas P. Brady, an attorney and judge in Mississippi, authored *Black Monday: Segregation or Amalgamation, America Has Its Choice.*[3]

In grotesque appeals that were less emotional but equally unyielding, James Jackson Kilpatrick, the influential editor of the Richmond *News Leader,* published defenses of segregation in national magazines, and newspapers across the South reprinted or echoed Kilpatrick. Senator Richard B. Russell of Georgia called the decision "a flagrant abuse of judicial power," and Senator James O. Eastland of Mississippi declared that "the South will not abide by, or obey, this legislative decision by a political court." In 1954 Marvin Griffin was elected governor of Georgia on the pledge: "Come hell or high water, races will not be mixed in Georgia schools." After George Wallace lost the 1958 Alabama governor's race to stridently racist John Patterson, he said he would never be "out-niggered" again, and he wasn't—starting with the campaign in 1962, when Wallace denounced the legendary, popular Folsom as "soft on the nigger question." These political leaders, whether ideologues or just power-hungry charlatans, fanned the flames of fear and hatred.[4]

Demagogues applied pressure for resistance at the grassroots level. Membership in a reemergence of the Ku Klux Klan mounted. Hangings, shootings, drownings, and church burnings were epidemic. Local and state enforcement agents had little interest in finding the culprits—and, indeed, some of these agents were the culprits. More popular among "moderates" was the Klan's better-dressed counterpart, the White Citizens' Councils, which used the businessman's pen to inflict economic damage more widespread and effective than the Klansman's gun. Formed in 1955 in Indianola, Mississippi, to maintain segregation and suppress dissent, the organization soon had chapters across the South.[5]

S. E. Rogers, a Summerton attorney for the Clarendon County defendants in *Briggs v. Elliott,* was also a recruiter for the Citizens' Council in

South Carolina. In a visit to the town of Lake City, South Carolina, on August 26, 1955, he reminded the white people that their city harbored Reverend Joseph A. De Laine (whom we met in Chapter 6), the man who had started the whole education mess in South Carolina, and that they should do something about it. Immediately, suspicious incidents, attacks, including drive-by shootings, and harassment of De Laine and his family commenced. After a complaint to the local sheriff, De Laine was instructed to "mark the car" of the perpetrators. On October 5 the church he pastored in Lake City was destroyed by arson, and three days later, he received an anonymous note reminding him of what had happened in Lake City in 1898 when vigilantes had killed African American postmaster Frazier B. Baker and his two-year-old daughter as they fled their burning home. The note gave De Laine ten days to get out of town or die. On October 10, only two days after receiving the threatening letter, De Laine was subjected to more drive-by shootings. He fired back; he "Marked The Car In Jesus Name." De Laine recalled, "The Lord said unto me, 'It's time for you to leave here,'" and that night in a dramatic escape, he fled to New York. On October 11 law enforcement issued a warrant against him for shooting at his attackers. De Laine was never bitter: "It's worth some suffering—it's even worth a man's life, if he can start something that will lead to a little more justice for people."[6]

Between January 1, 1955, and January 1, 1959, the Southern Regional Council (SRC) counted 225 separate acts of violence in the wake of *Brown*. The interracial SRC, formed in 1943, opposed white supremacist groups like the KKK and White Citizens' Councils, but it was slow to advocate structural changes to southern culture. At the behest of author and teacher Lillian Smith, the SRC denounced segregation in 1949. This act cost the organization about half of its white members, but the group has continued to work toward racial justice.[7]

After the Supreme Court announced the *Brown* decision, Governor Thomas B. Stanley of Virginia issued a statement saying that he expected the state to uphold the law peacefully, and in August 1954 he appointed a thirty-two-member all-white commission whose task was to make integration limited and slow. The commission's report in November 1955 recommended that broad authority be given to local school boards to assign pupils to appropriate schools and that tuition grants be set up so that white residents facing integrated schools might flee to private schools. By allowing token integration while shifting the burden of initiation to individual schoolchildren in hundreds of localities, Virginia made rapid integration virtually impossible.

As clever as this plan was, it did not meet the ideological needs of US Senator Harry F. Byrd of Virginia and his allies in the Virginia state legis-

Rev. Joseph A. De Laine, leader of the Clarendon County case that led to *Brown v. Board of Education,* with his family at their burned-out home in Summerton, South Carolina, in 1951. The burning of his home was one of many violent incidents of retaliation against him.

lature. Resurrecting John C. Calhoun's "interposition," a word Calhoun preferred to "nullification," the legislature passed an Interposition Resolution in February 1956. This doctrine supposedly would allow states to ignore federal law. Closely related was "Massive Resistance," which entered the national vocabulary in February 1956, when Senator Byrd issued a statement: "If we can organize the Southern States for massive resistance to this order [*Brown*] I think that in time the rest of the country will realize that racial integration is not going to be accepted in the South."[8]

Another term was "Southern Manifesto," a document denouncing *Brown v. Board*. Senators John Stennis of Mississippi, Richard Russell of Georgia, Sam Ervin of North Carolina, and Strom Thurmond of South Carolina drafted the manifesto, and Byrd rounded up the senators and representatives from the eleven former Confederate states to sign this Massive Resistance offensive. The 1956 manifesto claimed that the US Supreme Court had abused its judicial powers and declared that the justices "planted hatred and suspicion where there had been heretofore friendship and understanding." It pledged to use "all lawful means to bring a reversal of this decision which is contrary to the Constitution, and to prevent the use of force in its implementation." From these eleven states, 101 members signed the document, including 19 out of 22 senators (all but Senators Albert Gore and Estes Kefauver of Tennessee and Lyndon Johnson of Texas), and 82 members of the House of Representatives (most of the Democrats but only a minority of the small number of Republicans). Oregon senator Wayne Morris rebuked the southern senators who spoke in support of the manifesto: "You would think today Calhoun was walking and speaking on the floor of the Senate." In the gallery, Senator Walter George's wife, Lucy, told Jean Thurmond the comparison to Calhoun was a compliment.[9]

Massive Resistance had several components, including a legal strategy using state laws and lawsuits and an extralegal strategy that enlisted or encouraged economic and physical harassment and violence. These all fit together. New state and local anti-integration laws and spurious libel suits against national media reporting about the South were common. Many states had special state commissions, typically with secret functions like tapping telephones and "fixing" jury verdicts. Massive Resistance was eventually adopted by Alabama, Georgia, Louisiana, Mississippi, and South Carolina, as well as Virginia. Within three years of the *Brown* decision, not one school district had desegregated in these Massive Resistance states.[10]

In July 1958 the first Black children filed their applications for transfer to previously all-white high schools in Norfolk, Virginia. The Norfolk school board examined the 151 applications of the high school students, who had been carefully recruited and trained by the NAACP, and decided that none of them met the necessary criteria for pupil transfers. After federal judge Walter Hoffman ordered the school board to reconsider, it grudgingly approved 17 applications. In response, Governor Lindsay Almond ordered the Norfolk high schools closed. He followed that up by ordering grammar schools closed too.

In Norfolk, parents who wanted an education for their children, and business interests who feared economic damage to Virginia, opposed the all-out supporters of segregation. In 1959, when the federal court and the Virginia Supreme Court ruled that closing the schools violated the federal and state constitutions, Massive Resistance was broken, at least fractured in its formal dress. After that, the fight against integration would be fought by other, no less effective means.[11]

NAACP

Of all the components of Massive Resistance, the favorite by far was attacking the NAACP. Every southern state took part in this campaign; a dozen cases reached the Supreme Court. Southern politicians blamed the organization as the chief "outside agitator" and, along with its supposed ally, the Communist Party, as the chief "mastermind" of Jim Crow's woes. Variant attacks included laws restricting NAACP litigation, trumped-up legislative investigations of Communism or of organized crime within the NAACP, and laws that barred NAACP members from public employment such as teaching school. These efforts required little preparation because a special legislative session could be quickly called and almost as quickly could enact a battery of dubious but oppressive laws or issue a committee subpoena. State or local officials could also file a suit or issue a subpoena demanding NAACP compliance with some law or regulation. Most of the suits and subpoenas were simply subterfuges for obtaining lists of local NAACP members' names, which could be publicized in order to make them targets for economic pressure and violent attack.[12]

Alabama Drama in Four Acts

Alabama led the war against the NAACP. Its tactics set off an eight-year-long, Kafkaesque chain of events. It would take four decisions by the US Supreme Court before the defiance of the State of Alabama and the Alabama Supreme Court ended. In the process, Alabama's scheme would lead the US Supreme Court to major rulings protecting the First Amendment and the right of privacy.

Alabama's campaign against the NAACP began on June 1, 1956, when its attorney general filed suit in state court to make the New York–based NAACP register as an out-of-state corporation doing business in Alabama. Alabama's registration law was typical of most states' laws, but it was generally assumed that the law did not apply to nonprofit corporations like the NAACP. When the attorney general filed a lawsuit seeking a ruling that even nonprofit organizations must register, that was legitimate. What he and the judges of Alabama did after that was not.

Once the suit was filed, the ordinary next step would be to deliver a copy of the complaint to the NAACP, which would then have thirty days to contest the suit by filing an answer. Or, instead of contesting the suit, the NAACP could simply choose to register. Registration was not complicated; it involved a $100 fee and basic information like the organization's bylaws, office address, and chief officers' names.

Instead of events following this ordinary course, Alabama officials soon showed that having the NAACP register was not their real goal. Once the complaint was filed, and before the NAACP knew it had been sued, the state attorney general went to see a state judge to ask for an immediate injunction. Without notifying the NAACP of this visit or asking for the NAACP's position, the state judge obligingly issued an injunction barring the NAACP from engaging in any activity in Alabama, even trying to register, while the case was pending.[13]

Because the NAACP had not been heard from, this was what is called an "*ex parte* injunction," meaning an injunction issued after hearing only one side of a case. *Ex parte* injunctions are very rare, reserved for extreme emergencies where the risk of harm is so great and immediate that there is not even enough time to get the other side on the telephone. In the circumstances of this case, the judge's action was lawless; it was entered by Judge Walter B. Jones, who just weeks earlier had ordered the Montgomery bus company to keep segregating passengers. The type of injunction Jones issued was a "temporary restraining order." This is a short-term stopgap usually limited to no more than ten days, or twenty days in some cases. In this case it remained in effect for eight years.[14]

As the case before Judge Jones went forward, the Alabama attorney general moved to obtain certain records from the state NAACP. Some were appropriate—organization charter, bylaws, officers' names—but another item was what the attorney general really wanted: the Alabama NAACP's membership list. That list bore no conceivable relevance to the question whether the NAACP was required to register.

When the NAACP agreed to produce all the records except the membership list, Judge Jones imposed a fine of $10,000 and ordered that the records be produced within five days. Within the five days, the NAACP produced all the records except the membership list, whereupon Jones raised the fine to $100,000. He then ruled that because the fine was outstanding, the underlying issue of whether the NAACP was required to register would not be heard, nor would the NAACP be allowed to register even if it wanted to. The NAACP appealed to the Alabama Supreme Court, which refused to consider the appeal on that court's familiar ground that the NAACP had used the wrong procedure.

At this point the NAACP petitioned the US Supreme Court, which agreed to hear the case. The heart of the case was the NAACP's argument that providing the membership list would violate members' rights of free speech and association because public knowledge of NAACP membership in a state like Alabama would subject members to economic and physical threats, and possibly even death. In *NAACP v. Alabama* (1958), the Supreme Court unanimously agreed, which also eliminated the $100,000 fine. The massive evidence of economic reprisal and physical violence showed a real danger if members' names were released. The Supreme Court found a "vital connection between the First Amendment freedom to associate and privacy in one's associations," especially because Alabama showed no legitimate need for the membership list.[15]

The US Supreme Court also made short work of the Alabama Supreme Court's dodge, its rejection of the NAACP appeal for supposedly using the wrong procedure. The US Supreme Court spent five pages reviewing the Alabama Supreme Court's previous cases, which showed that the NAACP appeal was fully compliant. This was a repeat of Alabama's performance in the Scottsboro case of *Patterson v. Alabama* (1935).

That US Supreme Court decision turned out to be more of a beginning than an end. The case went back to the Alabama courts, where supposedly the NAACP would have a trial on the registration issue or, more likely, would simply register and end the dispute. But the Alabama attorney general put up a new roadblock. Now he said the US Supreme Court decision about the membership list was irrelevant because—although he had not mentioned this previously—there were *other* records the NAACP had failed to produce, so the NAACP was still in violation and still subject to a $100,000 fine, and could neither have a trial nor voluntarily register. The Alabama Supreme Court again complaisantly agreed with this hoax and ruled against the NAACP.

The US Supreme Court reversed again, in *NAACP v. Alabama* (II) (1959). The unanimous Court pointed out that the Alabama attorney general had conceded that all records besides the membership list had been produced, so the state could not tell one story in Washington and then "change its stance" in Montgomery. When this decision went back to the Alabama courts, they simply sat on their hands, doing nothing for two years, leaving the NAACP still barred from operating or registering in the state. In 1961 the NAACP took its third trip back to the US Supreme Court, which, in *NAACP v. Gallion* (1961), gave the Alabama courts a short deadline (seventy days) to make a ruling.[16]

Back in Alabama again, Judge Jones finally held a hearing and issued a ruling on December 29, 1961, three days before the deadline. This time he ruled against the NAACP because he found its actions were "a usurpation and abuse" and "detrimental to the State of Alabama." The Alabama Supreme Court again found a "procedural" excuse for ignoring the NAACP's arguments—this time apparently the paragraph breaks in the brief were misplaced. When the US Supreme Court reversed the Alabama Supreme Court a fourth time, in *NAACP v. Alabama* (IV) (1964), it devoted fourteen pages to showing that the Alabama Supreme Court had simply invented an imaginary rule about paragraph breaks.[17]

In August 1964 the Alabama Supreme Court finally conceded. After eight years of obstruction, the NAACP registered in Alabama. Judge Jones did not live to see it, having died in 1963.[18]

The Rest of the South versus the NAACP

Besides Alabama, the US Supreme Court struck down anti-NAACP schemes from Arkansas, Florida, Louisiana, Mississippi, South Carolina, and Virginia, while lower courts struck down similar schemes in other southern states. The anti-NAACP schemes of two states—Florida and Virginia—came close to being upheld by the Supreme Court.[19]

Florida's system was a variation of going after NAACP members' names; the Virginia scheme involved regulating lawyers in a way that threatened the NAACP's entire litigation program. These two cases arrived at the US Supreme Court at about the same time, and were argued in late 1961. The justices' tentative votes, confidential at the time, were 5–4 to uphold the state in both cases. These would have been the first civil rights setback in the Supreme Court in years.

The writing of the opinions was assigned and the opinions were being prepared as the spring of 1962 arrived. Justices' notes show that Harlan was writing the majority opinion upholding Florida. Frankfurter had the majority assignment upholding Virginia. Then suddenly a bitter battle over a different case, not involving race or the NAACP, resulted in the Court's losing two of the five justices who formed a majority against the NAACP in both cases.[20]

The precipitating case was *Baker v. Carr* (1962), the soon-to-be-famous "one-person-one-vote" case. Tempers on the Court flared over the case. Frankfurter bitterly opposed federal courts getting into the "political thicket" of reapportionment. A main target of his harangues was Justice Charles Evans Whittaker. On the Court for only four years, Whittaker was plagued by indecision in this and other cases. In early March 1962 he was admitted to Walter Reed Army Hospital in a state of acute depression. He would never return to the Court.

On Monday, March 26, 1962, in *Baker v. Carr* (1962), the Court ruled that reapportionment cases could be brought in federal court. The vote was 6–2, with Brennan writing the majority opinion and Frankfurter writing an emotional sixty-four-page dissent joined by Harlan. Whittaker did not participate in the decision. On Sunday, April 1, he officially retired.[21] On Monday, April 2, the Court issued orders listing ten cases to be "restored to the calendar for reargument." Both NAACP cases—Florida and Virginia—were on the list. Three days later, on Thursday, April 5, another shoe dropped: seventy-nine-year-old Justice Frankfurter had a massive stroke. Although he did not retire until August, he never came back to the Court, and he died in 1965.

As in 1953, when newcomer Earl Warren heard the segregation cases, critical NAACP cases would be reargued before a Supreme Court with new faces on the bench—both appointed by President John F. Kennedy. The new appointees would make all the difference in the two NAACP cases.

Frankfurter's replacement, Arthur Goldberg, voted for the NAACP in both cases. Byron White, who replaced Whittaker, voted against the NAACP in Florida, as Whittaker had, but voted for the NAACP on most issues in the Virginia case. That turned a pair of 5–4 decisions against the NAACP into a pair of NAACP victories, one by 5–4, the other by 6–3, and that is how the Florida and Virginia cases came down.

The Florida case broke no new ground because, like the Alabama case, it was an attempt to get membership information. The newest member, Justice Goldberg, wrote the majority opinion in *Gibson v. Florida Legislative Investigating Committee* (1963), following the Alabama case and rejecting Florida's argument that its approach through a legislative committee was different. The Virginia case, however, was different. The case involved one of Virginia's 1956 Massive Resistance laws. Ostensibly regulating certain kinds of agreements between lawyers and clients, the law in fact was carefully crafted to block civil rights cases and almost nothing else. But in *NAACP v. Button* (1963) the Supreme Court announced a major expansion of the First Amendment. The Court held that litigation to achieve "the lawful objectives of equality of treatment" is a classic "form of political expression" protected by the First Amendment. Virginia claimed its regulation of law practice was a traditional state function outside the First Amendment's protection, but the Supreme Court majority ruled that "the State cannot foreclose the exercise of constitutional rights by mere labels."[22]

With the Florida and Virginia cases in early 1963, the major Supreme Court rulings involving assaults on the NAACP were wrapped up (except for the last Alabama case in 1964). The attacks had a significant effect, cutting NAACP membership and income by one-third just in the single year between 1956 and 1957. But the effect could have been much worse. If any state's tactic had succeeded in the US Supreme Court, other southern states would have rushed to use the successful tactic—just as states at the turn of the century had rushed to adopt disfranchising laws and constitutions after the Supreme Court decision in *Williams v. Mississippi* (1898).[23]

New York Times v. Sullivan

The NAACP was not the only "outside agitator" hated and feared by white demagogues—there was also the press. The Supreme Court addressed that hatred too.

Segregation and Massive Resistance fared better with no witnesses, especially no news stories and no photos. Using the media, however, made a difference. When fourteen-year-old Emmett Till was brutally murdered in Money, Mississippi, in 1955, and his killers were acquitted within minutes, Till's mother insisted on keeping the funeral casket open, and *Jet* magazine showed his horribly mutilated body to an astonished and appalled nation. Silence and apathy ended. The press's role in spotlighting evil was duly noted in the South. Reporters and photographers were marked for violence nearly as much as the Black students who were integrating the schools. This was true of the mob in Little Rock, and equally true of the larger mob when James Meredith entered Ole Miss—where the first fatality of the riot in Oxford, Mississippi, was a French reporter.[24]

As segregation and civil rights became major national stories covered by national newspapers and magazines and, increasingly, radio and television, southern officials seized on a more effective weapon than mere violence: spurious libel suits to scare the press away. A publication can be sued for libel wherever it is circulated, so the *New York Times* could be sued in Alabama even though its sales in that state were only 400 copies. Once a publication was in the Alabama legal system, a complaisant judge and jury could be counted on to deliver an astronomical financial verdict.

The major show trial began with a full-page advertisement in the *New York Times* on March 29, 1960, captioned "Heed Their Rising Voices." The ad listed dramatic events that drew a picture of racial oppression and the civil rights struggle in Alabama. Eighty-nine prominent Americans, including Eleanor Roosevelt and a dozen Alabama ministers, sponsored the ad. Although the ad did not mention the names of any Alabama officials, one official, L. B. Sullivan, sued the *New York Times* and four of the ministers. Sullivan claimed that the ad referred to him (a requirement of libel law) because he was the city commissioner in charge of the Montgomery Police Department. He claimed that some of the statements were false (also a requirement of libel law), and he listed the inaccuracies.[25]

The ad did include some inaccuracies, but the Supreme Court later labeled them inconsequential. For example, one paragraph of the ad read as follows: "In Montgomery, Alabama, after students sang 'My Country, 'Tis of Thee' on the State Capitol steps, their leaders were expelled from school, and truckloads of police armed with shotguns and tear-gas ringed the Alabama State College Campus." The facts were that the students sang the national anthem—"The Star-Spangled Banner"—and not "My Country, 'Tis of Thee"; that only nine students were expelled; and that, although large numbers of heavily armed police were deployed near the campus on three occasions, they did not actually "ring" the campus. Another error in the ad was listing the number of Dr. King's arrests as seven when the actual number was four.

The trial judge was none other than Judge Walter B. Jones, of the Montgomery bus case and the NAACP registration case. The jury quickly returned a verdict of $500,000 for damages to Commissioner Sullivan's reputation. The Alabama Supreme Court affirmed the judgment against the newspaper, and the case went to the US Supreme Court. The Court reversed the libel verdict in a ruling that stands as one of the most important cases on freedom of the press under the First Amendment, *New York Times Co. v. Sullivan* (1964). Observing that criticism of public officials and official policy is the heart of the First Amendment, the Court said that such criticism cannot be restricted even if it is "vehement, caustic, and sometimes unpleasantly sharp." The Court then emphasized a significant point: "What a State may not constitutionally bring about by means of a criminal statute is likewise beyond the reach of its civil law of libel."[26]

Existing libel law already provided limited protection by immunizing a statement if it was true, but the Court said that was insufficient protection for the First Amendment because it would be too easy for even statements that are essentially correct and made in good faith to contain some error. Writing for a unanimous Court, Justice Brennan announced a rule limiting the ability of public officials to sue for defamation. When public officials sue for libel, they cannot recover damages unless they prove that an allegedly defamatory statement was made "with knowledge that it was false or with reckless disregard of whether it was false or not." This rule applies to public officials (later extended to "public figures"), but it does not affect libel suits by ordinary private citizens.[27]

The Supreme Court sent the case back to Alabama, and the case never surfaced again. The *New York Times* case, along with the end of Alabama's eight-year war against the NAACP, meant that Massive Resistance in the form of legal strategies against the NAACP and the press essentially ended by late 1964.[28]

The period of Massive Resistance in the 1950s and 1960s was a terrifying time. There was also an irony of timing: legal tools for combating Massive Resistance were both too late and too early. They were too late, because federal arrests and prosecutions might have stemmed or prevented mob violence in Little Rock, Oxford, Birmingham, and elsewhere, but that power had been removed by the nineteenth-century Supreme Court. On the other hand, they were too early, because the doctrine that laws intended to discriminate are invalid would have swept aside hundreds or even thousands of bad-faith laws in the 1950s and 1960s, but that doctrine was not developed until 1976 (Chapter 11).

The Civil Rights Movement

Massive Resistance fueled a counterforce—the Civil Rights Movement. With roots reaching far back, and with strong but isolated efforts in the mid- and late 1950s, the first half of the 1960s saw a passionate Civil Rights Movement. In that half decade, dozens of cases involving sit-ins, marches, and mass arrests were decided by the Supreme Court, and the Court kept ruling for "the Movement."

On the evening of January 31, 1960, Ezell Blair Jr., a freshman at North Carolina A&T College in Greensboro, warned his parents that he and three other students might be getting into some trouble the next day and he hoped they would not be embarrassed. The next day, February 1, Blair joined Franklin McCain, Joseph McNeil, and David Richmond, all A&T freshmen, to take direct action against Jim Crow. They entered the Woolworth store at 132 South Elm Street and made some routine purchases in the general merchandise departments. Carefully keeping their receipts, they then sat down at the lunch counter and waited for service, which did not come. One of the students asked, "I beg your pardon, but you just served us at [that] counter. Why can't we be served at the counter here?" Finally, they left.[29]

They came back the next day, along with about twenty additional friends. About sixty more students came the next day, and more the next, and white hecklers also arrived. By week's end, the idea was spreading to other stores, to other cities, and soon to other states. It was a hot news item. The *Greensboro Recorder* called it the "sit-down move." Claude Sitton of the *New York Times* reported that "much more might be involved than the matter of the Negro's right to sit at a lunch counter for a coffee break." After six months of sit-ins and boycotts, profits at the Greensboro Woolworth were off by 50 percent and the store ended its policy of "whites only" at its lunch counter.[30]

The protests against Jim Crow were largely nonviolent, which was an important element of the Civil Rights Movement's paradigm for change. Martin Luther King Jr. had become interested in radical nonviolence in the early 1950s. As a student of Gandhi's teachings and of African American theologians Howard Thurman and Benjamin E. Mays, King advocated nonviolent direct action as consistent with the Christian concept of

Sit-in in Talladega, Alabama, April 1962.

love. Nonviolence as a reaction to assault goes against human nature; it was no easy technique to learn. During the Montgomery bus boycott, Black Americans Bayard Rustin and James Lawson, as well as Glenn Smiley, who was white—peace advocates who had worked with the Fellowship of Reconciliation—taught weekly workshops on nonviolence as a strategic tactic. Activists in the movement also took classes at Highlander Folk School in Tennessee and Penn Center in South Carolina. Participants in sit-ins at lunch counters that began in 1960 also practiced nonviolence.

The hope was that through nonviolent protest, people reared in segregation would come to realize that their defense of segregation was untenable and they would reevaluate their prior lives, acknowledge their sinfulness, and work toward reconciliation with their former enemies. It would be a lasting and transformational change.[31]

Actual experience on the local level did not match the hope of the sit-in demonstrators. Southern white segregationists reacted to the sit-in movement with puzzlement, and then hostility. Sometimes proprietors ignored the protestors and with little commotion simply put "Closed" signs on their counters. Other times, angry white crowds gathered to punch and kick the sit-in protestors or pour condiments and beverages on their heads. The determination and discipline of the civil rights participants, including children, often attracted support. The violence of white reaction drew in the press. The contrast between the nonviolent protests and the violent reaction elicited sympathy outside the South for the peaceful demonstrators.

The sit-in movement gained momentum. In Rock Hill, South Carolina, nine students from Friendship Junior College were arrested on January 1, 1961, for sitting at McCrory's lunch counter, but they implemented a new tactic in the Civil Rights Movement. They refused to post bail, preferring to remain in jail until their trial. The "Jail-No-Bail" tactic caught on, and in some places, such as Birmingham, Alabama, the number of arrests overwhelmed the jail system.

When the fight against racial discrimination moved into lunch counters and the streets in the 1960s, it did not leave the courts behind. Tens of thousands of protesters were met with mass arrests for disorderly conduct, trespassing, parading without a permit, and so on. The cases would be tried in local courts and could be appealed to a state supreme court. Although a case can theoretically go all the way to the US Supreme Court, the Court chooses which cases it will hear, selecting only a fraction of all cases presented to it—10 to 15 percent in the 1960s and a far lower percentage today. And yet, during the first half of the 1960s the Supreme Court chose to take almost every sit-in or demonstration case—more than thirty appeals, most involving multiple demonstrators. Because of time delays in appealing through the state system and then to the US Supreme Court, most of the Supreme Court decisions came in 1963–1965 even though they involved arrests in 1960 and 1961.

A Supreme Court decision in 1961 was a sign of things to come. On March 29, 1960, just two months after the first sit-ins, Jannette Hoston and six other students at Southern University in Baton Rouge were arrested for sitting in at the lunch counter of Sitman's Department Store. Two other groups of Southern University students were arrested that day for sitting in at other lunch counters in Baton Rouge. All the students were convicted, and all the convictions were affirmed by the Louisiana Supreme Court. The charge against each student was "disturbing the peace."

When the case reached the US Supreme Court, both sides prepared for arguments on the momentous constitutional question whether a private lunch counter operator had the right to choose customers based on their race. Was anything different from the *Civil Rights Cases* (1883), when the Supreme Court held that the federal government had no power to prevent private citizens from discriminating? The Supreme Court did not answer that question. The Court used a precedent of a different kind, from a case decided the year before. That case involved "Shuffling Sam" Thompson of Louisville, Kentucky. It had nothing to do with sit-ins or segregation, but in its own way it had a lot to do with African Americans and law enforcement.

"Shuffling Sam" was a Black laborer who stopped in at a café early one Saturday evening in 1959 to wait for a bus. He whiled away the time by idly dancing—tapping his feet, or "shuffling." A policeman on a routine check noticed him and determined that he had been there for half an hour and had bought nothing. The policeman arrested Thompson for loitering. The policeman added a disorderly conduct charge when Thompson argued with him. The episode may have been a habit for the police, because Sam had been arrested fifty-four times previously.

In police court, Thompson faced the possibility of a small fine (not so small for him) and a few days in jail on each charge. He asked for time to get a lawyer and found one who agreed to represent him for a small fee. There was a continuance. By the time the case came up again, there was a second lawyer present for Sam Thompson—a prominent Louisville lawyer named Louis Lusky. Twenty years earlier, Lusky had been a law clerk for US Supreme Court Justice Harlan Fiske Stone. It was obvious that Lusky had something in mind. He made certain there was a court reporter present. The evidence was presented and the judge found Thompson guilty on both counts and fined him $10 on each charge.

The Kentucky courts held that there was no right to appeal convictions for these "petty offenses," at which point Lusky petitioned the US Supreme Court. He was now joined by two other former US Supreme Court law clerks. The US Supreme Court has jurisdiction to take cases from the state's highest court, and in this case, because there was no appeal in the Kentucky court system, the original police court was "the highest state court." The Supreme Court took Sam Thompson's $20 case and unanimously reversed the conviction. The Court said there was no evidence at all that Thompson had been loitering or disorderly, and a conviction based on no evidence at all was a denial of due process of law in violation of the Fourteenth Amendment. This case, *Thompson v. Louisville* (1960), would prove decisive in the first Supreme Court sit-in decision.[32]

In the Baton Rouge sit-in cases the Supreme Court went no further than the recent "Shuffling Sam" case to reverse the sit-in convictions. The charge in each sit-in case was "disturbing the peace," but the evidence showed otherwise. In the Sitman's Drug Store case, which was typical of the other cases, the students sat down at the exclusively white lunch counter, where the store manager himself happened to be sitting and eating his lunch. The manager asked a waitress to request them to leave, which the students refused to do. The manager kept eating, and when he finished his lunch, he telephoned the police to tell them that "Negroes were in his store sitting at the lunch counter reserved for whites." He did not say they were disorderly or were disturbing anyone. The police came and arrested the students. The students had done and said nothing except for one who asked for a glass of iced tea. In *Garner v. Louisiana* (1961), the Supreme Court ruled that without some conduct that was at least loud or boisterous, or that could logically have provoked disorder, the convictions were "totally devoid" of any evidence, and were thus doomed under the recent "Shuffling Sam" case. The state argued that the students were guilty of the crime of trespass by staying on the premises after being asked to leave. The Supreme Court rejected this argument because the students had not been charged with trespass. A fundamental principle of due process prohibits convicting a person for a crime not charged.[33]

This case was a sobering look into the reality of southern justice. Before the Warren Court, southern states (and some other states) had long been accustomed, especially in race cases, to simply charging whatever crime came to mind, convicting on whatever evidence was presented, if any, and having their appellate courts rubber-stamp those convictions. The shining of an outside light on these practices, as in this case and the Shuffling Sam case, was a shock.

The Supreme Court's decision in this and later sit-in cases had little immediate practical effect. In the Deep South, thousands of arrests and uncounted acts of violence mushroomed in the first half of the 1960s. Nevertheless, the Court kept its eye on constitutional protections. Throughout, civil rights demonstrators kept up the pressure, braving arrest, firehoses, attack dogs, and intense violence.

Another decision sparked another movement. In *Boynton v. Virginia* (1960), the Supreme Court reversed Howard Law student Bruce Boynton's 1958 conviction for refusing to leave the white section of the Richmond bus terminal snack bar; his arrest violated the Interstate Commerce Act. Then in the spring of 1961, dozens then hundreds of integrated passengers started boarding Greyhound and Trailways buses to ride through South Carolina, Georgia, Alabama, and Mississippi. They called themselves Freedom Riders. Of course, rigid segregation was still the rule in interstate facilities, even airport lounges, and the Freedom Riders aimed to end it.

As the integrated buses moved into the South, white thugs attacked the Riders in South Carolina. Then, in Anniston, Alabama, rioters burned a bus and beat the passengers exiting the wreckage. In Birmingham and Montgomery, police cooperated with local mobs, who were swinging lead pipes and baseball bats. Some of the Freedom Riders were severely beaten and hospitalized. Instead of ending the Rides, though, that violence brought an influx of new Riders, many of them African American students from Nashville. Many people tried to dissuade the students from the dangerous undertaking. John Seigenthaler, with the Kennedy Justice Department, called Diane Nash, a student at Fisk University in Nashville, to warn her that Riders' lives would be in danger. She knew that; she responded quietly, "We all wrote our wills tonight."[34]

In Jackson, Mississippi, group upon group of Freedom Riders descended on the state capital from all over the country. The city kept arresting, and Freedom Riders kept coming, eventually totaling more than three hundred in dozens of separate groups. Most of the Freedom Riders opted for "jail, no bail." Many spent a month or more at Parchman Penitentiary, a notoriously dehumanizing institution, but they were not physically assaulted because the nation was watching Mississippi.[35]

The courtroom drama played out slowly at the state level. An attempt to transfer the trials to federal court was unsuccessful, partly because of the nineteenth-century Supreme Court's rulings that restricted federal jurisdiction. Even sympathetic judges on the Fifth Circuit and the Supreme Court held that the cases first had to go forward in Mississippi's state courts. The city segregation ordinances and the arrests were later held to be unconstitutional, but the events were long in the past by then.[36]

On another front, however, Attorney General Robert Kennedy, who had originally opposed the Freedom Rides, was spurred into action as wave after wave of Freedom Riders kept the pressure on. On May 29, 1961, Kennedy filed a petition with the Interstate Commerce Commission (ICC), seeking to put teeth into the ban on interstate segregation, and on September 22, 1961 (speedy by agency standards), the ICC issued a sweeping order requiring every interstate bus line, airline, and railroad to enforce the ban on segregation at all the facilities they owned or used. The ICC order had an immediate effect. Although the order was not issued by the Supreme Court, it did bring to life the decisions the Supreme Court had issued in 1940, 1946, 1950, and 1960. At great human cost, the Freedom Riders had brought long-overdue change.[37]

The Pivotal Year of 1963

It was 1963 before the Supreme Court ruled directly on the civil rights of demonstrators on public or private property. First came a major case about marching on public property, where the First Amendment right of free speech applied. In March 1961 a group of several hundred African American high school and college students in Columbia, South Carolina, marched onto the South Carolina Capitol grounds, an area traditionally open to the public. The group carried signs protesting state segregation policies. Police were present and described the marchers as orderly and polite. A crowd of onlookers gathered, reflecting some tension but no disorder. At a certain point, the police told the marchers they had fifteen minutes to disperse. Instead of dispersing, the demonstrators engaged in what a city official called "boisterous, loud and flamboyant" conduct. When the official was quizzed about specifics, he elaborated that one of the leaders gave a religious "harangue" and the demonstrators loudly sang "The Star-Spangled Banner" and other patriotic and religious songs. After fifteen more minutes, the police arrested 187 demonstrators.[38]

All were convicted of "breach of the peace," and their convictions were affirmed by the South Carolina Supreme Court. The US Supreme Court reversed, in *Edwards v. South Carolina* (1963). The Court held that the conduct of the demonstrators shown by the record was classic First Amendment activity, specifically the right of free assembly to petition for redress of grievances. The fact that the opinions the demonstrators expressed were controversial and attracted a hostile crowd did not diminish their constitutional right to express themselves in this peaceful way. Again in pivotal 1963, the Supreme Court turned its attention to a collection of sit-in cases from five states across the South, all involving arrests in 1960 and 1961. These convictions did not have the "no evidence" problem of the first sit-in case because the charge in each case was trespass, which required no evidence of disorder, just a refusal to leave when requested. This time, however, all the cases had another wrinkle. The lead case was typical of the other cases in the group. The defendants were ten African American high school students who sat in quietly at a white lunch counter in a Kress store in Greenville, South Carolina. The manager asked them to leave and when they did not, he called the police, who also asked them to leave and then arrested them on trespass charges. The wrinkle was that Greenville had a local ordinance that prohibited mixed-race eating. The ordinance provided that a restaurant could not serve the two races in the same room, with an exception allowing same-room eating as long as the races were thirty-five feet apart and used separate utensils and dishes, with different color schemes, and which must be washed separately.[39]

At trial, the Kress manager said he asked the African Americans to leave because integrated service was "contrary to local customs" and also was against the law, meaning the Greenville ordinance. Based on this, the Supreme Court held, in *Peterson v. City of Greenville* (1963), that the city inserted itself into the decision of whom to serve. This changed the segregation policy from private "free choice" to "state action," and thus it was subject to the prohibition of the equal protection clause of the Fourteenth Amendment. Therefore, the rule of the *Civil Rights Cases* (1883) did not apply.[40]

These cases showed graphically how so-called private behavior was controlled by official state segregation policy, with no room for any alleged "freedom" to choose otherwise. Four other cities—Birmingham, Durham, Arlington, and Lynchburg—involved in this group of cases segregated their dining areas by local ordinance. The fifth city, New Orleans, carried out the segregation function by a proclamation of the mayor and police chief. Greenville argued that the manager might have made the same choice to segregate on his own, so state action was not necessarily involved. The Supreme Court rejected that argument, saying the state's criminal enforcement of racial segregation was a "palpable violation of the Fourteenth amendment [that] cannot be saved by attempting to separate the mental urges of the discriminators." The city's notion that the owner or manager could choose "freely" whether or not to segregate was a fantasy. Long-standing, pervasive segregation laws, and the rigid community control created by those laws, eliminated any choice but segregation. Indeed, as the testimony of the Kress manager in the Greenville case showed, proprietors or managers rarely said they personally opposed serving African Americans; they usually blamed the segregation policy on ordinances, local hostility, or corporate policy (which in turn was dictated by local law and custom).[41]

These cases were decided in the first half of 1963. What a tumultuous year! In Birmingham, police set fire hoses and police dogs on peaceful demonstrators, and in one day, May 3, the sheriff incarcerated over 900 children. By May 6 more than 2,500 demonstrators of all ages were in the Birmingham jail. On June 10, 1963, President Kennedy federalized the National Guard to protect Vivian Malone and James Hood, two African American students who were trying to enter the University of Alabama. Late that night, after listening to President Kennedy's speech asking for support for his proposed civil rights legislation, Medgar Evers attended an organizational meeting of the Mississippi NAACP, of which he was state field secretary. Then he headed home. His wife, Myrlie, and his children, who had waited up to see him when he arrived home after midnight, heard the gunshot that killed him. A member of the White Citizen's Council ambushed and shot Evers with a high-powered rifle. In August, 250,000 people participated in the March on Washington, and Martin Luther King Jr. gave his iconic "I Have a Dream" speech to commemorate the centennial of Lincoln's Emancipation Proclamation. In September 1963, Klansmen in Birmingham set off a bomb in the 16th Avenue Baptist Church on a Sunday morning, murdering Carole Robertson, Cynthia Wesley, Addie Mae Collins, and Denise McNair, three fourteen-year-olds and one eleven-year-old. Thirteen-year-old Sarah Collins lived but lost an eye. Sixteen others were injured when simply walking past the church.[42]

Also during 1963 President Kennedy sent Congress an omnibus civil rights bill especially targeting segregated lunch counters and restaurants, hotels, and motels. It was to be a reprise of the Civil Rights Act of 1875, which had been struck down in the *Civil Rights Cases* (1883). It could probably pass constitutional muster this time, under Congress's power to regulate interstate commerce, but the bill faced an uphill battle from filibuster-ready southern senators.[43] On November 22, 1963, President Kennedy was shot and killed in Dallas, Texas. Lyndon B. Johnson of Texas became president, and he decided that passage of Kennedy's civil rights bill, which was bottled up in Congress, was a top priority.

The Last of the Sit-In Cases

As the civil rights bill was percolating in Congress, a new set of sit-in cases came to the Supreme Court. They were argued in October 1963 and, under invariable Supreme Court practice, were due to be decided by the end of the term in June 1964. This collection consisted of cases from five states. Most of the cases had easy grounds for reversal, like the earlier sit-in cases had—lack of evidence, or state government involvement in the discrimination.

One of the cases, *Bell v. Maryland* (1964), however, did not share such defects, and it looked like the era of easy ways to decide sit-in cases was over. It looked like the era of Supreme Court decisions reversing all sit-in convictions might be over, too, with possibly huge consequences. Several justices believed the sit-ins at these places of "public accommodation" were constitutionally protected. They argued that innkeepers and the like had no right to deny admission to any persons conducting themselves in a proper manner. A powerful brief from the Justice Department made this argument, detailing the long history of state laws and state enforcement of segregation that only seemed private. On the other hand, five justices, a majority, were firmly convinced that the federal Constitution had no application to the private property of the restaurant owner, and the convictions should be upheld. Ironically, one who supported the convictions was Harlan, grandson of the first Justice Harlan who had dissented in the *Civil Rights Cases* (1883).[44]

Hugo Black of Alabama, as senior justice for affirmance, assigned himself to write the majority opinion. Black in the past had been a strong supporter of civil rights lawsuits seeking the enforcement of the Constitution, but his position altered as civil rights direct action brought more extreme reactions and disorder. It was not just disorder that troubled him; he became quite emotional about the sit-ins, believing that they had gone too far. His "pappy," he said, ran a country store and would never have dreamed he could not choose his customers. Trying to explain why Justice Black, who fully supported African American rights and then quite suddenly did not, his friend, Justice Brennan, said, "Hugo changed right before our eyes." Another opinion was offered by his brother-in-law, Clifford Durr: He "was a desegregationist, not an integrationist."[45]

As 1964 dawned, Justice Black's majority opinion to affirm the conviction of sit-in demonstrators in *Bell v. Maryland* was circulating among the justices. At the same time, the legislation that would make segregated lunch counters illegal was moving into the longest filibuster in Senate history, with no one betting on the outcome. Some justices were concerned about the effect a Supreme Court decision might have on the bill: If the Supreme Court announced a ruling against the sit-ins, would that strengthen the hand of opponents of the civil rights bill? At the Court, with a decision looming squarely on the constitutional issue, Justice Brennan now tried a strange procedural quirk in the case that could avoid a direct decision on the validity of these Maryland convictions. It had been there all along but no one had been interested. Now Brennan dusted it off for a try.

The quirk had to do with new city and state law in Maryland. The Maryland convictions of the protestors in a 1960 sit-in at Hooper's Restaurant in Baltimore had been affirmed by Maryland's highest court. After the affirmance, however, both Baltimore and the State of Maryland had passed laws against discrimination by restaurants and other such places. This meant that restaurants like Hooper's could no longer exclude African Americans, and in the future there would be no sit-ins and no sit-in convictions in Maryland. But what about *these* convictions? The legal rules governing what happens to convictions that are still on appeal when the law changes are complicated and often uncertain. Still, Brennan thought that needle could be threaded.[46]

Brennan circulated an opinion that would send the case back for the Maryland courts to decide what to do. Avoiding decision on a major constitutional issue when a case can be decided on another ground is usually—almost always—the preferred course, but some of the justices believed that a ruling on the competing constitutional claims in the sit-in cases was overdue. In any event, the justices were now considering three proposed opinions: Black's opinion upholding the convictions, Douglas's opinion reversing the convictions, and Brennan's compromise, which did not decide the constitutional issue either way. Among the three, Black still had the majority. It looked like the internal debate was over. As the Court began its scheduled conference at 10 a.m. on the morning of Friday, May 15, 1964, the opinions were ready. Black's majority decision to uphold the sit-in convictions at Hooper's Restaurant would be announced the following Monday, May 18, 1964.

Then suddenly, that Friday morning, the plan was upended, as were the convictions that were about to be affirmed. In the Court's conference, shortly after 10 a.m., Justice Clark said he had changed his mind, which he had told Black shortly before the conference. Now he agreed with Brennan's approach of avoiding the constitutional issue. Clark had been President Truman's attorney general and was generally on the conservative side of the Warren Court. On the other hand, he had written an important decision ordering a café to integrate because it was located in a city garage. As a political appointee, he may also have had a sense of the arc of history, especially some qualms about stepping into this issue when Congress might be about to solve it.[47]

The decision scheduled for Monday, May 18, was postponed. Black's majority was gone. Before the dust settled, Brennan's compromise had six votes. On June 22, in *Bell v. Maryland* (1964), the Supreme Court decided to send the case back to Maryland. By that time, the seventy-three-day filibuster (March 30–June 10, 1964) in the Senate had been broken, and ten days later, on July 2, President Johnson signed into law the Civil Rights Act of 1964.[48]

Black turned his former majority opinion into a bitter dissent, joined by Harlan and White. All the other sit-in cases that day were either sent back to the state court or were reversed outright. In all the sit-in cases it decided during three tumultuous years, the Supreme Court did not affirm a state criminal conviction in a single one.[49]

The new law meant there would be no more arrests for sit-ins, and indeed, no need for sit-ins. Thousands of sit-in cases still lingered in 1964, either convictions still on appeal or arrests still awaiting trial. They were like hostages awaiting repatriation after war's end. Based on the new law, the Supreme Court issued two decisions ending all those cases. Anyone in jail was released and all bond money was returned. By 1966 all of the sit-in hostages had been retrieved.[50]

The Civil Rights Movement also underwent a transformation. With the new Civil Rights Act of 1964 and the Voting Rights Act of 1965 (discussed in the next two chapters), the battle against Jim Crow's twin pillars of segregation and disfranchisement began to recede from the streets; mass marches and sit-ins were largely replaced by voter registration drives. Reverend James Bevel of SCLC (Southern Christian Leadership Conference) explained, "There is no more civil rights movement. President Johnson signed it out of existence when he signed the voting-rights bill." Actually, of course, the movement continued, but it became geared to political power and elections.[51]

Robert Mack Bell, whose case was the centerpiece of the *Bell* case, was a high school student who was in the protest at the invitation of students from Morgan State College, a historically Black state school. He went on to graduate from Harvard Law School, and, after some years in private practice, he became a judge, eventually becoming chief judge of Maryland's highest court. Hooper's Restaurant closed and the corner where it stood became the anchor for Baltimore's downtown commercial center. The law did what no individual or even group of business owners could have done. G. Carroll Hooper, owner of the restaurant, said he did not favor discrimination, "[but] I am at the mercy of my customers." Realistically, no owner could have chosen individually to break the local segregation pattern; only Law, with uniform rules for all establishments, could have overcome the rigid uniform custom that centuries of law had created.[52]

Miss Mary Hamilton

If a single act captures the tone of the Civil Rights Movement, it might be a small gesture of Miss Mary Hamilton.

A tenet of white supremacy was the social taboo against using courtesy titles like "Mr." or "Mrs." for African Americans. Instead, they were called by first names or "Boy," or, if elderly, by a euphemism like "Auntie." The practice served as a constant reminder that African Americans were not equal citizens. The tenacity with which this custom was maintained by white southerners is beyond comprehension today, but it was a true badge of slavery.

In 1964 this ingrained practice came to the Supreme Court via the appeal of Miss Mary Hamilton. She was cited for contempt of court for the following dialogue while she was on the stand in an Alabama court:

> Q: What is your name, please?
>
> A: Miss Mary Hamilton.
>
> Q: Mary, I believe—you were arrested—who were you arrested by?
>
> A: My name is Miss Hamilton. Please address me correctly.
>
> Q: Who were you arrested by, Mary?
>
> A: I will not answer a question—your question until I am addressed correctly.

Miss Mary Hamilton, a Freedom Rider from Cedar Rapids, Iowa, and later the southern regional director of CORE. Alabama courts convicted her of contempt of court for refusing to answer questions until she was addressed as "Miss," just as white women were.

THE COURT: Answer the question.

THE WITNESS: I will not answer them unless I am addressed correctly.

THE COURT: You are in contempt of court—You are in contempt of this court, and you are sentenced to five days in jail and a fifty dollar fine.

Around the country, contempt citations for minor misconduct are too numerous to count, and the Alabama Supreme Court upheld the conviction with no difficulty. On appeal, however, the US Supreme Court saw it differently. The Court took the case, an act that was a marvel in itself, and, without wasting time on oral argument or an extended opinion, simply reversed the contempt conviction, in *Hamilton v. Alabama* (1964). Waiving a five-day sentence and $50 fine was not the usual Supreme Court fare, but in light of the history and reality of Jim Crow, this small case expressed the meaning of freedom and the Supreme Court's understanding of that meaning.[53]

CHAPTER NINE

A New Birth of Freedom, Again

When Abraham Lincoln called for a "new birth of freedom" in 1863, Congress and the Supreme Court soon found themselves at odds. Congress answered Lincoln's call with three new constitutional amendments and a host of civil rights laws, but the nineteenth-century Supreme Court quickly began neutering the constitutional amendments and striking down major parts of the laws. For eighty years Democratic senators who represented the white South made sure that no new civil rights laws would be enacted, even while anti-lynching and anti-poll-tax bills passed repeatedly in the House of Representatives.[1]

In 1954 *Brown v. Board of Education* delivered a second "new birth of freedom," and Congress and the Supreme Court this time found themselves in sync. Beginning in 1957, after years of legislative futility, Congress repeated its Reconstruction-era harvest of new civil rights laws, with five in eleven years—1957, 1960, 1964, 1965, and 1968. The Supreme Court of the 1960s chose to give these new laws and the remaining old laws a positive reception—so different from the destructive treatment given to similar laws by the Supreme Court of the late nineteenth and early twentieth centuries. As always, the Supreme Court had choices, but the Warren Court made those choices in line with effective enforcement of the Constitution and laws.

New Civil Rights Laws of the Twentieth Century

The Supreme Court led the way forward with its school desegregation decision, and it was soon joined by other branches of the federal government. Both political parties favored desegregation. Speaking in 1956, Vice President Richard Nixon spoke words much like those Dr. King would use at the March on Washington in 1963: "Most of us here will live to see the day when American boys and girls shall sit, side by side, at any school—public or private—with no regard paid to the color of their skin."[2]

In early 1957 President Eisenhower's attorney general was Herbert Brownell, a strong civil rights supporter. He sent an administration bill to Congress, which easily passed the House of Representatives, 286–126. But the House had passed civil rights bills before, and they never even reached the Senate floor. There were pro-civil-rights majorities in both parties, but southern Democrats had assets—they controlled most of the committee chairmanships, and if it came to a filibuster, many of the non-southerners believed in the Senate tradition of unlimited debate. On the other hand, President Eisenhower wanted a civil rights bill and so did Senate Majority Leader Lyndon Johnson of Texas, who had presidential ambitions.

After some compromise, there was no organized filibuster except for a 24-hour, 18-minute, one-man show by South Carolina senator Strom Thurmond. The Senate vote for the weakened bill was 72–18 in favor, supported by every non-southern senator and Lyndon Johnson of Texas (all 43 Republicans and 29 out of 47 Democrats). Both President Eisenhower and Senator Johnson took credit for getting a bill passed. Even though the bill was relatively weak, passage showed there was a new political reality: for the first time in American history, a majority of both major political parties was in favor of civil rights.[3]

Three main provisions in the new Civil Rights Act of 1957 authorized the Justice Department to bring civil suits and obtain injunctions against voting registrars who engaged in racial discrimination. The nineteenth-century laws focused on enforcement by criminal prosecutions, which involved local juries and proof beyond a reasonable doubt. The new 1957 act provided for injunctions to be issued by judges after civil trials, with contempt of court charges facing any registrar who disobeyed an injunction. To help bring these new suits, the act also upgraded the small civil rights section in the Department of Justice to the Civil Rights Division, which meant increased power, personnel, and budget. Finally, this new act put a spotlight on civil rights by establishing a Civil Rights Commission with power to hold hearings and subpoena witnesses. Using its authority under the 1957 act, the Justice Department brought lawsuits against registrars in recalcitrant southern counties. Three cases had been lost or stalled in the lower federal courts, and the Justice Department promptly appealed to the US Supreme Court.[4]

First was a case against the registrar of Terrell County, Georgia, who routinely registered white applicants and rejected Black applicants, using cards of different colors to keep track of who to accept and who to reject. The district judge dismissed the Justice Department lawsuit and held that the new Civil Rights Act of 1957 was unconstitutional. His rationale was the crippling rule of the Court in 1876 that a law that might conceivably be applied against a private citizen would be unconstitutional. Although the Terrell County registrar was obviously engaged in state action, the district judge considered a hypothetical other case, and therefore, found the entire law unconstitutional.

Second was a case against the White Citizens' Council in Washington Parish, Louisiana, which had carried out a massive campaign to challenge the qualifications of voters already on the rolls and which removed 85 percent of the African American registrants along with 0.7 percent of the white registrants. An injunction had been issued against the Citizens' Council but was stayed because of uncertainty about enjoining a private organization.

Third, in Macon County, Alabama, the board of registrars, having registered virtually all the white citizens of the county, simply resigned so that it would not have to register any African Americans. The district judge dismissed the lawsuit because there were no registrars to sue.

The three cases all came to the Supreme Court in 1960. At about the same time, Congress supplemented the Civil Rights Act of 1957 with a new law, the Civil Rights Act of 1960. With strong bipartisan support again led by Republican president Eisenhower and Democratic senate majority leader Johnson, and with some inevitable compromises with southern Democratic senators, the final votes in both the House and the Senate were almost identical to the votes on the 1957 law. The new law plugged gaps in the voting provisions of the 1957 law that had been highlighted in the Justice Department's cases. After an eighty-year drought of civil rights legislation, the 1957 and 1960 acts were predictably modest. Still, they put the federal government back in the business of enforcing civil rights and opened the way for far-reaching new laws in future years.[5]

In all three cases the Supreme Court unanimously upheld the constitutionality of the 1957 act and removed the lower courts' roadblocks. Regarding Terrell County, Georgia, the Supreme Court overruled the doctrine of *United States v. Reese,* citing numerous cases that told courts to decide the cases in front of them, not other, hypothetical cases. In the

Louisiana case, the Court said the registrar's involvement made this an obvious exercise of state action and thus justified an injunction against all participants. As to the Alabama "resigning registrars," the new Civil Rights Act of 1960 came into being just in time to provide a solution. One section of the new act, specifically aimed at the Alabama ploy, provided that the state itself would become a defendant if local registrars resigned. Based on that section of the 1960 act, the Supreme Court reinstated the case to go forward against the State of Alabama.[6]

The Supreme Court chose to move unusually fast with these cases. Supreme Court cases typically take a year or two from lower-court decision to Supreme Court decision. In the Louisiana case, the Court took the case directly from the district court and skipped the court of appeals stage, a rare procedure. The total time from the district court decision to the Supreme Court decision—including court of appeals stay order, petition for certiorari, briefs (allowed typewritten instead of printed), oral argument, and final decision—was thirty-nine days: January 21 to February 29, 1960. In the Alabama case, the Court heard oral argument on May 2, 1960, the new 1960 act was signed into law four days later, and the Court issued its decision ten days after that, on May 16, 1960.

Buoyed by these Supreme Court decisions on the Civil Rights Acts of 1957 and 1960, the Justice Department multiplied the number of voting suits it brought. Each suit could take thousands of hours to analyze the individual voting records, each county had to be sued separately, and there were 288 counties in these three states alone. These suits graphically illuminated the problem of relying on lawsuits to cope with an entire region's insistence on keeping African Americans from voting by any means necessary. Clearly a different approach was needed. Before Congress passed new legislation, though, the Supreme Court looked back at a previously ignored section of one of the Reconstruction laws.

Revival of the Ku Klux Act

The case that brought the Ku Klux Act of 1871 to life involved, not a southern outrage, but instead a police search and interrogation in Chicago in the late 1950s. The outcome put the federal courts fully into the business of protecting federal constitutional rights. The case, *Monroe v. Pape* (1961), made a major change in the federal-state relationship.

The events that led to the landmark ruling began at 5:45 a.m. on the morning of October 29, 1958, when thirteen Chicago police officers investigating a murder broke into the home of James and Flossie Monroe. As the Supreme Court described it, the officers woke the couple with flashlights and forced them at gunpoint to stand naked in the living room with their six children while they ransacked the house. They called James Monroe "nigger" and "Black boy." They then took Monroe to the station, interrogated him, and placed him in lineups. Many hours later, they released him with no charges.[7]

The search and interrogation were without warrants, illegal under both Illinois law and the federal Constitution. The Monroes, foreseeing poor prospects in state court, sued in federal court, but federal courts have only the jurisdiction Congress gives them. In this case the only possible federal suit was under Section 1 of the Ku Klux Act of 1871, one of the few surviving Reconstruction laws. It provided for a suit in federal court for any violation of federal rights committed by a person acting "under color of" state law. "Under color of" is a legal term that has nothing to do with pigment or race. Rather, acting "under color of law" is equivalent to acting in the name of the law, or acting with state authority. In the Monroe case, the police were misusing that authority and acting illegally, but the Supreme Court held that the police were still acting "under color of state law." The Court said, "Misuse of power, possessed by virtue of state law and made possible only because the wrongdoer is clothed with the authority of state law, is action taken 'under color of' state law." The policemen were acting "under color of" state law because the power they exercised—properly or not—had been given them by the authority of the state.[8]

This was no mere technicality. Although the Supreme Court had never interpreted this provision, it had always been assumed that "under color of law" was limited essentially to the small number of cases where a state law itself was unconstitutional, like the grandfather clause. The new interpretation was a major change in the relationship between the states and the federal government. Previously, state officials whose acts violated both state and federal law could be sued only in state court, just as if their violations had been committed by private individuals. This case, however, held that state officials were *ordinarily* engaged in "state action," which allowed the federal government to step in to protect citizens' rights and to provide redress for victims of state wrongs.

These cases, widely known today, are called "Section 1983" cases. Before this decision, the number of cases brought in federal court under this statute was minuscule. Cases under the section were limited to those alleging that a state law itself, such as a grandfather clause or white primary law, was itself unconstitutional. Today tens of thousands of Section 1983 cases are filed in federal court each year alleging violation of federal rights "under color of state law."

Justice Felix Frankfurter wrote a fifty-eight-page dissent in *Monroe v. Pape,* saying this interpretation was out of keeping with the older Supreme Court cases and their view of federalism. He was undoubtedly correct in his reading of the older cases, but this was a new century, and no other justice joined in his dissent.

The Civil Rights Act of 1964

In 1960 Democrat John F. Kennedy narrowly defeated Republican Richard M. Nixon in the presidential election. Helpful to Kennedy was support from the Black community after he made a phone call in October 1960 to Coretta Scott King expressing concern over Martin Luther King's incarceration. Also helpful were Robert Kennedy's telephone calls to a judge and other officials in Georgia encouraging them to release King from jail. It is estimated that 70 percent of African Americans voted for Kennedy.[9]

President Kennedy's actual performance after the election disappointed many civil rights supporters. Defiance in the South, however, kept pushing him, and on June 11, 1963, Kennedy spoke to the nation over national television, describing civil rights as a moral imperative, "as old as the Scriptures" and "as clear as the American Constitution." He proposed a bill to ban racial discrimination in public accommodations, but Congress was not ready for such a strong bill, and it remained bottled up in congressional committees.[10]

It was not until the assassination of President Kennedy in November 1963, when Vice President Lyndon B. Johnson became president, that the civil rights bill moved forward. In his first State of the Union address, in January 1964, President Johnson set an ambitious agenda. In addition to declaring "all-out war on human poverty and unemployment in these United States," he also pronounced: "Let this session of Congress be known as the session which did more for civil rights than the last hundred sessions combined."[11]

President Johnson had a talent for political pressure. Warned by aides that pushing for the bill might use up "political capital," Johnson responded: "Then what the Hell's the Presidency for?"[12]

Even so, the road to passage of what became the landmark Civil Rights Act of 1964 was strewn with obstacles. The House of Representatives Rules Committee, which decides which bills will go forward to the House for discussion and vote, was headed by Virginia's Howard Smith. He was an archconservative and a racist who in 1957 said that "the colored race" did not have "equal intelligence." Smith made a major change to the bill, banning discrimination on account of sex. He may have thought this would mean the bill's defeat, but the civil rights bill passed Congress with Smith's addition. That change has turned out to be a fundamental advance in the law, which forbids discrimination based on an "individual's race, color, religion, sex, or national origin."[13]

On the Senate side, the bill was pried out of committee by presidential cajolery and arm-twisting, only to meet the longest debate in history—seventy-three days of unrelenting debate, maneuvering, and more debate. The only way to end a senate filibuster is by cloture, which at that time required a vote of two-thirds of the Senate. Never before had cloture succeeded in stopping an anti–civil rights filibuster. Working behind the scenes to end the filibuster were the Democratic Senate whip, Hubert Humphrey of Minnesota, and the Republican Senate minority leader, Everett Dirksen of Illinois. Dirksen called upon his fellow Republicans to remember Abraham Lincoln, and he evoked the French novelist Victor Hugo, author of *Les Misérables,* who said that nothing is stronger than an idea whose time has come: "The time has come for equality of opportunity in sharing in government, in education, and in employment. It will not be stayed or denied. It is here!" Finally, in June 1964, the Senate voted 71–29 (4 votes over the then-needed 67) to impose cloture. Passage soon followed (73–27 in the Senate; 289–126 in the House), and the Civil Rights Act of 1964 became law on July 2, 1964.[14]

The immediate center of attention was Title II, which banned discrimination in "places of public accommodation"—hotels, restaurants, movies, and such, the types of places that ordinarily welcomed all orderly patrons. The Civil Rights Act of 1875 had a similar provision, but the Supreme Court had ruled it unconstitutional in *Civil Rights Cases* (1883), rejecting both the Thirteenth and Fourteenth Amendments as possible supports. This time, however, Title II of the Civil Rights Act of 1964 covered the same types of establishments covered by the 1875 act if their operations "affect commerce"—which included virtually all of them. Congress's power to regulate interstate commerce was a constitutional support that had not been available for nineteenth-century civil rights laws because the constitutional definition of "interstate commerce" was so limited in those days. The Supreme Court expanded the meaning of interstate commerce, subject to congressional regulation, in a series of New Deal cases beginning in 1937 that upheld federal laws regulating minimum wages, farm price supports, and so on.

Also based on Congress's interstate commerce power was the other revolutionary part of the 1964 act: Title VII, which banned discrimination in private employment, that is, by private employers, labor unions, and employment agencies.

Other significant parts of the 1964 act tightened protection against voting discrimination, banned discrimination by any recipient of federal funds (intending to rectify the problem of discrimination in the federally assisted housing boom of the postwar years), facilitated removal of civil rights cases from state to federal court, and expanded Justice Department authority to bring race discrimination suits, especially those involving school segregation. This last provision had initially been in the 1957 bill, but a price of passage in 1957 had been striking it and limiting Justice Department suits to voting discrimination.

The Supreme Court gave speedy consideration to the public accommodations part (Title II) of the Civil Rights Act of 1964 and unanimously upheld it. The Court noted that Congress had ample information that obstructions and restraints resulting from racial discrimination in public accommodations were not just an injustice to the victims but significantly affected the flow of goods, services, and persons in commerce. The lead case, *Heart of Atlanta Motel v. United States* (1964), involved a large motel that advertised widely and attracted a high volume of interstate travelers. In a companion case the same day, *Katzenbach v. McClung* (1964), the Court said the same principles applied to very local establishments, upholding the act's application to Ollie's Barbecue, an off-the-beaten-track Birmingham café.[15]

The Court was emphatic in holding that the ruling in the *Civil Rights Cases* (1883) limiting Congress's powers under the Thirteenth and Fourteenth Amendments was "inapposite and without precedential value" in analyzing Congress's power under the interstate commerce clause. Because that issue had never been considered in the 1883 case, the Court was unusually blunt in saying that the 1883 decision had "no relevance" and was "devoid of authority" in considering the new statute.[16]

The Supreme Court listed thirty-two states whose laws already banned discrimination in public accommodations. And although the constitutional rationale was economic, the Court left no doubt that the act was a moral issue:

> The primary purpose of the Civil Rights Act of 1964 . . . is the vindication of human dignity and not mere economics. . . . Discrimination is not simply dollars and cents, hamburgers and movies; . . . It is equally the inability to explain to a child that regardless of education, civility, courtesy and morality, he will be denied the right to enjoy equal treatment.[17]

Several follow-up cases extended the spirit of the Civil Rights Act of 1964 to decide issues that Congress had not specifically addressed, including ending cases that were still ongoing, facilitating private lawsuits by awarding legal fees to victims of discrimination, and blocking attempted evasions of the law. In each of these cases, the Supreme Court had choices, and in each one it chose the route of more vigorous enforcement of the new law. Outlawing discrimination in public accommodations eliminated the single most visible form of racial segregation in the country. The change succeeded with amazing speed and thoroughness.[18]

Of course, it was not uneventful. Many businesses, usually very local ones, tried to resist, but in general the public accommodations part of the act was very effective. One notable holdout was Lester Maddox, who chose to close his Atlanta restaurant rather than integrate. Maddox campaigned for governor of Georgia with the ax handle he had used to keep African American customers away. He won and later also served a term as lieutenant governor. The issue could also have deadly consequences. In 1968, highway patrol officers shot and killed three students and injured twenty-seven others at South Carolina State College in Orangeburg at demonstrations that grew out of picketing at a still-segregated local bowling alley.[19]

Within a few short years, keeping African Americans out of inns, hotels, restaurants, cafés, bowling alleys, bars, and the like was almost unknown. A scar that had once been Jim Crow's most visible sign disappeared almost without a trace. The end of Jim Crow eating and sleeping also undercut a major Cold War propaganda weapon against the United States, because these segregated hotels and restaurants had worldwide impact.

The "public accommodations" and employment provisions of the 1964 law (Title II and Title VII) banned racial discrimination by private individuals and companies, going beyond "state action." From the seventeenth century on, it was colonies, states, and voluminous state law that created and sustained Jim Crow. Now the US Supreme Court ruled that indeed the Constitution supported a law to fight private Jim Crow.

The Voting Rights Act of 1965

After President Johnson signed the new Civil Rights Act of 1964 on July 2, 1964, he almost immediately privately directed his acting attorney general, Nicholas Katzenbach, to begin work to prepare "the goddamndest, toughest voting rights act that you can devise."[20]

In November Johnson won a landslide election over Republican Barry Goldwater (who had opposed the 1964 law). With that victory, Johnson prepared his agenda: first, Medicare and an education bill. Johnson thought the timing was not yet ripe for a voting rights bill. Time and events, however, were not within the power of the presidency. In December 1964, when Dr. Martin Luther King Jr. returned from his trip to Oslo, Norway, to accept the Nobel Peace Prize, he was invited to visit President Johnson at the White House. Johnson spoke of his priorities, but King wanted first and foremost a voting bill that would really work. King and others were tired of the obstacles put up by voting registrars in too many places. He was probably thinking of Selma, Alabama.[21]

In 1960, Dallas County, with its county seat in Selma, had a voting-age population of 30,000 people—15,500 Black and 14,500 white. Registration figures were radically different, with nearly 10,000 white registered voters compared with 170 African American registered voters (1 percent of the Black eligible population). African Americans stood at the registrar's door day after day in long lines that never moved. The Justice Department pressed a lawsuit that in four years increased Black registration only from 1 percent to 2 percent. Meanwhile, many of the registered white voters were plainly illiterate, as the Justice Department showed by introducing more than 5,000 voting records, a task that took thousands of hours of work.[22]

In 1963 the Student Nonviolent Coordinating Committee (SNCC) started a new voter registration campaign in Selma. SNCC, formed in 1960, was heavily involved in voting rights in rural areas. Bitter county opposition was led by the tyrannical sheriff Jim Clark, carrying his pistol, rope, and an electric cattle prod. At a Freedom Day rally held on October 7, 1963, there were 300 people standing in line all day without any being allowed to register. SNCC volunteers who brought food and water were beaten at Sheriff Clark's orders, as were some reporters and observers taking photographs.

Years of effort produced no results. C. T. Vivian of the Southern Christian Leadership Conference (SCLC), among others, organized many demonstrations, but the outcome was only to infuriate the local police. Breaking up a protest in February 1965 the police pursued some of the demonstrators, including Jimmie Lee Jackson, his sister, their mother Viola, and their grandfather as they fled into an African American–owned restaurant. In the altercation, Jackson, a deacon in the Marion, Alabama, Baptist church, tried to stop the police from beating his mother, but the police shot and killed him.[23]

As the situation grew more violent, Reverend Martin Luther King Jr. and others planned to conduct a very large demonstration for voting rights in Selma. The march was to begin on Sunday, March 7, 1965, at Brown Chapel, the African Methodist Episcopal (AME) church in Selma, and proceed to the state capital of Montgomery, fifty-four miles away. After a prayer by Andrew Young of SCLC, 600 people began the march, walking quietly in a column behind John Lewis of SNCC and Hosea Williams of

Hosea Williams and John Lewis leading marchers across the Edmund Pettus Bridge in Selma, Alabama, on March 7, 1965, moments before rampaging police on horseback turned the event into "Bloody Sunday," almost killing John Lewis and others and ultimately leading to the Voting Rights Act of 1965.

SCLC. At the Edmund Pettus Bridge, however, Major John Cloud, the state trooper in charge, commanded the group to halt, declaring, "This is an unlawful assembly." The marchers refused to turn back and knelt to pray, but within minutes the next order was given: "Troopers, advance." And advance they did—with billy clubs and tear gas. But blocking any retreat and closing in on the demonstrators from behind was Sheriff Jim Clark's posse. Some of the attackers carried whips, clubs, and rubber hoses wrapped with barbed wire. Demonstrators heard Sheriff Clark yell, "Get those goddamned niggers! And get those goddamned white niggers!" Police on horseback rode into the crowd to continue the beatings. Police chased, knocked down, and beat fleeing demonstrators, much of which the press captured on film. Cheering on the violence were at least a hundred white spectators, some flying Confederate flags.[24]

Among the injured, John Lewis took a severe blow to the head, which almost killed him. Lewis remembered, "I saw death. I really thought I was going to die." At Brown Chapel, volunteers with medical supplies cared for a hundred injured marchers. Good Samaritan Hospital, one of the few hospitals that would accept African Americans, took seventy to eighty people who were more seriously injured, with wounds ranging from broken teeth and severe head gashes to fractured ribs and wrists.[25]

The gruesome events of Bloody Sunday did not silence the protesters. Instead, with more determination than ever, SNCC set the next demonstration for March 9. In the meantime, Federal District Judge Frank Johnson, hoping to avoid more violence, issued a temporary restraining order. Would the marchers disobey a court injunction against the demonstration? King, in accordance with some behind the scenes negotiations, led the protesters across the bridge, guided the group in prayer, and turned back without moving on to Montgomery.[26]

Johnson was a University of Alabama Law School classmate of Governor George Wallace. Nevertheless, he had been one of the judges ruling against bus segregation in Montgomery and had ordered statewide desegregation of Alabama's public schools. The KKK had burned a cross on his lawn following the Rosa Parks decision, and his mother's house was bombed in 1967.[27]

After a four-day hearing, Judge Johnson rendered a decision in *Williams v. Wallace* (1965) that laid out Alabama's abuses in detail. He described a constant pattern of harassment and intimidation "for encouraging people to attempt to register to vote." He described "brutal treatment," including illegal mass arrests followed by long "forced marches" of demonstrators prodded by electric cattle prods and police night sticks.[28]

Relying on *Edwards v. South Carolina* (1963), Judge Johnson allowed the march along US Highway 80. The court recognized that approving the march was a far-reaching constitutional decision, but it was justified by the gross constitutional wrongs inflicted by officials. Johnson ordered that the marchers receive full protection. President Lyndon Johnson then did what Presidents Eisenhower and Kennedy had done—he federalized the Alabama National Guard.[29]

The order was issued on Thursday, March 17, 1965, and the march, now led by Reverend King, began again on Monday, March 21, as thousands of supportive Americans poured in from around the nation. At night Black and white demonstrators camped on the side of Highway 80, on land owned by African American farmers. By the time the marchers entered Montgomery on Friday morning, they were 25,000 strong. A climactic rally was held at the State Capitol, just up the hill from Reverend King's Dexter Avenue Baptist Church. The courage and determination of the demonstrators meant that Selma and Alabama would never be the same.

As the throng dispersed to return to their homes, it did not take long to realize that evil was still present. Later on the day of the rally in Montgomery, Viola Liuzzo, a thirty-nine-year-old white mother of five and a civil rights supporter who had come from Michigan, was shot and killed by Ku Klux Klansmen while she was driving other marchers back to Selma.[30]

A week after "Bloody Sunday," President Johnson, in one of his most inspiring speeches, addressed a joint session of Congress on the evening of Monday, March 15, and promised a new voting rights act. He accepted Dr. King's avowal of the previous December and declared that all races must "overcome the crippling legacy of bigotry and injustice." And, drawing the words out slowly, he added the anthem of the Civil Rights Movement, "And we *shall* overcome."[31]

An effective voting rights bill would have several goals—the elimination of current tricks that kept African Americans from voting and a guard against future tactics yet unknown. The remedies had to be targeted at the problem, and they could not rely on endless litigation. A bill to do all this was quickly introduced and after extensive hearings that detailed the "dirty tricks" certain states instituted to keep African Americans from voting, President Johnson signed the Voting Rights Act on August 6, 1965.[32]

Logically enough, solving the problem involved going back to its origin: the disfranchising state constitutions of the late nineteenth century. The main engine of discrimination in those constitutions was the fake literacy test used only as a subterfuge to allow registrars arbitrarily to reject African American applicants. As one local registrar in South Carolina bragged to a newspaper reporter in 1940: "If a coon wants to vote in the primary, we make him recite the Constitution backward, as well as forward, make him close his eyes and dot his t's and cross his i's. We have to comply with the law, you see."[33]

To target these sham tests while allowing states to use fair literacy tests, which were constitutionally permissible, Congress adopted a presumption that abnormally low voting turnout indicated a sham test. The act's dividing line was 50 percent of the voting-age population registering or voting. This formula turned out, unsurprisingly, to cover seven former Confederate states that adopted a literacy test in a disfranchising state constitution between 1890 and 1908: Alabama, Georgia, Louisiana, Mississippi, South Carolina, Virginia, and North Carolina (40 of 100 counties). For these states and their local governments, the major remedy for the present evil was that they could not use a literacy test at all; the protection against future evils was "preclearance," meaning they could not change their voting rules without first showing that the new law or rule was not discriminatory. The ban on literacy tests and the requirement of preclearance initially applied for five years, but these periods were extended several times in later years after congressional hearings showed continuing discrimination. The Voting Rights Act also directed the attorney general to sue states that had a poll tax. The poll tax was eliminated nationwide for federal elections by the Twenty-Fourth Amendment (1964) and for all elections when the Supreme Court held in *Harper v. Virginia State Board of Elections* (1966) that requiring payment for the fundamental right to vote violated the Fifteenth Amendment.[34]

The Voting Rights Act of 1965 received quick attention in the Supreme Court. Within seven weeks of the act's passage, the State of South Carolina filed a suit directly in the Supreme Court, seeking to block the Voting Rights Act as unconstitutional. Five southern states participated as amici curiae in support of South Carolina, and twenty-one states were on the opposite side, as amici curiae supporting the statute. In *South Carolina v. Katzenbach* (1966), the Supreme Court firmly held the far-reaching law constitutional. The chief justice stated, "The constitutional propriety of the Voting Rights Act of 1965 must be judged with reference to the historical experience which it reflects."[35]

The Supreme Court pulled no punches. Its words were blunt. The Court described two central realities that Congress faced:

> First: Congress felt itself confronted by an insidious and pervasive evil which had been perpetrated in certain parts of our country through unremitting and ingenious defiance of the Constitution.
>
> Second: Congress concluded that the unsuccessful remedies which it had prescribed in the past would have to be replaced by sterner and more elaborate measures in order to satisfy the clear commands of the fifteenth amendment.[36]

Among South Carolina's arguments, all rejected by the Supreme Court, one argument was reminiscent of the states' rights arguments of antebellum days. South Carolina complained that singling out certain states violated a so-called doctrine of equality of the states. The Court rejected this argument categorically. The Court responded that there is no such doctrine in the Constitution, except for the terms of admission of a state: "That doctrine applies only to the terms upon which States are admitted to the Union, and not to the remedies for local evils which have subsequently appeared." The Court closed its opinion, "Hopefully, millions of nonwhite Americans will now be able to participate for the first time on an equal basis in the government under which they live."[37]

The Voting Rights Act went into effect on August 6, 1965, and worked like magic. African American voters lined up in droves at the offices of local registrars or, in the fifty-five most recalcitrant counties, at the offices of the federal examiners who had taken over the registration process. With the elimination of spurious literacy tests used in the covered jurisdictions, aided also by court injunctions against the poll tax, more than a million African Americans registered to vote in just two years. Black registration doubled in Georgia and Louisiana, tripled in Alabama, and multiplied by almost ten times in Mississippi—from 28,000 to more than a quarter of a million.[38]

The numbers made an electoral difference. Even Sheriff Jim Clark campaigned for reelection in Selma's African American churches, trying to get the parishioners to forget Bloody Sunday. He lost. Black candidates started running and winning. In Mississippi, the 1967 statewide elections saw twenty-two Black candidates win offices in twelve counties, including the first to be seated in the Mississippi House of Representatives in the twentieth century. In 1968 Henry Frye became the first African American elected in the twentieth century to the North Carolina legislature. Back in 1956, North Carolina had used the literacy test to deny voter registration to this college graduate, but Frye, who served in the US Air Force during the Korean War, went from the state legislature to serve as chief justice of the North Carolina Supreme Court.[39]

Applying the Voting Rights Act

White officials did not sit idly by; they shifted tactics. Unable to keep African Americans from voting, they manipulated the rules and election machinery to maintain control and keep African Americans from exercising influence or winning office. In heavily Black counties, in an old ploy, offices were changed from elective to appointive. In Charleston County, South Carolina, for example, where there were eight school districts, a new state law changed the method of choosing the board of trustees from elected to appointed, but only in the two districts with African American population majorities, while the majority white districts—identical in every other way—kept electing their board members. Gerrymandering was rampant. A Mississippi legislator introduced one of these bills with the words, "This is needed to preserve our southern way of life."[40]

The preclearance remedy of the Voting Rights Act was Congress's way of trying to anticipate future discriminatory tactics. Somewhat surprisingly, new tactics did not focus on registration—that process seemed to go very smoothly very quickly. Instead there were new tactics designed to keep the new large numbers of African American voters from gaining real political power, methods now called "vote dilution." These measures included changing district lines, changing officeholders' responsibilities, and the like. Congress's solution of requiring preclearance was effective.

Cases arose quickly. In 1966, Fannie Lou Hamer and other members of the Mississippi Freedom Democratic Party (MFDP), which had unsuccessfully challenged the regular Mississippi delegation to the 1964 Democratic National Convention, decided to run as independent candidates rather than in the Democratic primary. The Mississippi legislature promptly passed a set of laws making it all but impossible to run as an independent: requiring more signatures, requiring them earlier, disqualifying many signatories, and so on.

The MFDP filed suit alleging that these changes were subject to the preclearance requirement of the Voting Rights Act, meaning that they could not go into effect without receiving advance federal approval. The lower court rejected the claim, holding that because the act's focus was on literacy tests and other direct barriers to registering and casting a ballot, the challenged types of changes—which did not interfere with registration or casting a ballot—were too far afield. The case, *Allen v. State Board of Elections* (1969), went to the US Supreme Court, along with several others involving similar tactics.

The key words in the statute said a covered jurisdiction must get advance approval of any change in a "voting qualification or prerequisite to voting, or standard, practice or procedure with respect to voting." What did those words include? The legislative history indicated that Congress was thinking primarily of tricks relating to registration and casting a ballot, but the words in the law were open-ended. The Supreme Court observed that the covered states had a history of "simply enacting new and slightly different requirements with the same discriminatory effect." Restricting the act's coverage to the problems that were foreseen at the time would be "underestimating the ingenuity of those bent on keeping Negroes from voting." The Court had a choice, and it chose an expansive interpretation that supported the act's "laudable goal" of making the Fifteenth Amendment "finally a reality for all citizens."[41]

The Voting Rights Act also affected the political system itself. Race-baiting subsided, and lines of communication opened. In 1974 Andrew Young, a civil rights activist with SCLC who would be elected mayor of Atlanta in 1982, addressed the Association of Southern Black Mayors: "It used to be that Southern politics was just 'nigger' politics: who could 'out-nigger' the other. Then you registered 10 to 15 percent in the community and folk would start saying 'Nigra.'" After registration numbers went to 35 to 40 percent, "it's amazing how quick they learned how to say 'Nee-grow.'" And when registration increased to 70 percent of the Black votes registered in the South, "everybody's proud to be associated with their black brothers and sisters."[42]

A different provision of the Voting Rights Act opened a new frontier for Americans of different native languages. It was designed primarily to benefit Puerto Ricans (who are US citizens) who moved to the mainland. Because the main teaching language in Puerto Rico was Spanish, they often were literate in Spanish but not necessarily in English. The act allowed such US citizens to qualify under state voting literacy laws. New York, with a literacy test and a large Puerto Rican–born population, challenged this provision. The state argued that the test was not discriminatory so Congress had no constitutional power to bypass it. In *Katzenbach v. Morgan* (1966), a majority of the Supreme Court disagreed, recognizing Congress's broad power to enforce the guarantees of the Fourteenth Amendment. In particular, the Court stressed that the vote is the most effective way to secure equality of treatment and rights. This was the beginning of laws recognizing rights of language minority people.[43]

New Reaction to Demonstration Cases

With passage of the 1964 Civil Rights Act and 1965 Voting Rights Act, marches and sit-ins subsided, but the Supreme Court was still deciding demonstration cases stemming from the first half of the decade. By this time, the justices' near-unanimity in the early demonstration cases was gone, replaced by a series of 5–4 decisions, including the first Supreme Court decisions upholding state convictions of demonstrators.[44]

In 1965 and 1966, 5–4 decisions reversed convictions for demonstrating peacefully near a Baton Rouge courthouse and sitting in at a segregated public library in Clinton, Louisiana. Justice Black became so exercised in the public library case that, in his dissent, he said, "It is high time to challenge the assumption" that groups had a constitutional right to protest on public property "whatever, wherever, whenever they want."[45]

The pattern of reversing civil rights demonstrators' convictions came to an end with two 5–4 decisions in 1966 and 1967 upholding old convictions. The first of these upheld convictions for picketing too near the Tallahassee jail, and the second upheld convictions in Birmingham in 1963 for marching in violation of an injunction. In this case, the dissenters argued that the terms of the injunction were surely unconstitutional; the majority did not disagree but held that unconstitutionality was no excuse for disobeying a court order.

The Warren Court closed out its movement cases in a visit to the past. In Birmingham during the awful year of 1963, filled with police dogs and a church bombing, civil rights leaders planned to march on Easter weekend. As required by city ordinance, march planners requested a parade permit, but the city official in charge, the infamous Theophilus Eugene "Bull" Connor, responded, "No, you will not get a permit in Birmingham, Alabama, to picket. I will picket you over to the city jail." March planners responded with a press conference where they denounced the injunction as "raw tyranny under the guise of maintaining law and order."[46]

Hundreds marched peacefully on Good Friday and were arrested and convicted for parading without a permit in violation of the city ordinance. It took six years for their appeals to reach the US Supreme Court, but the Court unanimously reversed the convictions for violating the city ordinance. In *Shuttlesworth v. Birmingham* (1969), the Court said the ordinance violated free speech because it gave city officials complete discretion to grant or deny a parade permit. There was a bittersweet quality to the ruling for the Good Friday marchers of 1963 because other peaceful marchers that weekend—on Easter Sunday—had been charged with violating an injunction, not the city ordinance, and their convictions had been upheld, as described earlier. Nevertheless, the Warren Court closed out its demonstration cases by finding consensus as in earlier days.

There was a highlight to the Good Friday arrests in Birmingham. In addition to march leader Rev. Fred Shuttlesworth, who had been arrested in Birmingham almost more times than one could count, another of those arrested was Rev. Martin Luther King Jr. That same day the newspaper published "A Call for Unity," an open letter from a group of Birmingham clergymen expressing support for civil rights but urging a slower pace. Earlier, college student Catherine George, working at a local church, had been given a draft of the letter to type. She had misgivings about the letter and suggested to the minister that sending this letter might not be a good idea. He disagreed, the letter was sent, and it was shown to Rev. King in jail. That letter sparked King's iconic "Letter from Birmingham Jail," with its inspiring theme soon reflected in his book titled *Why We Can't Wait*.[47]

Federal Criminal Prosecutions for Violation of Civil Rights

Civil rights laws, like other laws, were of two major types: *civil* statutes that provided remedies like injunctions or money damages, and *criminal* statutes that could put violators in federal prison. Thus far the Warren Court had been interpreting civil statutes. Two Supreme Court cases in 1966, however, involved criminal prosecutions brought by the Justice Department under Reconstruction-era statutes aimed at white supremacist violence. The question was whether the Supreme Court's interpretation of these laws would allow murderers to go free in the twentieth century as they had in the nineteenth century.

Both cases involved gruesome murders motivated by race hatred, but lower federal courts had dismissed the indictments on the sadly familiar ground that the charge of murder was a state responsibility and was beyond the constitutional power of Congress. According to this familiar interpretation, no civil rights law protected any American from being murdered.

One case involved the Neshoba County murders. In 1964 at the beginning of Freedom Summer, a project bringing young people from the North and West to Mississippi to work on voter registration, three volunteers—James Chaney (African American), Mickey Schwerner, and Andrew Goodman (both Jewish)—were brutally murdered in Mississippi by a gang that included Neshoba County Deputy Sheriff Cecil Price and several private individuals. The three civil rights workers had been arrested one day on their way to look at a burned-out church. They were released late that night, but the release was just a pretext to accost them not far away and murder them. Local law enforcement did nothing. Then the FBI, which had been criticized for its lack of enforcement of civil rights, invaded Mississippi in force, got someone to talk, and found the bodies in an earthen dam not far away. Mississippians who had joked that the young men's disappearance was a publicity stunt were shocked into silence as they saw the nation's outrage and contempt for Mississippi law enforcement and often for all white Mississippians as well.

At almost the same time in mid-1964, in Georgia, Colonel Lemuel Penn, a decorated World War II veteran who was driving home to Washington from Army Reserve duty, was shot and killed on the highway by Klansmen who just wanted to shoot a Black person. Federal grand juries, using surviving Reconstruction-era laws, indicted all the perpetrators in both incidents for conspiring to violate their victims' constitutional rights. When federal judges in lower courts dismissed the charges against all the private individuals in both cases, the Justice Department appealed to the Supreme Court. There had been a small number of criminal prosecutions for civil rights violations, but they were all of state law enforcement officials, not private individuals.[48]

The Supreme Court reinstated the federal criminal charges unanimously in both cases on the same day. In the Neshoba County killing, in *United States v. Cecil Price* (1966), the Court held that the private participants could be prosecuted for acting "under color of law" because they had acted in concert with public officers. In the Lemuel Penn killing, in *United States v. Herbert Guest* (1966), the Court found that Congress had power to act because the killing had occurred on an interstate highway.

The Thirteenth Amendment Rediscovered

In June 1968, a hundred years after the end of slavery, the Supreme Court brought the Thirteenth Amendment back to life. It did that by holding that racial discrimination in property transactions, *whether by state action or a private actor,* is a "badge of slavery" and, further, by interpreting the Civil Rights Act of 1866 to make discrimination in property transactions (such as buying, selling, or leasing) illegal for anyone, public or private.

The case that brought about this renewal of the Thirteenth Amendment began in 1965, when St. Louis residents Joseph and Barbara Jones decided to look for a home in the suburbs. They liked an advertisement for a new suburban development called Paddock Woods, with a plan for several hundred homes, a golf course, and other amenities. They visited and decided on a model house in the "Hyde Park" style with a price tag of $28,195. Then reality struck. The real estate developer would not sell a home to the Jones family. Barbara Jones was white, but Joseph Jones was African American. By coincidence, the Paddock Woods development was only a few minutes' drive away from the Labadie Avenue house that J. D. and Ethel Lee Shelley could not buy until 1948, when the Supreme Court decided *Shelley v. Kraemer* (see Chapter 6).

The Joneses brought a lawsuit. When the Jones complaint was filed in 1965, new federal laws were on the books against racial discrimination in hotels and restaurants, jobs, and voting, but not yet housing. Section 1 of the Civil Rights Act of 1866 guaranteed an equal right to buy and sell property regardless of race, but most people thought it aimed only at state laws, not private conduct. The Jones suit was dismissed in the district court on that ground. In the court of appeals, the case came before a panel headed by Circuit Judge Harry Blackmun, who was three years away from his Supreme Court appointment. Judge Blackmun's opinion observed that recent Supreme Court decisions seemed to signal a coming change in direction. Blackmun thought the Supreme Court might be about to do something with the Thirteenth or Fourteenth Amendments and what he called "the shackles of the state action limitation." It was not up to a lower-court judge to take that bold step, so he ruled against Joseph and Barbara Jones. On appeal, the Supreme Court did take that bold step, in *Jones v. Alfred H. Mayer Co.* (1968).[49]

There was also a more immediate background to the *Jones* case in 1968—the Kerner Commission Report and the new Fair Housing Act of 1968. At this time, fair housing was a national issue. In 1967 President Johnson had created the Kerner Commission to study the reasons for the intense rioting in urban African American communities. National grief and dismay increased in 1968 when the nation witnessed two assassinations: Martin Luther King Jr. in Memphis on April 4, and Robert F. Kennedy in Los Angeles on June 8. The Kerner Commission reported that a major responsibility for disorder was racial discrimination that determined urban conditions: "What white Americans have never fully understood—but what the Negro can never forget—is that white society is deeply implicated in the ghetto. White institutions created it, white institutions maintain it, and white society condones it." The commission especially emphasized housing.[50]

Soon after that report, Congress passed the Fair Housing Act as part of the Civil Rights Act of 1968. The Fair Housing Act was a comprehensive measure banning discrimination, not only in buying and renting housing, but in advertising, financing, and other aspects of the modern housing "process." It covered not only race and sex discrimination but other types of discrimination encountered in seeking housing, and it set up an administrative structure to provide effective remedies.[51]

In a decision announced on June 17, 1968, in *Jones v. Alfred H. Mayer Co.* (1968), the Supreme Court took the step that Judge Blackmun had foreseen. There had never been an explicit holding on whether Section 1 of the 1866 act applied to private conduct—because there had always been an assumption that it did not. Now the Court examined the legislative debates of 1865 and 1866. Those debates were inconclusive; some in 1866 wanted the law to apply to all conduct, reacting to the Black Codes, but others indicated a different attitude. Faced with conflicting legislative history, the Court in 1968 read the words of the statute in accordance with what it saw as the dominant purpose of the time.

That act of a century earlier stated that all citizens have the same rights as white citizens to "inherit, purchase, lease, sell, hold, and convey real and personal property." The Supreme Court of 1968 held that the act was valid under the Thirteenth Amendment, which has no state action requirement but imposes obligations on all persons, public and private. The Court, therefore, held that the right to equal treatment in property transactions applied not only to state laws but also to private transactions; in other words, the statute made it illegal for a private citizen to refuse to sell property to another person on account of race.[52]

The Supreme Court in the late 1960s. Front row, left to right: John Marshall Harlan II, Hugo Black, Chief Justice Earl Warren, William O. Douglas, William Brennan. Back row, left to right: Abe Fortas, Potter Stewart, Byron White, Thurgood Marshall.

Justice Potter Stewart, appointed in 1958 by President Eisenhower, wrote the majority opinion, in which he extolled the Thirteenth Amendment: "History leaves no doubt that, if we are to give [the law] the scope that its origins dictate, we must accord it a sweep as broad as its language." Stewart emphasized, "The Thirteenth Amendment authorized Congress to do more than merely dissolve the legal bond by which the Negro slave was held to his master; it gave Congress the power rationally to determine what are the badges and the incidents of slavery and the authority to translate that determination into effective legislation."[53]

Affirming the intended broad reach of the Thirteenth Amendment, the 1968 Court said Congress had the power to fulfill the Thirteenth Amendment's "promise of freedom." That promise included "the freedom to buy whatever a white man can buy, the right to live wherever a white man can live." It concluded, "If Congress cannot say that being a free man means at least this much, then the Thirteenth Amendment made a promise the Nation cannot keep."[54]

The reliance on the Thirteenth Amendment in the *Jones* case indicated a bright hope for the future. Powerful amicus briefs from across the country supported the idea of racial justice in housing and beyond. In the years between 1954 and 1968—the mere twinkling of an eye in judicial time—the Supreme Court ended separate-but-equal, brought the Reconstruction Amendments to life, and confirmed Congress's power to help overcome the legacy of slavery and race discrimination. It was a real beginning of a new birth of freedom. Or so it seemed.

CHAPTER TEN

Change in the Court

In 1952 a young Supreme Court law clerk wrote a memo to his judge, Justice Robert Jackson, about *Brown v. Board of Education* and the other school segregation cases pending before the Court. He said he knew his position was "unpopular and unhumanitarian," but he thought the Supreme Court should stand by the rule of separate but equal: "I think *Plessy v. Ferguson* was right and should be reaffirmed." Twenty years later, that law clerk, William Rehnquist, was on the Supreme Court, and for more than thirty years (including nineteen as chief justice), he would lead a dramatic turnaround in Supreme Court jurisprudence, not least in the law of race.[1]

None of this could have been foreseen when Thurgood Marshall joined the Court in 1967, climaxing a storied career. The Supreme Court had just upheld interracial marriage, and in 1968 it ordered school desegregation "now" and also resurrected the Thirteenth Amendment. With Marshall, the Supreme Court had a solid majority of five justices committed to strong civil rights enforcement, with the other four justices agreeing more often than not. Any vacancies would be filled by President Lyndon Johnson, winner of a landslide election only four years earlier.

It looked like the Supreme Court's direction was set for a long time. The three branches of government—executive, legislative, and judicial—were committed to equality and civil rights, and many Americans were feeling pride in what had been accomplished. And yet, behind the rosy horizon of dismantling Jim Crow, clouds were gathering. The United States was fighting an increasingly unpopular war, fueling an antiwar movement led by college students that brought chaos into the streets as well as generational conflicts into peoples' homes. Accompanying a fear of anarchy, white acceptance of racial progress was stopped short with two words: "Black Power." The words emerged in Greenwood, Mississippi, on June 16, 1966, in a fiery speech by the chairman of SNCC, Stokely Carmichael (later Kwame Ture). The words captured new themes: frustration at the numerous killings of nonviolent civil rights workers, impatience with "turning the other cheek," and despair at intractable race problems in the North, seemingly more entrenched than in the South. Also gaining national attention were movements like the Nation of Islam and the Black Panthers. Malcolm X articulated a powerful language in contrast to the southern civil rights movement's nonviolent integration, calling instead for separatism and revolutionary violence.[2]

The social upheavals of the Vietnam War, protests, assassinations, and urban riots combined to drive Johnson from the 1968 presidential race. The 1968 platforms of both the Republican and the Democratic Parties supported civil rights and the need for community order. In the campaign, however, Republican Richard Nixon pounded away on the theme of "law and order," combined with a "southern strategy." In stark contrast to law and order was the pandemonium in Chicago as police and protesters clashed at the Democratic National Convention. Vice President Hubert Humphrey, the Democratic nominee, was derided by antiwar liberals and abandoned by many of them in the campaign. There was irony in this because Humphrey had always been the party's liberal champion for equal rights. Nixon's vote margin over Humphrey was deceptively slim because Alabama segregationist George Wallace won nearly ten million votes as a third-party candidate and carried five Deep South states.

In President Nixon's first few months in office in 1969, he was handed two Supreme Court vacancies when Justice Abe Fortas was forced to resign and Chief Justice Earl Warren retired. Warren Burger, a judge on the federal appeals court in Washington, DC, was quickly named and confirmed as chief justice, but the other vacancy proved harder to fill. After the Senate rejected the nominations of federal appeals court judges from South Carolina and Florida (Clement Haynsworth and G. Harrold Carswell), Nixon gave up looking for a southerner. He named Harry Blackmun, a federal appeals judge from Minnesota and a lifelong friend of new Chief Justice Burger. Blackmun was swiftly confirmed and joined the Court in 1970.

The appointments of Burger and Blackmun were only the beginning of a long one-party run of Supreme Court appointments. From Nixon's election in 1968 through 1992, Republicans held the White House for twenty out of twenty-four years, and in that time appointed ten Supreme Court justices in a row. Every one of the ten new justices was less supportive of civil rights than his or her predecessor; only the fact that three of the ten eventually came to be strong civil rights supporters (albeit still not as strong as their predecessors) mitigated the outcome of one party's ten straight appointments.[3]

This chapter and the rest of this book tell the story of the Court's half century since 1969 under three chief justices: Warren Burger (1969–1986), William Rehnquist (1986–2005), and John Roberts (2005–present). The chapters cover different aspects of the same period—overview (this chapter), discriminatory purpose and effect (Chapter 11), affirmative action (Chapter 12), and criminal justice (Chapter 13). All show the same trajectory. Under Burger, with an often-divided Court, civil rights momentum slowed and some gains were eroded. Then, under Rehnquist and Roberts, the moderately conservative current grew into a dramatic wave washing away major civil rights protections—even rejecting some useful decisions of the Burger Court.

The Burger Court

With *Brown v. Board of Education* the Court ended official Jim Crow, but the United States needed to overcome the repercussions of years of official discrimination. Bigotry and the myriad ways that American culture disadvantaged racial minorities were far from over, but both political parties supported civil rights advances. A new form of coalition politics, unique except during a period in the early 1870s, seemed to be emerging in the South: large numbers of white voters—though not necessarily a majority of them—joined with newly enfranchised Black voters to elect moderate white candidates as well as the first African American officeholders in the South in the twentieth century. In 1970, moderate white Democrats John West (South Carolina), Jimmy Carter (Georgia), and Reubin Askew (Florida), with the support of enfranchised Black voters, defeated segregationist candidates to become governors of their states. In 1976 Jimmy Carter relied on the same coalition to win the presidency—with a sizable share (though a minority) of the white vote and a heavy Black vote. Meanwhile, a small but growing number of African Americans were being elected into the formerly all-white southern legislatures for the first time in the twentieth century. The new reality was a society that included African American officeholders, jurors, TV personalities, customers in integrated restaurants, and employees in previously all-white jobs. With all this progress, however, extremely different perceptions remained about how to handle the task ahead.[4]

During the 1970s, race cases ceased to be a southern monopoly. Major new issues included school segregation outside the South (that is, schools not previously segregated by law) and employment discrimination (made illegal for the first time by Title VII of the Civil Rights Act of 1964). During its seventeen years, the Burger Court decided more than a hundred civil rights cases, both major and minor. Half of them involved employment discrimination, and most of the rest involved school desegregation or voting. Signaling the awareness of race issues throughout the nation, the new cases were no longer clustered in the South—except for the voting cases. The sheer volume signaled the vast changes in American life and society that the new civil rights laws were helping to bring about. Because the Supreme Court had rarely faced race cases outside southern or border states, the Burger Court had a clean slate as it fashioned a jurisprudence for race as a nationwide issue. Because the issues in some ways turned out to seem more intractable than those the Warren Court had faced, the clean slate facing the Burger Court was both an opportunity and a burden.

As an appeals court judge, Warren Burger had criticized the Warren Court, most vehemently for its criminal procedure decisions but generally for what he saw as its "social engineering." When Burger was named chief justice by President Nixon, Burger set out to change the Supreme Court's direction. Soon after taking his seat, he wrote Judge Harry Blackmun (soon to join him on the Supreme Court), complaining about "some of the idiocy that is put forth as legal and constitutional profundity" at the Court, which, he said, might make him want "to shoot myself."[5]

Warren Burger espoused a philosophy of judicial restraint, which meant, among other things, putting limits on court enforcement of civil rights and especially halting new civil rights frontiers. On the appeals court, however, he wrote two bold opinions upholding a biracial religious group's challenge to blatantly distorted, racist programming of a Jackson, Mississippi, TV station. In *Office of Communication of United Church of Christ v. Federal Communications Commission* (1966, 1969), Burger's opinions ordered the racist broadcaster's license stripped away.[6]

The first two years of the new Court, when the only additions were Warren Burger and Harry Blackmun (sometimes referred to as the "Minnesota Twins," after the baseball team), the Supreme Court retreated in some civil rights cases but also made some major civil rights advances.

One dramatic retreat was a decision in *Palmer v. Thompson* (1971) allowing Jackson, Mississippi, to close all five of its public swimming pools

The Supreme Court in the late 1970s. Chief Justice Burger is flanked by four Warren Court holdovers in the front row, while four appointees of Presidents Nixon and Ford are in the back row. Front row, left to right: Byron White, William Brennan, Chief Justice Warren Burger, Potter Stewart, Thurgood Marshall. Back row, left to right: William Rehnquist, Harry Blackmun, Lewis Powell, John Paul Stevens.

(four white, one Black) when a court ordered the pools desegregated. The city's decision reflected the deepest psychoses of race and was part of a wave of swimming pool closings across the South. It was obvious that the pools had been closed to avoid white and Black people swimming together, but the city argued that it would lose money because patrons would not come to integrated pools. A 5–4 Supreme Court majority held there was no denial of equal protection since both races were affected. If there was a discriminatory purpose, that did not matter. This was a major victory for resistance to civil rights, after nearly two decades of Supreme Court decisions moving toward racial integration. The African American press was outraged; one editor called it a "dangerous" decision that "invites state and local governments to close public services for racist reasons."[7]

On the other hand, the Court handed down a string of major civil rights victories in Chief Justice Burger's first two years. In 1969, when the Nixon administration sought to repay its southern supporters by asking to delay school desegregation orders, the Court rejected the request with lightning speed. In *Alexander v. Holmes County Board of Education* (1969), the Court said desegregation must proceed "at once."[8]

In 1971 the Court turned to the Thirteenth Amendment to revive a long-defunct remedy. In 1966, with racial violence still present in Mississippi, Eugene Griffin and several other African Americans were driving in Kemper County, Mississippi, when white men stopped their car, forced them out, and beat them, out of racial hatred. The Supreme Court's nineteenth-century precedent said Congress had no power to create a remedy against private individuals in such a case. In *Griffin v. Breckenridge* (1971) the Court held that Congress had the power to enact the Ku Klux Act of 1871 against racially motivated violence. The power to do so was authorized by the Thirteenth Amendment—whether there was state action or not. The decision overruled nineteenth-century precedent, upheld Griffin's suit, and recognized a broad remedy against racial violence, public or private.[9]

Also in 1971, the Court faced its first school "busing" case, from Charlotte, North Carolina, in *Swann v. Charlotte-Mecklenburg School District* (1971). *Swann* began an ongoing story of the Supreme Court's grappling with school integration in an increasingly urban and suburban nation. Schools could no longer be legally segregated by race, but housing was so separated by race, and aggravated by racial economic differences, that a neighborhood school arrangement produced mostly segregated schools. One solution was transportation—busing students to create integrated schools. The school bus has long been an American institution, but busing for integration aroused fierce opposition among white people and a mixed reaction among African Americans. In *Swann* the Supreme Court upheld the busing order as a lower court's permissible tool to desegregate a large metropolitan school district. President Nixon expressed his disapproval in a message to Congress: "I am opposed to busing for the purpose of achieving racial balance in our schools."[10]

The same year also saw the Supreme Court's first two cases interpreting the employment discrimination law, Title VII of the Civil Rights Act of 1964. The first of these Title VII cases, *Phillips v. Martin Marietta Corp.* (1971), disallowed unjustifiable sex stereotyping of job assignments. The other case, *Griggs v. Duke Power Company* (1971), involved race discrimination in tests for promotions. *Griggs* was a landmark case that established far-reaching rules for deciding Title VII cases. This was novel territory; except for specialized laws protecting certain categories like military service members and some union workers, private employers had been unrestrained in hiring, firing, and other employment decisions. Title VII changed that system for employers and unions throughout the country.

At the beginning of 1972, two more Nixon appointees—Lewis F. Powell and William Rehnquist—joined the Court, after the deaths of Justices

Hugo Black and John Marshall Harlan II. Powell, a prominent corporate lawyer and former president of the American Bar Association, had also served on the Richmond and Virginia school boards during the desegregation struggles of the 1950s and 1960s. Rehnquist (author of the 1952 *Plessy v. Ferguson* memo) had practiced law in Phoenix and then served as assistant attorney general in the Nixon administration. After these appointments the Court's membership remained remarkably stable, with only two more changes in the fifteen years before Chief Justice Burger retired in 1986. The four Nixon justices, all conservatives until Justice Blackmun started drifting leftward in the late 1970s, joined five Warren Court holdovers—three liberals (William J. Brennan, William O. Douglas, and Thurgood Marshall) and two moderates (Potter Stewart and Byron White). Moderate John Paul Stevens (who eventually moved leftward) replaced Douglas in 1975, and conservative Sandra Day O'Connor replaced Stewart in 1981. The rightward drift was somewhat limited by the liberals' occasional ability to line up allies to moderate or even control a decision, but the center of gravity was conservative.

The Equal Protection Clause

The influence of Justices Rehnquist and Powell was felt immediately, especially in cases limiting the equal protection clause. Whereas the Warren Court had applied the equal protection clause to cover an increasing variety of unequal laws and regulations, the Burger Court ended that trend. Two particular examples of the change involved the doctrines of state action and strict scrutiny.[11]

The Burger Court's state action case arose out of an event that occurred one evening in 1968 when a small group of Pennsylvania state legislators went to a local Moose Lodge in Harrisburg for snacks and drinks. One of the legislators, a member of the lodge, took the others as his guests, but one of the group, Leroy Irvis, was turned away. Irvis was majority leader of the Pennsylvania House of Representatives, but he was denied entrance because he was an African American. The national constitution of the Moose Lodge limited members to "male persons of the Caucasian or White race above the age of twenty-one years, and not married to someone of any other than the Caucasian or White race."[12]

Irvis sued, arguing that the Moose Lodge could not discriminate because its liquor-dispensing license, heavily regulated by the state liquor commission, rendered the Moose Lodge's whites-only policy the equivalent of state action and therefore void. A lower court agreed with Irvis, saying the trend of cases supported a finding of state action, although it recognized that precedent had not yet gone this far. The Supreme Court reversed, 6–3, effectively stopping the trend. Justices Brennan, Douglas, and Marshall dissented.[13]

A year later the Supreme Court faced the issue of school funding. This was not a race case as such, but it had implications for issues of equity and school integration. As with some desegregation cases, this case originated with parent protests, in this instance protests against poor conditions in the Edgewood School District, a 90 percent Latino school district within the city of San Antonio. In 1968 sixteen Mexican American parents in the Edgewood district, headed by army veteran Demetrio Rodriguez, filed a class action suit over inequality in the financing system. Under Texas law, as in most states at the time, local property taxes were the main sources of school funding, which meant the per-pupil funding in each district depended on the per-pupil assessed value of taxable property located within the school district. For Edgewood, a poor area, that figure was $5,960, compared with $49,000 per pupil in Alamo Heights, a nearby high-income school district that was 80 percent white. Even though Edgewood residents had voted to tax themselves at the highest rate allowed by state law, a higher tax rate than Alamo Heights, the resulting difference in local funding was glaring. Other sources of funding, mostly federal funds, still left the disparity at 2:1.[14]

To decide whether the Texas law—or any state law—violated the equal protection clause, the Supreme Court looked at its two alternative methods: strict scrutiny and rational basis. If a state law divides people along lines of a "suspect classification" or affects a "fundamental right," the law is looked at with strict scrutiny. Under strict scrutiny, the law is assumed to be unconstitutional unless the state shows a "compelling interest" supporting the law. The other method of analysis, rational basis, is the opposite: the law is assumed to be valid unless the challengers show there is no conceivable rational basis for the law.

The difference between the two systems is illustrated by seeing the different way in which the lower court and the Supreme Court treated Texas's justification. The lower court in the *Rodriguez* case started by saying that strict scrutiny was the proper rule in this case, both because the Texas law divided children along lines of *wealth,* which the lower court held was a suspect classification, and because the law affected *education,* which the court said was a fundamental right. Then, using strict scrutiny, the lower court held the Texas school-funding law unconstitutional because Texas's justification was not a "compelling interest" for a law that produced such haphazard disparities.

The Supreme Court reversed, 5–4. The majority opinion by Justice Powell held that wealth (unlike race) is not a suspect classification and that

Demetrio Rodriguez, lead plaintiff in the Texas school finance case, *San Antonio Independent School District v. Rodriguez,* speaks to a graduate seminar in 1973 at the University of Texas at San Antonio.

education (unlike free speech) is not a fundamental right because it is not guaranteed in the US Constitution. Rather than using strict scrutiny, the Supreme Court used the standard of rational basis. The Court, therefore, ruled against the parents, saying that Texas's system was the same one used around the country, that almost every state depended on local property taxes, that the system promoted local control and involvement, and that each pupil was provided at least a basic education. The Texas law was rational and therefore constitutional. Justices Brennan, Douglas, Marshall, and White dissented on various grounds. Justice Marshall's dissent said the decision was an "abrupt departure from the mainstream" of recent cases and a "retreat from our historic commitment" to guaranteeing children "the chance to reach their full potential as citizens."[15]

During the 1970s a momentous, long-overdue new line of equal protection doctrine was created by the Supreme Court regarding sex discrimination. As of 1970, laws discriminating against women were not regarded as violations of equal protection. Responding to a new awareness, Congress approved the Equal Rights Amendment in 1972 and sent it to the states with a seven-year deadline for ratification. Although more than thirty states quickly ratified the amendment, the process then stalled, and the amendment failed before reaching the magic number of thirty-eight (three-quarters of the fifty states). Meanwhile, however, in several cases in five short years, 1971–1976, sex discrimination as unconstitutional state action became established Supreme Court doctrine. The ruling encompassed discrimination against men as well as women and by states as well as the federal government. Arguing several of the cases was Ruth Bader Ginsburg. At that time she was a Columbia University law professor and

ACLU attorney; in 1993, she would become the first Supreme Court justice appointed by a Democratic president in a quarter century, since Thurgood Marshall in 1967.[16]

The sex discrimination cases developed a new, different level of scrutiny, a "mid-level" scrutiny—more demanding than rational basis but not as stringent as strict scrutiny. That is, the Court may approve gender discrimination in some circumstances where discrimination would not be allowed on racial terms.

In several categories of cases, the Burger Court displayed a pattern of a vigorous start to enforcing civil rights, followed by a slowing or even backtracking. This pattern appeared in school desegregation, employment discrimination, and voting.

School Desegregation outside the South

The Burger Court inherited the task of desegregating the nation's schools, and the main focus quickly shifted to schools in large cities, especially in the North and West. A major fault line divided the justices—the question whether the segregated condition of neighborhoods and schools was the product of private choice and thus beyond the Constitution's reach, or whether that condition had been shaped by laws and government policies, thus bringing the Constitution into play.

In 1973 and 1974, one case opened a major door to desegregation in the North and West, and a second case largely closed that door. The background of northern school desegregation cases involved a pair of terms, "de jure" and "de facto." After years of dealing with southern schools segregated by law (de jure segregation), attention in the late 1960s began shifting to northern and western schools where there were no segregation laws but many schools were almost as segregated in fact (de facto segregation). As cases outside the South began percolating through the courts, it became increasingly clear that common, almost universal, patterns of actions by school and city officials created or aggravated segregation—choices like where to draw school attendance lines or where to build new schools. These actions often influenced real estate development and facilitated segregated housing patterns, which in turn stimulated more school segregation. It turned out that much of what was called de facto segregation was not coincidental after all.

The Supreme Court's first non-southern school segregation case involved Denver, where a single school district encompassed the whole city. The evidence showed that in Denver, which was two-thirds white, most of the African American and Latino students were concentrated in a handful of schools that were largely segregated. The evidence also showed that actions by the city and the school board had promoted that condition, and that the efforts to segregate schools in part of the city affected schools in the remainder of the city as well. This evidence led to a ruling, which the Supreme Court upheld in *Keyes v. School District No. 1 of Denver* (1973), ordering the Denver schools desegregated and, further, ordering that the plan cover the entire city-wide district. Justice Rehnquist was the only dissenter.

The justices' internal deliberations show that they almost produced a decision finding a violation based on the de facto segregation of the schools, but that did not come to pass. Instead, language in Justice Brennan's majority opinion implied, without quite saying so, that finding a violation depended on "segregative acts." The notion that de facto segregation by itself might violate the equal protection clause never resurfaced, and the phrase "de facto segregation" largely faded from the public vocabulary except as a historical curiosity. The Court's failure to rule that de facto segregation was unconstitutional would have fateful consequences, slamming the door on remedies for segregation.[17]

Denver was the first non-southern case; Detroit was next. The Denver decision was for integration; the Detroit decision was not. The situation in Detroit had become extremely segregated with the flight of white residents to suburbs in three surrounding counties. In those three counties, there were numerous separate school districts, mostly white. The lower court concluded that there was no way to achieve adequate relief by a remedy limited to Detroit itself. It therefore ordered a metropolitan plan that included busing some students between Detroit's outer areas and a group of nearby inner suburbs.

The Supreme Court, in *Milliken v. Bradley* (1974), blocked this remedy, 5–4, siding with the parents opposed to busing. The majority ruled that a violation of the Constitution was a prerequisite for imposing a remedy, and that this rule applied to each suburban school district separately. In other words, a suburban district could not be included in a desegregation plan unless that district itself had acted to create or maintain segregation. A majority of the Supreme Court now seemed to view a desegregation order less as a remedy for a condition of inequality than as a punishment to be visited only on those who had committed the actual wrong or caused the problem.[18]

The four dissenting justices charged that this was the death knell of any meaningful effort to desegregate America's urban core. Justice White in dissent said the state of Michigan was responsible for its entire education system because it had engaged in wholesale acts to promote Detroit's segregation. The majority, however, deemed these facts insufficient because the state had not directly manipulated suburban district lines. Justice Marshall echoed his dissent in the San Antonio school-funding case by calling the Court's decision a "giant step backwards." Three years later, in *Milliken v. Bradley II* (1977), the Court unanimously accepted a plan for school enhancements to help remedy some of segregation's ill effects. Marshall's dissent in *Milliken I* may have affected the decision. Brennan said that Marshall's presence on the Court "made all of us more sensitive to the legacy of discrimination."[19]

In 1979 the Court again approved desegregation orders in two Ohio cases, *Columbus School District v. Penick* (1979) and *Dayton School Board v. Brinkman* (1979). Because each of the cities had one school district and the cases did not involve suburbs, circumstances were analogous to the Denver case. One would surmise, then, that the justices would be as supportive of integration in the Ohio cases as they were in the Denver case. Instead, the vote was close. Clearly, the cause of school desegregation was in question. The Supreme Court did not rule on a school desegregation plan for the next dozen years. In the few cases thereafter, the Court has never approved a school desegregation plan since the two Ohio cases. The Court record on school desegregation followed the larger trend on civil rights: starting out with determination and vigor, and, over time, backing away.[20]

Employment and Voting Discrimination

The Burger Court decided many dozens of race employment discrimination cases under Title VII of the Civil Rights Act of 1964. Many involved the inevitable work of creating a new body of law, including routine procedure and issues of what kinds of evidence were allowed. A pair of cases in the mid-1970s showed the pattern of an initial ruling supporting broad relief for victims of discrimination followed by limits on that relief. The cases involved the question of how far a remedy for discrimination should reach when it hurts other employees hired after the discrimination occurred.

The two cases involved seniority systems and the issue of "retroactive seniority." If a person who was rejected because of discrimination is now entitled to be hired, should that person go to the end of the seniority line or be slotted in where he or she would have been, ahead of people hired afterward? The person who got the job is probably innocent of the discrimination, albeit a beneficiary of it. In many jobs, especially in industrial settings, seniority (or "competitive seniority") is the all-important determinant for promotions, layoffs, training, assignments, and so on. Either way, someone is going to lose out.

Both cases involved the trucking industry, where discrimination had long determined who got the more lucrative long-distance assignments. In *Franks v. Bowman Transportation Co.* (1976) the Supreme Court held that retroactive seniority was required. The majority held that denying retroactive seniority would simply perpetuate the effects of the illegal discrimination. The discrimination in this case all took place after 1964—in other words, after the date when discrimination became illegal. A year later the Supreme Court dealt with a slightly different scenario in *International Brotherhood of Teamsters v. United States* (1977). Here, unlike the previous case, the discrimination had taken place both before and after the 1964 act—that is, before and after employment discrimination became illegal. Here a majority split the two periods and held that retroactive seniority could be given only back to the date of the statute.[21]

As with schools and jobs, the Court moved forward, then back, in voting cases. The 1965 Voting Rights Act prohibited certain states and cities from making racially discriminatory voting changes, but two Virginia cities annexed large white population areas to maintain white city majorities. In *City of Petersburg v. United States* (1973) and *City of Richmond v. United States* (1975), the Supreme Court interpreted the Voting Rights Act broadly to block the annexations unless the cities also modified their methods of electing city council members from at-large elections to ward elections to mitigate any "dilution" of Black voting influence.

Soon after, however, the Supreme Court took a step backward when it approved a plan for city elections in New Orleans. The plan was racially discriminatory but no more so than the plan before the Voting Rights Act. In *Beer v. United States* (1976), the Court adopted a new, narrower interpretation of the Voting Rights Act. The act would not block a change even if it had a discriminatory effect—unless the discriminatory effect was worse than before. Thus, the Supreme Court replaced the act's no-discrimination rule with one that the Court called a "no-retrogression" rule.

Educating Children

In two cases, the Supreme Court made decisions that helped children of various ethnic and racial backgrounds. In *Lau v. Nichols* (1974), a suit brought on behalf of Chinese children in San Francisco, the Court held that under the Civil Rights Act of 1964, schools receiving federal funds must provide necessary language assistance to those children needing it. In *Plyler v. Doe* (1982), the Court struck down a Texas law barring "undocumented" children (those without legal immigration status) from attending public school. A 5–4 majority held that this law was a denial of equal protection. Most of the children were from Latin America, but as in the *Rodriguez* school-funding case from San Antonio, the decision was not based on race. Unlike the school-funding case, this case involved a complete denial of education. That seemed to make a difference to two of the justices (Blackmun and Powell), who had voted to uphold disparities in the state funding system but now joined in striking this law down. Powell, author of the majority opinion in the San Antonio funding case, now said this new case showed that there was not always a bright line between levels of scrutiny and which cases would fit within each level.

The Thirteenth Amendment

On a particularly notable issue, the Burger Court built on and expanded a major ruling of the Warren Court concerning the Thirteenth Amendment and the Civil Rights Act of 1866. The Warren Court held in *Jones v. Alfred H. Mayer Co.* (1968) that race discrimination in buying and selling property—even without state action—was a badge of slavery barred by the Civil Rights Act of 1866, which was constitutional based on Congress's power to enforce the Thirteenth Amendment. The issue came back to the Supreme Court in 1976, this time in a dispute over race discrimination in private contracts, which was also banned by the 1866 law.

The case involved two African American families' efforts to get their children off to a good start in life. Michael McCrary and Colin Gonzales were young African American boys whose parents tried to enroll them in two private schools in Fairfax, Virginia. Michael's application was for day camp, and Colin's was for nursery school. The schools rejected them, saying that the schools were for white children only. The lower court ruled for the African American families, recognizing that the Supreme Court had already given a broad interpretation to the Civil Rights Act of 1866. On appeal, the Burger Court, in *Runyon v. McCrary* (1976), reaffirmed its 1968 ruling and held that the 1866 act barred race discrimination in private contracts just as in private property transactions. This far-reaching decision covered all types of contracts, not only school admission but also buying and selling all manner of goods and services, including the right to be served without discrimination at lunch counters and, in this case, application for day camp and nursery school.

The 1976 *Runyon* opinion was written for a 7–2 majority by Justice Stewart, author of the *Jones* decision and two decisions giving life to the Ku Klux Act of 1871. Two of the justices in the majority, Justices Powell and Stevens, wrote concurring opinions. They doubted that the 1866 Civil Rights Act was really intended to cover discrimination by private citizens, but they joined in the ruling because the 1968 *Jones* decision was settled law and fundamental national policy. Justice Stevens wrote:

> The policy of the Nation as formulated by the Congress in recent years has moved constantly in the direction of eliminating racial segregation in all sectors of society. This Court has given a sympathetic and liberal construction to such legislation. For the Court now to overrule *Jones* would be a significant step backwards.[22]

Neither precedent nor fundamental national policy would get the same respect in the Rehnquist Court.

The election of President Ronald Reagan in 1980 signaled an ideological shift on civil rights. Reagan as a candidate had chosen to open his 1980 presidential campaign with a states' rights speech at the Neshoba County Fair in Mississippi. Neshoba County was notorious as the scene of the murder of three civil rights workers in 1964. That was either a blind spot or a welcoming signal to racist diehards. The new president brought—or reflected—a more ideological conservatism. During his first five years, his only appointment to the Supreme Court was Justice Sandra Day O'Connor, the first woman justice on the Supreme Court.[23]

The Court under Chief Justice Rehnquist

When Chief Justice Burger retired in 1986, President Reagan elevated Justice William Rehnquist to take the chief justice position. He then filled Rehnquist's vacated seat with the radically conservative Antonin Scalia. Chief Justice Rehnquist and Associate Justice Scalia were judicial activists ready to change the Court's interpretation on issues of race and civil rights. When Justice Powell retired a year later, it took another year to fill the seat (following the failed nominations of Robert Bork and Douglas Ginsburg), but by early 1988 Anthony Kennedy was on the Court. Although he expressed awareness of and concern for the nation's racial problems, Justice Kennedy was more conservative than his predecessor (except on gay rights, which Kennedy notably championed). With Justice O'Connor and Justice White, who by then was conservative on some issues, that made for a solid five-vote conservative majority after 1988.[24]

New justices fit largely in the mold of their predecessors. The only exception was in 1991, when President George H. W. Bush replaced Justice Marshall with the second African American Supreme Court justice, Clarence Thomas of Georgia. Thomas was Marshall's philosophical opposite. Fate had played a cruel trick on Thurgood Marshall. After a fabled quarter century as field marshal of the war against race discrimination, with wins in almost all of his Supreme Court arguments, he spent most of his last quarter century as the Court's Jeremiah, in almost constant dissent from a majority determined to dismantle Marshall's earlier work. Many spoke of his valiant service spotlighting the Court's steady retreat, but that service came at a huge personal cost. For years Justice Marshall said he had a lifetime appointment and expected to serve out his term. Moreover, he joked, "I expect to die at the age of a hundred and ten, shot by a jealous husband." But his health deteriorated, and with Justice Brennan's retirement in 1990, Marshall's only close friend on the Court was gone. With everyone expecting that President George H. W. Bush would be reelected handily in 1992, Justice Marshall retired for health reasons in October 1991. President Bill Clinton was inaugurated on January 20, 1993, and Justice Marshall died four days later, on January 24, 1993.[25]

Marshall's departure produced a final irony, affecting the history of the Supreme Court to this day. If Justice Marshall had not retired (and some ailing justices in the past had chosen not to retire), he would have been succeeded by a Clinton nominee rather than by President George H. W. Bush's nominee, Justice Thomas. With a Clinton nominee on the Court, one must wonder who would have won the 2000 case of *Bush v. Gore* (2000) and would thereby have become president. And who would have been president in 2005, to name the replacements of Chief Justice Rehnquist and Justice O'Connor, whose successors remain on the Supreme Court today? Of course, even a single Supreme Court appointment is often consequential, but it must be rare for one with such close timing to make this much difference for so long.[26]

With the Rehnquist Court in place, some of its sharpest opinions restricted civil rights. Moreover, it even overruled Burger Court decisions that were apparently deemed too moderate. The changes that took place on the Court were felt immediately and across the board.

The 1989 Employment Discrimination Cases

Once Justice Kennedy's arrival in 1988 created a solid five-vote majority to roll back the law on employment discrimination (including Justice White on this issue), it was not long before radical surgery began. At the end of the 1988–1989 term (Justice Kennedy's first full term), four decisions in ten days weakened Congress's fabric of protection against job discrimination.[27]

One of those cases was already at the Supreme Court and was argued soon after Justice Kennedy arrived. It was a suit by Brenda Patterson, who charged that her employer, McLean Credit Union of Raleigh, North

Carolina, had discriminated against her because she was African American. She said she had been harassed, denied a promotion by a supervisor who said, "Colored people don't work as fast," and finally forced out of her job of ten years. Patterson brought her claim, not as a modern-day Title VII case, but under the Civil Rights Act of 1866. Precedent supported Patterson's claim. In *Runyon v. McCrary* (1976), the Burger Court had held that the 1866 act banned race discrimination in contracts, private as well as public, and several other cases also made it clear that "contracts" included employment. In May 1988, in *Patterson v. McLean Credit Union* (I) (1988), the Court ordered reargument and added an issue that none of the parties had raised: whether the Court should "reconsider" *Runyon v. McCrary.* Four justices, those who had joined in *Runyon* in 1976, dissented vigorously from this procedural step. It seemed like an ominous sign, an unprompted threat against an important precedent that had become a staple of national policy.[28]

A year later, in *Patterson v. McLean Credit Union* (1989), the Court did not overturn *Runyon v. McCrary;* instead, the Court cut out much or most of the 1866 Civil Rights Act. In a 5–4 opinion by Justice Kennedy, the Court held that the 1866 act covers only discrimination in hiring and some promotions, but nothing else about the employer-employee relationship, and certainly not Patterson's claims of harassment and firing.

The words of the Civil Rights Act of 1866 (as presently codified as Section 1981) say, "All persons within the jurisdiction of the United States shall have the same right in every State and Territory to make and enforce contracts . . . as is enjoyed by white citizens." Patterson said this meant the law's protections spanned the entire employment relationship. She was supported by an amicus curiae brief filed by President Reagan's Justice Department (not a usual ally for a civil rights plaintiff), which said the words "make and enforce" apply to "the execution, definition, or performance of contractual opportunities and obligations."[29]

The Court majority thought differently. Justice Kennedy said the Court was simply interpreting the "plain terms" of the 1866 Act, but that is exactly what it did not do. Instead, the Court transformed the words into a bizarre version complete with four separate ellipses: "By its plain terms, the relevant provision in § 1981 protects two rights: 'the same right . . . to make . . . contracts' and 'the same right . . . to . . . enforce contracts.'" Having created two separate rights instead of Congress's one right (by leaving out the word "and"), the Court then defined each of the two words "make" and "enforce" separately and in isolation. The Court made another error. Its definition of "make" was sound, but its definition of "enforce" was not. The Court said "enforce" does not create any contract rights at all, but just "embraces protection of a legal process, and of a right of access to legal process." But that is impossible because another part of the same section of the law already gives all persons the right "to sue, be parties, give evidence." Thus, the law already includes the rights supposedly covered by Justice Kennedy's interpretation of "enforce," and it is a cardinal rule of interpretation to avoid giving the same meaning twice.[30]

Some of the justices, led by Justice Scalia, have espoused various forms of interpreting statutes, sometimes called "textualism" and "originalism," which look primarily or only at the words of a law, not at the legislative debates, and focus on what the words of the law meant when they were written. The *Patterson* decision failed on both counts. In addition to splitting up the words, the opinion paid no attention to what the words meant when they were written in 1866. The Civil Rights Act of 1866 was mainly a response to the most recalcitrant states' Black Codes and widespread cheating of freedpeople by their employers. Under the *Patterson* opinion's interpretation, one must believe that Republicans in 1866 drafted a statute to leave the freedpeople—once hired—at the mercy of their employers, who were often their former masters.

Finally, the Court seriously misquoted language that supposedly supported its interpretation of the 1866 act, but in fact did not support it. The quoted language came from *Georgia v. Rachel* (1966). In that case, decided almost exactly a century after passage of the Civil Rights Act of 1866, the Supreme Court was considering whether the right to remove a case from state to federal court (a procedure authorized by the 1866 act) applied to all federal rights, like free speech under the First Amendment, or only to *race-based* rights. The Supreme Court in *Georgia v. Rachel* chose the latter, more limited interpretation, saying, "The legislative history of the 1866 Act clearly indicates that Congress intended to protect a limited category of rights, specifically defined in terms of racial equality." The *Patterson* majority opinion quoted the first nineteen words of the passage, ending with the words "limited category of rights," and indicated that this quotation supported its view that the law covered only limited contract functions, like hiring. But the *Patterson* opinion left out the crucial last seven words of the *Georgia v. Rachel* quotation ("specifically defined in terms of racial equality"), which show that the *Georgia v. Rachel* use of the word "limited" had nothing at all to do with the issue in *Patterson*.[31]

The Court's opinion closed with an odd statement that was belied by the result of the case: "Neither our words nor our decisions should be interpreted as signaling one inch of retreat from Congress's policy to forbid discrimination in the private, as well as the public, sphere." Justice Brennan's dissent had a different view of "not one inch of retreat." He said: "What the Court declines to snatch away with one hand, it takes with the other."[32]

The *Patterson* case did not stand alone but was one of a blizzard of major employment discrimination cases decided by the Supreme Court in the 1988–1989 term. All the cases cut back on congressional protections for minority and women workers. The string of Supreme Court decisions eviscerating federal statutes provoked angry responses in Congress and led to passage of the Civil Rights Act of 1991 (after President Bush vetoed a 1990 version). This act responded to no fewer than a dozen Supreme Court decisions that had restricted civil rights enforcement. One section of the new Civil Rights Act responded to the *Patterson* case by defining the words "make and enforce contracts" to include "the making, performance, modification, and termination of contracts, and the enjoyment of all benefits, privileges, terms, and conditions of the contractual relationship." Senator John C. Danforth, a Missouri Republican, announced that everyone could claim victory with the bill: "Democrats, Republicans, liberals, conservatives." He called it "a victory for our country."[33]

School Desegregation Again

By the time Justice Rehnquist became chief justice, school desegregation cases had been essentially absent from the Supreme Court for almost a decade, but many school districts were still under supervision by lower federal courts. The Court largely shut these cases down in a trio of cases in the 1990s.

Before these cases arrived, there was a preview of sorts in a school desegregation case in 1988, when the Court first stayed and then, by 5–4, reversed contempt citations for several outrageously recalcitrant officials in Yonkers, New York. The Court's return to school desegregation cases came in 1991 and 1992. In cases from Oklahoma City and Atlanta, schools had been operating under court orders for years but still, or again, had substantial segregation. Nevertheless, said the Supreme Court, it was time to end those cases.[34]

That set the stage for a very large blow to desegregation. In Kansas City, Missouri, the city school district was ringed with suburban districts that had committed no violation and therefore could not be subjected to any desegregation plan for the city (as per the Detroit case of 1974). Instead, after earlier desegregation efforts in the city had failed and city schools remained segregated and unequal, the district court ordered a major educational enhancement program for city schools. The program, to be funded largely by the state of Missouri, included higher teacher pay, unique programing, and other features such as air-conditioned classrooms in high schools. The twofold purpose was to improve city students' opportunities and to attract white students from nearby suburban districts to make *voluntary choices* to attend city schools for magnet programs.

The state of Missouri objected to paying for the expensive Kansas City plan. In *Missouri v. Jenkins* (1995), the Supreme Court ruled against the city's use of magnet schools to attract suburban students. Chief Justice Rehnquist's opinion did not find fault with the Kansas City enhancements, but took aim at the goal of integration itself, inventing the label "interdistrict goal" and thereby calling it forbidden: "The District Court's pursuit of 'desegregative attractiveness' was beyond the scope of its broad remedial authority."[35]

In 1974 the Supreme Court said that a plan to integrate Detroit's schools could not force suburban children to attend city schools. In Kansas City, in 1995, the Court said a desegregation plan could not even encourage suburban children to attend city schools. The chief justice's view was in line with his 1952 memo supporting *Plessy v. Ferguson*. He further reflected this view in another part of the opinion. The Kansas City school board argued that the all-white schools in the suburbs were in part a "vestige" of segregation, that "white flight" was ultimately traceable to Missouri's long-standing segregation laws. The chief justice rejected this view by saying that "white flight may result from desegregation, not *de jure* segregation." Of course, it is true that desegregation can be an immediate stimulus for white flight, but denying that white flight has its roots in de jure segregation is a common nostrum of pro-segregation thinking. In dissent, Justice David Souter made the obvious point that "there is in fact no break in the chain of causation linking the effects of desegregation with those of segregation."[36]

There was a touch of irony in the doomed concept of "desegregative attractiveness" in Kansas City. Just three years earlier the Court had been almost unanimous in supporting a form of desegregative attractiveness in higher education, in *United States v. Fordice* (1992). That case, which involved Mississippi's system of public colleges and universities, held that a state that had maintained a segregated system had not only the obligation to remove formal racial barriers but also an affirmative obligation to root out every "vestige" or "remnant" of the segregated system in place for so long. The case was brought jointly by the Justice Department and a coalition of Mississippians, with Jake Ayers of Leland, Mississippi, as the lead class member. Part of the goal was to enhance historically Black schools.

One witness, Professor Leslie McLemore of Jackson State University, testified that when the federal agency threatened to cut off funds to the historically white schools, program enhancements and money suddenly started flowing into Jackson State and other Black schools. "It was like Christmas in July," he testified.[37]

In an opinion by Justice White, who maintained his strong support for desegregating public institutions, the Court identified a number of vestiges of segregation, especially the limitations on the programs that the historically Black schools were allowed to offer—such as no PhD programs. These limitations, according to the Supreme Court, made the historically African American schools unequal for their students and unlikely to attract white students. The Court did not use the term "desegregative attractiveness," but that was what the Supreme Court ordered in that case. It seems curious, at least, to deny a remedy in Kansas City that the Supreme Court itself ordered in Mississippi.

The Roberts Court

Seven changes in Court membership occurred early in the new century. In 2005 Chief Justice Rehnquist died and Justice O'Connor retired. John Roberts, a former Rehnquist law clerk and a judge serving on the DC Circuit, was quickly confirmed to succeed Rehnquist as chief justice. Replacing Justice O'Connor was not as easy. President George W. Bush first nominated his White House counsel, Harriet Miers. Opponents feared she might be too moderate, and a blowback from conservative voices, along with a concern about her limited experience, forced Miers out. President Bush then appointed the very conservative Samuel Alito in 2006. The appointments did not change the 5–4 strong conservative tilt.[38]

Several years later President Barack Obama replaced Justices Souter and Stevens (both appointed by Republican presidents) upon their retirements from the Court. Obama appointed Sonia Sotomayor, a judge on the Second Circuit Court of Appeals, in 2009, and Elena Kagan, a former law clerk for Justice Marshall, in 2010. Justice Sotomayor, of Puerto Rican background, was the first Latina Supreme Court justice. Justice Kagan, who was serving as solicitor general when she was named to the Court, was the first member of the Court in nearly thirty years (since Justice O'Connor in 1981) who did not come from the ranks of federal appeals court judges.

After Donald Trump won the 2016 election, he named three Supreme Court justices. Neil Gorsuch (2017) replaced Scalia, and Brett Kavanaugh (2018) replaced Kennedy. Both new justices clerked for Kennedy and both seemed to represent little change. His third nomination, Amy Coney Barrett

(2020) to replace Justice Ginsburg, was a different matter. Justice Barrett, previously a judge on the US Seventh Circuit Court of Appeals, clerked for Justice Scalia and is strongly conservative, the polar opposite of her liberal predecessor, Ruth Bader Ginsburg. Barrett became the sixth justice on the Court who was or had been a member of the conservative Federalist Society, along with Chief Justice Roberts and Justices Alito, Gorsuch, Kavanaugh, and Thomas.

The timing of Barrett's confirmation was extremely controversial because it was a stark contrast with events that followed Justice Scalia's death on February 13, 2016, early in that election year. On March 15, 2016, then-president Obama nominated Merrick Garland, a Washington, DC, Circuit judge, who was regarded as a moderate. The Republican majority in the Senate boycotted the nomination of Garland, stating repeatedly that a Supreme Court vacancy in an election year should be kept open to be filled by whoever is elected president in the upcoming election. When Justice Ginsburg died on September 18, 2020, Barrett was nominated eight days later and confirmed a month after that, on October 26, 2020, one week before the election on November 3, 2020.[39]

Democrats cried "foul" about the display of political power in this election-eve selection, but it was nothing new. In 1801, two months after incumbent John Adams was defeated for reelection, the lame duck president nominated John Marshall to be chief justice, and the Federalist majority in the Senate, also lame duck, quickly confirmed Marshall. The only thing that may have been new in 2020 was the Republican majority's pious pretense in 2016 that it was acting out of principle, not raw politics.[40]

The election of 2020 brought to office Joe Biden. His choice for vice president symbolized the vast change in America's population in the past half-century. Kamala Harris is the daughter of an immigrant mother, a biologist from India, and an immigrant father, an economics professor of African descent from Jamaica. As a child she lived in a Black neighborhood and was bused to a recently integrated white school in another neighborhood. Harris was the first woman vice president and the first identified as non-white (Charles Curtis, vice president under Herbert Hoover, 1929–1933, was part Kaw Indian but was generally identified as white).

Population numbers had changed remarkably since the Immigration Act of 1965 (Chapter 7), including the reduction of the white, non-Hispanic percentage of the US population from 80 percent in 1965 to less than 60 percent in 2019. Climbing steadily, the number of immigrants lawfully admitted for permanent residence has been about a million a year since 2000, and the number of naturalizations, people who become US citizens, has been almost that. The 1965 act opened a wide spectrum in the immigration of people of color in the current United States. More than 30 percent of both totals, new residents and new naturalized citizens, were born in Asia and more than 30 percent were born in the Western Hemisphere including the Caribbean. Ten percent of both new residents and new citizens were born in Africa, a large increase from this continent. Just 10 percent were from Europe.[41]

The Voting Rights Act

By the beginning of the Roberts Court in 2005, the volume of civil rights cases had dwindled, but not the importance or variety of issues. A major new civil right emerged: gay rights, led by Justice Kennedy on a bitterly divided Court. After the Rehnquist Court held in *Lawrence v. Texas* (2003) that consensual homosexual acts could not be made a crime, the Supreme Court struck down the federal Defense of Marriage Act in *United States v. Windsor* (2013), recognized a right to gay marriage in *Obergfell v. Hodges* (2015), and ruled, *Bostock v. Clayton County* (2020), that job discrimination against gay employees was discrimination on account of sex in violation of the Civil Rights Act of 1964. Protecting gay employees was not what Virginia representative Howard Smith had in mind when he added the ban on sex discrimination to the civil rights bill in 1964, but the words were plain and the text left no room for principled debate.

The highest-profile ruling of the Roberts Court in the area of race gutted the 1965 Voting Rights Act. The act had been an immediate success in ending gross disfranchisement in the covered states. Since then, the "preclearance" section had been the main part of the act. By the early 2000s, preclearance had blocked a thousand voting changes, large and small, each one the equivalent of a successful lawsuit.[42]

Special provisions of the act were initially enacted for just five years, but Congress realized that discrimination does not end so quickly, and so extended the life of these provisions four times, in 1970, 1975, 1982, and 2006. Each time, extensive hearings and massive records confirmed that the covered jurisdictions, while improving, still had significant problems of voting discrimination. The original act and the first three extensions of the preclearance remedy were upheld as valid exercises of Congress's Fifteenth Amendment power to remedy a still-existing problem.[43]

In 2006, as the most recent extension of preclearance was due to expire, Congress extended it again for twenty-five years. The extension followed lengthy hearings and a massive record that showed, as before, some improvement but also the need to continue the remedy. Congress confirmed that long-entrenched patterns of discrimination do not quickly disappear, and it committed to keeping an effective remedy until the problem was solved, not just ameliorated. Both houses of Congress voted for the extension, including members from the covered states, and President George W. Bush signed the extension in a Rose Garden ceremony.[44]

When John Roberts became chief justice of the US Supreme Court in 2005, he was no stranger to the Voting Rights Act. In 1981–1982, Roberts was special assistant to William French Smith, the attorney general in the Reagan administration. As one of his assignments, Roberts wrote memoranda opposing key parts of the Voting Rights Act. Although most of the debate at that time was about other provisions of the act, Roberts was also skeptical about the preclearance remedy. By the time the newest extension of the act was passed, Roberts was chief justice and in a position to make his views on the Voting Rights Act the law of the land.[45]

A new challenge to the constitutionality of the Voting Rights Act, *Northwest Austin Mun. Util. Dist. v. Holder* (2009), soon reached the Supreme Court. The Court sidestepped the constitutional issue on a technical statutory ground, that Northwest Austin district might be eligible for an exemption from the act's preclearance requirement. It was clear, though, that the act was living on borrowed time. The decision in *Northwest Austin* may have seemed uncontroversial, but the opinion by Chief Justice Roberts was anything but routine. The main feature of the opinion was the invention of a doctrine that the chief justice called "equality of the states" or "equal sovereignty." Such a doctrine had already been tried by South Carolina and thoroughly rejected by the Supreme Court in *South Carolina v. Katzenbach* (1966).[46]

In the *Northwest Austin* case Chief Justice Roberts resurrected South Carolina's "states' rights" vision and declared it to be constitutional doctrine, even "fundamental." He claimed support from the Supreme Court's 1966 decision, but only by leaving out key words and thus changing the meaning of the quotation. Thus, his doctrine rested on a basis that really did not exist.[47]

The actual quotation from *South Carolina v. Katzenbach* is as follows, with brackets around the words omitted in the *Northwest Austin* opinion:

> The doctrine of equality of States, invoked by South Carolina, does not bar [this approach, for that doctrine applies only to the terms upon which States are admitted to the Union, and not to the] remedies for local evils which have subsequently appeared.[48]

The words left out by Roberts change the meaning of the quotation. Read fairly, the *Katzenbach* quote says there is no doctrine of "equality of states" except when a state is initially admitted to the Union, whereas Chief Justice Roberts's quote says there is such a doctrine. Leaving these words out created a general doctrine of equality of states that did not exist before he created it with this misquotation.[49]

The chief justice's opinion was joined by everyone except Justice Thomas, who would have held the Voting Rights Act unconstitutional. Unaccountably, although the four liberal justices surely did not believe there was an "equal sovereignty" doctrine, none of them wrote a separate opinion. By the time any justice did take issue, when the Voting Rights Act came back to the Supreme Court four years later, it was too late; the near-unanimous decision in the *Northwest Austin* case had given the concept a pedigree, no matter how unearned.

The *Northwest Austin* case also showed an attitude toward Congress that was the opposite of the respect and deference that is traditionally professed. Notable was Justice Scalia's disdain. When the solicitor general pointed out that the 2006 extension of the act was adopted by overwhelming majorities in both the Senate and House of Representatives, Justice Scalia simply dismissed congressional concerns: "Do you ever expect, do you seriously expect Congress to vote against a re-extension of the Voting Rights Act? Do you really think that any incumbent would, would vote to do that?"[50]

After the *Northwest Austin* case, ideological opponents of the Voting Rights Act canvassed covered states, counties, and cities looking for a likely candidate to bring another lawsuit to a seemingly receptive Court. The candidate turned out to be Shelby County, Alabama, located in the suburbs of Birmingham. In *Shelby County v. Holder* (2013), the Supreme Court took the next step, actually striking down the entire preclearance procedure as carried out under the Voting Rights Act. The Supreme Court held that Congress had acted unconstitutionally in 2006 when it extended the preclearance remedy. This was the first race-based civil rights law to be held unconstitutional in more than a hundred years.[51]

Chief Justice Roberts's opinion for the 5–4 majority in *Shelby County* was the bitter fruit of the seeds planted four years earlier. The majority opinion in *Shelby County* quoted or cited the *Northwest Austin* case no fewer than twenty-six times. The "equal sovereignty" doctrine was the centerpiece of the *Shelby County* decision, and those words were repeated seven times. The chief justice did not repeat his misquotation of *South Carolina v. Katzenbach,* but he did rely on the defective doctrine supposedly supported by that case. Justice Ginsburg challenged the new doctrine, but she had only four votes.

Scholarly disapproval was swift. One scholar said the doctrine prompted "savage criticism not only from the left, but also from the right." Stanford Professor Michael McConnell, who had been a court of appeals judge appointed by President George W. Bush, said of the equal sovereignty concept, "This is a nice idea; it might be on my list of desirable constitutional amendments. But it is not in the Constitution we have." Richard Posner, a conservative appeals court judge appointed by Ronald Reagan, joined in:

"This is a principle of constitutional law of which I had never heard—for the excellent reason that . . . there is no such principle." If his point had not been clear, he added, "It rests on air."[52]

The doctrine of equal sovereignty shifted focus away from the Fifteenth Amendment. The question in the case should have been whether the Voting Rights Act, as extended in 2006, was within—or was still within—Congress's enforcement power under the Fifteenth Amendment. That would have been an easy question to answer because 200 years of constitutional doctrine make it clear that where the Constitution gives Congress certain power, the Supreme Court does not second-guess whether Congress's use of that power is necessary or effective, only whether Congress has done something which is *prohibited* by the Constitution. In overruling a major portion of the Voting Rights Act, the Court was careful not to suggest that Congress was exceeding its Fifteenth Amendment power. Instead the Court changed the subject to equal sovereignty and there found a "*prohibition*" that enabled it to override Congress's Fifteenth Amendment power. The doctrine of equal sovereignty thus became a weapon against the right to vote.[53]

That was neither the end of the case nor the end of the Court's errors. There was still a second issue. Equal sovereignty did not necessarily end the case, because the voluminous record compiled by Congress of continuing voting discrimination in the covered states might have been sufficient to justify their special coverage even under equal sovereignty. The Court disposed of that possibility by saying that the record was simply irrelevant because the types of voting discrimination (such as gerrymandering or city annexation of white but not Black neighborhoods) did not match the type of violations (barriers to registration and casting a ballot) on which the act's coverage formula was based.

The majority failed to recognize that vote discrimination methods are not in separate compartments but form a spectrum or continuum of variations (whatever works). In 1965 Congress identified covered jurisdictions based on one type of discrimination, but Congress knew that variations—then unknown—would be coming along, and the preclearance procedure reflected Congress's determination to block any new, substitute types of discriminatory changes. New and different methods of discrimination are precisely what preclearance was designed for. The Warren Court called it "the extraordinary stratagem of contriving new rules of various kinds for the sole purpose of perpetuating voting discrimination . . . in order to evade the remedies of the Act itself." The Burger Court noted as early as 1971 that "gerrymandering and boundary changes had become prime weapons for discriminating against Negro voters." It continued, "the history of white domination in the South has been one of adaptiveness, and the passage of the Voting Rights Act and the increased black registration that followed has resulted in new methods to maintain white control of the political process"—methods that were still being used when Congress renewed the act in 2006. The Burger Court recognized that literacy tests were quickly replaced by methods still common today, and the extensions of the act in 1970, 1975, and 1982—all upheld by the Court—were based on the same type of congressional record that the *Shelby County* majority said was irrelevant. The linchpin of the majority opinion, that "40-year–old facts" about voting discrimination have "no logical relation to the present day," could not be more wrong.[54]

The *Shelby County* majority correctly said, "the Act imposes current burdens and must be justified by current needs." Congress, filled with men and women whose political life depends on knowing "current needs," assessed those needs in 2006 and concluded the act was still needed because generations-long patterns of discrimination were not yet uprooted. That should have been enough for the Court. Instead, the Court far overstepped its role, contradicting Alexander Hamilton, who said, in Federalist 78, that even if "judiciary encroachments" should occur, they "could never be so extensive as to . . . affect the order of the political system."

Justice Ginsburg, from the bench, remembered Martin Luther King Jr.'s statement about the "arc of the moral universe," which supposedly "bends toward justice." Ginsburg added that it can do so only "*if* there is a steadfast commitment to see the task through to completion." In dissent, she also had a pithy rejoinder to the majority's notion that voting problems were all but wrapped up: "Throwing out preclearance when it has worked and is continuing to work to stop discriminatory changes is like throwing away your umbrella in a rainstorm because you are not getting wet."[55]

Within hours after the Supreme Court decision freed it from the Voting Rights Act, Texas announced a revival of its voter ID law, which the federal court had blocked under the Voting Rights Act for discriminating against minority voters. With the Voting Rights Act out of the picture because of the decision in *Shelby County,* minority plaintiffs had to file a traditional constitutional lawsuit, and a different federal court again found the Texas voter ID law to be discriminatory—purposefully discriminatory against African American and Mexican American voters. That lawsuit took five years and produced only limited results. It was the type of lawsuit whose inadequacy led to passage of the Voting Rights Act, and it shows why the Voting Rights Act remedy was so important.[56]

The Court that struck down the Voting Rights Act was certainly different from earlier Courts—not just the Warren Court, but the Court as led by Chief Justices Hughes, Stone, and Vinson. Those Courts consistently read the Constitution and laws broadly, even expansively, to favor civil rights claims to equality. It was even different from the Burger Court, where major rulings rejecting civil rights claims were leavened with some favorable rulings.

In 1989, in a dissenting opinion, Justice Blackmun made an observation that has seemed more prophetic with each passing day: "One wonders whether the majority still believes that race discrimination—or, more accurately, race discrimination against nonwhites—is a problem in our society, or even remembers that it ever was."[57]

CHAPTER ELEVEN

The War of Words

"Purpose" and "Effect"

Three hundred people were gathered in the East Room of the White House on June 29, 1982, as President Ronald Reagan picked up his pen to sign the Voting Rights Act amendments. Still fresh in the minds of many was the intense political battle that had led up to the festive occasion. The struggle over the Voting Rights Act had stretched out for two years, having been fought in Washington, the South, and even nationwide. Passage of the renewal in 1982 was an overwhelming civil rights victory, but that was neither the beginning nor the end of the battle.[1]

It was and remains a war fought largely over two words: *purpose* and *effect*. Those two words occupy a full chapter here because, although the issue was essentially nonexistent before 1970, the two words have come to occupy so much of the civil rights agenda in the age of the Burger, Rehnquist, and Roberts Courts. As the cases will illustrate, those two words often become proxies in the justices' debate over fundamental concepts like equality and discrimination.[2]

Some hypothetical illustrations show why the difference between the two words is so crucial. For example, suppose a state civil service rule gives veterans a preference in hiring. Should that be upheld because rewarding military service is sound policy? Or should it be thrown out because the military is overwhelmingly male and the *effect* is unfair to women? Or should it be thrown out only if there is proof that legislators' *purpose* was to prefer a mostly male workforce? What about the type or degree of preference?

What if the civil service rule not only gives veterans a hiring preference but also adds an automatic 5 percent wage differential in starting salary? What about a permanent 5 percent differential? What if a law claims to have one purpose but has another, hidden purpose? How does someone prove what a law's "purpose" really is, especially if different lawmakers have different purposes or give different explanations? What if a law has several or many purposes, some open and some hidden, some benign and some not so benign?[3]

Ascertaining and considering the purpose(s) and effect(s) of a law or other action, public or private, is what courts routinely do. Here, however, we will discuss those situations involving questions of discrimination, where the real purpose of an action may be hidden, or where purpose and effect might not match.

For more than 150 years the Supreme Court refused to look at any supposed hidden purpose of a law. The policy was adopted in an 1810 case involving the "Yazoo land frauds." In 1795, when Georgia owned or claimed all the land westward to the Mississippi River, the governor and legislators, all thoroughly bribed, sold 35 million acres of its western lands—about half of present-day Alabama and Mississippi—for about two cents per acre. As soon as a new legislature came into office, it passed the Rescinding Act, calling the deal off. This led to a decade of litigation that ended with the US Supreme Court, in *Fletcher v. Peck* (1810), saying a deal is a deal and the state was not allowed to rescind it because the Constitution prohibits a state from passing a law "impairing the obligation of contracts." Important for our purposes, the Supreme Court said it would not look behind the original law to see if it was crooked.

The judicial policy of taking state laws at face value protected many illegitimate laws over the years. Prime examples were laws to maintain white supremacy after it was supposed to have been ended by the Reconstruction Amendments to the Constitution. Thus, laws with consequences such as keeping African Americans from voting or serving on juries were immunized because the laws' words were neutral or benign. Yet on rare occasions the evil was so obvious that the Supreme Court did step in. In those cases, the concepts of discriminatory purpose and discriminatory effect were used almost interchangeably.[4]

The era of Massive Resistance during the 1950s and 1960s gave Congress and the Supreme Court a growing awareness of government actions with a hidden racial *purpose*, and of other actions having a discriminatory *effect*, even if not accompanied by a discriminatory purpose. Congress incorporated that lesson in the Voting Rights Act of 1965 by making certain voting procedures invalid if they had *either* a discriminatory purpose *or* a discriminatory effect. In several cases the Supreme Court struck the same note as Congress by indicating that certain voting procedures could be unconstitutional if, "designedly or otherwise," they would "operate to minimize or cancel out" racial or political voting minorities.[5]

The modern development begins with two employment discrimination cases, in 1971 and 1976, that are still at the heart of the "purpose versus effect" story half a century later. Notably, the first case involved a private company and the second case involved a government agency. Thereafter, similar though not identical standards would be applied in judging claims of discrimination against public and private actors.

Adopting a Discriminatory Effect Rule

In 1971, in *Griggs v. Duke Power Co.* (1971), the Court decided its first race discrimination case under the new employment discrimination law, Title VII of the Civil Rights Act of 1964. The decision made far-reaching rulings about what constituted discrimination and how to prove it. The main question in *Griggs* was whether a test used to select employees for promotion was racially biased. That question turned out to depend on whether any such discrimination would be measured by "purpose" or "effect."

Before the new law, Duke Power Company, like many employers, had openly restricted African American employees to the lowest-ranking department and barred their transfer into other departments. When Title VII of the Civil Rights Act of 1964 made it illegal to discriminate or classify employees because of their race or color, Duke's racial bars to transfer and promotion ended. But Duke also had rules, originating in the 1950s, that applicants for transfer or promotion had to pass a test. African American employees disproportionately failed it.[6]

In 1966 Willie Griggs and other African American employees sued, charging that Duke Power Company's test unfairly locked them out of better jobs. They alleged that the test was not job-related—that it did not measure the skills needed for work in Duke's plant. As proof of this claim, they pointed out that the test requirement had not applied to people already in the departments when the test requirement began, which meant that many white workers and even supervisors were successful in the advanced departments without ever having taken the test.

Some of the test questions seemed far afield, as, for example: "Does B.C. mean 'before Christ?'" Another question asked if the meanings of two sentences were similar, contradictory, or neither similar nor contradictory. The sentences to compare were: "All good things are cheap; all bad things very dear" and "Goodness is simple; badness is manifold." These may be interesting academic questions, but they did not seem to measure someone's on-the-job ability in an industrial plant. The lawsuit charged that the test was an irrelevant and unnecessary barrier to promotion.[7]

The lower courts upheld the test requirement, finding that Duke had acted in good faith with no discriminatory purpose. Duke's rule was thus approved even though the test requirement limited promotion opportunity for African Americans. At the Supreme Court, however, the plaintiffs were successful. Chief Justice Burger wrote the unanimous opinion. The statute made it illegal to "discriminate against" or "adversely affect" anyone with respect to conditions of employment "because of such individual's race, color, religion, sex, or national origin." The chief justice described the goal of the Civil Rights Act, which, he said, was "plain from its language": "It was to achieve equality of employment opportunities and remove barriers that have operated in the past to favor an identifiable group of white employees over other employees." The Court said Congress's chosen rule was an "effect" test: "Congress directed the thrust of the Act to the consequences of employment practices, not simply the motivation."[8]

The Court added: "Under the Act, practices, procedures, or tests neutral on their face, and even neutral in terms of intent, cannot be maintained if they operate to 'freeze' the status quo of prior discriminatory employment practices." But an "effect" test did not mean that numbers alone (racially different results, a difference in white and Black percentages of successful candidates) established a "discriminatory effect." Once the plaintiffs proved that an employment practice (Duke's test) produced racially different results, there was another step in deciding the case. The test could still be allowed if it was justifiable. To answer that question, the Court turned to a traditional procedural mechanism used to help decide cases: burden of proof. For an overall case and for separate issues in a case, the burden of proof determines *what* has to be proved and *which side* has to prove it. The burden of proof is usually decisive because whoever has the burden of proof must persuade the Court or lose that issue or the entire case.[9]

Analyzing the case under a two-step framework, the Court said the plaintiffs had the initial burden of proving racially different results on the test. They did so, based on statistics and the historical pattern. The question then became whether the test was sufficiently job-related for the racial difference in performance to be justifiable. But which party had the burden of proof on whether the test was job-related? Did the plaintiffs have the burden of proving the test *was not* job-related? Or did Duke have the burden of proving the test *was* job-related?

The Court answered unambiguously that the company had the burden of proof: "Congress has placed on the employer the burden of showing that any given requirement must have a manifest relationship to the employment in question." The specific requirement, according to the Court, was to show the "business necessity" of the test. Completing this second step of the analysis, the Court found that Duke did not meet its burden of proving business necessity, largely because of the satisfactory performance records of white employees and supervisors who had never taken the test. The Court added that "tests are useful servants" but Congress mandated that they not be "masters of reality."[10]

The Court concluded by emphasizing that its rule would not threaten employers' ability to seek and demand high performance, but would instead advance that goal: "Far from disparaging job qualifications as such, Congress has made such qualifications the controlling factor, so that race, religion, nationality and sex become irrelevant." Most remarkable about the *Griggs* decision was how unremarkable it seemed. The decision was unanimous, the opinion just twelve pages long.[11]

Title VII of the Civil Rights Act had an immediate impact on the workplace. Jobs, departments, even entire companies that had been virtually all white a decade earlier were showing progress toward at least a partially integrated workforce. Even the upper ranks were affected. Between 1966 and 1972, African American officials and managers in the workforce more than doubled their (admittedly small) numbers, from less than 1 percent to 2.4 percent. That progress toward racial integration was further spurred by *Griggs*'s interpretation of the new law. With an "effect" test and a shifting burden of proof, lower courts struck down practices with a discriminatory effect. Also, whereas *Griggs* involved a violation of a congressional statute, lower courts in nearly a dozen cases extended the "effect" rule in *Griggs* to claims brought under the equal protection clause of the Constitution.[12]

Adopting a Discriminatory Purpose Rule

In 1976 the Supreme Court decided a case, *Washington v. Davis,* that kept the *Griggs* "effects" rule for certain cases but adopted a "purpose" requirement for other cases. The case, like *Griggs,* involved a test, this time a language-skills test for selection of police officers in the Washington, DC, police department. African American applicants who failed the test alleged that it had a racially discriminatory effect and was not job-related. Because the case arose before the statute (Title VII) was extended to government employees in 1972, the case was brought under the equal protection clause of the Constitution. The difference seemed unimportant at the time. The district court in this case, applying the *Griggs* effects test, found the test sufficiently job-related, but the court of appeals found that the test was not job-related and reversed the district court.

The Supreme Court surprised everyone by paying little attention to the job-relatedness issue. Instead, the Court focused on the fact that the case was brought under a constitutional provision (equal protection clause) rather than a congressional statute (Title VII). The near-universal belief, reflected in numerous lower-court decisions in other cases, was that the same standards—including the *Griggs* "effect" rule—applied to employment discrimination cases whether they were brought under Title VII of the Civil Rights Act or under the equal protection clause of the Constitution. Now, in *Washington v. Davis,* the Court fashioned a different rule for cases alleging a *constitutional* violation, a rule holding that any claimed violation of the equal protection clause of the Constitution must rest upon proof of a discriminatory purpose.[13]

No one anticipated this new rule. All the parties, lawyers, and lower-court judges had tried the case from the beginning on the theory, based on the precedent of *Griggs,* that discriminatory effect was enough to show discrimination in equal protection cases. It was not until oral argument that several justices raised the issue. At that point one of the lawyers turned to another and said, "Now we know why they took the case." The outcome in *Washington v. Davis* was a rule that proof of discriminatory effect, which was sufficient for cases under the statute, Title VII, was insufficient in cases under the Constitution. No justice suggested that there had been a discriminatory purpose in creating or using the test, so the Court held that the test did not violate the equal protection clause. The result was a blanket Supreme Court rule that discriminatory purpose was now a requirement for proving an equal protection violation under the Constitution.[14]

To further complicate the issue, the Court did not undo the *Griggs* rule for cases under Title VII of the Civil Rights Act. The Court specifically said that Congress has power to make a law that can reach beyond a specific clause of the Constitution. But this created two directly opposite standards—an "effect" rule for a case under Title VII, and a "purpose" rule for an all-but-identical case under the equal protection clause. This meant that proof of discriminatory effect without purpose would win a case brought under the Civil Rights Act but lose a case brought under the equal protection clause of the Constitution. The two rules were obviously in tension, and that tension would linger and grow.[15]

The new purpose rule of *Washington v. Davis* was a radical change. The discriminatory purpose rule applied to all discrimination cases under the equal protection clause of the Constitution, not just—and not even primarily—employment discrimination cases. Even before *Brown v. Board of Education,* but especially since that case, the equal protection clause had been the main judicial engine for challenging race discrimination of all types. Now the prospect in all these types of cases of having to prove the purpose behind a law or other official action was daunting. Moreover, lawmakers who in the past had bragged about supporting white supremacy had learned to be more subtle. When subtlety and obfuscation ruled, proving intent was problematic.[16]

To moderate the new rigor of proving discriminatory purpose, the Supreme Court in *Washington v. Davis* said proof of discriminatory purpose need not be direct evidence, like a confession, but could use circumstantial evidence. In *Village of Arlington Heights v. Metropolitan Housing Development Corp.* (1977), the Court showed how this could be done. A development company sued Arlington Heights, a Chicago suburb, after being denied a rezoning permit for land where it planned to build racially integrated low- and moderate-income housing. The question was whether the denial amounted to racial discrimination. Because the case was tried before the decision in *Washington v. Davis,* no proof of discriminatory purpose had been presented, so the Supreme Court ruled against the rezoning. In the opinion, though, the Court established a script for using circumstantial evidence to prove discrimination. It used a two-step process and shifting burdens of proof, much like the approach in *Griggs.* Step 1 required the plaintiff to prove that race played a part—not necessarily the major part or a significant part, but a part among "the numerous competing considerations" that usually play a part in any law or governmental action. If indeed race were "a motivating factor in the decision," then in Step 2, the "burden of proof" *shifted* to the officials or official body to prove they would have made the same decision even if race had not factored into it. The Court explained that shifting a burden of proof is unusual but would be called for if race played a part because "racial discrimination is not just another completing consideration," but was important enough to taint the law or action.[17]

The *Arlington Heights* case came to stand for much more than its specific result. The case established a procedure that held out a possibility of proving racial purpose and thus ameliorated, at least to some extent, the difficulty of proving discriminatory purpose. The procedure became the central feature of cases involving discrimination claims under the equal protection clause—that is, where no statute was available. The *Arlington Heights* opinion also listed some types of circumstantial evidence that could help show that race played a part, including discriminatory effect of the challenged decision (still highly relevant even though no longer enough by itself), historical background, sequence of events in the decision-making process, and anything else that might logically suggest a discriminatory purpose for an action. This relevant evidence is "circumstantial."

The concepts of direct evidence and circumstantial evidence can be confusing. Direct evidence is what one sees or hears, whereas circumstantial evidence refers to any other evidence that is relevant but not direct. Contrary to common belief, neither is inherently stronger than the other; they are simply different types of evidence. For example, if you see someone breaking into a house, your identification of that person is direct evidence of who the burglar was. But if it was nighttime and raining, and you were a block away without your eyeglasses on, that is obviously weak evidence, even though direct. In this case, circumstantial evidence, such as the burglar's wallet or fingerprints left behind at the scene, would be the stronger evidence.

The new rule on the necessity for a racial purpose raised obvious questions: Why should discriminatory conditions be allowed just for inability to find a perpetrator with a guilty intent? Does the Fourteenth Amendment really mean what it says, or, to use Justice Harlan's words in the *Civil Rights Cases* (1883), is it just "a splendid bauble"? At first the questions were largely confined to lawyers and judges, but then a new case extended the rule to voting discrimination and the purpose rule took on a more public face.[18]

Discrimination in Voting Procedures

In 1980, in *Mobile v. Bolden*, the Supreme Court faced the issue of discriminatory purpose in a voting case claiming that elections for city commissioners in the Deep South city of Mobile, Alabama, were racially discriminatory. The specific problem addressed in this case was at-large elections. Since 1911 Mobile's elections had been at-large, meaning that each commissioner was voted on by all voters city-wide rather than by just the voters in a particular district or ward. Under this system, Mobile, whose one-third Black population was concentrated in one part of the city, had never elected an African American city commissioner.[19]

The Supreme Court had a recent precedent directly on the subject, the unanimous 1973 Texas decision striking down at-large elections in Dallas and San Antonio, *White v. Regester*. In that case the Court made no finding on purpose or effect; it ruled against at-large elections because the "totality of circumstances" showed discrimination in the local history and structure of the community. Evidence included recent official racial discrimination, aggravating features of the election law, a white-controlled slating process, and more, all adding up to a history of consistent defeat of candidates supported by minority voters. "Totality of circumstances" became the way to present evidence in cases involving vote discrimination, such as gerrymandering.

The Mobile case shared another distinction with the Texas case; they both reflected community mobilization by minority voters to achieve a political voice. The Texas case involved two minority groups and two counties. African Americans had experience working with legal organizations and used that in presenting the case against the Dallas County district. For Mexican Americans in Bexar County (San Antonio), it was more of a beginning. The Supreme Court had only once before decided a case based on a claim of discrimination against Latino people as a class—the jury discrimination case of *Hernandez v. Texas* (1954), decided by the Supreme Court two weeks before *Brown v. Board of Education*. The Bexar County portion of the Texas challenge was the first Supreme Court case for the new legal organization Mexican American Legal Defense and Education Fund (MALDEF). Organized on the model of the NAACP Legal Defense and Education Fund, and led at first by General Counsel Mario Obledo, MALDEF would go on to play a major role in many cases involving the rights of Latino people. Fittingly enough, its lawyer in *White v. Regester* was Ed Idar, who as a young lawyer twenty years earlier had assisted in *Hernandez v. Texas*. The unanimous victory for San Antonio voters in *White v. Regester* was an important milestone, especially coming just months after the defeat in the Texas school financing case, *San Antonio Independent School District v. Rodriguez* (1973) (in which MALDEF was not involved).

The *Mobile* case also reflected local organization. John Leflore worked in the Mobile post office, which gave him a degree of independence. In the 1920s he organized the Mobile branch of the NAACP, and when the state shut down the NAACP in Alabama in the 1950s, he organized a new group in Mobile called the Non-Partisan Voters League. The League combined organization and litigation, including the Mobile school desegregation case. Then Leflore turned his attention to the local elections, and in 1975 a lawsuit was filed challenging the at-large elections for city commission and county school board.

The lead plaintiff was Wiley Bolden, long active even in the leanest years of Alabama's racial history. Fifty years earlier, as he testified during the trial, he had fought in World War I, and when he was discharged he received a certificate from President Woodrow Wilson thanking him for his service to the country. When he returned to Mobile, he went down to the registrar's office with his certificate, but it didn't matter—he was still not allowed to register to vote. Other testimony showed that when one of the white incumbents in Mobile attracted African Americans' votes, that became a campaign issue and led to his defeat. The city's own expert witness testified that African American support was the "kiss of death" in Mobile elections.[20]

The lower courts said the totality of the circumstances in Mobile, Alabama, added up to a classic *White v. Regester* case and also provided strong circumstantial proof of racially discriminatory purpose satisfying the rule of *Washington v. Davis.* At the Supreme Court, Justice White agreed that Mobile's at-large election system was unconstitutional, because the proof met the requirements of both *White v. Regester* and *Washington v. Davis*—both opinions he had written. But Justice White was in dissent. The Supreme Court majority reversed the lower courts' rulings and upheld the at-large election system.[21]

The principal opinion by Justice Stewart did more than simply reverse this case. The opinion made clear that voting discrimination claims under the Constitution require proof of discriminatory purpose, and in addition, made the task of proving discriminatory purpose exceptionally difficult. The Supreme Court's repeated promises that discriminatory purpose could be proved by circumstantial evidence were nowhere in sight. "Totality of the circumstances," which had been sufficient to prove discrimination for a unanimous Court in *White v. Regester,* was not even mentioned. Neither was the *Arlington Heights* circumstantial evidence formula, with its shifting of the burden of proof. Circumstantial evidence was mentioned only to equate it with tenuous evidence. The *City of Mobile* opinion gave officials a wider field for discrimination, with little to fear from the courts. As the *Washington Post* reported, those who opposed any Supreme Court interference with local discriminatory rules for voting saw the case as good news: "White city officials, . . . who say they have waited a generation for a favorable omen from the justices, said they now believe they have one."[22]

Supporters of voting rights saw a possible solution in a statute prohibiting voting discrimination: the 1965 Voting Rights Act. Section 2 of the act was patterned on the language of the Fifteenth Amendment, prohibiting racial discrimination in voting. The Supreme Court in the *Mobile* case therefore interpreted Section 2 to require proof of discriminatory purpose, just like the Fifteenth Amendment. But as shown by the different rules of *Griggs* (effects test) and *Washington v. Davis* (purpose test), a statute could have a different rule than the Constitution. Thus, unlike the Fifteenth Amendment, Congress could amend Section 2 of the Voting Rights Act to eliminate the requirement of proving discriminatory purpose.

By sheer coincidence, the time for seeking a change was already at hand. Scheduled for congressional renewal were certain sections of the Voting Rights Act. The preclearance provision had been extended twice and was due to expire in August 1982 if Congress did not extend it again. Also scheduled for renewal was a section requiring that voter assistance be available in Spanish and several other minority voters' languages. With voting discrimination still a problem, as verified by congressional hearings, civil rights and congressional leaders were already gearing up for renewal of those sections. They channeled their dismay over the Supreme Court's 1980 *Mobile* decision into planning for congressional action. Early in 1981 the House of Representatives introduced legislation to accomplish three major tasks: extend preclearance, extend language assistance, and amend Section 2 to clarify that proof of purpose was not necessary for a claim of discrimination. Although putting the three together might have been expected to make the task harder, the combination actually strengthened the effort by making the bill a platform for what amounted to a national referendum on the right to vote.[23]

A broad coalition backing the bill included not only traditional civil rights organizations like the NAACP, but supporters like the League of Women Voters, national labor unions, and religious groups. They provided detailed information to their members nationwide, who found ready audiences in their senators, representatives, and local media. A dozen Fortune 500 companies signed a full-page ad captioned "Do You Remember Your First Vote?" and ran it in major daily newspapers across the country. It was not difficult to explain what was wrong with the Supreme Court decision and a purpose rule for voting. Two main problems with the purpose rule resonated with people, and the *Mobile* case illustrated them both. First, it seemed illogical. Average citizens knew, for example, that city councils in the Deep South had always been kept all white, and they had no trouble understanding that that was wrong and that a city council should not still be all white fifteen years after the Voting Rights Act. The Supreme Court's notion that the city council could stay all white unless some specific guilty perpetrator was found made no sense. Second, people could see that proving discriminatory purpose would be difficult or even nearly impossible, especially if the critical event was far in the past—like an old city ordinance. As one newspaper put it pungently, "It would be quite a trick for anyone to subpoena the legislators from their graves to testify about their racial motivations."[24]

The right to vote was not yet a strongly partisan issue, and both major parties supported the Voting Rights Act. Nevertheless, there were some opponents. One was newly elected Republican president Ronald Reagan, a longtime adversary of civil rights laws. His election in 1980 also put Republicans in control of the Senate and therefore of Senate committees.

A disheartened Justice Brennan asked his friend Thurgood Marshall, "Is it really true that Strom Thurmond is going to be chairman of the Judiciary Committee?" Yes, it was true. The committee assigned to hear any voting rights bill was chaired by the Dixiecrat nominee for president in 1948, instead of strong civil rights supporter Ted Kennedy of Massachusetts.

The chief opposition to the Voting Rights Act came from philosophical or ideological conservatives. One strong opponent, a prolific defender of the purpose requirement, was a young John Roberts, serving as special assistant to the attorney general. In that role, Roberts wrote a stream of memoranda opposing the new legislation. "In essence it would establish a quota system in electoral politics," he wrote; "Just as we oppose quotas in employment and education, so too we oppose them in elections."[25]

To respond to these fears, several provisions of the renewal efforts were designed to ensure that, even without a "discriminatory purpose" test, voting discrimination would depend on the totality of circumstances, not just an imbalance of election results. First, the bill used the term discriminatory "result" instead of the already-controversial "effect." Second, key language from *White v. Regester,* the original "totality of the circumstances" case, was included in the bill itself.

In the Senate, the two floor leaders on the bill, Democrat Ted Kennedy and Republican Bob Dole, agreed on some useful changes. The result was called—depending on who was speaking—the Kennedy-Dole bill or the Dole-Kennedy bill. There were some efforts to derail the bill by substituting a toothless version. Senator Thurmond, who had an ongoing relationship with a group of mayors of small, mostly Black towns in South Carolina, scheduled a meeting with them for one Saturday morning in Columbia in April 1982. One of the bill's supporters heard about the meeting, surmised that Thurmond's major purpose was to lobby the mayors for the toothless substitute, and called one of the mayors on Friday afternoon to alert him. The next morning, when Senator Thurmond started talking about voting rights with the mayors, he was met with a chorus of voices all saying, "We want the Kennedy-Dole bill."[26]

Senator Thurmond may not have been chastened or even surprised, but he voted for the bill in the end, along with almost every other representative and senator. The House vote to approve the bill was 389–24, and the Senate vote was 85–8. President Reagan signed it with great fanfare, as described at the beginning of this chapter. The purpose (intent) test was puckishly interred, at least for that day, by Senator Russell Long of Louisiana. As he prepared to cast his vote, a reporter asked him what he thought of the "intent" test. Long replied, "The road to Hell is paved with good intentions." With that, he walked into the Senate chamber and cast his vote for the bill.[27]

When the new voting law came before the Supreme Court in a districting case from North Carolina, the Court interpreted the results test more or less as written, and for the last half dozen years under Chief Justice Burger, there were no major changes on the purpose-versus-effects front regarding voting. In 2013, as discussed in Chapter 10, the Supreme Court did eliminate the preclearance procedure of the Voting Rights Act. But the Court has not hurt Section 2—so far.[28]

Griggs under Assault—*Wards Cove Packing Co.*

A major rollback of the law of employment discrimination came after William Rehnquist became chief justice. Emblematic of the change was the string of four cases in ten days in 1989. One of those four cases, *Patterson v. McLean Credit Union,* was described in Chapter 10. A second important case involved the issue of purpose versus effect, actually bringing to an end the somewhat peaceful coexistence of the two rules in employment cases. More precisely, the very existence of the effects test came under challenge, as it continues to be challenged to this day.

That case, *Wards Cove Packing Co. v. Atonio* (1989), was an assault on Burger's unanimous opinion in the 1971 *Griggs* case. *Griggs* not only adopted a discriminatory effect rule, but set up rules on procedures and burdens of proof to make the effects test a powerful tool against discrimination. Now, in 1989, the *Wards Cove* decision dismantled each rule. Like many other cases where a precedent is not formally overruled, the damage was somewhat obscured. The headline of the story was that *Griggs* remained alive, but the fine print said "just barely."

Wards Cove involved three salmon canneries operated for the summer months at a remote location in Alaska. The canneries had two separate and stratified workforces—non-cannery jobs, which were mostly skilled and mostly held by white employees, and cannery jobs, which were lower-paid, unskilled, and held almost entirely by nonwhite employees, mostly Filipinos and Alaska Natives. The two groups not only filled different jobs but also lived and ate in segregated housing and mess halls, all of which the employer contended was a function of the isolated location and the need to operate efficient work shifts.

The case had been bouncing up and down the lower courts for several years and was scheduled for another trial when the Supreme Court stepped in to set ground rules for the new trial. The Supreme Court made three changes in the *Griggs* rules, all dealing with the burden of proof, and all making discrimination harder to prove.[29]

The first change was in defining the plaintiffs' initial burden. The court of appeals had ruled that the Wards Cove employees met their initial burden

Cannery crew, mostly consisting of nonwhite employees, at Wards Cove Packing Co., Ketchikan, Alaska, 1940, site of *Wards Cove v. Atonio* (1989).

of proof. They met that burden by showing that the employer's overall recruiting and hiring process had a racial result—keeping the composition of Wards Cove's skilled workforce mostly white. The Supreme Court, however, now said that the method of analysis approved by the court of appeals was not satisfactory. Rather, the employees' evidence had to break down the overall process into its constituent parts—nepotism, separate hiring channels, rehiring preference, ad hoc subjective hiring, and so forth—and demonstrate a separate statistical showing of racially different results for each one of these particular hiring practices. Of course, employment practices typically, as here, blend together, making such a proof requirement both meaningless and impossible.

The Supreme Court continued. Its second change abolished the shifting of the burden that *Griggs* had ordained. The Supreme Court now said that if the employees met their initial burden of proving that the employment practice produced racially different results, the burden of proof would not shift to the employer (as had been done in *Griggs*) to show that the business practice was justified. Instead, the plaintiff had the burden of proving that the practice was *not* justified.

Finally, a third change made the particular employment practice easier to justify and harder to challenge. In *Griggs* the Court said an employment practice, if it produced racially different results, had to meet the "business necessity" standard to be valid, but now *Wards Cove* said it just had to meet an employer's "legitimate business goals"—a far more employer-friendly standard. And of course, with the burden now on the employees, they had to prove the negative—that the hiring process did *not* meet legitimate business goals.

The Court's ruling meant essentially that the Wards Cove company was not obliged to justify its hiring practices. The case went far toward negating any chance to fight employment discrimination in the courts. The vote was 5–4. Stevens and Blackmun, joined by Brennan and Marshall, were in dissent. Stevens called the majority's rulings a "sojourn into judicial activism." Blackmun said the discriminatory effect rule might still be technically alive, but the Court's rulings "immunize these practices from attack" under that rule. He summarized, "Today a bare majority of the Court takes three major strides backwards in the battle against race discrimination."[30]

Congress promptly enacted the Civil Rights Act of 1991 (see Chapter 10). The new law amended Title VII to undo each of the Court's holdings in *Wards Cove* and restore the previous understanding of the burden of proof based on *Griggs*. Unhappily for Frank Atonio and his fellow workers, the new 1991 law contained a particular thorn for them and a gift for Wards Cove Packing Company. A unique section of the 1991 law made its new changes not applicable to cases filed before 1975 and first decided after 1983—meaning just one case, *Wards Cove v. Atonio*. In the end, the case dragged on for a decade under the Supreme Court's 1989 rules that no longer applied to anyone else in the country. It finally came to an end in 2001, with a final district court ruling against the plaintiffs. Since then the fishing industry has changed, and the Wards Cove cannery is now closed.[31]

Ricci v. DeStefano

The Supreme Court continued to limit the effects rule after John Roberts became chief justice in 2005. In *Ricci v. DeStefano* (2009), a case involving New Haven firefighters, the concepts of discriminatory purpose and discriminatory effect were pitted directly against each other. Justice Scalia called it a "war." The Court decision essentially declared purpose the winner and effect the loser.

The case had a curious origin: the employer, the New Haven Fire Department, was claiming that its own test for promoting firefighters was unfair. Fire departments have long been some of the most segregated institutions in America. New Haven was no exception. In recent years, with a 60 percent minority population in the city, the department's line levels integrated, but not the officers' ranks. In 2003 the city announced openings for fifteen lieutenants and captains. It aimed to fill these slots according to a plan in the collective bargaining agreement: first, a test—60 percent written and 40 percent oral—followed by interviews of the highest-scoring candidates. Test results showed that almost all those who qualified for interviews were white, with few Latino or Black candidates. The results were extreme enough to meet the initial burden of proof required in a discriminatory effect case. Concerned by the test's apparent discriminatory effect, the city conducted hearings that produced evidence both for and against the validity of the test. Knowing it would be sued by one group or the other no matter which way it decided, the city chose to reject the test results. Thereupon, a group of candidates who had scored high on the test, seventeen of them white and one Hispanic, sued the city and the mayor, John DeStefano. They claimed that canceling the results after seeing that white candidates passed and minority candidates failed was purposeful racial discrimination in violation of Title VII of the Civil Rights Act of 1964.

The lower courts upheld the city in its cancellation of the test, but the Supreme Court reversed the decision in a 5–4 opinion by Justice Kennedy. The majority opinion barely acknowledged Chief Justice Burger's unanimous 1971 opinion in *Griggs*. The crux of the Court's opinion was that discriminatory purpose was "the original, foundational prohibition of Title VII," whereas the discriminatory effect rule, not expressly included in the original statute, was a judicial interpretation added in *Griggs,* and not occupying the same priority. Justice Ginsburg, in dissent, saw a very different relationship between discriminatory purpose and discriminatory effect. She saw discriminatory effect as a "central" part of Title VII. It stood on an "equal footing" with discriminatory purpose, and together they aimed at "ending workplace discrimination and promoting genuinely equal opportunity."[32]

The practical question was how to reconcile the purpose and effect claims. This boiled down to the question of how strong the evidence of the test's discriminatory effect had to be to withstand the white firefighters' claim of discriminatory purpose. The lower courts, as Ginsburg had done, treated the outcomes of discriminatory purpose and discriminatory effect as equivalent. If fewer job opportunities or fewer college admissions result from a policy, should it matter if the policy itself was based on intent? In the lower courts' view, the evidence of discriminatory effect (the results plus evidence at the city's hearing) gave the city "good cause" to cancel the test.

The Supreme Court majority said good cause was not good enough. Discriminatory effect is not as important as discriminatory purpose. To justify canceling the test, they said, the city had to show that there was "a strong basis in evidence" to believe there was a discriminatory effect. The phrase "strong basis in evidence" sounds reasonable and not so different from "good cause," but in reality there is a radical difference. "Strong basis in evidence" is a formula almost impossible to meet. The Supreme Court devised this measure for judging any race-based plan. Indeed, the majority seemed to view the effects test in a highly disfavored category.[33]

The case illustrated two fundamentally different views of discrimination. Kennedy and Ginsburg both saw a familiar-looking test and promotion process that produced results that were racially very different, with no overt signs of anyone's racially discriminatory purpose. To Ginsburg, that was the beginning of the inquiry, whereas to Kennedy it was the end of the inquiry.[34]

Fair Housing Act

Six years later a fair housing case seemed primed for another assault on the discriminatory effect rule (equivalent to the Court's phrase "disparate impact"). In *Texas Department of Housing and Community Affairs v. Inclusive Communities Project, Inc.* (2015), the Supreme Court would decide whether the Fair Housing Act of 1968 allowed suits challenging discriminatory effect or whether the act required proof of discriminatory purpose.

The Fair Housing Act of 1968 used the same "because of" words that conservative justices had increasingly been equating with "purpose." True, lower courts had been allowing discriminatory effect cases under the Fair Housing Act for more than forty years, but the Supreme Court had never decided the issue. The Court's hostility to *Griggs* and its rulings in the *Wards Cove* case and the New Haven firefighters case (*Ricci*) suggested that it might be about to end all discriminatory effect cases completely.[35]

Everyone knew the stakes were high. This was the third year in a row that the Supreme Court had taken a case to decide whether the Fair Housing Act allowed lawsuits based on discriminatory effect. The first two cases had been promptly settled when the Supreme Court announced it would hear them. But there had been no way to scuttle this third case. More than fifty amicus curiae briefs were filed on both sides, supplemented by the usual public opinion blitz, with editorials and op-eds on both sides. This Texas case involved allocation of federal funds to build low-income housing. The state housing authority concentrated these funds in African American neighborhoods. While such a distribution helped the housing situation in these neighborhoods, it perpetuated segregated housing, keeping low-income families out of white neighborhoods. The Inclusive Communities Project sued for a distribution that would spur more integrated housing.[36]

On January 21, 2015, Justice Kennedy delivered the Supreme Court opinion. On one hand, he was the author of the New Haven firefighters opinion that was dismissive of *Griggs;* on the other hand, he was the one member of the five-vote conservative bloc who sometimes broke ranks. This time, analyzing the legislative history of the Fair Housing Act and several other statutes, he ruled for a 5–4 Court that the suits under the Fair Housing Act could be based on discriminatory effect. *Griggs* was still alive. Kennedy relied heavily on *Griggs,* and he found other words in the complex structure of the Fair Housing Act ("otherwise make unavailable") to leaven the purpose-sounding words "because of." A critical part of his reasoning was government's long complicity in promoting segregated housing patterns, ranging from judicial enforcement of restrictive covenants to federally subsidized mortgage redlining. Kennedy also referred to events that formed some of the background of the Fair Housing Act, including the assassination of Martin Luther King Jr. and issuance of the report of the 1968 Kerner Commission, which outlined the deep racial divisions in the country and helped lead to Congress's adoption of the Fair Housing Act in 1968.[37]

In response to Kennedy's opinion, the four conservatives joined in a vehement dissent by Alito, while Thomas added an even more strident separate dissent. Both dissenting opinions made it clear that *Griggs* was their target, attacking it by name forty-three times in their two dissenting opinions. Thomas derided the discriminatory effect theory as "made of sand" and said that in *Griggs* the 1971 Supreme Court had simply been hoodwinked by an administrative agency (EEOC, the Equal Employment Opportunity Commission) that had an agenda of its own.[38]

The bottom line in the *Inclusive Communities* case was that "effects" cases were alive under the Fair Housing Act. It was not an unalloyed victory for supporters. Kennedy put enough restrictions in the opinion to ensure that such cases would be few and narrow, but the overall concept had survived. The opinions in the *Inclusive Communities* case show that "effect" and *Griggs* hang by a thread. Five justices viewed racially segregated neighborhoods as shaped by governmental policy decisions, and therefore subject to challenge by law. Four justices in the minority could not see that state involvement created separate and unequal housing opportunities. The view that "fair housing opportunities for all" should be limited to "eradicating intentional discrimination" did not prevail.[39]

Losing Ground on Discriminatory Purpose

Although the modern Court has deprecated discriminatory effect as compared to discriminatory purpose, minority plaintiffs who do bring claims of discriminatory purpose fare no better. In 2000, even before preclearance was ended in *Shelby County v. Holder* (2013), the Supreme Court weakened the Voting Rights Act by exempting a major category of intentionally discriminatory voting changes from the act's coverage. The case that did this began in the 1990s, when the school board of Bossier Parish, Louisiana, redrew the lines for electing its twelve members. Louisiana was one of the states that had to preclear its voting changes, so the parish school board had to show that the new plan did not have the purpose or effect "of denying or abridging the right to vote on account of race or color." Although 20 percent of the parish was African American, and that population was mainly concentrated in one area, no African American had ever been elected as a school board member. The parish's new plan, like the previous one, had no majority-Black districts. In *Reno v. Bossier Parish School Board* (2000), the Supreme Court did not apply the law as written. Instead it held that a purposely discriminatory plan would not violate the Voting Rights Act unless it also had a purpose to make the discrimination worse than before. The 5–4 opinion was written by Justice Scalia, ordinarily the justice most wedded to reading the words of a law exactly as written. Constricting the no-discriminatory-purpose rule had no support in the words of the statute, and it contradicted previous Supreme Court cases under the Warren Court and also the Burger Court. Both previous Courts recognized that "Congress intended that the Act be given 'the broadest possible scope.'" Evidence in Bossier Parish showed a "tenacious determination to maintain the status quo," and that evidence would have blocked the change as the Voting Rights Act was written. But there was no proof that the parish wanted to make discrimination worse, so the Court approved the plan.[40]

Two other cases, in 2018 and 2020, combined to undermine, or even abandon, procedures that had become fundamental tools enabling minority challengers to meet the Court's demanding requirement of proving discriminatory purpose. In 1977 in *Village of Arlington Heights v. Metropolitan Housing Development Corp.*, the Supreme Court established two rules: first, that discriminatory purpose can be proved by circumstantial evidence; second, that there is a two-stage process with a shifting burden of proof in the second stage. In the two recent cases, the Supreme Court took aim at both rules.

In 2018, the Supreme Court reversed a lower court for conducting exactly the kind of examination that *Arlington Heights* prescribed. The lower

The Supreme Court in the late 1990s. The nine justices include appointees of five of the last six presidents of the twentieth century—all except Jimmy Carter, the only president to serve a full term and have no Supreme Court appointments. Front row, left to right: Antonin Scalia, John Paul Stevens, Chief Justice William Rehnquist, Sandra Day O'Connor, Anthony Kennedy. Back row, left to right: Ruth Bader Ginsburg, David Souter, Clarence Thomas, Stephen Breyer.

court had struck down several districts in a Texas redistricting plan after concluding they had been drawn with racially discriminatory purpose. One factor considered by the lower court was the Texas legislature's readoption of those districts from a previous, questionable plan without giving these districts any new consideration. The language of *Arlington Heights* specifically approved this category of inquiry, saying, "The specific sequence of events leading up to the challenged decision also may shed some light on the decisionmaker's purposes." Yet, in *Abbott v. Perez* (2018), in a 5–4 opinion written by Justice Alito, the Supreme Court harshly criticized the lower court for this inquiry. Even though the lower court had (as required) carefully kept the burden of proof on the challengers to prove their case, the Supreme Court said the lower court's inquiry forced the state to defend itself and that this was putting the burden of proof on the state. This mistaken accusation that the lower court had put the burden of proof on the wrong side was no mere technicality; under the rules of evidence, it allowed the Supreme Court to take the factual issue of "purpose" completely out of the lower court's hands, decide the factual issue for itself (something that the Supreme Court as a reviewing court would ordinarily not be allowed to do), and make its own finding that these Texas districts were free of discriminatory purpose and were perfectly valid.[41]

The second case ignoring the *Arlington Heights* rules came before the Supreme Court in 2020. A small group of Black owners of TV outlets was denied a contract for space on a cable network, and, in a suit under the Civil Rights Act of 1866, claimed it was denied because of race. The lower court found enough substance for the case to go forward. In *Comcast Corp. v. National Association of African American–Owned Media*, however, the Supreme Court ordered the case dismissed. The lower court had used the standard method of a shifting burden of proof in cases involving discrimination. The Court bluntly rejected this standard method. Declaring that it is a "textbook" rule that a plaintiff bears the burden of proof throughout a case, the Supreme Court was seemingly unaware of its own *Arlington Heights* rule that specifically includes a two-stage process that shifts the burden of proof when race is shown in the first stage.[42]

With the *Abbott v. Perez* and *Comcast* cases, it increasingly seems that discriminatory effect does not matter, and discriminatory purpose is beyond proof. The debate over two words, *purpose* and *effect*, represents major discord about the very nature of discrimination. The resolution of that debate might determine if the bright promise reflected in the Reconstruction Amendments and Congress's civil rights laws will be realized.

CHAPTER TWELVE

Affirmative Action

Color Blind or Color Conscious

In the early 1970s, at a time of wide support for affirmative action, two young minority students entered Ivy League schools and set out on paths that would lead them far from their roots. The young African American man, from rural Georgia, graduated from the College of the Holy Cross in Massachusetts and entered Yale Law School in 1971; the young Latina woman, from the Bronx, started her undergraduate work at Princeton University in 1972, after which she too went on to Yale Law School. Both spent part of the 1980s in law enforcement, he as head of an agency enforcing civil rights law, and she as a criminal prosecutor. Their careers paralleled each other again when President George H. W. Bush named them both to judgeships in 1991, he to the US Supreme Court, and she to a district court in Manhattan. The young man, Clarence Thomas, became the Supreme Court's most vigorous opponent of affirmative action, while the young woman, Sonia Sotomayor, who would join the Supreme Court in 2009, became affirmative action's most vigorous supporter.[1]

For more than fifty years, since the 1970s, the issue of affirmative action has been a central battleground in America, and it is still part of the ongoing "culture wars." The past fifty years, however, are only part of the story of affirmative action in modern America. Affirmative action on a far more massive scale than anything imagined today dates back to the desperate needs during the Great Depression of the 1930s. Government response focused on the needs of white people, and that focus continued on through the war and postwar years. In the 1940s–1960s, the United States saw a massive affirmative action program, funded by federal and state laws and other government assistance, that created a class of 35 million new home-owning families. Affirmative action created a middle class and new suburbs. In rural areas, government affirmative action helped farmers keep family land.[2]

The new suburbs were highly segregated and mostly white. African Americans were frequently left behind in increasingly crowded and declining urban rental housing, where redlining defined the neighborhood. Even the GI Bill helped many more white than Black veterans. Farm programs saved white farmers while allowing evictions of Black farmers off the land. So too with major laws benefiting workers—Social Security, minimum wage, and unemployment insurance. All were written in ways that covered most white workers but excluded two-thirds of all Black workers. Charles Houston, who successfully challenged segregated law schools, white labor unions, and restrictive covenants, found the many federal laws and regulations frustrating. Testifying before Congress, he said they were "like a sieve with holes just big enough for the majority of Negroes to fall through." Truly, it was an age, as characterized by historian Ira Katznelson, "when affirmative action was white."[3]

The consequences of affirmative action for white people are visible today. As discrimination has gradually decreased, the racial gap in current *income* has narrowed, but the racial gap in *wealth,* or net worth—which is so heavily dependent on the past—is still astronomical. Data from 2017 show that white *income* is now less than twice as much as Black income (actual ratio of 1.7 to 1). The same 2017 data, however, show that the ratio of white to Black *wealth* remains at a staggering 9.7 to 1. This history and these data do not decide the constitutional or other questions involved in today's affirmative action debate. But they do show that favoring white people did not end in the long-ago past. Race-based affirmative action is not new—the only new aspects are the race of the beneficiaries and the keen debate about it.[4]

The Bible (Exodus 12:35–36) tells us that when the Egyptians freed the Hebrew slaves, they gave them gold, silver, and fine garments in addition to freedom. No such gifts went to America's freed slaves—no forty acres, no mules. Instead, for generations, efforts were made to keep them shackled to white people's land and out of white people's businesses. Finally, after 300 years of slavery and Jim Crow, when the good jobs, land, housing, schools, business opportunities, and—not least of all—money, had been going to white people, the United States made a commitment of sorts to a national policy of freedom and racial equality.

The goal of overturning centuries-long patterns of racial hierarchy and institutional exclusion was monumental. Generations of rigid law and custom had created a deeply rooted caste society, with signs of inequality and separation everywhere. This was universally understood at a personal level. One of the authors recalls a party, in the days before the Vietnam War, celebrating an African American soldier's retirement from a twenty-year career in the relatively integrated US Army. Asked what he planned to do next, the veteran said he would like to use his military experience to join a city fire department. There was a stunned silence among the guests, followed by shrieks and guffaws of unending laughter. "You? A fireman? Do you know what color you are? Why don't you try something more reasonable, like flying to the moon or becoming head of General Motors? Firefighting—that's a white man's job."

Nor was the field of fighting fires unique. The United States has always faced a conflict between ideal and reality. America's ideals of justice, equality, and liberty are for the individual rather than a group; yet the nation's institutions, led by the state and federal governments, have long violated that ideal, enslaving a group, denying opportunity to a group. This has created a present-day reality that is far from the ideal. The question for the nation is how to undo that reality. The particular question here concerns the proper role of the Supreme Court—which helped to entrench that reality with its interpretation of the Constitution and in the culture. Part of that question involves "race-conscious decision making," including what is called affirmative action.

This chapter traces the movement of the US Supreme Court from a tenuous support for some color-conscious remedies under Chief Justice Burger to a near-rejection of affirmative action under Chief Justices Rehnquist and Roberts. The Court has addressed cases involving traditional forms of affirmative action, but has also chosen to expand its anti-affirmative-action theory to other areas of the law as well.

Notably, the Supreme Court debate has been framed in terms of the Fourteenth Amendment, which so often is called "color-blind." Many people use the term "color-blind" to mean free from prejudice, a good thing when serving all customers, when being kind to one's neighbors and compassionate to strangers. On the other hand, if color is the root of a problem—segregated schools, voting, or redistricting, for example—then being color-blind means not seeing the problem. Some justices say that color-conscious decision making is constitutionally permissible and is one essential tool for overcoming entrenched racial discrimination. Other justices say that the Constitution mandates color blindness; justices in this group seem to hold either that color blindness is the way to overcome racial inequality or that this question is irrelevant to their work of applying the Constitution and laws.[5]

Origins

Many early civil rights efforts, especially desegregation, focused on dismantling the governmental structures that kept African Americans "in their place." This was not the same as achieving equality, or even equal opportunity. In 1965 President Lyndon Johnson recognized the limits of abstract freedom: "You do not wipe away the scars of centuries by saying, 'now you are free.' You do not take a person who for years has been hobbled by chains and liberate him, bring him up to the starting line of a race, and say, 'you are free to compete with all the others,' and still justly believe that you have been completely fair." Johnson followed up on September 24, 1965, with Executive Order 11246, which forbade government contractors from discriminating on the basis of race and required them to take affirmative action to ensure against race discrimination. He was the fifth consecutive president to sign an executive order barring race discrimination by government contractors, and he was the second one (after President Kennedy) to use the phrase "affirmative action."[6]

When President Richard Nixon took office in 1969, his administration continued to enforce the antidiscrimination executive orders and even put teeth into them. A new order targeted the notoriously all-white construction industry in several large cities. Called the "Philadelphia Plan," the order required federal government contractors to set specific goals and timetables for hiring African Americans (and later, women) to overcome entrenched discrimination in construction jobs.

By the 1970s many white people and predominantly white institutions began to question previously accepted standards and practices that effectively gave opportunities only to white people. Some abandoned unnecessary and unfair practices, like the practice of recruiting new employees by word-of-mouth references from current (white) employees. In other instances, special—and for the first time, positive—attention was paid to Black applicants. For example, some universities began considering African American applicants by favorable standards like those used for evaluating some other categories, such as "legacies" (children of alumni).[7]

This was also the period that acknowledged the historic and continuing discrimination against women, especially in the workplace and the professions. In a series of cases beginning in the early 1970s, several of which were argued by future justice Ruth Bader Ginsburg, the Supreme Court fashioned a body of law on the subject of sex discrimination. Opportunities for women increased, whether in law or medical schools, construction work, or female-headed contracting companies. Overall, women took advantage of new opportunities.[8]

At first, increasing minority opportunities was a widely popular goal. Then, as white people for the first time faced competition from African Americans for jobs, college admission, and business contracts, opposition mounted. Some white people objected that African Americans were getting favored treatment in the competition—favored treatment that used to go only to white men.

Even the Constitution pointed in two directions. The Thirteenth Amendment not only destroyed slavery but outlawed its "badges and incidents" in a still-living commitment to bring freedom and undo slavery's harm to the formerly enslaved race and their descendants. The Fourteenth Amendment, instituted to guarantee citizenship and equal protection to African Americans, used universal language that applies to all persons without regard to race. Advocates and opponents of race-conscious decision making could all find support for their positions in the Constitution.

Because the efforts toward affirmative action overtly treated people differently based on race (or sex), legal issues arose from the start, and moral and historical issues along with them. In this country and elsewhere, separating people by race or religion has often or typically been done for evil purposes. America's past history of slavery and Jim Crow was race discrimination in only one direction—against African Americans, both enslaved and free.

As public debate swirled, the Supreme Court stayed out of it for a decade. In 1970, when contractors and unions challenged the goals and timetables in the Philadelphia Plan, the lower courts upheld the plan and the Supreme Court skipped the case by denying review. Another case, brought by a white student after being rejected by a law school, did reach the Supreme Court but was then dismissed on a procedural ground. The wait for a Supreme Court decision on affirmative action ended in 1978 with the *Bakke* case involving student admissions to medical school, followed quickly in 1979 and 1980 by the *Weber* and *Fullilove* cases involving employment and government contracts.[9]

The Burger Court

The history of US education confirms deliberate racial discrimination at every step of the way. Keeping Black people uneducated had a long tradition, from laws prohibiting teaching enslaved people (and even free African Americans in some cases) to read and write, to restricting African Americans to vocational or "industrial" education, to keeping them out of higher education. Even after legal barriers were struck down in several higher education cases and the 1954 *Brown v. Board of Education* desegregation decision, little happened to correct the virtual absence of African Americans from graduate and professional schools.[10]

By 1970 many graduate and professional schools saw a need for change, among them the new medical school at the Davis campus of the University of California. Its first entering class in 1968 had no African Americans and very few other minority students. The school then created a set-aside program in admissions as a way of increasing minority students' enrollment. Of the 100 seats available for the class, 16 seats were set aside for minority applicants (African American, Latino, American Indian, and Asian). The first five years of the special program brought in 26 African Americans along with additional minority students. Those selected met all entrance standards, but their admission under the extremely competitive regular admission program would have been uncertain or unlikely.

Allan Bakke was a white engineer for NASA, but he wanted to be a doctor. After attending night classes to fulfill his prerequisites, he applied to eleven medical schools and was rejected by all of them. One problem may have been that he was thirty-eight years old, much older than the usual medical school applicant. One of the rejections was from the University of California at Davis, where Bakke had been one of 3,737 applicants for 84 regular places. Bakke brought a lawsuit in 1974 against the UC-Davis 16-seat special program. He did not challenge his rejection by UC-Davis from its 84 regular admission slots, nor did he sue any of the other schools that rejected him. His suit charged that setting aside 16 slots for which he as a white person was ineligible was race discrimination and was unconstitutional under the equal protection clause of the Fourteenth Amendment.[11]

Bakke won in the California Supreme Court, and then the school appealed the case to the US Supreme Court, in *Regents of the University of California v. Bakke* (1978). After receiving more than 100 amicus briefs on all sides, the justices split 4–4–1, with six separate opinions totaling 155 pages and 165 footnotes. The UC-Davis plan and the theory of affirmative action were accepted by four justices and rejected by four justices. That left the deciding vote to Lewis F. Powell, who split his own vote, agreeing partly with each side.[12]

The four justices who categorically rejected the UC-Davis program and the school's use of race joined in a single opinion that almost, but not quite, said race could never be considered. Their approach was straightforward.

They essentially relied on the first Justice Harlan's famous dissent, which they quoted, in the segregation case *Plessy v. Ferguson* (1896): "Our Constitution is color-blind." Harlan penned the words in defiance of the majority opinion. Although he was expressing the view that the Constitution is open to Black citizens, his words are now sometimes used to invalidate proposed remedies.[13]

The other five justices (including Powell) said that race could be considered, and that a race-based affirmative action program could be constitutional if it met certain conditions. The basic condition accepted by all five of these justices was that a race-based affirmative action plan must satisfy strict scrutiny, meaning that it must be supported by a compelling interest. That was the end of the consensus between Powell and the other four justices who supported some use of race. They disagreed over what qualified as a compelling interest. Only four justices (Warren Court holdovers Brennan, White, and Marshall, plus Nixon appointee Blackmun) found a compelling interest because the affirmative action plan was essential to change the historic and enduring patterns of racial discrimination. This group did not have Powell as a fifth vote. Marshall recited chapter and verse of the hundreds of years of governmental and private race discrimination—including 100 years while there was supposedly an equal protection clause in the Constitution—years that brought about the near-all-white schools that the UC-Davis program was hoping to rectify. He said that without efforts to bring African Americans into the mainstream of society, "America will forever remain a divided society." He added, "During most of the past 200 years, the Constitution, as interpreted by this Court, did not prohibit the most ingenious and pervasive forms of discrimination against the Negro." Now, Marshall pronounced, the Court was setting up a barrier to any remedy. Blackmun wrote dramatically, "In order to get beyond racism, we must first take account of race. There is no other way. We cannot—we dare not—let the Equal Protection clause perpetuate racial supremacy." Blackmun also noted the irony of the controversy over race-conscious admissions while colleges routinely give preferences to athletes, alumni connections, potential donors, and the well-connected. The views of these justices were summed up in an opinion by Justice Brennan that used the term "societal discrimination" to describe the comprehensive array of historical and continuing race discrimination in society.[14]

The term "societal discrimination," however, was where Justice Powell departed from the group supporting the UC-Davis affirmative action plan. Powell agreed that the UC-Davis program was an attempt to overcome societal discrimination, but for him that disqualified the program rather than justifying it. He said a race-based affirmative action plan could be justified to overcome "the disabling effects of identified discrimination," but he distinguished "identified discrimination" from "societal discrimination." Identified discrimination was limited to specific findings by a court, legislature, or similar body, whereas societal discrimination could not justify affirmative action because it was "an amorphous concept of injury that may be ageless in its reach into the past." Powell did not deny the existence of societal discrimination, but he said that for this case it was insufficient. The first Supreme Court appearance of the term "societal discrimination," a concept of continuing importance, occurred in the *Bakke* case. The term originated in about 1970 to describe the concentration of race discrimination in seemingly limitless forms—pervasive, obvious, and mutually reinforcing. By the time of the *Bakke* case, the term was in such wide use that it appeared in dozens of the amicus briefs filed in that case.[15]

The two justices who used the term in their *Bakke* opinions—Brennan and Powell—had very different answers about what remedies, if any, could flow from societal discrimination. Because Powell had the swing vote in the *Bakke* case, his view prevailed. Although the two justices voted together in several later affirmative action cases, the difference was quite significant. Brennan's view was open-ended. Powell's approach, on the other hand, seemed to exclude race-based programs in all but the most extreme cases.

In *Bakke,* reliance on societal discrimination to justify the UC-Davis plan was hampered by a lack of specifics, which for Powell made it quite different from "identified discrimination." In fact, though, the specifics were abundant. Just as "de facto" segregated schools turned out almost invariably to rest heavily on official acts of purposeful discrimination and segregation, the same was true in other areas, and the overwhelmingly white medical profession at issue in *Bakke* was no different.

The case was tried in 1974, figuratively the dawn of jurisprudence facing the court on issues of equal protection. There was virtually no law yet to guide thinking about affirmative action doctrine. As a consequence, the case on behalf of the UC-Davis plan was skeletal. The facts presented in *Bakke* omitted almost everything we now know about how the profession was kept so white. The evidence presented to show the need for the affirmative action program was primarily the tiny proportion (2 percent) of African American doctors and medical students, the fact that almost all of them came from just two medical schools (Howard and Meharry), and the bleak history of segregated and unequal education. For Powell, these particulars of societal discrimination could be ignored, as opposed to identified discrimination, which implies intent or purpose and which would require attention.[16]

The reality, however, does not fit into that dichotomy. Societal discrimination depends on government action for its formation and its perpetuation; it is part of, and not in opposition to, identified discrimination. Maintenance of medicine as a white preserve was a product of intentional, long-running acts by every actor—public and private—with a role in shaping the medical profession, intentional acts that extended to the very eve of the UC-Davis program and the *Bakke* case. This included state and private hospitals, medical schools, licensing agencies, state and local medical societies, the American Medical Association (which in 2008 issued a formal apology for its previous racially discriminatory actions). Most striking, Congress and the federal government, from the mid-1940s through the mid-1960s, had poured billions of dollars into building and supporting an industry of segregated hospitals, including teaching hospitals. A section of the Hill-Burton Act of 1946 specifically authorized spending federal dollars for segregated medicine and produced the familiar separate-but-not-equal result.[17]

If these facts had been presented, it might or might not have changed the *Bakke* decision, but Justice Powell could hardly have dismissed the specifics as just societal discrimination, something long-ago and far-away. The argument for affirmative action was also undercut because it was tied to no constitutional anchor, but looked like just a freehand exception to the Supreme Court doctrine that the Fourteenth Amendment applied to white people as well as minorities. And yet there was a constitutional basis for the public interest in "overcoming the legacy of past discrimination"—it was firmly rooted in the Thirteenth Amendment, which remains a continuing obligation and a compelling interest as long as its promise remains unfulfilled. As with other missing ingredients in the *Bakke* debate, this is not to say the outcome would or should have changed, just that the debate was incomplete.

Having rejected the UC-Davis plan, however, Powell then took a sharp turn that opened a window for affirmative action. Although UC-Davis had shown no compelling interest to support a race-based program, he said, colleges and universities have a separate compelling interest in student diversity; it flows from the right of colleges and universities to enjoy academic freedom. Race, he said, could be considered as one type of student diversity as long as a plan included other types of diversity, such as musical talent or unique life experience. Under this approach, the UC-Davis program in the *Bakke* case still failed because it considered only race. Still, it was a blueprint for UC-Davis and other schools to devise new programs that might pass muster with the Supreme Court.

In the end, Allan Bakke was ordered admitted; he eventually graduated and practiced medicine until he retired, without ever saying much about his case. UC-Davis lost its race-based affirmative action program, but it learned how to design a valid diversity-based program. The question the *Bakke* case was supposed to answer—Can a race-based affirmative action program be constitutional?—was left unsettled, but the answer seemed to be a cautious "sometimes."

Powell's opinion has been criticized by affirmative action supporters for failing to acknowledge the tangible harm inflicted by discrimination, and by affirmative action opponents for letting racial criteria slip in by indirection. Nevertheless, Powell's blueprint for colleges and universities, but only for colleges and universities, has survived to this day.[18]

Positive Signals for Affirmative Action: The *Weber* and *Fullilove* Cases

In the two years after *Bakke* the Burger Court decided two affirmative action cases, and in each one it upheld a racial set-aside not so different from the plan rejected in *Bakke*. The first case, *United Steel Workers v. Weber* (1979), involved a factory department that had once been all white and was still virtually all white years after the Civil Rights Act of 1964 banned employment discrimination. To address that situation, the Kaiser Aluminum Company and the United Steel Workers Union voluntarily signed a collective bargaining agreement that allocated half the new openings in the department to African Americans until the racial composition of the department matched that of the local labor force. A 7–2 majority of the Supreme Court (including three justices who had voted against the UC-Davis plan in *Bakke*) upheld the plan. The 1964 Civil Rights Act contained language saying that promotions and assignments could not be made "on account of race," but the Court held that this language did not apply to a privately negotiated plan to overcome severe, entrenched patterns of discrimination. Brennan's opinion for the Court said, "It would be ironic indeed if a law triggered by a Nation's concern over centuries of racial injustice" were interpreted to preserve "patterns of racial segregation."[19]

A year later, in 1980, the Supreme Court issued a sweeping decision in support of minority contractors in *Fullilove v. Klutznick* (1980). The ruling squarely upheld the constitutionality of a federal contracting set-aside. The Public Works Act of 1977 provided that 10 percent of its construction contracting funds were to be awarded to minority contractors and subcontractors. Extensive congressional hearings detailed the problems faced by minority contractors, including incidents of race discrimination. Those hearings had shown that minority businesses received less than 1 percent of federal contracts. The hearings described refusals by prime contractors to hire minority subcontractors and actions by public agencies to favor white applicants. The hearings also showed other barriers that hit African Americans hardest, such as lack of working capital, lack of a visible track record, and lack of access to informal networks. These hearings supplied the type of detail that UC-Davis had not presented in the *Bakke* case.

The main opinion upholding the federal contracting set-aide was written by Chief Justice Burger. He emphasized Congress's documentation of the problems that African American contractors faced. Based on this background, Burger found that the set-aside program was justified by the need to overcome the history of discrimination against minority contractors. Burger rejected head-on the argument that affirmative action is unfair. He acknowledged that some nonminority contractors might lose contracts but said that was permissible as an "incidental consequence" of the law, not its objective: "When effectuating a limited and properly tailored remedy to cure the effects of prior discrimination, such 'a sharing of the burden' by innocent parties is not impermissible." He noted that some of the nonminority contractors might well have gained from past discrimination—even if they did not cause it—through "business as usual" by governmental bodies and other contractors.[20]

Burger's opinion did not apply any specific standard of review, nor use words like "strict scrutiny" or "compelling interest," but Justice Powell's did. In a separate concurring opinion, Powell explained that he was joining because the decision was consistent with his opinion in *Bakke*. The federal law in this case met the strict scrutiny requirement of showing a compelling interest—specifically, evidence in the hearings that discriminatory acts had affected minority contractors, a condition he said was missing in *Bakke*.

Three dissenters again referred to the first Justice Harlan's opinion in which he had described the Constitution as color-blind. One of these dissenters, Justice Stewart, said the majority's decision was wrong for the same reason that allowing segregation in *Plessy v. Ferguson* (1896) was wrong: "The equal protection standard of the Constitution has one clear and central meaning—it absolutely prohibits invidious discrimination by government." But at that time Stewart's was a dissenting view. Thus, as of 1980 the Supreme Court favored a narrow variant of affirmative action in higher education and approved affirmative action in private-sector jobs and government contracts. The traffic light facing affirmative action was not green, but it was a cautious yellow.[21]

New Political Winds

A growth of racial division that came with the election of Ronald Reagan in 1980 was especially pronounced in the area of affirmative action. President Reagan was a committed opponent of affirmative action, and his determination to end it was shared by his key civil rights appointments: William Bradford Reynolds, as assistant attorney general for the Civil Rights Division of the Department of Justice, and Clarence Thomas, as chair of the Equal Employment Opportunity Commission. The new appointees swiftly and sharply changed the direction of both agencies, in some cases even changing sides and challenging affirmative action plans the agencies had previously supported.[22]

In a particularly high-profile case, *Bob Jones University v. United States* (1983), where the Internal Revenue Service had revoked the charitable tax exemptions of schools that had explicit policies of racial discrimination, the Reagan administration suddenly abandoned the IRS position and switched sides in the midst of Supreme Court consideration of an appeal. Reynolds argued to the Supreme Court that these schools should be allowed to keep discriminating and still be granted a charitable tax exemption. The administration's position and the schools' tax exemptions were rejected, 8–1, with Burger writing the opinion and Rehnquist in dissent.[23]

The Supreme Court did not change as quickly as the executive branch of government. Six Supreme Court cases, all involving employment, gave mixed signals. Lower courts had upheld the affirmative action plans in all six cases, but the Reagan administration filed amicus briefs in all of them—each time opposing the affirmative action plan and urging reversal of the lower court. Of the six affirmative action plans brought before the Supreme Court, the Court upheld four involving hiring or promotion. It rejected the other two plans, both of which involved layoffs—that is, laying off white employees while keeping less-senior African American employees.[24]

An ominous sign for future efforts was the opinion rejecting the Michigan school district's affirmative action layoff plan, *Wygant v. Jackson Board of Education* (1986). The Supreme Court used this case to set an extremely high burden of proof needed to justify *any* affirmative action plan. The specific burden was to prove there was a "strong basis in evidence" for concluding that an affirmative action was a necessary remedy. These words in this 1986 Michigan case essentially put affirmative action plans favoring African Americans in the same category as laws or practices explicitly discriminating against them. The mixed results in these cases left the future unclear, but the yellow traffic light facing affirmative action plans was about to turn a blinking, though not a solid, red.[25]

The Rehnquist Court

The occasion for the radical rollback was a case that looked like a replay of a Supreme Court case from nine years earlier, *Fullilove v. Klutznick* (1980). After *Fullilove* had upheld the federal set-aside for minority contractors, many cities and states adopted similar plans. One of those was the city of Richmond, Virginia. Richmond had shifted from at-large to ward elections for city council as a result of the Supreme Court's Voting Rights Act ruling in *City of Richmond v. United States* (1975), and by the early 1980s there was an African American majority on the Richmond City Council. Adoption of the set-aside ordinance followed a meeting of the council where there was testimony that, in a city more than 50 percent black, less than 1 percent of the city's $124 million in contracts had gone to minority businesses.

A lawsuit quickly followed adoption of the ordinance. The dispute was over a $125,000 project to build toilets for the city jail. J. A. Croson Company prepared to bid as the general contractor, and looked for a minority subcontractor to order and install the fixtures. With some difficulty Croson located one minority contractor, Continental, but Continental had trouble finding a supplier for the fixtures. This was just the kind of problem minority contractors faced, as the Supreme Court had described in the *Fullilove* case. One supplier contacted by Continental simply refused to make a bid, and another said that because it was unfamiliar with Continental, it would first have to run a lengthy credit check. When Continental still had no supplier lined up by the bid deadline, Croson submitted its overall bid with an estimate for the subcontracting cost. When Continental did finally obtain a supplier, the price was $7,000 higher than the estimate Croson had included in its bid. Croson was the sole bidder and had been awarded the contract, subject to complying with the minority subcontracting clause.

Croson asked the city if it could simply raise its bid price by $7,000. The city said it could not grant that request, but would rebid the project; since Croson would likely again be the only bidder, it would be awarded the contract again, at the higher price, and the drama would be over. Instead of taking that course, Croson sued the city for requiring minority participation. In defense, the city relied on the Supreme Court's *Fullilove* decision allowing such a set-aside.

After a six-year journey through the courts, the case, *City of Richmond v. J. A. Croson Co.,* was decided in early 1989, three days after President Reagan left office. A majority of the Court, with three new justices and a new chief justice, ruled that the *Fullilove* precedent was simply irrelevant. According to the Court, the previous case rested on power possessed by Congress but not by states and cities.

Even after the Court set differing standards for the federal and state affirmative action plans, Richmond still believed its history of gross race discrimination gave it the compelling interest needed to support its set-aside program. Richmond pointed to the nationwide discrimination in contracting recognized in *Fullilove,* undoubtedly at its worst in Richmond. It showed that African Americans had been systematically excluded from construction unions in Richmond, and thus were denied the experience and contacts that were the usual springboard to becoming contractors. Added to this was Richmond's almost-unmatched record of race discrimination.

The city believed that these facts, the totality of circumstances, showed that its plan was justified by its need to remedy its past discrimination. In a majority opinion by Justice Sandra Day O'Connor, however, the Court rejected all the city's evidence as irrelevant or vague. The Court agreed that overcoming the effects of racial discrimination in Richmond could be a compelling interest, but said the city needed to show specific proof that minority contractors had suffered discrimination in the Richmond area, at the hands of the city itself or of nonminority contractors. Evidence of other discrimination or barriers did not count, nor did the evidence that Congress had compiled about nationwide discrimination and barriers suffered by minority contractors. The Court said the almost complete absence of African Americans from local and state contractors' associations did not show discrimination. Instead it might have resulted from mere societal discrimination in education and economic opportunities, or, as O'Connor speculated (with phrasing that looked like racial stereotyping), African Americans might simply be less interested in the construction industry: "Blacks may be disproportionately attracted to industries other than construction."[26]

Marshall filed an angry dissent: "As much as any municipality in the United States, Richmond knows what racial discrimination is." He called the majority "myopic" to think the dismaying pattern of national exclusion which Congress so painstakingly identified had somehow bypassed segregated Richmond. Blackmun also dissented: "I never thought that I would live to see the day when the city of Richmond, Virginia, the cradle of the Old Confederacy, sought on its own" to remedy past discrimination. And yet the Supreme Court, "the supposed bastion of equality, strikes down Richmond's efforts as though discrimination had never existed or was not demonstrated in this particular litigation."[27]

The uncompromising rejection of Richmond's plan and the denial of Richmond's evidence of discrimination signaled that state and local affirmative action programs had little future. Many cities and counties around the country began dismantling their plans: If Richmond could not justify such a plan, what city or state could? And if states and cities could not, how long would the federal government be allowed to have affirmative action programs? Or would the Supreme Court overrule its own precedent in the *Fullilove* decision?

A case involving a federal program soon came to the Supreme Court. *Metro Broadcasting, Inc. v. Federal Communications Commission* (1990) concerned a program giving licensing preference to minority broadcasters. Four justices voted in effect to overrule *Fullilove v. Klutznick,* but White voted to uphold the program. That created a 5–4 majority for a Brennan opinion upholding federal affirmative action. The *FCC* opinion was the last one ever written by Brennan. This Eisenhower appointee retired in 1990 after thirty-four years on the Supreme Court.[28]

To replace Brennan, President George H. W. Bush appointed David Souter. To many people, Souter was an unknown quantity, now a rarity in these days of increasing research on any nominee. Justice Souter soon began voting with the Court's liberal wing. Not so for Bush's other appointment, Clarence Thomas, who remained an avowed opponent of affirmative action. He wrote in 1987, as Ronald Reagan's chair of the Equal Employment Opportunity Commission (EEOC), "I think that preferential hiring on the basis of race or gender will increase racial divisiveness, disempower women and minorities by fostering the notion they're permanently disabled and in need of handouts."[29]

The *Adarand* Case

Changes in the Supreme Court's makeup meant that by 1995, the *Fullilove* case (1980), which upheld a federal contracting affirmative action law, was in trouble. None of the six justices who supported *Fullilove* was still on the Court; more relevant, four current justices had, in *Metro Broadcasting* (1990), voted to overrule *Fullilove* (Rehnquist, O'Connor, Scalia, and Kennedy). Now Thomas had joined the Court, replacing Marshall, and was a likely fifth vote to end *Fullilove*. The denouement on federal affirmative action came in 1995.

After the Supreme Court in *Fullilove* approved set-aside programs to provide opportunities for minority contractors, similar programs had been incorporated in statutes and regulations of other federal contracting agencies. Congress also had broadened affirmative action to cover categories of disadvantaged people beyond racial minorities. The new case arose when a company classified as "disadvantaged" gained a Department of Transportation subcontract for highway guardrails in Colorado. Adarand Constructors, a disappointed subcontractor that was not classified as disadvantaged, filed a lawsuit against the Department of Transportation, *Adarand Constructors v. Pena* (1995).

The lower courts followed the Supreme Court precedent in *Fullilove* and *Metro Broadcasting* and upheld the federal law. As the Supreme Court had determined, the stringent standards of set-aside programs (*City of Richmond v. J.A. Croson*) applied only to the states, not to the federal government. In this case, however, the Supreme Court 5–4 majority reversed. O'Connor, whose opinion in the *Richmond* case had emphasized that the rules for federal and state affirmative action plans were different, now held that they were the same.

The actual rule of law governing federal affirmative action plans took little space in the opinion. The Court simply reiterated for federal statutes the restrictive rule it had applied to state laws in *City of Richmond*. The Court recognized that *Fullilove* had upheld the same type of federal plan, but said *Fullilove* had used the wrong standard. The careful distinctions drawn in the *City of Richmond* case were left behind, and the recent decision in *Metro Broadcasting* was overruled. The decision expressed the Court's skepticism of all governmental affirmative action programs and sent the *Adarand* case back to the lower court to reconsider the decision under the Supreme Court's new rule.[30]

At the heart of the case was a debate between Thomas and Stevens about the fundamental nature of affirmative action. Thomas said firmly that "government-sponsored racial discrimination based on benign prejudice is just as noxious as discrimination inspired by malicious prejudice." Stevens said with equal firmness that there was "no moral or constitutional equivalence" between "invidious discrimination," which is "an engine of oppression," and the remedies for such discrimination, which seek to "foster equality in society"—"the difference between a No Trespassing Sign and a welcome mat."[31]

Since the Rehnquist Court tightening of the rules, affirmative action battles have largely quieted down. Large-scale or highly publicized programs have receded, but many federal agencies and some local and state governments still have affirmative action rules that apply in awarding contracts. These programs are mostly based on "disadvantage," a broad heading that includes race and typically recognizes that race often means disadvantage. These affirmative action plans have been tested in several federal appellate courts and have been upheld in all but one of those courts. The Supreme Court has stayed out of the fray.[32]

A significant feature of these cases has been the growing awareness of the depth of race discrimination in parts of the nation and in episodes of our history. The post-*Adarand* affirmative action plans, federal and state, have relied on new, detailed studies that show pervasive contracting discrimination. The white affirmative action programs of the mid-twentieth century (housing, suburbs, GI Bill, Social Security, minimum wage) have been studied extensively only since the 1980s; the medical profession has been the focus of attention only since the 1990s; even the slave-trading activities of northern philanthropists have emerged from obscurity or archives only in recent years and under the gaze of a new generation of scholars. Ironically, this explosion of knowledge owes a lot to the Supreme Court. By insisting that only purposeful discrimination and proof of guilt can support remedies, the Court has spurred an awareness among all Americans that racism has been far more pervasive and infectious than they had ever realized.[33]

Back to *Bakke*: Diversity Admissions at Michigan and Texas

One form of affirmative action that stayed alive is the type of student admissions program based on diversity that Powell prescribed in 1978 in *Bakke*. In the years since *Bakke,* these types of programs have spread throughout academia. Challenges have come to the Supreme Court twice, in 2003 involving the University of Michigan and in 2016 involving the University of Texas. Each time, the Court's general antipathy to affirmative action roused anticipation, or fear, that the Court would end such programs. Both times, however, the programs survived, by one-vote margins.

The University of Michigan had two separate programs. In the law school case, *Grutter v. Bollinger* (2003), O'Connor picked up Powell's mantle and reaffirmed the diversity-based affirmative action outlined in the *Bakke* case. She supplied the fifth vote to uphold the Michigan law school program, which gave each applicant an individual evaluation that included race among other types of diversity. At the same time, in *Gratz v. Bollinger* (2003), the Court ruled against the affirmative action program for admitting first-year students to the undergraduate college. To consider 20,000 applicants a year, the college used a point system, which was struck down for not making individualized determinations.[34]

The *Grutter* decision turned out to be only a short reprieve for the law school's affirmative action program. In 2006, voters in Michigan, following several other states, adopted a state constitutional amendment that banned any public body in the state (including universities) from any "discrimination" or "preference" based on race, sex, ethnicity, or national origin, in public education, employment, or contracting. The US Supreme Court upheld the Michigan amendment in *Schuette v. Coalition to Defend Affirmative Action* (2014). A line of earlier cases had struck down state provisions that prevented passage of local antidiscrimination ordinances, but the majority here said this case was different. Whereas the state laws that had been struck down in the earlier cases had interfered with the state's obligation to provide "equal protection," the Michigan referendum restricted only affirmative action—a voluntary policy of the state, not its constitutional obligation. Justice Sotomayor, who has said she would not be where she is today except for the opportunity she received as "a product of affirmative action," dissented. She pointed out that shifting power from one level of government to another was a classic form of manipulation used by white majorities to keep power away from African Americans.[35]

In the next decade the Supreme Court looked at another *Bakke*-style program twice, in *Fisher v. University of Texas* (2013, 2016), first sending it back to the lower court for another look, and then upholding it. With O'Connor gone, Kennedy now stepped in to provide the decisive vote to uphold the Texas program—which was somewhat surprising because Kennedy had voted to strike down the University of Michigan law school plan in the *Grutter* case. No single issue accounted for the Texas decision, but Kennedy emphasized how limited the program was, saying Texas used race only as "a factor of a factor of a factor."[36]

Recently a new front has opened up in affirmative action, Asian American lawsuits against college admissions. One claim is a standard challenge of affirmative action, alleging that the regular admission slots are reduced because of an affirmative action program that the suits claim is race-based and therefore improper. The second claim is a classic "quota" claim, that these colleges simply minimize the number of highly qualified Asian American applicants they admit—just as many colleges did with Jewish students in former days. In late 2020 a federal appeals court affirmed a district court ruling that Harvard College's diversity-based affirmative action program met the strict standards first established in the *Bakke* case and that statistical evidence

President Barack Obama nominates Sonia Sotomayor to be associate justice of the US Supreme Court, 2009. Vice President Joseph Biden is on Obama's right. Sotomayor is the first Latina and third woman on the Court.

did not show a bias or quota system restricting admission of Asian American students.[37]

At the same time, college admission fraud scandals have erupted, sending some movie stars to prison. These scandals have subjected the entire college admission process to a level of scrutiny more stringent than strict scrutiny—cynical or derisive scrutiny.

Color Blindness

The Rehnquist and Roberts Courts have expanded the rule of color blindness beyond standard affirmative action cases. Two areas in particular where color blindness is now the rule are school desegregation and legislative redistricting. In 2007 the Court held that public school districts could not voluntarily use race in assigning students to schools, not even to overcome patterns of segregation. Two school districts, in Seattle and Louisville, adopted student assignment plans that contained modest racial "tie-breaker" criteria for assignment if other criteria left some schools overcrowded. Neither district was subject to a desegregation order—Seattle never had been sued, and Louisville had recently been released after making progress. Still, school officials in both cities were concerned about increased segregation in housing and its effect on school enrollment; hence, the racial tie-breaker plans.

Some parents in Seattle and in Louisville were dissatisfied with their children's school assignments and instituted lawsuits. The two cases were decided together in *Parents Involved in Community Schools v. Seattle School District 1* (2007). The Supreme Court's 5–4 ruling used new anti-affirmative-action rules against school integration. Chief Justice Roberts held that the school districts were forbidden to use race in any way—including for integration—unless they met the strict scrutiny rules applicable to race-based affirmative action plans. Justice Thomas added in a concurring opinion that this required "a strong basis in evidence," the standard that is all but impossible to meet. The chief justice went on to say that this was the meaning he drew from *Brown v. Board of Education.* This seemed to amount to a principle that it is no more legitimate for a government officer or body to work for integration than it would be to work for segregation. The decision took on added significance because the principle was not limited to schools but became a rule that extends to eliminating all use of race in governmental decision making of any kind.[38]

Kennedy joined the majority holding that the Seattle and Louisville plans were unconstitutional, but he drew back from what he called Roberts's "all-too-unyielding" position. Kennedy said that race might be used at least indirectly in some instances. He acknowledged a continued national problem of racial inequality and a national goal of racial integration. None of the other four justices in the majority joined his views. Breyer captured the great significance of the case in a sentence he added orally to the presentation of his dissent: "It is not often in the law that so few have so quickly changed so much."[39]

This case also opened a debate about how to achieve racial equality. Roberts closed his opinion by saying, "The way to stop discrimination on the basis of race is to stop discriminating on the basis of race." Sonia Sotomayor, who was not on the Court at the time of this decision, responded in a later case: "The way to stop discrimination on the basis of race is to talk openly and candidly on the subject of race."[40]

The Supreme Court under Chief Justice Rehnquist had effectively put the courts out of the business of racial integration; this case put school districts out of that business also.

Redistricting

One significant application of the color-blindness rule is in redistricting of state legislatures and congressional districts, especially in the South beginning in the 1990s. Historically, election district lines have been manipulated to discriminate against Black voters and against Latino and Indian voters in some western states or counties. The usual method has been to divide up minority population concentrations so as to keep white voters in the majority in all or most districts. In the 1990s, though, largely to comply with the Voting Rights Act, southern states began doing the opposite, creating some districts with Black voting majorities (or Latino majorities in Texas) by combining rather than dividing minority populations.[41]

This development had great consequences in both racial and partisan politics. When minority voting populations were dispersed, they typically joined in supporting candidates of the Democratic Party (in modern times), who were most often white unless a district had a Black majority. Creating more majority-Black districts meant probably electing more Black representatives but, conversely, could mean electing fewer white Democrats. Democrats, white and Black, applauded the election of more African Americans, but were concerned about the potential overall drop in Democratic seats; Republicans were delighted. Another change was in the type of Republican who was elected. When district lines were drawn to make some districts more Black and others more white, the representatives elected in white districts often turned out to be more conservative, even radically so, and far less concerned with issues facing Black voters.[42]

The creation of Black (or other minority) majority districts turned into a constitutional issue as well. Redistricting occurs after each census and usually produces many legal challenges in every state, but the new minority districts produced a new type of lawsuit—suits brought by white voters alleging that the race-conscious districts discriminated against their equal right to vote. There was some irony in these suits. Each plaintiff's right to vote, like all constitutional rights, was personal, not dependent on a group. Yet white voters as a group were already overrepresented in each state; a successful lawsuit would further increase the overrepresentation of white voters. For example, in North Carolina, with a 75 percent white population, the plan had ten majority-white districts out of twelve (83 percent), and the lawsuit challenged one of the two majority-Black districts.

It was undisputed that the majority-Black districts had been drawn to make them majority Black, in other words, with a predominantly racial purpose. In a series of cases beginning with *Shaw v. Reno* (1993) in North Carolina, the Supreme Court began holding that if districts are drawn with race as a predominant factor, the plan is subject to strict scrutiny with all the strict scrutiny rules: the redistricting must be supported by a compelling interest and have a "strong basis in evidence." Under this theory the Supreme Court quickly struck down a number of state redistricting plans for discriminating against white voters. In this group were the North Carolina plan, as well as plans for Georgia and Texas. In each of these states, the long-running and recent history of voting discrimination should have sufficed as a "strong basis in evidence" to show a compelling interest for a race-based measure. Nevertheless, the Supreme Court rejected all these states' plans by the same 5–4 vote that struck down the federal affirmative action plan in *Adarand Constructors v. Pena* (1995). The Court's analysis in these cases seemed to bear out Justice Brennan's fear (expressed in *Bakke*) that strict scrutiny would become "strict in theory, and fatal in fact."[43]

A perverse new version of this issue surfaced in the state redistricting plans that followed the 2010 census. Southern legislatures, now dominated by Republicans, decided that if small efforts could reduce the overall number of Democrats, larger efforts could achieve larger reductions. If more African American or Latino voters were packed into fewer districts, the total number of Democratic officeholders would drop—without increasing the number of minority officeholders. Doing this of course required focusing on race in drawing the new plans. The result has been a series of cases in which the Supreme Court has rejected these partisan attempts to hide race-motivated plans in Alabama, Virginia, and North Carolina, but the decisions have been limited, and it is not clear how issues of race, partisanship, and redistricting will develop. The next round of redistricting will follow the 2020 census.[44]

Back to the Land's First Occupants

Perhaps it is appropriate to close this chapter with a case that involves the preservation, or the disappearance, of the "race" of people who originally occupied this land. About three million people identify as Native American or American Indian, and 700,000 of them live on reservations.

In *Adoptive Couple v. Baby Girl* (2013) the Supreme Court devoted 155 pages in five opinions to a child custody case. The reason for this close attention was that the father of the child was a member of the Cherokee Nation, a fact that brought into play the provisions of the federal Indian Child Welfare Act of 1978 (ICWA). Designed to maintain Indian families and preserve children's Indian heritage, that law implements certain federal protections and preferences for state agencies and state courts to follow in cases of child custody, adoption, and termination of parental rights. The act gives affirmative preference to Indian families in the fundamental decision of which family gets to raise the child. Families would shape the children's identities and ultimately their heritage.[45]

Treatment of Indians by many states and by the United States has been mainly a history of massacre, broken treaties, discrimination, and misguided forms of paternalism. The Indian Child Welfare Act was one of a series of laws that tried a different direction in the latter twentieth century, addressing issues like health care, joblessness, religious freedom, and others. These laws were responses to the long-standing practice of removing Native American children from their homes and from their Indian identity. A century earlier the federal Bureau of Indian Affairs forced Indian children to attend boarding schools (like the famous Carlisle Indian School attended by athlete Jim Thorpe) to eliminate "negative" family influences. A common view of Indians historically was described in a 1913 Supreme Court case that depicted Indians as "inferior," "ignorant," "immoral," "degraded," and "primitive." Race discrimination against Native Americans continued in modern times. That prejudice, plus high rates of Indian poverty and alcoholism, could influence otherwise well-meaning state agencies who thought that Indian children would be better off in white families. The result was very large numbers of Indian children removed from Indian parents and an attempt to turn them into non-Indians. ICWA was designed to stop this.[46]

Adoptive Couple v. Baby Girl involved parents who had planned to marry but broke up before the baby's birth in 2009. The case was a custody dispute between the child's Indian father and her foster parents, a white couple from South Carolina. The couple who were raising the baby wanted the father to relinquish his parental rights so they could adopt the child. The South Carolina courts ruled that the Indian Child Welfare Act supported the father's custody and that this result was also in the best interests of the child, including maintaining her Indian heritage. The two year old went to live with her father in Oklahoma.[47]

The US Supreme Court reversed, 5–4. The decision rested on the specific words of the law. Justice Alito for the majority said the specific wording of ICWA did not cover the father in this case. Justice Scalia for the dissenters was equally confident the words did cover the father. The main dispute was over Section 1912(f) of ICWA, which says Indian parents' rights may not be terminated unless there is strong proof that "continued custody" would seriously damage the child. Alito said "continued" could only apply where there was a preexisting custody, which the father in this case did not have, but Scalia said that nothing in the word "continued" required previous custody. On remand, with ICWA now out of the picture, the South Carolina Supreme Court in 2013 terminated the father's parental rights and approved the adoption. The little girl moved back to South Carolina.[48]

When the case was before the Supreme Court, it did not decide any constitutional questions, but it did have a warning for the future. An expansive interpretation of ICWA could put the law at risk: "Such an interpretation would raise equal protection concerns." Justice Alito did not elaborate, but he likely was referring to racial aspects of the law. An affirmative action program for Indians had already been approved by the Supreme Court in *Morton v. Mancari* (1974), four years before *Regents v. Bakke* (1978). There, the Supreme Court faced a provision of the Indian Reorganization Act of 1934, which created certain preferences for Indians in employment at the Bureau of Indian Affairs. Relying on Congress's special relationship with Indians, and the special role of the Bureau, the Court unanimously upheld the employment preferences, saying the law was directed to aid "participation by the governed in the governing agency." That case, however, may not be a solid foundation for future cases, because the Court also made two other points that may look different to the Supreme Court of today or tomorrow. First, the Court said the preference "is granted to Indians not as a discrete racial group, but, rather, as members of quasi-sovereign tribal entities whose lives are governed by BIA in a unique fashion." Second, the Court used a "rational basis" level of scrutiny: "Here, where the classification is rationally designed to further Indian self-government, we cannot say that Congress's classification violates due process."[49]

In recent years the Supreme Court has decided at least two cases that may suggest trouble ahead for ICWA. In 1996 the Court held a federal Indian law (the Indian Gaming Act) unconstitutional because it interfered with state prerogatives. In 2000 the Court struck down a Hawaii law that allowed only native Hawaiians to vote for trustees of a state trust operated for the benefit of native Hawaiians. The Indian Child Welfare Act may be an upcoming test of how far the Supreme Court will pursue its opposition to race-based laws.[50]

The future of affirmative action is uncertain, and that uncertainty breeds ongoing, passionate debate. But the questions being argued cannot be about the goal; that is already known: "All men are created equal." The questions are about how to achieve that goal. In one of the darker days in US history, just after the *Dred Scott* decision of 1857 and not long before the Civil War began, Frederick Douglass declared that the Declaration of Independence and the Constitution together "give us a platform broad enough, and strong enough, to support the most comprehensive plans for the freedom and elevation of all the people of this country without regard to color, class, or clime." History instructs us that more *was* required: three powerful Reconstruction Amendments, supporting civil rights laws from Congress, and, equally important, a Court committed to interpret and apply these laws so as to guarantee liberty and equality. A century later, Thurgood Marshall was less optimistic. He worried whether the Constitution, even with the Reconstruction Amendments, was sufficient to the task. He warned against letting the Constitution stand "as a barrier" to ending "the effects of that legacy of discrimination." Time will tell.[51]

CHAPTER THIRTEEN

The Color of Criminal Justice

Throughout slavery and Jim Crow, "law enforcement" and the "criminal law process" were often means of controlling and even terrorizing African Americans, particularly in the South. After a twentieth century in which the Supreme Court led the way to moderating the worst of the excesses, the nation faced a twenty-first-century version of law enforcement and a criminal process that has certain protections. And yet the protections are uneven, and the new century has also been one of mass incarceration.[1]

On May 24, 2020, George Floyd, an African American man, was killed by a white Minneapolis police officer who pressed his knee on Floyd's neck for more than eight minutes until Floyd was dead. The story would likely have ended there, just like countless similar tales—except that a young bystander filmed the entire episode. A new reality of police conduct is the police bodycam and the now-ubiquitous cellphone camera videos.

What else was different about George Floyd's death was the reaction: protestors of all races demonstrated across the country, with the rallying call "Black Lives Matter." That slogan dated back half a dozen years earlier to the killing of Trayvon Martin, a seventeen-year-old African American, by George Zimmerman, a self-appointed, armed neighborhood guard or vigilante. When Zimmerman was acquitted of charges, one television observer, Alicia Garza, brokenhearted, posted on Facebook on July 13, 2013: "Stop saying we are not surprised. . . . I continue to be surprised at how little Black lives matter. . . . Our lives matter." Black Lives Matter became a movement that has fueled new awareness by people across the color spectrum.

Crime and punishment have been with us since Eve and Adam ate the forbidden fruit, since Cain murdered Abel. This chapter looks at three major areas of present-day concern involving the intersection of race and the Supreme Court with law enforcement and the criminal law process: the death penalty, juries, and prisons. It concludes with a look at remedies for official violation of civil rights.

Death Penalty

One of the most dramatic episodes of the Burger Court was the sudden end of the death penalty, followed soon by its reappearance in altered form. Always an issue, the death penalty grew more controversial as the twentieth century progressed. By the early 1970s the death penalty had been under increasing pressure in many states and the US Supreme Court. As of 1972 no executions had been carried out in the United States since 1967. Then, in three appeals of African Americans from death sentences imposed by Georgia and Texas, the US Supreme Court ruled, in *Furman v. Georgia* (1972), that the death penalty was cruel and unusual punishment in violation of the Eighth Amendment to the US Constitution. The vote was 5–4, with the five Warren Court justices in the majority and the four Nixon appointees in dissent. Three of the majority, Justices Douglas, Brennan, and Marshall, said the death penalty was cruel and unusual without qualification, but the other two, Justices Stewart and White, said it was unconstitutional because it was haphazardly applied. The four dissenting justices said the death penalty could not conflict with contemporary standards of decency because it was in the statute books of a majority of the states. All nine justices wrote separate opinions. The ruling emptied out death rows in prisons around the country, to mixed reactions. Senator Strom Thurmond of South Carolina, who as a state judge had sentenced four men to death (three Black, one white), said the issue should be left to "each sovereign state." But the governor of Thurmond's state, John West, said, "I cannot accept the premise that man can end a life that God has created." Because two of the majority justices thought the problem with the death penalty was its haphazard application, several states enacted new laws designed to limit arbitrariness. Four years after striking down all existing death penalty laws in *Furman v. Georgia,* the Supreme Court, in *Gregg v. Georgia* (1976), upheld a group of new state laws that specified "aggravating" and "mitigating" factors that judges or juries must consider in deciding who would live and who would die.[2]

A year after reinstating the death penalty, the Supreme Court, in *Coker v. Georgia* (1977), closed a brutal page of race history by holding that the death penalty may not be imposed for rape. The Court held that, notwithstanding the horrible consequences of rape, the penalty of death is "grossly disproportionate" to the offense, and is therefore cruel and unusual in violation of the Eighth Amendment. Eventually the Court held that, with rare exceptions, the death penalty can be imposed only for a crime where a life is taken. The Court has also made the death penalty unavailable in some other situations, such as for defendants of limited capacity (juvenile or mentally ill), or defendants who did not have competent legal representation, and, not surprisingly, where race discrimination invades the process. The Supreme Court's decisions, especially restricting discretion, have essentially eliminated systemic discrimination based on the race of the defendant. Since death row is populated mostly by poor people, however, it is bound to have a disproportionate number of people of racial minority groups.[3]

In 1987, in *McCleskey v. Kemp,* the Supreme Court rejected a major systemic challenge based on statistical evidence of a somewhat indirect form of race discrimination. The challenge was not that the process singled out African American defendants, but that it singled out defendants—of any race—who killed white victims. The issue arose in the death penalty case of Warren McCleskey, an African American man who killed a white police officer while acting as the lookout in a store robbery in Atlanta. McCleskey relied on a detailed study led by sociologist David C. Baldus of 230 factors in 2,000 Georgia murder cases, including 128 death sentences. The study found only one clear race-related pattern—death sentences were much more likely with a white victim than a black victim, no matter what color the killer was. McCleskey argued that the presence of race as a factor denied him equal protection of the law.

A lower court said the study seemed to show race prejudice was "at work" in the Atlanta area but upheld the sentence. The Supreme Court, 5–4, also rejected the equal protection claim, saying the proof was too diffuse because the study showed nothing about McCleskey's own jury or his case, but simply spread unspecific responsibility over a host of actors in the Georgia system, from prosecutors to jury commissioners to jurors and others without proving a discriminatory purpose by anyone. Thus, McCleskey lost because he failed to show a discriminatory purpose, as the Court now requires in order to prove a violation of the equal protection clause (*Washington v. Davis*). Notwithstanding the "discriminatory purpose" theory on which the majority relied, it seems unlikely that the Court would have upheld McCleskey's death sentence if the Baldus study had shown a statistically significant bias in the race of the sentenced defendant.[4]

From the death penalty's resumption in 1976 through the end of 2020, there were 1,529 executions. Executions have been declining in the twenty-first century, with about twenty annually in recent years. Most significant are widespread moral concerns. The death penalty also has political, financial, and emotional drawbacks, even for victims' families—especially compared to an alternative of life in prison without parole. Advocacy groups oppose every death sentence and have shown that more than a few people on death row were innocent.[5]

A shocking set of events in early 2021 shows that the death penalty does not lack supporters. After the federal government executed ten people in 2020 (its first in seventeen years), the government rushed to execute three more in the second week of January 2021. In *United States v. Higgs* (2021), a 6–3 Supreme Court swept aside its usual inflexible procedures to accommodate the lightning schedule. Without question, the crimes were horrible, but the process that was short-circuited is especially important before administering death. Justice Sotomayor said in dissent: "This is not justice." The Justice Department's reason for rushing was political and obvious—to ensure the executions took place before the incumbent president left office, for fear the new president might call them off. But what could justify the Supreme Court's complicity in this process?[6]

Racial Fairness in Juries

The Supreme Court has dealt with the issue of all-white juries since 1880 and has done so seriously since 1935. By the 1970s discrimination in summoning jury pools—from which jurors are selected—had largely ended. Still, many juries remained all white or mostly white, often because of a procedure called the "peremptory challenge" or "jury strike." The peremptory challenge is a centuries-old procedure in which each side is entitled to "strike" (remove) a set number of potential jurors (usually about four to ten for each side, although in federal death penalty cases each side gets twenty strikes) with no explanation required. Actual reasons for striking a juror could range from a paid consultant's study of the juror's background to the lawyer's guesswork, or "hunch." (These strikes are in addition to a judge's removal of jurors for "cause"—such as being related to a lawyer or party in the case, or obvious partiality.) Many prosecutors, not just in the South, routinely struck minority jurors, especially in cases involving minority defendants. This was usually based on a generalized belief that minority jurors were likely to be more skeptical of police officers and more receptive to the defendant's testimony.

A Warren Court decision, in *Swain v. Alabama* (1965), declined to interfere with prosecutors' use of this practice, but the issue returned to the

Burger Court two decades later with *Batson v. Kentucky* (1986). James Batson's 1982 burglary trial in Louisville ended in a hung jury when one Black female juror held out for acquittal. In a retrial Batson was convicted by a jury that was all white because four African American potential jurors were all struck by the prosecutor. In Batson's appeal, the US Supreme Court—now fortified by its new "discriminatory purpose" jurisprudence of the 1970s—rejected the *Swain v. Alabama* precedent and reversed Batson's conviction. The Court's new holding was that jury strikes based on race deny a defendant a fair trial (Batson was not tried again). The Court established a new procedure requiring a prosecutor to explain the reasons, other than race, for a challenge and having the judge decide if the reasons are valid or a pretext. Justice Marshall, concurring, agreed that this decision was a step forward, but urged the complete abolition of peremptory challenges because, he warned, jury strikes would continue to be racial no matter what kind of proof was required to defend them. (Reactions were split, with many arguing that a *defendant's* jury challenges were essential to getting a fair jury.)[7]

Cases since then show that race-based strikes have not gone away, though presumably they have decreased. Trial judges typically accept prosecutors' nonracial explanations, even improbable ones. A recent study listed some dubious examples of claimed nonracial reasons for striking African American jurors: the juror wore glasses, was single, married, or separated, was too old (age forty-two) or too young (age twenty-eight), had relatives who attended historically Black colleges, walked a certain way, chewed gum, or lived in a "bad" part of town.[8]

Recently the Supreme Court tightened its rule against race-based peremptory challenges, reversing death sentences in a pair of decades-old murder cases where all-white or nearly all-white juries sentenced African American defendants to death. In Timothy Foster's trial in Georgia in 1986, an unusual piece of evidence threw new light on the jury strikes. The prosecutors struck four Black prospective jurors but offered nonracial explanations, which the judge accepted. After years of unsuccessful appeals, Foster (or his lawyers) made a simple request under Georgia's Open Records Law. The records he received contained, amazingly enough, the prosecutor's original file including handwritten notes highlighting each Black prospective juror's name in green, marked with a "B" and with other racial signals. Georgia state courts rejected Foster's new claim, but in 2016 the US Supreme Court reversed. In a 7–1 opinion by Chief Justice Roberts, the Court said, "the now-revealed notes" showed that two of the prosecution's jury strikes "were motivated in substantial part by race." "Two peremptory strikes on the basis of race are two more than the Constitution allows."[9]

The Supreme Court, 2020. Front row, left to right: Stephen Breyer, Clarence Thomas, Chief Justice John Roberts, Ruth Bader Ginsburg, Samuel Alito. Back row, left to right: Neil Gorsuch, Sonia Sotomayor, Elena Kagan, Brett Kavanagh.

Three years later, in 2019, the US Supreme Court again ruled against race-based jury strikes. Curtis Flowers, an African American man charged with murder in 1996, had been tried six times, resulting in two hung juries and four convictions with death sentences. The Mississippi Supreme Court reversed the first three convictions, but it upheld the fourth. The US Supreme Court noted that forty-one of the forty-two Black potential jurors had been struck by the county prosecutor in the various trials, including five of six in the last trial. Finding that at least one of the five had been struck because of race, the Court reversed the conviction. Mississippi attorney general Lynn Fitch inherited the case after the US Supreme Court ruling, and, after reviewing the file, announced on September 4, 2020, that the charges against Flowers were dropped.[10]

The peremptory challenge cases involved fairness in selecting the jury. In two other cases the Court took steps to ensure racial fairness in the jurors' deliberations and verdicts. One case, *Pena-Rodriguez v. Colorado* (2017), involved the conviction of Miguel Angel Pena-Rodriguez, a

Mexican American man, on charges of sexual assault. After the verdict, two jurors told the defense lawyer, who reported it to the judge, that another juror had expressed clear anti-Mexican bias against the defendant, including statements such as that "Mexican men had a bravado that caused them to believe they could do whatever they wanted with women." This juror also dismissed the defendant's alibi witness because he was "an illegal." The Supreme Court majority, 5–3, acknowledged the bedrock rule against jurors "impeaching" their verdict (rejecting a verdict based on jurors' testimony about their deliberations), but held that there must be an exception for racial bias. Justice Kennedy, joined by the four liberal justices, said this case called upon "our Nation to rise above racial classifications." He added, "This imperative to purge racial prejudice from the administration of justice was given new force and direction by the ratification of the Civil War Amendments."[11]

Another case, *Ramos v. Louisiana* (2020), held that jury verdicts of guilt must be unanimous, and the Court reversed Evangelisto Ramos's 10–2 murder conviction. Nonunanimous jury verdicts were still used in only two states, Louisiana and Oregon, and the Court pointed out that in both states, the practice had a discriminatory origin. The Louisiana rule was adopted by the disfranchising convention in 1898 to ensure that, if Black jurors had to be allowed, they could not interfere with the white majority's preferred verdict. (Louisiana voters ended the practice in 2018, but this case predated the change.) The Court said Oregon adopted its practice in the 1930s under the influence of the Ku Klux Klan.

While the foregoing shows there has been progress in reducing discrimination in administering the death penalty and in operation of the jury system, other areas of criminal justice tell a different story.

Explosion in Prison Population

By the time of the Burger Court, the criminal justice system included constitutional protections against warrantless searches, forced confessions, trials without lawyers, and trials by all-white juries. The Burger, Rehnquist, and Roberts Courts interpreted the protections quite narrowly but maintained the basic constitutional rules. One notable case that illustrates this involved the *Miranda* case ("read him his rights"), the most famous hallmark of the Warren Court's criminal procedure cases. After the Supreme Court decided *Miranda v. Arizona* (1966), Congress enacted a law rejecting that rule. In 2000 the Supreme Court declared that law unconstitutional. The opinion by Chief Justice Rehnquist said, "*Miranda* has become embedded in routine police practice to the point where the warnings have be-

Work detail from Louisiana State Penitentiary at Angola, 2011. In the latter twentieth century, Angola Prison was found to be run under grossly unconstitutional conditions, as were the main prison or entire prison systems of ten of the eleven former Confederate states (all except Virginia).

come part of our national culture." He added, however, that subsequent Supreme Court cases "have reduced the impact of the *Miranda* rule on legitimate law enforcement while reaffirming the decision's core ruling."[12]

The past fifty years have witnessed an explosion in the prison population, especially concentrated among African Americans and other racial minorities. There were about 200,000 people in state and federal prison in 1970, a number that had been relatively constant over the previous two decades. Beginning in 1970 and accelerating after 1980, however, the number began to climb at a dizzying rate, until it reached approximately 1.6 million in 2010, before leveling off somewhat. (In addition, other people are serving time in county and city jails, sometimes merely waiting for trial, without having been convicted but still in confinement because they cannot afford bail.) Did the United States become eight times more lawless in forty years (or five times more lawless, if accounting for population growth)? That seems unlikely.[13]

Many factors played into this rush to imprison, but a useful place to start is the law enforcement push of the late 1960s, including the Omnibus Crime Control and Safe Streets Act of 1968 (signed by President Johnson) and the "law and order" campaign of that same year, which helped put Richard Nixon in the White House.

A Warren Court case paved the way. Its ruling in *Terry v. Ohio* (1968) put an asterisk into the Fourth Amendment of the Constitution, which requires "probable cause" for a search or arrest. On October 31, 1963, in Cleveland, when two African American men, John Terry and Richard Chilton, were stopped and frisked, the police officer found guns; he arrested them for having concealed weapons without a permit. In the *Terry* case the Supreme Court decided that a police officer can stop a person (not quite an arrest) on "reasonable suspicion" (not quite probable cause) and, for the officer's safety, can conduct a limited pat-down for weapons (not quite a search). This decision, joined by liberal icons Earl Warren, Thurgood Marshall, and William Brennan, was the beginning of "stop and frisk" and has become a universal policing practice, accounting for many millions of formerly illegal stops each year. These "*Terry* stops" have overwhelmingly targeted African Americans and their neighborhoods. Since the 1980s the Supreme Court has upheld more and more intrusive uses of the *Terry* stop. In many of the cases the Supreme Court reversed state courts that the Court held were restricting the police too much. Thus, the Warren Court unlocked the door, and subsequent Supreme Court decisions have pushed it wide open.[14]

A second and related major factor in driving up prison numbers is the war on drugs, which President Nixon declared in 1971 with strong bipartisan support. Then in June 1986 a tragic event practically in Congress's backyard spurred legislative action. Len Bias, a basketball superstar at the University of Maryland, died of a cocaine overdose on the day after he was drafted to play pro basketball for the Boston Celtics. That event prompted Congress to pass the Anti-Drug Abuse Act of 1986—with strong bipartisan and biracial support—and further amendments in 1988. In 2019 the number of people in prison for drug offenses was almost 300,000—more than the entire American prison population in 1970.[15]

There has been a racial cast to these developments. For example, the *Charlotte Observer* stated in 1968, "To many North Carolinians, law and order means 'keep the niggers in their place.'" John Ehrlichman, who was President Nixon's White House counsel and domestic policy advisor, recalled that they used the country's anti-drug efforts with a political and a racial tinge; by concentrating on the Black community and the antiwar movement, they could "disrupt" those groups.[16]

The racial tilt in the war on drugs is obvious in the disparate punishments. The law punishes "crack" cocaine (thought to be favored by minority users) far more harshly than "powder" cocaine (thought to be white users' choice). The penalty for possessing 5 grams of crack cocaine (little more than an amount for personal use) was established at the same level as the penalty for possessing 500 grams of powder cocaine. In 2010 Congress reduced the ratio from 100:1 to a still disparate 18:1.[17]

These developments dovetailed with trends to harsher laws and sentences: laws with mandatory minimum sentences or mandatory life sentences, "truth-in-sentencing" laws (longer incarceration rather than parole or probation), "three-strikes" laws (longer sentences, including life imprisonment, for repeat offenders), and other get-tough measures. Challenges to these laws have met with little success in the Supreme Court. For example, the Court has held 5–4 that a life sentence for three nonviolent check or credit card crimes is not "cruel and unusual" in violation of the Eighth Amendment. The Court said such sentences "may be cruel, but they are not unusual in the constitutional sense." The Supreme Court has decided five cases involving such long or life sentences and upheld all but one of these sentences.[18]

Although three-strikes laws were primarily intended for violent criminals, the net also caught people like Leandro Andrade. A nine-year army veteran with three children, Andrade had a history of drug use and a record of several nonviolent offenses. In 1995 he was caught shoplifting several children's videos from a K-Mart and a few weeks later was caught stealing more videos at another K-Mart. Each group of videos was worth less than $100. These were "petty theft," a misdemeanor (minor crime), and would not have invoked California's three-strikes law, which covers only "violent" or "serious" criminals. But because Andrade had prior convictions, his petty theft became the more serious "petty theft with a prior," which is a felony (major crime). The prior convictions, which had already been counted in turning his petty thefts into felonies, were counted again as "two strikes." That made the petty theft of videos into a third strike. Not just once, but twice, since the prosecutor used his discretion to charge the two K-Mart incidents as two separate crimes, amounting not only to a third strike but also a fourth strike. The sentence for each of these third and fourth strikes was twenty-five years to life, which under California law had to be sentenced consecutively rather than concurrently as would ordinarily have been done.[19]

The appeal went to the US Supreme Court, which in 2003 upheld the California statute and Andrade's sentence, 5–4. The dissenters argued that it was unconstitutional because it was grossly disproportionate to the offenses, but the majority held that the state had the power to impose such a sentence. By the time Andrade is eligible for release, he will be eighty-seven years old. Cascading penalties, such as Andrade's, give a false image of a violent crime wave, while swelling the prison population with lesser offenders. White-collar criminals, convicted of stealing millions of dollars, are not given such drastic sentences.

The overcrowding of the prison system through mass incarceration has had severe consequences. One is the distortion of political redistricting with "prison gerrymandering." Some prisons are large enough to skew one-person, one-vote districting, leading to overrepresentation of the surrounding area, often sparsely populated, at the expense of other areas, often urban. With a new awareness of this issue, some state legislatures are addressing this problem.[20]

Another consequence is the rise of private prison companies, some with publicly traded stock. When private companies build and run prisons, they create an industry with a vested financial interest in keeping the prison population high. The US Bureau of Justice Statistics reported that the number of people incarcerated in private prisons in 2018 was 128,000, up almost 50 percent since 2000.[21]

Yet another consequence is that there are very few trials. More trials would break the system because there are not enough judges, prosecutors, or defense lawyers (usually public defenders) to handle today's huge volume of cases. Those shortages apply pressure to dispose of cases quickly; the pressure comes from every corner, including people and corporations whose civil cases are delayed because criminal cases usually have priority. The result is that now, more than ever, almost all cases end in guilty pleas—plea bargains. Defendants, even those who may be innocent, are pressured to accept a plea bargain because it saves the time and cost of a trial and gives the defendant a sure sentence instead of the risk of a far stiffer sentence after a trial and conviction.

All of the foregoing factors have severe racial aspects. Countless examples are played out on national news of racial profiling: stopping African Americans who are driving vehicles on the highways, and targeting Black neighborhoods. Critics who call today's incarceration practices "the new Jim Crow" can find sad support for that argument in the nature and numbers of current practices. Ironically, national disasters seem to provide some relief. The prison population has declined somewhat since the financial crisis of 2008, and the coronavirus pandemic of 2020 may also highlight a realization that many prisoners do not need to be in prison.[22]

Ex-Felon Disfranchisement

People with prison records often cannot find a job or decent housing. Another offshoot of incarceration is the inability to vote, although the number of states with long-term or permanent disfranchisement of ex-felons has decreased in recent years. Historically, most states disfranchised people who had been convicted of certain crimes, and in the late nineteenth and early twentieth centuries, many former Confederate states deliberately and openly manipulated this device to disfranchise African Americans. As of late 2020, forty-plus states allow ex-felons to vote either after release from prison or after completion of parole and probation—which can be a significant delay. The remaining states still impose lifetime bans for selected crimes or require significant payments, which effectively amount to a lifetime ban.[23]

The imposition of bans on ex-felons as a way of disqualifying voters has been tested in three major Supreme Court cases. In 1898 in *Williams v. Mississippi,* the Supreme Court upheld the deliberately racial felon disfranchisement provision in Mississippi's 1890 constitution, and that ugly scar, with slight cosmetic changes, remains in the Mississippi Constitution today. In 1985 in *Hunter v. Underwood,* the Supreme Court struck down a similar racial provision in the Alabama Constitution on the grounds that it was purposely discriminatory. Absent such obvious race discrimination, "felony disfranchising laws" as a category were upheld in *Richardson v. Ramirez* (1974). The Court's theory was that such laws are somehow not subject to the equal protection clause because a different section of the Fourteenth Amendment amounted to an "affirmative sanction" for disfranchising those convicted of crime. Dissenting justices argued that a clause designed to deal with the ex-Confederate states should not have this present-day application. The majority's term "affirmative sanction" was a play on words rather than a reasonable basis for minimizing the fundamental right to vote.[24]

A new issue concerns a poll tax in the guise of an ex-felon law. Florida disfranchises all ex-felons for life—currently about a million people. In 2018 the people of Florida amended the state constitution to provide, as about twenty other states now do, that "voting rights shall be restored upon completion of all terms of sentence including parole or probation." The Florida legislature passed a law to require payment of any fines or fees imposed with the conviction as a condition of regaining the right to vote. A federal district judge held this unconstitutional as a form of poll tax, but the court of appeals reversed the district court and upheld the Florida legislature's restrictive law. During these events, which preceded the November 2020 elections, the Supreme Court declined to intervene, so the pay-the-fines requirement stayed in effect. Justice Sotomayor, joined by Justices Kagan and Ginsburg, dissented, saying that "nearly a million otherwise-eligible citizens cannot vote unless they pay money."[25]

Redress for Police Violation of Civil Rights: Section 1983

The public's reaction to the death of George Floyd in 2020 was immediate and emotional. For much of the nation it was profoundly educational, shaking many people out of their faith that racial justice, though long deferred, was progressing well. The incident also prompted officials and citizens to look for necessary reforms, and for remedies for wrongs done. Remedies are no panacea, as they do not make up for a life lost; but for all injuries, large and small, remedies are one place to begin.

One set of remedies is governmental. Local, state, and federal governments can reform police policies and practices, they can take employment action, and in extreme cases they can bring criminal prosecutions against a police officer or other government employee. All these actions are rare, though less so than they were formerly. In 2014, when Eric Garner, an African American man, was killed by a police officer's chokehold in New York, the officers involved were fired and the city's civil service commission upheld the firing. In 2015, when Walter Scott, an African American man in South Carolina, was shot in the back while fleeing, the officer was prosecuted by both local and federal governments. He pleaded guilty to violating federal civil rights laws and received a twenty-year sentence.[26]

Those remedies are in governmental hands, but what remedies are available to private citizens—the victims themselves? Every state provides a state court remedy, typically through a "tort claims act," but in many states and at many times these have been regarded as inadequate or futile. Therefore, the pressing question is, what federal court remedies are available if state or local police or other officials violate the Constitution? And how effective are those remedies? The answer to those questions goes back to 1871. In that year, soon after adoption of the Reconstruction Amendments, Congress created an open-ended authorization for civil suits by private individuals in Section 1 of the Ku Klux Act. That section is still on the books today, as Section 1983 of Title 42 of the US Code, often called simply "Section 1983." It provides that when any person acting with state authority deprives any person of a federal constitutional right, the victim can sue the violator in federal court for damages for the injury or an injunction to prevent future violations.[27]

For many years Section 1983 was interpreted narrowly and was used rarely—mainly in situations where a state or local law itself violated the federal Constitution. The case of *Monroe v. Pape* (1961) (discussed in Chapter 9) changed that. Since that time, Section 1983 has been interpreted to cover any violation of federal rights committed by any person or agency acting with state or local authority ("under color of law"), whether the wrong is done by an official policy or by a single act. Since then, Section 1983 cases of many types have mushroomed, but the Supreme Court has added severe limitations on who can be sued under Section 1983 and under what circumstances. These limitations leave many or even most victims with nobody to hold responsible for constitutional wrongs, a condition not so different from the pre-1961 rule.[28]

Individual Liability

The most obvious remedy, and the one specifically recognized in *Monroe v. Pape,* is a suit against the person who actually caused the injury. Soon after *Monroe,* however, the Supreme Court, in *Pierson v. Ray* (1967), interpreted Section 1983 to grant state and local personnel a degree of "immunity" in Section 1983 suits. The case arose in 1961, when police in Jackson, Mississippi, arrested an interracial group of Episcopal priests for trying to integrate the bus terminal in violation of a city segregation ordinance. The ordinance was later struck down in the Freedom Rider cases, but this was not until after the ministers were arrested. The ministers were never convicted, but they sued the policemen for arresting them under an unconstitutional law. The Supreme Court dismissed the suit, saying the police officers should be immune from suit because the segregation law they were enforcing had not been held unconstitutional at the time when they made the arrests. (The Supreme Court called this "qualified immunity," as opposed to "absolute immunity," because it depended on the circumstances.)

The immunity rule in suits against individuals is today governed by the words "clearly established"—that is, officials are immune from damages unless they violate a clearly established constitutional rule. A simple way of expressing this is that "officials are not liable for bad guesses in gray areas; they are liable for transgressing bright lines." The Supreme Court, however, has shown how nearly impregnable this immunity is. For a rule to be clearly established, there must be existing precedent involving similar facts and circumstances, similar enough to put the question "beyond debate." This means, in the Supreme Court's words, that the rule protects "all but the plainly incompetent or those who knowingly violate the law." Under this standard the Court has ruled for the public officer, usually by unanimous vote, in almost every one of approximately thirty immunity cases over the past several decades.[29]

However, in late 2020, the Supreme Court did reject qualified immunity in a case it called "egregious." Trent Taylor, a Texas prison inmate, alleged that for six full days he was confined to two shockingly unsanitary cells, one with walls covered from floor to ceiling with feces and the second frigidly cold with no toilet but only a clogged drain that spewed out refuse. The Fifth Circuit (which was the heroic court in the civil rights days) agreed these conditions were cruel and unusual punishment, but granted immunity to the correctional officers because, as the Fifth Circuit said, the unconstitutionality of such punishment was not clearly established. The Supreme Court reversed, saying no reasonable correctional officer could have thought this was proper. Justice Thomas dissented, and Justice Alito, while agreeing with the decision, said he did not understand why the Supreme Court took the case.[30]

The immunity doctrine is not the only barrier to recovering from individual wrongdoers, because even those few victims who overcome the immunity rule and get to trial often find unreceptive juries. A graphic illustration is a case, *Graham v. Connor* (1989), involving a man who did nothing wrong but was seriously roughed up by police who thought he was acting suspiciously. On November 12, 1984, Dethorne Graham, a state maintenance worker who was a diabetic, was in great need of a sweet to avoid going into insulin shock. Driven to a convenience store by a friend, he dashed into the store but immediately ran out because of the long line. This quick in-and-out by a Black man was suspicious enough for nearby police to pull the car over, ignore explanations, manhandle Graham, and throw him into their squad car, saying (as rendered in the Court opinion), "Ain't nothing wrong with the M.F. but drunk. Lock the S.B. up." The police quickly learned there had been no crime at the convenience store, and they released a badly bruised Graham, with cuts and a broken foot. The Supreme Court held that Graham's allegations showed a constitutional violation (use of unreasonable force in a police stop, in violation of the Fourth Amendment) and that the case should indeed go to trial. With the case finally cleared to go to trial, however, attorneys for Graham still had to persuade the jury. Juries tend to support the police officers, and in this case, true to form, the jury ruled for the policemen and against Graham.[31]

Municipal and State Liability

In trying to find a remedy, the injured person might look to the local or state government that employs the individual who caused the injury. Throughout the legal system, when an employee injures someone, the employer is ordinarily held liable under a principle called *respondeat superior* ("let the master answer"). This principle reflects an obvious view that injuries to victims ought to be redressed, and that the employer is in the best position to control the activities of employees and to cover costs—

typically through insurance. The Supreme Court, however, has adopted a judicial interpretation rejecting the rule of *respondeat superior* for Section 1983 cases.

Where the violator is an employee of a local government (such as a city, county, or school district), the Supreme Court has followed a tortuous path that leaves only a small window open for a Section 1983 suit against such an entity. In *Monroe v. Pape,* while allowing Monroe to sue the Chicago police officers who conducted the search, the Court ruled unanimously that he could not sue the City of Chicago—indeed, the Court ruled that governmental bodies could not be sued under Section 1983 at all. The Court's theory was that the wording of the statute—specifically the word "person"—was not intended to cover governmental bodies.

Then in 1978 the Supreme Court decided that its 1961 opinion was wrong on this point, and that cities and other local governments are covered by the statute's word "person." The new rule came in the case of Jane Monell, an employee of the New York City Department of Social Services who became pregnant in 1970. Under rules that were common in the 1970s, the Department required pregnant employees to take leave immediately, unpaid and without being medically necessary. Monell turned to her husband, Oscar Chase, who happened to be a law professor, and he sued the city department under Section 1983, in *Monell v. New York Dept. of Social Services* (1978).

After lower courts said the city and its departments could not be sued under Section 1983, the Supreme Court reversed. It overruled *Monroe v. Pape* on this one point and held that the city and its departments were "persons" and could be sued under Section 1983. The change was only partial; the Court said a city could be sued if a violation stemmed from an actual law or policy, but it could not be sued just because a wrong was committed by one of its employees—in other words, no *respondeat superior.* That is still the current law, but with an important qualification: the concept of a policy is not limited to formal policies, but can be interpreted broadly in some circumstances to cover both formal policies like the pregnancy policy in the *Monell* case and an informal "custom or usage" (words in the statute). For example, a local government could be held liable for injuries inflicted by a police officer or other employee who was defectively trained or supervised.[32]

Curiously enough, the *Monell* rule allowing suits against cities over their policies does not apply to states and state agencies. In *Will v. Michigan Dept. of State Police* (1989), a 5–4 Supreme Court decision retained *Monroe v. Pape*'s complete ban, ruling that even if cities and counties are "persons" under Section 1983, states and state agencies are *not* persons and cannot be sued under Section 1983 at all.

Solving the Liability Problem

The issue of compensation for constitutional wrongs may seem trivial when considering the large issues of racial justice, often a matter of life and death. But financial compensation is an important redress for many injuries, and it can also play a critical role in prompting reform. As noted by Booker T. Washington in 1895, one of the color lines in America is the color of money. When government agencies have to fork over they start paying more attention to preventive measures—or the insurance companies do. Injuries by an official or a police officer working on our behalf, whether inflicted accidentally or purposely, have a cost that we collectively ought to bear.[33]

Under current interpretations, Section 1983 is a remedy for virtually nothing but intentionally unconstitutional misconduct, which means the great mass of injuries go unremedied. Changing or even abolishing qualified immunity for individual officials might not change that condition very much, but applying a rule of *respondeat superior* for all state and local governments would do so. Under current law, when local governments are liable under Section 1983, there is no immunity, and that should of course remain the same, and should apply to states as well.[34]

The reality is that states and cities already deal with *respondeat superior* liability because that is the rule under state tort claims acts. States and cities are also familiar with paying for injuries caused by their employees, because they routinely do so (usually by means of an insurance policy) whenever an employee is or may be required to pay for causing an injury. The Ku Klux Act of 1871 should provide a remedy. It is unlikely (though not impossible) that the Supreme Court would reinterpret Section 1983. But Congress can make that change, amending the Ku Klux Act to make it the comprehensive remedy it should be.

Thus, the major consequence of *respondeat superior* for Section 1983 would be to provide an effective—though familiar—remedy for the many injuries that currently go unredressed. As the English historian Frederic W. Maitland said more than a century ago, "It is a wholesome sight to see the Crown sued and answering for its torts."[35]

Injunctions

Section 1983 specifically authorizes a "suit in equity," which is a legal term for an injunction. Courts have issued injunctions over the years to curb specific police practices, but more wide-ranging injunctions issued by lower courts in the 1970s were blocked by the Supreme Court. In *City of Los Angeles v. Lyons* (1983) the Supreme Court blocked an injunction that banned chokeholds in Los Angeles. Adolph Lyons, a twenty-four-year-old Black man, was pulled over for a traffic violation and wound up in a police officer's chokehold that left him unconscious. He sued for damages and for an injunction against the chokehold, which he alleged was a routine practice in the city police force even though it had produced a number of fatalities. Lower federal courts banned chokeholds while the case was proceeding. At the Supreme Court, however, the ban was reversed, 5–4. The Court said Lyons might have a valid claim for damages against the officers but could not sue for the injunction because there was no proof that Lyons himself might again be the victim of a chokehold. How many lives might have been saved since 1983 if the Supreme Court had not reversed the ban?[36]

Most law enforcement officers are honorable professionals doing a hard and often dangerous job on behalf of society, and at times called on to make split-second life-and-death decisions. They deserve respect and support. That is not incompatible with insisting on needed reforms to minimize things going wrong and realistic modes of redress when things do go wrong. It is also not inconsistent with recognizing that race is at the root of much of what goes wrong in law enforcement, including the killing of unarmed citizens. African American poet Claudia Rankine expressed grief and frustration: "I don't know how to end what doesn't have an ending." White circuit judge Henry Floyd of South Carolina expressed his grief and frustration in an opinion (issued two weeks after the death of George Floyd), which involved Wayne Jones, a man who was shot by police twenty-two times while in their custody: "This has to stop."[37]

Conclusion

This book is personal for the authors. Vernon Burton grew up near the segregated cotton mill town of Ninety Six, South Carolina, and has spent a career writing about a past that we must overcome. Armand Derfner, whose family escaped the Nazis when he was a baby, has spent a career as a civil rights lawyer challenging discrimination. We both know that all Americans are enriched when everyone is a full-fledged member of society. Albion Tourgée, who was a novelist as well as Homer Plessy's lawyer in the separate-but-equal case, had a fictional character remind us that we should never forget "what the law *ought* to be, in trying to find out what it was." We have tried to do both.[1]

The Supreme Court in 2021 is said to be divided between liberals and conservatives. It is not always clear what those terms mean. Definitions boil down to choices that justices make in a particular case or type of case. The civil rights and antidiscrimination cases in this book suggest a dividing line: on one side, interpreting and applying those laws in the broadest interpretation, to mean the *most* they can mean; on the other, treating such laws narrowly, to mean the *least* they have to mean. Those methods of interpretation define the line that divides today's Supreme Court justices on race issues, and historically, that has always been the dividing line.

That division was evident as early as 1842, when an African American woman was seized without a judge's certificate that federal law required. One justice took the law seriously, saying the seizure was illegal, but the majority ruled the certificate was just optional. In 1872, in the

Supreme Court's first major civil rights case after the Reconstruction Amendments, the Court majority minimized the Civil Rights Act of 1866 by making its guarantee of African Americans' equal right to testify and be witnesses inapplicable to Black victims of crime. In 1876 the Court reduced the Enforcement Act of 1870 by ignoring the word "aforesaid" in the statute, thus eliminating the law's protection against widespread schemes to disfranchise African Americans. In 1898 the Supreme Court unanimously agreed that the Fifteenth Amendment contained a "field of permissible action" where race discrimination was allowed, opening the door to disfranchisement provisions across the South. In other cases around the turn of the twentieth century, the Court reduced all three Reconstruction Amendments and all four of Congress's major civil rights laws to mean as little as they could conceivably mean for racial justice.[2]

Other racial minorities fared no better. With the notable exception of the Chinese laundry case, the Supreme Court of that era adopted similar narrow interpretations of the Constitution, civil rights law, and foreign treaties, all to the detriment of Native Americans and American residents of Chinese ancestry.[3]

The justices had choices, and in making those choices they consistently rendered narrow interpretations that left the laws as mere shadows and set African Americans and other nonwhite people adrift. Yet while the Court was contracting the Fourteenth Amendment into a useless provision for formerly enslaved people, it was expanding the same amendment as a powerful weapon for business to wield against state regulation.[4]

The Supreme Court started turning around under Chief Justices White and Taft. In 1911 the Court read the Anti-Peonage Act of 1867 broadly to strike down part of Alabama's convict-leasing system. In two shocking state criminal convictions, the Court found a basis in the due process clause to begin overturning unfair state criminal trials.[5]

The Supreme Court of the late 1930s and 1940s, under Chief Justices Hughes, Stone, and Vinson, became more consistent in reading protections for the most they could mean, not the least. In 1938 the Court interpreted "federalism" to increase rather than decrease a state's obligation to provide equal educational opportunities, and in 1950, the Court followed up by holding that graduate schools with comparable facilities were not equal if they differed in reputation and prestige. In 1944 and 1948 the Court expanded its view of the equal protection clause and overruled its previous decisions allowing restrictive covenants and all-white primaries. During World War II, however, the Court's record was seriously marred when it held that the equal protection clause did not prevent the internment of 120,000 people of Japanese ancestry, two-thirds of them American citizens.[6]

In the 1950s and 1960s, under Chief Justice Warren, the Court extended the pattern of reading the Reconstruction Amendments and both old and new civil rights laws for the most they could mean, rather than the least. In 1961 the Court's interpretation of the words "under color of law" in the Ku Klux Act of 1871 created a remedy for constitutional violations. In 1968 the Court unleashed the power of the Thirteenth Amendment when it read the Civil Rights Act of 1866 to bar race discrimination in private property transactions by private individuals, not just by the state. In 1969 the Supreme Court read the Voting Rights Act broadly to cover discrimination in voting systems, not just interference with registration and casting a ballot.[7]

The broad-interpretation approach that began in 1911 and prevailed since the 1930s largely continued when Chief Justice Burger first arrived. In 1971 the Court gave broad readings to both old and new civil rights laws—the Ku Klux Act of 1871 (reversing nineteenth-century precedents) and the employment discrimination rules in the Civil Rights Act of 1964.[8]

After the arrival of Justices Powell and Rehnquist, the Court began to narrow its interpretations, but not always. In 1973 the Court took a restricted view of the equal protection clause when it upheld wide disparities in Texas's school-financing system. In 1977 it gave a narrow interpretation of "full relief" under the Civil Rights Act of 1964 in a seniority case. A monumental decision in 1976 erected a high hurdle for discrimination claims by establishing a rule requiring proof of discriminatory purpose for any claimed violation of the equal protection clause (somewhat tempered by a 1977 decision explaining how discriminatory purpose could be proved). On the other hand, there were some decisions that did give broad readings to civil rights protections. In 1976 the Court extended the reach of the Civil Rights Act of 1866 by banning race discrimination by private schools and other private contracts. In 1982 the Court also read the First Amendment broadly to uphold demonstrators' rights in a classic civil rights boycott.[9]

Since Justice Rehnquist became chief justice, the pattern of reading civil rights provisions to mean the most they could mean has been reversed. In a set of early decisions, the Court sharply reduced the reach of both old and new laws against employment discrimination. One case in 1989 hollowed out the meaning of the words "make and enforce contracts" in the Civil Rights Act of 1866. Another 1989 case stripped away almost all of the "discriminatory effects" rule of the Civil Rights Act of 1964. A 2001 case made it harder to use the Civil Rights Act of 1964 to stop recipients of federal funds from discrimination. All three decisions effectively reversed decisions of the Burger Court. In 2000 the Rehnquist Court also severely restricted the types of violations prevented by the Voting Rights Act.[10]

The Roberts Court has continued to read civil rights protections in constitutional amendments and civil rights laws for as little as they can mean.

Twice, once in 2018 and then in 2020, the Court has decided cases that seemingly involved only questions of evidence, but in fact seriously eroded the protection of civil rights previously afforded. The 2018 decision made it harder to prove a violation of the equal protection clause (in sex discrimination as well as race discrimination cases), and the 2020 case did the same weakening for race discrimination cases under the Civil Rights Act of 1866. These cases reversed pro–civil rights decisions of the Burger Court. Most notable was the decision in the *Shelby County* case (2013), where the Court found that the Fifteenth Amendment did not confer enough power on Congress to continue the extraordinarily effective preclearance process under the Voting Rights Act. This was the first time a federal law against race discrimination had been held unconstitutional by the US Supreme Court in more than a hundred years.[11]

The justices who have made these recent decisions are usually called "conservative," but there is no inherent reason why "conservative" should mean a justice disposed to minimizing civil rights provisions of the Constitution and laws. Justices who are considered conservative often read other constitutional amendments for the most they can mean. In protecting the First Amendment's right to "free exercise" of religion, justices give a very broad interpretation, even exempting giant retailers and corporations from general laws to suit religious preferences of their owners. In protecting citizens from an abridgment of freedom of speech, they rule against regulation of money in politics on the theory that giving full value to the First Amendment requires an expansive view of "free speech," even though the original framers in 1791 did not imagine that "free speech" meant money or included corporations, which were essentially unknown at the time. Likewise, "conservative" justices read the Second Amendment's "right to bear arms" for the most that clause can mean, even if the interpretation ignores the beginning words: "A well regulated Militia, being necessary to the security of a free State." These examples are not complaints: they simply note that conservative justices, like others, give a broad value to some constitutional provisions.[12]

Surely, the Thirteenth, Fourteenth, and Fifteenth Amendments, for which a horrible civil war was fought, call for full value rather than decisions draining them of content. The Reconstruction Amendments became part of the Constitution—the fundamental law of the land—to overcome our country's original sin. Redeeming the unfinished promise of those amendments surely calls for expansive readings. So do the laws enacted in the nineteenth century and the twentieth century to carry out those amendments. That is signaled by their text, which gives civil rights laws the extra imprimatur of special enforcement clauses in each of the Reconstruction Amendments themselves.

An expansive reading of civil rights constitutional amendments and laws is also faithful to the origin and text of the amendments, a matter that would be of interest to those who espouse current doctrines of originalism and textualism as modes of interpretation. A Supreme Court description soon after passage of the amendments and several laws emphasized both the origin and the text of the Reconstruction Amendments:

> We repeat, then, in the light of this recapitulation of events, almost too recent to be called history, but which are familiar to us all; and on the most casual examination of the language of these amendments, no one can fail to be impressed with the one pervading purpose found in them all, lying at the foundation of each, and without which none of them would have been even suggested; we mean the freedom of the slave race, the security and firm establishment of that freedom, and the protection of the newly-made freeman and citizen from the oppressions of those who had formerly exercised unlimited dominion over him. It is true that only the fifteenth amendment, in terms, mentions the negro by speaking of his color and his slavery. But it is just as true that each of the other articles was addressed to the grievances of that race, and designed to remedy them as the fifteenth.[13]

The Thirteenth Amendment was a fundamental redirection of the nation's future. It still is. A bold stance in 1865, the Thirteenth Amendment continues its promise to remove all the badges and incidents of slavery and the oppression of twelve generations. A broad reading of the Thirteenth Amendment shows that its principle is still alive, that its obligation is still far from met, and meeting that obligation will benefit all Americans.

The nation is very different today than when the Thirteenth Amendment changed the Constitution just over 150 years ago. Then, the vast majority of African American people in this country were formerly enslaved, almost all tied to the land in a region largely hostile to them. Today, the nation as a whole has, for at least the last fifty years, expressed a goal of racial equality, however uncertain or halting. Laws that created segregation and maintained a color line are gone—though unwritten laws of extreme wealth disparity and entrenched residential segregation can be more powerful than written codes. Time moves away from the past, generation by generation, but as Ta-Nehisi Coates has explained, "A nation outlives its generations." A generation from now, no living person will remember a time when segregation was the law of the land, but the legacy remains. A myth of the past was that law could not change human attitudes or behavior. The events in this book show otherwise; discriminatory laws did just that. As Thurgood Marshall declared in 1966, "There is very little truth in the old refrain that one cannot legislate equality. Laws not only provide concrete benefits, they can even change the hearts of men—some men, anyhow—for good or evil." Others may see less promise or be more focused on present failures than the prospect of far-future improvement. But new generations will continue the work. Historical awareness provides the encouragement and incentive to keep working for change.[14]

Judge Matthew J. Perry Jr. (1921–2011), South Carolina's leading civil rights attorney of his generation, and an African American, took unpopular and courageous stands during his career and experienced scorn from many in power, but now the federal courthouse in Columbia bears his name, honoring his advocacy for others. Judge Perry once told the authors, "I have seen things I never dreamed I would live to see." He also spoke of the great distance yet to go, but understanding that positive change had occurred made him realize that more could and would be achieved. Progress was an inspiration to work harder for change, not an excuse to relax.

The progress toward achieving racial justice today seems to be at a crossroads—perhaps it always is. One would like to think it will continue, and accelerate, but progress is not inevitable. Progress toward racial equality varies; it moves swiftly when the three branches of the federal government work together, as they did in the mid-twentieth century. Progress is also influenced by presidential appointment of Supreme Court justices, and here the coincidences of Time can make a difference. William Howard Taft had six appointments (including a chief justice) in his four-year term, and Warren Harding had four in two years before his early death; Jimmy Carter had none. Franklin D. Roosevelt had none in his first term and five in his second term. Timing of appointments matters even more now because Supreme Court justices stay longer than they used to, averaging twenty-five years nowadays, compared to half that long even fifty years earlier.[15]

In a 1951 poem, the Harlem Renaissance bard Langston Hughes asked, "What happens to a dream deferred?" History, shaped by the Court's unfolding interpretations and limitations on rights, tells us that Justice has been deferred too long.[16]

Abraham Lincoln challenged us: "Determine that the thing can and shall be done, and then we shall find the way." We take inspiration from the young people who will be writing the next chapter. In 2019–2020 the US Youth Poet Laureate, Amanda Gorman, gave readings around the country of a poem she had been commissioned to write for Independence Day. In her performance at the American Academy of Arts and Sciences, Gorman, an African American woman from Los Angeles who was a student at Harvard, explained that she sees American democracy not as "something that's broken," but as "something that's unfinished." Rather than falling prey to discouragement, she speaks of being "audacious" in "taking up the mantle" of our founders and playing her role in finishing their work. In her poem, "Believers' Hymn for the Republic," she declares, "Every day we write the future together."[17]

Notes

See the Index of Cases for full case citations.

Introduction

1. *Ozawa v. United States* (1922) and *U.S. v. Thind* (1923).
2. On defining the South, see Orville Vernon Burton, "The South as Other, the Southerner as Stranger," *Journal of Southern History* 79 (2013): 7–50. In 1860, slavery was still legal in fifteen states (and the District of Columbia). Eleven of these joined the Confederacy: Virginia, North Carolina, Tennessee, South Carolina, Georgia, Florida, Alabama, Mississippi, Louisiana, Texas, and Arkansas. The slave states of Kentucky, Missouri, Maryland, and Delaware remained in the Union. Historians have generally defined the South after the Civil War and in the first half of the twentieth century as the eleven Confederate States, Kentucky, and Oklahoma, and sometimes Missouri. US Census Bureau, Department of Commerce, Economics and Statistics Division, "Race and Hispanic Origin in 2003," 1–9, see esp. table 1: Population by Race and Hispanic Origins: 2—and 2003, 2, and summary 2–3. Population profile of the United States: Dynamic Version: Living Working and Growing in the USA, and "Population Distribution in 2003," 1. For definitions of "South" and minority population changes in the United States, see http://justice-deferred.clemson.edu.
3. *Confirmation Hearing on the Nomination of John G. Roberts, Jr. to Be Chief Justice of the United States: Hearing before the S. Comm. on the Judiciary,* 109th Cong. 56 (2005).
4. For the number of generations, we are using the dates 1668 and 1968 as the marker dates, with the following slightly arbitrary justifications. 1668: Although Africans arrived here in 1619, historians generally agree that the system of hereditary slavery as opposed to bonded or indentured service arose early in the second half of the 1600s. 1968: passage of the Fair Housing Act, the third major civil rights law of the 1960s, after the Civil Rights Act of 1964 and the Voting Rights Act of 1965.
5. Massachusetts chief justice Lemuel Shaw, in *Roberts v. City of Boston* (1849). Two justices who have expressed this idea in modern times are William Rehnquist in *Missouri v. Jenkins* (1995) at 95, and Clarence Thomas in *Parents Involved v. Seattle School Dist.* (2007) at 750. George Orwell, *1984* (Signet Classics, 1961), 75.
6. Justice Felix Frankfurter quote in Jeffrey Rosen, *The Supreme Court: The Personalities and Rivalries That Defined America* (Henry Holt, 2006), 9.

7. Admission of new states increased the need for more Supreme Court justices to ride circuit and hear cases. The number of justices never actually dropped to five because in 1802 the new Jefferson administration raised it back to six. Act of September 24, 1789, 1 Stat. 73 (original: six); Act of February 19, 1801, 2 Stat. 89 (five); Act of April 29, 1802, 2 Stat. 156 (six); Act of February 24, 1807, 2 Stat. 420 (seven); Act of March 3, 1837, 5 Stat. 176 (nine); Act of March 3, 1863, 12 Stat. 794 (ten); Act of July 23, 1866, 14 Stat. 209 (seven); Act of April 10, 1869, 16 Stat. 44 (nine).
8. Alexander Hamilton, *Federalist* No. 78, in *The Federalist Papers,* ed. Clinton Rossiter (New American Library, 1961), 427–435.
9. Other cases: *Fletcher v. Peck* (1810); *Martin v. Hunter's Lessee* (1816).
10. Charles Evans Hughes, *Addresses and Papers of Charles Evans Hughes, Governor of New York, 1906–1908* (G. P. Putnam's Sons, 1908), 139. Hughes meant the statement as praise, not condemnation, for he went on to say, "and the Judiciary is the safeguard of our liberty and our property under the Constitution." Number of unconstitutional laws: Congressional Research Service, *Constitution of the United States of America: Analysis and Interpretation,* Senate Document 112-9 (2017), 2253.

1. The Constitution, the Supreme Court, and the Road to Civil War

1. James Brewer Stewart, *William Lloyd Garrison and the Challenge of Emancipation* (Harlan Davidson, 1992), 164.
2. Jamestown colonist John Rolfe letter to the Virginia Company of London, approx. 1619/1620, in Susan Myra Kingsbury, ed., *The Records of the Virginia Company of London,* 3 (US Government Printing Office, 1933), 3: 241–247.
3. Fewer white indentured servants came to the New World as the economic and political situation in England changed. The English Civil War and the Commonwealth disrupted immigration, and the improving economy in Britain affected emigration. David W. Galenson, "The Rise and Fall of Indentured Servitude in the Americas: An Economic Analysis," *Journal of Economic History* 44 (March 1984): 1–26; Edmund S. Morgan, *American Slavery, American Freedom: The Ordeal in Colonial Virginia* (Norton, 1975), argued that class conflict led to slavery as the lifetime status for African Americans. John C. Coombs, "Beyond the 'Origins Debate': Rethinking the Rise of Virginia Slavery," in *Early Modern Virginia: Reconsidering the Old Dominion,* ed. Douglas Bradburn and John C. Coombs (University of Virginia Press, 2011), 239–278; Alan Gallay, *The Indian Slave Trade: The Rise of the English Empire in the American South, 1670–1717* (Yale University Press, 2002). See http://justice-deferred.clemson.edu.
4. Trans-Atlantic Slave Trade Database, at Emory University, https://www.slavevoyages.org/voyage/database. See http://justice-deferred.clemson.edu.

5. A. Leon Higginbotham, *In the Matter of Color* (Oxford University Press, 1978), 58; Edgar J. McManus, *A History of Negro Slavery in New York* (Syracuse University Press, 1966), 72–74, 88–92, 122–126, 146; Peter Hoffer, *Cry Liberty: The Great Stono River Slave Rebellion of 1739* (Oxford University Press, 2010).

6. Higginbotham, *Matter of Color,* 43–44; Laws against enslaving Christians also were changed. William McKee Evans, *Open Wound: The Long View of Race in America* (University of Illinois Press, 2009), 7–20.

7. Thomas D. Morris, *Southern Slavery and the Law, 1610–1860* (University of North Carolina Press, 1996), 23–24, 40–41, 44–45, 303–304; Peggy Pascoe, *What Comes Naturally: Miscegenation Law and the Making of Race in America* (Oxford University Press, 2009), 165.

8. Black Code, Sec. 40, 188–190; Judith Kelleher Schafer, *Becoming Free, Remaining Free: Manumission and Enslavement in New Orleans, 1846–1862* (Louisiana State University Press, 2003), 97–98.

9. Orville Vernon Burton, *The Age of Lincoln* (Hill and Wang, 2007), 4–8, 18–21, 36–49.

10. Scholars argue that the slave states gained a 25 percent bonus in the House. David A. Bateman, Ira Katznelson, and John S. Lapinski, *Southern Nation: Congress and White Supremacy after Reconstruction* (Princeton University Press, 2018), 8. On the 1800 election: Some assert Adams would have won because the electoral votes attributable to the slave count exceeded Jefferson's eight-vote victory margin (73–65). As we have analyzed the vote, however, Maryland and North Carolina split their electoral votes, making it impossible to tell how many votes each man would have lost and thus impossible to tell who would have won.

11. Sean Wilentz, in *No Property in Man: Slavery and Antislavery at the Nation's Founding* (Harvard University Press, 2018), esp. xiii, 2, 11, 262, 286, argues that Madison prevented the Constitution from ever affirming the right of "property in man." He believes a vibrant antislavery constitutional tradition emerged from the constitutional convention, a similar position to that articulated by Abraham Lincoln.

12. Quotation was by George Mason. Robert A. Rutland, ed., *The Papers of George Mason* (University of North Carolina Press, 1970), 173 and 966; see also Wilentz, *No Property in Man,* 82–83. Mason was one of those curious people who owned slaves and yet wrote about the evils of slavery. Gerald Leonard and Saul Cornell, *The Partisan Republic: Democracy, Exclusion, and the Founders' Constitution, 1780s–1830s* (Cambridge University Press, 2019), 20–21, 61–62, 146–177.

13. Henry Walcot Farnam, *Chapters in the History of Social Legislation in the United States to 1860* (Lawbook Exchange, 2000); Roger D. Bridges, "Historical Research and Narrative," 1, https://www.lib.niu.edu/1996/iht329602.html; Robert R. Dykstra, "White Men, Black Laws," *Annals of Iowa* 46 (Fall 1982): 407; M. Scott Heerman, *The Alchemy of Slavery: Human Bondage and Emancipation in the Illinois Country, 1730–1865* (Univer-

sity of Pennsylvania Press, 2018), 88, 123. Black people in Illinois were required to register themselves at the county courthouse and to pay a fee of $500, which increased to $1,000 after the passage of the Fugitive Slave Law. Naturalization Act of March 26, 1790, 1 Stat. 103.

14. Act of March 2, 1807, 2 Stat. 426; Southern state courts freeing slaves: *Dred Scott* at 558. Missouri Compromise: Act of March 6, 1820, 3 Stat. 545.

15. Paul Finkelman, *Supreme Injustice: Slavery in the Nation's Highest Court* (Harvard University Press, 2018), 52, and see chaps. 2 and 3; R. Kent Newmyer, *John Marshall and the Heroic Age of the Supreme Court* (Louisiana State University Press, 2001), 424–434; Morris, *Southern Slavery and the Law,* 418–419.

16. Eric Foner, ed., *Nat Turner* (Prentice Hall, 1971), 1–10; Heather Andrea Williams, *Self-Taught: African American Education in Slavery and Freedom* (University of North Carolina Press, 2005), 203–213. South Carolina initiated the slave states' anti-literacy codes in 1740 and made its law harsher in the act of 1834. John Belton O'Neal, *The Negro Law of South Carolina* (John G. Bowman, Publisher, 1848), 23; see also North Carolina Legislative Papers, 1830–1831, Session of the General Assembly, https://docsouth.unc.edu/nc/slavesfree/slavesfree.html.

17. William Lee Miller, *Arguing about Slavery* (Knopf, 1996), 115–129, 146–149; Peter Charles Hoffer, *John Quincy Adams and the Gag Rule, 1835–1850* (Johns Hopkins University Press, 2017), 26–27, 67–69.

18. Register of Debates, 24th Congress, 2nd Sess., 721–722. See also Robert Elder, *Calhoun: American Heretic* (Basic Books, 2021), 337–340.

19. Article I, Sections 2 and 8.

20. Alexis de Tocqueville, *Democracy in America* (1835), trans. Arthur Goldhammer, ed. Olivier Zunz, vol. 1 (Literary Classics of the United States, 2004), part 2, 365–366.

21. Jackson to John Coffee, April 7, 1832, in Tim Alan Garrison, *The Legal Ideology of Removal: The Southern Judiciary and the Sovereignty of Native American Nations* (University of Georgia Press, 2002), 193–194; Newmyer, *John Marshall,* 434–458.

22. Claudio Saunt, *Unworthy Republic: The Dispossession of Native Americans and the Road to Indian Territory* (Norton, 2020), 278. Harry L. Watson, *Andrew Jackson vs. Henry Clay: Democracy and Development in Antebellum America* (Bedford/St. Martin's Press, 1998), 75, 166. Michael D. Green and Theda Perdue, *The Cherokee Nation and the Trail of Tears* (Penguin Books, 2007), 126–140.

23. For good overviews on the "dire consequences," see Saunt, *Unworthy Republic* and Frederick E. Hoxie, *This Indian Country: American Indian Activists and the Place They Made* (Penguin Books, 2012).

24. Howard Jones, *Mutiny on the Amistad: The Saga of a Slave Revolt and Its Impact on American Abolition, Law, and Diplomacy* (Oxford University Press, 1987), 4–5; Marcus Rediker, *The Amistad Rebellion: An Atlantic Od-*

yssey of Slavery and Freedom* (Penguin Books, 2012), 1, 29–30. Before the Africans took the ship there had been forty-nine men and four children.

25. Death penalty: Act of May 6, 1820, 3 Stat. 600.

26. *Amistad* at 596–597.

27. US Congress, House, The Chevalier de Argaiz to Mr. Forsyth, 26th Cong., 1st sess., *House Documents, Otherwise Publ. as Executive Documents,* vol. 4., doc. no. 185, 18; on Argaiz, see Jones, *Mutiny on the Amistad,* 87, 91, 93, 111, 140–141, 160–162, 184, 206.

28. H. Robert Baker, *Prigg v. Pennsylvania: Slavery, the Supreme Court, and the Ambivalent Constitution* (University Press of Kansas, 2012), 101–126.

29. Quote attributed to Theophilus Harrington in John J. Duffy, Samuel B. Hand, and Ralph H, Orth, *The Vermont Encyclopedia* (University Press of New England, 2003), 151; Carol Wilson, *Freedom at Risk: The Kidnapping of Free Blacks in America, 1780–1865* (University Press of Kentucky, 1991).

30. Baker, *Prigg v. Pennsylvania,* 79, 101–126, and 79; Finkelman, *Supreme Injustice,* 140–141.

31. Paul Finkelman and Joseph Story, "Story Telling on the Supreme Court: Prigg v. Pennsylvania and Justice Joseph Story's Judicial Nationalism," *Supreme Court Review* 1994 (1994): 277.

32. *Prigg v. Pennsylvania* (1842) at 612.

33. *Prigg v. Pennsylvania* (1842) at 668.

34. Act of Sept. 9, 1850, 9 Stat. 446.

35. *Roberts v. Boston* (1849) at 198; J. Morgan Kousser, *Dead End: The Development of Nineteenth-Century Litigation on Racial Discrimination in Schools* (Clarendon Press, 1986); David Donald, *Charles Sumner and the Coming of the Civil War* (Knopf, 1967), 180–181.

36. The eight cases were listed in the dissenting opinion in *Scott v. Emerson* (1852) at 590.

37. *Scott v. Emerson* (1852) at 586.

38. *Scott v. Emerson* at 591.

39. If the Scotts had appealed directly from the Missouri Supreme Court, the US Supreme Court would automatically have affirmed the Missouri decision under the rule of another slave case, *Strader v. Graham* (1850).

40. On the notoriety of *Dred Scott,* see Jamal Greene, "The Anticanon," *Harvard Law Review* 125 (2011): 379–475, esp. 406–412; Kelly Marie Kennington, *In the Shadow of Dred Scott: St. Louis Freedom Suits and the Legal Culture of Slavery in Antebellum America* (University of Georgia Press, 2017), 172. According to Timothy S. Huebner, *Liberty & Union: The Civil War Era and American Constitutionalism* (University Press of Kansas, 2016), 91, the case contains the "most infamous lines in Supreme Court history." The classic study is Don Edward Fehrenbacher, *The Dred Scott Case: Its Significance in American Law and Politics* (Oxford University Press, 1978); see also Earl M. Maltz, *"Dred Scott" and the Politics of Slavery*

(University Press of Kansas, 2007); and for a political scientist's argument that there was more controversy over whether a slaveholder's rights in the territories was absolute than over Black citizenship, see Mark Graber, *Dred Scott and the Problem of Constitutional Evil* (Cambridge University Press, 2006).

41. Timothy S. Huebner, "Roger B. Taney and the Slavery Issue: Looking Beyond—and Before—Dred Scott," *Journal of American History* 97 (June 2010): 17–38.

42. The Kansas-Nebraska Act of 1854, Act of May 30, 1854, 10 Stat. 277.

43. James Buchanan, "Inaugural Address," March 4, 1857, online at Gerhard Peters and John T. Woolley, *The American Presidency Project,* http://www.presidency.ucsb.edu/ws/?pid=25817.

44. Fehrenbacher, *The Dred Scott Case,* 309–314; Finkelman, *Supreme Injustice,* 173–184, 201–204.

45. *Dred Scott* at 125–126 (Justice McLean, dissenting), citing *Pease v. Peck* (1856).

46. Kenneth Stampp, *America in 1857* (Oxford University, 1990), 80–90. Neither McLean nor Curtis were Democrats.

47. *Dred Scott* at 405.

48. Carl B. Swisher, *Roger B. Taney* (Macmillan, 1935), 152–154.

49. *Dred Scott* at 407.

50. *Dred Scott* at 407. Taney argued that the Framers' words should be interpreted as they were *originally* understood, even if that was different from current (1857) understanding: "It is difficult at this day to realize the state of public opinion in relation to that unfortunate race . . . when the Constitution of the United States was framed and adopted." *Dred Scott* at 405. Cass R. Sunstein, "Constitutional Myth-Making: Lessons from the Dred Scott Case," Occasional Papers No. 37, Harvard University, 1996.

51. Curtis: *Dred Scott* at 576; Taney, 416–417.

52. Earlier extremist views: Wilentz, *No Property in Man,* 201–205. "Power coupled with the duty," *Dred Scott* at 452.

53. Not like other property: *Prigg v. Pennsylvania* at 612. Entry of slaves banned in Virginia: *Dred Scott* at 627; banned in Mississippi: *Groves v. Slaughter* (1841).

54. Northwest Ordinance: Act of August 7, 1789, 1 Stat. 50. The Northwest Ordinance is usually dated in 1787, the date it was enacted under the Articles of Confederation, before being reenacted by the First Congress under the new Constitution. Taney: *Dred Scott* at 446–448.

55. *Dred Scott* at 407.

56. Lea Vandervelde, "The 'Dred Scott' Case as an American Family Saga," *OAH Magazine of History* 25 (April 2011): 24–28.

57. *The Liberator,* March 13, 1857; *New York Tribune,* March 7, 1857. Quotation: William Preston, in the Charleston *Daily Courier,* June 4, 1860.

2. A New Birth of Freedom

1. J. David Hacker, "A Census-Based Count of the Civil War Dead," *Civil War History* 57 (December 2011): 307, 348, and "Recounting the Dead," *New York Times,* September 20, 2011.

2. Abraham Lincoln, "Address at Sanitary Fair, Baltimore Maryland: April 18, 1864," in *The Essential Lincoln: Speeches and Correspondence,* ed. Orville Vernon Burton (Hill and Wang, 2019), 165.

3. Abraham Lincoln "Gettysburg Address," November 19, 1863, in Burton, *The Essential Lincoln,* 253–254.

4. See http://justice-deferred.clemson.edu for more information on the five Freedmen's Bureau Acts, four Reconstruction Acts, two Civil Rights Acts, two Enforcement Acts, six Readmissions Acts, the Ku Klux Act, the Anti-Peonage Act, and a number of other laws.

5. On emancipation and the meaning of freedom in and coming out of the Civil War, see Joseph P. Reidy, *Illusions of Emancipation: The Pursuit of Freedom and Equality in the Twilight of Slavery* (University of North Carolina Press, 2019).

6. Reverend James W. Hood, quoted in Steven Hahn, *A Nation under Our Feet: Black Political Struggles in the Rural South from Slavery to the Great Migration* (Harvard University Press, 2003), 121.

7. Timothy Huebner, "'The Unjust Judge': Roger B. Taney, the Slave Power, and the Meaning of Emancipation," *Journal of Supreme Court History* 40 (2015): 253–255; Harold M. Hyman and William M. Wiecke, *Equal Justice under Law: Constitutional Development, 1835–1875* (Harper and Row, 1982), 252–255, 268, 274, 305, 397.

8. Eric Foner, *Reconstruction; America's Unfinished Revolution, 1863–1877* (Norton, 2019), 31, 34–37; Michael Vorenberg, *Final Freedom: The Civil War, the Abolition of Slavery, and the Thirteenth Amendment* (Cambridge University Press, 2001), 210.

9. Roy Basler, ed., *The Collected Works of Abraham Lincoln* (Rutgers University Press, 1953), 8:254; *New York Times,* February 1, 1865; David E. Kyvig, *Explicit and Authentic Acts: Amending the U.S. Constitution, 1776–1995* (University Press of Kansas, 1996), 162.

10. On the Thirteenth Amendment's exception for crimes, see Chapter 5. Willie Lee Rose, *Rehearsal for Reconstruction: The Port Royal Experiment* (Bobbs-Merrill, 1964).

11. Freedman's Bureau: Act of March 3, 1865, 13 Stat. 507; Claude F. Oubre, *Forty Acres and a Mule: The Freedmen's Bureau and Black Land Ownership* (Louisiana State University Press, 1978), 67–68, 188; Donald G. Nieman, *To Set the Law in Motion: The Freedmen's Bureau and the Legal Rights of Blacks, 1865–1868* (KTO Press, 1979), xix–xv, 46; Stephen R. Wise and Lawrence S. Rowland, with Gerhard Spieler, *Rebellion, Reconstruction, and Redemption, 1861–1893,* vol. 2 of *The History of Beaufort County* (University of South Carolina Press, 2015), 157–159, 182–184, 253–274.

12. Abraham Lincoln, "Second Inaugural," March 4, 1865, in Burton, *The Essential Lincoln,* 170.

13. Quote, "now if ever," by Black minister Henry McNeil Turner, in Paul D. Escott, *The Worst Passions of Human Nature: White Supremacy in the Civil War North* (University of Virginia Press, 2020), 2–3.

14. Lincoln formulated a plan for Louisiana when that state came under Union control. In his "Proclamation of Amnesty and Reconstruction" (December 8, 1863), he would allow Louisiana into the Union when 10 percent of those who voted in 1860, excluding Confederate government and military leaders, took an oath of allegiance to the United States and accepted emancipation. Peyton McCrary, *Abraham Lincoln and Reconstruction: The Louisiana Experiment* (Princeton University Press, 1979), 6–10, 185–193; James G. Hollingsworth, *An Absolute Massacre: The New Orleans Race Riot of July 30, 1866* (Louisiana State University Press, 2004); Steven V. Ash, *A Massacre in Memphis: The Race Riot That Shook the Nation One Year After the Civil War* (Hill and Wang, 2013).

15. Orville Vernon Burton, *Penn Center: A History Preserved* (University of Georgia Press, 2014), 9, 11–12, 19–20, 29, 31; Rose, *Rehearsal for Reconstruction,* 196, 201–202, 276, 278, 285, 291, 294, 380, 402; Blake McNulty, "William Henry Brisbane: South Carolina Slaveholder and Abolitionist," in *The Southern Enigma: Essays on Race, Class, and Folk Culture,* ed. Walter J. Frazier and Winfred B. Moore Jr. (Greenwood Press, 1983), 119–129, esp. 125; J. Brent Morris, "'We Are Verily Guilty Concerning Our Brother': The Abolitionist Transformation of Planter William Henry Brisbane," *South Carolina Historical Magazine* 111 (2010): 118–150; Wise and Roland, *Rebellion, Reconstruction, and Redemption,* 157–159; Wisconsin case: *Ableman v. Booth* (1859). See Robert Cover, *Justice Accused: Antislavery and the Judicial Process* (Yale University Press, 1975), 185–188.

16. Abraham Lincoln, "Speech . . . April 11, 1865," in Burton, *The Essential Lincoln*, 171–177.

17. Proclamation Establishing Government for North Carolina, May 29, 1865, in *The Papers of Andrew Johnson,* vol. 8, ed. LeRoy P. Graf, Ralph W. Haskins, and Paul H. Bergeron (University of Tennessee Press, 1967–1999), 4, 136–138; Hans L. Trefousse, *Andrew Johnson: A Biography* (Norton, 1997), 216–218; O. O. Howard, *Autobiography of Oliver Otis Howard: Major General, United States Army* (Baker and Taylor, 1907), 2:236; Rose, *Rehearsal for Reconstruction*, 346–357.

18. South Carolina Black Citizens to Andrew Johnson, June 29, 1865, in Graf et al., *Papers of Andrew Johnson,* 8:317–319; "Speech of B. F. Perry," *Journal of the People of South Carolina, Held in Columbia, South Carolina, September 1865* (Julian A. Selby, 1865), 14. 42d Congress, 2d Sess., House Report 22: Testimony Taken by the Joint Committee to Enquire into the Condition of Affairs in the Late Insurrectionary States; 43d Congress, 2d Sess., House Report 262: Affairs in Alabama, June 9, 1971, 93 (Parson's quote), https://archive.org/details/reportofjointselo8unit/page/92/mode/2up; Albert Castell, *The Presidency of Andrew Johnson* (University Press of

Kansas, 1979), 101–102; McCrary, *Abraham Lincoln and Reconstruction*, 312. See Foner, *Reconstruction*, 176–227, esp. 215, 182–183, and 187–190 on Johnson's appointments of provisional governors. Southern opinion in the aftermath of Johnson becoming president is discussed in Michael Perman, *Reunion without Compromise: The South and Reconstruction, 1865–1868* (University of Cambridge Press, 1973), 13–53, 61–64, 68–81; LaWanda Cox and John H. Cox, *Politics, Principle, and Prejudice, 1865–1866: Dilemma of Reconstruction America* (Atheneum, 1969), 151–171.

19. T. B. Wilson, *Black Codes of the South* (University of Alabama Press, 2000); "Laws in Relation to the Freedmen," 39 Cong. 2 Sess., Senate Exec. Doc. 6, *Freedmen's Affairs*, 170–230; *Laws of Mississippi*, 1865, 82 ff; Florida State Constitution, 1865, chap. 1467, sec. 1, "An Act to punish Vagrants and Vagabonds"; Laura F. Edwards, *A Legal History of the Civil War and Reconstruction: A Nation of Rights* (Cambridge University Press, 2015), 143 argues that white Southerners retained the antebellum legal order; Amy Dru Stanley, *From Bondage to Contract: Wage Labor, Marriage, and the Market in the Age of Slave Emancipation* (Cambridge University Press, 1998), 59 notes the "contract served as a legitimating symbol for social relations in which inequality was either cloaked by exchange or said to arise from consent."

20. *National Anti-Slavery Standard* (New York, NY), January 5, 1867; *Wilmington Daily Dispatch* (Wilmington, NC), May 26, 1866; *Congressional Globe*, 39th Congress, 2d Sess., 324 (1867); "Congressional Proceedings," *Charleston Daily Courier* (Charleston, SC), January 8, 1867.

21. "Black Codes of Mississippi," *Chicago Tribune*, December 1, 1865.

22. Eric L. McKitrick, *Andrew Johnson and Reconstruction* (University of Chicago Press, 1960), 258; Foner, *Reconstruction*, 239.

23. Congressional Globe, 39th Cong. 1st Sess. 322 (January 29, 1866).

24. S. 60, 39th Cong., 1st Sess. vetoed February 19, 1866. Charles Fairman, *History of the Supreme Court of the United States: VI, Reunion and Reaction, Part One* (Macmillan, 1971), 1153–1167.

25. Foner, *Reconstruction*, 159–162; Oubre, *Forty Acres and a Mule*, 53–54; Donald G. Nieman, *To Set the Law in Motion*, 108–115; and "Andrew Johnson, the Freedmen's Bureau and the Problem of Equal Rights, 1865–1866," *Journal of Southern History* 44 (1978): 399–420.

26. Civil Rights Act of April 9, 1866, 14 Stat. 27, § 1; Christian G. Samito, ed., *The Greatest and Grandest Act: The Civil Rights Act of 1866 from Reconstruction to Today* (Southern Illinois University Press, 2018); Foner, *Reconstruction*, 243–245. Little noticed at the time was a provision for schools in Washington, DC, that were segregated by race.

27. Exclusion of "Indians not taxed" continued the notion, largely academic by then, that the Indian tribes were sovereign nations. Citizenship was finally granted in 1924 by the Indian Citizenship Act, Act of June 2, 1924, 43 Stat. 253. Before then, Native Americans had US citizenship in limited circumstances; *Elk v. Wilkins* (1884).

28. Richard H. Fallon Jr. et al., Hart and Wechsler's *The Federal Courts and the Federal System,* 5th ed. (Foundation Press, 2003), 826–829; Act of July 16, 1866, 14 Stat. 173.

29. "Burglariously": *US v. Rhodes* at 785, 786.

30. David Mayer Silver, *Lincoln's Supreme Court* (University of Illinois Press, 1998), 103–106; Timothy S. Huebner, *The Taney Court: Justices, Rulings and Legacy* (ABC-CLIO Supreme Court Handbooks, 2003), 103–106; James Simon, *Lincoln and Chief Justice Taney: Slavery, Secession, and the President's War Powers* (Simon and Schuster, 2016), 336.

31. *United States v. Rhodes* (1867) at 793.

32. Discussion in *Civil Rights Cases,* 109 U.S. 3 (1883); *Congressional Globe,* 38th Congress, 1st Sess., 1313, 1439–1440, 2989, on "Incidents of Slavery."

33. Based on the votes of residents, the measure on the Maryland constitution would have been defeated, but Maryland soldiers serving in the US Army voted their support and the state amendment passed. See James D. Schmidt, *Free to Work: Labor Law, Emancipation, and Reconstruction* (University of Georgia Press, 1998) for a brief discussion of the case. See Barbara Jeanne Fields, *Slavery and Freedom on the Middle Ground: Maryland during the Nineteenth Century* (Yale University Press, 1985), 139–142, 148–149, 151, 153–156, on apprenticeship of Black children. For Chief Justice Chase's role, see Harold M. Hyman, *The Reconstruction Justice of Salmon P. Case: In Re Turner and Texas v. White* (University Press of Kansas, 1997), 109.

34. Quote on "strong arm of power" in James M. McPherson, "Lincoln and the Millennium," Jefferson Lecture, March 27, 2000; Eric Foner, *The Second Founding: How the Civil War and Reconstruction Remade the Constitution* (Norton, 2019), 55–92.

35. Burke A. Hinsdale, ed., *The Works of James Abram Garfield,* vol. 1 (James R. Osgood and Co., 1882), 249.

36. The Reconstruction Act became law on March 2, 1867 (14 Stat. 428) and was amended several times: March 23, 1867 (15 Stat. 2), July 19, 1867 (12 Stat. 14), February 18, 1869 (15 Stat. 344). Charles Sumner to Theodore Tilton, April 18, 1867, in The *Selected Letters of Charles Sumner,* ed. Beverly Wilson Palmer (Northeastern University Press, 1990), 2:394.

37. *United States v. Louisiana* (1963) at 353n49; Richard Engstrom, Stanley A. Halpin Jr., Jean A. Joll, and Victoria M. Caridas-Butterworth, "Louisiana," in *The Quiet Revolution in the South: The Impact of the Voting Rights Act, 1965–1990,* ed. Chandler Davidson and Bernard Grofman (Princeton University Press, 1994), 104; James M. McPherson, *Ordeal by Fire: The Civil War and Reconstruction* (Knopf, 1982), 535; Foner, *Reconstruction,* 314; Donald G. Nieman, *Promises to Keep: African-Americans and the Constitutional Order, 1776 to the Present* (Oxford University Press, 1991), 71–72.

38. After Georgia was readmitted, it promptly expelled its elected Black legislators, at which point Congress reimposed military rule, required reversal

of the expulsion, and required Georgia to ratify the Fifteenth Amendment before again readmitting the state by Act of July 15, 1870, 16 Stat. 363. Vikram David Amar, "Jury Service as Political Participation Akin to Voting," *Cornell Law Review* 80 (1995): 203, 230–232. Tennessee was not put under military Reconstruction because it promptly ratified the Fourteenth Amendment and was readmitted July 24, 1866, 14 Stat. 364. Other Readmission Acts were on June 22, 1868, 15 Stat. 72 (Arkansas); Jan. 26, 1870, 16 Stat. 62, amended Feb. 1, 1870, 16 Stat. 63 (Virginia); Feb. 23, 1870, 16 Stat. 67 (Mississippi); Mar. 30, 1870, 16 Stat. 80 (Texas); July 15, 1870, 16 Stat. 363 (Georgia); and June 25, 1868, 15 Stat. 73 (the other six states, including Georgia's first abortive readmission). Congress added another condition for readmission of the last three states, Virginia, Mississippi, and Texas. They had to guarantee in their new state constitutions equal education for Black and white students.

39. Alexander Keyssar, *The Right to Vote: The Contested History of Democracy in the United States* (Basic Books, 2000), tables A2 and A5.

40. Xi Wang, *The Trial of Democracy: Black Suffrage and Northern Republicans, 1860–1910* (University of Georgia Press, 1997), 39–48, 52–57. Senator Sherman, speaking on Suffrage Constitutional Amendment, on February 9, 1869, 40th Congressional 3rd sess., *Congressional Globe* 61, pt. 2: 1039. Frederick Douglass, in *Proceedings of the National Convention of Colored Men, held in The City of Syracuse, N.Y., October 4, 5, 6, and 7, 1864; with the Bill of Wrongs and Rights and the Address to the American People* (J.S. Rock and Geo L. Ruffin, 1864), 60, on voting, 22, 34, 42, 47, 55–60.

41. Robert R. Dykstra, *Bright Radical Star: Black Freedom and White Supremacy on the Hawkeye Frontier* (Harvard University Press, 1993), 227.

42. James M. McPherson, *Struggle for Equality: Abolitionists and the Negro in the Civil War and Reconstruction* (Princeton University Press, 1964), 424–430; Faye E. Dudden, *Fighting Chance: The Struggle over Woman Suffrage and Black Suffrage in Reconstruction America* (Oxford University Press, 2012). Tennessee ratified the Fifteenth Amendment in 1997.

43. Eric Foner, *Freedom's Lawmakers: A Directory of Black Officeholders during Reconstruction* (Oxford University Press, 1993); P. B. S. Pinchback served as governor of Louisiana for just over one month, from December 9, 1872, to January 13, 1873.

44. "A Reform Absolutely Complete," April 9, 1970, in *The Papers of Frederick Douglass*, ed. John W. Blassingame et al., ser. 1, vol. 4 (Yale University Press, 1991), 259–265, quotation at 260.

45. Joel Williamson, *After Slavery: The Negro in South Carolina during Reconstruction, 1861–1877* (University of North Carolina Press, 1965), 260; Foner, *Freedom's Lawmakers*, 32.

46. Michael A. Ross, *Justice of Shattered Dreams: Samuel Freeman Miller and the Supreme Court during the Civil War Era* (Louisiana State University Press, 2003), 147. Ross footnotes a letter to William Pitt Ballinger, an attorney in Galveston, dated February 6, 1867; George C. Rable, *But There*

Was No Peace: The Role of Violence in the Politics of Reconstruction (University of Georgia Press, 1984); Elaine Frantz Parsons, *Ku-Klux: The Birth of the Klan during Reconstruction* (University of North Carolina Press, 2016).

47. Enforcement Act, Act of May 31, 1870, 16 Stat. 140. Section 6 allowed imprisonment of up to ten years, but section 7 provided that the penalty could even be death if the conspiracy resulted in a crime that would carry the death penalty under state law.

48. Ku Klux Act, Act of April 20, 1871, 17 Stat. 13; Lou Falkner Williams, *The Great South Carolina Ku Klux Klan Trials, 1871–1872* (University of Georgia Press, 1996); Everette L. Seinney, "Enforcing the Fifteenth Amendment, 1870–1877," *Journal of Southern History* 26 (May 1962): 421–440.

49. Federal oversight of federal elections was first provided in Section 6 of the Naturalization Act of July 14, 1870, 16 Stat. 254. It was then provided in detail in the Second Enforcement Act of February 28, 1871, 16 Stat. 433.

50. Act of March 1, 1875, 18 Stat. 385. The law was passed a year after the death of Senator Charles Sumner, who had long been the chief advocate for such a law. Amy Dru Stanley, "Slave Emancipation and the Revolutionizing of Human Rights," in *The World the Civil War Made,* ed. Gregory P. Downs and Kate Masur (University of North Carolina Press, 2015), 271 argues that this act marked "a turning point in both the death of slavery and the emergence of human rights."

3. The Supreme Court in Reconstruction

1. The correspondence is described in Justice Goldberg's concurring opinion in *Bell v. Maryland* (1964) at 309 and note 29. The case holding that the Bill of Rights controlled only the federal government was *Barron v. Baltimore* (1833).

2. Xi Wang, *The Trial of Democracy: Black Suffrage and Northern Republicanism, 1860–1910* (University of Georgia Press, 1997), 135–144; Richard White, *The Republic for Which It Stands: The United States during Reconstruction and the Gilded Age, 1865–1896* (Oxford University Press, 2017), 282–284.

3. Victor B. Howard, "The Black Testimony Controversy in Kentucky, 1866–1872," *Journal of Negro History* 58 (1973): 140–141, and notes 3 and 4 (end of the no-Black-testimony rule in other states).

4. An earlier decision, *United States v. Ortega* (1825), interpreted the word "affecting" to mean only the parties to a case, but that decision had nothing to do with the rights of witnesses or the Civil Rights Act and therefore did not justify the majority's holding in *Blyew.*

5. *Blyew* at 599 and 601. Chief Justice Chase did not participate in the decision.

6. Howard, "Black Testimony Controversy," 164–165n30; Charles Fairman, *History of the Supreme Court of the United States: Reconstruction and Reunion, 1864–88,* vol. 1 (Macmillan, 1971), 846.

7. La. Acts of 1869, Act 118, March 8, 1869.

8. Compiled Service Records of Confederate Soldiers Who Served in Organizations Raised Directly by the Confederate Government, NARA microfilm publication M258, 123 rolls, ARC ID: 586957, War Department Collection of Confederate Records, Record Group 109, The National Archives at Washington, DC, https://www.nps.gov/civilwar/soldiers-and-sailors-database.htm; "Saturated": Samuel Freeman Miller to William Pitt Ballinger, Oct. 15, 1877, Samuel Freeman Miller Papers, box 2, folder 2, Library of Congress, Washington, DC; Michael A. Ross, "Obstructing Reconstruction: John Archibald Campbell and the Legal Campaign against Louisiana's Republican Government, 1868–1873," *Civil War History* 49, no. 3 (2003): 251.

9. The best-known summary of "privileges and immunities" was in a lower court opinion by Supreme Court Justice Bushrod Washington in *Corfield v. Coryell,* 6 Fed. Cas. 546 (Lower court, 1823). Article IV used "and" while the Fourteenth Amendment used "or," but this was simply grammatical. Another possible definition of "privileges or immunities" could have been the Bill of Rights, as Judge Woods thought in *U.S. v. Hall.* See http://justice-deferred.clemson.edu on *Slaughter-House.*

10. New Orleans *Daily Picayune,* June 7, 1870 (at earlier stage of the case).

11. Michael A. Ross, *Justice of Shattered Dreams: Samuel Freeman Miller and the Supreme Court during the Civil War Era* (Louisiana State University Press, 2003), 115.

12. *Slaughter-House Cases* at 113 and 129. The other dissenters were Justice Field, who favored the businessmen but had no love for African Americans, and Chief Justice Chase, who did not write a separate opinion because he was very ill and died three weeks later. See Harold M. Hyman, *The Reconstruction Justice of Salmon P. Chase: In Re Turner and Texas v. White* (University Press of Kansas, 1997), 158.

13. Act of May 31, 1870, 16 Stat. 140.

14. Charles Lane, *The Day Freedom Died: The Colfax Massacre, the Supreme Court, and the Betrayal of Reconstruction* (Henry Holt and Company, 2008), 124.

15. Judge Woods apparently delivered his opinion orally, so he had no written opinion.

16. *Cruikshank* at 550. A recent canvassing of what the *Cruikshank* case did to the US Constitution is James Gray Pope, "Snubbed Landmark: Why United States v. Cruikshank (1876) Belongs at the Heart of the American Constitutional Canon," *Harvard Civil Rights-Civil Liberties Law Review* 49 (2014): 385.

17. The words "war of race" come from Justice Bradley's lower-court opinion at 714.

18. *Dred Scott* at 417.

19. *Cruikshank* at 555. The opinion also said, puzzlingly, that Count 4 did not allege a racial purpose, although the words of that count plainly did. *Cruikshank* at 554. Note that the Court rejected Count 4, alleged violation of the equal protection clause, twice on two separate grounds.

20. *Jones v. van Zandt* (1847); *Ableman v. Booth* (1859). Bradley's lower court opinion did discuss *Prigg* (1842).

21. Pamela Brandwein, *Rethinking the Judicial Settlement of Reconstruction* (Cambridge University Press, 2011), 28–59. She has argued that the Supreme Court actually left open a way to prosecute private individuals if, as was often the case, a state defaulted on its obligation to enforce the law on behalf of the freedmen. Her theory of "state neglect" is intriguing but does not excuse the Court's errors in *Cruikshank*.

22. Nicholas Leman, *Redemption: The Last Battle of the Civil War* (Farrar, Straus and Giroux, 2006), 26.

23. Act of May 31, 1870, 16 Stat. 140; see Robert Michael Goldman, *Reconstruction and Black Suffrage: Losing the Vote in Reese and Cruikshank* (University Press of Kansas, 2001), esp. 60–107.

24. *Reese* at 220, 242.

25. *Kitchen v. Randolph* (1876). A possible explanation for Waite's opinion is suggested by Brandwein, *Rethinking the Judicial Settlement,* 122–123, and Leslie Goldstein, "The Specter of the Second Amendment," *Studies in American Political Development* 21 (2007): 121–148. These two scholars present cogent arguments for a view of the Reconstruction Court quite different from the one presented here. True, there were justices sympathetic to the freed people, opinions with eloquent language, and decisions upholding large verdicts for victims of race discrimination—*Railroad Company v. Brown* (1873) and *Walker v. Sauvinet* (1876)—just weeks after *Cruikshank* and *Reese.* The mystery remains how the Court could have rendered decisions so technically flawed and producing results so disastrous then and for the future.

26. See discussions of *United States v. Raines* (1960) in Chapter 9 and *Griffin v. Breckinridge* (1971) in Chapter 10. The classic discussion of the subject shows that the *Reese* Court had ample authority in both directions, that is, whether to strike the entire statute or not. Robert L. Stern, "Separability and Separability Clauses in the Supreme Court," *Harvard Law Review* 51 (1937): 76.

27. Leman, *Redemption,* 100–172, esp. 148–161, 170–172. Gary corresponded with James Z. George and Sam W. Ferguson, two leaders of the 1875 Mississippi Plan. Patrick Dean Kent, "Red Shirt Revisited: The Politics of Martin Gary, 1868–1881" (MA thesis, Clemson University, 2015), 53; "Plan of the Campaign of 1876," Papers of Martin Witherspoon Gary, South Caroliniana Library, University of South Carolina. *Charleston News and Courier,* September 22, 1876.

28. Benjamin R. Tillman, "The Struggle of 1876: How South Carolina Was Delivered from Carpet-Bag and Negro Rule," speech delivered at the Red

Shirt Reunion at Anderson, South Carolina, 1909; the wearing of "red shirts" may have been copied from Guiseppe Garibaldi's troops' use of Red Shirts in the Italian wars of 1870.

29. June 22–23, 1879, 9 Cong. Rec. 2292, relating to House Bill 2252. All of Hayes's vetoes were sustained because the Democrats did not have the two-thirds majorities to override them.

30. This jurisdiction was enhanced because federal elections were defined to include elections for state offices if they were conducted together with the election for federal officers. Sections 20–22 of the Enforcement Act of 1870.

31. *Ex parte Yarbrough* at 657. Prosecution of state officials for civil rights violations at a federal election had been upheld in *Ex parte Siebold* (1880).

32. *Terry v. Adams* (1953); Leslie Anne Lovett, "The Jaybird-Woodpecker War: Reconstruction and Redemption in Fort Bend County, Texas, 1869–1889" (MA thesis, Rice University, 1994). An example of similar violence took place in 1886 in Washington County, Texas. Donald G. Nieman, *Promises to Keep: African-Americans and the Constitutional Order, 1776 to the Present* (Oxford University Press, 1991), 78–79.

33. Ann. Rep. of the Attorney General, 1890, xiii, quoted in Paul Freund et al., *Constitutional Law,* 2nd ed. (Little Brown and Co., 1961), 927. "Several assassinations of officers and witnesses, with the purpose of impeding the execution of the laws and orders of the United States courts, have occurred during the past year." Prosecution dismissed: *U.S. v. Sanges* (Lower court, 1891) appeal dismissed on procedural grounds, *U.S. v. Sanges* (1892).

34. By the time of his release, Strauder had been incarcerated for nine years. Christopher Waldrep, *Jury Discrimination: The Supreme Court, Public Opinion, and a Grassroots Fight for Racial Equality in Mississippi* (University of Georgia Press, 2010), 164.

35. Christopher Waldrep, *Racial Violence on Trial: A Handbook with Cases, Laws and Documents* (ABC Clio, 2001), 172–174. *Ex parte Reynolds* (Lower court, 1878).

36. *Virginia v. Rives* at 322.

37. Anthony Amsterdam, "Criminal Prosecution Affecting Federally Guaranteed Civil Rights: Federal Removal and Habeas Corpus Jurisdiction to Abort State Criminal trial," *University of Pennsylvania Law Review* 113 (1965): 793.

38. *Ex parte Virginia* at 347. No prosecutions since then: Benno Schmidt, "Juries, Jurisdiction and Race Discrimination: The Lost Promise of Strauder v. West Virginia," *Texas Law Review* 61 (1983): 1401, 1475.

39. Michael Les Benedict, "Preserving Federalism: Reconstruction and the Waite Court," *Supreme Court Review* 39 (1978). Benedict has pointed out a number of Supreme Court decisions during this period that rejected arguments that would have made conditions far worse.

40. Justice John Marshall Harlan did not dissent, but later, in *Baldwin v. Franks* (1887), he said he disagreed with the *U.S. v. Harris* decision. The Thirteenth Amendment might have been inapplicable anyway, because the victims were

apparently white, as Pamela Brandwein has convincingly shown: Brandwein, *Rethinking the Judicial Settlement,* 154–155. A contemporaneous newspaper article seems to bear this out, suggesting the incident was part of a feud between white families: "The Enforcement Act," *Daily American (Nashville Tennesseean),* August 6, 1876, 1.

41. In another coincidence, Woods had been through a "dress rehearsal" of the *Harris* case just months earlier. Sitting as a circuit justice in Texas, he had dismissed an almost identical prosecution, *U.S. v. Le Grand* (Lower court, 1882). His opinion in *Harris* was almost a carbon copy of his opinion in the Texas case.

42. Act of March 1, 1875, 18 Stat. 335; Paul Finkelman, "The Hidden History of Northern Civil Rights Law and the Villainous Supreme Court, 1875–1915," *University of Pittsburg Law Review* 79 (2018): 357, 369–389. Under a Louisiana law of this type, the US Supreme Court upheld a $1,000 verdict for an African American who was turned away from a coffeehouse in New Orleans, *Walker v. Sauvinet* (1876).

43. *Civil Rights Cases* at 17.

44. *Civil Rights Cases* at 20.

45. *Civil Rights Cases* at 24. "It would be running the slavery argument into the ground to make it apply to every act of discrimination . . . ," at 24–25.

46. *Civil Rights Cases* at 25.

47. Loren P. Beth, *John Marshall Harlan: The Last Whig Justice* (University Press of Kentucky, 1992), 53–67, 69, 119–129; Linda Przybyszewski, *The Republic According to John Marshall Harlan* (University of North Carolina Press, 1999), 15, 27, 35–38, 41–42, 73–75, 201–202.

48. *Civil Rights Cases* at 27.

49. *Civil Rights Cases* at 49.

50. Editorial, *New York Globe,* October 20, 1883. "Civil Rights: The Opinions of Two Leading Colored Lawyers on the Recent Decision; Deep Game Being Played by Arthur Politicians—What Next?—Hon. John P. Green Gives His Views," *Christian Recorder,* November 1, 1883. A thorough survey of African American reactions to the decision is in Marianne L. Engelman Lado, "A Question of Justice: African-American Legal Perspectives on the 1883 Civil Rights Cases," *Chicago-Kent Law Review* 70 (1995): 1123.

51. *Civil Rights Cases* at 26, 40.

52. The Court recognized Congress's power to punish racial violence under other constitutional provisions; *Logan v. U.S.* (1892) (murder of a prisoner held in federal custody and thus entitled to federal protection); *Waddell v. U.S.* (1884) (interference with a homesteader).

53. *Yick Wo v. Hopkins* (1886) at 358–359; Of 310 wooden laundries in the city, 240 were operated by Chinese people. There were several laundries made of brick or stone, which were exempt from the permit requirement.

54. *Yick Wo* at 373–374 and 370–371. The Court appears also to have held that the ordinance violated the due process clause because it had no standards and thus allowed the city free rein to grant or deny a permit at will.

55. "Twin pillars" is a biblical reference to King Solomon's temple: 1 Kings 7:15. Other writers have used it in connection with Jim Crow; see Robert Volney Riser, *Defying Disfranchisement: Black Voting Rights Activism in the Jim Crow South, 1890–1908* (Louisiana State University Press, 2010), 2.

56. J. Morgan Kousser, *The Shaping of Southern Politics, 1880–1910: Suffrage Restriction and the Establishment of the One-Party South* (Yale University Press, 1974), 29–31; Xi Wang, *The Trial of Democracy,* esp. 207–259.

57. Robert Smalls, "Election Methods in the South," *North American Review* 151 (1890): 599; Albion Tourgee, "Shall White Minorities Rule?," *The Forum,* April 1889, 150.

58. Homer Socolofsky and Allan Spetter, *The Presidency of Benjamin Harrison* (University of Kansas, 1987), 60–65; David A. Bateman, Ira Katznelson, and John S. Lapinski, *Southern Nation: Congress and White Supremacy after Reconstruction* (Princeton University Press, 2018), 198–208; Kousser, *Shaping of Southern Politics,* 29–31; Richard E. Welch Jr., "The Federal Elections Bill of 1890: Postscripts and Prelude," *Journal of American History* 52 (1965): 511; Richard M. Valelly, *The Two Reconstructions: The Struggle for Black Enfranchisement* (University of Chicago Press, 2004), 131, 247; Sarah A. Binder and Steven S. Smith, *Politics or Principle? Filibustering in the United States Senate* (Brookings Institution Press, 1997), 129–135. The bill came to the Senate floor in the lame duck session in early 1891, but it was finally pulled in the face of an unyielding Democratic filibuster.

59. Gilbert Thomas Stephenson, "The Separation of the Races in Public Conveyances," *American Political Science Review* 3 (May 1909): 180–204. For the period leading up to segregated railroad cars, see Kenneth W. Mack, "Law, Society, Identity, and the Making of the Jim Crow South: Travel and Segregation on Tennessee Railroads, 1875–1905," *Law and Social Inquiry* 24 (1999): 377.

60. The US Supreme Court said there was a difference in the cases because the Mississippi Supreme Court interpreted its law to apply only within the state, but this supposed difference made no sense because the issue involved what happened at the state border, where the burden under the two states' laws, large or small, was identical.

61. *Louisville, N.O. & T.R.R. v. Mississippi* at 594. Justice Harlan had joined the Supreme Court just before the *Hall v. DeCuir* decision (1878), but did not participate. See Reporter's Memorandum in *U.S. Reports,* vol. 95. Justice Bradley's dissent was one of his last votes before he died in 1892. Curiously, the actual passage in Justice Harlan's opinion in *U.S. Reports* has the wording of the sentence backward. Here is the actual, mistaken sentence as it appears in *U.S. Reports:* "It is difficult to understand how a state enactment requiring the separation of the white and black races on interstate carriers of passengers is a regulation of commerce among the states, while a

similar enactment forbidding such separation is not a regulation of that character." Justice Harlan's actual, transposed words make it appear that the Court was striking down the Mississippi law but had upheld the Louisiana law—the opposite of what actually happened in the two cases. It is unknown whether anyone has noticed this transposition in the 130 years since the decision. But as the Roman poet Horace said about an error in *The Iliad*, "Even Homer nods."

62. *Blyew v. U.S.* (1872); *Virginia v. Rives* (1880); *U.S. v. Reese* (1876); *U.S. v. Cruikshank* (1876); *U.S. v. Harris* (1883); *Baldwin v. Franks* (1887); *Civil Rights Cases* (1883).

4. The Supreme Court and the Jim Crow Counterrevolution

1. Leon F. Litwack, *Trouble in Mind: Black Southerners in the Age of Jim Crow* (Knopf, 1999), xiv–xv; Brian Roberts, *Blackface Nation: Race, Reform, and Identity in American Popular Music, 1812–1925* (University of Chicago Press, 2017).

2. See Chapter 3 for *Hall v. De Cuir* (1878) and *Louisville RR* (1890).

3. Gilbert Thomas Stephenson, "The Separation of the Races in Public Conveyances," *American Political Science Review* 3 (May 1909): 180–204; Kenneth W. Mack, "Law, Society, Identity, and the Making of the Jim Crow South: Travel and Segregation on Tennessee Railroads, 1875–1905," *Law and Social Inquiry* 24 (1999): 377.

4. Vernon Lane Wharton, *The Negro in Mississippi, 1865–1899* (Harper, 1965), 199–215; for a recent study, see Dorothy Overstreet Pratt, *Sowing the Wind: The Mississippi Constitutional Convention of 1890* (University Press of Mississippi, 2018).

5. Jackson *Clarion-Ledger*, July 31, 1890; Wharton, *The Negro in Mississippi*, 210–211.

6. R. Volney Riser, *Defying Disfranchisement: Black Voting Rights Activism in the Jim Crow South, 1890–1908* (Louisiana State University Press, 2010), 39.

7. Neil R. McMillen, *Dark Journey: Black Mississippians in the Age of Jim Crow* (University of Illinois Press, 1989), 39, 41, 43, 49.

8. Jackson *Clarion-Ledger*, October 30, 1890; Wharton, *The Negro in Mississippi*, 210–211, 214–215.

9. W. Roy Smith, "Negro Suffrage in the South," in *Studies in Southern History and Politics, Essays in Honor of William Archibald Dunning* (Columbia University Press, 1914), 242; US Commission on Civil Rights, *Political Participation* (1967), 244–247.

10. Act of February 8, 1894, 28 Stat. 36.

11. *Journal of the Constitutional Convention of the State of South Carolina* (Charles A. Calvo Jr., 1895), September 10, 1895, 1–2. Tillman quotation: October 31, 1895, 464; David Duncan Wallace, *The South Carolina Con-*

stitution of 1895, Bureau of Publications, no. 197, University of South Carolina, February 15, 1927, 35; "The South Carolina Constitutional Convention of 1895," *Sewanee Review* 4 (May 1896): 346–360.

12. *Mills v. Green* at 832 (Lower court, 1895); Lewis Henry Reece IV, "Pure Despotism: South Carolina's Route to Disfranchisement, 1867–1895" (PhD, Bowling Green University, 2001), 263–296; Riser, *Defying Disfranchisement*, 19–22, 24–28, 33–34.

13. Booker T. Washington, "The Standard Printed Version of the Atlanta Exposition Address," in *The Booker T. Washington Papers: Volume 3, 1889–1895*, ed. Louis Harlan (University of Illinois Press, 1972), 583–587, quote 586; Washington modeled Tuskegee after Virginia's Hampton Institute, where he had received his own education.

14. The railroad company seems to have cooperated in allowing Plessy to buy the ticket. Railroad companies typically opposed separate car laws because of the inconvenience and expense, but were reluctant "to array themselves against" the law. Letter from Louis Martinet to Albion Tourgée, quoted in Charles A. Lofgren, *The Plessy Case* (Oxford University Press, 1987), 32. For a modern analysis of this landmark case, see Williamjames Hull Hoffer, *Plessy v. Ferguson: Race and Inequality in Jim Crow America* (University Press of Kansas, 2012); and for a more recent account, see Steve Luxenberg, *Separate: The Story of Plessy v. Ferguson, and America's Journey from Slavery to Segregation* (Norton, 2019).

15. *Ex parte Plessy* (State court, 1893) at 951; Hoffer, *Plessy v. Ferguson*, 2–3, 67–68.

16. Mark Elliott, "Race, Color Blindness, and the Democratic Public: Albion W. Tourgée's Principles in *Plessy v. Ferguson*," *Journal of Southern History* 67 (May 2001): 289–290; Otto H. Olsen, *Carpetbagger's Crusade: The Life of Albion Winegar Tourgée* (Johns Hopkins University Press, 1965); Luxenberg, *Separate*, 70–88, 153–173, 237–258, 312–340; Albion W. Tourgée, *A Fool's Errand: A Novel of the South during Reconstruction* (Fords, Howard and Hulbert, 1879).

17. *Plessy v. Ferguson* (1896) at 543–544. The words "exactly the same" come from *Virginia v. Rives* (1880) at 318.

18. *Plessy v. Ferguson* at 544–545.

19. *Plessy v. Ferguson* at 548.

20. *Railroad Co.* at 449.

21. *Plessy v. Ferguson* at 551.

22. William Graham Sumner, *Folkways: A Study of the Sociological Importance of Usages, Manners, Customs, Mores, and Morals* (Ginn, 1907), 77. To Sumner the demise of Reconstruction was "the proof that legislation cannot make mores." See also C. Vann Woodward, *The Strange Career of Jim Crow* (Oxford University Press, 1955), 88. *Plessy v. Ferguson* at 551. Contrary to Justice Brown, a "badge of inferiority" was not simply in their own minds but was stamped in Louisiana law, which held that a white

person was entitled to damages for slander for being called a Negro. *Spotorno v. Fourichon* (1888).

23. *Ferguson v. Gies* (1890) at 368.

24. *Plessy v. Ferguson* at 559.

25. *Plessy v. Ferguson* at 559, 562.

26. "A Damnable Outrage," Parsons (Labette County, Kansas) *Weekly Blade,* May 30, 1896; "Black Men for the White Metal," *Chicago Daily Tribune,* August 13, 1896; "The 'Jim Crow' Case," *Indianapolis News,* May 18, 1896; "Three Louisiana Cases Decided," *Times-Picayune,* May 19, 1896. The *New York Times* carried a small story about the case on an inside page under the heading "Railway News," and a keyword search for "Plessy" found only one other mention before 1950, a mention unrelated to civil rights, on January 17, 1903. The *Washington Post, Los Angeles Times,* and *Atlanta Constitution* did somewhat better, with short articles about the case in 1896. Four major African American newspapers (the *Pittsburgh Courier, Afro-American, Chicago Defender,* and *Amsterdam News*) were only marginally better than the *New York Times,* with no references before 1937 and 1938—in reference to the ongoing NAACP litigation in *Missouri ex. Rel. Gaines v. Canada* (1938) and other cases.

27. "Like the Measles," Springfield, Massachusetts, *Republican,* May 20, 1896.

28. Benjamin E. Mays, "The New Negro Challenges the Old Order," in Asa H. Gordon, *Sketches of Negro Life and History in South Carolina,* 2nd ed. (University of South Carolina Press, 1971), 194; Richard Kluger, *Simple Justice: The History of Brown v. Board of Education and Black America's Struggle for Equality* (Knopf, 1976), 88.

29. J. Clay Smith, *Emancipation: The Making of a Black Lawyer* (University of Pennsylvania Press, 1993); W. Lewis Burke, *All for Civil Rights: African American Lawyers in South Carolina, 1868–1968* (University of Georgia Press, 2019).

30. Riser, *Defying Disfranchisement,* 38–39; McMillen, *Dark Journey,* 54; Smith, *Emancipation,* 294–295, 303; Pratt, *Sowing the Wind,* 180–186, 188, 205; Wharton, *The Negro in Mississippi,* 202–203.

31. Riser, *Defying Disfranchisement,* 40–41.

32. Smith, *Emancipation,* 131; *Gibson v. Mississippi* (1896); *Smith v. Mississippi* (1896).

33. *Ratliff v. Beale* (1896) at 868.

34. *Ratliff v. Beale* (1896) at 868.

35. This case was carefully staged, as shown by the fact that the taxpayer complaining about a two-dollar poll tax was represented by S. S. Calhoon, chairman of the 1890 convention, and J. Z. George, Mississippi's US senator and former chief justice. At the heart of the case was most likely the not-quite-ended battle for domination between the majority-white counties and the planters in the Black Belt counties who still wanted to "harvest" votes from the African Americans they controlled on their plantations and farms.

36. *Williams v. Mississippi* at 221–222 (quoting passages from the Mississippi Supreme Court).

37. *Williams v. Mississippi* at 222.

38. *Williams v. Mississippi* at 225.

39. Scott Zesch, "Chinese Los Angeles in 1870–1871: The Makings of a Massacre," *Southern California Quarterly* 90 (2008): 109–158; T. A. Larson, *History of Wyoming* (University of Nebraska Press, 1978), 141–144. The Rock Springs, Wyoming, massacre in 1885 took somewhere between twenty-eight and fifty lives. John Higham, *Strangers in the Land: Patterns of American Nativism, 1860–1925* (Atheneum, 1965), 25.

40. Act of March 3, 1875, 18 Stat. 477; Act of May 6, 1882, 22 Stat. 58. The Burlingame Treaty of July 1868, 16 Stat. 739, allowed free immigration, though not naturalization, but the Angell Treaty of November 17, 1880, 22 Stat. 826, allowed the United States to stop immigration by laborers (who accounted for almost all the Chinese immigration). Quotations in Iris Chang, *The Chinese in America* (Viking Press, 2003), 13.

41. Act of July 5, 1884, 23 Stat. 115; Act of October 1, 1888, 25 Stat. 504; Act of May 5, 1892, 27 Stat. 25; Act of August 18, 1894, 28 Stat. 390; Act of April 29, 1902, 32 Stat 176. One impetus for restricting reentry certificates was said to be the practice of "paper names," in which—in those preidentification days—a new Chinese immigrant might impersonate one who was already a US resident.

42. *Chy Lung v. Freeman* (1876). This case arose when a California port official designated twenty Chinese passengers as "debauched women," so, under the disputed state law, they could not enter without posting a $500 bond in gold for each. Pigtail ordinance: *Ho Ah Kow v. Newnan* (Circuit Court, 1879). Early Chinese Exclusion Act cases: *Chew Heong v. United States* (1884); *Jung Ah Lung* (1888).

43. *Baldwin v. Franks* at 695; *Chae Chan Ping v. U.S.* (1889); *Fong Yue Ting v. U.S.* (1893); *Lem Moon Sing v. U.S.* (1895).

44. United States citizenship was a longstanding issue. In the *Dred Scott* case (1857), Chief Justice Taney wrote that the descendants of Africans, even if born in the United States, could not be US citizens and that Congress had no power to make them citizens, even though Article I of the Constitution gives Congress power "to establish an uniform rule of naturalization." Even after the Fourteenth Amendment, the Supreme Court held that someone who was a member of an Indian tribe at birth but who later left the tribe was still not a US citizen, *Elk v. Wilkins* (1884).

45. Chief Justice Fuller wrote a dissent, joined by Justice Harlan. Rag tag quote: Erika Lee, "Birthright Citizenship, Immigration and the U.S. Constitution, The Story of *United States v. Wong Kim Ark*," in *Race Law Stories*, ed. Rachel Moran et al. (Foundation Press, 2008), 89, 98. The victory in *Wong Kim Ark* was soon watered down. The 1894 amendment to the Chinese Exclusion Act gave immigration officers final authority and eliminated an immigrant's right to appeal to a court. That law initially did not

bar court hearings for claims of citizenship, but in *U.S. v. Ju Toy* (1905), a lamentable opinion by Justice Holmes held that even claims of citizenship could be shut off from the courts. If that interpretation had been adopted in the 1890s, Wong Kim Ark would simply have been sent back to China with no court case. *Ju Toy* was effectively overruled in *Ng Fung Ho v. White* (1922).

46. Magnuson Act, Act of December 17, 1943, 57 Stat. 600. Even then, the immigrant quota for China was set at an insulting 105 per year when it should have been 2,148 (based on the statutory formula of two percent of the nationality's 1890 population, which was 107,475). A special irony of the Chinese cases was the seeming anti-Chinese view of Justice John Marshall Harlan, in contrast to his strong support for African American rights. Gabriel Chin, "The Plessy Myth," *Iowa Law Review* 82 (1996): 151; Earl Maltz, "Only Partially Color-Blind: John Marshall Harlan's View of Race and the Constitution," *Georgia State Law Review* 12 (1996): 973; Loren P. Beth, *John Marshall Harlan: The Last Whig Justice* (University Press of Kentucky, 1992), 236–237; Linda Przybyszewski, *The Republic According to John Marshall Harlan* (University of North Carolina Press, 1999), 120–112.

47. The agreement was never formally written. The Japanese commitment was described in correspondence from the Japanese ambassador to Secretary of State Charles Evans Hughes and reprinted in the Congressional Record. 68th Cong., 2d Sess., vol. 65, p. 6073 (1924). Paul Finkelman, "Coping with a New 'Yellow Peril': Japanese Immigration, the Gentlemen's Agreement, and the Coming of World War II," *West Virginia Law Review* 117 (2015): 1446. Some important cases involved Japanese immigrants. In *Yamataya v. Fisher* (1903), the Supreme Court held that in deportation (removing a noncitizen from the country), as opposed to exclusion (barring entry), there is a constitutional right to at least minimal due process.

48. *U.S. v. Sioux Nation of Indians* (1979) at 470.

49. *Congressional Record,* 56th Cong., 2d Sess., vol. 34, pt. 2 (US Government Printing Office, 1901), 1635, 1636, 1638.

50. James C. Cobb, *The Most Southern Place on Earth: The Mississippi Delta and the Roots of Regional Identity* (Oxford University Press, 1992), 91; Armand Derfner, "Racial Discrimination and the Right to Vote," *Vanderbilt Law Review* 26, no. 3 (1973): 523, 536n46; on disfranchisement and voting, see J. Morgan Kousser, *The Shaping of Southern Politics, 1880–1910: Suffrage Restriction and the Establishment of the One-Party South* (Yale University Press, 1974); Canter Brown Jr., *Florida's Black Public Officials, 1867–1924* (University of Alabama Press, 1998), 59, 63.

51. Paul Lewinson, *Race, Class, and Party: A History of Negro Suffrage and White Politics in the South* (Oxford University Press, 1932), 86; Michael Perman, *Pursuit of Unity: A Political History of the American South* (University of North Carolina Press, 2010), 177.

52. Matthew J. Shott, "Progressives against Democracy: Electoral Reform in Louisiana, 1894–1921," *Louisiana History* 20 (Summer 1979): 247–260;

Kousser, *The Shaping of Southern Politics,* 43–44, 47–50, 59, 60–62, 68–71, 83–86, 191, 236–250, 246–249; and see chart 239.

53. Riser, *Defying Disfranchisement,* 101. Smith had actually won a Supreme Court case in 1900 (*Carter v. Texas*). Louis R. Harlan, *Booker T. Washington: The Making of a Black Leader, 1856–1901* (Oxford University Press, 1972), 245–246; Robert J. Norrell, *Up from History: The Life of Booker T. Washington* (Belknap Press of Harvard University Press, 2009), 298.

54. Owen Fiss, *Troubled Beginnings of the Modern State* (Cambridge University Press, 2006), 372–379.

55. *Giles v. Harris* at 488.

56. *Giles v. Harris* at 486. The Court said its opinion did not decide whether the Alabama scheme was valid or not, Giles at 487, a pointless statement because the Court gave Alabama a clear go-ahead.

57. The Alabama court's theory was as follows (as the US Supreme Court explained it): "Conceding the allegations of the petition to be true . . . [that the Alabama constitution] has for its purpose to prevent negroes from voting and to exclude them from registration for that purpose, no damage has been suffered by the plaintiff, because no refusal to register by a board thus constituted in defiance of the Federal Constitution could have the effect to disqualify a legal voter." *Giles v. Teasley* at 164.

58. *Jones v. Montague* (1904); *Selden v. Montague* (1904); Smith, "Negro Suffrage in the South," 254–255.

59. *Cumming v. Richmond County School Board* at 545. Justice Harlan also said, mistakenly, that the plaintiffs had chosen the wrong remedy. The decision of the Georgia lower court granted the plaintiffs' requested remedy, saying it was appropriate. J. Morgan Kousser, "Separate but Not Equal: The First Supreme Court Case on Racial Discrimination in Education," *Journal of Southern History* 46 (February 1980): 17–44; Michael Klarman, *From Jim Crow to Civil Rights: The Supreme Court and the Struggle for Racial Equality* (Oxford University Press, 2004), 46–47. Klarman found only six public high schools for African Americans in the whole South. The fact that the schools were segregated was not raised or challenged.

60. Klarman, *From Jim Crow to Civil Rights,* 43, 45. J. Morgan Kousser, "Progressivism for Middle-Class Whites Only: The Distribution of Taxation and Expenditures for Education in North Carolina, 1880–1910," *Journal of Southern History* 46 (1980): 169–194; Kluger, *Simple Justice,* 88. Horace Mann Bond, *Negro Education in Alabama: A Study in Cotton and Steel* (1939; repr. Atheneum, 1969); Forty-Second Annual Report of the State Superintendent of Education of the State of South Carolina, South Carolina Department of Education, 1910, "Per Capita Expenditure According to Enrollment by Counties 1909–'10," in *The South Carolina General Assembly Reports and Resolutions* (The State Company, 1910), 3:837, and Forty-Third Annual Report of State Superintendent (1911), 395, 398, 399, 401.

61. Kluger, *Simple Justice,* 87.

62. *Berea College v. Kentucky* at 69. David E. Bernstein, "Lochner vs Plessy: The Berea College Case," *Journal of Supreme Court History* 25, no. 1 (2008); Ronald Rauschberg, "*Berea College v. Kentucky:* Scientific Racism in the Supreme Court," *Journal of Supreme Court History* 48 (2020): 262–286.

63. *Santa Clara County v. Southern Pacific RR* (1886); Adam Winkler, *We the Corporations: How American Businesses Won Their Civil Rights* (Liveright, 2018), 158. Charles Wallace Collins, *A Study of the Operation of the Restraint Clauses of Section One of The Fourteenth Amendment to the Constitution of the United States, 1912* (De Capo Press, 1974): 129–138. Blocking state regulation: *Minnesota Rate Case* (1890) (railroad rates), *Allgeyer v. Louisiana* (1897) (insurance), *Lochner v. New York* (1905), and *Coppage v. Kansas* (1915). Berea instituted a separate school, called the Lincoln Institute, for African Americans.

64. Harlan dissented in both cases, joined by one other justice each time (two different justices).

65. In *Clyatt v. U.S* (1905), the Supreme Court upheld the constitutionality of the Peonage Act of 1867 but even here the Court narrowed the statute.

66. *Tarrance v. Florida* (1903); *Brownfield v. South Carolina* (1903); *Martin v. Texas* (1906); *Thomas v. Texas* (1909); *Franklin v. South Carolina* (1910).

67. Montgomery County, Alabama, put some African Americans on juries after *Rogers v. Alabama*. Robert J. Norrell, *Up from History,* 299.

68. Smith, *Emancipation,* 291–292; McMillen, *Dark Journey,* 167, 169; Christopher Waldrep, *Jury Discrimination: The Supreme Court, Public Opinion, and a Grassroots Fight for Racial Equality in Mississippi* (University of Georgia Press, 2010), 31, 103–104.

69. In 1945 President Truman appointed Mollison's son, Irvin Mollison, to the US Customs Court, one of the first two African American federal judges.

70. *Lewis v. State* (State court, 1908); Waldrep, *Jury Discrimination,* 226–227.

71. Alfred M. Waddell, "The Story of the Wilmington, North Carolina, Race Riots," *The Farmer and Mechanic* (Raleigh, NC), November 29, 1898; David S. Cecelski and Timothy B. Tyson, eds., *Democracy Betrayed: The Wilmington Race Riot of 1898 and Its Legacy* (University of North Carolina Press, 1998).

72. Benjamin E. Mays, *Born to Rebel: An Autobiography* (University of Georgia Press, 1987), 329–335; George Brown Tindall, *South Carolina Negroes, 1877–1900* (University of South Carolina Press, 1952), 256–258, Charleston newspaper quote on 256.

73. Yorkville *Enquirer,* August 19, 1899; Tindall, *South Carolina Negroes,* Tillman quote on 258; People did attempt to kill some of the Tolberts, but the family and others in the area continued as Republicans to work for Black people's rights. In 1900 in Georgetown, South Carolina, a similar four-day white riot ended the sharing of county offices between white Democrats and African Americans (mostly Republicans).

74. Deborah Davis, *"Guest of Honor": Booker T. Washington, Theodore Roosevelt, and the White House Dinner That Shocked a Nation* (Atria, 2012); Kenneth M. Hamilton, *Booker T. Washington in American Memory* (University of Illinois Press, 2017), 61–62.

75. *The Colored American Magazine,* Editorial and Publishers' Announcements, November 1901, 78.

76. Terence Finnegan, *A Deed So Accursed: Lynching in Mississippi and South Carolina, 1881–1940* (University of Virginia Press, 2013), 50–55; Tindall, *South Carolina Negroes,* 255–256; Joel Williamson, *The Crucible of Race: Black-White Relations in the American South since Emancipation* (Oxford University Press, 1984), 116. When the postmaster general reopened the Indianola post office the next year, he downgraded it from third to fourth class on the grounds that the previous year's receipts had been so low. Today the Indianola post office is named after Minnie Cox.

77. Springfield, Illinois, *Independent,* August 20, 1908, and September 3, 1908. Gregory Mixon, *The Atlanta Riot: Race, Class, and Violence in a New South City* (University Press of Florida, 2005).

78. Mary White Ovington, *Black and White Sat Down Together: The Reminiscences of an NAACP Founder* (Feminist Press, 1995), 56–57, originally published as a series in the Baltimore *Afro-American,* 1932–1933; Patricia Sullivan, *Lift Every Voice: The NAACP and the Making of the Civil Rights Movement* (New Press, 2009), 5–6.

79. Charles Flint Kellogg, *N.A.A.C.P.: A History of the National Association for the Advancement of Colored People, 1909–1920* (Johns Hopkins University Press, 1967), 9–19; James M. McPherson, *The Abolitionist Legacy: From Reconstruction to the NAACP* (Princeton University Press, 1975), 368–393; Jerold S. Auerbach, *Unequal Justice: Lawyers and Social Change in Modern America* (Oxford University Press, 1981), 65–66.

80. Michael J. Pfeifer, "At the Hands of Parties Unknown? The State of the Field of Lynching Scholarship," *Journal of American History* 101 (December 2014): 837; Lester Frank Ward, *Pure Sociology: A Treatise on the Origin and Spontaneous Development of Society* (Macmillan, 1921), 359; Ibram X. Kendi, *Stamped from the Beginning: The Definitive History of Racist Ideas in America* (Nation Books, 2016), 296.

81. Rayford Logan, *The Negro in American Life and Thought: The Nadir, 1877–1901* (Dial Press, 1954); James W. Loewen, *Sundown Towns: A Hidden Dimension of American Racism* (New Press, 2005); Katherine C. Mooney, *Race Horse Men: How Slavery and Freedom Were Made at the Racetrack* (Harvard University Press, 2014); Ryan A. Swanson, *When Baseball Went White: Reconstruction, Reconciliation, and the Dream of a National Pastime* (University of Nebraska Press, 2014); David Zang, *Fleet Walker's Divided Heart: The Life of Baseball's First Major Leaguer* (University of Nebraska Press, 1995).

82. W. E. B. Du Bois, *The Souls of Black Folk* (A. C. McClurg and Co., 1903), 12.

5. Beginning the Long, Slow Turnaround

1. Adam Domby, *The False Cause: Fraud, Fabrication, and White Supremacy in Confederate Memory* (University of Virginia Press, 2020), 23, and see 13, 16–17, 19, 28; Karen Cox, *Dixie's Daughters: The United Daughters of the Confederacy and the Preservation of Confederate Culture* (2003; University of Florida Press, 2019), xxii.
2. Walter F. Wilcox, "Negro Criminality," in Alfred Stone, *Studies in the American Race Problem* (Doubleday, Page and Co., 1908). Frederick Hoffman, a renowned statistician who served as president of the American Statistical Association in 1911, used census data to show "without exception" that "the criminality of the negro exceeds that of any other race of any numerical importance in this country." Hoffman, *Race Traits and Tendencies of the American Negro* (American Economic Association, 1896), 217–234; Madison Grant, *The Passing of the Great Race* (1918; Arno Press, 1970). On historians, see John David Smith and J. Vincent Lowery, eds., *The Dunning School: Historians, Race, and the Meaning of Reconstruction* (University Press of Kentucky, 2013). Racist historians included Harvard professor Albert Hart, described at that time as the "grand old man" of United States history, Samuel Elliot Morrison, "Hart, Albert Bushnell," *Dictionary of American Biography,* Supplement 3, *1941–1945* (Charles Scribner's Sons, 1973), 337; Khalil Gibran Muhammad, *The Condemnation of Blackness: Race, Crime and the Making of America* (Harvard University Press, 2010).
3. Michele K. Gillespie and Randal L. Hall, *Thomas Dixon Jr. and the Birth of Modern American* (Louisiana State University Press, 2006); Linda Gordon, *The Second Coming of the KKK: The Ku Klux Klan of the 1902s and the American Political Tradition* (Liveright Publishing, 2017); Kenneth T. Jackson, *The Ku Klux Klan in the City, 1915–1930* (Oxford University Press, 1967); Nancy MacLean, *Behind the Mask of Civility: The Making of the Second Ku Klux Klan* (Oxford University Press, 1995).
4. James N. Gregory, *The Southern Diaspora: How the Great Migrations of Black and White Southerners Transformed America* (University of North Carolina Press, 2007). Historians and the US Census usually date the Great Migration as occurring approximately 1910 to 1970 (these were the years when more African Americans moved out of the American South than moved in).
5. Mark Curriden and Leroy Phillips, *Contempt of Court: The Turn of the Century Lynching That Launched a Hundred Years of Federalism* (Faber and Faber, 1999).
6. "Judge Technicality: The Lawyers Worked Every Point to Save Johnson," *Chattanooga Times,* March 5, 1906; Kittrell Rushing, "The Case of Ed Johnson [1906]," in *Illusive Shadows: Justice, Media, and Socially Significant American Trials,* ed. Lloyd Chiasson (Greenwood, 2003), 71. The petition was for a "writ of habeas corpus," an alternative method of appeal for constitutional issues, discussed later in this chapter in *Moore v. Dempsey* (1923).

7. *Chattanooga News,* March 19, 1906. Mark Curriden, "A Supreme Case of Contempt," *ABA Journal* 95, no. 6 (2009): 39; Philip Dray, *At the Hands of Persons Unknown: The Lynching of Black America* (Random House, 2002), 158.

8. *United States v. Shipp* (I) (1906) at 573.

9. Curriden and Phillips, *Contempt of Court,* 334 (Holmes), 234–235 (preacher and attorneys).

10. Pete Daniel, *The Shadow of Slavery: Peonage in the South, 1901–1969* (University of Illinois Press, 1972), chap. 4, 65–81; August Meier, *Negro Thought in America, 1880–1915: Racial Ideologies in the Age of Booker T. Washington* (University of Michigan Press), 110–114.

11. Booker T. Washington to Oswald Garrison Villard, Sept 7, 1908, in the Papers of Booker T. Washington, Manuscript Division, Library of Congress, box 41, published in Louis R. Harlan and Raymond W. Smock, eds., *The Booker T. Washington Papers,* vol. 9 (University of Illinois Press, 1980), 618; On Washington's pivotal role, see Daniel, *The Shadow of Slavery,* 67–78.

12. Anti-Peonage Act of 1867: Act of March 2, 1867, 14 Stat. 546.

13. *Bailey* at 244. Following the Bailey case, the Supreme Court struck down another Alabama law that was an aggravated form of the convict-leasing system that kept the convict "chained to an ever-turning wheel of servitude." *United States v. Reynolds* (1914) at 146–147.

14. *Lynch v. Alabama* (2011): *Lynch v. State,* 2011 U.S. Dist. LEXIS 155012 at 834–837; Matthew J. Mancini, *One Dies, Get Another: Convict Leasing in the American South, 1866–1928* (University of South Carolina Press, 1966); Scott Reynolds Nelson, *Steel Drivin' Man: John Henry, the Untold Story of an American Legend* (Oxford University Press, 2006).

15. Charles Sumner to George William Curtis, April 13, 1864, in *The Selective Letters of Charles Sumner, 1859–1871,* ed. Beverly Wilson Palmer (Northwestern University Press, 1990), 2:233–235. One delegate at the South Carolina constitutional convention in 1865, a white unionist Republican from upstate, objected to the clause because it could allow states "to reestablish the condition of slavery by a system of crimes and punishments." Sidney Andrews, *The South since the War* (1866; Houghton Mifflin, 1971), 323–324; John Richard Dennett, *The South as It Is, 1865–1866* (University of Alabama Press, 2010), originally published as a series of articles in *The Nation* between July 8, 1865, and April 11, 1865. *Ruffin v. Commonwealth* (State court, 1871) at 796.

16. Eric Foner, *The Second Founding: How the Civil War and Reconstruction Remade the Constitution* (Norton, 2019), 45–51, 110.

17. Harland and Holmes were on opposite sides in both appearances of *Bailey v. Alabama* (1908, 1911). A striking portrait contrasting these two justices in *Bailey* and other cases is Jeffrey Rosen, *The Supreme Court: The Personalities and Rivalries that Defined America* (Henry Holt and Co., 2007), 71–125. Also fascinating is the contrast (oversimplified) between Harlan

(the most pro-Black, but anti-Chinese) and Brewer (the most pro-Chinese, but anti-Black).

18. State laws: *Louisville, N.O. & T.R.R. v. Mississippi* (1890) (discussed in Chapter 3); *Chesapeake & O.R.R. v. Kentucky* (1900). Interpretation of the state laws was the function of the state supreme courts, but the same approach those state courts followed should have led the US Supreme Court to uphold the federal law. The issue was highly technical; see discussion of the *Butts* case in Robert L. Stern, "Separability and Separability Clauses in the Supreme Court," *Harvard Law Review* 51 (1937): 76. The federal ban on discrimination on trains and boats was still alive because the Supreme Court had not fully dealt with that issue when it struck down the inns and theaters portion of the law in the *Civil Rights Cases* (1883).

19. *McCabe* at 161.

20. *Guinn v. U.S.* (1915) at 364–365.

21. *Myers v. Anderson* (1915). Chicago *Defender,* July 1, 1915; Patricia Sullivan, *Lift Every Voice: The NAACP and the Making of the Civil Rights Movement* (New Press, 2009), 48.

22. *Guinn v. U.S.* at 365. For *Washington v. Davis,* see Chapter 11.

23. *Harris v. Louisville* (State court, 1915) at 559; Richard Rothstein, *The Color of Law: A Forgotten History of How Our Government Segregated America* (Liveright, 2017), 44–45.

24. John R. Howard, *The Shifting Wind: The Supreme Court and Civil Rights from Reconstruction to Brown* (SUNY Press, 1999), 185–193.

25. *New York Age,* November, 10, 1917; *Literary Digest,* November 24, 1917; Howard, *The Shifting Wind,* 192, 365.

26. *Harmon v. Tyler* (1927) (New Orleans); *City of Richmond v. Deans* (1930).

27. Rothstein, *The Color of Law,* 77–81.

28. Rothstein, *The Color of Law,* 44–45.

29. *Civil Rights Cases* at 25–26, said "the wrongful acts of individuals" do not violate the federal Constitution if "unsupported by State authority in the shape of laws, customs, or judicial or executive proceedings."

30. James Kushner, "Apartheid in America," *Howard Law Journal* 22 (1979): 563n38; Jeffrey D. Gonda, *Unjust Deeds: The Restrictive Covenant Cases and the Making of the Civil Rights Movement* (University of North Carolina Press, 2015), 4–6, 93–97, 134–136.

31. When an NAACP lawyer tried to argue that Gong Lum did not approve school segregation, Justice Frankfurter took him to task. Kluger, *Simple Justice,* 567–569; Adrienne Berard, *Water Tossing Boulders: How a Family of Chinese Immigrants Led the First Fight to Desegregate Schools in the Jim Crow South* (Beacon Press, 2016), 59–61, 89.

32. Virginia's Racial Integrity Act of 1924, described as an expression of nativism in *Loving v. Virginia* (1967) at 5–6; John Higham, *Strangers in the Land: Patterns of American Nativism, 1860–1925* (Atheneum, 1965).

33. Immigration Act of 1924, Act of May 26, 1024, 43 Stat. 153. With three million recent immigrants from Italy, an Italian quota based on the 1920 census would have been 60,000, but the actual quota based on the 1890 census was 3,845. The quota for England and Ireland, which were sending few immigrants by then, was 62,574. *Statistical Abstract of the United States.*

34. Act of July 14, 1870, 16 Stat. 254.

35. *Ozawa v. U.S.* (1922) at 194.

36. *Ozawa* at 198.

37. *U.S. v. Thind* (1923) at 215.

38. *Toyota v. U.S.* (1925) at 412.

39. *Buck v. Bell* (1927) at 208. Eighteen years later, at the Nuremberg war crimes trials after World War II, testimony and records showed that the Nazis had long called attention to this US Supreme Court decision.

40. Howard Thurman, "A 'Native Son' Speaks" (1940), in *The Papers of Howard Washington Thurman,* ed. Walter Earl Fluker (University of South Carolina Press, 2012), 2:250–251.

41. "For Action on Race Peril," *New York Times,* October 5, 1919.

42. Red Summer: James Weldon Johnson, *Along This Way* (Da Capo Press, 1933), 241; Johnson also wrote "Lift Every Voice," which became the Black National Anthem. *New York Times,* October 5, 1919; Robert Whitaker, *On the Laps of Gods: The Red Summer of 1919 and the Struggle for Justice That Remade a Nation* (Random House, 2008); Cameron McWhirter, *Red Summer: The Summer of 1919 and the Awakening of Black America* (St. Martin's, 2011); Sullivan, *Lift Every Voice,* 89; Benno Schmidt, *Red Scare: FBI and the Origins of Anticommunism in the United States, 1919–1943* (Museum Tusculanum Press, University of Copenhagen, 2000), 24–28; Tim Madigan, *The Burning: Massacre, Destruction, and the Tulsa Race Riot of 1921* (St. Martin's Press, 2001). B. C. Franklin was the father of renowned historian John Hope Franklin. Buck Colbert Franklin, *My Life and an Era: The Autobiography of Buck Colbert Franklin,* ed. John Hope Franklin and John Whittington Franklin (Louisiana State University Press, 1997), 196–202; John Hope Franklin, *Mirror to America: The Autobiography of John Hope Franklin* (Farrar, Straus and Giroux, 2005), 4, 15–16, 24–27, 30, 372–373. Interview with Franklin, May 17, 2004, with Georganne and Vernon Burton, Urbana, Illinois. "Tulsa Race Riot: A Report by the Oklahoma Commission to Study the Tulsa Race Riot of 1921," February 28, 2001, updated December 13, 2014, https://archive.org/details/ReportOnTulsaRaceRiotOf1921/page/n1/mode/2up and https://www.tulsahistory.org/exhibit/1921-tulsa-race-massacre/. David R. Colburn, "Rosewood and America in the Early Twentieth Century," *Florida Historical Quarterly* 76, no. 2 (Fall 1997): 175–192; Michael D'Orso, *Like Judgement Day: The Ruin and a Redemption of a Town Called Rosewood* (G. P. Putnam's Sons, 1998).

43. *The Gazette* (Arkansas), October 3, 1919; Grif Stockley Jr., *Blood in Their Eyes: The Elaine Race Massacre of 1919* (University of Arkansas Press, 2001).

44. Michael J. Klarman, *From Jim Crow to Civil Rights: The Supreme Court and the Struggle for Racial Equality* (Oxford University Press, 2004), 120–121. An earlier appeal was also rejected by the US Supreme Court in *Ex parte Frank* (1914). See Steve Oney, *And the Dead Shall Rise: The Murder of Mary Phagan and the Lynching of Leo Frank* (Pantheon Books, 2003); Leonard Dinnerstein, *The Leo Frank Case* (University of Georgia Press, 1987); Jeffrey Paul Melnick, *Black-Jewish Relations on Trial: Leo Frank and Jim Conley in the New South* (University Press of Mississippi, 2000). Based on overwhelming evidence of innocence, Leo Frank received a full pardon in 1986, more than seventy years after he was killed.

45. The Supreme Court had already rejected a "direct appeal" of the decision of the Arkansas Supreme Court, *Moore and Hicks v. Arkansas* (1920). This case, *Moore v. Dempsey,* was a second try in the form of a "habeas corpus" petition. Unlike a direct appeal, which is generally limited to issues raised in the trial itself, a habeas corpus petition could go beyond the actual trial into surrounding circumstances like intimidation, threats of lynching, and inflammatory newspaper influence. Although the habeas corpus procedure had been used to reverse state court convictions where a state law itself was unconstitutional, it does not appear that any federal court had ever granted a habeas corpus petition to reverse a state court conviction on the ground of unconstitutional *procedures* in or surrounding the state court trial. Such a petition was about to be considered in *U.S. v. Shipp* (1906, 1909), the Chattanooga case discussed earlier in this chapter, but of course the lynching of Ed Johnson ended that possibility. Habeas corpus petitions to challenge state court criminal convictions have mushroomed in later years and have been the subject of many controversial cases from the early 1950s to the present day.

46. *Moore v. Dempsey* at 89–90. Justice Holmes was describing the prisoners' allegations, which had not yet been proved. The habeas corpus procedure begins with a petition that describes the unconstitutional events that the prisoner says occurred, but those facts must be proved at a hearing. In this case, the lower court dismissed the petition without a hearing—the universal practice before this case. The question before the Supreme Court was whether the facts, if they turned out to be accurate, added up to an unconstitutional conviction. If so, the Supreme Court would order the lower court to hold a hearing.

47. Klarman, *From Jim Crow to Civil Rights,* 118; Michael Klarman, "The Racial Origins of Modern Criminal Law," *Michigan Law Review* 99 (2000): 48.

48. Dan T. Carter, *Scottsboro: A Tragedy of the American South* (1969, Louisiana State University Press, 2007); James Goodman, *Stories of Scottsboro* (Vintage Books, 1994). The defendants were Olen Montgomery (age 17), Clarence Norris (19), Haywood Patterson (18), Ozie Powell (16), Willie Roberson (16), Charlie Weems (16), Eugene Williams (13), and brothers Andy (19) and Roy Wright (12). Several of the Scottsboro defendants also wrote their stories; Haywood Patterson and Earl Conrad, *Scottsboro Boy* (Collier

Books, 1969), see note 58 below. Also see James R. Acker, *Scottsboro and Its Legacy: The Cases That Challenged American Legal and Social Justice* (Greenwood, 2007). James A. Miller, *Remembering Scottsboro: The Legacy of an Infamous Trial* (Princeton University Press, 2009).

49. Carter, *Scottsboro,* 215 and 238.

50. Glenda Elizabeth Gilmore, *Defying Dixie: The Radical Roots of Civil Rights, 1919–1950* (Norton, 2008), 118–119; Goodman, *Stories of Scottsboro,* 267.

51. The doctrine, sometimes called "selective incorporation," began with the First Amendment in *Girtlow v. New York* (1925), but *Powell v. Alabama* was the first case involving criminal trial procedure. A most recent incorporation was the rule of unanimous jury verdicts implied in the Sixth Amendment, *Ramos v. Louisiana* (2020).

52. Carter, *Scottsboro,* 235, 237.

53. Carter, *Scottsboro,* 340, 284.

54. *Norris v. Alabama* (1935) at 589–590. Supreme Court review of facts: *Cedar Rapids Gaslight Co. v. City of Cedar Rapids* (1912); *Union Pacific Ry. Co. v. U.S* (1941).

55. *Norris v. Alabama* at 591–595.

56. *Strauder v. West Virginia* (1880); *Neal v. Delaware* (1881); *Bush v. Kentucky* (1883).

57. Patterson was convicted again, and this time his conviction was affirmed and the Supreme Court denied review (1937).

58. Acker, *Scottsboro and Its Legacy*; Miller, *Remembering Scottsboro;* Haywood Patterson and Earl Conrad, *Scottsboro Boy* (Collier Books, 1969). Clarence Norris and Sybil D. Washington, *The Last of the Scottsboro Boys: An Autobiography* (Putnam, 1979). For the fate of the Scottsboro defendants after the trials, see http://justice-deferred.clemson.edu.

59. Art. 3093a, Texas Laws of 1923. A challenge to the white primary in Houston in 1921 (before the rule was put into state law) was disposed of without reaching constitutional issues, *Love v. Griffith* (1924).

60. *Nixon v. Herndon* at 540–541; Darlene Clark Hine, *Black Victory: The Rise and Fall of the White Primary in Texas* (KTO Press, 1979); Michael Klarman, "The White Primary Rulings: A Case Study in the Consequences of Supreme Court Decisionmaking," *Florida State Law Review* 29 (2001): 55.

61. David Danelski and Joseph Tulchin, eds., *The Autobiographical Notes of Charles Evans Hughes* (Harvard University Press, 1973), 299; "Roosevelts Visit Holmes Who Is 92," *Washington Post* (Washington, DC), March 9, 1933; G. Edward White, *Justice Oliver Wendell Holmes: Law and the Inner Self* (Oxford University Press, 1995), 469–470; "Kennedy Pays Courtesy Call on Frankfurter at Home," *Washington Post,* July 27, 1962; Dean Acheson, *The President's Call on Justice Frankfurter, Thursday, July 26, 1962,* n.d. (carbon copy of six-page typed document), in Felix Frankfurter Papers, Library of Congress, Manuscript Division, Washington, DC, box 124, Folder: "Get Well Messages—Illness April 1962 A–K."; Felix Frankfurter Oral History Interview—JFK #1, 6/10/1964, Kennedy Library; John Q. Barrett,

"The President Visits the Justice at Home (1933 & 1962)," 2–6; *The Robert H. Jackson Center* (2012).

6. Breaking New Ground

1. As with many striking quotes, the original source will probably never be conclusively identified. For example, one contemporary source said it was Justice Sutherland, but he denied it. Drew Pearson and Robert Allen, *Nine Old Men* (Riverhead Books, 1936), 15; John Keefe, "The Marble Palace at 50," *American Bar Association Journal* 68 (October 1982): 1229. The first Monday in October has been the start of the term since 1917; it had been the second Monday in October since 1873.
2. Leon Higginbotham and William C. Smith, "The Hughes Court and the Beginning of the End of the 'Separate but Equal' Doctrine," *Minnesota Law Review* 76 (1992): 1104.
3. James N. Gregory, *The Southern Diaspora: How the Great Migrations of Black and White Southerners Transformed America* (University of North Carolina Press, 2007); *Negro World* (New York), July 21, 1923, 6; Langston Hughes, *Big Sea: An Autobiography* (1940; Hill and Wang, 1963), 33; see also Melvin G. Holli and Peter d'A. Jones, eds., *Ethnic Chicago: A Multicultural Portrait* (1977; Grand Rapids: Eerdmans, 1995), 317.
4. "Black Americans in Congress" (Office of History and Preservation, Office of the Clerk, US House of Representatives).
5. Patricia Sullivan, *Lift Every Voice: The NAACP and the Making of the Civil Rights Movement* (New Press, 2009), 156–157; Kenneth W. Mack, *Representing the Race: The Creation of the Civil Rights Lawyer* (Harvard University Press, 2012), 83–85, 106–109; Genna Rae McNeil, *Groundwork: Charles Hamilton Houston and the Struggle for Civil Rights* (University of Pennsylvania Press, 1983), 31–32, 49–54.
6. *Crawford v. Hale* (1933); Mack, *Representing the Race,* 83–85, 106–109; McNeil, *Groundwork,* 89–95, 102–106. Many, including Walter White, executive secretary of the NAACP, praised Houston's work, but some, including W. E. B. Du Bois, were critical. The disagreement was only part of a major rift in the leadership of the NAACP. Du Bois resigned as editor of *The Crisis* in 1933. One of the lawyers was Howard law professor Leon Ransom.
7. McNeil, *Groundwork,* 135–138; Sullivan, *Lift Every Voice,* 164–168.
8. James F. Simon, *FDR and Chief Justice Hughes: The President, the Supreme Court, and the Epic Battle over the New Deal* (Simon and Schuster, 2012), 180; William G. Ross, *The Chief Justiceship of Charles Evans Hughes, 1930–1941* (University of South Carolina Press, 2007), 206–207.
9. *Brown v. Mississippi* (1936) at 282. *Canty v. Alabama* (1940); *Chambers v. Florida* (1940); *Hale v. Kentucky* (1938); *Pierre v. Louisiana* (1939); *Lomax v. Texas* (1941); *Smith v. Texas* (1940); *White v. Texas* (1940).
10. Herndon's case was unusual because the Supreme Court had already dismissed his direct appeal, *Herndon v. Georgia* (1935), but now took a second look on a habeas corpus petition and this time ruled for Herndon.

11. *Missouri ex rel Gaines* at 350, 351. Unlike Donald Murray, who graduated from the Maryland Law School and had a long career, Lloyd Gaines never attended Missouri Law School. By the time the case ended he had disappeared, and he never reappeared.

12. *Mitchell v. United States* (1941) at 90.

13. *Mitchell v. United States* (1941) at 97. In a very unusual step, the Department of Justice, usually assigned to defend federal agencies and departments, opposed the decision of the Interstate Commerce Commission.

14. *Lane v. Wilson* at 275.

15. Robert G. Weisbord, *Racism and the Olympics* (Routledge, 2015), 25–54.

16. *San Francisco News,* February 14, 1938; *Dallas Times,* March 16, 1938; Raymond Arsenault, *The Sound of Freedom: Marian Anderson, the Lincoln Memorial, and the Concert That Awakened America* (Bloomsbury Press, 2009), 91, 109, and 129.

17. Oral interview with Lt. Col. William Thompson by Georganne and Vernon Burton at their home in Urbana, Illinois, February 3, 2006. Other Tuskegee Airmen attended the gathering. J. Todd Moye, *Freedom Flyers: The Tuskegee Airmen of World War II* (Oxford University Press, 2010), 50–53.

18. Eric Arnesen, *Brotherhood of Color: Black Railroad Workers and the Struggle for Equality* (Harvard University Press, 2001), 200–202, 249.

19. Sullivan, *Lift Every Voice,* 249.

20. *Smith v. Allwright* at 664–665, 666; Darlene Clark Hine, *Black Victory: The Rise and Fall of the White Primary in Texas* (KTO Press, 1979).

21. *Elmore v. Rice* (Lower court, 1947) at 528.

22. *Brown v. Baskin* (Lower court, 1948) at 936–937; Tinsley E. Yarbrough, *A Passion for Justice: J. Waties Waring and Civil Rights* (Oxford University Press, 1987), 62–80.

23. *Steele* at 198.

24. *Steele* at 204. To increase his chances of getting a Supreme Court ruling, Houston had filed two cases against the union, this case in Alabama and a similar case in federal court in Virginia. Houston's approach succeeded, as the Supreme Court ruled for the Black firemen the same day. *Tunstall v. Brotherhood of Locomotive Firemen* (1944); Arnesen, *Brotherhood of Color,* 201, 206–210, 219, 224–225, 234.

25. Richard Reeves, *Infamy: The Shocking Story of the Japanese American Internment in World War II* (Henry Holt, 2011), 98–99; Jim Newton, *Justice for All: Earl Warren and the Nation He Made* (RiverHead Books, 2006), 121–142.

26. President Roosevelt, Executive Orders 9066 and 9102; Act of March 21, 1942, 56 Stat. 173.

27. *Hirabayashi* at 111; Peter Irons, *A People's History of the Supreme Court* (Penguin Books, 2006), 360. See also Peter Irons, *The Courage of Their Convictions: 16 Americans Who Fought Their Way to the Supreme Court* (Free Press, 1988), 37–62.

28. Wendy Ng, *Japanese American Internment during World War II: A History and Reference Guide* (Greenwood Press, 2002), 83; Greg Robinson, *By Order of the President: FDR and the Internment of Japanese Americans* (Harvard University Press, 2001), 213–219, and Greg Robinson, *A Tragedy of Democracy: Japanese Confinement in North America* (Columbia University Press, 2009), 219–225, 297–298.

29. *Korematsu v. U.S.* at 216.

30. *Korematsu v. U.S.* at 216 and 219.

31. *Oyama v. California* (1948) (land ownership); *Takahashi v. Fish & Game Commission* (1948) (fishing licenses). *Korematsu v. United States* (Lower court, 1984); *Hirabayashi v. United States* (Lower court, 1987).

32. David Falkner, *Great Time Coming: The Life of Jackie Robinson, from Baseball to Birmingham* (Simon and Schuster, 1995).

33. David M. Robertson, *Sly and Able: A Political Biography of James F. Byrnes* (Norton, 1984), 355.

34. *Screws v. United States* at 92.

35. *Screws v. United States* at 140. The dissenters were Roberts, Frankfurter, and Jackson. No specific author is identified, but it seems to have been Frankfurter. Robert K. Carr, *Federal Protection of Civil Rights: Quest for a Sword* (Cornell University, 1947), 111–112; Christopher Waldrep, *Racial Violence on Trial: A Handbook with Cases, Laws and Documents* (ABC Clio, 2001), 75–76. See also Armand Derfner, "Why Do We Let Judges Say Anything about History When We Know They'll Get It Wrong?," *Public Historian* 27 (2005), 9, 11–13.

36. Richard Gergel, *Unexampled Courage: The Blinding of Sgt. Isaac Woodard and the Awakening of President Harry S. Truman and Judge J. Waties Waring* (Sarah Crichton Books, 2019); Richard Kluger, *Simple Justice: The History of Brown v. Board of Education and Black America's Struggle for Equality* (Knopf, 1975), 298–299; Carr, *Federal Protection of Civil Rights,* 161–162.

37. Gergel, *Unexampled Courage,* 131; Truman letter to Ernest W. Roberts, August 18, 1946, in *Off the Record: The Private Papers of Harry S. Truman,* ed. Robert H. Ferrell (Harper and Row, 1980), 146. Charles Lloyd Garretson III, *Hubert H. Humphrey: The Politics of Joy* (Transaction Publishers, 1993), 90–98.

38. Robert C. Weaver, *The Negro Ghetto* (Harcourt, Brace, 1948); Clement Vose, *Caucasians Only: The Supreme Court, the NAACP, and the Restrictive Covenant Cases* (University of California Press, 1967); Michael J. Klarman, *From Jim Crow to Civil Rights: The Supreme Court and the Struggle for Racial Equality* (Oxford University Press, 2004), 261; Jeffrey D. Gonda, *Unjust Deeds: The Restrictive Covenant Cases and the Making of the Civil Rights Movement* (University of North Carolina Press, 2015), 1–14, 34–37, 45–69, 189–196.

39. The Hansberry house at 6140 South Rhodes Avenue, has been designated a landmark by the City of Chicago.

40. George B. Stafford, "St. Louis Scene," *Pittsburgh Courier,* July 5, 1947, 2; Vose, *Caucasians Only,* 160.

41. *Shelley v. Kraemer* at 14.

42. *Shelley v. Kraemer* at 21n26; *Amicus Brief of American Indian Citizens League of California,* filed in *Shelley v. Kraemer* at 4. These covenants were so common that the Court had only six sitting justices—Reed, Jackson, and Rutledge recused themselves, apparently because their own house deeds had restrictive covenants: Del Dickson, *The Supreme Court in Conference, 1940–1985: The Private Discussion behind Nearly 300 Supreme Court Decisions* (Oxford University Press, 2001), 698; Richard Rothstein, *The Color of Law: A Forgotten History of How Our Government Segregated America* (Norton, 2017), 77–91.

43. James Kushner, "Apartheid in America: An Historical and Legal Analysis of Contemporary Racial Residential Segregation in the United States," *Howard Law Journal* 22 (1979): 547.

44. On the complicated history of the development of the suburbs, the standard work is Kenneth T. Jackson, *Crabgrass Frontier: The Suburbanization of the United States* (Oxford University Press, 1985); see also Kevin M. Kruse and Thomas J. Sugrue, *The New Suburban History* (University of Chicago Press, 2006). On the South, and especially the remarkable story of Black suburbs, which increased by 5.5 million people between 1960 and 2000, see Andrew Wiese, *Places of Their Own: African-American Suburbanization in the Twentieth Century* (University of Chicago, 2004), and "African-American Suburbanization and Regionalism in the Modern South," in *The Myth of Southern Exceptionalism,* ed. Matthew D. Lassiter and Joseph Crespino (Harvard University Press, 2010), 210–233. In 1940, 46 percent of Americans lived in small towns and rural areas, 34 percent in cities, and 19 percent in the suburbs. By 1960, 35 percent lived in the suburbs, 34 percent in cities, and 31 percent in rural areas. US Census, "Tracking the American Dream: 1940–1990," Housing ownership. According to the US Census, the largest increase in the percentage of all homeowners was an increase of 11.4 percent from 1940 to 1950, and the second largest was from 1950 to 1960, an increase of 6.9 percent. Dickson, *Supreme Court in Conference,* 680, quotes Lewis F. Powell in conference discussion of *Keyes v. School District No. 1 of Denver.*

45. Jackson, *Crabgrass Frontier,* 190–218, "adverse influences" at 207, "inharmonious" at 209.

46. Ira Katznelson, *When Affirmative Action Was White: An Untold History of Racial Inequality in Twentieth-Century America* (Norton, 2005), 113–141.

47. Martha Biondi, *To Stand and Fight: The Struggle for Civil Rights in Postwar New York City* (Harvard University Press, 2003), 121–136; Samuel Zipp, *Manhattan Projects: The Rise and Fall of Urban Renewal in Cold War New York* (Oxford University Press, 2010), 73–154; David Margolick, "Lee Lorch, Desegregation Activist Who Led Stuyvesant

Town Effort, Dies at 98," *New York Times,* March 1, 2014; Sullivan, *Lift Every Voice,* 384–388; Rothstein, *The Color of Law,* 274. See Lorch family in Chapter 8.

48. Sullivan, *Lift Every Voice,* 386. Publicity about the case caused an ongoing furor, and New York City responded by insisting on a nondiscrimination clause in any future projects. Met Life responded by building a housing project for African Americans in Harlem. Shortly after the case ended, Met Life began accepting Black tenants in Stuyvesant Town. "Stuyvesant Town to Admit Negroes after a Controversy of Seven Years," *New York Times,* August 25, 1950, 1. In 2020, African Americans made up 4 percent of the Stuyvesant Town residents. Rothstein, *Color of Law,* 107.

49. *Sweatt v. Painter* at 634.

50. Michael D. Davis and Hunter R. Clark, *Thurgood Marshall: Warrior at the Bar, Rebel on the Bench* (Carol Publishing Group, 1992), 147; *Sweatt v. Painter* at 651.

51. Jaybird primary: *Terry v. Adams* (1953); restrictive covenants: *Barrows v. Jackson* (1953); yellow-ticket jury: *Avery v. Georgia* (1953); DC restaurants: *District of Columbia v. John R. Thompson Co.* (1953).

52. *Bob-Lo Excursion Co v. Michigan* (1948). Just two years earlier, the Court had held in *Morgan v. Virginia* (1946) that a Virginia law requiring segregated seating on interstate buses was an unconstitutional interference with interstate commerce. It could seem like a Supreme Court rule that state-ordered segregation interferes with interstate commerce, but state-ordered integration does not. What a far cry from the nineteenth century (see Chapter 3), when the Supreme Court seemed to have the opposite rule, favoring segregation and disfavoring integration.

53. South Carolina Advisory Committee for Commission on Civil Rights, Transcript of Proceedings, Manning, South Carolina, May 22, 1964, 7–8 in the Papers of Joseph A. De Laine, folder 5, 13439, South Caroliniana Library, University of South Carolina; Kluger, *Simple Justice,* 16.

54. Orville Vernon Burton et al., "Seeds in Unlikely Soil: The *Briggs v. Elliott* School Segregation Case," in *Toward the Meeting of the Waters: Currents in the Civil Rights Movement of South Carolina during the Twentieth Century,* ed. Orville Vernon Burton and Winfred B. Moore Jr. (University of South Carolina Press, 2008), 177. See Chapter 4.

55. *AME Christian Recorder,* June 20, 1967, 2; *AME Christian Recorder,* August 29, 1967; "Eliza and Harry Briggs Seek Refuge in N.Y. after S.C. 'Economic Pressure,'" *Afro-American,* January 13, 1962; Burton et al., "Seeds in Unlikely Soil," 183; *AME Christian Recorder,* May 23, 1967; "Things That Happened since Nov. 11, 1949" and "South Carolina Advisory Committee for Commission on Civil Rights," 36 and 47. One of the original 107 petitioners, William Ragin stated, "In town they cut us all off from anything; a few of my good white folks [did] stand by me, but they couldn't let it be known." Another signer of the original petition, Mr. Thelmar Bethune, who "signed the petition so that my children could get a better edu-

cation than I had," was denied loans. White neighbors pressured him to take his name off the petition, but he told them, "I couldn't take it down."

56. Burton interviews with Joseph. A. De Laine Jr., March 5 and 6, 2003, Charleston, SC; April 2, 2004, Urbana, IL; April 22, 2004, Columbia, SC; and February 14, 2019, Charlotte, NC; Georganne and Vernon Burton telephone interview with J. A. De Laine Jr., September 10 and November 26, 2020; Ophelia De Lane Gona, *Dawn of Desegregation: J. A. De Laine and Briggs v. Elliott* (University of South Carolina Press, 2011), 126–133, 167. J. A. De Laine Jr. thought the bishop transferred Reverend De Laine to stop his activities on the case.

57. Kluger, *Simple Justice,* 302–303.

58. Gergel, *Unexampled Courage,* 218–219. Michael D. Davis and Hunter R. Clark, *Thurgood Marshall: Warrior at the Bar, Rebel on the Bench* (Birch Lane Press, 1992), 150–151, 219; Kluger, *Simple Justice,* 304.

59. David Robertson, *Sly and Able,* 504.

60. *Briggs v. Elliott* (Lower court, 1951) at 548.

61. Gergel, *Unexampled Courage,* 185.

62. *Briggs v. Elliott* at 548.

7. The End of Separate but Equal

1. Jeffrey Rosen, *The Supreme Court: The Personalities and Rivalries That Defined America* (Henry Holt, 2006), 9; Richard Kluger, *Simple Justice: The History of Brown v. Board of Education and Black America's Struggle for Equality* (Knopf, 1975), 656.

2. Heather Cox Richardson, *To Make Men Free: A History of the Republican Party* (Basic Books, 2014), 250.

3. Jack Greenberg, *Crusaders in the Courts: How a Dedicated Band of Lawyers Fought for the Civil Rights Revolution* (HarperCollins, 1994), 189–193; William H. Harbaugh, *Lawyers' Lawyer: The Life of John W. Davis* (Oxford University Press, 1973), 96, 481–519; on Davis's views of race and African Americans, and his support of segregation, see 492–495.

4. Reed: Jim Newton, *And Justice for All: Earl Warren and the Nation He Made* (Riverhead Books, 2006), 235. Juan Williams, "Marshall's Law," in *Thurgood Marshall: Justice for All,* ed. Roger Goldman and David Gallen (Carroll and Graff, 1992), 151.

5. Newton, *And Justice for All,* 279–291. Recess appointment of a federal judge or justice could raise serious problems because the appointment is temporary, whereas the Constitution says federal judges have life tenure. Some justices in the past began with recess appointments, but now that the Senate is usually in session year-round, there have been no recess appointments to the Supreme Court since President Eisenhower's three (Earl Warren, William Brennan, and Potter Stewart).

6. Noah Feldman, *Scorpions: The Battles and Triumphs of FDR's Great Supreme Court Justices* (Twelve, 2010); James F. Simon, *The Antagonists: Hugo Black, Felix Frankfurter and Civil Liberties in Modern America* (Simon and Schuster, 1989).
7. Cal. Educ. Code §§ 8003-04 (West 1945), repealed by 1947 Cal. Stat. 1792, ch. 737 (June 14, 1947). Juan F. Perea et al., *Race and Races: Cases and Resources for a Diverse America,* 2nd ed. (West, 2007), 333–336; As California attorney general during World War II, Warren had been an enthusiastic proponent of the Japanese internment program. He later regretted his position.
8. Kluger, *Simple Justice,* 605–606.
9. Kluger, *Simple Justice,* 698.
10. *Botiller v. Dominguez* (1889), involving a dispute under an 1851 federal law concerning land claims predating the War with Mexico.
11. Calhoun: *Congressional Globe,* January 4, 1848; Perea, *Race and Races,* 295.
12. *Lopez v. Seccombe* (Lower court, 1944) (swimming pool); *Mendez v. Westminster School Dist.* (Lower court, 1946), *aff'd* (Lower court, 1947) (schools).
13. *Rice v. Sioux City* at 71. Del Dickson, *The Supreme Court in Conference, 1940–1985: The Private Discussion behind Nearly 300 Supreme Court Decisions* (Oxford University Press, 2001), 703–705.
14. "Truman Sets Arlington Interment for Indian Vet Denied 'White' Burial," *New York Times,* August 30, 1951, 1; "Rice, Sergeant John R.," Sioux City History, http://www.siouxcityhistory.org/notable-people/8-sergeantjohnrrice.
15. *Brown v. Board* (1954) at 492, 494.
16. *Brown v. Board* at 494, 495.
17. *Brown v. Board* at 495.
18. Gunnar Myrdal, *An American Dilemma: The Negro Problem and Modern Democracy,* 2 vols. (Harper & Bros., 1944); Kluger, *Simple Justice,* chap. 26; Peter Irons, *Jim Crow's Children: The Broken Promise of the "Brown" Decision* (Viking, 2002), 173; James T. Patterson, *Brown v. Board of Education: A Civil Rights Milestone and Its Troubled Legacy* (Oxford University Press, 2001).
19. Juan Williams, *Eyes on the Prize: America's Civil Rights Years, 1954–1965* (Viking, 1987), 20. These doll studies may seem unsophisticated. But they asked the right questions, got true answers, and drew sound conclusions. No serious person would question that today, and no serious person would have questioned it at that time if not for the mass delusion that the system of white supremacy created and demanded.
20. Mays, "Educators Comment on School Decision," *Chicago Defender,* May 22, 1954, 5; Bethune and Bond, "Nat'l Leaders Laud Ban on School Segregation: Supreme Court's Decision Called 'Long Overdue,'" *Courier* (Pittsburgh), May 29, 1954, 31.

21. The words "all deliberate speed" are in *Brown II* (1955) at 300. The *Briggs v. Elliott* (Lower court, 1955) quote is at 777.

22. Expressing early frustration: Loren Miller, *The Petitioners: The Story of the Supreme Court of the United States and the Negro* (World Publishing Co., 1966), 347–364. More recent, no less frustrated: Justin Driver, *The Schoolhouse Gate: Public Education, the Supreme Court and the American Mind* (Random House, 2018), 253–264; Derrick Bell, "Preface to the Sixth Edition," in *Race, Racism and American Law* (Aspen, 2008), xix–xxiv; Charles Ogletree, "Conclusion," *All Deliberate Speed: Reflections on the First Half-Century of Brown v. Board of Education* (Norton, 2004), 310–316.

23. Juan Williams, *Thurgood Marshall: American Revolutionary* (Random House, 1998), 229. The two congressmen were William Dawson (D-IL) and Adam Clayton Powell (D-NY); a third, Charles Diggs (D-MI), was elected in November 1954. One federal judge was Hon. William Hastie, appointed to the district court of the Virgin Islands in 1937 and to the court of appeals for the Third Circuit in 1949. The other federal judge was Hon. Irvin Mollison, appointed to the US Customs Court in 1945. Hastie had preceded Charles Houston as valedictorian at Amherst College, earned a law degree from Harvard, and succeeded Houston as dean of Howard Law School. Mollison was a prominent Chicago lawyer and the son of Willis Mollison, the turn-of-the-century Mississippi lawyer described in Chapter 4. Both had won important civil rights cases in the US Supreme Court, Mollison in *Hansberry v. Lee* (1940) and Hastie in *Morgan v. Virginia* (1946).

24. Mary L. Dudziak, *Cold War Civil Rights: Race and the Image of American Democracy* (Princeton University Press, 2000). In addition, information flowed more freely across the United States and was more accessible on national television. A new interstate highway system brought regions of the nation, including the South, closer together. Air conditioning brought more business and more visitors to the South. Raymond Arsenault, "The End of the Long Hot Summer: The Air Conditioner and Southern Culture," *Journal of Southern History* 50 (November 1984): 597–628.

25. *Muir v. Louisville Park Theatrical Assn* (1954); *Hawkins v. Board of Control of Florida* (1954); *Tureaud v. Board of Supervisors of L.S.U.* (1954); *Dawson v. Mayor and City Council of Baltimore* (1955); *Holmes v. City of Atlanta* (1955).

26. 48 Ala. Code of 1940 § 301 (31a, b, c); Mont. City Code of 1952, Ch. 6, Secs. 10–11. J. Mills Thornton III, *Archipelagoes of My South: Episodes in the Shaping of a Region, 1830–1965* (University of Alabama Press, 2016), 191.

27. Jeanne Theoharis, *Rebellious Life of Mrs. Rosa Parks* (Beacon Press, 2013), 62, 64; David J. Garrow, *Bearing the Cross: Martin Luther King, Jr., and the Southern Christian Leadership Conference* (William Morrow, 1986), 13.

28. Jo Ann Gibson Robinson, *Montgomery Bus Boycott and the Women Who Started It: The Memoir of Jo Ann Gibson Robinson* (University of Ten-

nessee Press, 1987); Danielle L. McGuire, *At the Dark End of the Street: Black Women, Rape, and Resistance—A New History of the Civil Rights Movement from Rosa Parks to the Rise of Black Power* (Knopf, 2010), 80.

29. *South Carolina Electric & Gas Co. v. Flemming* (1956); Montgomery bus company memorandum is printed in the opinion of Judge Walter B. Jones, *Race Relations Law Reporter* 1 (1956): 535, and the reference to other cities is in the transcript of the hearing that follows at page 545.

30. "City of Montgomery v. Montgomery City Lines, Inc.," *Race Relations Law Reporter* 1 (1956): 535.

31. Fred Gray, *Bus Ride to Justice: The Life and Works of Fred Gray*, rev. ed. (New South Books, 2012), esp. 90–93.

32. Jack Bass, *Unlikely Heroes: The Dramatic Story of the Southern Judges of the Fifth Circuit Who Translated the Supreme Court's Brown Decision into a Revolution for Equality* (Simon and Schuster, 1981); Frank T. Read and Lucy S. McGough, *Let Them Be Judged* (Scarecrow Press, 1978); Armand Derfner, "The Friendly Judicial Climate," in *Voice of Civil Rights Lawyers: Reflections from the Deep South, 1964–1980*, ed. Kent Spriggs (University Press of Florida, 2017), 249–254. At that time the Fifth Circuit included Florida, Georgia, Alabama, Mississippi, Louisiana, and Texas.

33. Frankfurter letter quoted in Gerald Gunther, *Learned Hand: The Man and the Judge* (Knopf, 1992), 577. A professor who admired Frankfurter called the Court's grounds "wholly without basis in the law." Herbert Wechsler, "Toward Neutral Principles of Constitutional Law," *Harvard Law Review* 73 (1959): 1, 34. For more on Frankfurter and Hand, see also Jane Dailey, "Is Marriage a Civil Right?," in *The Folly of Jim Crow: Rethinking the Segregated South*, ed. Stephanie Cole and Natalie J. Ring (Texas A&M University Press, 2012), 198.

34. *Williams v. Georgia* (1955) at 391. The earlier, yellow ticket case, was *Avery v. Georgia* (1953), discussed in Chapter 6.

35. *Williams v. State* (State court, 1955) at 763. Law clerk Barrett Prettyman quoted in Del Dickson, *Supreme Court in Conference, 1940–1985*, 244, n. 63.

36. Del Dickson, "State Court Defiance and the Limits of Supreme Court Authority: *Williams v. Georgia* revisited," *Yale Law Journal* 103 (1994): 1423–1481. The US Supreme Court took a similar approach when the Alabama Supreme Court said Haywood Patterson's appeal came too late, but in that case, the Alabama Supreme Court changed its previous ruling and granted a new trial. *Patterson v. Alabama* (1935).

37. *Arkansas Gazette* (Little Rock), September 2, 1957, 1; Gene Roberts and Hank Klibanoff, *The Race Beat: The Press, the Civil Rights Struggle, and the Awakening of a Nation* (Vintage Books, 2006), 151–152.

38. Roberts and Klibanoff, *Race Beat*, 154, 158.

39. Daisy Bates, *The Long Shadow of Little Rock* (McKay, 1962), 69–72; Roberts and Klibanoff, 161; Herbert Shapiro, *White Violence and Black Response: From Reconstruction to Montgomery* (University of Massachusetts Press, 1988), 413–14. The crowd tormented Lorch also, calling her a "nigger-lover." After repeated harassment, including terrorists' attempt to bomb their garage, the Lorches ultimately had to move to Canada to feel safe. "Grace Lonegran Lorch," *Encyclopedia of Arkansas History and Culture.* A decade earlier, Lorch and her husband, Lee Lorch, had been evicted from their apartment in Stuyvesant Town (discussed in Chapter 6) for having a Black family live with them in violation of the project's white-tenants-only rule. Anthony B. Newkirk, "'The Long Reach of History': The Lorches and Little Rock, 1955–1959," *Arkansas Historical Quarterly* 76 (Autumn 2017): 248–67. Bombing: 260; Stuyvesant: 250; David Margolick, "Lee Lorch, Desegregation Activist Who Led Stuyvesant Town Effort, Dies at 98," *New York Times,* March 1, 2014.

40. Roberts and Klibanoff, *Race Beat,* 175; Roy Reed, *Faubus: The Life and Times of an American Prodigal* (University of Arkansas Press, 1997), 219.

41. Richardson, *To Make Men Free,* 250–251.

42. Gilbert C. Fite, *Richard B. Russell, Jr., Senator from Georgia* (University of North Carolina Press, 1991), 344.

43. *Cooper v. Aaron* at 16, 4, 17, 18.

44. *Faubus v. Aaron* (1959). The events and litigation in Little Rock are detailed by Jack Greenberg, Thurgood Marshall's successor as director-counsel of the NAACP Legal Defense Fund. Greenberg, *Crusaders in the Courts,* 228–243.

45. *U.S. v. Louisiana* (1960) at 501. This was an order denying Louisiana's request for a stay pending appeal. The Supreme Court soon thereafter gave its final approval of the lower court's decision. *Louisiana v. United States* (1961).

46. *Meredith v. Fair* (1962) (Justice Black, acting as circuit justice).

47. Dan T. Carter, *The Politics of Rage: George Wallace, the Origins of the New Conservatism, and the Transformation of American Politics* (Simon and Schuster, 1995), 83–84, 140–153.

48. *Gomillion v. Lightfoot* at 340, 347. See Robert J. Norrell, *Reaping the Whirlwind: The Civil Rights Movement in Tuskegee* (Knopf, 1985), 71, 91–111, 118–119, 123–124.

49. *Louisiana v. U.S.* (1965) at 154. The Court took similar action the same day in *U.S. v. Mississippi* (1965).

50. Sam J. Ervin Jr., "Proposed Amendment Is Unwise," *Asheville Citizen-Times,* October 1, 1959, 4; Daniel M. Berman, *A Bill Becomes a Law: The Civil Rights Act of 1960* (Macmillan, 1962).

51. The Civil Rights Act of 1964, Title VI; 1965 Elementary and Secondary Education Act Title I. Such a provision could have made the difference in the

housing boom discussed in Chapter 6 by banning discrimination in the activities of the Federal Housing Administration (FHA) and New York City's assistance to the building of a segregated Stuyvesant Town.

52. Act of October 3, 1965, 79 Stat. 911. Meiklejohn quote from Jia Yang, *One Mighty and Irresistible Tide: The Epic Struggle over American Immigration, 1924–1965* (Norton, 2020), 239. For the 1965 Immigration Act see Roger Daniels, *Coming to America: A History of Immigration and Ethnicity in American Life* (HarperCollins, 1990), 336–345.

53. The Fourth Amendment had already been held applicable to the states in *Wolf v. Colorado* (1949), but that ruling was without teeth because the all-important "exclusionary rule" (illegally seized evidence may not be used at trial) was not applied to the states until *Mapp v. Ohio* (1961).

54. Women: *Hoyt v. Florida* (1961). Peremptory challenges: *Swain v. Alabama* (1965). Police stops: *Terry v. Ohio* (1968). See the criticism by Justin Driver, "The Constitutional Conservatism of the Warren Court," *University of California Law Review* 100 (2001): 1101, 1130–1139.

55. Senator Strom Thurmond spoke for many when he blamed the Court for "crime in the streets" and for advocating "a free rein of communism, riots, agitation, collectivism and the breakdown of moral codes." Columbia, *The State,* June 28, 1957.

56. Morton J. Horwitz, *The Warren Court and the Pursuit of Justice* (Hill and Wang, 1998), 65; Walter Murphy, *Congress and the Court: A Case Study in the American Political Process* (University of Chicago Press, 1962), 182–225.

57. *McLaughlin v. Florida* at 190.

58. The five other states were Delaware, Kentucky, Missouri, Oklahoma, and West Virginia.

59. Peter Wallenstein, *Tell the Court I Love My Wife: Race, Marriage, and Law—An American History* (Palgrave Macmillan, 2002), 216. Judge's quote: *Loving v. Virginia* at 3.

60. *Loving v. Virginia* at 3, 7.

61. *Loving v. Virginia* at 11.

62. *Griffin* at 233; Brian J. Daugherity, *Keep On Keeping On: The NAACP and the Implementation of Brown v. Board of Education in Virginia* (University of Virginia Press, 2016). Reopening and funding the public schools in Prince Edward County did not integrate the public schools, because the white children did not return, but at least the African American students again had schools to go to.

63. Victor Navasky, *Kennedy Justice* (Atheneum, 1971), 285. Juan Williams, "Marshall's Law," in *Thurgood Marshall: Justice for All,* ed. Roger Goldman and David Gallen (Carroll and Graf, 1992), 153–154; Michael D. Davis and Hunter R. Clark, *Thurgood Marshall: Warrior at the Bar, Rebel on the Bench* (Carol, 1992), 236. An often told story is that Committee Chairman James Eastland of Mississippi instructed Robert Ken-

nedy to tell President Kennedy that Eastland would "give him the n——" if Kennedy would nominate conservative judge Harold Cox of Mississippi to a district court; after Kennedy nominated Cox, Marshall was confirmed by the Senate. Juan Williams calls the story apocryphal, as Cox had been confirmed to federal judgeship before Kennedy's nomination of Marshall to the bench. Williams, *Thurgood Marshall,* 299. President Johnson created a vacancy on the Court by appointing Justice Tom Clark's son, Ramsey Clark, as attorney general, after which Justice Clark felt compelled to resign to avoid any conflict of interest. Wil Haygood, *Showdown: Thurgood Marshall and the Supreme Court Nomination That Changed America* (Vintage Books, 2015), 15. Marshall argued thirty-two Supreme Court cases for the NAACP and the Legal Defense Fund, and nineteen more as solicitor general, probably exceeded only by Justices Stanley Reed and Robert Jackson, each of whom argued frequently as solicitor general under President Franklin D. Roosevelt.

64. Daugherity, *Keep On Keeping On;* see also Julie Roy Jeffrey, *Education for Children of the Poor: A Study of the Origins and Implementation of the Elementary and Secondary Education Act of 1965* (Ohio State University, 1978); *Green v. New Kent County* at 437–438, 439, 442.

65. On what was given up and the costs to the Black community, see Lani Guinier, "From Radical Liberalism to Racial Literacy: *Brown v. Board of Education* and the Interest Divergence Dilemma," in *Remembering Brown at Fifty: The University of Illinois Commemorates Brown v. Board of Education,* ed. Orville Vernon Burton and David O'Brien (University of Illinois Press, 2009), 149–182.

8. Opposing Forces

1. Laura Barre, "7 Atlanta Ministers Urge Churches Help Carry Out Segregation Ruling," *Atlanta Constitution,* July 13, 1954, 1; Gareth D. Pahowka, "Voices of Moderation: Southern Whites Respond to Brown v. Board of Education," *Gettysburg Historical Journal* 5, no. 6 (2006); Grant Wacker, *America's Pastor: Billy Graham and the Shaping of a Nation* (Belknap Press of Harvard University Press, 2014), 125; Billy Graham, "Billy Graham Makes Plea for the End to Intolerance," *Life,* October 1, 1956; Graham, "No Color Line in Heaven," *Ebony,* September 1957. See also Graham, *Just As I Am: The Autobiography of Billy Graham* (Harper, 1997), 425–427; Southern Baptist Convention Annual Meeting, 1954, 56, quoted in Edward L. Queen, *In the South the Baptists Are the Center of Gravity: Southern Baptists and Social Change, 1930–1980* (Carlson, 1991), 83; David L. Chappell, *A Stone of Hope: Prophetic Religion and the Death of Jim Crow* (University of North Carolina Press, 2004), 137–138. Denominational leaders and especially foreign missionaries argued that segregation at home was a hindrance to their evangelistic efforts around the world.

2. New Orleans *Times-Picayune,* May 4, 1956; Numan V. Bartley, *The Rise of Massive Resistance: Race and Politics in the South during the 1950s*

(Louisiana State University Press, 1969), 280; Roy Reed, *Faubus: The Life and Times of an American Prodigal* (University of Arkansas Press, 1997), 169; "The Little Man's Big Friends," *Economist*, February 11, 2017, 25.

3. David Sansing, "John Bell Williams: Fifty-Fifth Governor of Mississippi: 1968–1972," *Mississippi History Now*, January 2004, http://www.mshistorynow.mdah.ms.gov/articles/265/index.php?s=extra&id=152; Tom P. Brady, *Black Monday: Segregation or Amalgamation, America Has Its Choice* (Association of Citizens' Councils, 1955), 88, "the social, political, economic, and religious preferences of the negro remain close to the caterpillar and the cockroach."

4. James Jackson Kilpatrick, "Conservatism and the South," in *The Lasting South: Fourteen Southerners Look at Their Home*, ed. Louis D. Rubin and James Jackson Kilpatrick (Regnery, 1957), 188–205; Kilpatrick, *The Sovereign States: Notes of a Citizen of Virginia* (Regnery, 1957); Kilpatrick, *The Southern Case for School Desegregation* (Crowell-Collier, 1962); Gilbert C. Fite, *Richard B. Russell, Jr.: Senator from Georgia* (University of North Carolina Press, 1991), 331; Kevin J. McMahon, *Reconsidering Roosevelt on Race: How the Presidency Paved the Road to Brown* (University of Chicago Press, 2010), 224n9 for Russell and Eastland quotations; Charles P. Roland, *The Improbable Era: The South since World War II* (University of Kentucky Press, 1975), 36; Stephen G. N. Tuck, *Beyond Atlanta: The Struggle for Racial Equality in Georgia, 1940–1980* (University of Georgia Press, 2003), 99; "Little Man's Big Friends," 25.

5. Neil R. McMillen, *The Citizens' Council: Organized Resistance to the Second Reconstruction* (University of Illinois Press, 1994); Stephanie R. Rolph, *Resisting Equality: The Citizens' Council, 1954–1989* (Louisiana State University Press, 2018).

6. *AME Christian Recorder*, June 13, 1967, 4; *AME Christian Recorder*, in the Papers of Joseph A. De Laine, South Caroliniana Library, University of South Carolina. The events are carefully chronicled by De Laine's daughter in Ophelia De Laine Gona, *Dawn of Desegregation: J. A. De Laine and Briggs v. Elliott* (University of South Carolina Press, 2011), 168–169, 171, 175, 185–187, 189; Joseph A. De Laine Jr., speaking at the Citadel Conference on Civil Rights in South Carolina, March 5, 2003. Telephone interview with Joseph A. De Laine Jr., September 9, 2020; Burton interviews with Joseph A. De Laine Jr., March 5 and 6, 2003, Charleston, SC; April 2, 2004, Urbana, IL; April 22, 2004, Columbia, SC; and February 14, 2019, Charlotte, NC; and Georganne and Vernon Burton telephone interview with Joseph A. De Laine Jr., September 10 and November 26, 2020. Many have noted the leadership and level of endurance of Reverend De Laine in bringing to fruition the first of the five cases that ended segregation in the United States. John Egerton, *Speak Now against the Day: The Generation before the Civil Rights Movement in the South* (Knopf, 1994), 589. The warrant was not removed from the books until 2000 *posthumously*.

7. Southern Regional Council Papers, 1944–1968, from ProQuest.

8. John C. Calhoun, *A Disquisition on Government,* ed. Richard K. Cralle (1853; Peter Smith, 1943), 57, 81; Gerald Robinson, "Freedom of Choice: Brown, Vouchers, and the Philosophy of Language," in *Educational Reform in Urban America: Brown v. Board after Half a Century,* ed. David Salisbury and Casey Lartigue Jr. (Cato Institute, 2004), 19.

9. *Congressional Record,* Senate, March 12, 1956, 4462; *Greenville News,* March 13, 1956; Brent J. Aucoin, "The Southern Manifesto and Southern Opposition to Desegregation," *Arkansas Historical Association* 55, no. 2 (Summer 1996): 173–193; Joseph Crespino, *Strom Thurmond's America* (Hill and Wang, 2012), 105–107; Bartley, *Rise of Massive Resistance,* 116–117.

10. Gene Roberts and Hank Klibanoff, *The Race Beat: The Press, the Civil Rights Struggle, and the Awakening of a Nation* (Vintage Books, 2006), 191. North Carolina had only 3 districts integrated, out of 172 with biracial populations, Tennessee had only 3 out of 141, and Florida had none.

11. *James v. Almond* (Lower court, 1959); *Griffin v. Prince Edward County Board of Education* (1964); Brian J. Daugherity, *Keeping On Keeping On: The NAACP and the Implementation of Brown v. Board of Education in Virginia* (University of Virginia Press, 2016), 1, 31–32, 47–48, 57–60, 69, 72–75.

12. Patricia Sullivan, *Lift Every Voice: The NAACP and the Making of the Civil Rights Movement* (New Press, 2009), 425–426. Attorney General J. P. Coleman of Mississippi (later governor, then a US circuit judge) said that any legislature could pass new laws faster than a court could strike the old ones down. David Sansing, "James Plemon (J.P.) Coleman: Fifty-Second Governor of Mississippi: 1956–1960," *Mississippi History Now,* January 2004, http://www.mshistorynow.mdah.ms.gov/articles/265/index.php?s=extra&id=149.

13. *Alabama ex rel. Patterson v. NAACP, Race Relations Law Reporter* 1 (1956): 707. Alabama may have chosen this illegitimate procedure after seeing Louisiana's efforts to do the same thing to the NAACP. Louisiana had filed a similar suit seeking NAACP registration, but the state properly served the complaint. That gave the NAACP time to "remove" the case to federal court. "Removal" blocked further state proceedings and protected the NAACP until the Louisiana suit was thrown out, *Louisiana ex rel. Gremillion v. NAACP* (1961). Alabama, then, chose not to use proper legal procedures and instead sought and obtained an immediate injunction.

14. The Alabama attorney general was John Patterson, who won the 1958 race for governor by running a more racist campaign than his opponent, George Wallace, and who was complicit in the beating of the Freedom Riders in 1961.

15. *NAACP v. Alabama* (1958) at 462.

16. Although it was the US Supreme Court's decision in *NAACP v. Alabama* (II) (1959) that was prompted by Alabama's "change its stance," those words

actually come from the US Supreme Court's decision in *NAACP v. Alabama* (IV) (1964) at 290.

17. Judge Jones's decision of December 29, 1961, is titled *Alabama ex rel. Gallion v. NAACP,* and is reported in *Race Relations Law Reporter* 7 (1962–63), 221.

18. The state supreme court opinion is titled *NAACP v. State* (1964) (state court).

19. One case that was not a state-sponsored attack—at least on the surface—was an award of damages to a white Savannah grocer for losses his store suffered during a boycott. The US Supreme Court granted certiorari on the single question whether the national NAACP shared in the liability, then changed its mind and decided, 5–4, not to take the case after all (certiorari "dismissed as improvidently granted"). *NAACP v. Overstreet* (1956).

20. Justice Brennan Papers and Justice Douglas Papers, Library of Congress.

21. J. Douglas Smith, *On Democracy's Doorstep: The Inside Story of How the Supreme Court Brought "One Person, One Vote" to the United States* (Hill and Wang, 2014), 67–93, 91–92 on Whittaker and Frankfurter.

22. *NAACP v. Button* (1963) at 429; Daugherity, *Keeping On Keeping On,* 60–61, 88–91.

23. Peter F. Lau, "From the Periphery to the Center: Clarendon County, South Carolina, *Brown,* and the Struggle for Democracy and Equality in America," in *From the Grass Roots to the Supreme Court: Brown v. Board of Education and American Democracy,* ed. Peter F. Lau (Duke University Press, 2004), 118–121; Sullivan, *Lift Every Voice,* 425–436: Bartley, *Rise of Massive Resistance,* 211–232; Adam Fairclough, *To Redeem the Soul of America: The Southern Christian Leadership Conference and Martin Luther King, Jr.* (University of Georgia Press, 1987), 22–23, 45–46. Some states' NAACP membership dropped even further; in South Carolina between 1955 and 1957, NAACP membership declined from 8,266 members to 2,202.

24. *Jet,* September 15, 1955, 6–9. Roberts and Klibanoff, *Race Beat,* 66.

25. J. Mills Thornton III, *Archipelagoes of My South: Episodes in the Shaping of a Region, 1830–1965* (University of Alabama Press, 2016), 202.

26. *New York Times Co. v. Sullivan* (1964) at 277; David E. Marion, *The Jurisprudence of Justice William J. Brennan, Jr.: The Law and Politics of "Libertarian Dignity"* (Rowman and Littlefield, 1997), 61; Anthony Lewis, *Make No Law: The Sullivan Case and the First Amendment* (Vintage Books, 1992).

27. *New York Times Co. v. Sullivan* at 280.

28. Papers of M. Roland Nachman, Alabama Department of Archives and History, Montgomery, AL. Another libel case disposed of was a $40,000 verdict won by Eugene "Bull" Connor of Birmingham for articles written by reporter Harrison Salisbury. The case was dismissed by the federal Fifth Circuit court of appeals in *New York Times Company v. Connor* (Court of Appeals, 1966).

29. William H. Chafe, *Civilities and Civil Rights: Greensboro, North Carolina, and the Black Struggle for Freedom* (Oxford University Press, 1981), 82–83.

30. Chafe, *Civilities and Civil Rights,* 97; Marvin Sykes, "Woolworth Made Target for Demonstration Here," *Greensboro Recorder,* February 2, 1960; Claude Sitton, "Negro Sitdowns Stir Fear of Wider Unrest in South," *New York Times,* February 14, 1960.

31. Clayborne Carson, *In Struggle: SNCC and the Black Awakening of the 1960s* (Harvard University Press, 1981), 11–12, 19–25, 38, 61, 65, 68, 164, 237; Martin Luther King Jr., *Stride toward Freedom: The Montgomery Story* (Harper, 1958). Orville Vernon Burton, *Penn Center: A History Preserved* (University of Georgia Press, 2014), 70–98; Myles Horton, with Herbert and Judith Kohl, *The Long Haul: An Autobiography* (Teachers College Press, 1997); Aldon D. Morris, *The Origins of the Civil Rights Movement: Black Communities Organizing for Change* (Free Press, 1984), 62.

32. The factual details are from the Transcript of Record in the Supreme Court. The other former Stone law clerk was Harold Leventhal, who later became a federal appellate judge. The third lawyer was Eugene Gressman, an eminent Washington lawyer who had been a law clerk for Justice Frank Murphy. Twenty years earlier, Angelo Herndon, an African American man, had won his freedom in *Herndon v. Lowry* (1937), with representation from two other former Stone law clerks and a future president of the American Bar Association (see Chapter 6).

33. *Garner* at 171.

34. Raymond Arsenault, *Freedom Riders: 1961 and the Struggle for Racial Justice* (Oxford University Press, 2006), 182–186. On first encounter with violence, see Arsenault, "Five Days in May: Freedom Riding in the Carolinas," in *Toward the Meeting of the Waters: Currents in the Civil Rights Movement of South Carolina during the Twentieth Century,* ed. Orville Vernon Burton and Winfred B. Moore Jr. (University of South Carolina Press, 2008). Nash quote is from the PBS documentary "Freedom Riders," produced by Stanly Nelson (2011).

35. Arsenault, *Freedom Riders,* 349–363, esp. 352 and 360.

36. Jurisdiction: *Matter of Wyckoff* (1961); *Bailey v. Patterson* (1962); held unconstitutional: *Abernathy v. Alabama* (1965); *Thomas v. Mississippi* (1965).

37. Arsenault, *Freedom Riders,* 367, 476. Kennedy filed a Petition for Rule Making. The ICC rule was *Discrimination in Operations of Interstate Motor Carriers of Passengers,* No. MC-C-3358 (Sept. 22, 1961). It supplemented an earlier Order in *Sarah Kets v. Carolina Coach Co.,* No. MC-C-1564 (Nov. 7, 1955).

38. *Edwards v. South Carolina* (1963) at 233.

39. Greenville Code of 1953, amended in 1958, sec. 31-8.

40. Other sit-in cases decided that day included *Avent v. North Carolina* (1963), *Gober v. Birmingham* (1963), *Lombard v. Louisiana* (1963), and *Shuttlesworth v. Birmingham* (1963). Convictions were also reversed on slightly different grounds in *Wright v. Georgia* (1963). Three weeks later the Supreme Court vacated four Virginia cases and sent them back for reconsideration in light of *Peterson v. Greenville: Henry v. Virginia* (1963), *Randolph v. Virginia* (1963), *Thompson v. Virginia* (1963), and *Wood v. Virginia* (1963).

41. *Peterson v. Greenville* at 263.

42. Dan T. Carter, *The Politics of Rage: George Wallace, the Origins of the New Conservatism, and the Transformation of American Politics*, 2nd edition (Louisiana State University Press, 2000), 124–127, 147, 150. Charles Payne, *I've Got the Light of Freedom: The Organizing Tradition and the Mississippi Freedom Struggle* (University of California Press, 1995), 288; Taylor Branch, *Pillar of Fire: America in the King Years 1963–65* (Simon & Schuster, 1998), 76–78. For the story of the children demonstrators in Birmingham, see Taylor Branch, *Parting the Waters: America in the King Years 1954–63* (Simon & Schuster, 1988), chap. 20.

43. Julian E. Zelizer, *The Fierce Urgency of Now: Lyndon Johnson, Congress, and the Battle for the Great Society* (Penguin Books, 2015), 346–352.

44. Peter Irons, *The Courage of Their Convictions: Sixteen Americans Who Fought Their Way to the Supreme Court* (Free Press, 1988), 129–152.

45. Gerald T. Dunne, *Hugo Black and the Judicial Revolution* (Simon and Schuster, 1977), 392–393; Roger K. Newman, *Hugo Black: A Biography* (Pantheon Books, 1994), 550. Peter Charles Hoffer, Williamjames Hull Hoffer, and N. E. H. Hull, *The Supreme Court: An Essential History* (University Press of Kansas, 2007), 355.

46. The Maryland attorney general had told the Supreme Court that the issue was "no longer significant" because Baltimore had adopted an ordinance banning discrimination in restaurants. Brief in Opposition to Certiorari, 3, filed October 1, 1962.

47. *Burton v. Wilmington Parking Authority* (1962). The behind-the-scenes events at the Supreme Court relating to this case have been widely reported. See Justice Brennan's Clerks' Summary of October Term 1963, in Justice Brennan's papers at the Library of Congress; Del Dickson, *Supreme Court in Conference (1940–1985): The Private Discussions behind Nearly 300 Supreme Court Decisions* (Oxford University Press, 2001), 717–725.

48. *Bell v. Maryland* (1964). A vote for cloture, aided by Republican senator Dirksen of Illinois, ended the long debate.

49. Other cases in which convictions were reversed or remanded that day, on various grounds, were *Davis v. Maryland* (1964), *Griffin v. Maryland* (1964), *Barr v. City of Columbia* (1964), *Bouie v. City of Columbia* (1964), *Fox v. North Carolina* (1964), *Green v. Virginia* (1964), *Harris v. Virginia* (1964), *Mitchell v. City of Charleston* (1964), *Robinson v. Florida* (1964), and *Williams v. North Carolina* (1964).

50. Convictions pending on appeal were ended by *Hamm v. City of Rock Hill* (1964). Cases awaiting trial were essentially all ended by *Georgia v. Rachel*

(1966), which upheld their removal to federal court, where they were dismissed. See Chapter 9.

51. August Meier and Elliott Rudwick, *CORE: A Study in the Civil Rights Movement, 1942–1968* (University of Illinois Press, 1973), 329.

52. Irons, *The Courage of Their Convictions,* 132.

53. The transcript is quoted in the state court decision. *Ex parte Hamilton* (State court, 1963). See also *Johnson v. Virginia* (1963), where the Supreme Court reversed a contempt conviction for violating a segregated seating rule in a state courtroom.

9. A New Birth of Freedom, Again

1. David Bateman, Ira Katznelson, and John Lapinski, *Southern Nation: Congress and White Supremacy after Reconstruction* (Princeton University Press, 2018).

2. Heather Cox Richardson, *To Make Men Free: A History of the Republican Party* (Basic Books, 2014), 250–252; John A. Ferrell, *Nixon: A Life* (Double Day, 2017), 252. This was in a speech for the Al Smith dinner in New York City in 1956.

3. William S. White, "Eisenhower Lauds Civil Rights Plan," *New York Times,* June 20, 1957; "Senate Approves Rights Bill, 72–18, with Jury Clause," *New York Times,* August 8, 1957, 1; Robert Caro, *Master of the Senate: The Years of Lyndon Johnson* (Knopf, 2002), chap. 39.

4. Act of September 9, 1957, 71 Stat. 634.

5. Act of May 6, 1960, 74 Stat. 86.

6. Georgia: *United States v. Raines* (1960); Louisiana: *Thomas v. United States* (1960) (two orders); Alabama: *United States v. Alabama* (1960).

7. *Monroe v. Pape* at 203.

8. *Monroe v. Pape* at 184. This broad interpretation of "under color of law" was first adopted in a case interpreting a criminal section of a Reconstruction-era law, *United States v. Classic* (1941).

9. Malcolm Lee Cross, "Kennedy, John Fitzgerald," in *Civil Rights in the United States,* ed. Patricia Sullivan and Waldo E. Martin Jr., 2 vols. (Macmillan, 2000), 1:403.

10. Andrew Hoberek, ed., *The Cambridge Companion to John F. Kennedy* (University of Missouri Press, 2015), 85; Julian E. Zelizer, *The Fierce Urgency of Now: Lyndon Johnson, Congress, and His Battle for the Great Society* (Penguin Press, 2015), 46–60.

11. State of the Union, January 8, 1964, Lyndon B. Johnson Speeches, Presidential Speeches, Miller Center, University of Virginia, https://millercenter.org/the-presidency/presidential-speeches/january-8-1964-state-union; Zelizer, *The Fierce Urgency of Now,* 80.

12. Randall B. Woods, *LBJ: Architect of American Ambition* (Free Press, 2006), 434.

13. Smith 1957 quote from Charles Euchner, *Nobody Turn Me Around: A People's History of the 1963 March on Washington* (Beacon Press, 2010), 88. If, as many people believe, Smith intended the provision as a "poison pill" (something that would drag the main bill down to defeat), it turned out to have the opposite effect, prompting additional enthusiastic support. Katherine Turk, *Equality on Trial: Gender and Rights in the Modern American Workplace* (University of Pennsylvania Press, 2016), 3–4, 215n11.

14. E. W. Kenworthy, "Action by Senate: Revised Measure Now Goes Back to House for Concurrence," *New York Times,* June 20, 1964, 1; "President Signs Civil Rights Bill: Bids All Back It: Approves Sweeping Measure 5 Hours after Passage in House 289–126," *New York Times,* July 3, 1964; Edward L. Schapsmeier and Frederick H. Schapsmeier, *Dirksen of Illinois: Senatorial Statesman* (University of Illinois Press, 1985), 158. Schapsmeier and Schapsmeier cite Victor Hugo's diary for the quote.

15. Tomiko Brown-Nagin, *Courage to Dissent: Atlanta and the Long History of the Civil Rights Movement* (Oxford University Press, 2011), 214, 232, 243.

16. *Heart of Atlanta Motel v. United States* (1964) at 252.

17. *Heart of Atlanta Motel v. United States* (1964) at 292.

18. Ending cases: *Hamm v. City of Rock Hill* (1964) and *Georgia v. Rachel* (1966). Legal fees: *Newman v. Piggie Park Enterprises* (1968). "Private club" dodge: *Daniel v. Paul* (1969).

19. Brown-Nagin, *Courage to Dissent,* 222, 349, 301, 346; Bob Short, *Everything Is Pickrick: The Life of Lester Maddox* (Mercer University Press, 1999); Cleveland L. Sellers Jr., Jordan M. Simmons III, Jack Bass, and William C. Hine, "The Orangeburg Massacre," in *Toward the Meeting of the Waters: Currents in the Civil Rights Movement of South Carolina during the Twentieth Century,* ed. Winfred B. Moore Jr. and Orville Vernon Burton (University of South Carolina Press, 2008); Adam Parker, *Outside Agitator: The Civil Rights Struggle of Cleveland Sellers, Jr.* (Hub City Press, 2018), 121, 138–143, 199–200; Jack Nelson and Jack Bass, *The Orangeburg Massacre* (World, 1970).

20. Gary May, *Bending toward Justice: The Voting Rights Act and the Transformation of American Democracy* (Basic Books, 2013), 48; Ari Berman, *Give Us the Ballot: The Modern Struggle for Voting Rights in America* (Picador, 2016), 14–16. This was very early to begin work on voting rights, and Katzenbach was sorry not to have a bit of a break.

21. David J. Garrow, *Bearing the Cross: Martin Luther King, Jr., and the Southern Christian Leadership Conference* (Vintage Books, 1988), 368. May, *Bending toward Justice,* 47–48.

22. May, *Bending toward Justice,* 1.

23. Taylor Branch, *Pillar of Fire: America in the King Years, 1963–65* (Simon and Schuster, 1998), 151–152 (Freedom Day rally October 7, 1963); Clayborne Carson, *In Struggle: SNCC and the Black Awakening of the 1960s* (1981; Harvard University Press, 1995), 158; Townsend Davis, *Weary Feet,*

Rested Souls: A Guided History of the Civil Rights Movement (Norton, 1998), 121–123.

24. Nick Kotz, *Judgment Days: Lyndon Baines Johnson, Martin Luther King Jr., and the Laws That Changed America* (Houghton Mifflin, 2005), 282–285; Gene Roberts and Hank Klibanoff, *The Race Beat, the Press, the Civil Rights Struggle, and the Awakening of a Nation* (Knopf, 2006), 385–386; Carson, *In Struggle*, 158–161; Garrow, *Bearing the Cross*, 397–398.

25. May, *Bending toward Justice*, 89; Garrow, *Bearing the Cross*, 399; Lewis quote in Berman, *Give Us the Ballot*, 5. That Sunday evening, March 7, 1965, news reports of the bloody attack in Selma reached the general public. It so happens that ABC interrupted a movie to tell the news. The movie was *Judgment at Nuremberg*, about Nazi atrocities, and many viewers saw the parallel with racial hatred and violence closer to home.

26. Murdered that day was white minister James Reeb from Boston. Zelizer, *The Fierce Urgency of Now*, 210–211.

27. Garrow, *Bearing the Cross*, 400; Dan T. Carter, *The Politics of Rage: George Wallace, the Origins of the New Conservatism, and the Transformation of American Politics*, 2nd ed. (Louisiana State University Press, 2000), 4–48, 51, 99–104, 255–256; Jack Bass, *Taming the Storm: The Life and Times of Judge Frank M. Johnson, Jr., and the South's Fight over Civil Rights* (Doubleday, 1992), 236–254, 257–259.

28. *Williams v. Wallace* at 104.

29. *Williams v. Wallace* (Lower court, 1965); May, *Bending toward Justice*, 130.

30. Mary Stanton, *From Selma to Sorrow: The Life and Death of Viola Liuzzo* (University of Georgia Press, 1998). In Montgomery the marchers stayed on the grounds of the City of Saint Jude Catholic Church. Heather Gray, "Black Farmers' Lives Matter," *Counterpunch*, October 14, 2015.

31. Zelizer, *The Fierce Urgency of Now*, 213–214.

32. On the problems and trickery the Voting Rights Act had to overcome, see Brian K. Landsberg, *Free at Last to Vote: The Alabama Origins of the 1965 Voting Rights Act* (University Press of Kansas, 2007), 104–107, 154, 159–160, 162, 168–172, 188–189; Abigail M. Thernstrom, *Whose Votes Count: Affirmative Action and Minority Voting Rights* (Harvard University Press, 1987), 15–17; Frank R. Parker, *Black Votes Count: Political Empowerment in Mississippi after 1965* (University of North Carolina Press, 1990).

33. Francis W. White to Harold C. Booker Jr., August 3, 1940, in the Papers of Sam Latimer, South Caroliniana Library, University of South Carolina, Columbia.

34. A few scattered counties in other states, for example in New Hampshire, were swept in because they had literacy tests and abnormally low voter turnout resulting from weather conditions, but the act had a "bail-out" procedure allowing states or counties to show they had not discriminated in administering their literacy test. Other jurisdictions covered in the 1965 Act were the State of Alaska, which "bailed out" in 1966, and a few counties in

Arizona, Hawaii, and Idaho, some of which (Elmore, Idaho; Apache, Navaho; and Coconino, Arizona) were also able to bail out. Laughlin McDonald, *A Voting Right Odyssey: Black Enfranchisement in Georgia* (Cambridge, 2003), 125. When there is no proof of discrimination, the Supreme Court has upheld literacy tests, in *Lassiter v. Northampton County Board of Elections* (1959), and poll taxes, in *Breedlove v. Suttles* (1938). On the "bailout" provision, see Paul F. Hancock and Lora L. Tredway, "The Bailout Standard of the Voting Rights Act: An Incentive to End Discrimination," *The Urban Lawyer* 17 (1985): 379–425.

35. *South Carolina v. Katzenbach* (1966) at 308, 310n9.

36. *South Carolina v. Katzenbach* (1966) at 309. The Court catalogued the failure of Congress's efforts to expedite judicial remedies, such as the need to spend as much as 6,000 work hours on a single case. The new civil rights laws of 1957 and 1960 left African American registration virtually unchanged, increasing from only 31.7 to 31.8 percent of the eligible African American population in Louisiana, 14 to 19 percent in Alabama, and 4.4 to 6.4 percent in Mississippi, while white registration in each of those states was more than 50 percentage points higher.

37. *South Carolina v. Katzenbach* (1966) at 328–29, 338.

38. Chandler Davidson and Bernard Grofman, eds., *Quiet Revolution in the South: The Impact of the Voting Rights Act, 1965–1990* (Princeton University Press, 1994), 38–154; see the chapters on Alabama, Georgia, and Mississippi.

39. Frank R. Parker, David C. Colby, and Minion K. C. Morrison, "Mississippi," in Davidson and Grofman, *Quiet Revolution;* Howard Covington, *Henry Frye: North Carolina's First African American Chief Justice* (McFarland, 2013), 50. See Henry Frye interview, Southern Oral History Project, University of North Carolina, https://dc.lib.unc.edu/cdm/compoundobject/collection/sohp/id/7856/rec/4; "Literacy Test Proposal Loses," *News and Observer* (Raleigh, NC), November 5, 1970; Rob Christensen, *The Paradox of Tar Heel Politics: The Personalities, Elections, and Events That Shaped Modern North Carolina* (University of North Carolina Press, 2010), 264.

40. School board law: Act. No. 890 of 1956, "An Act to Amend Section 21-1631 of the Code of Laws of South Carolina, 1952, Relating to the Election or Appointment of Trustees of School Districts in Charleston County, So as to Make Further Provision for the Appointment of the Trustees of St. John's School District No. 9 and St. Paul's School District No. 23, in the County," adopted 19 April 1956. "Southern way of life": state senator Bill Carraway, US Congress, House of Reps., *Committee on the Judiciary, Extension of the Voting Rights Act: Hearing before the Subcommittee on Civil and Constitutional Rights of the Committee on the Judiciary,* 94th Cong., 1st sess., 1975, 1267; see catalog of two dozen methods of discrimination in Armand Derfner, "Racial Discrimination and the Right to Vote," *Vanderbilt Law Review* 26 (1973): 552–558.

41. *Allen v. State Board of Elections* (1969) at 548, 556.

42. Jack Bass and Walter DeVries, *The Transformation of Southern Politics: Social Change and Political Consequence since 1945* (Basic Books, 1976), 47; David S. Broder, *Changing of the Guard: Power and Leadership in America* (Simon and Schuster, 1980), 367.

43. *Katzenbach v. Morgan* (1966) at 652.

44. August Meier and Elliott Rudwick, *CORE: A Study in the Civil Rights Movement, 1942–1968* (University of Illinois Press, 1973), 329.

45. *Cox v. Louisiana* (1965) (2 cases); *Brown v. Louisiana* (1966) at 162; *Adderly v. Florida* (1996); *Walker v. Birmingham* (1967). Gerald T. Dunne, *Hugo Black and the Judicial Revolution* (Simon and Schuster, 1977), 393.

46. Gen. Code of Birmingham, Sec. 1159. Connor quote: *Walker v. City of Birmingham* (1967) at 317n9, 325, 335, 339; *Shuttlesworth v. City of Birmingham* (1969) at 157. Austin Sarat, "Keeping Civility in Its Place: Dissent, Injustice, and the Honor Lessons of History," in *Law, Society, and Community: Socio-Legal Essays in Honor of Roger Cotterrell*, ed. Richard Nobles and David Schiff (Routledge, 2014), 302.

47. Andrew Manis, *A Fire You Can't Put Out: The Civil Rights Life of Birmingham's Reverend Fred Shuttlesworth* (University of Alabama Press, 1999); Armand Derfner interview with Catherine G. Boykin, January 1, 2021.

48. Howard Ball, *Murder in Mississippi: United States v. Price and the Struggle for Civil Rights* (University Press of Kansas, 2004); William Shipp, *Murder at Broad River Bridge: The Slaying of Lemuel Penn by Members of the Ku Klux Klan* (Peachtree Press, 1981); Branch, *Pillar of Fire*, 398–400.

49. Hugh Davis Graham, *The Civil Rights Era: Origins and Development of National Policy 1960–1972* (Oxford University Press, 1990), 374–376, for discussion of the *Jones* case.

50. *Report of the National Advisory Commission on Civil Disorders* (New York Times Publications, 1968), 1–2, 389; Ibram X. Kendi, *Stamped from the Beginning: The Definitive History of Racist Ideas in America* (Nation Books, 2016), 404.

51. The Fair Housing Act is Title VIII of the Civil Rights Act of 1968, Act of April 11, 1968, 82 Stat. 81.

52. Two dissenters, Harlan and White, disagreed about the interpretation of the 1866 statute without addressing the reach of the Thirteenth Amendment. They also questioned why the case should be decided at all, since the Fair Housing Act of 1968 had already been enacted by the time the case was decided. The majority's explanation was not entirely clear. The decision was analogous to *Bell v. Maryland* (1964), discussed in Chapter 8, which was on a parallel track with the Civil Rights Act of 1964. Unlike the 1964 law, the 1968 Housing Act was already law well before the Supreme Court decision.

53. *Jones* at 437, 440.

54. *Jones* at 443.

10. Change in the Court

1. Nomination of Justice William Hubbs Rehnquist to be Chief Justice of the United States, Hearings before the S. Comm. on the Judiciary, 99th Cong. 324–325 (July 31, 1986), memo, titled "A Random Thought on the Segregation Cases," in *The Supreme Court of the United States: Hearings and Reports on Successful and Unsuccessful Nominations of Supreme Court Justices by the Senate Judiciary Committee, 1916–1986,* ed. Roy M. Mersky and J. Myron Jacobstein (William S. Hein, 1989), 634–635. The memo can also be found at https://www.govinfo.gov/content/pkg/GPO-CHRG-REHNQUIST/pdf/GPO-CHRG-REHNQUIST-4-16-6.pdf. Justice Rehnquist later said the memo did not reflect his views, a statement that has drawn mixed reactions. See Adam Liptak, "The Memo That Rehnquist Wrote and Had to Disown," *New York Times,* September 11, 2005.
2. Clayborne Carson, *In Struggle: SNCC and the Black Awakening of the 1960s* (Harvard University Press, 1981), 3, 209–210; Charles M. Payne, *I've Got the Light of Freedom: The Organizing Tradition and the Mississippi Freedom Struggle* (University of California Press, 1995), 227, 313–314, 366–380, 393–397, 435–436; Taylor Branch, *At Canaan's Edge: America in the King Years 1965–68* (Simon and Schuster, 2006), 486, 608–609.
3. The three civil rights supporters were Blackmun, Stevens, and Souter, who replaced Fortas, Douglas, and Brennan.
4. See especially Chandler Davidson and Bernard Grofman, eds., *The Quiet Revolution in the South: The Impact of the Voting Rights Act, 1965–1990* (Princeton University Press, 1994); Gavin Wright, *Sharing the Prize: The Economics of the Civil Rights Revolution in the American South* (Harvard University Press, 2013); Wright, "Voting Rights and Economics in the American South" in *Lincoln's Unfinished Work: From Generation to Generation,* ed. Orville Vernon Burton and Peter Eisenstadt (Louisiana State University Press, forthcoming 2021); Kevin M. Kruse and Julian E. Zelizer, *Fault Lines: A History of the United States since 1974* (Norton, 2019).
5. Anthony Lewis, "Supreme Court Enlarging Role as Instrument of Social Change," *New York Times,* May 17, 1964; see also James E. Moliterno, *The American Legal Profession in Crisis: Resistance and Response to Change* (Oxford University Press, 2013), 63. Quote from Blackmun Papers, in Michael Graetz and Linda Greenhouse, *The Burger Court and the Rise of the Judicial Right* (Simon and Schuster, 2016), 4. Warren Burger was campaign manager for Minnesota's liberal Republican governor Harold Stassen when Stassen ran for president in 1952. President Eisenhower put Burger on the US Court of Appeals for the DC Circuit, where he was especially conservative on criminal law issues. On the Supreme Court, he became more conservative after the arrival of Justices Rehnquist and Powell in 1972, and drifted to the right as his longtime friend, Justice Blackmun, drifted to the left.
6. One of the station's practices was to cut off network news about race matters and show a screen saying "Out of Order."

7. Aaron Henry, "No Slow Down Seen in Rights Suits," *Delta-Democratic Times* (Greenville, MS), June 15, 1971, 7. The city's claim of economic risk was an obvious pretext, because it had made no attempt to keep operating even one of the five pools before closing them. White people might not come, but integrated pools were what African Americans had been seeking.
8. *Alexander v. Holmes County* at 20.
9. The nineteenth-century cases were *U.S. v. Reese* (1876) and *U.S. v. Harris* (1883).
10. C. Vann Woodward, *The Strange Career of Jim Crow,* 3rd ed. (Oxford University Press, 1974), 214.
11. An example is a pair of contrasting decisions involving state regulations limiting payments under the federally sponsored AFDC program (Aid to Families with Dependent Children). In *Rosado v. Wyman* (1970), with seven Warren Court holdovers, a Harlan majority opinion blocked a New York regulation. In *Jefferson v. Hackney* (1972), with four Nixon appointees aboard, a Rehnquist majority upheld a similar Texas regulation.
12. *Moose Lodge No. 107 v. Irvis* (1972) at 181.
13. After the case ended, the Moose organization deleted the whites-only clause from its constitution at its next national convention.
14. *San Antonio Independent School District v. Rodriguez* (1973) at 11–13. Cynthia E. Orozco, "Rodriguez v. San Antonio ISD," Handbook of Texas Online, https://www.tshaonline.org/handbook/entries/rodriguez-v-san-antonio-isd; "San Antonio School District," in *Future Directions for School Finance Reform,* ed. Betsy Levin (Lexington Books, 1974); Elaine Ayala, "Rodriguez, Who Fought for Equality, Dies at 87," April 23, 2013, mysanantonio.com; Peter Irons, *The Courage of Their Convictions: 16 Americans Who Fought Their Way to the Supreme Court* (Free Press, 1988), 281–303.
15. *San Antonio v. Rodriguez* at 70–71. Rejection of a federal constitutional claim shifted cases to state courts, where state constitutions universally guarantee free public education. Such cases have since been filed everywhere, including Texas, with varying effectiveness.
16. On the ERA see Marjorie J. Spruill, *Divided We Stand: The Battle over Women's Rights and Family Values That Polarized American Politics* (Bloomsbury, 2017). Congress passed a number of laws against sex discrimination in this period: Equal Pay Act of 1963, Title VII of the Civil Rights Act of 1964 (employment), Fair Housing Act of 1968, Title IX of the Education Amendments of 1972 (education programs), and the Pregnancy Discrimination Act of 1976. Prior to these decisions, the Supreme Court had several times upheld laws that explicitly discriminated against women: *Bradwell v. Illinois* (1873) (practicing law); *Minor v. Happersett* (1875) (voting); *Goesaert v. Cleary* (1948) (bartending); *Hoyt v. Florida* (1961) (jurors).

17. John Jeffries, *Justice Lewis F. Powell, Jr.* (Scribner's, 1994), 298–307; Justin Driver, *The Schoolhouse Gate: Public Education, the Supreme Court, and the Battle for the American Mind* (Vintage, 2019), 274–284; Bernard Schwartz, *The Ascent of Pragmatism: The Burger Court in Action* (Addison-Wesley, 1990), 259–266.

18. The lineup was the same as in the San Antonio school financing case—the majority consisted of the four Nixon justices plus Justice Stewart. See discussion in Gary Orfield, Susan E. Eaton, and the Harvard Project on School Desegregation, *Dismantling Desegregation: The Quiet Reversal of Brown v. Board of Education* (Free Press, 1996), 10–16 and 143–178.

19. *Milliken v. Bradley* at 762.

20. Burger and Stewart technically concurred in the *Dayton* case, but their views were almost the equivalent of dissents.

21. The difference came from interpretation of words in the law. Title VII requires that a victim of discrimination be "made whole," but another section of the statute immunizes a seniority system if it is "bona fide." In the first case, the majority held that a seniority system cannot be "bona fide" if it locks in illegal discrimination. In the second case, the majority held that a seniority system can be "bona fide" if the discrimination predated the law—at a time when discrimination was "wrong" but not yet illegal.

22. *Runyon v. McCrary* (1976) at 191. Justice Stewart's two major opinions on the Ku Klux Act of 1871 were *U.S. v. Guest* (1966), and *Griffin v. Breckinridge* (1971).

23. James C. Cobb, *Away Down South: A History of Southern Identity* (Oxford, 2005), 319; Rick Perlstein, *Reaganland: America's Right Turn, 1976–1980* (Simon and Schuster, 2020), 833.

24. David G. Savage, *Turning Right: The Making of the Rehnquist Supreme Court* (Wiley, 1992). The rightward turn sputtered in the 1986–1987 and 1987–1988 terms, gaining full speed only when Justice Kennedy arrived. Justice Kennedy wrote the opinions in major gay rights cases: *Romer v. Evans* (1996) (anti-gay initiative); *Lawrence v. Texas* (2003) (sodomy); *Obergefell v. Hodges* (2015) (gay marriage).

25. Mark Tushnet's two books chronicle the two phases of Marshall's career: *Making Civil Rights Law* (Oxford University Press, 1994) (covering 1936–1961) and *Making Constitutional Law* (Oxford University Press, 1997) (covering 1961–1991). See also Juan Williams, *Thurgood Marshall: American Revolutionary* (Random House, 1998), 387.

26. President Bush was popular after the successful military operation "Desert Storm." In the Clinton victory in the 1992 presidential election, the third-party candidate, Ross Perot, siphoned votes from President Bush. To a lesser degree Perot also took some votes from Bob Dole in the 1996 election.

27. *Patterson v. McLean Credit Union* (1989); *Martin v. Wilks* (1989); *Lorance v. AT&T Technologies, Inc.* (1989). Patterson is discussed in this chapter. *Wards Cove Packing Co. v. Atonio* (1989) is discussed in Chapter 11.

28. The events are described in Savage, *Turning Right*, 184–192.

29. This part of Section 1 of the 1866 act has been broken into two sections, which today are 42 U.S. Code Section 1981 (contracts and court proceedings) and 42 U.S. Code Section 1982 (property). Brief for the United States as Amicus Curiae Supporting Petitioner, in *Patterson v. McLean Credit Union* at 10.

30. *Patterson v. McLean Credit Union* at 176, 177.

31. *Patterson* at 176, quoting from *Georgia v. Rachel* (1966) at 791. *Georgia v. Rachel* was the last of the sit-in cases. The Supreme Court held that the Civil Rights Act of 1964 was phrased in terms of racial equality, which therefore allowed removal of all remaining sit-in prosecutions from state courts to federal courts, where they were promptly dismissed.

32. *Patterson v. McLean Credit Union* at 188, 189.

33. Adam Clymer, "Senate Approves Civil Rights Bill, 95–5," *New York Times,* October 31, 1991.

34. New York: *Spallone v. U.S.* (1988) (stay order); (1990). The Court upheld a contempt citation against the city, which the majority said should have been and in fact turned out to be sufficient to gain compliance. Oklahoma City: *Board of Educ. of Oklahoma City v. Dowell* (1991); Atlanta: *Freeman v. Pitts* (1992).

35. *Missouri v. Jenkins* (1995) at 94.

36. *Missouri v. Jenkins* at 94–95 and note 8. The Court provided support for the unsurprising proposition that desegregation can prompt white flight, but its "supposition" that a background of segregation plays no role was just wrong, *Missouri v. Jenkins* at 164.

37. Testimony of McLemore in the *Fordice* case. Derfner was the attorney questioning McLemore in the courtroom when McLemore made the statement.

38. George Will, "Can This Nomination Be Justified?" *Washington Post,* October 5, 2005.

39. Adam Liptak and Sheryl Gay Stolberg, "Shadow of Merrick Garland Hangs Over the Next Supreme Court Fight," *New York Times,* September 19, 2020.

40. "Amy Coney Barrett Sworn In as Supreme Court Justice, Cementing Conservative Majority," *New York Times,* October 26, 2020, updated November 8, 2020.

41. Immigration figures come from the US Department of Homeland Security, Yearbook of Immigration Statistics, published annually; naturalization statistics come from the US Department of Homeland Security, Annual Flow Report, also published every year.

42. Preclearance objections: All the objections are listed by state on the Department of Justice website: https://www.justice.gov/crt/section-5-objection-letters.

43. Statute and extensions upheld: *South Carolina v. Katzenbach* (1966); *Georgia v. United States* (1973); *City of Rome v. United States* (1980); *Lopez v. Monterey County* (1999). Literacy tests were initially suspended temporarily and only in certain states, but by 1975 they were banned permanently and

nationwide. The 1975 law also included Section 203 providing foreign language election assistance in areas of high non-English-speaking population concentrations.

44. Not long before the renewal, a majority opinion by Justice O'Connor projected that a twenty-five-year period would be needed for affirmative action programs to be effective. *Grutter v. Bollinger* (2003) at 343.

45. See John Roberts's memoranda dated 11/6/81, 12/22/81, 1/22/82 (2 memos), 1/25/82, 1/26/82 (2 memos), 2/8/82, 2/17/82. For a specific reference to Section 5 (preclearance), see page 5 of "Talking Points" attached to Roberts Memorandum of 1/25/82. In the Papers of John Roberts, Justice Department Files, Library of Congress; Ari Berman, *Give Us the Ballot: The Modern Struggle for Voting Rights in America* (Picador, 2015), 147–152. See Chapter 11 for discussion of the debate over the 1982 amendment to Section 2 of the Voting Rights Act.

46. The Court avoided the constitutionality of preclearance by holding that the act allowed local governments with good records of compliance to "bail out"—that is, to move for exemption from the act's coverage. Carol Anderson, *One Person, No Vote: How Voter Suppression Is Destroying Our Democracy* (Bloomsbury Publishing, 2018), 38–40.

47. *Northwest Austin* at 203. The principal support for the "equal sovereignty" theory was several cases recognizing an "equal footing" doctrine—i.e., that states enter the union on an equal footing.

48. *South Carolina v. Katzenbach* at 328–329.

49. *Northwest Austin* at 203.

50. *Northwest Austin* Oral argument, April 29, 2009, 56:12 (Oyez Project), https://www.oyez.org/cases/2008/08-32.

51. Strictly speaking, the Court struck down only the "coverage formula" of Section 4 of the Act, which identified those jurisdictions that were covered—but with no states or counties covered, anywhere, the entire Section 5 preclearance remedy was obviously at an end. Past civil rights law held unconstitutional: *James v. Bowman* (1903). In *Adarand v. Pena* (1995), the Supreme Court raised constitutional doubts about federal affirmative programs but did not hold any laws or regulations unconstitutional. Berman, *Give Us the Ballot,* 9–10, 273–278, 280–285; Anderson, *One Person, No Vote,* 25–26, 123–127.

52. Thomas Colby, "In Defense of the Equal Sovereignty Principle," *Duke Law Journal* 65 (2016): 1087, 1089, 1167–1170 (Colby lists a few of the critics in his notes 4–9); "Town Hall Debate: McConnell and Rosen on the Voting Rights Act," *Yahoo News,* June 25, 2013, http://news.yahoo.com/town-hall-debate-mcconnell-rosen-voting-rights-act-184607340.html; Richard A. Posner, "The Voting Rights Act Ruling Is about the Conservative Imagination," *Slate,* June 26, 2013. One article drew a connection between "equal sovereignty" and the *Dred Scott* decision: James Blacksher and Lani Guinier, "Free at Last: Rejecting Equal Sovereignty and Restoring the Right to Vote," *Harvard Law and Policy Review* 8 (2014): 39. Some few scholars agreed that there is a principle of equal sovereignty, but they declined to

defend the Supreme Court's use of it to strike down the Voting Rights Act. See Jeffrey Schmitt, "In Defense of Shelby County's Principle of Equal State Sovereignty," *Oklahoma Law Review* 68, no. 2 (2016): 262; Anthony Belia and Bradford Clark, "The International Origins of American Federalism," *Columbia Law Review* 120 (2020): 940.

53. *McCulloch v. Maryland* (1819) at 424: "But where the law is not prohibited and is really calculated to effect any of the objects intrusted [*sic*] to the government, to undertake here to inquire into the degree of its necessity, would be to pass the line which circumscribes the judicial department and to tread on legislative ground." For example, Prohibition in *James Everard Breweries v. Day* (1924).

54. *Perkins v. Matthews* (1971) at 38; *Shelby County v. Holder* at 554. Even within the strictures of the equal sovereignty doctrine, the lower court pointed to a record that showed a difference between the covered and uncovered states. *Shelby County* (Lower court, 2012) at 873–879, which hardly constituted "40-year-old facts."

55. *Shelby County v. Holder* at 590, 592. On Ginsburg's oral statement, see Joan Biskupic, *The Chief: The Life and Turbulent Times of Chief Justice John Roberts* (Basic Books, 2014), 272.

56. Preclearance denied under the Voting Rights Act: *Texas v. Holder* (DC district court, 2012). Discriminatory purpose found again, *Veasey v. Perry* (Texas district court, 2014). No court ever found the Texas law free of discriminatory purpose, but Texas substituted a law that burdened voters less, and it was upheld, *Veasey v. Abbot* (Court of appeals, 2018).

57. *Wards Cove Packing Co. v. Atonio* (1989) at 662.

11. The War of Words

1. Lani Guinier, *Lift Every Voice: Turning a Civil Rights Setback into a New Vision of Social Justice* (Simon and Schuster, 1998), 71–85; William L. Taylor, *The Passion of My Times: An Advocate's Fifty-Year Journey in the Civil Rights Movement* (Carroll and Graf, 2004), 131–146; Michael Pertschuk, *Giant Killers* (Norton, 1986), 148–180.

2. Cases often use synonyms. Thus, "purpose" is the same as "intent," and "effect" is the same as "impact." Another word often encountered is "disparate," simply meaning "different."

3. The first of these hypotheticals, a veterans' hiring preference, was upheld in *Personnel Administrator v. Feeney* (1979) at 279, 278, on the ground that proof of a purpose to discriminate against women was lacking.

4. *Guinn v. U.S.* (1915) (grandfather clause for voting); *Gomillion v. Lightfoot* (1960) (changing boundaries of Tuskegee, Alabama, from a square to "an uncouth 28-sided figure").

5. Section 5 of the Voting Rights Act, 42 U.S.C. 1973c. "Designedly or otherwise": *Fortson v. Dorsey* (1965) at 439; *Burns v. Richardson* (1966) at 88; *Whitcomb v. Chavis* (1971) at 179.

6. *Griggs* at 430–431. As an alternative to the test, an applicant could present a high school diploma. The Supreme Court held that this part of the requirement was discriminatory because the historically unequal schooling had left disproportionate numbers of African Americans without high school diplomas in midcentury North Carolina.

7. Amicus Brief of United Steelworkers of America filed in *Griggs v. Duke Power Co.* (1971) at 3.

8. *Griggs* at 429–430. The testing requirement—though not the particular test—had been adopted several years before the new law, when it initially applied only to white employees, so it did not seem like a sudden, suspect response to the Civil Rights Act. Section 703(a) of the Civil Rights Act of 1964, 42 U.S.C. 2000e(a).

9. *Griggs* at 430.

10. *Griggs* at 432, 433.

11. *Griggs* at 436.

12. Melvin Urofsky, *The Affirmative Action Puzzle: A Living History from Reconstruction to Today* (Pantheon Books, 2020), 126–129; Ruth G. Blumrosen, "Wage Discrimination, Job Segregation, and Title VII of the Civil Rights Act of 1964," *University of Michigan Journal of Law Reform* 12 (1979): 402–502; Richard B. Freeman, "Changes in the Labor Market for Black Americans, 1948–72," *Brookings Papers on Economic Activity* 1 (1973): 67–131; Mitra Toossi and Leslie Joyner, "Blacks in the Labor Force," US Bureau of Labor Statistics, Spotlight on Statistics, February 2018, https://www.bls.gov/spotlight/2018/blacks-in-the-labor-force/home.htm. The number of African American officials and managers in the workforce plateaued at near 7 percent in 2002 until 2013, technicians as a group were 4 percent in 1966 and 13 percent in 2013, office and clerical workers increased from about 3.5 percent to about 16 percent in 2013, and Black laborers actually decreased from 21 percent in 1966 to about 17 percent in 2013. See US Equal Employment Opportunity Commission website for statistics and graph, https://www.eeoc.gov//eeoc/statistics/reports/american_experiences/african_americans.cfm.

13. Lower court cases: *Washington v. Davis* at 244n12. A majority of the Court also did find the test to be job-related, referring to a statute covering the District of Columbia.

14. Armand Derfner, oral interview with Richard T. Seymour, October 11, 2018. There had been conflicting suggestions in recent cases about whether proof of discriminatory purpose was important in an equal protection case. Suggesting that proof of purpose was necessary: *Keyes v. Denver School District* (1973); *Jefferson v. Hackney* (1972). Unnecessary: *White v. Regester* (1973); *Palmer v. Thompson* (1971).

15. The Supreme Court had upheld statutes giving more leeway to congressional action—e.g., *Katzenbach v. Morgan* (1966). This was a stark contrast to *U.S. v. Cruikshank* (1876).

16. In *Personnel Administrator v. Feeney* (1979), the Court said the proof must show that a certain course was chosen "because of," not "in spite of," likely

discriminatory consequences; the Court also ruled that "awareness" of a likely discriminatory consequences is not enough.

17. *Arlington Heights* at 265.

18. *Civil Rights Cases* (1883) at 48.

19. See the history of discriminatory intent in adoption of the ordinance in 1911, see "Final Arguments in Voting Rights Case," *Associated Press,* May 26, 1981; "Mobile Voting Rights Case Awaiting Judge's Decision," *Associated Press,* May 28, 1981; Art Harris, "In Much of South, Voting Rights Act Remains Key to Racial Politics," *Washington Post,* June 19, 1981.

20. Ari Berman, *Give Us the Ballot: The Modern Struggle for Voting Rights in America* (Picador, 2016), 222–223. Kiss of death: Brief for Respondents filed in *Mobile v. Bolden* (1980) at 78–79.

21. At-large elections for the Mobile County school board were upheld in the companion case of *Williams v. Brown* (1980). Justice Blackmun dissented, making the vote 5–4, whereas he concurred in upholding at-large elections in the City of Mobile (making that vote 6–3), because he viewed the city's commission form of government as incompatible with ward elections.

22. Fred Barbash, "High Court May Have Derailed Voting Drive by Blacks in South; Supreme Court Slows Blacks' Political Drive," *Washington Post,* April 24, 1980.

23. Preclearance and bilingual elections were provided, respectively, in Sections 5 and 203 of the Voting Rights Act, 42 U.S. Code Sections 1973c and 1973aa1a, now transferred to 52 U.S. Code Sections 10304 and 10503. Section 203 required assistance in a foreign language if that language was used by a certain percentage of voters in a given area. The course of the legislation through 1981–1982 is described in detail in Thomas M. Boyd and Stephen J. Markham, "The 1982 Amendments to the Voting Rights Act: A Legislative History," *Washington and Lee Law Review* 40 (1983): 1347–1428.

24. *New York Times,* May 18, 1982, 8; *Washington Post* and *Los Angeles Times,* May 20, 1982; Gary May, *Bending toward Justice: The Voting Rights Act and the Transformation of American Democracy* (Basic Books, 2013), 214–231; Berman, *Give Us the Ballot,* 135–142, 145, 152–157. *Birmingham Post-Herald,* in op-ed quoted in Bowd and Markham, "The 1982 Amendments to the Voting Rights Act," 1404n279.

25. Stephen L. Carter, "Living without the Judge," in *Thurgood Marshall: Justice for All,* ed. Roger Goldman and David Gallen (Carroll and Graff, 1992), 203. "Talking Points" attached to Roberts Memorandum to Attorney General, January 25, 1982, 4; Roberts Memorandum to Attorney General, January 26, 1982, 2; in the Papers of John Roberts, Justice Department Files, Library of Congress. Quotas ("numerus clausus") are devices to exclude certain groups. Quotas were used in European countries to limit or exclude Jews from universities or professions, and quotas were used in American immigration laws in the period 1924–1965.

26. Derfner made one of the phone calls, to Mayor Ross of Lincolnville, SC, April 23, 1982.

27. Two days after the bill was signed, the Supreme Court ruled in *Rogers v. Lodge* (1982) that at-large elections in a Georgia county were unconstitutional under the *Mobile* "purpose" standard. Personal recollection by Armand Derfner, who heard this exchange. Berman, *Give Us the Ballot,* 150–151, 156–157.

28. *Thornburg v. Gingles* (1986). The Court has a Section 2 case in 2021, *Brnovich v. DNC*. It is an appeal from *DNC v. Hobbs* (Lower court, 2020), which held that several Arizona laws discriminated against minority voters.

29. David Savage, *Turning Right: The Making of the Rehnquist Supreme Court* (Wiley, 1992), 272–276.

30. *Wards Cove* at 661, 662, 663.

31. "Wards Cove Hires Firm to Sell Nine Seafood Processing Plants in Alaska," *Juneau Empire, Associated Press,* December 18, 2002.

32. Scalia's use of the word *war* in *Ricci* at 595. *Ricci* at 581, 625.

33. *Ricci* at 585. The stringency of that standard was reflected in a procedural ruling that ended the case. The ordinary course when a new rule of evidence is announced is to remand the case for new proceedings under the new rule, and the majority could have done that here. Instead the Court said the lack of evidence was so clear that a remand was not needed.

34. As an indicator of problems with the test, Justice Ginsburg noted that this type of test had been abandoned in many fire departments.

35. Justice Kennedy cited cases from nine of the twelve circuits holding that the FHA allows cases based on "disparate impact" (discriminatory effect). *Texas Department of Housing and Community Affairs* (2015) at 2519.

36. The two cases disposed of by settlement were listed in Justice Alito's dissent, *Texas Department* at 2532n1.

37. Justice Kennedy said, "In April 1968, Dr. Martin Luther King, Jr., was assassinated in Memphis, Tennessee, and the nation faced a new urgency to resolve the social unrest in the inner cities. Congress responded by adopting the Kerner Commission's recommendation and passing the Fair Housing Act." *Texas Department* at 2516.

38. *Texas Department* at 2526.

39. *Texas Department* at 2537.

40. Tenacious: *Bossier Parish* (Lower court, 2000) at 29. Burger Court case: *Perkins v. Matthews* (1971) at 387. The majority said its ground for adopting a retrogression rule was to be consistent with *Beer v. U.S.* (1976), which added a retrogression rule to the "effect" portion of the law. But *Beer* itself rejected the rule adopted in *Bossier Parish,* saying retrogression would not apply where a change was *unconstitutional,* which purposeful discrimination is.

41. Circumstantial evidence: *Arlington Heights* (1977) at 267. The lower court in *Perez* said at least seven times that the challengers had the burden of proof and rejected several challenges to other districts for failing to meet their burden. *Perez v. Abbott* (Lower court, 2017), 267 F.Supp.3d at 765, 773, 794; and 274 F.Supp.3d at 643, 646, 668, 673, 675.

42. Textbook rules: Comcast Corp at *Comcast Corp* at 1014; shifting burden of proof: *Arlington Heights* at 270n21. The *Arlington Heights* rules apply

to cases, like this one, under the Civil Rights Act of 1866. *General Building Contractors Assn. v. Pennsylvania* (1982) at 389–391.

12. Affirmative Action

1. Clarence Thomas, *My Grandfather's Son: A Memoir* (HarperCollins, 2007). Sonia Sotomayor, *My Beloved World* (Knopf, 2013). This chapter is not about arguments for and against affirmative action. Three of the countless sources that discuss this topic are Melvin Urofsky, *The Affirmative Action Puzzle: A Living History from Reconstruction to Today* (Pantheon, 2020); Randall Kennedy, *For Discrimination: Race, Affirmative Action and the Law* (Pantheon, 2013); and John David Skrentny, *The Ironies of Affirmative Action: Politics, Culture, and Justice in America* (University of Chicago Press, 1996).
2. This development of affirmative action for white people has received increasing attention in recent years. Ira Katznelson, *When Affirmative Action Was White: An Untold History of Racial Inequality in Twentieth-Century America* (Norton, 2005); Richard Rothstein, *The Color of Law* (Norton, 2017); Kenneth Jackson, *Crabgrass Frontier: The Suburbanization of America* (Oxford University Press, 1985); James Kushner, "Apartheid in America: An Historical and Legal Analysis of Contemporary Racial Residential Segregation in the United States," *Howard Law Journal* 22 (1979): 547; George Lipsitz, *How Racism Takes Place* (Temple University Press, 2017); Lipsitz, *The Possessive Investment in Whiteness: How White People Profit from Identity Politics* (Temple University Press, 2006); Keeanga-Yamahtta Taylor, *Race for Profit: How Banks and the Real Estate Industry Undermined Black Homeownership* (University of North Carolina Press, 2019).
3. Houston quote: Katznelson, *When Affirmative Action Was White*, 48. There are many studies of particular laws and agencies. For farm programs, see US Commission on Civil Rights, *Equal Opportunity in Farm Programs* (1965). On discrimination against Black farmers, see *Pigford v. Glickman*, (Lower court, 2000); Pete Daniel, *Dispossession: Discrimination against African American Farmers in the Age of Civil Rights* (University of North Carolina Press, 2013); Valerie Grim, "Between Forty Acres and a Class Action Lawsuit: Black Farmers, Civil Rights, and Protest against the USDA, 1997–2010," in *Beyond Forty Acres and a Mule: African American Landowning Families Since Reconstruction*, ed. Debra Ann Reid and Evan P. Bennett (University Press of Florida, 2012), 271–297; Adrienne Monteith Petty, *Small Farmers in North Carolina since the Civil War* (Oxford University Press 2013). On the GI Bill, see Juan F. Perea, "Doctrines of Delusion: How the History of the G.I. Bill Undermines the Supreme Court's Affirmative Action Jurisprudence," *University of Pittsburgh Law Review* 75 (2014): 583.
4. The figures are from the Federal Reserve Board 2017 report: a median household income of $61,200 for white people and $35,400 for African Americans, but a median household net worth of $171,000 for white households and $17,600 for African American households. The ratio varies little by education level. For households headed by a person with a bachelor's degree or higher, the ratio is 10.2 to 1 ($375,500:$36,800), while for

households without a bachelor's degree, the ratio is 8.5 to 1 ($87,100:$10,300). Board of Governors of the Federal Reserve Board, "Recent Trends in Wealth-Holding by Race and Ethnicity: Evidence from the Survey of Consumer Finances," FEDS Notes, September 27, 2017, https://www.federalreserve.gov/econres/notes/feds-notes/recent-trends-in-wealth-holding-by-race-and-ethnicity-evidence-from-the-survey-of-consumer-finances-20170927.htm.

5. Justice Blackmun, in *Regents of the University of California v. Bakke* (1978) at 507. Chief Justice Roberts in *Parents Involved in Public Education v. Seattle School Dist.* (2007) at 747; Justice Thomas in *Parents Involved* at 751.

6. "To Fulfill These Rights," Public Papers of the Presidents of the United States, Lyndon Johnson, 1965 (US Government Printing Office, 1966), 2:635–640. The previous executive orders were E.O. 8802 (Roosevelt, June 25, 1941), E.O. 9980 (Truman, July 26, 1948), E.O. 10479 (Eisenhower, August 13, 1953), E.O. 10925 (Kennedy, March 6, 1961).

7. Jennifer Giancola and Richard D. Kahlenberg, "True Merit: Insuring Our Brightest Students Have Access to Our Best Colleges and Universities" (Jack Kent Cooke Foundation, January 2016); Elyse Ashburn, "At Elite Colleges, Legacy Status May Count More than Was Previously Thought," *Chronicle of Higher Education*, January 5, 2011.

8. The first major case was *Reed v. Reed* (1971), striking down an Idaho law that automatically preferred a male over a female in selecting an estate administrator when there was no will.

9. Philadelphia Plan: *Contractors Assn of Eastern Pennsylvania v. Secretary of Labor* (1971) (denying certiorari). Law school: *DeFunis v. Odegaard* (1974). Marco DeFunis was ordered admitted to the University of Washington Law School while the lawsuit was pending; by the time the Supreme Court was ready to decide, he was about to graduate, so the Supreme Court dismissed the case as moot. Two early cases are often overlooked: *Morton v. Mancari* (1974) (upheld hiring preference for Indians at the Bureau of Indian Affairs) and *Hughes v. Superior Court of California* (1950) (held picketing for quota hiring was not protected as free speech because the goal of the picketing—quota hiring—was illegal under California law).

10. In 1965, 4.9 percent of college undergrads were African American. In 1970, 800 African Americans were enrolled in medical schools, but only 211 of those students attended schools that were predominantly white. Howard Ball, *The Bakke Case: Race, Education, and Affirmative Action* (University Press of Kansas, 2000), 3, 5, 49. See James D. Anderson, *The Education of Blacks in the South, 1860–1935* (University of North Carolina Press, 1988); Henry Allen Bullock, *A History of Negro Education in the South from 1619 to the Present* (Praeger, 1967); Heather Andrea Williams, *Self-Taught: African American Education in Slavery and Freedom* (University of North Carolina Press, 2005), 179–186; Christopher M. Span, "Learning in Spite of Opposition: African Americans and Their History of Educational Exclusion in Antebellum America," *Counterpoints* 131 (2005): 25–53, esp. 27.

11. John W. Johnson and Robert P. Green Jr., *Affirmative Action* (Greenwood Press, 2009), 64.

12. Bernard Schwartz, *Behind Bakke: Affirmative Action and the Supreme Court* (NYU Press, 1988). See also Ball, *The Bakke Case;* Nancy MacLean, *Freedom Is Not Enough: The Opening of the American Workplace* (Harvard University Press, 2006), 222–223, 251, 315.

13. *Bakke* at 284–285 (Opinion of Justice Stevens, joined by Chief Justice Burger and Justices Stewart and Rehnquist).

14. Marshall: *Bakke* at 396, 387; Blackmun: *Bakke* at 407. Some of Blackmun's wording apparently was borrowed from articles by McGeorge Bundy and Alexander Heard. Linda Greenhouse, *Becoming Justice Blackmun* (Henry Holt, 2005), 132–133.

15. *Bakke* at 407. Antonia Chayes, Christopher Kaufman, and Raymond Wheeler, "The University's Role in Minority Group Hiring in the Construction Industry," *University of Pennsylvania Law Review* 119 (1970): 91, 100, 120–121 and note 116. George Frederickson discussed societal racism in 1971 in *The Black Image in the White Mind: The Debate in Afro-American Character and Destiny, 1817–1914* (Oxford University Press, 1971).

16. Ball, *Bakke Case,* 48–49. In 1970 Meharry and Howard had over 70 percent of minority medical students. Urofsky, *Affirmative Action,* 355–358.

17. Harriet A. Washington et al., "Segregation, Civil Rights and Health Disparities: The Legacy of African American Physicians and the American Medical Association, 1910–1968," *Journal of the National Medical Association* 101 (2009): 513; Robert B. Baker, "The American Medical Association and Race," *AMA Journal of Ethics* 16 (2014): 479; Larry T. Menefee, "Are Black Americans Entitled to Equal Health Care? A New Research Paradigm," *Ethnicity and Disease* 6 (1996): 56; Todd Savitt, "Abraham Flexner and the Black Medical Schools," *Journal of the National Medical Association* 98 (2006): 1421. See, e.g., *Simkins v. Moses H. Cone Mem. Hosp,* (Lower court, 1963); *Cypress v. Newport News Non-Sectarian Hosp. Assn* (Lower court, 1967); *United States v. Medical Society of South Carolina* (Lower court, 1969). Hill Burton Act of August 13, 1946, 60 Stat. 1041, Section 622.

18. Kennedy, *For Discrimination,* 187–189. Urofsky, *Affirmative Action,* 350–361.

19. *United Steelworkers of America v. Weber* at 203 (because this case involved a private corporation, not the government, the constitution did not apply, only the statute); MacLean, *Freedom Is Not Enough,* 226–227, 249–256, 304.

20. *Fullilove* at 484.

21. *Fullilove* at 523.

22. Joel L. Selig, "The Reagan Justice Department and Civil Rights: What Went Wrong," *University of Illinois Law Review* (1985): 785. Assistant Attorney General Brad Reynolds responded to this article but did not disagree with the facts. William Bradford Reynolds, "The Reagan Administration and Civil Rights: Winning the War against Discrimination," *University of Illinois Law Review* (1986): 1001. See also Department of Justice Press Release (April 2, 1985) at 1–3. Manning Marable, *Race, Reform, and Rebel-*

lion: The Second Reconstruction and Black America, 1945–2006 (University Press of Mississippi, 2007), 196.

23. Charles Fried, *Order and Law: Arguing the Reagan Revolution: A First-hand Account* (Simon and Schuster, 1991), 102–104; Lincoln Caplan, *The Tenth Justice: The Solicitor General and the Rule of Law* (Knopf, 1987), 101–109; "Top Lawyer Dissents in Brief on Tax Exemptions," *New York Times,* February 27, 1982, sec. 1, p. 8. The administration's sudden abandonment of its case led the Supreme Court to appoint William T. Coleman, who had been the Supreme Court's first African American law clerk (for Justice Frankfurter in 1949) as amicus curiae to argue the government's original position on behalf of the IRS and against the schools' tax exemptions. Katherine Shaw, "Friends of the Court: Evaluating the Supreme Court's Amicus Invitations," *Cornell Law Review* 101 (2016): 1533, 1553–1554.

24. Fried, *Order and Law,* 110–118. The two cases where the Court rejected the layoff plans were *Memphis Firefighters Local 1784 v. Stotts* (1984) and *Wygant v. Jackson Bd. of Education* (1986). The four hiring or promotion cases where the Court upheld the plans were *Local 28, Sheet Metal Workers v. EEOC* (1986), *Local 93, Firefighters v. City of Cleveland* (1986), *United States v. Paradise* (1987), and *Johnson v. Transportation Agency* (1987). On retreat from affirmative action, see MacLean, *Freedom Is Not Enough,* 213–214, 218–219, 222–224, 268, 299, 302–314.

25. *Wygant v. Jackson Bd of Educ.* at 277.

26. *City of Richmond* at 506–508 The Court also held the plan was not "narrowly tailored" because it required a 30 percent set-aside (compared to *Fullilove's* 10 percent) and covered other minority populations even though there was no suggestion of any discrimination against them in or by Richmond. The Court did expand the range of permissible justification, by holding that a plan could seek to overcome discrimination by others in its market area, not just its own discrimination. In *Johnson v. Transportation Agency* (1987), Justice O'Connor expressed opposition to a similar stereotyping of women workers.

27. Marshall: *City of Richmond* at 529, 530; Blackmun: *City of Richmond* at 561.

28. The decisive vote in *Metro* was Justice White, who a year earlier had voted to strike down Richmond's affirmative action plan but had supported the federal plan in *Fullilove.*

29. Kevin Merida and Michael A. Fletcher, *Supreme Discomfort: The Divided Soul of Clarence Thomas* (Doubleday, 2007), 256.

30. 15 U.S.C. 637(d)(2) and (3). Although the dispute arose under a particular law relating to the Small Business Administration, there was sufficient confusion about how various statutes and regulations operated that the Supreme Court made no ruling on any of them.

31. Thomas: *Adarand Constructors* at 241; Stevens: *Adarand Constructors* at 245.

32. Steven K. DiLiberto, Comment, "Setting Aside Set Asides: The New Standard for Affirmative Action Programs in the Construction Industry," *Villanova Law Review* 42 (1997): 2039n3 (list of federal affirmative action programs). As of 2020 it appeared that affirmative action programs have been upheld in several circuits and struck down in one. See cases cited in the opinion of Rehnquist and Scalia dissenting from the denial of certiorari in *Concrete Works of Colorado v. City and County of Denver* (2003).

33. Craig Steven Wilder, *Ebony and Ivy: Race, Slavery, and the Troubled History of America's Universities* (Bloomsbury Press, 2013); Leslie Harris, Alfred Brophy, and James T. Campbell, *Slavery and the University* (University of Georgia Press, 2019); James T. Campbell, "Confronting the Legacy of Slavery and the Slave Trade: Brown University Investigates Its Painful Past," *UN Monthly Chronicle* 44, no. 3 (2007). See also *Seeking Abraham: A Report of Furman University's Task Force on Slavery and Justice,* 2nd ed. (Furman University, 2019); and, on Georgetown, Rachel L. Swarns, "272 Slaves Were Sold to Save Georgetown: What Does It Owe Their Descendants?," *New York Times,* April 16, 2016.

34. Nearly a hundred amicus briefs were filed in the *Grutter* case, and nearly a hundred again in the *Fisher* cases. See also *Gratz v. Bollinger* (2003). Nick Anderson, "How Harvard Set the Model for Affirmative Action in College Admissions," *Washington Post,* June 21, 2016; Adam Harris, "The Supreme Court Justice Who Forever Changed Affirmative Action," *Atlantic,* October 13, 2018; Matthew Chigos and Victoria Lee, "40 Years after the Bakke Decision, What's the Future of Affirmative Action in College Admissions?," Urban Wire: Education and Training, Blog of the Urban Institute, https://www.urban.org/urban-wire/40-years-after-bakke-decision-whats-future-affirmative-action-college-admissions. See especially three papers published in 2005 by the Association of American Colleges and Universities' Making Excellence Inclusive Initiative—Preparing Students and Campuses for an Era of Greater Expectations: Jeffrey F. Milem, Mitchell J. Chang, and Anthony Lising Antonio, "Making Diversity Work on Campus: A Research-Based Perspective"; Georgia L. Bauman, Leticia Tomas Bustillos, Estela Mara Bensimon, M. Christopher Brown II, and RoSusan D. Bartee, "Achieving Equitable Educational Outcomes with All Students: The Institution's Roles and Responsibilities"; and Damon A. Williams, Joseph B. Berger, and Shederick A. McClendon, "Toward a Model of Inclusive Excellence and Change in Postsecondary Institutions."

35. On Sotomayor: Meg Greene, *Sonia Sotomayor: A Biography* (ABC-CLIO, 2012), 37; Bill Mears, "Sotomayor Says She Was the 'Perfect Affirmative Action Baby,'" CNN Politics, June 11, 2009; Sotomayor, *My Beloved World.*

36. *Fisher v. University of Texas II* at 2207.

37. *Students for Fair Admission v. President and Fellows of Harvard University* (Court of Appeals, 2020). The suits against private colleges have been filed under Title VI of the Civil Rights Act of 1964, which prohibits race discrimination by anyone receiving federal funds; the suits against public

colleges have been filed (as in *Bakke*) under that statute and the equal protection clause.

38. Strict scrutiny: *Parents Involved* at 720; strong basis: *Parents Involved* at 754–755 (Justice Thomas concurring).

39. All-too unyielding: *Parents Involved* at 787 (Justice Kennedy concurring); Breyer oral statement: Oyez Project: https://www.oyez.org/cases/2006/05-908 (Opinion Announcement, at 19:02).

40. Roberts: *Parents Involved* at 747; Sotomayor: *Schuette v. Coalition to Defend Affirmative Action* (2014) at 381.

41. Bernard Grofman, ed., *Race and Redistricting in the 1990s* (Agathon Press, 1998); J. Morgan Kousser, *Colorblind Injustice: Minority Voting Rights and the Undoing of the Second Reconstruction* (University of North Carolina Press, 1999), 46, 195, 243–316, 366–455.

42. One may wonder why it makes any difference whether a district is majority-Black or not. Historically, few white voters vote for a Black candidate or for any candidate that is the preference of Black voters, so a Black candidate usually could not win an election unless a district was majority or near-majority Black.

43. Georgia: *Miller v. Johnson* (1995); Texas: *Bush v. Vera* (1996); North Carolina: *Shaw v. Hunt* (1996). See also *Shaw v. Reno* (1993); Ari Berman, *Give Us the Ballot: The Modern Struggle for Voting Rights in America* (Picador, 2015), 201–202, 237–238. Strict in theory and fatal in fact: *Bakke* at 361–362.

44. Alabama: *Alabama Legislative Black Caucus v. Alabama* (2015); Virginia: *Bethune-Hill v. Virginia State Board of Elections* (2017); North Carolina: *Cooper v. Harris* (2017). A seemingly contrary result came in Texas, where the Supreme Court rejected minority voters' challenge to a redistricting plan. *Abbott v. Perez* (2018), discussed in Chapter 11.

45. Indian Child Welfare Act is the Act of November 8, 1978, 92 Stat. 3069. The law requires certain protections before terminating Indians' parental rights (section 1912) and lists certain Indian preferences in adoption of Indian children (section 1915).

46. The disparaging words are in *United States v. Sandoval* (1913) at 39, 43, 44, 45 and 47. The case is prominently featured in Walter Echo-Hawk, *In the Courts of the Conqueror: The Ten Worst Indian Cases Ever Decided* (Fullerton Publishing, 2010), chap. 8. Laws enacted by Congress during that period include the Indian Civil Rights Act of 1968, the American Indian Religious Freedom Act of 1978, and the Indian Health Care Improvement Act of 1976. Statutes affecting Native Americans and Alaskan Natives are listed and described in David S. Case and David A. Woluck, *Alaska Natives and American Laws,* 2nd ed. (University of Alaska Press, 2002).

47. The birth mother was not a party to the case but filed an amica brief in the US Supreme Court supporting the adoptive couple. The brief also highlighted the greater complexity of ICWA issues when the parents of a child disagreed, as they did here.

48. *Adoptive Couple v. Baby Girl* (State court, 2013).

49. Kathryn E. Fort and Adrian T. Smith, "Understanding the Hurdles: Indian Child Welfare Act and Litigation," *Federal Bar Journal* 67 (2020): 52, 54–57; *Morton v. Mancari* at 555.

50. *Seminole Tribe v. Florida* (1996); *Rice v. Cayetano* (2000).

51. Frederick Douglass, "The Dred Scott Decision: Speech Delivered in New York on the Occasion of the Anniversary of the American Abolition Society, May, 1857," in *Two Speeches by Frederick Douglass . . .* (Rochester, New York, August 4, 1857), 34, Frederick Douglass Papers, Library of Congress, https://www.loc.gov/item/mfd.21039; Marshall: *Bakke* at 387.

13. The Color of Criminal Justice

1. Mary Frances Berry, *Black Resistance, White Law: A History of Constitutional Racism in America* (Penguin, 1994); Randall Kennedy, *Race, Crime and the Law* (Pantheon, 1997); Michael Klarman, "The Racial Origins of Modern Criminal Procedure," *Michigan Law Review* 99 (2000): 48; Ibram X. Kendi, *Stamped from the Beginning: The Definitive History of Racist Ideas in America* (Nation Books, 2016), 501–502; Khalil Gibran Muhammad, *The Condemnation of Blackness: Race, Crime, and the Making of Modern Urban America* (Harvard University Press, 2010).

2. Armand Derfner represented a death row inmate whose death sentence was voided, *Yates v. Cook* (1972). Thurmond quote: "Death Penalty Ban Saves Lives of 11 S.C. Inmates," *Greenville News,* June 30, 1972; West quote: "West Heeds Conscience, Vetoes Death Penalty Bill," *Charlotte Observer,* July 2, 1974. The court upheld guided sentencing laws in *Proffitt v. Florida* (1976) and *Jurek v. Texas* (1976), and it struck down mandatory sentencing laws (because there was still discretion in the decision of what crime to charge or convict of) in *Woodson v. North Carolina* (1976) and *Roberts v. Louisiana* (1965).

3. *Coker v. Georgia* (1977); *Kennedy v. Louisiana* (2008); *Buck v. Davis* (2017) (admission of racist testimony held to be prejudicial); Bryan Stevenson, *Just Mercy: A Story of Justice and Redemption* (Spiegel and Grau, 2014), 295–297 (juveniles).

4. Prejudice "at work" quote: *McCleskey* at 289 and 353. David C. Baldus, Charles Pulaski, and George Woodworth, "Comparative Review of Death Sentences: An Empirical Study of the Georgia Experience," *Journal of Criminal Law and Criminology* 74, no. 3 (1983): 661–753.

5. Of executions, 52 percent of defendants were white, African American defendants were 34 percent, Latino defendants were 8 percent, Native American 1 percent, and Asian 0.5 percent. Terry L. Snell, BJS Statistician, "Capital Punishment, 2017: Selected Findings," July 23, 2019, Bureau of Justice Statistics; Deborah Fins, "Death Row U.S.A., Winter 2020," quarterly report by the NAACP Legal Defense and Educational Fund, Inc., https://www.naacpldf.org/wp-content/uploads/DRUSAWinter2020.pdf. There are still more than 2,000 inmates on death row nationwide, although the number

is declining and most of them will never be executed. See the Death Penalty Information Center website, https://deathpenaltyinfo.org/.

6. Halley Fuchs, "U.S. Executes Dustin Higgs for Role in 3 1996 Murders," January 16, 2021. The Court granted certiorari before judgment in the court of appeals, exceedingly rare, and decided the case immediately with no argument and no opinion.

7. The *Batson* rule was soon extended to bar gender-based as well as race-based jury strikes, *J.E.B. v. Alabama ex rel. T.B.* (1994), in civil as well as in criminal cases, *Edmonson v. Leesville Concrete Co.* (1991), and by criminal defendants as well as prosecutors, *Georgia v. McCollum* (1992). William T. Pizzi, "*Bason v. Kentucky:* Curing the Disease but Killing the Patient," *Supreme Court Review* (1987): 97–156.

8. *Miller-El v. Dretke* at 268–269 (2005) (Justice Breyer concurring opinion); amicus brief filed by Joseph diGenova and others in *Foster v. Chatman* (2016) at 6.

9. *Foster v. Chatman* (2016) at 1765.

10. *Flowers v. Mississippi* (2019). Robert Barnes, "Charges Dropped against Man Who Was Prosecuted Six Times for Murder," *Washington Post,* September 4, 2020; Nicholas Bogel-Burroughs, "After 6 Murder Trials and Nearly 24 Years, Charges Dropped against Curtis Flowers," *New York Times,* September 4, 2020.

11. *Pena-Rodriguez v. Colorado* (2019) at 855.

12. *Dickerson v. U.S.* (2000) at 443. Sharp cut backs on Warren Court precedents are federal habeas corpus review of state court criminal convictions, e.g., *Wainwright v. Sykes* (1977), *Rose v. Lundy* (1982). Jonathan Weiss, "A Road Not Taken," *Seton Hall Legislative Journal* 26 (2002): 415.

13. Inmate Statistics (race, ethnicity) and Population Statistics, Federal Bureau of Prisons, Statistics, https://www.bop.gov/about/statistics/; Robert T. Chase, "We Are Not Slaves: Rethinking the Rise of the Carceral States through the Lens of the Prisoners' Rights Movement," *Journal of American History* 102 (June 2015): 80–81; Muhammad Hernández and Heather Ann Thompson, "Introduction: Constructing the Carceral State," *Journal of American History* 102 (June 2015): 18.

14. E.g., *Florida v. Bostick* (1991); *Illinois v. Wardlaw* (2000). Of the 5 million "stop-and-frisks" conducted by the New York Police Department in 2015, less than 12 percent resulted in arrests, but nearly 90 percent were performed on young Black and Latino men. Hernández and Thompson, "Introduction: Constructing the Carceral State," 18–21. See the litigation in *Floyd v. New York* (2013) (lower court), including Judge Shira Sheindin's finding.

15. Act of October 27, 1986, 100 Stat. 3207; amended by Act of November 18, 1988, 102 Stat. 418. 20 U.S. C. § 841; Sentencing Project, "Trends in U.S. corrections (June 2019), 1, https://perma.cc/SY6B-4QQW. In 2017 the US Department of Health and Human Services declared opioid addiction a public health emergency. Whereas the opioid crisis of the twenty-first century, which affects more white than Black people, prompted a search for medical solutions,

the abuse of other drugs was viewed as a problem of crime and punishment. Drug arrests, convictions, and long sentences all climbed dramatically.

16. Dan Baum, "Legalize It All," *Harper's,* April 2016; J. A. C. Dunn, "Law and Order Depends . . . ," *Charlotte Observer,* October 27, 1968.

17. Joseph Palamar et al., "Powder Cocaine and Crack Use in the United States: An Examination of Risk for Arrest and Socioeconomic Disparities in Use," *Drug and Alcohol Dependence* 15 (April 2015): 111; National Institutes of Health, Patrick A. Langan, "The Racial Disparity in U.S. Drug Arrests," US Department of Justice Bureau of Justice Statistics (October 1, 1995), https://www.bjs.gov/content/pub/pdf/rdusda.pdf. The Fair Sentencing Act of 2010 is the act of August 3, 2010, 124 Stat. 2372.

18. *Harmelin v. Michigan* (1991) at 994. The three other cases are *Rummel v. Estelle* (1980), *Ewing v. California* (2003), and *Lockyer v. Andrade* (2003). *Solem v. Helm* (1983) is the one case where the sentence was held to be disproportionate to his crimes. See William Pizzi, *The Supreme Court's Role in Mass Incarceration* (Routledge Books, 2020), chap. 8 on proportionality.

19. *Lockyer v. Andrade* (2003). Erwin Chemerinsky, "Cruel and Unusual: The Story of Leandro Andrade," *Drake Law Review* 52 (2003): 1–2, 8. In California in 2003, there were 344 people serving long sentences, some for life, for "petty theft with a prior." The article adds that "African-Americans and Latino defendants are much more likely to have the three strikes law used against them than white defendants."

20. *Davidson v. City of Cranston, Rhode Island* (Court of Appeals 2016); *Calvin v. Jefferson County Board of Commissioners* (District Court 2016); "Prison Gerrymandering: Ghost Constituents, Counting the Incarcerated Counts," *The Economist,* April 11, 2020, 37; Heather Ann Thompson, "Why Mass Incarceration Matters: Rethinking Crisis, Decline, and Transformation in Postwar American History," *Journal of American History* 97, no. 3 (2010): 733.

21. Office of the Inspector General, "Review of the Bureau of Prisons Monitoring of Contract Prisons" (U.S Department of Justice, 2016); Kara Gotsch and Vinay Basti, "Capitalizing on Mass Incarceration: U.S Growth in Private Prisons" The Sentencing Project, August 2, 2018, https://www.sentencingproject.org/publications/capitalizing-on-mass-incarceration-u-s-growth-in-private-prisons/.

22. Michelle Alexander, *The New Jim Crow: Mass Incarceration in the Age of Colorblindness* (New Press, 2010).

23. Current and changing state laws are reported at the website of the Brennan Center for Justice, https://www.brennancenter.org/. Alexander Keyssar, *The Right to Vote* (Basic Books, 2000), tables A6 and A15; Pippa Holloway, *Living in Infamy: Felon Disfranchisement and the History of American Citizenship* (Oxford University Press, 2014).

24. Section 2 of the Fourteenth Amendment penalized a state for disfranchising any adult males, "except for participation in rebellion, or other crime." Justice Rehnquist, for the majority, said this showed that the equal protection

clause of the Fourteenth Amendment was not intended to guarantee the right to vote of men who had committed crimes. True enough, but the equal protection clause was not at that time intended to protect anyone's right to vote. Calling section 2 an "affirmative sanction" was no logical basis for excluding this category of men from all the other categories of people whose right to vote is protected by the equal protection clause. The phrase "affirmative sanction" was a play on words rather than a reasoned basis for a decision.

25. *Raysor v. De Santis* (2020) at 2600 (Justice Sotomayor dissenting); the final decision is in *Jones v. De Santis* (Lower court, 2020). Holloway, *Living in Infamy,* x; Christopher Uggen, Ryan Larson, and Sarah Shannon, "6 Million Voters Lost: State-Level Estimates of Felony Disenfranchisement, 2016" (The Sentencing Project, October 6, 2016), https://www.sentencingproject.org/publications/6-million-lost-voters-state-level-estimates-felony-disenfranchisement-2016/; Ruth Marcus, "On the Eve of John Lewis's Death, a Cruel Supreme Court Blow to His Legacy," *Washington Post,* July 19, 2020.

26. Andrew Knapp, "Michael Slager's Sentencing to Mark End of Still-Contested Courtroom Battle in Walter Scott Killing," *Charleston Post and Courier,* December 2, 2017; Ashley Southall, "Daniel Pantaleo, Officer Who Held Eric Garner in Chokehold, Is Fired," *New York Times,* August 19, 2019.

27. Section 1983 is broader than the 1871 law in an important respect: it adds the words "and laws" and thus protects not only constitutional rights but also rights created by federal statute. Section 1983 reads as follows: "Every person who, under color of any statute, ordinance, regulation, custom, or usage, of any State or Territory or the District of Columbia, subjects, or causes to be subjected, any citizen of the United States or other person within the jurisdiction thereof to the deprivation of any rights, privileges, or immunities secured by the Constitution and laws, shall be liable to the party injured in an action at law, suit in equity, or other proper proceeding for redress."

28. For acts committed by federal personnel, suits in federal court are authorized by the federal Tort Claims Act, and in some instances additional remedies may be sought directly under the Constitution. *Bivens v. Six Unknown Named Agents* (1971).

29. Bright line: *Estate of Jones v. City of Martinsburg* (Court of Appeals 2020), at 667; existing precedent and "beyond debate": *White v. Pauly* (2017) at 551–552; "plainly incompetent": *Malley v. Briggs* (1986) at 341; recent cases: William Baude, "Is Qualified Immunity Unlawful?," *California Law Review* 106 (2018): 88.

30. *Taylor v. Rioja* (2020) at 54. On earlier prison rights cases see Malcolm M. Feeley and Edward L. Rubin, *Judicial Policy Making and the Modern State: How the Courts Reformed America's Prisons* (Cambridge University Press, 1998) and John J. DiIulio Jr., *Courts, Corrections and the Constitution: The Impact of Judicial Intervention on Prison and Jails* (Oxford, 1990).

31. *Graham v. Connor* (1989) at 389. The Supreme Court opinion shows the swear words in this abbreviated form.

32. Seriously inadequate training as a basis for city liability: *City of Canton v. Harris* (1989).

33. Booker T. Washington, "The Standard Printed Version of the Atlanta Exposition Address," in *The Booker T. Washington Papers, Volume 3: 1889–1895*, ed. Louis Harlan (University of Illinois Press, 1972), 583–587.

34. The Supreme Court has held that when municipal policy violates Section 1983, the municipality has no immunity: *Owen v. City of Independence* (1980).

35. West Publishing Co., "Authorization or Requirement for Insurance," in *Civil Actions against State and Local Government* (West Publishing Co., 2020), section 3:9. A few types of suits might be barred by the Eleventh Amendment, but most suits, including those for police conduct, would be plainly constitutional under the Fourteenth Amendment. Maitland quoted in Justice Frankfurter's opinion in *Great Northern Life Ins. Co. v. Read* (1944) at 59.

36. *O'Shea v. Littleton* (1974) at 502; *Rizzo v. Goode* (1976) at 366; Alexander, *The New Jim Crow,* 103–107, 128–129.

37. Claudia Rankine, *Citizen* (Graywolf Press, 2014), 159. *Estate of Jones v. City of Martinsburg* (4th Cir. 2020) at 673.

Conclusion

1. Albion W. Tourgée, *With Gauge and Swallow, Attorneys* (Lippincott, 1889), 112.

2. *Prigg v. Pennsylvania* (1842); *Blyew v. U.S.* (1872); *U.S. v. Reese* (1876); *Williams v. Mississippi* (1898).

3. *Yick Wo v. Hopkins* (1886); *Baldwin v. Franks* (1887); *Lone Wolf v. Hitchcock* (1903).

4. *Allgeyer v. Louisiana* (1897); *Lochner v. New York* (1905).

5. *Bailey v. Alabama* (1911); *Moore v. Dempsey* (1923); *Powell v. Alabama* (1932). There were still backward steps. *Corrigan v. Buckley* (1926); *Grovey v. Townsend* (1935).

6. *Missouri ex rel. Gaines v. Canada* (1938); *Sweatt v. Painter* (1950); *Mitchell v. U.S.* (1941); *Smith v. Allwright* (1944); *Shelley v. Kraemer* (1948); *Korematsu v. U.S.* (1944).

7. *Monroe v. Pape* (1961); *Jones v. Alfred H. Mayer Co.* (1968); *Allen v. State Board of Elections* (1969).

8. *Griffin v. Breckinridge* (1971); *Griggs v. Duke Power Co.* (1971).

9. *San Antonio Independent School Dist. v. Rodriguez* (1973); *International Brotherhood of Teamsters v. U.S.* (1977); *Washington v. Davis* (1976); *Village of Arlington Heights v. Metropolitan Housing Development Corp.*

(1977); *Runyon v. McCrary* (1976); *NAACP v. Claiborne Hardware Co.* (1982).

10. *Patterson v. McLean Credit Union* (1989); *Atonio v. Wards Cove Packing Co.* (1989); *Alexander v. Sandoval* (2001); *Reno v. Bossier Parish School Board* (2000).

11. *Abbott v. Perez* (2018); *Comcast Corp. v. National Assn of African American–Owned Media* (2020); *Shelby County v. Holder* (2013). The previous case was *James v. Bowman* (1903).

12. *Citizens United v. Federal Election Commission* (2010); *Burwell v. Hobby Lobby Stores, Inc.* (2014); *District of Columbia v. Heller* (2008).

13. *Slaughter-House Cases* (1873) at 71–72.

14. Ta-Nehisi Coates, "The Case for Reparations," *Atlantic Monthly*, June 2014; Gilbert King, *Devil in the Grove: Thurgood Marshall, the Groveland Boys, and the Dawn of a New America* (HarperCollins, 2012), 4. Two scholars with gloomier outlooks are Derrick Bell, "Preface to the Sixth Edition," *Race, Racism and American Law* (Aspen, 2008), xix–xxiv; Charles Ogletree, "Conclusion," *All Deliberate Speed: Reflections on the First Half-Century of Brown v. Board of Education* (Norton, 2004), 310–316. For a mixed view, see Orlando Patterson, preface to *The New Black: What Has Changed—And What Has Not*, ed. Kenneth Mack and Guy-Uriel E. Charles (New Press, 2013), ix.

15. This is a comparison of the length of service of the eleven justices appointed between 1970 and 2000 with the twenty justices appointed between 1920 and 1950.

16. Langston Hughes, "Harlem," *Montage of a Dream Deferred* (Holt, 1951), 71.

17. Abraham Lincoln, "Speech in the United States House of Representatives on Internal Improvements," June 20, 1848, in *The Collected Works of Abraham Lincoln*, ed. Roy P. Basler (Rutgers University Press, 1953), 1:489; Gorman: "Convening on the Practice of Democratic Citizenship: Special Performances," February 7, 2020, American Academy of Arts and Sciences, https://www.youtube.com/watch?v=9cZUl3hRBB4.

Acknowledgments

The genesis of this book dates back forty years, although the two authors didn't realize it at the time. When a voting rights decision by the Supreme Court—*Mobile v. Bolden,* 1980—created the need to prove intent, it became clear that attorneys and historians needed to work together for that proof. Our relationship began then, and, as Rick said in *Casablanca,* it was "the beginning of a beautiful friendship." For many years since 1980, we have discussed the issues in this book. Formal plans began in 2014 at a meeting at Penn Center in South Carolina. Over the next six years, we have become indebted to so many who have helped us with this book, and it is a pleasure to acknowledge their contributions.

First and foremost, we thank our spouses for love, support, and inspiration. Our utmost appreciation goes to Georganne Burton, who has assisted at every step of the way with her questions and her insistence on clarity. In addition, her editing skills are reflected in every chapter as she melded the two voices of an attorney and a historian. Vernon would like to say that, in addition to her demand for topic sentences and thesis statements, she is his soulmate in faith and love. Armand expresses the same love and appreciation to his own soulmate, Mary Giles, whose sharp archivist's and editor's eye has made a real contribution.

We give a special thank you to the Supreme Court archivist Matt Hofstedt and Supreme Court photographer Fred Schilling. Librarians are a historian's best friend. And in the era of COVID-19 and without access even to books in one's own office, let alone the library, we in particular appreciate the heroic efforts of Anne Grant, librarian for the History Department, and Rodger Bishop, Maggie Mason Smith, and Grendel J. Williams, library specialists at Clemson University, for obtaining books for us to check quotes and page numbers, and the librarians at Charleston School of Law, Katie Brown, Deborah Turkewitz, and Melissa Strickland, who is now at Louisiana State University. In addition, librarians throughout the country, especially at the Library of Congress, the National Archives, and the University of South Carolina, have aided us in our search for sources. Special thanks to Ed Bridges, emeritus director of the Alabama Department of Archives and History, for his help, especially for introducing to us to Meredith McDonough, their digital assets coordinator. Harlan Gradin, scholar emeritus at the North Carolina Humanities Council, and Robert Anthony, curator of the North Carolina Collection and director of the North Carolina Digital Heritage Center at the University of North Carolina at Chapel Hill, both helped us locate an elusive photograph of an "Impeach Earl Warren" sign, and we owe a particular thank you to our dear friend Bill Ferris for his generosity in allowing us to use his photo.

With pleasure we acknowledge those who read this manuscript and enriched it with their brilliant suggestions. A special thank you to Joel Derfner and Jeremy Derfner (the best writers, and Armand's sons).

The originally anonymous reviewers of the draft manuscript gave an intense look at the manuscript, and their criticism forced us to tighten up the arguments in the book. Thank you to Paul Finkelman, J. Morgan Kousser, and Louis Michael Seidman. We also have benefited from ongoing conversations with Morgan Kousser for clarifications. We give special thanks to proofreader extraordinaire Doliene Slater, the one person other than Armand, Vernon, and Georganne who has read the manuscript more than four times. We are grateful for her proofreading and for her insistence that we clarify basic themes across chapters (not to mention her work encouraging us to minimize parentheses).

Thank you to those who read portions of the manuscript and provided advice and special insight: Chandler Davidson, Dan Edelman, David Ellenhorn, Robert P. Green Jr., Gerry Hebert, David Herr, Timothy Huebner, Jim Lewis, Henry Lippmann, Edward Menefee, Larry Menefee, Henry Monaghan, Barbara Phillips, Terry Ann Rickson, Michael Tigar, Billy Want, Jonny Weiss, and Lee Wilson. In addition, we are especially grateful to our friends Peter Eisenstadt and Steve Hoffius for their careful reading of an early draft of the book.

A number of experts answered email questions or chatted on the phone with us to help with specific issues or points that needed clarifying. Of those we can remember, we thank Jonathan Altman, Sam Altman, Eric Franklin Amirante, Abraham Arditi, Ray Arsenault, Rims and Judy Barber, Jack Bass, Jim Blacksher, John Blume, David Case, Bill Chafe, Oscar Chase, Pete Daniel, Larry Derfner, Laurie Dill, Susan Dunn, Monica Gisolfi, Harlan Greene, Philip and Bryanna Griswold, Shirene Hansotia, George Korbel, Jim Kushner, Dan Littlefield, Jim Loewen, Eileen Ma, Ray McClain, Peyton McCrary, Larry McDonnell, David Moltke-Hansen, Gary Orfield, Aaron Polkey, Michael Ross, Richard Rothstein, John Ruoff, Herman Schwartz, Tom Sugrue, Brook Thomas, Peter Wilborn, and Suzanne Zaharoni. On Native American history, we appreciate the guidance from Fred Hoxie and from Vernon's former students Troy Smith and Rosemary Stremlau. For help on understanding and using the amazing Emory University Slave Voyages databases and estimating the number of enslaved people and when and from where they were brought to the United States, the authors would like to thank Jorge Felipe, Gwen Hall, Kathy Hilliard, Patrick Manning, Philip Misevich, Greg O'Malley, and Randy Sparks. We would also like to recognize the helpful feedback of scholars in seminars in 2016 at the University of Edinburgh, Oxford University, and the University of London, and in 2018 at the Lincoln's Unfinished Work conference, Clemson University.

We also appreciate the office help of Jan Spicher, Patricia McCurdy, and Rachel Savini. Both authors had computer emergencies, and we appreciate the Clemson IT specialists, especially Jonathan Clayton, Karen Parker, and Curt Russell, for rescue. J. Tucker Morris went to Armand's home to resolve computer issues.

The dedicated website for this book, http://justice-deferred.clemson.edu, is designed for readers who want more detail on particular topics, as well as for those interested in the twists and turns of academic debate. We greatly appreciate Eduardo Nieves, the amazing web developer for Clemson University's College of Arts, Architecture, and Humanities; he and Clemson master's student Anna Maria Nieves helped us set up the website. We also acknowledge the research assistants who have worked on the website and are continuing to do so.

Thank you to Clemson University for its support. We also acknowledge our gratitude to the students who helped with this book (and hope we have not inadvertently forgotten someone). In Armand's class at Charleston School of Law, Race and the Supreme Court, students gave new ways to look at the cases. Vernon's classes at Clemson University wrestled with ideas and historiography. We would like to thank our research assistants: Harris Bailey, Alexandra Bethlenfalvy, Alexander Bowen, Randi Brandoon, Dominick Bucca, Kelcey Eldridge, Megan Gaston, Bijan Ghom, Shirene Hansotia, John Kozelski, Tim Nicolette, Ben Parten, Anderson Rouse, Adam Schmidt, Matthew Clark Simmons, Jason Whitley, Trevor Woods, and Hanan Zaki.

As we often have needed to consult an index in our research, we have seen the difference a careful index can make. We appreciate the thorough indexing of Beatrice Burton and Human Enterprises. Also, her editing advice has been superb. We thank Alice Burton Traetto for visiting with Joe De Laine Jr. to get materials for us during the COVID-19 lockdown.

Thank you to our editor at Harvard University Press, Kathleen McDermott, executive editor for history. Her cheerful encouragement helped to keep us on target, which is no easy matter. Thanks also to our previous editor, Thomas LeBien, who helped us launch the project. We also thank project manager and senior editor Louise Robbins, and we give a special shout out to jacket designer Cymone Wilder. We are also appreciative of the work of copyeditor Wendy Nelson and the patience and professionalism of Kimberly Giambattisto, senior production editor at Westchester Publishing Services.

With all this help, there should not be any errors of fact, judgment, or interpretation. If there happen to be any, however, blame us, and not our friends listed above, or those who were our friends, before this book was published.

Illustration Credits

4 Photograph by Cecil Williams. Cecil Williams South Carolina Civil Rights Museum, Orangeburg, SC, https://www.cecilwilliams.com/. Used by permission.

27 Library of Congress, Prints and Photographs Division, LC-DIG-ds-12470.

54 Library of Congress, Prints and Photographs Division, LC-DIG-pga-02595.

60 Photograph by Samuel M. Fassett. Collection of the Supreme Court of the United States.

68 Billy Hathorn/Wikimedia/CC BY-SA 3.0.

89 Library of Congress, Prints and Photographs Division, LC-DIG-ds-04383.

91 Library of Congress, Prints and Photographs Division, LC-USZ62-56711.

105 Library of Congress, Prints and Photographs Division, LC-USZ62-69314.

126 Delta State University Archives and Museum.

127 Library of Congress, Prints and Photographs Division, LC-DIG-npcc-16218.

131 National Archives, photo no. 45503132.

134 Library of Congress, Prints and Photographs Division, LC-H25-16484-A.

136 Alabama Department of Archives and History.

144 Library of Congress, Prints and Photographs Division, LC-USZ62-101029.

151 National Portrait Gallery, Smithsonian Institution; gift of the Fred T. Korematsu Family.

158 Reproduced from the Mapping Prejudice Project, University of Minnesota.

161 Library of Congress, Prints and Photographs Division, LC-USZ62-116927.

165 Joseph A. De Laine Papers, South Caroliniana Library, University of South Carolina.

170 Photograph by Hessler Photographers. Collection of the Supreme Court of the United States.

173 Courtesy of the Sioux City Public Library, Sioux City, Iowa.

176 Library of Congress, Prints and Photographs Division, LC-USZ62-130574.

184 Everett Collection Inc./Alamy Stock Photo.

192 Photograph by William Ferris. William Ferris Collection, Southern Folklife Collection, Wilson Library, University of North Carolina at Chapel Hill.

201 Photograph courtesy of Joseph A. De Laine Jr.

211 Alabama Department of Archives and History. Donated by Alabama Media Group. Photo by Hill, Birmingham News.

222 Alabama Department of Archives and History.

233 Alabama Department of Archives and History. Donated by Alabama Media Group. Photo by Tom Lankford, Birmingham News.

244 Oyez.org. CC BY-NC 4.0.

250 Library of Congress, Prints and Photographs Division, LC-USZ62-60135.

254 Gil Barrera Photographs of the University of Texas at San Antonio, MS 27, University of Texas at San Antonio Libraries Special Collections.

287 University of Washington Libraries, Special Collections, SOC5009.

293 Oyez.org. CC BY-NC 4.0.

313 Photograph by Chuck Kennedy. Barack Obama Presidential Library, National Archives.

325 Oyez.org. CC BY-NC 4.0.

327 AP Photo/Gerald Herbert.

Index of Cases

Medical Society of South Carolina, United States v., 298 F.Supp. 145 (D.S.C. 1969), 409n17
Memphis Firefighters Local 1784 v. Stotts, 467 U.S. 561 (1984), 410n24
Mendez v. Westminster School District, 161 F.2d 774 (9th Cir. 1947), 382n12
Meredith v. Fair, 83 S.Ct. 10 (1962) (Justice Black), 385n46
Metro Broadcasting, Inc. v. FCC, 497 U.S. 547 (1990), 309, 310
Miller-El v. Dretke, 545 U.S. 231 (2005), 414n8
Miller v. Johnson, 515 U.S. 900 (1995), 412n43
Milliken v. Bradley, 418 U.S. 717 (1974); 433 U.S. 267 (1977), 256–257, 400n19
Mills v. Green, 67 Fed. 818 (D.S.C. 1895); 159 U.S. 651 (1895), 88
Minor v. Happersett, 88 U.S. 162 (1875), 399n16
Miranda v. Arizona, 384 U.S. 436 (1966), 326
Mississippi, United States v., 380 U.S. 128 (1965), 385n49
Missouri ex rel. Gaines v. Canada, 305 U.S. 337 (1938), 143–144, 364n27, 377n11, 417n6
Missouri v. Jenkins, 515 U.S. 70 (1995), 265–266, 345n5, 401nn35–36
Mitchell v. Charleston, 378 U.S. 551 (1964), 392n49
Mitchell v. United States, 313 U.S. 80 (1941), 145, 377n12–13, 417n6
Mobile v. Bolden, 446 U.S. 55 (1980), 281–283, 405n20
Monell v. New York Dept. of Social Services, 436 U.S. 658 (1978), 335
Monroe v. Pape, 365 U.S. 167 (1961), 226–228, 332–333, 335, 393nn7–8, 417n7
Moore v. Dempsey, 254 U.S. 630 (1920) [*Moore v. Arkansas*]; 261 U.S. 86 (1923), 130–131, 137, 368n70, 370n6, 374n45, 417n5
Moose Lodge No. 107 v. Irvis, 407 U.S. 163 (1972), 399n12
Morgan v. Virginia, 328 U.S. 373 (1946), 380n52, 383n23
Morton v. Mancari, 417 U.S. 535 (1974), 318, 408n9, 413n49
Muir v. Louisville Park Theatrical Association, 347 U.S. 971 (1954), 383n25
Myers v. Anderson, 238 U.S. 368 (1915), 372n21
NAACP v. Alabama, 1 Race Relations Law Reporter 707 (Montgomery County Circuit Court, 1957) [*Alabama ex rel. Patterson v. NAACP*]; 357 U.S. 449 (1958); 360 U.S. 240 (1959); 368 U.S. 16 (1961) [*NAACP v. Gallion*]; 377 U.S. 288 (1964); 277 Ala. 89 (Ala. 1964) [*NAACP v. State*], 203–206, 389–390nn15–18
NAACP v. Button, 371 U.S. 415 (1963), 207, 390n22
NAACP v. Claiborne Hardware Company, 458 U.S. 886 (1982), 418n9
NAACP v. Overstreet, 384 U.S. 118 (1966), 390n19
Naim v. Naim, 350 U.S. 891 (1955); 350 U.S. 985 (1956), 181, 192
Neal v. Delaware, 103 U.S. 370 (1883), 74, 375n56
Newman v. Piggie Park Enterprises, 390 U.S. 400 (1968), 394n18
New Negro Alliance v. Sanitary Grocery Co., 303 U.S. 552 (1938), 143
New York Times Co. v. Connor, 365 F.2d 567 (5th Cir. 1966), 390n28
New York Times Co. v. Sullivan, 376 U.S. 254 (1964), 208–209, 390nn26–27
Ng Fung Ho v. White, 259 U.S. 276 (1922), 365n42
Nixon v. Condon, 286 U.S. 7 (1932), 138
Nixon v. Herndon, 273 U.S. 536 (1927), 138, 375n60
Norris v. Alabama, 294 U.S. 587 (1935), 135–136, 375nn54–55
Northwest Austin Municipal Utility District v. Holder, 557 U.S. 193 (2009), 269–270

Obergefell v. Hodges, 576 U.S. 644 (2015), 400n24
Office of Communication of United Church of Christ v. FCC, 359 F.2d 994 (D.C. Cir. 1966), 425 F.2d 543 (D.C.Cir. 1969)., 249
Oklahoma City, Board of Education v. Dowell, 498 U.S. 237 (1991), 401n34
Ortega, United States v., 24 U.S. 467 (1825), 356n4
O'Shea v. Littleton, 414 U.S. 488 (1974), 417n36
Owen v. Independence, 445 U.S. 622 (1980), 417n34
Oyama v. California, 332 U.S. 633 (1948), 378n31
Ozawa v. United States, 260 U.S. 178 (1922), 125–126, 345n1, 373n35–36

General Index

Italicized page numbers refer to illustrations.